HISTORY

OF THE

OBERLIN-WELLINGTON RESCUE.

VIEW OF THE JAIL AT CLEVELAND, OHIO, WHERE THE PRISONERS WERE CONFINED.

COMPILED BY

JACOB R. SHIPHERD.

WITH AN INTRODUCTION BY

PROF. HENRY E. PECK, AND HON. RALPH PLUMB

NEGRO UNIVERSITIES PRESS
NEW YORK

Originally published in 1859
by J. P. Jewett and Company

Reprinted from a copy in the collections
of the Brooklyn Public Library

Reprinted 1969 by
Negro Universities Press
A DIVISION OF GREENWOOD PRESS, INC.
NEW YORK

SBN 8371-2729-7

PRINTED IN UNITED STATES OF AMERICA

TO THE

THIRTY-SEVEN INDICTED,

and to all

WHO WITH THEM BELIEVE IN THE DOCTRINES OF THE
DECLARATION OF AMERICAN INDEPENDENCE,

This Volume

IS AFFECTIONATELY INSCRIBED,

BY

THE COMPILER.

(3)

TABLE OF CONTENTS.

(iv)

CHAPTER FOURTH.

CHAPTER FIFTH.

INTRODUCTORY NOTE.

NINE years ago the moral sense of the better part of our nation, not to say of the civilized world, was shocked by the passage by Congress of the Fugitive Slave Act. The iniquities of this new device of oppression, — its assault upon personal rights in the virtual suspension of *Habeas Corpus*, its daring invasion of States-rights, its summary and cruel process of recaption, its arbitrary requirement that all citizens shall serve the man-hunter at his call, and the vindictive penalties which it denounced against any who might be constrained by self-respect or humanity to disregard its infamous precepts, — these peculiarities made this composing draught* as "molten lead to a mint-julep" in comparison with all previous pro-slavery Federal enactments. Language could not describe the terror which this villany framed into law carried to the souls of the colored people scattered through the North, who saw that now, whether free or not, they might, at any moment, be spirited away under nominally-legal forms, and consigned to hopeless slavery. Nor could words express the profound apprehension with which the friends of Freedom foresaw in this new and abject concession to the slave-holding power its final predominance in our country.

But the horror with which this so-called law was very generally regarded in the Free States was qualified, and almost, if not quite appeased by the conviction that so infamous an enactment would not and could not be enforced. Alas, for the hopes based on this conviction! The carrying into slavery of several persons afterwards proved to be free, and the recaption of one poor fugitive from oppression after another, soon proved that the cruel statute was not a dead letter. It has been from its enactment a living, as well as terrible, reality.

---

* The illustration is borrowed from a Speech made by a celebrated Cleveland divine soon after the passage of the Fugitive Slave Act.

What this ordinance, misnamed law, is; what its purposes, what its demands, and what its penalties are, and what the measures by which it enforces itself against the conscience and sense of justice which everywhere in the North oppose it, — all these points have been well illustrated in the now celebrated Oberlin-Wellington Rescue trials. These trials occurred on the Western Reserve — a name honorable for the reputation for love of Freedom which is coupled with it, and may, therefore, be supposed to exhibit a fair encounter on a fair field between the despotic enactment, and the outraged sense of right which protests against it. They engaged on both sides, and at the bar of both the Federal and Supreme State Courts, the highest legal talent in the State. A correct history of them will, therefore, show clearly what the Fugitive Slave Act is, and what measures its enforcement requires.

Such a history is presented in this volume. Its compiler is a young man of excellent ability who has had more than common experience in reporting public events, and it has been made up, as the undersigned know from constant communication with the compiler, and from a careful review of his materials, with religious fidelity to truth.

In closing this Introduction, we beg leave to urge the readers of this volume to inquire, in the light of what is here presented, whether the fact that the Fugitive Slave Act can exist, and be in form enforced, does not prove that regard for Freedom no longer presides in the councils of our Government; that the slave-holding power has smitten down the personal rights of freemen, and trampled on the honor and rights of the States; and whether, if the Free States do not speedily, by judicial and legislative action, assert their rights, our whole country will not soon, under the operation of the Dred Scott decision, be embraced in the arms of a gigantic tyranny which shall know no law but its own despotic will.

Especially would we ask our fellow-citizens of Ohio, whether they are willing longer to allow arbitrary encroachments on the part of the Federal Government, and timid deference to precedent on the part of our State Judiciary, to make our noble State a mere province of an overshadowing empire of centralized and malignant power.

H. E. PECK,
RALPH PLUMB.

CUYAHOGA COUNTY JAIL,
Cleveland, Ohio, July 1, 1859.

FIRST WORDS.

The digest of the testimony in Mr. Bushnell's case was made during the progress of the trial, and with such care that it is believed it will be found more accurate and comprehensive than any hitherto published. The arguments of Messrs. Riddle, Spalding, Griswold, Backus, and Wolcott were reported phonographically, and are published with the sanction of their authors. Every effort was made to secure equally full and accurate reports of the arguments of the counsel for the Government, but, unfortunately, without success. For such use as has been made of the materials of others, it has been endeavored to accord due acknowledgment elsewhere, save that it remains to mention here the kind offices of Mr. J. H. Kagi, of Mr. J. M. Greene, and of one whose modesty forbids the mention of her name. To Mr. Greene, the reader is indebted for the stereoscopic view which is found engraved upon the title-page.

The materials with which the writer has wrought, have been superabundant. Much that seemed scarcely less important than the rest, and at first none less, has been necessarily omitted. Necessarily, lest the general reader should feel burdened. To the people of Ohio, it is believed that every link of this remarkable chain of events has surpassing significance and interest. But, lest it may not be so abroad, the best judgment of the compiler has been taxed to omit nothing essential, while accepting nothing trivial. If others would have chosen more wisely, no one can regret more sincerely than himself that their counsel was not seasonably at his command.

Such typographical errors as may have escaped notice in the proofs, the reader is asked to be patient with, in consideration of the urgency with which the work has been pressed; the last page being in type within eight days after the Reception of Mr. Bushnell.

Quietside, }
Oberlin, July 20, 1859. }

(viii)

HISTORY

THE OBERLIN-WELLINGTON RESCUE.

CHAPTER FIRST.

THE modest village of WELLINGTON, which of late seems to have had greatness — or, better, perhaps, notoriety — thrust upon it, is by no means a locality of pretentious claims. It is a plain, thriving village, in a flourishing and populous township of the same name, and lies upon the Cleveland, Columbus, and Cincinnati Rail Road, thirty-six miles south-west of the city first named. It is, therefore, within the bounds of that part of Northern Ohio widely known as the "Connecticut Western Reserve," which was first settled some forty-five or fifty years ago by the representatives of Puritan New England, and has ever since been noted for the characteristics of the men who founded and shaped its social, political, and religious institutions.

OBERLIN is a village of some 3,000 permanent inhabitants, to which, for nine months in the year, may be added 800 students, who seek the advantages afforded in the various departments, academic, collegiate, and theological, of OBERLIN COLLEGE. It lies upon the Southern Division of the Cleveland and Toledo Rail Road, nine miles due north of Wellington, and thirty-three miles nearly west of Cleveland. Both these communities are within the county of Lorain, of which the village of Elyria, sixteen miles distant from Wellington and eight from Oberlin, is the county seat.

THE RESCUE has been variously called, in different prints, "The Oberlin Rescue," "The Wellington Rescue," and "The Oberlin-Wellington Rescue." It is sufficient to remark, that the alleged fugitive was a resident of Oberlin, was arrested near home, and taken to Wellington, whence, with the aid of friends, he is said to have made his escape. These friends were from Oberlin as well as from Wellington, and very naturally, perhaps, the Oberlin friends were the more active in his behalf. But since the locality of THE RESCUE was Wellington, it seems natural, without entering into any comparative analysis of the assistance contributed by the citizens of either place to the release of our hero, to denominate it, as for the purposes of this volume we shall, "THE OBERLIN-WELLINGTON RESCUE."

Before ushering the reader into the labyrinthical mazes of this necessarily multitudinous volume, benevolence would seem to dictate an outline sketch of the ground which is so disconnectedly and repetitiously beaten by the thousand feet of witnesses, counsel, court, and compiler, in the progress of these pages.

Know, then, gentle reader, that some time in the month of January, in the year of our Lord one thousand eight hundred and fifty-six, we are told that a negro slave, called John, about eighteen years of age, was missing from the

1

plantation of Mr. John G. Bacon, a citizen of the northern part of Mason county, Kentucky. Late in August, 1858, Mr. Anderson Jennings, a neighbor and personal friend of this bereaved planter, taking a northerly tour in pursuit of some escaped chattels belonging to his uncle's estate, to which he sustained the relation of an administrator, stopped a few days in Oberlin, and while there became possessed of information which induced him to write at once to his friend Bacon that the long lost John was undoubtedly in Oberlin, and that with the assistance of a witness and the authority of a power of attorney, the writer would quite likely be able to capture and return him to the domestic hearth. Omitting intervening details, let it suffice to say that on Wednesday the eighth of September following, Mr. Jennings found the wish of his neighborly heart gratified, by pressing the hand of Richard P. Mitchell, a gentleman whom he had known as an employee of Mr. Bacon, and receiving at his hand a document purporting to be a duly drawn and certified power of attorney, authorizing Anderson Jennings to capture and return to the State of Kentucky, one negro slave called John, who, owing service to John G. Bacon in said State, had unlawfully, knowingly, and willingly escaped therefrom—together with the assurance that he, Mr. Mitchell, could identify the truant beyond the possibility of mistake. To make assurance doubly sure, Mr. Jennings next day took the cars for Columbus, possibly not being aware that he was travelling from one judicial district into another, and obtained a warrant from one Sterne Chittenden of that place, who certifies himself to be a U. S. Commissioner, and authorized by an act of Congress approved Sept. 18, 1850, to issue such warrants,—commanding the U. S. Marshal, or any deputy U. S. Marshal of the Southern District of Ohio, to apprehend, etc., the boy John; which warrant was intrusted for execution to Jacob K. Lowe, who is said to be a deputy of the U. S. Marshal for the said Southern District. Mr. Lowe engaged the assistance of Samuel Davis, Esq., an acting Deputy-Sheriff of Franklin county, and the trio set out for Oberlin, where they arrived on the evening of Friday.

The suspicions of the good people of Oberlin having been aroused by the strange conduct of Mr. Jennings during his previous protracted stay at the Russia House, and the colored people having become alarmed for their personal safety, by an attempt only a few days before to kidnap at midnight an entire family, Mr. Jennings and his party, as he tells us, were advised by their landlord and other sympathizing friends, that an attempt at arrest within the bounds of the village might not impossibly be attended with difficulties, and perhaps fail of complete success. Inquiry for "a man whom a fellow could put confidence in," to quote the gentleman's own affecting words, introduced him to the acquaintance of Mr. Lewis D. Boynton, a gentleman-farmer, whose residence is some three miles north of the College. As the result of a visit extending from Saturday evening to Sabbath evening, a son of this Mr. Boynton, aged thirteen years, and bearing no less a name than that of the Bard of Avon, was engaged for a stipulated price to decoy John into a ride out of town the next day, and at a specified place to deliver him into the bosom of his old friends, who had so long sought him sorrowing.

This plan, after a slight amendment, proved successful, and John was arrested on Monday, the 13th of September, at about 11 o'clock, A. M., some one and three fourths miles north-east of Oberlin, by Jacob K. Lowe, Richard P. Mitchell, and Samuel Davis; Mr. Jennings prudently declining to expose the head of the expedition to unnecessary peril.

The successful posse, with their prisoner, took a road which passed at a safe distance to the east of Oberlin toward Wellington, where in due time they arrived, and took quarters at the hospitable house of one Wadsworth, at that time the proprietor of the Wadsworth House. Young Shakespeare, returning from the place of capture to the Russia House, hastened to relieve Mr. Jennings's painful anxieties, and was rewarded with twice the promised fee. Making a hasty and slender meal, as we may well suppose, Mr. Jennings was soon being rapidly expressed toward Wellington, his affectionate heart overflowing with a tumult of the tenderest emotions at the prospect of once more embracing his long-lost sable friend, and speedily restoring him to home and happiness.

But the ways of Providence are inscrutable.

As Marshal Lowe and his party were entering Pittsfield on their way Wellington-ward, two young men met them. These young men hastened to Oberlin with a description of the party, and a few moments sufficing to ascertain that John was missing — that he had been last seen driving toward New Oberlin with Shakespeare Boynton — that Shakespeare had returned without him — and that the Southerners had all left town — an intense excitement seems to have become manifest, and to have taken the shape of pursuing parties. A large crowd lingered about the hotel until late in the afternoon, and then suddenly dispersed. What happened and what did not happen inside this crowd and between it and the parties having John in custody, the reader must glean as best he can from the testimony. He will find much that is contradictory, some things impossible, some improbable, and some, we think, worthy of credit, there stated; all of which has with much care and labor been written out from the witnesses' mouths for his eye, and is submitted to him as a member of that Great Jury, before which all prisoners are tried, and to which they look for condemnation or acquittal with far greater anxiety than to the twelve men who render the special verdict in Court.

THE GRAND JURY. So flagrant a protection of the rights of a citizen of a Free State may well be supposed to have appealed in no uncertain tones to the powers that be — id est of course, the Federal Administration. The U. S. District and Circuit Court for the Northern District of Ohio straightway assembles a Grand Jury, and the Judge thereof breaks to them his woes in the following painful strains :

" He remarked, that in consequence of occurrences which had recently transpired in an adjoining county, he had been requested by the District-Attorney to call the attention of the Jury to this act of Congress. He said this section prohibits the obstruction of every species of process, legal or judicial, whether issued by a Court in session, or a Judge, or a United States Circuit Court Commissioner, acting in the due administration of this law of the United States. It matters not whether the warrant is being served by the United States Marshal himself, his deputies, or any one else lawfully empowered to serve such writ.
" The offence of obstructing process does not necessarily consist of acts of rude violence. It may consist in refusing to give up possession, or opposing, or obstructing the execution of the writ by threats of violence, which it is in his power to enforce, and thus preventing the offi-

cer from executing his writ. To warrant the charge, however, of unlawfully obstructing the arrest of a fugitive from labor, some act of interference on the part of the person accused must be proved, tending to impair the right of recaption secured by the statute. Mere obstruction, hinderance, or interruption is no offence unless made to prevent a seizure in the first instance or a recaption in case of escape. Yet it is not necessary, to constitute an obstruction in the sense of the term used in the statute, that force or violence should be actually resorted to, to defeat an arrest. The refusal to permit an arrest on the premises of another, after notice that the person sought to be taken is a fugitive from labor, and a demand of permission to arrest such person is, under the law, an obstruction. And so is the removal of the alleged fugitive by the direction of another, when done to prevent an arrest. And this is for the reason that the officer, in executing the writ, is under no obligation to commit a trespass or a breach of the peace in carrying out his purpose.
" There are some who oppose the execution of this law from a declared sense of conscientious duty. There is, in fact, a sentiment prevalent in the community which arrogates to human conduct a standard of right above, and independent of, human laws; and it makes the CONSCIENCE of each individual in society the TEST of his own ACCOUNTABILITY to the laws of the land.
" While those who cherish this dogma claim and enjoy the protection of the law for their own lives and property, they are unwilling that the law should be operative for the protection of the constitutional rights of others. It is a sentiment semi-religious in its development, and is almost invariably characterized by intolerance and bigotry. The LEADERS of those who acknowledge its obligations and advocate its sanctity are like the subtle prelates of the dark ages. They are versed in all they consider useful and sanctified learning — trained in certain schools in New England to manage words, they are equally successful in the social circle to manage hearts; seldom superstitious themselves, yet skilled in practising upon the superstition and credulity of others — FALSE, as it is natural a man should be whose dogmas impose upon all who are not saints according to HIS CREED the necessity of being hypocrites — SELFISH, as it is natural a man should be who claims for himself the benefits of the law and the right to violate it, thereby denying its protection to others — more attached to his own peculiar theories of government than to his country, and constantly striving to guide the politics of the nation with a view of overthrowing the Constitution and establishing instead a Utopian government, or rather no government at all, if based on the Federal Union.
" Gentlemen, this sentiment should find no place or favor in the Grand-Jury room. Its

tendency leads to the subversion of all law, and a consequent insecurity of all the constitutional rights of the citizen. The Fugitive Slave Law may, and unquestionably does, contain provisions repugnant to the moral sense of many good and conscientious people. Nevertheless, it is the law of the United States, and as such should be recognized and executed by our Courts and Juries until abrogated or otherwise changed by the legislative department of the Government. Ours is a government of laws, and it is by virtue of the law that you and I, and every other citizen, whether residing north or south of the Ohio River, enjoys protection for his life and security for his property."

The names of the gentlemen composing this Grand Jury were as follows : —

Foreman, DANIEL P. LEADBETTER.

GORDIAS H. HALL,   LEWIS D. BOYNTON,
OTIS REED,   EDSON T. STICKNEY,
HENRY H. GREGG,   ANDREW W. MORRISON,
RICHARD WILSON,   ASHAEL MEDBURY,
PHILO SCOVILL,   FRENCH W. THORNHILL,
ROBERT CARRON,   JOHN FRIEND,
ANSON HAYDN,   SAMUEL CLARK.

After several weeks of severe labor they brought forth bills, whereupon warrants were issued to the Marshal, on the 7th of December, against the following persons, most of them residents of Oberlin or Wellington : —

John H. Scott,
John Watson,
Simeon Bushnell,
James R. Shepard,
Ansel W. Lyman,
Henry Evans,
Wilson Evans,
David Watson,
Wm. E. Scrimeger,
Henry E. Peck,
James M. Fitch,
William Watson,
Thomas Gena,
Oliver S. B. Wall,
Walter Soules,
William Sciples,
Ralph Plumb,
John Mandeville,
Matthew De Wolfe,
Franklin Lewis,
John Hartwell,
Abner Loveland,
Lewis Hines,
Matthew Gillett,
Chauncey Goodyear,
Lorin Wadsworth,
Daniel Williams,
Henry D. Niles,
Eli Boies,
Charles Langston,
James Bartlett,
Robert Windsor,
William E. Lincoln,
Jeremiah Fox,
John Copeland,
James H. Bartlett,
Robert L. Cummings.

The same day Marshal JOHNSON appeared in Oberlin, accompanied by a single attendant. He called first at Prof. Peck's study, and as gently as possible broached his errand, concluding with an exhibition of the huge packet of warrants, and requesting introduction to such of the persons attached as were residents

of Oberlin. To this, polite assent was given, and the two set out for the purpose. Fifteen of the twenty-one sought were found, and arrested. The Marshal protesting that he felt as safe with the word as with the bond of any one of them, and that he wished to go on to Wellington without delay, they would oblige him by remaining at their places of business as usual until the morning train next day, when they might set out alone for Cleveland, where he would await them in the *depôt*, — it was unanimously decided, after consultation, to do so, and Mr. Johnson departed in peace. At Wellington, having no Prof. Peck to assist him, he succeeded in finding only a few individuals, and obtained from such as he found but qualified promises of voluntary appearance. Content with such success as he met, however, he took the evening train homeward, as empty handed as he came. The occurrences of the day following are accurately detailed by the correspondent of the *New York Tribune :* —

STARTING FOR COURT. — At 10:42 this forenoon, fifteen of the twenty-one residents of Oberlin for whom warrants were issued left the Oberlin station, amid the shouts and huzzas of a large crowd of ladies and gentlemen who had assembled to see them off. A considerable number of the most prominent men of the village, including Mayor Beecher, volunteered to accompany the prisoners and see them comfortably quartered or safely returned. Marshal Johnson was in waiting as they left the cars, and pointing the prisoners to omnibuses bound for the Bennett House, directed them to take good care of themselves and be ready for a call at 2 o'clock. After dinner, the Hon. R. P. Spalding, the Hon. A. G. Riddle, and S. O. Griswold, Esq., who had volunteered their services for the defence, free of charge, were called in for consultation. Soon after 2 o'clock, the parties proceeded to the court-room.

THE TRIAL BEGUN. — The MARSHAL read the names of the persons upon whom he had served processes at Oberlin, with the number of the bills in which their names severally stood. Judge SPALDING, acting for the defence, entered a plea of Not Guilty, in behalf of all.

Those who responded were as follows : —

Name.	No. of Bill.	Charge.	Plea.
John H. Scott,	78	Rescuing.	Not Guilty.
Henry E. Peck,	95	Aiding & Abetting.	Not Guilty.

Name.	No. of Bill.	Charge.	Plea.
John Watson,	72	Rescuing.	Not Guilty.
William Watson,	94	Rescuing.	Not Guilty.
Henry Evans,	84	Rescuing.	Not Guilty.
Wilson Evans,	85	Rescuing.	Not Guilty.
David Watson,	86	Rescuing.	Not Guilty.
Ansel W. Lyman,	80	Rescuing.	Not Guilty.
James M. Fitch,	96	Aiding & Abetting.	Not Guilty.
Simeon Bushnell,	74	Rescuing.	Not Guilty.
James R. Shepard,	77	Rescuing.	Not Guilty.
Oliver S. B. Wall,	84	Rescuing.	Not Guilty.
Wm. E. Scrimmager,	88	Rescuing.	Not Guilty.
James Bartlett,	60	Rescuing.	Not Guilty.

Pleas of abatement were entered for misnomer in the cases of the persons arrested as James R. Shepard, Oliver S. B. Wall, and William E. Scrimmager. James Bartlett was in town, but not present in the court-room when his name was called. Ralph Plumb was allowed a few days to complete business engagements, pledging his parole to appear with as little delay as possible. The representatives from Wellington are expected to-morrow.

Judge SPALDING gave notice that the accused were ready for, and requested trial immediately. The DISTRICT-ATTORNEY begged continuance for time to send to Kentucky for witnesses. Should need at least two weeks.

Judge SPALDING thought that citizens of Ohio might think two weeks some time to lie in jail for the convenience of citizens of Kentucky.

The COURT remarked that it was not necessary for them to lie in jail. They could be liberated on bail.

Judge SPALDING was not sure of that, by any means. He was not authorized to believe that all of them could furnish bail, and it was that very question which he wished settled. He wished to know if bail would be required.

The DISTRICT-ATTORNEY said it would.

The COURT thought all might find bail at $500 each, which would be very moderate.

Mr. GRISWOLD informed the Court that only a portion of his clients could find bail in any amount.

Judge SPALDING received permission to retire for consultation with his clients, and returning, informed the Court that no bail would be given. The accused were ready for, and demanded immediate trial. The United States had summoned them to appear for trial, and it was the business of the United States to be ready to proceed with the trial without any delay. If a continuance was ordered, they were willing to enter into a recognizance to appear when called, but would do nothing farther.

The Court conferred with the District-Attorney.

The COURT announced that individual recognizances in the sum of $1,000 would be sufficient.

These recognizances were accordingly made, and the trial thus adjourned until the second Tuesday in March, 1859.

At various dates within the few days following severally appeared others of the arrested, and entered into their personal recognizances as above. Such were:—

Walter Soules, John Mandeville,
William Sciples, Abner Loveland,
Matthew De Wolfe, Matthew Gillett,
Lewis Hines, Lorin Wadsworth,
Chauncey Goodyear, Henry D. Niles,
Daniel Williams, Eli Boies,
Ralph Plumb, Charles Langston.

THE FELONS' FEAST.

An occurrence of much interest, and the next one of public concern which properly finds place in these records, is happily narrated by the senior editor of the *Cleveland Morning Leader*, in the following terms:—

"FELONS' FEAST" AT OBERLIN.—A strange and significant scene for this enlightened and Christian age, and in our boasted free Republic, transpired at the peaceful and God-fearing and God-serving village of Oberlin, on the afternoon of Tuesday, the 11th of January, 1859. It was literally the "Feast of Felons," for the thirty-seven good citizens of Lorain county, indicted by the Grand Jury of the United States District Court of Northern Ohio under the Fugitive Slave Act, for the crime of a conscientious and faithful observance of the higher law of the Golden Rule, sat down with their wives and a number of invited guests to a sumptuous repast at the Palmer House. It was in the best sense a good social dinner, followed by a real "feast of reason and flow of soul." The entertainment was given by the indicted citizens of Oberlin to their brethren in bonds, as will be seen by the following

Card of Invitation.—At a meeting of the citizens of Oberlin, who had been indicted by the Grand Jury of the U. S. District Court at Cleveland, charged with rescuing the negro boy John Price, held on the evening of January 4, 1859, it was

Resolved, That it is expedient for the whole number of the citizens of Lorain county who have been thus indicted to meet for the purpose of consultation and agreement as to the course

to be pursued in the present emergency and for mutual comfort, and for this purpose to meet at the Palmer House on Tuesday, January 11th, at 2 o'clock, P. M., for dinner, and such other good things as may follow, and that we invite the citizens of Wellington, implicated with us, to participate on the said occasion as our guests.   JAMES M. FITCH, *Chairman.*
JACOB R. SHIPHERD, *Secretary.*

The Indicted Present. — Prof. H. E. Peck, Hon. Ralph Plumb, J. M. Fitch, O. S. B. Wall, James Bartlett, William D. Scrimgeour, David Watson, Wilson Evans, Henry Evans, John Watson, John H. Scott, Simeon Bushnell, Jacob R. Shipherd, Ansel W. Lyman, Oberlin; Wm. Sciples, Matthew Gillett, Abner Loveland, Lewis Hines, Eli Boies, Matthew DeWolf, John Mandeville, Daniel Williams, Loring Wadsworth, Walter Soules, Wellington; Henry D. Niles, Pittsfield; Chauncey Goodyear, Penfield.

This list embraces all of the thirty-seven who have been arrested.

The balance, we understand, were away on business when the Marshal came to arrest them.

The following ladies, wives of the indicted, were also present: — Mrs. O. S. B. Wall, J. M. Fitch, J. H. Scott, James Bartlett, Ralph Plumb, David Watson, H. E. Peck, Henry Evans, John Watson.

The above ladies have been heard to say that their acquaintance shall be renewed at the trials of their husbands, whenever that affair shall occur.

These were the honored Men and Women of the "Felons' Feast." Among them were venerable gray-headed men, some of the early settlers of Lorain county — men who had felled the forest and built the humble log-cabins, school-houses, and churches of the wilderness — noble men, good men, and true men — men of Puritan and Covenanter stock, of Revolutionary blood, of spotless reputation — indicted criminals! and for what? for violation of the Bible injunction, "Whatsoever ye would that others should do unto you, do ye even so unto them."

At the table the Divine blessing was impressively invoked by the beloved Patriarch of Oberlin, Rev. JOHN KEEP; and after the good things so abundantly provided had been discussed, Prof. PECK announced that the "criminals" had invited SAMUEL PLUMB, Esq., to officiate as President. The President in a brief and happy manner stated the object of the social gathering, and referred to the deep sympathy felt by the men and women of Lorain for their brethren in bonds. He said the reading of letters from invited, but absent guests, would be first in order.

Prof. Peck read the following

Letter from George A. Benedict, Esq.

HERALD OFFICE, }
Cleveland, Jan. 11, 1859. }

Prof. PECK AND OTHERS, Com. — *Gentlemen:* At the latest moment I am compelled to decline your polite invitation to your festival of to-day. Business that cannot be postponed is my excuse. Allow me to say that the spirit which dictates the festival, and which gave rise to it, meets my heartiest sympathy.

Yours, etc.,
GEO. A. BENEDICT.

Mr. Horr read the following

Letter from John M. Vincent, Esq.

ELYRIA, Jan. 10, 1859.

HONORED "37." — DEAR SIRS: I regret that previous engagements will prevent me from joining in your festivities to-morrow. My heart is with you, and any other "aid and comfort" which I can in the future render, is at your service.

Your position is a proud one. To be charged with the crime (?) of loving Liberty too well, enrolls your names with that immortal band of *Patriots* who gave us the "Declaration of Independence," and the foundation of a free government.

Their sacrifices and sufferings, their firmness and resolution, we were early taught to admire and imitate. It has been left for our "latter day" rulers to teach us that all our cherished ideas of freedom are vagaries, and that the liberty of the American Union is only that of the *white* man to enslave the *black*.

This will never do; such rank perversion of God's truth we will never allow. We will say to these rulers, as Arnold the poet said to Barlow, who had been composing a revised edition of Watts' psalms and hymns: —

"You've proved yourself a sinful *cretur*,
You've murdered Watts, and spoiled the meter.
You've tried the Word of God to alter,
And for your pains deserve a halter."

"Brethren in bonds," let nothing drive you from the right. Iniquity shall not always triumph, and reason and justice shall not always be driven before might.

"As our fathers have fought, and our grandfathers bled,
And many a hero now sleeps with the dead,
Let us nobly defend what they bravely maintained,
Nor suffer our sons to be fettered and chained."

As one in bonds with you, I remain yours,
JOHN M. VINCENT.

Prof. Peck then read the following

Letter from S. Burke, Esq.

ELYRIA, January 7, 1859.

GENTLEMEN: Your esteemed favor of the 5th instant, inviting me to meet with you at the Palmer House in Oberlin on the 11th instant, for the purpose of manifesting our sympathy and partaking of a dinner with the "thirty-seven criminal" citizens of Lorain county, recently indicted in the United States Court at Cleveland, came duly to hand. In answer, permit me to say, that I shall endeavor to do myself the honor to meet with you and those whom you represent, at the time mentioned. Circumstances may transpire, however, that will render it impossible for me to meet you, in which event, permit me to reassure you and the other accused citizens of Lorain county, who may be present with you, that I have a deep and abiding sympathy with the oppressed and down-trodden race to which the fugitive John belongs, and that it is a part of my business, and in accordance with my nature, to resist tyranny and oppression in all its forms. If there is any doctrine or creed to which I give my full and unqualified consent, it is the doctrine of political equality and individual freedom; the right of man, black or white, native or foreigner, to carve out, under God, his own destiny, and choose his own rulers. Much as I feel flattered by the kind manner in which you have been pleased to refer to the fact that I have been chosen to aid in the defence of the parties indicted in the United States Court, I am not insensible of the fact that my known sympathy with the cause and the accused had much more to do with my selection than any probable service I could render you upon trial. Be that as it may, I can assure you I have watched with much interest the proceedings of the Government in these cases, and have been led to the conclusion that very few if any of the numerous persons indicted would be put on their defence, but I may be mistaken in this. It is said that "whom the gods would destroy they first make mad," and that symptoms of madness have recently appeared in high places, cannot be denied. What may be determined on, therefore, by the ruling madmen, I know not. Nor can I tell what farther sacrifices it may yet become necessary for the lovers of freedom to make, to render our own beloved and beautiful Ohio, indeed and in truth the land of the free and the home of the brave — to deliver our people from the demoralizing spectacle of slave-catching and slave-hunting in our midst — to render it safe for the humanely disposed among us to feed the hungry, clothe the naked, or relieve the distressed, without fear of Government spies, or running the risk of fines, forfeitures, and prison bars and bolts. But whatever the sacrifice may be, I feel that our people are prepared to make it, and that Ohio will yet be free — that when the panting fugitive from oppression shall breathe the air and tread the soil of our noble State, his chains will fall off, and his natural, inalienable rights of personal liberty, personal security, and the right to enjoy the fruits of his own labors be restored to him.

Allow me, in conclusion, to say, that whatever aid I can render you and those whom you represent, either *before* or *after* Judgment, in or out of Court, shall be freely and cheerfully given.

I am, Gentlemen, very respectfully, etc.,
S. BURKE.

To H. E. PECK and others, Committee, Oberlin, O.

REGULAR TOASTS.

1st. *The Inalienable Rights of Man* — Founded in Nature as constituted by God, and well recited by our Fathers in the Declaration of Independence.

Geo. G. Washburn, Esq., editor of the Lorain Independent Democrat, ably responded to this sentiment. He spoke of the extraordinary fact, that in the middle of the 19th century, American citizens have met to ask whether man has any inalienable rights. He referred to man's inalienable rights, to the higher law, the law of the Creator of all, and to the hoary-headed men around him who had been arraigned as criminals for violating the Fugitive Slave Act. Mr. W. declared that the detested law never could be enforced in Lorain, and closed by offering the following sentiment, which met with a hearty response: —

The Fugitive Slave Act — Making war as it does upon all that is manly in man, we will hate it while we live, and bequeathe our hatred to those who come after us when we die. No fines it can impose or chains it can bind upon us, will ever command our obedience to its unrighteous behests.

2d. *Good Will to Man* — The best bond of Society; the surest support of Government; and never more fully developed than when at the call of the weak and oppressed it resists the tyranny of wicked rulers.

Father Keep said he could not discuss such a sentiment. We all know what good-will to man means. It embodies that sweetest element of human life. It is eulogized. Why is it eulogized? It is the best bond of society. — What is the other part of the eulogy? It is the strength of government. What is the strength of government? It is truth, integrity, charity, humanity, love. This is the eulogy pronounced on good-will to man.

The best development of this sentiment is when, at the call of the weak and the oppressed, it resists tyranny. Good-will is forbearing, long suffering, and, through kindness, heaps coals of fire on the head of the oppressor; but, said the Christian of nearly four-score, with the energy of '76, there is a point where forbearance ceases to be a virtue. When that is reached, let the tyrant perish! [Great applause.]

3d. *Loyalty to God and loyalty to human Government when it is loyal to God* — The Patriotism which inspired our Fathers and shall prompt us and our children.

To this sentiment Prof. Peck responded. He said : —

There is current in society an idea that there is no patriotism where there is not an acknowledgment of the maxim, " our country, right or wrong." But such was not the doctrine of our noble fathers. They esteemed patriotism a cardinal virtue. They were to the last degree *loyal* men. King and country never rightfully asked of them any sacrifice that they did not cheerfully render it. They loved to offer even life itself for the protection of the realm against its foes. But their loyalty enjoined of king and country one imperative condition — that the State itself should recognize Divine law. " GOD and our country" was their maxim. They held that when the State refused the behests of God by assuming prerogatives which did not belong to her, or by enacting laws which contradicted justice, she did that which disgraced and dishonored herself, and that patriotism could render to her no other service so useful as that of compelling, by steadfast resistance of her usurpations, her return to her broken allegiance. So was it that they never esteemed themselves more loyal than when they brought the Stuart to the block for arrogating to himself powers which belonged to God alone. So was it, too, that they thought they were acting as patriots when they turned their backs on home because liberty was restrained there, and sought freedom in a savage land ; and so was it, too, that they felt that loyalty itself required them to enter armed protest against the royal encroachments on right which followed them to their wilderness retreat, and to try the chances of war with Fatherland, which they loved as their own firesides were hardly loved.

And the doctrine of patriotism which our fathers nobly illustrated has come down to us and is *our* doctrine. We hold that our prayers, our labor, and our blood are due to our country when she needs them. We mean to make patriotism a part of our religion, and to be behind none in prompt and earnest service for the honor and good of the commonwealth. But we hold that the commonwealth can prosper only when she is loyal to God, and that when by "framing iniquity into law" she puts herself in the place of God, she does that which must, sooner or later, bring ruin upon herself, and hence that we are no traitors but rather truest liege-men when we declare that we will obey no law in which impiety is thus flaunted in the face of Heaven. We cannot obey the fugitive slave act, not because we do not love and honor our country, but because we cannot do that which will reflect deepest dishonor and disgrace upon her.

And the faith we have got from our fathers we mean to hand down to our children. We mean to rear them in devout allegiance to God and fervent patriotism to the country and institutions given us of God. We mean to teach them to respect law and its ministers, to pro-

mote by every possible means the dignity and well-being of the noble commonwealth of which we are a happy part. But we also mean to teach them that they will not be dutiful to the State, if they do not hold her to her duty to God ; that they will be *traitors* if they obey laws which break the laws of Heaven.

And we trust that they will have sufficient self-respect to stand to such patriotism as was our inheritance and as shall be their patrimony, even if in so doing they encounter bonds or death itself.

4th. *Personal Sacrifices* — The seed of to-day which brings the harvest for to-morrow.

Mr. John M. Langston eloquently responded to this sentiment. He inquired — what is the work of the American citizen of to-day to accomplish ? It is this. He is to reinstate the Declaration of Independence, and to reinstate the Constitution of the United States. American Slavery has stricken down the first; the Fugitive Slave Law the latter. Shall we meet this duty ? To do it we must make sacrifices — go to prison, or, if necessary, go out on the battle-field to meet the Slave Oligarchy. Mr. L. closed with the following sentiment : —

The Rescuers of John Price — the Rescuers of Benjamin Rice — the Rescuers of the Bells — Their conduct should immortalize their names.

5th. *The sovereign authority of the State, and the voice of the people* — The refuge of American citizens from the tyrannies of federal enactments not sanctioned by justice and the Constitution.

R. G. Horr, Esq., ably discussed the sovereignty of the State, and the voice of the people. They will be felt. They have been felt in Wisconsin, and thirty-seven is a good number for the Supreme Court of Ohio to commence on. Mr. H. made many happy hits and several hard ones. He said the Fugitive Slave Law sometimes sunk men below the depths of manhood, and they became a *Dayton!* [Much laughter and applause.] He had no sentiment to offer — he read the right sentiment in the face of every man and woman in the assembly.

6th. *The Alien and Sedition Law of* 1798 *and the Fugitive Slave Act of* 1850 — Alike arbitrary, undemocratic, and unconstitutional. As did the one, so may the other rouse the country to a political and moral revolution which shall restore the doctrines of Personal Liberty and State Rights which centralizing power has wantonly violated.

R. Plumb, Esq., rose and said : —

MR. PRESIDENT — The sentiment you have just read carries us back in our national history to the early days of the republic, to the very infancy of our Constitution.

The year 1798 was memorable for producing the Alien and Sedition laws of federalism. The alien laws, as you well know, conferred upon the President the power to remove, in a summary manner, any alien or foreigner who might be deemed by him unsafe to the government — while the sedition laws made criminal and punished with fine and imprisonment any one who might dare to oppose any measure of the Government of the United States, or any of its laws, or to intimidate or prevent any officer under that government from undertaking or performing his duty. It was also enacted, that if any person should write, print, utter, or publish any false, scandalous, or malicious writing against the Government, Congress, or President of the United States, or aid in doing so with intent to defame them or bring them into disrepute, or to excite any unlawful combinations for opposing any law of the United States, etc., he should be liable to fine and imprisonment. Under this famous sedition law, Matthew Lyon, a member of Congress from Vermont, was indicted for using the following words in a letter to a Vermont newspaper: — " Whenever I shall, on the part of the Executive, see every consideration of the public welfare swallowed up in a continual grasp for power, in an unbounded thirst for ridiculous pomp, foolish adulation and selfish avarice ; when I shall behold men of merit daily turned out of office for no other cause but independence of sentiment; when I shall see men of firmness, years, and ability discarded in their application for office for fear they possess that independence, and men of meanness preferred for the ease with which they take up and advocate opinions, the consequences of which they know but little of; when I shall see the sacred name of religion employed as a State engine to make men hate and persecute each other — *I shall not be their humble advocate.*"

Yes, fellow-citizens, this true man, this loyal citizen, was dragged before a District Court of the United States, upon this indictment tried, found guilty, fined $1,000, and imprisoned four months.

But what was the effect of these laws and of this and kindred indictments and trials under them?

The pen that drafted the immortal Declaration of Independence, was again wielded by Thomas Jefferson in defence of the Declaration, the Constitution, the sovereignty of the States, and the rights of the people.

In 1798, the Legislature of Kentucky passed the resolutions drafted by Jefferson, while the next year the Legislature of Virginia passed similar setiments from the pen of James Madison. Mr. President, I hold in my hand a copy of the Kentucky resolutions as Jefferson penned them, the second of which reads as follows: —

" 2. *Resolved*, That the Constitution of the United States, having delegated to Congress the power to punish treason — counterfeiting the securities and current coin of the United States — piracies and felonies committed on the high seas, and offences against the laws of nations, *and no other crimes whatever*, and it being

true, as a general principle, and one of the amendments of the Constitution having also declared that 'the powers not delegated to the United States by the Constitution, nor prohibited by it to the States, are reserved to the States respectively, or to the people ' — therefore the Act of Congress passed July 14th, 1798, entitled 'An Act in addition to an Act for the punishment of certain crimes against the United States,' *and all other of the Acts which assume to create, define, or punish crimes* other than those enumerated in the Constitution, are altogether VOID and of NO FORCE, and that the power to create and define such other crimes is reserved, and of right appertains solely and exclusively to the respective States, each within its own territory."

These resolutions, the whole of them, ladies and gentlemen, will repay a faithful perusal by us all, women as well as men, — because of the importance of the doctrines which they contain, and the appropriateness to the times in which we live.

This brings us to the Fugitive Slave Act of 1850.

That act was conceived in sin and brought forth in iniquity.

The slave power not only demanded the passage of the Act, but they also required the greatest statesmen of our land, then living, should give their voice and their vote for the infamous measure — not caring that the voice and vote demanded should consign to infamy those who but for this and similar debasements would have been embalmed in the grateful memories of the latest generations.

But the Act was passed, and now mark the similarity between the Act and that of its illustrious predecessors.

The sedition law of 1798 defined crimes *unknown to the Constitution*, and authorized the Courts of the United States to punish those pretended crimes by imprisonment and fines.

The Fugitive Act of 1850 defines crimes *unknown to the Constitution*, makes it a crime to feed the hungry, clothe the naked, and help the weary traveller on his journey, and authorizes the U. S. Courts to punish those pretended crimes by imprisonment and fine.

Jefferson and Madison, those illustrious founders of genuine Republicanism, whose labors were blessed to the complete rout of the Federalism of their day, held that such enactments were VOID and of NO BINDING FORCE, and so do we, the thirty-seven criminals of Lorain.

Ladies and gentlemen—since I had the honor to appear before the august tribunal that is to try us in March next, and enter my plea as a criminal, I have endeavored to look over my past life with becoming seriousness, that I might, if possible, find in what my crime consists. I find many things for which I ought to be condemned, but surely the wrong things of my life were not included in what I did on the 13th of September, 1858.

My sins of that day were sins of omission, and not of commission. I did not go to Wellington, but I confess to you all (don't tell any of the witnesses what I say), that my whole being was stirred when the news came suddenly upon us that a man had been stolen from our midst at mid-day, and when the noble band of rescuers wended their way towards Wellington, my heart went up in prayer to Almighty God for the success of their enterprise, and when the news came back that in some way, I know not how, the man-thieves had been despoiled of their prey, my heart went up again to God with such emotions of gratitude to Him as I hope often to feel hereafter.

This is my crime. You may call it treason if you like, and the courts may punish me if they will — " they may drag me to prison, and from prison to death ; yea, let me die a felon's death, but let me die a man."

Fellow-citizens, we have met to-day to feel each other's hearts — to understand better the common impulse that hitherto has moved us, and to prepare for whatever awaits us in the future.

For one I had rather sit among you as I do to-day, reading as I do in your calm countenances, your dignified bearing, the puritan purpose of your lives, with the sure prospect of speedy poverty before me, than to exchange the privilege for all the gold of California.

Mr. President, we may well turn from the present to a glorious future that awaits us.

Our country needs deliverance from the galling yoke of the Slave power, and it is near at hand.

A second Jefferson must soon appear of such qualities of head and heart as shall enable him to take command of our noble ship of State — one who by a firm adherence to the doctrines of the Republican resolutions of 1798, will secure to the States their sovereign rights, the people the enjoyment of the blessings of liberty, and keep the Federal Government and the Federal Courts clearly within the limits prescribed by the Constitution.

That man is already born, a man of executive experience, and, if I mistake not, has more than once stood upon the soil consecrated to freedom by the ordinance of '87, and breathed the free air of our own Ohio — who shall bring the good ship of State out from the rocks and shoals that beset her, into the ocean of a glorious future which shall bless the world.

Fellow-citizens, God reigns !

It is He who speeds on their way the ever-moving tides of population from all the East, even from beyond the broad ocean, to our vast unoccupied domain ; to build them there new homes, and yearly as the swelling tide rolls on, countless new altars and firesides shall be consecrated to freedom for universal man.

It is His will, since the avarice of man has torn the negro from his home and thrust him upon American soil, to make his presence here the occasion upon which the problem of personal freedom, that second revolution, more important than the first, shall be worked out by the American people, for the good of the world.

VOLUNTEER SENTIMENTS.

By J. M. Fitch. *The Prosecution* — Will it " subdue " us ? — shall it " clear the town of us ? " — can it " crush us out ? "

The " No ! No ! No ! " in response, " settled. the question," and Mr. Fitch, in a few thrilling sentences, spoke of his own indictment for no cause, unless for his " poor prayers " [laughter] in behalf of the oppressed ; and of the liberty-loving men and women who have been amerced in fines and cast into prison, for manifesting active sympathy " for the least of one of these."

Mr. F. Shipherd was called out, and gave as a sentiment — *The Felons' Feast !* Mr. S. spoke in high commendation of the present feast, and happily of ancient feasts in commemoration of important events. He thought the present one auspicious, for Roman history informs us that the best preparation for successful battle is a good dinner ! [Laughter.]

Mayor A. N. Beecher, of Oberlin, in response to a call, offered the following sentiment, which was warmly cheered : —

The Thirty-seven Criminals of Lorain — Men of true grit, and " hale fellows well met." May we never fall into worse company ; and should the bloodhounds of Slavery again visit our county, may they find a *Wall Plumb* before them, *De Wolf* after them, and get well *Peck*-ed in the bargain.

This brought up R. Plumb, Esq., who, after some happy pleasantry, referred to the ruthless murder of young Brown, son of the famous " Ossawatomie " Capt. John Brown, in Kansas, by the pro-slavery Border Ruffians, and to the just retribution which had since overtaken two of his murderers, G. W. Clark and Martin White. He then read a thrilling letter of sympathy from Mr. John Brown, Jr., brother of the Kansas victim, and formerly an old neighbor of Mr. Plumb in Ashtabula county, upon hearing through the papers that Mr. P. was one of the " honored thirty-seven." A single extract will show the " spirit of '76 " transmitted from sire to son :

" Friend Plumb, would you say, ' Oh ! but that would be *Treason*.' Well, thank God ! ' I've been there.' I have for months at a time had before me the brilliant prospect of ' standing on nothing, and looking through a halter ! ' — The cry of ' Treason ! ' I have become accustomed to ; indeed it has become so familiar that I confess I rather like the music."

" Step by step the Slave power is driving us on to take one or the other horn of the dilemma, either to be *false* to *Humanity* or *traitors* to the *Government.* If we ' would ordain and establish Justice,' and maintain our Constitution not only in its essential spirit but its letter, strange to say we are *forced* into the *attitude of resistance to the Government.* I am glad the work of Judicial ' crushing out' is progressing not only out of Kansas but in Ohio — on the Western Reserve, the New England of the West. This is bringing the war home to

> ' The green graves of our sires,
> To our altars and our fires.' "

Prof. Peck said he thought he heard his name associated with others in the toast given by Mr. Beecher. He should return the compliment, and gave

When those slaveholders come again, may we have a Beecher for *mare* [Mayor] to give them a trot! [Much merriment.]

By J. R. Shipherd. *The Press* — While we have so intrepid *Leaders,* so faithful *Heralds,* and so undegenerate *Democrats,* we fear neither slaveholders at the South, nor slave-hunters here.

The editor of the *Leader* was called out, and acknowledged the compliment to the independent press of Cuyahoga and Lorain. He refreshed the " honored 37 " with the sketch of a former " indictment " in Erie county, New York, to be more widely published in due season. It is unnecessary to add that the narrative was heard with attention.

The President said a descendant of the old tyrant-hating Covenanters was among the indicted, and called on Mr. Wm. Douglas Scrimgeour. Mr. S. responded in one of the most effective off-hand speeches of the festival, and showed himself no degenerate son of the noble race. His words glowed and burned with the fervor of true freedom and manly spirit. His venerated father had sent him words of high cheer. 'He blessed his son, and would have so acted himself had he been present. He was ready to meet fines and imprisonment for such a son, and for such a discharge of duty to God and his fellow man. Mr. S. was warmly applauded, and concluded by offering the following sentiment : —

Our Fathers and our Mothers — Free themselves, and bequeathing Freedom to their children ; they have shown by their words and actions that they desire " Liberty to be proclaimed through all the land to all the inhabitants thereof."

The President announced that he understood we had a Hunter in our midst, not a miserable hunter of the panting fugitive, but a noble Nimrod and man, the Hon. John Hunter, of Cleveland, the colleague from Columbiana of Messrs. Plumb and Monroe in the House at the session when good and humane legislation closed the jails of Ohio against persons not charged with crime, and further protected the rights of the people by Habeas Corpus ; enact-

ments since repealed by the slave-cringing Democracy. Mr. Hunter was called out, and electrified his hearers for a few moments. The hour for consultation and business having arrived ; the "Felons' Feast" closed with the following heartily applauded sentiment : —

By the Company. *Our Hostess* — If Uncle Sam shall take us to board, may we have her for " help ! "

The social festival at Oberlin will long be pleasantly remembered by those who participated. It was just what might be expected of sincere, earnest, devoted men and women — earnest, cheerful, orderly. The men in bonds were more closely knit together by the association, and the opposition to the execution of an unrighteous law is tenfold strengthened by the persecutions set on foot under it. The spirit manifested was temperate and religious. There was no railing at the officers of the law — only denunciation of the law itself. The " criminals," meeting by themselves, appointed a staunch committee, vested with full powers to make every arrangement for the details of the defence in March, and attend to *certain other items* not yet made public, but which some time may be, to the inconsolable astonishment of a few individuals, and their friends, if they have any. The committee is as follows : —

Prof. H. E. Peck, Hon. R. Plumb, W. D. Scrimgeour, Oberlin ; Matthew De Wolfe, Esq., Loring Wadsworth, Esq., Wellington.

THE ARREST OF LINCOLN.

On Friday, the 14th of January, Wm. E. Lincoln, who had left town for the winter vacation several weeks before any bills were found, was engaged in the duties of a school-teacher in the town of Dublin, twelve miles from Columbus, when a rap was heard at the door, and a moment after two men entered, who subsequently proved to be Samuel Davis, the deputy-sheriff that assisted deputy marshal Lowe in the capture of John, and some constable of the vicinity employed for the occasion. Mr. Davis, stepping forward much excited, demanded the school teacher's name, and being answered truly, declared him to be " the very fellow he was after," and straightway, without further explanation of any sort, produced a pair of HANDCUFFS, and began to fasten them upon Lincoln's wrists. The teacher remonstrated earnestly, but altogether in vain ; with many oaths and immense bluster the considerate officer expressed his moderate confidence in abolitionists under any circumstances, and avowed the purpose of never again exposing himself to their power : — the occurrences at

Wellington having proved to him, as he hoped, a wholesome experience! After some difficulty Mr. Lincoln was allowed to exchange his gown and slippers for coat and boots, and then straightway thrust into a carriage for Columbus.

It would be doing serious injustice to the witnesses of this remarkable transaction to make no mention of their conduct. And to appreciate this conduct, it must be understood that the entire town was — with the exception of a few families — of unanimous political faith, and trusted to the powers that be as the adherents of a certain religious creed trust to their father-confessor. With a dread of "niggers" and a horror of "abolitionists" such as only children trained under similar influences could acquire, these representatives of the rising generation had, nevertheless, become devoted to their new teacher with an ardor of affection and respect that manifested itself in this trying hour in a most decisive manner. Only with difficulty could he persuade them — and particularly the older girls — from undertaking his defence *vi et armis*, and nothing could silence the emphatic expression of personal views of the Fugitive Slave Law in general, and of "Sam Davis" in particular. It is not necessary to quote "samples" of the expressions used; a lively imagination, familiar with the habits of a *naïve* child's mind, will readily supply them.

The ride to the city — Mr. Davis's assistant was at Mr. Lincoln's instance soon dismissed — was not so pleasant as rides have sometimes been. In the first place the road was exceedingly bad, and their progress necessarily slow to tediousness. And, in the other place, a careful comparison of views upon certain points did not reveal a very affectionate unity of opinions. Mr. Lincoln having conscientious scruples in regard to too frequent violations of the third commandment, was not always pleased with his companion's choice of language; and Mr. Davis, not making any pharisaical or other pretensions to personal piety, it may reasonably be feared, could not fully sympathize in some of his companion's "faithful" exhibitions of Gospel Truth. And then Mr. Davis ventured upon some confidential revelations of "what he would like to do" with his prisoner, and others of the "Rescuers," if he were not fettered by the forms of law; which, as this volume is designed for "general circulation" we will not repeat. Some time in the

course of the ride, Mr. Lincoln inquired if his captor had a legal process to authorize the arrest, and was condescendingly shown a "*capias*" signed by Frederick W. Green, Esq., Clerk of the U. S. District and Circuit Court for the Northern District of Ohio.

The arrest was made at about half past one in the afternoon. After dark they entered the Capital. Mr. Lincoln asked permission to be taken to some one of his several influential friends in the city, before being thrust into jail, but the request was promptly and emphatically denied. Arrived at the prison they found Marshal Lowe in waiting, and to him Mr. Lincoln repeated his natural desire to send for friends, but only to be again as emphatically refused. He was later in the evening allowed to send a letter to the post-office, when it had become long past business hours, and it was ascertained that the first train for Cleveland left at four clock in the morning, but this letter never reached its destination.

Before being shown to his cell, in the presence of Mr. Lowe and the jailer, Mr. Lincoln asked that his irons might be removed, since no escape could longer be feared, and his wrists were severely galled. But his crime was not trifling enough to allow of favors, and he was so informed.

Introduced to his new quarters and his new associates, the irons were removed, and he was left alone, to sit up or lie down as he chose, a liberty of choice which of course would not have been allowed, had there been any convenient way of withholding it. It is said that supper was ordered for him, but it is certain that none reached him. Driving the rats out of his straw pallet, and stuffing his nostrils to keep out "a little" of the stench, he was at length so fortunate as to woo the caresses of Morpheus, but had scarcely succeeded before a messenger came to say that it was car time, and Mr. Lowe was in waiting. At the *depôt* the Marshal provided his prisoner as well as himself with a cup of coffee and a piece of pie, the taste of which Mr. Lincoln avers will long remain bright in his memory. Not to multiply details, let it suffice to say that the prisoner, by providing a livery for himself and the marshal, succeeded in finding Judge WILSON, who received his recognizance and released him at four o'clock in the afternoon.

He had now been fasting twenty-eight hours

(excepting the morning lunch), with scarcely any rest, and subject, meanwhile, to such mental excitement as the occurrences above named would naturally induce, and found himself at liberty, thirty-three miles from a solitary acquaintance, with twenty cents in his pocket, and the Sabbath close upon him. Consider that his health is not strong, and a tolerably fair idea of the success of the Administration may be formed. Mr. Lowe on being appealed to, relented so far as to lend him a dollar, which brought him to Oberlin; whence friends returned him to his school.

Shortly previous to the first of March, Richard Winsor, indicted as Robert Windsor,* who was absent from town at the time of the first arrests, and had not been sought for since, presented himself before the Court at Cleveland, and asked to have the orthography of his name corrected, and to be bound over for trial; which was accordingly done.

* There are numerous errors in the orthography of the names, though not many of them so serious as this: the compiler follows the Clerk of the Court in this chapter.

Robert L. Cummings was arrested in Cleveland on the 5th of May following. The remaining six are still at large. These are : —

John Hartwell,   James H. Bartlett,
Jeremiah Fox,   Thomas Gena,
John Copeland,   Franklin Lewis.

About two weeks before the day set for the trials, which, as the reader may remember, was the 8th of March, the United States District-Attorney applied to the counsel for the defence for a further extension of the adjournment, pleading private professional engagements of importance. His request was granted, and the cases put over to Tuesday, the 5th day of April, 1859. It was agreed that the case of SIMEON BUSHNELL should be first taken up, and that the others should come on in the order of the docket, unless by mutual consent. At the request of the counsel for the defence the Court had granted Mr. Bushnell a "struck" jury, which is a panel of forty, from which each party strike twelve peremptorily, and the first twelve of the remainder drawn by the clerk are sworn in.

CHAPTER SECOND.

TUESDAY, APRIL 5, 1859. On the coming in of Court, at 10 o'clock in the forenoon, the case of SIMEON BUSHNELL was called, and the defendant responded in person and by counsel. In addition to the three gentlemen who had volunteered their legal services for the defence on the first appearance of the defendants, Mr. F. T. BACKUS now came forward in the same behalf. The District-Attorney associated with himself Hon. GEO. BLISS.

Before the organization of the jury, the District-Attorney informed the Court that he should need a writ of *Habeas corpus ad Testificandum* in behalf of Jacob K. Lowe, a material witness for the government, who, as he was informed, had been arrested at Grafton, the evening previous, on his way from Columbus to Cleveland, by Richard Whitney, a deputy-sheriff of Lorain county, under and by virtue of a warrant issued by the Lorain County Court of Common Pleas, on an indictment for *kidnapping*, which was found by the Grand Jury of that county at its last session, — and was now confined in Lorain county jail, at Elyria.

While the Court had the matter under advisement, however, Mr. Lowe made his appearance, having been discharged at an early hour on the bond of Mayor Sampsel [of Elyria], which was given as security in the sum of one thousand dollars for the defendant's appearance for trial on the 17th day of May following.

Twenty of the thirty indicted who had been arrested, were present at the bar of the Court, and being neither called on to renew their recognizances nor taken into custody, continued their regular attendance at Court, until ordered to jail, as we shall see by and by. Their counsel advised them that they were considered by the Court as continuing their recognizances until voluntarily surrendering them. Of the twenty thus in attendance, sixteen were from

Oberlin, and four from Wellington. Their names will be found in the next chapter.

THE TRIAL OF BUSHNELL. — *First Day.*

United States District Court, Northern District of Ohio. } WILLSON, Judge.

The United States
vs.
Simeon Bushnell. } Indictment for rescuing a fugitive from service.

GEO. W. BELDEN,
U. S. Dist. Att'y,
GEO. BLISS, } For the Government.

RUFUS P. SPALDING,
FRANKLIN T. BACKUS,
ALBERT G. RIDDLE,
SENECA O. GRISWOLD, } For the Defence.

Of the sixteen struck jurors, twelve answered to their names, as follows : —

GEORGE KNUPP, Tiffin.
JAMES G. HALEY, Napoleon.
SABERT SCOTT, St. Mary's.
EDWARD FOSTER, Bryan.
DANIEL P. RHODES, Cleveland.
ANDREW LUGENBEEL, Tiffin.
GEORGE W. SLINGLUFF, Canal, Dover.
JAMES JUSTICE, Tremont.
CHARLES N. ALLEN, Cadiz.
JOHN CASSELL, Marysville.
GEORGE HARPER, Upper Sandusky.
ANDREW SCOTT, Newton Falls.

It is but just to all concerned to remark, that although all parties connected with the prosecution were notoriously of one political faith, and all parties prosecuted of another, the Clerk of the Court, who had the making of the jury entirely in his own hands, summoning without restriction whom he chose, was able to find only ten men out of the forty who sympathized politically with the defendants, while he found thirty who sympathized with the Court. The ten were immediately "stricken" off by the District-Attorney, and the defence allowed their " choice " of the remaining thirty.

A series of similar acts, forming an unbroken chain from the beginning to the time of present writing, has doubtless induced the appellation somewhat widely used in the public prints of " The Political Trials at Cleveland."

Judge SPALDING, by permission of the Court, stated to the jury the nature of the case about to be tried, and then inquired of each juror, whether he had, in his own mind, formed any opinion of the guilt or innocence of the accused ; to which each responded for himself in the negative.

The DISTRICT-ATTORNEY requested the Clerk to call the names of the witnesses for the prosecution, which being done, and twenty-nine failing to respond, he asked an adjournment until afternoon.

Judge SPALDING asked that the jury might be sworn first. The trials were likely to be lengthy enough at best, and it was to be hoped that no time should be lost. He wished, also, and thought it only a matter of common prudence, that the jury should be put upon their oaths before going out to mingle with the community at large, where they would be constantly hearing the merits of the case discussed.

The DISTRICT-ATTORNEY thought an admonition from the Court would be sufficient safeguard, and answer every purpose, in which

The COURT concurred, and charged the jury to avoid all conversation among themselves upon the case they were about to try (as they would, of course, with other persons), and if any approaches were made to them, they would give immediate notice thereof to the Court.

And thereupon a recess until 2 o'clock was declared.

FIRST DAY — AFTERNOON SESSION.

Court convened at 2 o'clock.

Jury called.

Names of witnesses for the prosecution called. Thirteen failed to respond.

The COURT asked if the defence were ready to proceed.

Mr. RIDDLE asked leave to withdraw temporarily the plea of Not Guilty, in order to enter a motion to quash ; which being granted, the plea of Not Guilty was withdrawn, a motion to quash filed subject to future call and argument, and the plea of Not Guilty then resumed for the purposes of the trial.

Jury sworn.

Such of the witnesses for the prosecution as were present were then called, and, after being sworn, dismissed to the Grand-Jury Room, with an order from the Court not to enter the Court Room during the giving of testimony, until sent for.

The DISTRICT-ATTORNEY then stated the case to the jury as he expected to prove it, by reading to them the indictment, which runs as follows : —

United States of America
Northern District of Ohio } ss.

{ In the District Court of the United States, for the Northern District of Ohio, of the November term, A. D. 1858.

The Grand Jurors of the United States of America, empanelled, sworn and charged to inquire of crimes and offences within and for the body of the Northern District of Ohio, upon their oath, present and find, that, heretofore, to wit, on the first day of March, in the year of our Lord one thousand eight hundred and fifty-seven, a certain negro slave called John, a person held to service and labor in the State of Kentucky, one of the United States, the said John being the property of one John G. Bacon, of the said State of Kentucky, the person to whom such service and labor were then due, and the said negro slave called John, to wit, on the day and year last aforesaid, so being held to service and labor as aforesaid, and said service and labor being due as aforesaid, did escape into another of the United States, to wit, into the State of Ohio from the said State of Kentucky: — that afterwards, to wit, on the first day of October, in the year of our Lord one thousand eight hundred and fifty-eight, one Anderson Jennings, the agent and attorney of the said John G. Bacon, duly authorized for that purpose by power of attorney in writing, executed by the said John G. Bacon, to wit, on the fourth day of September, A. D. 1858, and acknowledged before him on said day, before Robert A. Cochran, Clerk of the County Court of the county of Mason, in said State of Kentucky, and on said day certified by said Robert A. Cochran, clerk as aforesaid, under the seal of said Mason County court, the said Robert A. Cochran then being a legal officer, and the said Mason County court then being a legal court — in the said State of Kentucky, in which said State said power of attorney was executed— did pursue and reclaim the said negro slave called John, into and in the said State of Ohio, and did, to wit, on the said first day of October, in the year last aforesaid, in said Northern District of Ohio, and within the jurisdiction of this Court pursue and reclaim the said negro slave called John, he then and there being a fugitive person as aforesaid, and still held to service and labor as aforesaid, by then and there on the day and year last aforesaid, and at the District aforesaid, and within the jurisdiction of this Court, seizing and arresting him as a fugitive person from service and labor, from the said State of Kentucky as aforesaid: — and that the said negro slave called John, was then and there, to wit, on the day and year last aforesaid, in the State of Ohio, at the District aforesaid, and within the jurisdiction of this Court, lawfully, pursuant to the authority of the statute of the United States, given and declared in such case made and provided, arrested, in the custody and under the control of the said Anderson Jennings, as agent and attorney aforesaid, of the said John G. Bacon, to whom the service and labor as aforesaid, of the said negro slave called John, were then and still due as aforesaid, — together with one Jacob K. Lowe, then and there lawfully assisting him, the said Anderson Jennings, in the aforesaid arrest, custody, and control of the said negro slave called John.

And the jurors aforesaid do further present and find that Simeon Bushnell, late of the District aforesaid, together with divers, to wit, two hundred other persons, to the jurors aforesaid unknown, heretofore, to wit, on the first day of October, in the year of our Lord one thousand eight hundred and fifty-eight, at the District aforesaid, and within the jurisdiction of this Court, with force and arms, unlawfully, knowingly, and willingly, did rescue the said negro slave called John, then and there being pursued and reclaimed, seized and arrested, and in the custody and control aforesaid, he, the said negro slave called John, being then and there a fugitive from, and held to service and labor as aforesaid, from the custody of the said Anderson Jennings, then and there the authorized agent of the said John G. Bacon as aforesaid, and the said Jacob K. Lowe then and there lawfully assisting the said Anderson Jennings, as aforesaid, he the said Simeon Bushnell then and there well knowing that the said negro slave called John, was then and there a fugitive person held to service and labor as aforesaid, and pursued and reclaimed, seized and arrested and held in custody as aforesaid: — to the great damage of the said John G. Bacon; contrary to the form of the Act of Congress in such case made and provided, and against the peace and dignity of the United States.

G. W. BELDEN, *U. S. Attorney.*

He informed them that this indictment was based exclusively on the Act of Congress approved Sept. 18, 1850, commonly known as the Fugitive Slave Law, which was passed as an amendment to the Act of Feb. 12, 1793.

He would read that portion of the Act of 1850 which authorizes the seizure of the fugitive from service with or without process.

"§ 6. And be it further enacted, That when a person held to service or labor in any State or Territory of the United States, the person or persons to whom such service or labor may be due, or his, her, or their agent or attorney, duly authorized by power of attorney in writing, acknowledged and certified under the seal of some legal officer or court of the State or Territory in which the same may be executed, may pursue and reclaim such fugitive person, either by procuring a warrant from some one of the courts, judges, or commissioners aforesaid, of the proper circuit, district or county, for the apprehension of such fugitive from service or labor, or by seizing and arresting such fugitive where the same can be done without process, and by taking or causing such person to be taken forthwith before such court, judge, or commissioner, whose duty it shall be to hear and determine the case of such claimant in a summary manner," etc.

The next section provides for the punishment of those who interfere with the arrest to prevent or violate it: —

"§ 7. And be it further enacted, That any

person who shall knowingly and willingly obstruct, hinder, or prevent such claimant, his agent or attorney, or any person or persons lawfully assisting him, her, or them, from arresting such a fugitive from service or labor, either with or without process as aforesaid, or shall rescue or attempt to rescue such fugitive from service or labor from the custody of such claimant, his or her agent or attorney, or other person or persons lawfully assisting as aforesaid, when so arrested pursuant to the authority herein given and declared, or shall aid, abet, or assist such person so owing service or labor as aforesaid, directly or indirectly to escape from such claimant, his agent or attorney, or other person or persons legally authorized as aforesaid, or shall harbor or conceal such fugitive, so as to prevent the discovery and arrest of such person, after notice or knowledge of the fact that such person was a fugitive from service or labor as aforesaid, shall, for either of said offences, be subject to a fine not exceeding one thousand dollars, and imprisonment not exceeding six months, by indictment and conviction before the District Court of the United States, for the district in which such offence may have been committed," etc.

He might also call attention to that clause in the Constitution of the United States, which clearly authorized the passage of this act.

Art. IV., Section 2. "No person held to service or labor in one State, under the laws thereof, escaping into another, shall, in consequence of any law or regulation therein, be discharged from such service or labor, but shall be delivered up on claim of the party to whom such service or labor may be due."

He said that he should show that this negro was rescued by the defendant and his associates, not only to the great detriment of the owner, and contrary to the wishes of the agent who made the arrest as authorized by this statute, but even against the earnest wishes of the *negro himself*, who expressed himself anxious to return to the service of his master. They should further show, on behalf of the Government, that this defendant, previous to going himself to Wellington, got up a great deal of excitement in the town of Oberlin; hitched up his own carriage, and exhorted others to do likewise; and when calling for volunteers to go to Wellington, rejected some, saying that he wanted *men*, not boys, as there would most likely be a fight. And that after the rescue he boasted of the success of the mob and of his share in its doings, and avowed his entire readiness to act a like part again on the first opportunity.

Judge SPALDING replied briefly in behalf of the defence, that they should contend that no such offence as that charged in the indictment could be perpetrated in the State of Ohio, so as to make the defendant liable to fine and imprisonment as a punishment therefor. The District-Attorney had fatally erred in not charging in his indictment, in compliance with the terms of Sect. 2, Art. IV. of the Constitution, that the negro John was held to service or labor in the State of Kentucky, "*under the laws thereof.*" The defence would therefore insist that by no law, human or divine, did the negro rescued owe service to any man living; that his arrest was kidnapping, procured by the use of the most scandalous and fraudulent deceit, and that, whether the defendant aided to rescue him or not, he was amenable to no criminal statute whatever.

The first witness called was

John G. Bacon. Reside in Kentucky, in Mason county. Have resided there four years. Was born and brought up in the State. Owned a negro boy named John from the Spring of 1847 to January 1856. Don't know who owns him now. He is still my property. Never parted with my interest in him. He is still mine, *bone and flesh.* He ran off from me in January, 1856; he and another slave named Frank, and a negro woman named Dinah, all ran off at the same time. They stole two horses from me to go off on. I finally got the horses again. Dinah was my —

Mr. BACKUS. No consequence about Dinah.

John went without my consent or direction. I executed a power of attorney to Anderson Jennings.

[The instrument referred to was here presented to the witness and identified by him. It runs as follows: —]

KNOW ALL MEN BY THESE PRESENTS, That we, Richard Loyd and John G. Bacon, of the county of Mason, and State of Kentucky, do hereby constitute and appoint Anderson Jennings of the county of Mason and State of Kentucky our attorney; for us and in our name and for our use, to capture and return to our service and possession in Kentucky, three negroes now at large in the State of Ohio:

Which negroes answer the following description, viz.: —

Frank, the property of Richard Loyd, is a large black negro, full six feet high, large pop eyes, rather thick tongued, about twenty-six years old. *John*, the property of John G. Bacon, is about twenty years old, about five feet six or eight inches high, heavy set, copper colored, and will weigh about 140 or 50 pounds. *Dinah*, the property of said Bacon, is a tall, slim negro woman, about twenty-one or two years old, dark copper color, very straight, holds high head, and very quick spoken.

Whatsoever our attorney shall lawfully do in the premises, we do hereby confirm the same, as if we were present and did the same in our own proper names.

IN WITNESS WHEREOF we have hereunto set our hands and seals, this 4th day of September, 1858.
                                    RICHARD LOYD,
                                    JOHN G. BACON.

State of Kentucky, ⎫ sct.
  Mason County, ⎰

I, Robert A. Cochran, Clerk of the County Court of the county aforesaid, do hereby certify that this power of attorney, from Richard Loyd and John G. Bacon to Anderson Jennings, was this day produced to me, and acknowledged by the said Richard Loyd and John G. Bacon to be their act and deed. The said parties are personally known to me, and the said acknowledgment is according to law.

Given under my hand and official seal, in the city of Maysville, this 4th day of September, 1858.   ROBERT A. COCHRAN, Clerk,
  by WILLIAM H. RICHARDSON, D. C.

Have never seen John since he left in January, 1856. John was born and raised on my father's farm in Mason county, Ky. He was eighteen years old, about five feet eight inches high, copper color, and heavy built. At the time of his escape he owed service to me, if to any one. Previous to his owing service to myself he owed service to my father and to his family. John's mother was a slave and is still; has been ever since I can remember. Have never relinquished my right to his service. [Objected to.]

Cross-examined. Father died in 1845 or 1846, leaving myself and five other children, who are all still living. Knew when John was born, because I was then on the farm and heard of the event within an hour after it happened. Was fifteen or sixteen years old at the time. Remember I was at home at the time; do not remember what time in the year it was. There were twenty or twenty-five other persons of both sexes on the place at the time, who were held as slaves. Others of them were born slaves, like John. Was gone from home to boarding school, more or less afterward. Do not remember how long I was at home after John's birth before I first went away to school. Was away two years or so in all. First went away something like a year or two after John's birth. Didn't recognize him from personal memory from time to time as I came home from abroad, but supposed him to be the same because he bore the same name, recognized the same mother, etc. The boy's mother was held by my father as a slave from my earliest recollection; that's all I know of my father's title to her. Also knew John's grandmother; she was held, too, as a slave. I was nineteen years old when my father died; never purchased the boy; claim him only by inheritance. Was not at home when John and Frank and Dinah went away. Was visiting my father-in-law about four miles distant. Had been gone two days. Left things in charge of an Irishman, who is still in my employ. He had no more general authority than any other hired hand. He and John had about equal authority. Neither could control the other. Own no slaves except John and Dinah. Never did own any others, and don't know as

I shall get any more. The Irishman's name is Peter. Left Dinah, John, and Peter when I went to father-in-law's. Locked up the house, taking all my family with me. They staid in their own cabins. They three were alone on the place when I left. Dinah is cousin to John. My place is about a quarter of a mile from the Ohio river. Ripley, in Brown county, is the nearest village on the opposite shore. I live about two miles above the Ripley ferry. Never heard of John's going over that ferry under any circumstances. Found the horses in Brown county, about twenty miles from home. The niggers had left them on purpose. The horses were all right when I found 'em; did n't seem to have been ill used in any way. John was in the habit of riding them. They were rather high-spirited. Don't know whether they ran off with him or he with them. Found the horses about a week after I missed John. I executed this power of attorney; signed it on the day of its date. Jennings was a neighbor of mine. At the date of this power of attorney he was in Ohio hunting a slave of his own. He wrote to me that he had discovered a nigger near Oberlin answering to the description of mine, and so I made him this power of attorney. He does n't follow the business of capturing niggers. Think John weighed about one hundred and fifty or one hundred and sixty pounds.

Mr. BACKUS: What was the arrangement between you and Mr. Jennings? what was you to give him if he got John back for you?

Judge BLISS objected, and argued his objection at length.

Mr. BACKUS urged the perfect propriety of the inquiry.

The COURT overruled the objection and directed the witness to answer the question.

Witness continued: If he brought him back, he was to have one half of what the nigger would sell for; I to sell him when and where I chose.

The DISTRICT-ATTORNEY filed the power of attorney as evidence, subject to the exceptions of the defence.

Robert A. Cochran, called. Reside in Maysville, Mason county, Ky. Have resided there fifteen years. On the 4th of September, 1858, was acting as clerk of the Mason County Court. Have been its clerk since 1851.

Judge SPALDING wished it understood that the testimony of this witness was received subject to exceptions.

The COURT assented.

Witness continued: This is not my signature. My name was written by a deputy. [These statements refer to the acknowledgment of the power of attorney.] The deputy was Wm. H. Richardson. The entire certificate of acknowledgment is in Richardson's handwriting. Am acquainted with John G. Bacon; have been for at least the last nine years. Do not know the negro John. Have no personal knowledge of this acknowledgment. Have no better evidence that it was ever made than the handwriting of my deputy. This is the seal of the Mason County Court.

[The counsel for the government here read the power of attorney and the certificate of acknowledgment.]

Anderson Jennings, called. Reside in Mason County, Ky. Was born and raised within about four miles of John G. Bacon. Live now about five miles from him. Knew John two or three years before he ran away. Had seen him ten or fifteen times, perhaps, in all. Bacon owned him. I mean he owned him as we'd own any property. Didn't see him run away. Don't know as he did run away. Heard he did. First went to Bacon's without seeing him several months after it was said that he had run away. Have seen him since then. Saw him at Wellington, in this State, on the 13th of September, 1858.

The DISTRICT-ATTORNEY: Did he recognize you?

Mr. BACKUS objected earnestly that the acts of this piece of property, this chattel, this *thing,* were nothing to charge the defendant by, unless he, the defendant, were a party to them. The recognition of his master's agent by this chattel, was no more than the recognition a dog might make by the wagging of his tail. It was absurd in the Government to attempt to charge the defendant by such frivolous and incompetent testimony as was sought to be introduced here.

DISTRICT-ATTORNEY: The question is one of identity. The question put to the witness is, Did he recognize you? I contend that, for the purpose of identifying this piece of property, if the gentleman prefers that title, it is competent to prove that the negro boy came up to the witness, shook hands with him, and expressed his desire to go back to his master, naming Bacon as his master.

The COURT sustained the objection, and ruled out the evidence.

The DISTRICT-ATTORNEY to the witness: Well, did you recognize him as the boy John, whom you had known in Kentucky, as the property of John G. Bacon?

Witness: I did. I had a power of attorney from John G. Bacon, authorizing me to arrest him. [Taking the paper offered him.] This is the one given me. Had this in my possession when I met John at Wellington. We meant to take him to Columbus. I met him first at Wellington, at Wadsworth's hotel. This was the first time I had seen him since I saw him in Kentucky before he was missing in January, 1856. Met him first in a room below stairs. Didn't like the looks of the room, because it was large, and there was folding doors, and there was no fastening to the door, and the people began to gather in with their guns. Found the landlord, and got him to give us a better room up stairs, in the top story. Lowe, Mitchell, and Davis were helping me, and went up stairs with us. Meant to take the nigger before United States Commissioner Chittenden, at Columbus. Did n't take him there, however. [Laughter.] Don't know the defendant. There was, I thought, as much as a thousand people around and in the house. [Great laughter.] A great many of them had arms; — rifles, shot-guns, etc. Should think there were five hundred guns in the crowd. [Renewed laughter.] First met John about two or three o'clock in the afternoon. The people began gathering in pretty soon after, and hung about till purty near dark. Took John up stairs purty soon after I first met him. Was up there with him some three hours. .Several got into the room up stairs. They brought in a sheriff, and tried to arrest us. They asked the negro if he was a slave, and whether he wanted to go back; to both of which questions he answered, Yes. He said he was the slave of John G. Bacon. The nigger and myself went out on to the platform to tell the crowd that he was a slave, and wanted to go back; but there was two or three rifles pointed at him, and it *skeert* the nigger so't he went back into the house. Purty soon after that the crowd broke in the window of the third story. I had fastened the door with a rope, and held on as well as I could. Purty soon they come up the stairway, and begun to pry at the door. Then the next I know'd I got a punch on the side o' my head, which went through my hat, and knocked me over. [Wounded hat exhibited.] It stunned me a good deal. They punched through a stove-pipe hole that was made through the partition, betwixt the little room at the head of the stairs, and the room't we was in. It was made through close by the door, and was right agin my head, as I stood a-holdin' the door. So I let go the rope when I was knocked down, and they come in and took the nigger out. The next I see of the nigger he was a paddlin' down stairs over the heads of the crowd, as it seemed to me. Then I went to the window, and saw 'em puttin' him into a wagon that stood in the middle of the square, in front of the house. After they got him in, the wagon was drove off towards Oberlin. They brought a man up they said was a lawyer, and we showed him the power of attorney, and all our papers, and fifteen or twenty others looked at 'em. We invited 'em to go to Columbus with us, and see that the nigger hed a fair trial, and promised 'em that if we didn't prove all we claimed, we'd let them fetch him back.

They said that was a little too fur south [Laughter]; they didn't like to trust it. I myself also told 'em that the nigger was a slave of Bacon. Have never seen John since. He went off at purty good speed. [Laughter.] Don't think I heard the name of the man that was in the wagon with him. Can identify only one man that was in the crowd, and he is a yaller man they call Watson. I see him sittin' over yonder now. Think there were fifteen or twenty niggers in the crowd, in all. The crowd come into the room and seized hold of the nigger, and with pullin' and pushin' took him out. They was all 'round him. He did n't go out of himself.

Cross-examined. Think Bacon has been living where he now does some ten or fifteen years. Am older than Bacon. Have known him fifteen or twenty years. Did n't go abroad to school with him; but know that he did go away to school somewhere; don't know where. Knew the niggers in my neighborhood better when I was young than I do now. Know Bacon's niggers. Bacon never owned more than two niggers that I knew of. One of these was John, and the other was a nigger woman they called — called — lemmesee, I can't think of her name now, but it seems to me I've heerd it.

Mr. BACKUS. Oh yes, you know all about *her;* her name was Dinah, wa'nt it? [Laughter.]

Witness: Well, I dunno; but I should rather think it was. I saw John hauling sand about a year before he put off. Saw him haul one load. His marster was buildin' a house then, and they wanted the sand for that. Had seen him several times before. Think he would weigh 165 or 170. He was twenty-one or twenty-two years old. Knew him well enough to recognize him at sight. Never made any arrangement with Bacon about pay for ketchin' the nigger. Never made no bargain with him about pay no-ways. Never heerd nothin' said about my havin' one half what the nigger would sell for. I set down at Oberlin and wrote to him that the nigger was there, and if he'd send me a power of attorney and a witness I would try and bring him back. Did this out of pure neighborly regard. Thought it was my duty to. Never tried nigger-catching before. Never asked nor was offered any pecuniary reward whatever. There was nothing passed between us about reward at any time, either by letter, by word, or by third parties. What I did I did all out of pure neighborly regard. Went to Oberlin after a nigger of my own. I wrote the letter a day or two after I got to Oberlin, and directed it to Mr. Reynolds, and directed him to send it out to Mr. Bacon. He sent Mr. Mitchell at once with the power of attorney. I met Mitchell first at Sandusky. I started from Sandusky to go home, and reached home, and saw Mr. Bacon. He told me that he had sent Mitchell, and that Mitchell had just started, and must have passed me on the river. So I started back and overtook Mitchell at Oberlin. Arrived at Oberlin on the Friday immediately preceding the Monday of the Rescue, which was the 13th of September; so the Friday must have been the — the — the — 10th. Found Mitchell, and asked him if he had seen the nigger. He said he had. Put up at Wack's tavern, and found Mitchell there. So the next morning I took the cars for Columbus, and found Lowe out of the city on the Fair Ground.

He went into the city with me, and found Mr. Chittenden. Mr. Chittenden give us a warrant. Lowe and I then come back to Oberlin. Got there about ten or eleven o'clock at night.

Mr. BACKUS: What day was this?

Witness: This was Friday.

Mr. BACKUS: But you went away on *Saturday;* it seems to me you must have made pretty good time! [Laughter.]

Witness: No; I was mistaken. Friday night was the night I got back from Columbus. I must have got back from Kentucky before that. Saturday all day did n't do much of any thing. Saturday night we went — me and Lowe — to Gen. Boynton's. There we made an arrangement with the General's little boy to come and get the nigger out of town, away from his house. The General was n't in the room when we made the bargain with the boy, but I told him what I wanted the boy for, and he made no objections. After I had made the arrangements with the boy I told him of it agin, and he said me and the boy must make our own arrangements; they was nothin' to him; the boy was capable of lookin' out for himself.

Mr. BACKUS: How did you come to go to Boynton's?

Witness: Wal, we was told that it would be dangerous to undertake to arrest the nigger in that town; so I went to old Mr. Warren, and asked him if he knowed of any one a man could put confidence in [great laughter], and he told me I could trust Boynton.

Mr. BACKUS: Who told you that there was danger?

Witness: I heard a good many talking about it; Mr. Warren for one.

Mr. BACKUS: So you heard Mr. Warren say there was danger, and so went to him for counsel. Well, what was the arrangement between you and the boy Boynton?

Witness: I engaged the boy to go and hire the nigger to come and dig potatoes on his father's farm, and if he brought the nigger I was to give him $20.

Mr. BACKUS: Well, then, you told the old man what you had promised the boy?

Witness: No, I did n't tell him any thing about it.

Mr. BACKUS: What, sir! do you remember what you told me within the last fifteen minutes?

Witness: Wal, I only told him I had got the boy to come down, I did n't tell him what for, and he said me and the boy must fix it up between us, he had nothin' to do with the boy's doins. I never made the old man Boynton any offer for his help. He knowed what I was goin' to use his boy for, for I told him myself before I said any thing to the boy. Then me and Lowe went back to Oberlin. This was Sunday, towards night. The boy was to come down on Monday morning, and see if he could hire the nigger to dig the potatoes, and after he had seen the nigger he was to come and tell us whether the nigger would go or not. So the next mornin' he come and told us that the nigger said he could n't go, for Frank had got cut, and he must stay and take care of him, — I wanted to get Frank too — but that there was a nigger down at New Oberlin that he thought would go and dig the potatoes, and he would go with Shakespeare and help him find that nigger. So we told Shakespeare that would do, and he went back with his buggy and took John in, and in about fifteen minutes Mr. Lowe, and Mr. Mitchell, and Mr. Davis started on after him, I staid at Wack's till Shakespeare come and told me that they'd got him.

Mr. BACKUS: Did Shakespeare tell you how they took him?

Witness: Yes; he said about a mile and a half or two miles out of town they overtook him, and drove alongside of his buggy, and then they took the nigger out of his buggy and put him into theirn, and drove off with him.

Mr. BACKUS: Did you give him the $20?

Witness: Yes, sir; I gin him the $20, and got my dinner, and started for Wellington. I hired Mr. Wack's buggy, and he sent a boy down with me to bring the buggy back. I started about one o'clock. Don't know whose horse and buggy Shakespeare had; supposed it was his daddy's. Paid the boy in good money; don't remember what sized bills. Saw no fire-arms along the road. Had two pistols in my pocket.

Court adjourned till next morning at 9 o'clock.

SECOND DAY. — 9 A. M.

Anderson Jennings. Cross-examination continued. Have had no conversation with Bacon since adjournment of Court yesterday. He told me in our conversation before I came after Mitchell, that he had said he would give $500, or one half the value of the nigger to any one that would catch him and bring him back. Never saw the nigger after he run off till I saw him at Wellington. Had two pistols with me. [Witness showed one of them, a five-shooter, and said the other was precisely like it.] Had no other weapons. Had two pairs of handcuffs. [The Court ruled out the evidence with respect to handcuffs.] Never informed any one at Oberlin of my business except under injunction of secrecy. Stopped nowhere between Oberlin and Wellington. Stopped at Wadsworth's hotel in Wellington. Found a good many people there. Did n't know any of them. Found Lowe, Davis, and the boy John in the hotel. Found them in a room on the first or second floor. Found where to go by the people crowding up the steps around the door. Fifty or sixty persons were about. Did n't see the defendant. The hall below stairs, and hall above were full with them. Had hard work to get up stairs. Not sure whether I found John on the first or second floor, but think it was the second. Don't know whether the stairs landed in a hall or in a room, but had to pass through a door after reaching the top of the stairs. Spoke to them that were inside, and they let me in. Had no occasion to show weapons going up. Said nothing to the people in the halls or on the stairs. Saw the people crowding in with guns, asking for *the men that had John*, and did n't stop to talk long! [Laughter.] Crowd made no opposition to my going up. The room in which John was had no good fastening, so I asked the boys [Lowe, Davis, and Mitchell] if we could n't get a better room. Landlord soon came in and I asked him. So he showed us up stairs. Crowd made no resistance or demonstration of any kind as we passed through the hall. Landlord led the way. Think I was next; all went out together. As many as two could go up the second stairs abreast. Am not positive whether I found John on the first or second floor. At the top of this second flight of stairs, the landlord showed us a safer room. Went in. Took my stand at the door. Landlord left without going into the room. Lowe, Davis, Mitchell, John, and self staid. Staid till about dusk. It was a front room. Recollect only one window. The window looked out upon the public square. Heard nothing from the crowd below distinctly enough to make out words. Some men came pretty soon and asked us to let them in. First along I let in every one that wanted to come in. The first that wanted to come in, come within fifteen minutes after we got in. They come in about two or three to a time. Would come and rap and ask if they might come in. I would ask 'em how many there was, and they would say, "two," or "three," or "four," as it happened to be, and then I would let them in. Did n't see defendant there. Did n't see him at all during the day. The sheriff come and wanted us to show our authority for taking that boy. We showed him our papers. He staid some time and talked about arresting us. This was about an hour after I got there. Sheriff passed out and in several times. He went away the last time within an hour of the time he first came. After the sheriff he come in and talked so about arresting us, concluded I would n't let in no more, 'cept such as had a right to come in. But there was three or four staid in the room all the time. One of the men inside was purty reckless, and hollered out to the crowd that they was d——d cowards and fools. I asked 'em why they did n't come up and take the man out. We told him to hush, but said nothing to the crowd outside; either to those below in the square, or to those in the hall. Those in the square could not have heard what I said, but those in the hall were perfectly still when any of us was talking inside, and might have heard. The punch against my head through the stove-pipe hole was about half an hour before John was taken out. This "lick" did n't knock me down, but would, if I had n't been braced. It broke the skin and made the blood run. Did n't let go the door till they broke in the window. They come into the window with a ladder. They got from the ladder on to the platform, and clumb from the platform into the window. Good many got in through the window; don't know how many; ten or fifteen piled in at least. Others come in at the door. After I see 'em come in at the window, I let go o' the door, was perfectly cool; know all that was done. They seized hold of nobody but John. Seized him and took him out. I made no demonstration to fight at all. They crowded all around John and moved toward the door. Think there were no persons of his color in the crowd that surrounded him. Did n't see anybody take hold of him, but they all surrounded him and moved along towards the door with him. Staid fifteen or twenty minutes after John had gone. Saw John but once after he was taken out, and that was just as they were landing him into the wagon. Was looking out of the window. See a right smart little bunch of men with John, and they took him and put him in the wagon. Saw him just as he got cleverly off the hotel steps below, and saw the crowd follow him and put him into the wagon. Saw him first when he had got within five or six feet of the wagon, and while he was being put into it. The wagon stood about in the centre of the square, and I saw him first when he was about half way from the house to the wagon. It might have been five or six yards from the house to the wagon. Could just see John's head. There was such a crowd about him that I could n't tell whether he was walking or the crowd carried him. He was put into the wagon. Several took hold of him. Could see plainly from where I stood. Cannot say whether he resisted the attempts to put him in or not. Very soon after he was put into the wagon, they put on the switch and run him off. Have never seen him since. Have never seen the wagon since. Cannot tell whether it was three years more or less before he ran off that I saw him hauling sand.

Direct examination resumed. John was a full blooded negro, not a drop of white blood in him. Recognized John when I found him in the room, to be the same boy I had known in Kentucky. There was no arrangement between me and Bacon about compensating me for fetching the nigger back. Did what I did towards it, and meant to do the whole, out of pure neighborly kindness. Thought it was my duty. Went direct from home to Oberlin the first time in pursuit of a nigger belonging to my uncle's estate, of which I was administrator; staid about a day and a half in Oberlin, wrote to Bacon, and went to Sandusky. From Sandusky went home, passing Mitchell on the Ohio river without knowing it at the time. Found Bacon, and he told me that Mitchell had just started with the power of attorney. I did not know at the time that Bacon had offered any kind of reward for his nigger, but in the course of the conversation he told me that he had said he would give five hundred dollars, or half the value of the nigger, to any one that would fetch him back. I tried to get him to go, but he said he could not, and so finally I told him that since I had caused him to send the power of attorney, I would go and use it if I could; but nothing was said by either of us about any reward to be given to me. Think the wagon was ten or fifteen yards from the hotel; don't know certain. It stood about in the centre of the square. Do n't know how large the square was.

Cross-examination resumed. We have different names for different colored niggers at the South. Some we call black, some yellow, and some copper-colored. Yellow is part white and part black blood, usually about half-and-half. Copper color is between black and light mulatto. Black is black — pure African. Some would call John copper color, but I should call him black. Have seen blacker niggers than him. Never saw a slave so white it was hard to tell him from a white person. Never saw, as I can remember now, but one that looked to me to be more than half white, and that was a free woman that come from Ohio. Saw some of these real white ones at Oberlin.

Seth W. Bartholomew called. Reside in Oberlin. Resided there in September, 1858. Was not at Wellington on the 13th. Recollects the occurrence. Saw the party start from Oberlin to go to Wellington. They left about four o'clock in the afternoon. The first went about four o'clock; and the rest kept stringing along afterwards. First saw the defendant coming out of Fitch's bookstore. Defendant is the man witness saw. Defendant inquired of some men on the street steps if "they had got John?" They said "they had." He (defendant) asked what had best be done. The men he asked were Professor Peck, Ralph Plumb, and James M. Fitch. One of them — can't remember which — told defendant to go out and get 'em ready, and they would come round and tell him. These were the words. Do n't know what was meant. Defendant started and went to the crowd. Crowd was sixty or eighty feet off. Next saw defendant coming up to a buggy with two men in it; one of them had a gun. Only two or three minutes intervened between the time he left the store steps and his coming up to the buggy. Do n't know who the men in the buggy were; think they were students. Defendant said to the one without a gun that he had no business in there, and wanted him to get out. That's about all witness heard defendant say. Don't think the man addressed got out. Saw defendant get into George Stevens's buggy a few minutes after, perhaps ten minutes. Quite a number had already gone. Heard defendant say nothing farther. Oliver S. B. Wall was in the buggy with defendant. They drove south toward Wellington. Wall had a gun. Wall's color is what I should call "mixed." Did n't see defendant have any. Never heard defendant make any statement afterward with reference to where he had been, or what was done at Wellington. This is all witness knows about defendant's part in the crowd. It was Stevens's horse as well as buggy. Did n't see the horse afterward. Don't know where the horse and buggy went to. Defendant was noisy in the crowd before he went away, but witness can't tell what he said. Have no idea what he said. Defendant went away about half an hour after the first of the party started. The conversation in the crowd was about getting off as soon as they could to rescue John. They reckoned Lowe would take him to Wellington, and catch the five o'clock train for Columbus. So they was in a great hurry. I met John. I met John and the officers on the road, and told of it, so a good many come to me to ask about it. I told 'em they 'd have to be quick if they overtook him. All the crowd were active. Defendant was active with the rest. The crowd was all over the street. They went off in buggies, wagons, hay-racks, wood-racks, etc. Could not state how many had arms. Saw guns sticking up all 'round.

Recess till 2, P. M.

SECOND DAY. — 2 P.M.

Seth W. Bartholomew, cross-examined. Have resided in Oberlin twenty-five years. Am twenty-six years old. Was in the show business (panorama) in Sept. 1858. Saw Jennings twice the day of the Rescue. First, in the morning, in front of Wack's tavern, and in the afternoon about two miles south of Oberlin, going towards Wellington, in Wack's buggy, with Wack's boy along. Witness had been to Pittsfield to post bills of his show, and met Jennings on his return. Also met the negro John. He was on the back seat of a carriage, three white men being in the carriage with him. Davis was one of them. Do not know the others. They were on the diagonal road from Elyria to Columbus, about two miles south of Oberlin. The first men I told about John, were Peck, Plumb, and Fitch. Had no conversation with any of the persons who were in the carriage. The carriage they were in was not an Oberlin carriage. Don't know where it belonged. Lyman was with me coming from Pittsfield, but did n't see John. Don't know that Lyman told any one before I told Peck, Plumb, and Fitch. One of them said — they were standing in the road a little north-east of Carpenter's store — that they had better go up to John's house and see whether he was gone. I told 'em they need n't be to that trouble, for I had met John on the road, headed towards Wellington. Followed these three men as far

as Fitch's store for the purpose of telling them more. Defendant came out of the store. They stood on the door-sill, and I stood on the sidewalk. Don't know that any one else was near. Defendant spoke first and asked if they 'd got him. One of them told him they had. [Witness repeated what followed precisely as on the direct examination.] Watson's buggy left for Wellington first of all. Was not surprised to find a crowd on my return to Oberlin, because it had been threatened that if any man was taken off he would be followed and brought back. When I first reached Oberlin, returning from Pittsfield, no crowd was gathered. Put out my horse without speaking to any one, and coming into the street some fifteen minutes after, found a crowd of twenty or thirty persons. Then spoke to Peck, Plumb, and Fitch, as before stated. Don't know what became of Lyman after he got out at his house in the lower part of the village. Told Lyman, coming up, that if he would n't say any thing about it till next day, I would n't, for John was a *poor louzy pup*, and I wished they would take him off. Lyman agreed to this.[*] I made the proposition to keep still. I once stole half a cheese to keep from starving, and was put through for it.

Direct resumed. It was Ansel Lyman.

Artemas S. Halbert, called. Resided in Oberlin in Sept. of last year. Also before and since. Was at Oberlin on the 13th of Sept. Left about 3 o'clock. Saw the people assemble at Oberlin. Think they began to assemble about 2 o'clock. Should think three hundred or more had gone before I went. I should rather say that three hundred or more had gathered, but probably not so many as three hundred went. Most who went at all went before I did. Saw defendant a few minutes before I left; he was talking with another man about going to Wellington. Defendant said something about getting a horse to go to Wellington; but did n't state on what business he was going. The man he was talking with was Mr. O. S. B. Wall. One of them, witness cannot say which, said they ought not to go without a gun, and the other, who witness thinks was defendant, said he knew where he could get a gun. Witness then went down street and was invited to go to Wellington, and accordingly went. Don't know what became of defendant. Witness went in a buggy. Just outside the village, defendant and Wall sitting together in a buggy, overtook and passed witness, and kept just ahead, most of the time in sight, all the way to Wellington. It was Harvey Whitney who asked witness to ride, and with whom witness did ride. It is nine miles to Wellington. We went in three quarters of an hour. Saw defendant after we got there. Found a crowd of five hundred, I should think, in front of

---

[*] Mr. LYMAN immediately published a card in the Cleveland *Herald*, flatly denying this story.

Wadsworth's hotel. Defendant was in this crowd. Crowd were talking about getting out a warrant to arrest some men that had a fugitive slave there, and defendant said that that would be the best way to do it, or something to that effect. He seemed to be pretty cool; cooler than the rest, and yet somewhat excited. Saw no arms in defendant's possession. Crowd talked about getting the fugitive out in some way or other; and did n't talk about much else. Saw some persons go into the house, and among them Ansel Lyman, Wilson Evans, Messrs. Lincoln, Winsor, Scott, and Lairie. Don't know as I remember any others. I was standing in the street in front of the hotel, with the crowd all 'round me. A good many went in. Some came out on to the porch of the second story, and made some report. They said if more men would come up they could get the man out. Did n't say who they meant by "the man." Heard defendant say nothing at this time. Don't know where he was. The information brought out to the crowd was —— [the opposite counsel submitted that the information brought out to the crowd was irrelevant, unless it was positively shown that this information reached the defendant. The Court overruled the objection. Exception was taken to the ruling]. Heard Patton say as he came out, that he had seen and examined the papers in the house, and that they were good. Then there was a sort of general discussion through the whole of the crowd about the papers, some thinking they were right, and others doubting it. Was there when the negro was brought down. Think it was about an hour after they began discussing the papers. Meantime, some said, " let 's go up and bring him down ; " others said, " he *must* come out of there." Could not tell who was most active in such talk and movements ; all were pretty much excited. Should think the crowd had two hundred or three hundred pieces of firearms, such as guns, pistols, etc. Don't know that I heard any threats. Heard nothing from defendant except what I have already stated. When they came out with the negro, I was in front of the hotel, near to it. Had been all about through the crowd before this. When the negro was brought down, defendant was sitting in a buggy near me. A horse was attached to the buggy.

Well, what was done with the *nigger ?*

He was put into the wagon in which defendant was sitting. There was quite a crowd between me and the wagon, and it was a little dusk. He seemed to be thrown in, or something like it, for his heels were higher than his head. The horse started towards Oberlin, somebody cracking the whip and driving.— Think defendant drove, but am not sure. There was another person in the buggy whom I did not know. Some time before the negro was brought down, some one asked defendant if that was the buggy which was to carry the nigger off, and he said, " it was," or, " he

s'posed it was." Heard defendant say nothing more about the buggy afterward. Have not seen John since. Think I have heard defendant say nothing about the Rescue since. Do not know who went up stairs inside, not going into the house at all myself. Did not see the negro come out on the piazza. The wagon stood, I should think, from eight to twelve rods from the house. Saw some go in by the second story windows from the second story piazza. Cannot tell how many.

Cross-Examined. Have lived in Oberlin about three years. Am a painter by trade. Went from Cincinnatus, Cortland Co., N. Y., to Oberlin. Was eighteen last December. Never served any time at my trade. Was not at work in September last. First heard of the excitement about one o'clock. Heard the crowd say that there had been a fugitive taken away by some Southerners. The crowd in which I was consisted of two or three persons beside myself, in front of Mr. Watson's grocery. Ansel Lyman was one of them. Remember names of no others. None of them had guns. It was Lyman who said they had got the fugitive. This was not more than two hours after I saw him returning to town with Bartholomew. There was another crowd in front of Mayor Beecher's store, about three rods distant. Saw no guns in it — about twenty-five in this crowd. There were other groups pretty much all over the street. There were five or six persons in front of Scott's shop. Staid around the corners some three hours before going to Wellington. Crowd became much larger than first found it. Saw the first gun about the time the crowd was largest. Saw revolvers at Oberlin. Had one myself. Mine was broken. Don't know but all the others were. The crowd at Wellington talked as though they thought the Southerners had *kidnapped* the negro, contrary to all law, and they wanted to arrest them for the purpose of an investigation. The garret and its window were one story above the piazza of the second story, and there was no covering above this second story piazza. Lyman and Winsor and Lincoln went into the house from the second story piazza. Wilson Evans went in at the front door below. Cannot tell what time in the afternoon either of them went in. Lairie went in below or above, can't say which. John Scott went in at the door above. Saw no one go in at the attic window. Saw no breaking in of said window. Staid pretty much in front of the door from the time the men went up till the negro was brought down. Some of the crowd thought they had best have Lowe come down and show his papers, if he had any. Such were Henry Evans and Mr. Wall. Others thought they had better go and take him any way. Don't know any names of such persons. Think I could identify two or three by sight. One of these said, "Let's go and bring the nigger out any how." This was a mulatto. He stopped at

Oberlin some little time. Does n't stop there now. Saw him last some time last winter. Have n't at any time told any of the officers of this Court what I was going to swear to. They have gone it pretty blind in putting me on the stand. Have had no particular or extended conversation — nothing more than a few general words — with any of them about this case or trial. Can't say that I ever told any one, under any circumstances, what I was going to swear to. Can't say who asked defendant if that was the buggy the nigger was going off in. Don't think I saw the person speaking and did not recognize the voice. The language was substantially, "Is this the buggy he 's going off in?" Defendant said, "It is," or "I suppose it is." The buggy did n't stand in the middle of the square; it stood in front of the hotel toward the North. Think it was not the same buggy that defendant went down in. Don't know whose buggy it was. The man who went off with defendant and the negro was not the man who went down (from Oberlin) with defendant. Don't know but he was the owner of the buggy. Don't know who he was. Think the buggy was a covered one. The cover partly up and partly down.

Direct resumed. Saw a ladder put up. Could not say where it reached to. It rested on the edge of the portico. Saw several persons on the ladder. Think one or two went up by the ladder to the portico. Think not much of any-thing was done with the ladder. Saw no one go into the attic window from the ladder.

Cross resumed. Saw Addison Wood go up on it to the portico. Mr. Wood and Mr. Marks put up the ladder. [Two administration democrats.] Don't know Marks's first name. Is the only Marks I know; he lives in Oberlin and keeps a meat market.

Norris Addison Wood, called. Resided in Oberlin last September. Was there on the 13th. The crowd began gathering about 1 or 2 o'clock. Large crowd. Don't know how many. Don't know that I saw defendant in the crowd. Was at Wellington that day. Started 2 or 3 o'clock. Marks and Wack went with me. Found a crowd there. There must have been 500 or 600. A large crowd at any rate. Saw defendant there. Don't know that I saw him running around in the crowd or elsewhere. Think I saw him in the buggy in front of Wadsworth's tavern. Did see him. Think it was an hour or two after I arrived that I saw defendant in the buggy. Think that only one team from Oberlin got to Wellington before mine. Think I did n't see defendant before I saw him in the buggy. Saw him afterward out of the buggy going towards the house. Don't know what he was doing or saying. There was a great deal of excitement. Everybody was excited. Was excited myself. Don't know as defendant was any more excited than the rest of us. There were a good many guns. Don't know how many. Saw a colored man

point and snap a gun at a white man, neither of them known to me. Some of the crowd said, "They'd have the boy or pull the house down," "pull the roof off," "would n't leave one brick on another," etc. The Southerners came out on the portico, and one of them said that if any one there wanted to ask the boy whether he wanted to go back, they had the privilege. I spoke first, and immediately two or three others. The boy replied that they had the papers, and *he s'posed he'd have to go.* Don't know as he said any thing else. The crowd around me then appeared to be very thick, sir — *very* thick. Think it was the tallest man of the two Southerners that spoke to the crowd; the same one that I had seen at Wack's that morning. Think there were some started to go and examine the papers, but can't say where they went to. Heard talk about papers and an examination that had been made, but could n't tell who went in or who came out. I mean the papers which were being made out to arrest the Southerners. Don't know any thing about an examination of the papers belonging to the Southerners. Don't know that any such examination was attempted or made. Heard it said that there could be no arrest without sending to Elyria. It was not a great while after they had been out on the portico before they brought him down. Can't tell how long. There was a great deal of excitement and noise and confusion; did n't take much note of time. Did n't hardly know it was night when it was night. There was a man hollered out of the attic window every once in a while, telling the crowd to come up there and not be such d——d cowards. Don't know who he was. Some of the crowd hollered back that they would come up; others that they must open the door and let him out. It was a very noisy time; a great deal of excitement and confusion. Saw a ladder put up and taken down, and after a little there was another ladder put up. Some went up on the second ladder. Saw no one go in at the attic window. Was up on the porch and heard the cry that they had got him. Rushed at once into the hall to try to get a sight at him. Could only get one glimpse as he was going down the stairs. Next I saw of him he was in the buggy. Don't know whether there was or was not some one in the buggy before the nigger was put in. Saw defendant in the buggy with the nigger. Don't know whether any one else got in. Did n't see them drive off. Don't know which way they went or who drove. Have never seen John since. He was generally reputed to be a fugitive.

Was there any thing said in the crowd about the *Higher Law?*

Don't know, unless that was what they meant to send to Elyria about. [Uproarious laughter, in which even the Court itself heartily joined.]

Cross-examined. First I heard of the excitement I was going down from dinner to my (livery) stable, and met Gaston and Bartholomew. They stopped me and told me the Southerners had got a negro and gone off with him. *Did n't want I should say any thing about it.* Went farther down town and found Lyman in front of Watson's grocery, telling the story. Some doubted the truth of it. I looked around, and Bartholomew stood right behind me. He spoke and said it was so. There was some little crowd then, which kept growing larger all the time. There was a fire at Wellington Sunday night or Monday morning (the Monday of the alleged rescue) within eight or ten rods of the hotel (Wadsworth's), which was not yet extinguished in the afternoon, and there was something of a crowd around it, looking at the ruins when I first reached Wellington. Some were talking about the fire, and some about the negro. Went from the fire to the saloon, and got some cigars. A good many Oberlinites were now coming in. Do n't know who put up the first ladder. After this was taken down, Marks and I went across the street and found a couple of ladies, and asked them if we might take a ladder there was there. They said yes. It was a very heavy ladder, but did n't seem heavy then. Seemed light. We were excited a good deal. Everybody was. We took it across the street and set it up against the portico. Several persons helped us. I went up on the ladder. A man threatened to shoot me if I came up. He cocked his gun at me. Do n't know who he was. He did n't fire. Saw no one go in at attic window. Believe no one tried to go in there. A colored man near me told John, who was at the attic window, to jump down, and if they tried to hinder him, he would shoot.

Did you invite the negro to jump down? No, sir.

Did you *beckon* to him to jump down? [Witness instantly colored scarlet and dropped his face, making no reply. Counsel therefore withdrew the question.] Adjourned till 9 o'clock next morning.

THIRD DAY.— 9, A. M.

Jacob Wheeler, called. Reside in Rochester, Lorain county, sixteen miles from Oberlin; six or seven from Wellington. [Is Postmaster of the place.] Was not at Oberlin on the 13th of September. Was at Wellington at the time of the rescue of the negro, John. Got to Wellington a little after noon. Remained till the slave was rescued. Could not tell how many people were there. Were a good many. Might be 400. A good many had guns with them. Was around in the crowd some of the time. They said they were after a slave that had been taken from Oberlin. The main talk was to rescue the man and take him back at any rate, if they had to tear the house down. See a good many go into the room where the negro was. Went in myself. Also Barnabas Meacham,

a constable, and Walter Soules, Hines, Mandeville, John Wheeler, Conrad Wheeler and Edward Wheeler, all three my brothers. All these were white men. Esquire Bennett was in the room adjoining; am not sure whether he went into the room where the negro was. Esquire Bennett and others examined Lowe's papers. A gentleman named Patton, from Oberlin, was with them. I saw the power of attorney; think Meacham was present when I saw it. The papers were exhibited by Lowe. Sciples had the same chance to see them that the rest of us did. Can't say that Sciples and Soules saw the papers. They two came in together. Lowe called upon all in the room to assist him. I might have been in the room in all three hours. I went first into the attic room. Staid in that room three hours or so. Went down for the purpose of trying to still the crowd. Told the crowd that it was not the better way to take such a course; that there was no question but that they had a legal right to take him, that they had shown their papers, that Bennett and others had seen the papers, and any that still doubted could go up and see them. Lowe said he was willing to go before a magistrate in the Town Hall or anywhere else and have the papers examined, if he could go safely. I did n't tell the crowd this last. Lowe said this in the room or in the hall, in the presence of a good many people. Believe they said they had a warrant to arrest Lowe. After Lowe had gone out to show his papers, two white men came in and took hold of John, and took him to the door and tried to get him out. The door was fastened, and those near it would not let them take him out. Don't know the names of these two men, but should know their faces; at least, one of them. The papers were shown and examined in a little small room, adjoining the one in which the nigger was. Esquire Howk, Esquire Bennett, and Mr. Patton examined Mr. Lowe's papers. Think Patton went out more than once on to the balcony, and tried to *peacify* the crowd, and make 'em keep order. He told them there was no doubt but that they had a right to retain him according to law, as the law was. If they done any thing, they would hev to take legal steps. Langston, of Oberlin, did likewise. When Patton made these statements the crowd was all around the house, but mostly in front of the portico. Think most of the crowd could hear him. He spoke loud, for the purpose of being heard. A good deal was said by the crowd in reply. Some of what I should call the *lower orders*, and some that I thought was a little intoxicated, made some *pooty hash* expressions. I mean they swore, and said they 'd hev the nigger anyhow, etc. The carriage stood within five or six rods of the door. Saw John pitched into the carriage, and the horse start. Don't know who was in the carriage at the time. Don't know defendant. Carriage went towards the North. Was not in the room at the time they took him out. Saw him first just as they got him down out of the door. Can't say whether I saw any one go in at the door. Was standing at the foot of the lower stairs, to keep the crowd from going up. Requested to do so by Mr. Wadsworth. Saw a ladder put up, and people going up on it. Pretty soon saw the hall above was full. After they got full above, I left the foot of the stairs and went out where I could have a chance to see. Had no conversation with defendant. Don't know him.

Cross examined. There was considerable of a crowd when I first got to Wellington. More came afterwards. A good many more. About sundown there were 400 or so. [By leave of counsel for defence.]

Direct resumed. Saw the negro go out on to the platform. I had asked and received permission of Lowe to put to the negro such questions as I saw fit. Asked him where he belonged. He said in Kentucky. Belonged to a man by the name of Bacon.

[Counsel for defence objected to testimony as to what this piece of property said. Objection overruled.] Asked him for what cause he had left his master. Asked if his master did n't use him well, and give him enough to eat and wear. Asked him if he had ever abused him. He rather hesitated, and appeared to hang back, as if he thought he was ,abused sometimes. Then I told him he had lived long enough in this part of the country to know that it was necessary for white folks here to correct their own children sometimes, for their good. [Much laughter.] He said yes. Asked him if his master had ever used him worse than some white folks punish their children here. Said he did n't know as he did. Said he had started to go back to Kentucky once; got as far as Columbus, and the folks from Oberlin overtook him and brought him back! [Great laughter.] Asked him if he did n't want to go back now. He said that he s'posed accordin' to the laws of the country, he was obleeged to go back. By the laws of the country he meant the laws of Ohio. [Laughter.] I told him that if he wanted to go back his best way was to let the people know it, for the crowd was getting to act like crazy people, some of 'em. He hesitated a good deal, but finally *partly said* he was willing to go, and was willing to tell the crowd so. He finally pretty much give me to think that that was his answer. Then I told Mr. Lowe that his best way was, if the nigger was willin' to go back, to take him out on to the platform, and have him tell the crowd so. Then Lowe and him and Mitchell, and several other gentlemen [laughter] went out on to the platform, and he began to tell his story. Some of the colored people below told him to come down, but finally order was restored so that he could go on with his story. Don't know as I can get his words. The substance was this: — The nigger requested of 'em fur to be peaceable a minnit, and said

he s'posed he should hev to go; they had arrested him, and accordin' to the laws of the State of Ohio, he supposed he should hev to go. After he had got through, some of the colored folks pointed their guns towards him, and told him to come down. Then Mr. Lowe and the rest of 'em that was on the platform, hurried him right back into the hall and shut the door. This was about a half an hour, perhaps, before the nigger was finally brought down. Was excited, and did n't notice much about time.

Cross resumed. Might have been thirty or forty colored people out of the four hundred. The rest were white. Went to Wellington to see about the fire. Fire was over when I got there. Good many went from Rochester besides myself; three of my brothers at any rate; and perhaps half a dozen others. No colored people among these. Overtook other people going in to see the fire. Saw people that I knew from all the towns about. Knew nothing of the negro affair till I got to Wellington. Nothing but the fire brought me there. Think nothing else brought others who were coming in from towns all about when I was. About one hundred in all were gathered in town when I came in. No stir was made till, it might have been, near about four o'clock. Didn't see the nigger brought in. Don't know when he was brought in. Had been there an hour or so before I heard of him. Heard then that some Kentuckians had a nigger there. Went and asked landlord if I might go and make their acquaintance. Wanted to see them because I have a brother in Kentucky, that I have n't seen but once in thirty years, and didn't know but these men might know him, or perhaps he might be one of 'em. Either the landlord or Fay went up and introduced me. Entered into conversation with Mitchell. Asked about my brother. Mitchell knew him well. He wondered if we were brothers. Could n't b'lieve we had the same father. Complexions aint much alike. My brother's hair is very black.

The first beginning of the breeze was when Watson's team drove up, Then they began to hurrah outside. Was introduced to all the *other* gentlemen except John. [Much laughter.] Think it was after four and might have been five o'clock when Watson drove up. John was up in the cock-loft when Watson drove up. The house has three stories above the ground. John was in the third story. Think there is an attic above that. But one window in the room. When I found these men knew my brother, I went down and got my other brothers, and took them up; so't they might have a chance to talk with 'em. My brothers and I staid till Watson drove up. Should think there was five or six, or more, fellows in the buggy with him. John, Edward, and Conrad are my brothers' names. About the time Watson drove up, Edward went down. The rest of us staid. Saw Watson when he drove up. Can't say whether any of those with him were white. The Kentuckians acted as though they were a little started when the buggy drove up, and Lowe immediately called upon all in the room to assist him. Think Fay was in the room. There might have been others in. There were persons passing in and out. Different persons; did not recognize every one. Pretty soon a mess more come marching up into the square, some of 'em white and some colored. More drove up in buggies and wagons, and then they surrounded the house; put a guard all 'round. It might have been a half an hour, more or less, after this before I went down. Went down and back several times. It was before I went down the first time that I catechized John. I talked with him before Watson came, and then again after the crowd got so excited I went and talked with him again. He told me, in the first conversation, that he was willing to go with Mitchell anywhere; he was a man that he was acquainted with; when they took him he did n't know the other men. By "the other men" he referred to Lowe, Jennings, and Davis. Closed up this first conversation with him, it might have been a half an hour or an hour before Watson came. All was quiet before Watson came, except an occasional remark that there was a slave in the hotel. The greater part of the Oberlin folks had got there when I went down. The door of the room in which the negro was, was fastened, I think, when I first came in, and when I went out was unfastened to let me out, and fastened after me. Found a large crowd down there all round the house, some three hundred or so. The house was surrounded with guards. The colored people seemed the most warlike. Think some of the younger lads among the white folks might have had guns too. Did see arms in hands of white men. Lincoln, the reporter yonder, was one of them. He had a nice rifle. Saw him pretty much the first when I got down, near the back door, outside. Went out the back door because the front door was fastened. Five or six colored men were with Lincoln, all bearing arms. He had a nice little rifle; don't know whether it was a Sharpe's. Told Lincoln he ought to have more sense than to crowd them colored men up where they might be dangerous. [Laughter.] Told him the passage was narrow, and if they tried to get up there would be difficulty, and if one gun was fired, more would be fired. Also that I was satisfied that accordin' to law Lowe was authorized to keep him, and if any one doubted it, they could go up and see his papers. Told the crowd that the negro had told me he once started to go home, got as far as Columbus, and the Oberlin people overtook and brought him back. [Much laughter.] Did n't tell them I was authorized to invite them to look at the papers. Lowe did not request or authorize me to do so. Told this to a crowd in the yard. Might have been one hundred and fifty in the yard, which is four rods square.

Then went around to the back side of the house to the L part, where the women stood at the windows, and they let me in. They were afraid there would be trouble. Went through the dining-room, around into the hall, to the foot of the stairs. A constable and the landlord stood guarding the back door of the hall, keeping the crowd out. Landlord asked me to stand at foot of stairs to keep the crowd from going up. Stood there half an hour or so. While I stood there the crowd broke in at the east door. Some of the crowd clinched with Fay [who seems also to have been one of the guard], and I went to his assistance. Saw a man strike towards him with a gun. Snatched the gun away, and threw it out into the street, through the dining-room window. Followed it into the street, picked it up, threw it against the wall, and broke it and jammed it up bad, and then flung it out again, further away into the street. Then passed 'round in front of the front door, and just about the time I got 'round, they came down with the darkie, and rushed him off.

Direct resumed. Lincoln answered me that he was a child of God, and had as lief die in a good cause as live. I told him that if he got in the way God would let a bullet go through him just as quick as through one of those black fellows. [Counsel submitted that this was purely a theological discussion, not relevant to the case; which, of course, provoked universal merriment.] If there were any crowd in front of the building they could not hear what I was saying to Lincoln and his crowd. The crowd was moving about all the time. Think that when I went round front side after throwing the gun away, might have been stopped by some person asking me something about the negro's wanting to go back.

Richard P Mitchell, called. Reside in Mason Co., Kentucky. Was born there in 1824. Always lived there. Know John G. Bacon. For last four or five years lived within quarter of a mile of him. Knew negro John. Known him since he was a small child. He was *hild* as the property of John G. Bacon from 1846 or 1847 to the time he left. Bacon got him from his father's estate by division of property. Knew his mother Louisa. She was a slave belonging to the estate of John G. Bacon, deceased, and is yet. I saw her last Friday evening. Think she now belongs to John G. Bacon's mother or his younger brother. Used to know nigger John at old man Bacon's, and have likewise known him since he came into the son's possession. Been with him a great deal of late years (prior to his alleged escape), almost constantly. Have worked on the same farm with him. This was in '48. After that worked for Bacon by the day a great deal, right alongside the boy. John left in Jan. '56. Don't know the day of the month. Did n't see him go. Don't know that he went away. Bacon was visiting at his father-in-law's when nigger left. Saw John first after he left, at

Oberlin, in Sept., '58. Went to Oberlin for Bacon. First time I saw John he passed the window of Wack's hotel. Knew him instantly. Next time I saw him was when we arrested him, one and a half or two miles east of Oberlin, on the 13th of September, 1858. Took him to Wellington. I was along with him. Took our dinner at the hotel, and went up into the second story. Jennings came and said he did n't like that room. He asked the landlord for, and received a better room in the third story. Went up to the third story about 3 o'clock. Several persons came into the room to see us and talk with us, Jacob Wheeler and others. Don't know names of others. Crowd pulled the door open, and took John out. No lock on the door. Jennings was holding it. I was standing close to the door; within a few feet of it. Was trying to assist Jennings. Think they come in and got hold of the nigger and led him out. They took him down stairs. Last I seen of him they put him into a wagon in the open space in front of the hotel. Power of attorney was exhibited to several persons who came in in the course of the afternoon. One I think called himself a lawyer; he took it and read it. Don't know that any one else did. Wheeler talked with the nigger. Am not sure that others did. Think they did, but did n't hear what was said, if any thing. Several persons outside asked by what authority the boy was held, and were told, By power of attorney. Several asked if he was a slave. We told 'em he was. They took John out on the platform (portico). John went out and told 'em he was going home. His master had sent for him and he was going home. Also that they had the papers for him and he'd hev to go home. Think he did n't say with whom he was going. Several persons in the room asked him if he was willing to go home. He observed that he was; would go with Mr. Mitchell anywhere. Some persons asked him why he was willing to go with Mr. Mitchell. He said he knew if he went with Mr. Mitchell he would get to see his massa John and his old mistress. Persons asked him if he wanted to see his mother. Said he did, but would *much rather see his old mistress!* [Laughter.] Think there was no Justice of the Peace in the room at the time, but several other persons might have been, besides our party and Jacob Wheeler. Told me he started to go home to Kentucky, got as far as Columbus, and was stopped there by persons who detained him a day or two, and then sent him back to Oberlin, paying his way in the *kyars.* Recess till 2, P. M.

THIRD DAY.— 2, P. M.

Richard P. Mitchell, examination in chief continued. Don't remember that any thing else passed between the negro and myself. Did n't notice any guns pointed at the negro while out on the platform.

Cross-examined. Am a farmer. Have been constable. Held that office two or three years. Been in Ohio frequently before coming to Oberlin last September. All that I know of Bacon's whereabouts when John was missed, is by hearsay. Know nothing personally. Know nothing about his leaving except by report, and the fact that I did n't see him about any more. Have been twice after John. In March, '56, went into Fayette county after him. Did n't see John then. Had been in Ohio after negroes before going first after John. Before going after him the second time, Bacon came and asked me to go out to Oberlin to act with Jennings as witness and assistant in taking John. Nothing was said about compensation. He gave me fifty dollars to pay my expenses. Expected to receive a dollar a day for my time. Only this, Bacon paid me eleven dollars when I got home for the eleven days I was gone. Think this good pay. But no bargain was made about pay. Had been in this state in pursuit of one slave before going after John first. Had the same pay then. No bargain made in that case about pay before starting. John was Bacon's slave, because he served and obeyed him as a slave. Know nothing about the right he had to the slaves, except by seeing them treated as slaves. Don't know as the old gentleman made any will. He died in 1847. Know nothing personally about the division of the property. Jennings has been in the witness' room telling what he had sworn to. I have also seen the report in the paper. I should call John a dark copper color, not a jet black. Have worked as a hand with John for Bacon many a day, since I was constable. Last time I remember to have seen John was about Christmas or New-Year's, 1856. John is about five feet eight or ten inches high; weighs about 150 or 160 pounds. Full face, good-looking. Some niggers are called black; these are the nigger blood; pure African. Copper color, the same blood, a little lighter color. There's a nigger behind you there I should call a mulatto, but could n't be sure that he was not pure African blood. We sometimes call full-blooded niggers mulattoes, because they are so light. Besides the black and copper we have mulattoes, sometimes called yaller; I never use that term. Have seen a *great many* niggers whiter than the counsel. Call them light mulattoes. So we have black, light and black copper, yaller, and light and dark mulattoes, which include all classes. I arrived at Oberlin on Monday, Sept. 6, 1858. Jennings came I believe two days after. I communicated my business to United States deputy-marshal Dayton. Bacon told me to inquire for him. Asked Wack, my landlord, if he knew Dayton. Said he did. Wrote to Dayton. Dayton came next day. After Jennings came, told Wack my business — looking for a nigger. He asked what nigger. Never saw Boynton till I met him as grand juror. Never talked with old

Mr. Warren. Heard Jennings talk with him. Never talk to men about my business unless I know who I am talking to. Never doubted the legality and sufficiency of the power of attorney. Came a day or two after the attempt to take Van Wagoner. Heard about it. Had no hand in procuring John to pass Wack's window when I first saw him.

Next saw John on Monday, Sept. 13th, in a buggy east of Oberlin. Expected to find him. Jennings told me the arrangement he had made. Davis and Lowe were with me. Davis got out and took hold of John. I got out and told him he must get in the carriage with us. I had a revolver and dirk. [Dirk exhibited.] Showed no arms to John. Saw no one show arms to John. Lowe showed power of attorney to John. I read it to him. Think Lowe gave John a chance to read it. Don't know. Think he can't read it if he had a chance. Saw Davis have a revolver the night before. Never saw — think I never did — Lowe have any weapons. We overtook the buggy in which John was, checked our horses, and Davis jumped out and took hold of John before Shakespeare stopped. John had a small knife. I told him to give it to me. He objected. I put my hand toward my inside pocket, and he dropped the knife right down on the ground. My revolver was in that pocket. I suppose he knew what the movement meant. John first said he did n't know me, but after we had driven a little piece, he laughed and said, he knew me as soon as he see me. This change of buggies happened a mile or two out of Oberlin. Last I saw of Shakespeare he was turning his horse around and heading toward Oberlin. Shakespeare started from Oberlin first, and we overtook him. I had nothing to do with making the plans. Simply followed Jennings's directions. Stopped at Wadsworth's hotel in Wellington. John sat on the back seat with me. Lowe drove. It was a two-seated, double, covered carriage. Told Wadsworth we had a nigger we had arrested, and were going to take to Kentucky, and wanted something to eat. In about thirty minutes he gave us some dinner. Took John up stairs while waiting for dinner. Took John down and had him eat dinner with us. That was the *first* time I ever eat with a nigger though. [Laughter.] First time I seen Jennings was after dinner. There was a consid'ble many people about the fire and in the streets when we first came on. First intimation of excitement we had, the landlady came to us at the dinner table, and told us the hall was pretty full of people that seemed to be excited, and she tho't it would n't be safe for us to try to go through the hall up them stairs. So she took us up by another pair of stairs. Jacob Wheeler came into the room on the second floor, and talked about a *half* brother of his in Kentucky. His half brother's name was not Wheeler, but Morgan. He talked to John. [Witness repeated what was said as given on the direct

examination.] Wheeler brought none of his brothers into this lower room. When Jennings came in, he began right off to say that there was a large crowd about, with a good many guns. Think his eyes did not protrude far. We in the room did not experience any trouble from the crowd while in this lower room. Helped Jennings hold the door part of the time. The upper room was next to the roof. We Southerners call it evening after 12 o'clock at noon. The first alarming demonstration I saw was the crowd outside with guns. [Witness confirmed various other statements made on direct examination.] The man who called himself a lawyer looked over the power of attorney and said, he supposed it was legal, *but did n't know:* did n't see any thing wrong in it. Can't say positively that any one beside our party was in the room when the lawyer read the power of attorney. Have no positive recollection whether Patton read the power of attorney or not. Can't say that anybody else read the papers. Don't know that any one else did. Have no recollection that any one else did. Think Patton read the power of attorney. No reason to think any one else did. John did n't try to get away at all. The window was about three feet above the floor. John did n't leave the upper room after he went in till he was taken out. He went out upon the balcony from the first room we were in, before we went up. Positively did not come down from the upper room. Jennings told John there were some persons out there who wanted to know whether he wanted to go back, and he might go out and tell them if he wanted to. He had not before manifested any special anxiety to make a farewell speech to that congregation. I went out with him, and I think Jennings and Lowe did. I had my "toothpick" and revolver, suppose John knew it. John said in substance, "My master has sent for me, and I am going home." Am not sure that John said any thing else. Saw no movement in the crowd inviting John to come down. There was no hurry to get John back. Jennings told him to come in after he had got done speaking, and he did. Don't know how many were on the platform when John spoke. Don't know that there were any on it beside our own party. I saw no ladder during the afternoon. The crowd hollered and laughed as though they were dreadful glad when the nigger was gone. Don't know that any one came in by the window. Think no one did. Still they might. Last I see of John, he was moving out of the room with the crowd. Made no attempt to hold on to him after the door was opened. Think the door was pulled open by the crowd outside. Neither of our party showed any of our weapons. Last I saw of John was from the window as he was being put into the buggy. Saw the buggy drive off from where it stood.

Chauncey Irish, sworn. Resided in Wellington in September, 1858. On the 13th, was about "the centre." Don't know defendant. Supposed he was a colored man.

Bela Farr, called. Resides in Oberlin. Was at Wellington on the day of the rescue. Reached Wellington about 1 o'clock. Anson P. Dayton rode with me. Saw nothing out of the way there. There had been a fire that morning, and some were out looking at the ruins. Remained some twenty-five or thirty minutes. Went thence to Ashland. Saw none of the party who were with the negro. Got back to Oberlin about 10 or 11 o'clock next day. Know defendant. Some two or three evenings after this, I heard defendant and another man talking as they passed my door. It was 9½ or 10 o'clock. Too dark to see him. Did n't see him. Caught but a few words. Only heard defendant say, that "if taking him and bringing him from Wellington is a crime, I suppose I am guilty." Don't know what they were talking about, or what they meant. Heard nothing else.

Barnabas Meacham, sworn. Resided in Wellington last September. Was present when the crowd assembled and rescued the negro John. Think they gathered pretty soon after dinner. Don't know defendant. Negro was carried from the steps and put into a buggy, and the man that was in the buggy drove off at pretty good jog. Saw only one in the buggy (beside negro). Went into the room where the negro was as many as three times. Should think there were from five hundred to one thousand in the crowd. Saw some men with guns. Quite a good many. The crowd urged me to go on and make the arrest. I had a warrant for the arrest of the men who had the negro. Esquire Bennett and Mr. Dixon went in with me. John Mandeville, William Soules, and William Sciples went in with me at my request. Saw in the room only the parties having the negro, perhaps the landlord, and the men I requested to go in with me. I went into the uppermost room. Examined the power of attorney. Told the crowd that if they would make me secure by bond I would make the arrest. I asked Lowe to go out and read his authority to the crowd. He at first declined, but I told him I would try and see him safe back in his room. So he went. We went down and out of the house, a little aside in the street, and got up on to some steps, perhaps two or three rods south of the hotel, and he begun to read his papers, and some one took hold and read it for him. This must have been an hour, more or less, before the negro was taken away. Then Lowe went back into the house. Some of the crowd said they was satisfied; others gave up that I had no power to act, and nothing farther to do. Could n't tell that others said any thing. When I went down, after examining the papers, told the crowd that they had a warrant, and I was satisfied I could do nothing. Said nothing about a power of attorney. Saw a ladder. Don't know who put it up. Saw three or four go up. B'lieve they

went up purty near the garret window. Mean the *ladder* went up near the garret window. Whether they got off on the porch, or went up to the window, I could n't say.

Cross-examined. I proposed to Lowe to go to the Town-House, and he declined. The hotel fronts west. Those standing in front, and east of the house, probably could not hear when the warrant was read. The *warrant* was read to the crowd. *No other paper was read.* Am constable, *and rather think* I know a warrant from a power of attorney. Heard no threats made by the crowd.

Direct resumed. Think no paper was shown me except the warrant. If I said so a little back, I was mistaken, I think. The paper I saw was signed, I believe, by a U. S. Commissioner. I called the attention of the crowd to the fact, that Lowe was about to read. Was about these premises all the afternoon.

Cross resumed. During the entire afternoon have no recollection that these men gave me to understand that they were attempting to carry this man back by virtue of any paper except the warrant. Think nothing was said about a power of attorney.

David L. Wadsworth, called. Reside in Wellington. Am not the landlord there. Was there on 13th September last. Should think there were from four hundred to one thousand in the crowd. The general topic of conversation was in relation to the slave. Some said they'd pull our house down if the slave didn't come out. Some said, "Bring him out." Some said, "Break in the house." Saw in the crowd Loren Wadsworth, Loveland, Sciples, Watson, Bushnell, the defendant, two or three Wheelers, Lovejoy, Warner, Bradner, Howk, Phelps, Bassett, Hines, Perkins, De Wolfe. First time I saw defendant, he came up and spoke to me. Don't know as he said more than to pass the time of day. This was in front of the hotel, sometime between 3 and 5 o'clock, and from one to three rods from the hotel. He was on foot at that time. The buggy which took off the negro was in front of the hotel, a few rods off. Should judge defendant was between buggy and hotel when I saw him. He was then on foot. Don't recollect of seeing him again till I saw him go off in the buggy. I am brother of the landlord. Saw the nigger put into the buggy. He was hurried along pretty lively. Could hardly tell whether he touched the ground or not. After the nigger was put in, defendant drove off. Did n't notice as there was any one else in the buggy. It was a noisy assembly. Good deal of hurrahing; most of it as the negro was driven away.

Cross-examined. Saw Lowe, as he was said to be reading a paper, but could not hear him. Two thirds of the crowd were as far, or farther, from Lowe than myself. Don't know what was read, of course.

Isaac Bennett, sworn. Reside in Wellington. Resided there in September last. Was present at the time of the crowd on the 13th. The most part of the gathering was in consequence of the fire that occurred there in the forenoon. Might have been two hundred or three hundred in all about the hotel. Might have seen fifty guns in the crowd. The remarks about in the crowd were, that they had come up there after a negro there was in the hotel. Some said they'd have him if they tore the house down. Some said that corner would be as bad as the other corner, — the one that was burnt. Saw a ladder put up. Think it was taken down. Previous to the ladder being set up, I was sent for to go up into the room where Lowe, Jennings, and others were. Mr. Meacham came down and asked me. Lowe told me it was said, out in the crowd, that he was holding the boy in custody without any legal process whatever. Told me that if I would go down and tell the people, and they would fall back, he would go to the Town-House and exhibit his papers. Went out on to the balcony and spoke to the crowd, and asked if they would n't hear me a minute. There was a colored man in the crowd spoke up and said, "Bring down the man," "We'll have the man," and pointed his gun up towards me. It did n't seem to be the intention of the crowd to listen. A ladder was set up. I went up and took hold of the ladder to throw it down. A man tried to come up on it, but was pulled back by some persons. I told him not to come up. Don't know whether the ladder was taken down or not. Then I went down stairs, and out ten or fifteen rods from the house. Lowe showed me, before I went down, a warrant issued by a U. S. Commissioner, and a power of attorney. When I went out on to the ground, told several persons what I knew about the papers. Recollect Esquire Howk was one of them, also a man called Langston, and Constable Meacham, and several others. Recollect, also, Esquire De Wolfe. Told them that, as far as I knew, the papers were legal. Think Langston urged the constable very strongly to execute a warrant which had been issued against Lowe, I think. Don't know who was most active in the crowd. Was n't in the crowd much. A good deal was said. A good deal of confusion. Saw the current that moved from the house to the carriage, and inferred from the movement that the negro was put into the carriage and driven off. Saw Lowe come down and mount the steps. Some one called the crowd to order, and said that Lowe would read the warrant. Crowd pretty generally attended. Think I was not near enough to hear the reading. There was something read. Could n't hear what it was. Think two hundred or three hundred were gathered round Lowe. Think Lowe himself read. Don't know. Did n't care to hear.

Court adjourned till 9 o'clock next morning.

FOURTH DAY. — 9, A. M.

Isaac Bennett, cross-examined. Think it was

Lowe showed me the paper. A paper purporting to have been signed by a U. S. Commissioner. In speaking of a warrant I mean this paper. Some person gave me a paper which he said was a power of attorney. Cannot now identify the man who gave it to me. Looked it over and saw it purported to be a power of attorney. In imparting the information I had gained to the crowd, think I confined myself to mention of the warrant.. Might have said "papers." Do not know what Lowe read. He said he was going to read the warrant. I understood it to be the warrant which he read. Saw no other paper read. Did not hear this. Was Justice of the Peace. My intention was to preserve the peace. I had a pistol. Standing at the head of the ladder I pointed the pistol down at the crowd. The talk in the crowd was that the man was kidnapped without legal process of any kind. Some insisted until the warrant was read that there were no papers. Supposed myself that it was *Mr. Lowe* who claimed to have control of the negro. Supposed so throughout the whole affair. It might have been held in the crowd that the papers were spurious. Did not hear it so held. Was not much in the crowd.

Direct resumed. Saw no address or manifestation from Mr. Lowe to the crowd except the reading of the warrant. Think Lowe began to read and some one else took the paper from him and finished. It was said in the crowd that the negro was a free man, taken by force and without legal process from Oberlin, and brought thus to Wellington. Did n't observe that information about the papers held by Lowe made any difference in the crowd. Heard a black man say the boy had been kidnapped. Did not tell this black man what I had discovered up in the room. Had no conversation with the boy John. Had no individual conversation with any colored man in the crowd.

E. S. Kinney, sworn. Was in Oberlin in September, 1858. Was at Oberlin on the day the negro was taken away from Wellington. There was considerable agitation in Oberlin. It commenced between the hours of one and two o'clock. The principal gathering seemed to be in front of Commercial Block. First discovered the crowd about two o'clock. The crowd was on Main street. Fitch's bookstore is on College street. Know defendant. Did n't see him in the crowd. Saw him passing around the corner of Main and College streets. He was walking. Don't recollect seeing any one with him. He was walking rapidly toward Fitch's bookstore. There were only a few about Fitch's bookstore. Saw him no more about there. About an hour after, think I saw defendant and Wall in a buggy, passing down Main street south, toward Wellington. Noticed nothing in their manner peculiar, except that I think Wall had a gun, which was nothing peculiar for that day. This was about 3 o'clock. I went south on foot part of the way, and in a two-horse wagon the rest of the way. There were nine in the wagon. Can name only one, Mr. Lang. Walked about a mile. Got to Wellington at sunset, or a little after. Saw defendant there. Met him in a buggy, just before reaching the square of the village. Winsor was in the buggy, I think, with defendant. Also a colored man they called, in Oberlin, John. Met them two or three rods north of N. E. corner of the Public Square. Think defendant drove. Horse was on the jump. Think Winsor had a gun swinging it, and think Winsor cried out, " all right!" Crowd wàs shouting loudly. Defendant's attention seemed directed mainly to the reining of the horse. Don't know where negro John was conducted to. Returned to Oberlin soon after.

Was there any public demonstration at Oberlin that night ?

Objected to.

Withdrawn.

Did n't see defendant again that night.

Cross-examined. About a week before this Rescue, heard that a family by the name of Wagoner narrowly escaped kidnapping. It was also universal town talk that there were several Southerners at Wack's tavern, whose business it was supposed to be to seize and carry off some of the citizens of the place. And the apprehension was that they would attempt to execute their business in the night, or when a considerable portion of the citizens were away. The talk of the crowd was, and their understanding was before starting, that a colored man had been decoyed ·out of town, kidnapped, and carried to Wellington. I understood that the object of the crowd, in pursuing, was to thwart an attempt at *kidnapping.* Was on the way to my recitation, which was at two o'clock, when I first heard and saw the crowd. Think defendant went among the last of the first parties, about an hour after two o'clock. After the first part of the crowd had gone, a message was sent back. One night, not long before, there was a cry of murder near my room.

Direct resumed. The rumor in the crowd was — I did not hear the person who brought the message — that the message was a call for more men. Don't know who brought the message. After the message the second part of the crowd went down. All went who could get conveyances. I knew that John told me he was a slave. Don't know what others knew about it. If the owner of the slave should come and take his negro without any papers, I should not call it an arrest. If an agent of the owner should come with power of attorney and proper warrant, I should call it an arrest. There was apprehension that fugitives *and free colored persons* would be taken away. Mr. John Lang and several other persons communicated these apprehensions to me, especially after the Wagoner affair. My purpose in going to Wellington was to put myself in a way to do by others as I would like to be done by [laughter] ; to rescue John from the persons who had seized him. Why, or for what purpose, they had seized him I do not know. Am confident the c_owd did *not* rescue John, supposing him to have been seized as a fugitive. The cry of murder referred to was a mile or more from where the negro Frank got his throat cut. Don't know what caused the cry of murder. It was said to come from the Wagoner family, It was supposed and said that *Southerners* had carried off John because Southerners are the men that usually carry off people ! [Laughter.]

Cross resumed. Those in the wagon knew by hearsay that John was a fugitive ; but I did not know, and think none of the others knew that John G. Bacon was the owner of John, that Jennings was the attorney, or that Lowe had any paper. I had no intention of obstructing the legal arrest of John by his owner or attorney, nor do I know of any person who by any act led me to suppose he had any such intention.

Direct resumed. I knew that a power of attorney would authorize a person to act as agent in making an arrest.

Chas. T. Marks, called. Was in the Court Room day before yesterday, a few minutes, while testimony was being given. Reside in Oberlin. Was there 13th September, 1858. Went to Wellington. Crowd began to assemble about one o'clock. Was in the crowd but a moment. Did n't see defendant at Oberlin at all. Started for Wellington about two o'clock, perhaps. Was probably about forty minutes making the nine miles. Wack and Wood were with me. Saw a crowd at Wellington. Put up my horse, staid ten or fifteen minutes in the crowd, and then went upon the other side of the street. Was at Wellington till the negro was taken away. Saw defendant. Heard no words from him. Saw him with a whip, on foot. Afterward saw him sitting in a buggy. Saw him on foot, in the crowd, half an hour to an hour before the Rescue. Did n't see him address anybody. Saw him only in front of the hotel, perhaps twenty feet from the portico. After John was taken away, saw something like Lowe making an address or reading to the crowd. Saw no such reading by Lowe or his party before the negro was taken away. Negro came out on the balcony, and said something to the crowd. Saw the negro brought out. Did n't see defendant before the negro was brought out on to the portico. Saw the negro brought out from the door. Did not see him put into the buggy. Don't know who was in the buggy.

Cross-examined. — Helped Wood put up a ladder.

For what purpose did you help put up the ladder ?

Objected to.

Court overruled testimony. [Just such testimony was drawn out by the Prosecution, ten minutes before.] Nothing was said between

Wood and self about the purpose for which the ladder was put up.

Chauncey Wack, *sworn*. [Defence asked leave to introduce testimony to show that the witness was in Court after the order was given by the Court that witnesses should retire and remain out till called. Court refused the petition, but directed the District-Attorney to ask the witness. Witness said he had been in the room, but heard *only a little* testimony. Had been told that witnesses must keep out of the Court Room, but did n't know it was an order of the Court. Was not present when the order was given. By leave of the Court, Ansel W. Lyman testified that the witness *was* in the Court Room when the Court gave the order. The Court ordered the examination to go on.] Reside in Oberlin. Keep public house. Was there on September 13th last. Went to Wellington. Staid till the negro was rescued. Did n't see Bushnell at Oberlin or Wellington. Was in the crowd at both places. A lawyer named Dickson came out of the hotel at Wellington and came into the crowd and said to those near him that he had examined the papers by which the men held the negro, and thought they were all right. Some replied they did n't care for papers or any thing; they 'd have the nigger anyhow. Mr. Patton, who sits yonder, came out, I think soon after Dickson, and stood on the lower porch in front, and seemed to be endeavoring to still the crowd, and told them that they *hed* papers which he thought were all right, and advised taking some legal course. Don't know what the crowd said to this. They listened a little while and purty soon got noisy again. Afterwards a good many advised breaking into the house and taking him out anyhow, and purty soon they did take him out. Got back to Oberlin about candle-light. Did n't see the buggy in which the nigger went off. Saw the rush when the nigger come out of the house. Buggy went north. Don't know as there was a meeting that night at Oberlin. Heard there was. Heard a great deal of cheering up that way. Have no reason to suppose defendant was at the meeting. Heard a great deal said in the crowd at Wellington. Some said they 'd tear the house down but that they 'd have the nigger ; they were Higher Law men, etc. They grew still about train-time, as I afterwards learned because they expected a despatch had been sent to Cleveland for U. S. troops, and they waited to see if they had come. Some advised to make a rush before train-time, but they wa'n't agreed enough. Think the train passed about five o'clock in the afternoon. Don't know what day of the month the Rescue took place. It took place about sundown or a little after, between five and six o'clock, I should think. Remember the Rescue was a few days after the tenth of September. Don't think Patton brought out any papers. Did n't see any one mount

steps and read papers. Was out of the crowd across the street perhaps half the time. Saw John come out on the balcony. He came out and a man with him and some one stated he was brought out for the purpose of telling the crowd whether he wanted to go back to Kentucky. He did commence telling his story, but did n't get through with it, because the crowd below told him not to say any thing, but to come down, jump down, and they would protect him. He did n't say he wanted to go back but I think he was *just a going to*, when they hollered to him. Saw a number as soon as he come out on to the porch lift their guns toward the balcony, cock them, and tell him to jump down and they would protect him. Was not in the room myself at any time. Saw a rush at the backside of the house with weapons. Some young men belonging to the house stood at the door and told them they could n't come in. One of these had a pistol and told 'em they could not come in there. Saw the rush which broke in by the front door just as the negro was brought out. Think some went up by the ladder, but some one stood at the top with a pistol to keep them back. A ladder was put up and a rush was made before the train come in, and again afterward. It was generally understood through the crowd that the men had papers. Some of the crowd advised peace, and some a rush.

Cross-examined. Have kept tavern at Oberlin some ten or twelve years. Had had no reason at all to anticipate a crowd that day. Jennings, Lowe, Davis, and Mitchell, put up at my house. Jennings had been there no longer than Lowe, I think. Don't know how long they had been about. They had generally been off daytimes, lodging with me. Did not know that there was an intention to run off a nigger. One of the men had asked me about Frank. Was surprised to see the crowd. Went to Wellington to return a $10 bill I had taken of Jennings, which all the money judges I found in Oberlin thought was counterfeit. At Wellington found the bill was perfectly good. Had some curiosity about what was to be done at Wellington, but should not hev gone if it had n't been for the bill. Saw people coming in from all quarters — not all Oberlinites by considerable. A good many had gathered to see the ruins of the fire which was still smoking just opposite the hotel. There was about fifty at the hotel and one hundred at the fire. I got out nearest to the nigger crowd. Did n't try to hear. Did n't think why the crowd was gathered just then. After standing around about half an hour went across the street and sat down to talk with some old friends. Sat there fifteen or twenty minutes and then went back to the vicinity of the hotel. Then went over to the fire. So kept moving about the square all the afternoon. Almost constantly in sight of the front of the hotel. Was in front of the tavern and heard the train come. Staid right there till the rush was made. Then I expected there would be some shootin' going on, and I did n't want to die just then, so I left. [Laughter.] Was in front of the hotel when the negro John was brought out on the balcony to talk to the crowd. This was very soon after I first got there. Am quite sure Davis was with him. Did n't see Jennings there, nor Lowe, that I remember. Don't remember any one but Davis. Did n't understand him to say exactly that he wanted to go back, but that he was in the hands of the law and s'posed he might as well go back. Dickson came out either a little before or a little after the train came in, and seemed remarkably cool for him, and said to those of the crowd near me that he had examined the papers, and as far as he could see they were all right. Defendant was not in the crowd. Saw nothing of defendant that day. Afterward Patton came out and said that he had seen papers which appeared to be all right, and he thought they had better take a legal course, and not be trying to get him off in this shape. Recess till 2, P. M.

Fourth Day. — 2, P. M.

Chauncey Wack. Cross-examination continued. [Witness repeated most that he had stated on direct examination.] Got hungry the latter part of the afternoon, and went around to the kitchen to try and get something to eat. The women was there, but would n't let us in; tho't we were part of the rescue crowd. Did n't know any thing about the plan to decoy the negro out of town. Mitchell told me a day or two before that he was lookin' for negroes. Mitchell kept very close in the house while he was stopping at my house. But Jennings was gone out most of the time.

Direct resumed. Warren's barn was burnt while Mitchell was at my house, but that night Jennings was gone. Think it was Saturday night. The negro's throat was cut while Mitchell was there, too. Don't remember what night that was. Don't remember which happened first. Heard that the throat cutting was in a fight between the niggers themselves.

Cross resumed. Jennings was frequently gone nights while stopping with me, from first to last. Warren's boy is part white. Lowe and Davis came to my house on Monday morning with their team, had it fed, but not unharnessed, and went off again at 10 or 11 o'clock. Have no recollection of their coming in the night of Sunday. They came Monday, to best of my recollection. Only one of the party staid with me Sunday night, I think. Think it was Mitchell, am not positive.

Oliver S. Wadsworth, sworn. Am not keeper of public house at Wellington, but was such last September. Was at home on the day of the rescue. Think the first of the rescuers came between three or four o'clock. Did n't know any of them. Some asked to see the negro, and I consented. Don't know who they were, or whether they went into the room. Was told that some of these persons were Watson, Patton, Lincoln, and Scrimgeour. Heard that the crowd were after a negro who was in the hands of the Marshal. Can't say what part or position Watson had in the crowd. Can't say what was said out doors. Was in the house most of the time. Should think there were somewhere near five hundred in the crowd. Might have been twenty to seventy-five bearing arms. Can't tell how many. Had some conversation with Mr. Lincoln. Think Lincoln said they was bound to have him any way. Told him there was a legal way to get at it without having a riot. Lincoln said what was done must be done before the train from Cleveland came, as there was a rumor that a despatch had been sent to Cleveland for United States forces. The train was due at 5:13. Lincoln was a stranger to me. Told him I did n't think any despatch had been sent. Had some conversation with Matthew Gillett. He told me that the best thing I could do was to open my house and let the crowd go in and take out the negro. I told him I did n't want my house ransacked by a mob. He proposed to have a committee of ten to twenty go in and confer with the men peaceably, and see what could be done in a proper manner. I told him I had no objections to such a committee going in; they might go in and confer. This was in the back yard; a good many persons being in hearing. Don't know whether any such committee was chosen. At his request, I mentioned several names of persons who I was perfectly willing should be on the committee. Armed men occupied positions all 'round the house. Don't know who stationed them. I was in the hall when the crowd rushed down; did n't identify the negro, but the cry was that John was gone.

William B. Worden, called. Live in Oberlin. Lived there in September last. Was at Oberlin on the return of the rescuers from Wellington. Did not see the negro John. Saw defendant. It was some dark when they came back. Heard defendant say nothing. A gentleman in the wagon in which defendant had been, said they had got John. Defendant had gone into the store. Don't know whether defendant heard the remark. Wagon stood in front of the store. Defendant had gone in. Don't know how far in. Store door stood open.

Richard K. Whitney, sworn. Reside in Oberlin. Remember the rescue day. Was in Oberlin. Don't know when John was brought back to Oberlin, or when taken away, or how, or any thing about it.

The prosecution here rested.

District Attorney asked leave to recall one more witness.

John G. Bacon, recalled. Direct examination. In conversation between Jennings and myself after his first return from Oberlin, Jennings asked me whether I thought Loyd would give him any thing for catching his nigger. Told him I did n't know any thing about that, *but I* had offered publicly one half of what the nigger would sell for, and he might consider this offer open to himself. He did n't say whether he would or would not accept these terms, but finally said he would go, and I considered myself thus obligated to pay him one half the nigger would sell for if he brought him back, but not any thing unless he brought him back. There was no other contract.

Prosecution rested.

Witnesses for the defence sworn.
Lewis D. Boynton, called. Reside in the town of Russia, about thirty rods over three and one half miles from Oberlin Church. Was at home on Sunday before the Rescue. Was not at home on Monday. Went to Ashland. S'pose I shall not be driven out of the Court House if I say I went as delegate to a Democratic convention. [Mr. RIDDLE: Not out of *this Court House*, certainly.] [Laughter.] Saw Jennings for the first time in my life on Sunday, 12th of September, 1858. Got home about 11 o'clock on Saturday night. Wife told me there were two gentlemen, strangers, in the house; she thought they had come to buy cows. Said she believed one of them was from Columbus. Told her they had n't come after cows then. After milking next morning, these gentlemen came down stairs. Lowe came and asked me if this was Mr. Boynton, etc. After breakfast, went out to water my cattle down at the creek, and they followed me out, and then for the first time Mr. Lowe told me his business. This was Sunday.

What did he say?

Objected to as immaterial. Argued by counsel on both sides.

Objection sustained. [*Jennings*, by special ruling, was allowed to give a detailed account of his visit to Boynton. It was understood by both counsel and Court that Boynton would *impeach* Jennings.]

Shakespeare Boynton, called. [Counsel still argued upon the point just decided, by leave of the Court, with reference to a reconsideration of the ruling. Judge Bliss for the prosecution, argued at length, that it was utterly immaterial whether the Rescue was made *knowingly* (that is knowing that the negro was legally arrested) or not. It was enough to show that a *rescue* of the negro from the hands of the men who had him in custody was made. The Court did not see fit to change the ruling.]

Am thirteen years old. *Expect* I am a son of last witness, but it's hard telling now-a-days! Remember the Rescue day. Last I saw of John, Lowe and Davis and Mitchell were putting him into their wagon, about one and three fourths miles northeast of Oberlin. Davis and Mitchell had hold of John. Lowe sat in the buggy. Just about as soon as they got even with my buggy, Davis had his arm right around John. John sat in my buggy. John was picking his teeth with his jackknife. Mitchell told him to give it to him. He objected. Mitchell put his hand to his inside pocket and John dropped the knife. Lowe says "bring him along." I saw them a few rods before they came up. I was driving on a slow walk, they were trotting. I was waiting for them. When Lowe said "bring him along," John said, "I 'll go with you," Davis and Mitchell kept hold till they got him in. Had seen all the men before at Wack's, and Lowe at my father's. Lowe gave me a card. I lost it. I went back to Wack's. Went from home to Oberlin that morning to get John to dig potatoes. Said he could n't go. Went with John because I was getting well paid for it. Knew what the men wanted to get John for. Was to have $20 for it. Jennings was to pay me. Did pay me $20. The bargain was made at Wack's on Monday morning. It was spoken of at my father's house. Got John to ride to another negro's who promised to come and dig potatoes. Then I told John he might as well have a good ride afterwards. Came back after they had got John, and told Jennings they had got him. So he paid me the $20; good money. Father knew nothing of this matter till afterward, that I know of. Told him of it soon afterward. I was to have $20 more if I got big Frank. Was sorry I could n't get him. The card had their address on, so I could write to them if I had any occasion to. Have had no occasion to write. Have never written. Lost the card.

Adjourned till next morning at 9 o'clock.

FIFTH DAY.— 9, A. M. SATURDAY.

District-Attorney rose to say that he was willing Messrs. Dickson, Peck, Fitch, and Plumb, of the witnesses for the defence should remain in the Court Room. Defence accepted the courtesy.

Henry E. Peck, called. Am Professor in Oberlin College. Reside at Oberlin. Remember the day of the alleged Rescue. Did *not* on the afternoon of that day meet defendant at or near the steps of Fitch's bookstore, either alone or with Plumb or Fitch. Heard no inquiry from defendant to any one, as to whether they had got John. Heard Bartholomew's testimony. Understood Bartholomew to say that defendant came up to witness, Fitch, and Plumb, and asked if they had got John; one of us replied they had; defendant asked what had best be done; one of us replied, "go and get them ready, and we will tell you." *No such or similar conversation took place on that day between such parties.* Knew negro John well. He was a decidedly black man. Five feet five inches in height; under, if any thing; could have been but a fraction over that. He had been sick just before being taken away. At that time would not weigh over one hundred and thirty-five pounds. In health would weigh one hundred and sixty pounds, or more. Was broad shouldered, stoutly built.

Cross-examined. Remember to have known John very well from the spring of 1858 up to the time he was taken away. May have known him before. Do not know what his employment was. Did not know him to be employed. He boarded with James Armstrong, who lives next to my farm, so that I saw him, with rare exceptions every day for some months. Never saw him after September 13th. Know nothing when ór how he left except by common rumor.

Did you ever have any conversation with defendant about John's leaving ?

Counsel inquired if Judge BLISS called that cross-examination.

Judge BLISS : I do. [Argued by both sides at some length.]

Judge BELDEN claimed that no principle in law is better settled than that any witness may be used by either party, either as witness-in-chief or in-cross. Judge SPALDING affirmed that, in the cross-examination, the witness must be confined to such topics as had been testified upon by him in direct examination.

The COURT ruled that Judge SPALDING was undoubtedly correct.]

Where did John go to from Wellington, on September 13th ?

Objected to.

The COURT inquired if the prosecution wished to ask witness such a question after witness had stated he knew nothing of him after September 13th ?

DISTRICT-ATTORNEY. Yes, your Honor.

The COURT. Proceed, sir.

Witness knew nothing about him on or after September 13th. Saw defendant on 13th September, in Oberlin, in a room over Mr. Ells's store. Saw him at no other time or place on that day.

What time of the day was this ?

Objected to, as incompetent on cross-examination.

The COURT decided that it was incompetent, unless to prove the conversation as being there, which was alleged by Bartholomew to be in front of Fitch's store.

Ralph Plumb, Samuel Plumb, J. M. Fitch were present in the room. Other persons were in, but whether at that moment or not, I cannot say. The windows were closed and curtained. About 3 o'clock, or later, this was. We staid together about an hour. Before going in there, had been near Fitch's store. This was just about a quarter past two. No crowd about this store. There was a crowd in and near Watson's store. Almost entirely there. Samuel Plumb, Ralph Plumb, and J. M. Fitch were with me. No others near, unless a customer or two passing. Am positive I did not see defendant there, and that he was

not there. The crowd was *all* rushing to Watson's, as the rallying point. Was somewhat excited, but perfectly in hand, as I am now. Can recollect perfectly and positively what I did, for I am extraordinarily sensitive about violations of the Fugitive Slave Law. Did not go to Wellington. About five minutes past two o'clock I went over toward Mr. Carpenter's store, and found Mr. Samuel Plumb. We stopped about sixty or eighty seconds, and Seth Bartholomew came up at my back, with the evident manner of an *eave-dropper.* I then went East, and met Mr. Fitch, who, coming up, made some expression of indignation. Within a few days after this, I heard that there were United States officers in town, ferreting out information, when and since when I have carefully retained what I knew of the circumstances. I am only testifying of what occurred at the points where I was with these gentlemen, always at a considerable distance from the crowd. I was led by a great singularity in John's appearance, frequently to note his height, weight, etc. Nothing but the singularity of his appearance led me so frequently to note him. He was evidently sick most of the time, and apparently sick in a way a man ought not to be. Should have noticed any one else who had a similar manner.

Ralph Plumb, called. Reside in Oberlin. Was at Oberlin on 13th September. Heard Bartholomew's testimony in this case. [Witness repeated that part of Bartholomew's testimony which related to the alleged conversation between defendant, witness, last witness, and Fitch, as stated by last witness.] No such conversation took place. Did n't see defendant there. Defendant was not there. Bartholomew was not there. Never saw John in my life, that I know of. Know of his existence only by hearsay.

Cross-examined. Fitch, Peck, and self were on Fitch's store steps. Defendant is clerk in this store. Think no other person was near. Have perfectly distinct recollection of persons present. Am positive defendant was not present. Think defendant was not in the store. Think I should have seen him if he was, for the store doors are glass, and should have seen him, unless he were far down in the store. But very few people were in sight. Watson's store is in another street, around the corner. Saw Bartholomew in the crowd. Had no conversation with him. The crowd was continuous from Carpenter's to Watson's. Passed through the crowd on the way to my office. May have said a word or two to some one in passing. Did not stop to converse.

James M. Fitch, called. Reside in Oberlin. Own the store called by my name. Heard Bartholomew's testimony. Was at home on September 13th. Was on the steps at the time Bartholomew speaks of. Defendant was not there. He was not at the store; had left some time before. Did not see Bartholomew there. No such conversation as Bartholomew alleges took place in my hearing.*

Cross-examined. A few words may have passed on the steps. Don't remember what, if any. Remember passing over the steps, but do not remember stopping on them. William Bushnell, another of my clerks, was in the store. My son, the third and only other clerk, was absent, and defendant had passed out of the store by the front door a few minutes before, and some minutes after our being on the steps, he came back. Do not know where he went, or for what. Defendant was not in the store all the afternoon. There was something of a crowd about the streets. Do not remember to have seen Bartholomew. Am one of the indicted for aiding and abetting the rescue of this negro, John. Professor Peck is also one.

Joseph H. Dickson, sworn. Reside in Wellington. Attorney-at-law by profession. Was at Wellington 13th September last. Should think two or three hundred were there at noon, attracted by the heavy fire of the early morning. About 1 o'clock we were trying a lawsuit in the town hall, and some person came in and said a negro had been kidnapped. Constable was sent to say that the Southerners wished to see me. Passed through the public square, which may contain two or three acres. The lawsuit was before Justice Bennett. The same crowd was there as in the morning. This was about half past one or two o'clock. Saw only one Oberlin man, Watson. Went up to the room where the Southerners were, in the attic. Now not far from two o'clock. Some persons in the halls and bar-room seemed excited. At the door, the constable gave some message, and the door was opened, and I went in, a young man, stranger to me, following us. No one came in except these three. Found three men and the negro in the room. No others. Lowe introduced himself and his official character. I asked if he had papers for holding the negro. Said he had. Showed me his warrant, — no other papers. No one else showed other papers. Read the warrant, and, being asked, said I saw no informality except the *lack of a seal.* Lowe said it was not customary for such papers to have a seal. I said I was not conversant with such papers. I then turned to one of the other men, supposing him to be the owner, and asked what he would take for the negro. He said fourteen hundred dollars. A third man, with red whiskers, said he'd better take twelve hundred dollars if he could get it. The man I bargained with is tall, dark complexion. [Witness identified Jennings in the audience as the bargainer.] Nothing was said about the authority by which he would sell the negro. Nothing said of power of attorney. No such paper shown or seen. Lowe, turning to the other two, said that, as this man was a

lawyer, they had better employ him. Lowe introduced the subject of the Greene County slave case, and asked me if I was aware of the decision in the court in that case. This young man who followed me in, sat down by my side and read the warrant with me. Have since been told his name was Scrimgeour. I staid in the room some fifteen or twenty minutes. Remember no other conversation than that stated. When I came down, noticed that the crowd had increased. Think I went out the back door. Found something of a crowd about. *Made no proclamation or address to the crowd whatever.* Conversed with several individuals, remarking that I had seen the warrant, but it lacked a seal. *Made no expression of opinion as to its efficacy or value, saying that I was not much conversant with such papers.* Did n't see Lowe out in the crowd at all. Did n't see the negro or those holding him in custody upon the balcony at all. Went home about four o'clock. Did not return to the crowd afterward. Going towards it about sunset, heard a great shout, and heard it said that the slave was carried off. Those in the crowd who spoke with me, spoke of the negro being *kidnapped,* and asked earnestly if something could not be done to save him. Stated to those who asked that I had seen the paper, but could not tell whether it was sufficient authority or not. Think I said to them that U. S. Marshal Lowe held the negro. Think I talked with but a few persons in the crowd. Think there were four or five hundred in the crowd. It was a promiscuous crowd. Saw no concerted movement. Can't say that I saw any common purpose manifested by the crowd. Think three hundred people at least were attracted by the fire. Think most that came after two or three o'clock, came from the north. Saw people with arms first after coming down. Think in all I did not see more than twenty guns. Observed none except in the hands of colored men. Understood from some persons that more or less of the guns were not loaded. No guns were discharged or attempted to be discharged in my presence, or to my knowledge. Know defendant. Did not see him there. Neither of the magistrates were in the room with myself and the southern gentlemen.

Cross-examined. Don't know how the negro went off. Was in sight of the hotel and heard the shout, and saw a general movement of the crowd. The warrant had *neither seal nor scroll.* The only impression I got from the warrant, and the party, was that *Jennings was the negro's owner.* No paper was shown me except the warrant by Lowe. I told them they could n't employ me. Think none came into the room while we were there. Remember no one coming in. Was not there when Esqrs. Bennett and Howk, or Mr. Wheeler were there. Don't remember more than three men with the negro. Remember nothing about Davis. Remember Lowe, a tall, dark-faced man, and a sandy-whiskered man.

---

* Mr. Bartholomew has since been indicted by the Grand Jury of Cuyahoga county, for *perjury.*

While talking with the individuals below, at one time there were four or five persons about me. Said to Mr. Wadsworth, I thought the crowd had better abstain from interference. They made no statement of the purpose for which they wished to employ me. This talk was cut short by my saying that they could not employ me. Think it was after I read the warrant that the offer to employ me was made. Nothing was said about my endeavoring to quiet or disperse the crowd. No request of that sort was made. No claim of authority was made except by showing the warrant.

James L. Patton, called. Resided in Oberlin in September, 1858. Belong, as a student, to the college there. Remember some of the occurrences of the 13th of that month. Saw a crowd that afternoon. My attention was first called to it between 1 and 2 o'clock. Can fix the time within half an hour. Had just seated myself to study after dinner. Some one came into the hall and said that some one had been carried off by slave-catchers, as they were called, I think. Took my hat and went to the crowd near Watson's store. Heard this rumor confirmed there. Did not stay at all, but left and went to Whitney's livery stable. Before going there I learned in the crowd some of the circumstances under which the man had been taken. In substance, that a man had been decoyed out of town and snatched up and taken away by parties lying in wait. The rumor had been about the town for several days that parties were lying in wait to make such an abduction. Don't know what brought the crowd together. I joined the crowd because I heard that the man had been carried off. Know others who joined the crowd for the same reason. I went to Wellington because I had information that the man had been caught up and carried in that direction. Wm. D. Scrimgeour and John G. W. Cowles went with me. A number were ahead of me; don't know how many. Drove to Wellington in about an hour. Might have been eighty or one hundred about the hotel. Did n't notice how many were about the fire — saw a crowd there. Passed 'round through the crowd half an hour or so, and then went into the room in the garret. Can't tell what time I got into that room, somewhere about 4 o'clock. Went to the back door which was guarded. Told a man, I took to be the landlord, that I wanted to see the marshal. He refused. Then said I wanted to see Scrimgeour; and he took me to the room in the garret. He knocked at the door, and Lowe came out. Landlord said I wanted to see Scrimgeour. Lowe took me by the arm and said he wanted to talk with me. Led me to a little room near by, and told me he had sent to Cleveland by telegraph for aid, which would come on the 4 o'clock train, and that his papers were all right. He then showed me his warrant, which I looked over somewhat, but did not read carefully. He showed me no other papers. He then asked me if I would go down and tell the crowd that he was legally authorized, and that he must return his warrant at Columbus, and make for him a proposition to the crowd to choose a committee, which should go with him to Columbus and see that the boy had a fair trial. I then went down to the crowd, and got up on the steps of the hotel and stated to the crowd that I had seen the warrant, and stated as nearly as I could the proposition of the marshal, adding that, as far as I could see, the warrant was right, and if they wished to proceed according to law, they would probably have to send to Elyria for a writ of *habeas corpus*. Was in the room with the marshal perhaps fifteen or twenty minutes. He said nothing to me of the manner of the arrest, or of any authority for the arrest, except the warrant. He said nothing about a power of attorney. *Neither heard any thing about, nor saw any thing of, a power of attorney till I heard of it in this Court Room.* Received no instructions to speak of a power of attorney to the crowd below. Saw others of Lowe's party while up stairs, but had no conversation with them.

Court adjourned at noon to Monday morning at 10 o'clock.

SIXTH DAY. — 10, A. M. — MONDAY.

James L. Patton, examination-in-chief continued. [Before proceeding with the testimony, Mr. RIDDLE wished to call the attention of the Court to a fact which had just come to his knowledge, namely, that *one of the Jurors,* Mr. Chas. N. Allen, *was an officer of the Court* — a deputy marshal. He did not wish to intimate any unfairness, but desired the Court to notice the fact. The Court did not see fit to take any action in regard to the matter.]

The examination therefore proceeded.

The warrant was spoken of in my interview with the marshal and his party, but no other paper. Saw no other. Lowe offered to go out and read his warrant to the crowd, if I would go along and protect him. He was afraid of violence if unprotected. I consented to go. We went out the back door, along the south side of the house into the square, thence a few rods south to some steps. Lowe and I mounted, he handed me the warrant, and I read it. We then proposed to the crowd that as they had heard his papers, they let him go about his business. Some one answered that the warrant made no difference, the crowd would have the boy any way. Just then, I heard a rush, and looking toward the hotel, saw the crowd pouring in at the front door. Lowe caught me by the arm, and we with a third gentleman returned to the room in the attic. Passed up the first flight of stairs without difficulty, but found something of a crowd on the second flight. We crowded through into the room. This was some ten minutes before the boy was taken out. No warrant was shown to me, or in my presence, except when

Lowe and I were alone in the adjoining room. *I asked Jennings if the boy belonged to him, and he said he did.* No other conversation or remark about the ownership of the boy was made in my hearing. Think no one beside Mandeville, and the parties who had the boy in custody, were present when I asked about the ownership of the boy. I saw nothing of defendant on this day, either at Oberlin, or at Wellington, or on the road between. On arriving at Wellington, heard that the boy had been out on the balcony. Did not see or hear of his being out there after my arrival. Heard at Wellington that a man had been kidnapped and was about to be taken away. Heard that he was a fugitive at Wellington; do not remember hearing him spoken of at Oberlin as a fugitive. Heard it said, not by the crowd, but by the marshal, that a telegram had been sent to Cleveland for assistance which would come by the 4 o'clock train. I did not make this fact known to the crowd; may have heard it spoken of in the crowd, but do not so remember. Was, perhaps, in the room with Lowe in first interview ten minutes. Remember the warrant declared the slave to be the property of John G. Bacon. Asked Jennings if he was the owner, because I had not learned his name, and he affirming himself to be the owner, I at once took him to be John G. Bacon.

Cross-examination. The crowd responded to the reading of the warrant by saying that they cared nothing for papers; they would have the boy anyhow; Columbus was too far south to go. During the afternoon heard threats that the roof should be torn off the house but that the boy should be rescued. Heard no such threats in response to the reading of the warrant. Some persons passed in and out during my first and second visits to the room; there were not many of these; cannot say how many. Think most of them belonged to the company I first found there. Saw Wheeler during the afternoon; can't tell where; can't say he was in the house; was not present when he had an interview with those in the room. Do not remember to have seen Esq. Howk or Esq. Bennett in the room. Know witness Wheeler only by face; know nothing of his brothers. Was in the room when negro was taken out. Did not see him put into the buggy.

Examination in chief resumed. Heard no threats after the warrant was read. Saw nothing like concerted action in the crowd. Knew of no concert in counsel among any acting as leaders.

Cross-examination resumed. The response to the reading of the warrant was made by *a single gentleman, who accompanied the marshal as his friend,* and declared himself a stranger in the place. The expression was, "The *crowd* care nothing for papers; they will have the nigger anyhow."

William Howk, sworn. Resides in the town of Wellington, three miles north of the village. Some time in the forenoon of the day of the Rescue, some one, passing my house, said, Wellington was burning up; and, although unwell, I immediately set out for the scene of the fire. Should think at noon there was a crowd of five hundred or more. Think some were then about going home. There was a case of assault and battery being tried there that day, to which I went; I think the case was appointed for 2 o'clock. Esquire Bennett asked me to sit with him (am Justice of the Peace), which I did. We got just through the case, when a man came in and said a man had been kidnapped, and was now in custody near by. Think he made oath to the fact; the affidavit was read aloud to those in the Town-House — one hundred or so — and a warrant was issued. Esquire Bennett then asked me, if there should be a trial, to sit with him, to which I assented. Those in the Town-House then went out. Do not know who came in and made the affidavit. This might now have been 4 o'clock. Esquire Bennett and myself then went toward the hotel. The Town-House stands south of the hotel ten or twelve rods, on the same side of the public square. Should think the crowd was now not less than at noon, and I noticed some individuals I had not before seen. Saw some guns, in all, perhaps twenty. Saw none except in the hands of colored men, except that I saw Mr. Wheeler throw a gun. Saw no leader or leaders. No concerted action. Heard a good many speak of the man in the attic as having been kidnapped; it was farther said that no papers had been used in the arrest of the man. These remarks were made by persons who were strangers to myself. Some whom I knew, standing upon the outskirts of the crowd, said they wondered if it was a case of kidnapping, adding that, to all appearances, it was. Did not see the negro on the balcony. Saw a man on the steps reading a paper. Could not hear what was read. I went into the building. Wm. Sciples came to me and said the marshal wanted to see me. This was the first I knew whether there was a marshal, or in what shape the case was. I went up and found Mandeville and David L. Wadsworth in the room. This was quite late, and dusky. A man came up to me, and speaking quite low, said he wanted to see me. He led the way out of the room to the head of the stairs, and there handed me a paper; I took it, and looking at it, told him I could not read it without glasses, and handed it back to him. He said nothing till then, but then said, "If half a dozen or so of your men will go with me to Columbus, and this thing isn't a straightforward thing, I'll let the boy come back." I told him I wanted nothing of the boy. Nothing was said by either of us concerning his name or office, or the character of the paper in any way. Nothing was said of another paper. The first I ever heard of a power of attorney, was in this Court House. Saw nothing that was on the paper. Thought I made out the word " Columbus," in large type. Could not tell whether the paper was written or printed. As I was passing up I heard some one say there was no seal on their papers, so I looked especially for that, and found nothing like a seal. Was not with this man more than a minute and a half, or so. No other conversation passed, except that I said to him, as I started to go down, that I thought the crowd did not know there was any marshal. The name of the gentleman who took me out was not mentioned in my hearing, or his official character. Nothing was said about any other person having any thing to do with the custody or ownership of the boy, except the gentleman with whom I spoke.

Cross-examined. Heard no statement that there were papers until, as I was passing up, just before entering the room, some one said the papers were good for nothing, having no seal. Heard nothing of a marshal, till Sciples came to say to me that the marshal wanted to see me. Don't know who it was came to get the warrant for the arrest of kidnappers. Kept mainly on the outskirts of the crowd. Heard something about a quarrel, a colored man having snapped a gun at a white man, or some such matter ; don't know what the quarrel was. Sciples, in presenting me to the gentleman in the room, barely mentioned my name, saying nothing else. Did not know, therefore, the man who took me aside, but supposed him to be the marshal, and his paper to be a warrant. But this was all supposition.

By what sort of a claim did you *understand* him to hold the negro ?

[Counsel for defence submitted that the witness's *understanding* was not competent evidence.

The Court ruled that it *was.*]

I understood it, or supposed it to be a legal claim. Asked Esq. Bennett if he had read the *papers*, referring to the one paper shown me. He said he had, and guessed they were all right. Mentioned to some persons that I had seen a paper, but took no pains to spread this information in the crowd, having so bad a cold as to be unable to speak loud at all. Said nothing to the crowd.

Direct resumed. In speaking with Esquire Bennett about the paper, I think I said, " the marshal's paper," having reference only to the warrant. Bennett said nothing to me of any other paper. Do not know that the crowd, as a whole, knew of any paper. The general cry of the crowd was that it was out and out *kidnapping,* there being no papers at all.

Lysander S. Butler, called. Reside at Oberlin ; was at Wellington on the day of the Rescue. Was not in the room where John had been, while John was there. Was next to Lowe and Patton during the reading of the warrant. There was nothing said, in my hearing, of any other paper. I looked over Patton's shoulder while he read. The paper purported to be a warrant issued and signed by a U. S. Commissioner. There was no seal upon it. Was a law student at that time, and have been since. On this account examined the paper with special interest. Heard nothing said by any one at any time about the existence of any other paper. Particularly asked some persons passing in and out of the room if they knew of any other papers, and was answered in the negative. Heard only one opinion in the crowd, and that was that the arrest was utterly illegal — absolute kidnapping. Knew John well. He was not to exceed five feet five inches, at the utmost. This is my own height, and I feel sure he was no higher, and probably not so high as myself. Am confident of this. Know Seth W. Bartholomew. Have known him for ten years intimately. His reputation for truth and veracity is not as good as that of men in general. If he had any prejudices or personal interests in a suit, I should very much dislike to believe him under oath.

Recess till 2 o'clock.

SIXTH DAY. — 2, P. M.

Lysander S. Butler, cross-examined. Have been reading law with the firm of Plumb & Plumb for a year or two past. First knew John something more than a year ago.

Have you ever heard that John was a fugitive ?

Objected to.

Objection sustained.

For what purpose did you go to Wellington ?

Objected to as improper on cross-examination, no such topic having been introduced on the examination-in-chief.

Objection overruled.

I heard that a man had been kidnapped, and taken toward Wellington. By kidnapping, I mean a seizure contrary to the laws of the United States. All that I heard was the simple statement that a man had been kidnapped.

When did you first hear that day that John was a fugitive ?

Objected to as travelling beyond the limits of cross-examination.

The Prosecution stated that it intended to use this witness to show the knowledge and opinion of the crowd.

Argued.

Objection overruled. Exception taken.

Q. When was it that you first learned or was informed that John was a fugitive slave ?

A. I do not know ; cannot remember at what time, and under what circumstances I first heard this. It is my impression, that it was not generally understood at Oberlin, that John was a fugitive slave. I went to Wellington in the regular stage plying between Oberlin and Wellington. Think there was not more than one person beside myself, and the usual passengers on board.

When were you in the room with the negro John?

I was not in the room.

But you testified on the examination-in-chief that you were in that room.

No, sir, I must have been misunderstood.

[The learned associate of the District-Attorney gave the witness such a "talking to" as brought the counsel for the defence to their feet to ask if witnesses had any rights in this court. In making this inquiry, they were so seriously interrupted, that the Court was obliged to command silence. This was a lamentable departure from the dignity and courtesy which had heretofore characterized the bearing of the prosecution. The Court promptly enforced order.]

I said to some individuals that I thought the warrant was good for nothing. Said so, because I supposed a seal to the warrant was necessary.

Did you not say to the crowd that you thought the papers were all right, and the only legal relief was by a writ of *habeas corpus?*

Objected to as new matter.

Argued.

Court first sustained, and then overruled the objection.

I have no recollection of ever making any such remark as my own opinion, but do remember *quoting* a remark like the one incorporated in the question. I quoted it to some one sitting in a buggy near the buggy in which I was then sitting. Am positive John was not over five feet five inches. Think he was about five feet four inches. Have had no conversation with any individuals concerning John's height since this case commenced, farther than barely remarking on reading the testimony of witnesses who thought him five feet eight or ten, that they had set him up pretty well.

J. J. Cox, sworn. Reside in Oberlin. Have resided there twenty years. Remember the occurrences of Sept. 13th. Was not at Wellington on that day. Knew John well. Am builder by occupation. John's height was up to my ear, five feet four or five inches. Have worked and scuffled with him an hundred times or more. Am pretty sure he would not in health weigh more than one hundred and forty pounds. Know Seth W. Bartholomew. Have known him from his cradle. Lived many years in the house with him. His reputation for truth and veracity from his boyhood up, among the large majority of the people of Oberlin, has been bad.

Cross-examined. If in a suit he had any prejudices or interests at stake, I should not believe him under oath. His reputation has always been bad. Could hardly find a man who would not agree that he was notoriously untruthful. John was very black, so black he shone.

Philo Weed, sworn. Reside in Oberlin;

have resided there fifteen or sixteen years. Knew John by sight. Knew him pretty well. He was a black, a very black negro. About five feet seven or eight inches high. Might weigh 130 or 140. Rather short and stout built. Know Seth W. Bartholomew. Have the means of knowing his general reputation for truth and veracity. It is not as good as that of men in general. Should not want to believe him under oath.

Cross-examination. Have known Bartholomew ever since I have been a resident there. His reputation has always been bad. Have heard the largest part of the inhabitants of Oberlin speak distrustingly of him. Among them Elliott, Pelton, Lowe, Beecher, Cox, and Brokaw. Some nine or ten years ago he was indicted for stealing money. He has been an apprentice of mine. These men named have spoken of him to me repeatedly as a thief and a liar. Did you not know that he was a candidate for constable at the late village election in Oberlin?

No, sir; never heard of it. But did hear that he got *two votes* for that office. [Laughter.] He stole ten dollars in money, and was tried before a Justice.

Brewster Pelton, sworn. Know Seth W. Bartholomew. Know his general reputation. That it is not as good for truth and veracity as that of men in general. Have known his reputation for truth and veracity to be thus bad from 1850 to the present time.

David Brokaw, sworn. Have resided in Oberlin seventeen years. Have been Mayor of the village. Known Bartholomew during these seventeen years. Would not believe him under oath, if he were interested or prejudiced. Do not know the boy John.

Clark Elliott, sworn. Do not know John. Have known Bartholomew thirteen years. Would not believe him under oath, if likely to be interested or prejudiced.

A. N. Beecher, sworn. Resided in Oberlin twelve years. Am Mayor of the village. Know Bartholomew. It would depend entirely on circumstances whether I should believe him under oath.

Dr. H. A. Bunce, sworn. Resided in Oberlin five years. Known Bartholomew five years. His reputation for truth and veracity is not as good as that of men in general.

Dr. H. Johnson, sworn. Am a physician. Have resided in Oberlin thirteen and a half years. Remember the incidents of September 13th last. Knew nothing of the crowd until after the return from Wellington. About 3 in the afternoon was going in the outskirts of the village to visit a patient, when a man met me going toward the centre of the village, and said that a negro had just been kidnapped.

What was the state of the public mind at this time with reference to the apprehended arrest or seizure of negroes?

Objected to as irrelevant.

Objection sustained. [The Court had previously repeatedly *ruled in* precisely this character of testimony.]

O. S. B. Wall affirmed. [Though a colored man, Judge WILLSON, forgetful of the Dred Scott decision, decided him to be a perfectly competent witness.]

Am resident of Oberlin. Have been since '53. Native of North Carolina. My father was a very extensive slaveholder. Knew the colors by which people of color were classified. There were black, blacker, blackest. [Laughter.] Then copper color, which is about the color of hemlock tanned sole leather. [Laughter.] Then there are dark, lighter, and light mulatto. Knew John very well. He was a decidedly black negro. Not over five feet and a half, and probably not over five feet four or five inches. His weight on the 13th of September last could not have been over 125 or 130.

Defence rested.

Defence asked leave to make three arguments. The Court refused.

At the request of the prosecution, the Court adjourned till the next morning at 9 o'clock.

SEVENTH DAY.— 9, A. M.

The prosecution resumed the examination of witnesses. Witnesses sworn.

Norris A. Wood, recalled. Have lived in Oberlin three or four years. Know Seth W. Bartholomew somewhat. Have had a good deal of deal with him since I have been there. Have taken his reputation for truth and veracity to be good. Would believe him under oath. Was at Wellington. Know L. S. Butler. Saw him at Wellington. Heard him say something about the papers. He came to me and I asked him what they was a going to do, and he said they couldn't do anything there. He said the papers was right; they'd got to go to Elyria and get a writ of *habeas corpus* to take John away from them. He wanted to get a horse and buggy of me, and I told him I had n't got any there. I come with Mr. Marks. He turned right about and went to Mr. Marks, who was standing about ten foot from me. This was about half an hour or more before the Rescue.

Cross-examined. I put up a ladder to go up by and see the fun. Expected there would be shooting up there, and wanted to see it. This was but a very few minutes before John was taken out. · Should not think it was more than five minutes. This was about three quarters of an hour after my conversation with Butler. Will swear positively to this.

M. P. Gaston, called. Resided in Oberlin twelve years. Have known Seth W. Bartholomew ever since I moved into the place. Have lived right across the road from his father's for four or five years.

Have you the means of knowing what his reputation for truth and veracity is?

Never heard aught against him.

Such an answer objected to.

Question repeated.

Same answer.

The COURT asked the witness if he understood the English language.

Question repeated.

I have. Would believe him under oath as soon as men in general.

W. B. Worden, recalled. Have lived in Oberlin five or six years. Know Seth W. Bartholomew. Have no reason to distrust his word under oath.

E. A. Munson, called. Am son of the present Postmaster at Oberlin. Reside in Cleveland. Have done so for the past five years. Previous to that, resided seven years in Oberlin. Knew Bartholomew intimately, as a schoolmate. As a boy, he was rather wild, but since coming to years of discretion, have understood his reputation to be as good as that of men in general. Would as soon believe him under oath as men in general. Knew that when he was thirteen or fourteen years old he was accused of stealing some change and something else, don't remember distinctly what it was. Never heard of his being under arrest. Heard that he paid back the money, and so the matter was settled.

Cross-examined. He was at work about Mr. Pelton's store, where I was employed at this time. This was about twelve years ago, *after* we had done going to school together. [Witness was evidently confused in dates, since it was but twelve years since he first came to Oberlin.]

E. P. Dodge, sworn. Live in this city. Left Oberlin two years ago. Was brought up there. Know Bartholomew. We grew up together as playmates. Should think his reputation for truth and veracity was as good as that of men in general. Would believe him under oath as readily as men in general.

Charles T. Marks, recalled. Lived in Oberlin about two years. Keep meat market there. Known Bartholomew for two years well. Never heard but that his reputation for truth and veracity was as good as that of men in general. Would believe him under oath as readily as men in general.

Richard P. Mitchell, recalled. Something was said between Dickson and myself about the seal to the *power of attorney.* Do not know whether he saw the warrant or not. The *power of attorney* was shown him, and he remarked that it had no seal, but he was not well enough acquainted with such papers [laughter] to know whether a seal was necessary, and I said that our laws did not require a seal. Jennings was standing close by.

Anderson Jennings, recalled. [This witness corroborated the statements of the last.]

Another list of witnesses sworn.

B. L. Pierce, called. Lived in Oberlin last twenty years. Known Bartholomew from his boyhood. Have not known him intimately, personally. Have known him as a citizen of the place. Have not the means of knowing his reputation so well as some. Could not say that his reputation for truth and veracity was as good as that of young men in general.

Harvey Dodge, called. Have lived in Oberlin last twenty-four years. Known Bartholomew from his cradle intimately. Never heard his reputation for truth and veracity questioned until now.

William E. Kellogg, called. Lived in Oberlin last ten years. Know Bartholomew tolerably well. About as well as most men. Don't think his reputation for truth and veracity is quite as good as that of men in general. Would believe him under oath.

George Dewey, called. Lived in Oberlin four years. Known Bartholomew thus long. His reputation for truth and veracity is as good as that of men in general.

E. F. Munson, called. Lived in Oberlin sixteen years. Know Bartholomew. Never knew his character for truth and veracity to be called in question. Quite a number of years ago while he was an apprentice to the tinning business, he was charged with stealing. Never heard a similar charge since that. [Is Postmaster at Oberlin].

John S. Dodge, called. Lived at Oberlin twenty-three years. Bartholomew and I grew up together. His reputation for truth and veracity is and has been as good as that of men in general.

Chauncey Wack, recalled. Have lived in Oberlin eighteen years. Know Bartholomew as well as I know any man in Oberlin. Would unhesitatingly believe him under oath. Am landlord of the Russia House.

Prosecution closed its testimony.

Defence closed its testimony.

The COURT gave the case to the Jury.

At the request of the prosecution, the Court adjourned at half past ten, till two o'clock in the afternoon.

[For the reports of the arguments of the counsel for the Government in this case, we are indebted to the *Cleveland Evening Herald*. Taking them as there published, we assume no responsibility for their accuracy. We believe them, however, to be faithful so far as they go.]

SEVENTH DAY. — AFTERNOON SESSION.

Court opened at 2 o'clock.
[The Marshal reserved the seats upon the east side of the Court Room for ladies, and they were speedily filled. The Judge's rooms, adjoining the Court Room, were also occupied by gentlemen and ladies. Every available spot was occupied by spectators, and nothing save the admirable ventilation and the lofty ceiling, rendered the air of the room tolerable.]
Judge BLISS opened for the Government.

He commented upon the crowd in attendance upon the Court, as proof of the interest the case has with the public, being novel as the first attempt to enforce the Fugitive Slave Law; this case excites interest because some wish to know if the Federal laws can be executed, and some desire to be permitted to pursue their rebellion against the laws of the country. Some people seem to suppose the States have the right to legislate on and repudiate the law of Congress in regard to reclamation of Fugitive Slaves; some States have passed laws in conflict with Federal laws on this subject; Ohio has laws subject to this objection, being in conflict with the Federal power, which is supreme over all the States.

Ohio has no right to legislate upon the subject of fugitives from labor.

Counsel quoted the clause in the Constitution under which fugitives are recaptured; that clause of the Constitution underlies the Federal Union; and impugned by any one is *ipso facto* a dissolution of the Union. Under that clause, independent of any law, the ownership of any slave escaping to Ohio, remained in the owner; it follows of necessity, that the master has a right to follow and recapture his slave in Ohio. This question was settled years ago, in the case of Prigg, of Pennsylvania. By that case it is the duty of Congress to carry out that clause; and counsel cannot imagine how any lawyer or statesman could hold that the State has any thing to do with it.

The Counsel then came to the facts in this case: Was John the slave of Bacon in Kentucky, at the time he escaped in 1856? On that question Bacon swears he was his slave, and knew John's mother, and the maternity establishes the status as a slave or free man; Jennings testifies that he knew John to be Bacon's slave, for a period of time; saw John in Oberlin, Sept. 13, 1858, and captured him. Mitchell also knew John as a slave of Bacon, and knew his mother to be a slave. This evidence is not contradicted, and it is all the law requires — the issue, so far, is established. The next fact to be considered, is John's escape, and that is proved by his being found in the common resort of fugitive slaves, to wit, in Oberlin; but a question of identity is endeavored to be made. Counsel read the description of John, as in the power of attorney: about twenty years old, about five feet six or eight inches high, heavy set, copper colored, weight one hundred and forty or one hundred and fifty pounds. The height and color are disputed by defence; they introduce three witnesses, who say John's height is less than five feet five or eight inches high. One says he is five feet four inches, and two others say he was five feet four inches; but might be five feet five inches; another says John was about five feet eight inches. The evidence does not show that John's height was misdescribed in the power of attorney; one witness says he was in the habit of embracing this negro, or of playing with him, and their bodies were often brought in contact, and he says John came just about up to his ear, and thus infers John's height from his own height. The next point is John's color, and is described as copper colored. Bacon, Mitchell, and Jennings say he was a full-blooded negro. Bacon says he is copper color. Jennings calls him black, and Mitchell would agree with Jennings rather than with Bacon. Witnesses on the other side say he was full-blooded, and call him black. At the same time there are blacker negroes than John, and the inhabitants of Oberlin have abundant opportunities of knowing, but those living in Kentucky have a better opportunity of knowing. John proclaimed that he was a slave, that he escaped from Bacon, and when a crowd of law violators were around him, he said he was Bacon's slave, and must go back to Kentucky; and he said he desired to go back and see his master and his mistress. The identity of John is placed beyond the reach of every question. As to his weight all counsel has to say is that he became a victim of a foul disease contracted by leaving Kentucky, and going to Oberlin; witnesses for the government estimated his weight when he was in health.

It is said that in order to be chargeable with rescuing a slave, it is necessary to show notice on the part of the claimant of the character of the person claimed. The Court will no doubt charge you that the defendant should have some notice as to the character of John as a fugitive from justice. What is sufficient proof? Any circumstance that a man of ordinary appreciation would notice is sufficient. The counsel read from Giltner v. Graham, 4 McLean, p. 418, being an action for a penalty of $1,000 for rescuing a slave as to the liability of persons who join in a rescue, and on the subject of the notice to rescuers, and the liability of the members of such a crowd.

The Oberlin people who came to the rescue of John, knew he was a fugitive, their language showed it; they assembled on receipt of information that a *fugitive* had been taken by *slave* catchers; all agreeing to the common fact that John was a fugitive and as such was captured. What other motive had they to assemble for his arrest except that he was a slave, and they intended to rescue him? Several answered that they went to Wellington to rescue a slave; some were in favor of getting a process for the claimants, others that they cared not for papers but would have him any way; a miscellaneous crowd of black, white, and *blue* — for some were drunk — crying out, tear down the house, tear off the roof, brandishing guns and weapons. Is there any doubt every one of that crowd knew John was a fugitive, legally held by due process, and their intention was to rescue the slave. It was known that he was held under a Commissioner's warrant to be taken to Columbus for examination, every person who knew that warrant knew that John was a fugitive

slave. The Marshal freely exhibited that warrant, showing almost an undue anxiety to impress on that crowd the sacred obligations they were under to let him alone in the execution of his duty; sending for the Justice, Constable, and the Lawyer, and Jennings shows his power of attorney, thus being doubly armed. Proclamation was made to the crowd, and the warrant read, and Mr. Patton summoned the people and read the paper, and they all gathered around and the warrant proclaimed to them that John was a fugitive slave from Bacon, and Jennings was authorized to arrest him. No information was conveyed by the warrant, for they all knew before that John was a fugitive. The negro voluntarily interfered to quiet that crowd, and attempted to speak to the crowd, and said his master had sent for him and he must go. If he had a master, of course he was a slave; the mob interfered and told him not to say he wanted to go back to Kentucky, and then the cry arose from that infuriated crowd they would have him any way. Now, shall that crowd say that they believed a free man was being kidnapped? We do not fear that Southerners will come to Ohio to kidnap free men.

There is no need of Higher Law; there is no need of the rallying of the children of God — as Lincoln says of himself — in the shape of a riot to protect free negro men of Ohio; the children of this world are adequate for such duty. When these Oberlin men went down to Wellington, they proclaimed that they did so under the Higher Law, for they knew they were outraging the law of the land.

It is a pity that all the good people of Oberlin had not behaved as well as Patton; had they, this indictment would not have been found; although Patton went from Oberlin to Wellington, and his motive might have been good or bad, his conduct there was honorable to him, and counsel would say to all his associate students at Oberlin, "Go and do likewise," and you will get the respect of all good men. He went out and told that crowd all about that warrant, and the power of attorney by which these men were armed, and that all that could be done was to try some process of law, by getting a writ of *habeas corpus*, which according to the Higher Law of Oberlin might have superior power to the United States Court.

A young man by the name of Butler, a lawyer, swore that he was in the crowd, but never heard of a fugitive slave in that crowd, but it is in proof that he did declare that John was held as a fugitive by lawful authority, and said so in the crowd, and went to a Mr. Marks to furnish a horse and buggy, that he himself might go and get a *habeas corpus* to get John away.

Look out for the forgetfulness of these men. You may expect that they will forget what took place in the crowd. Patton has told the whole truth, but Butler has forgotten.

Dickson says there was no seal upon the warrant, and spoke about it at the time ; and the marshal said it was not necessary. Mitchell says it was the power of attorney, about which this conversation took place, and Jennings says he took the power of attorney out of his coat pocket and handed it to Dickson to read. Here the power of attorney was openly proclaimed as the paper on which they claimed to hold John. Counsel does not say that Dickson means to testify falsely, but his memory is not so good in facts that tend to sustain the government, as those that tend to its defeat. The authority by which John was held, was the joint authority of the power of attorney and of the warrant. Lowe, Jennings, and Mitchell, all held possession. The indictment does not allege that he was rescued from a warrant, but was rescued from Jennings acting under a power of attorney, assisted by other persons.

The defence says the indictment is bad, because it does not aver that John owed service to his master in Kentucky under the laws thereof. But the indictment uses the words of the statute. Is not that sufficient? Such minds as Clay and Webster, in framing the act, did not think the words " under the law thereof" necessary, although they were in the act of '98.

The jury will be compelled to find that the crowd went to Wellington in defiance of the law, caring nothing for it, to rescue this fugitive, in the midst of his own protestations and against the right of his owner made evident to them. Mr. Bushnell was the principal one in that crowd at Wellington, having induced persons to go there armed, saying to one that he had no business there unless armed. Bushnell is proved to be in the crowd, and there is no contradiction of the fact that Bushnell was in the buggy, being the same buggy in which the negro was placed. It was not Bushnell's horse and buggy, and he therefore must have been selected for the purpose of carrying the negro off. Bushnell was in waiting according to his office, when John was put in the buggy, cracked the whip, and away he went. At Oberlin, this is thought to be a good joke. People around Oberlin think so little of their government and the statutes of the Federal Government, when they interfere with their sympathies with negro women and men, that they consider their violation a good joke. Is it right any people should impugn the laws of the land, knowing no law but their own consciences? This is a serious question. Any jury of undebauched minds will execute this statute in the same faith as in any civil or criminal case under statute law.

Judge Bliss spoke two hours and a half.

Mr. RIDDLE addressed the Court and Jury, in substance, as follows : —

May it please the Court; Gentlemen of the jury.

The progress of this case has reached a stage in which it becomes my duty and privilege to address you on behalf of the defence. In the discharge of that duty it is also my right, to discuss just such propositions, and in just such a manner as I may think proper. This announcement need create no apprehension, for I have no ambition to play moral heroics, nor do I design to pitch the key of my remarks above the plane, on which courts and juries are obliged to dispose of the every-day affairs of practical life, with which they must deal. And I trust that in bearing and deportment, I may not fall below the gravity of this high occasion.

It is no purpose of mine to make this Court Room the scene, and this trial the occasion for the expression of peculiar views and sentiments, any farther than they properly have to do with the issues.

I need spend no declamation on the importance of the case, in any of its aspects. The novelty of the issue, the character of the evidence, the argument of counsel, based on the central idea of property in man, mark this as standing strongly out from all the subject-matters ever before adjudicated in our courts. In the sort of neutral ground that ever stretches from the feet of the advocate as he arises to the actual case which he must discuss, there is usually found a variety of matters, usually more or less discussed, which I shall pass unnoticed.

There is one subject, however, lying partly in that neutral ground, and in part connected with the gist of the case, upon which I must remark; and in so doing, I may, and probably shall, advance sentiments with which you cannot sympathize ; and for the utterance of which, I only ask the toleration which, on all occasions I would extend to you. Whatever diversity of sentiments may exist among us, as citizens of this great free State, there can be no diversity of interests.

You are here merely and purely because you are such citizens. As jurors, you represent the only unqualified democratic element in our government. The path which leads from your citizens' seats to your seats as jurors, is straight and level, or rather you bring your citizens' seats with you, and sit with all your good vigorous sense, experience, feelings, sympathies, hopes, fears, passions, and prejudices as men upon you ; yet all chastened and elevated, subdued and toned by the oath which binds you to the duties of this present high calling.

As such citizens and such men only shall I address you.

And now, as to the matter referred to, the so-called dogma of the Higher Law, I am frank to say, gentlemen — and I never had a sentiment I was not ready to avow — I am perfectly frank to declare, *that I am a votary of that Higher Law!* And I here, in the face of this high tribunal, boldly proclaim, that he who has no higher regard for the right than that which is enforced by the penal code of the country which is so unfortunate as to number him with its citizens, — whose moral sense does not rise above the coerced observance of the criminal statutes, — is neither a good citizen, nor an honest man.

Right, and its everlasting opposite, *Wrong*, existed anterior to the feeble enactments of men, and will survive their final repeal — and must ever remain Right and Wrong, because they are such, unchanged and unqualified by your acts of Congress, and statutes of your Legislatures. Will any mortal say that there can be no right, no wrong, outside of the U. S. Statutes at Large? Dare any man arise here and say in the face of this sun, that the gossamer threads of human enactments, can break through or bind down the everlasting pillars of justice, as set up by the Almighty himself?

It is conceded that the will of one man cannot accomplish this. If one cannot, ten cannot, nor ten thousand; nor can they confer power on any man, or set of men, who can do it.

You may erase, expunge, exile and outlaw this thing, Right, from your Statutes, and denounce it as wrong, and still it is Right. Traduce it till it seems leprous — arraign, condemn, and execute it as felon, and it is still Right, Imperial Right! who will lord it right royally over the consciences of men, and punish their non-observance. And the wrong which you enthrone in the place of banished Right, is still wrong. No matter though it reign till proscription sanctify its usurpation, it is wrong. Jurors may be sworn by its authority, and learned courts so adjudicate as to uphold its supremacy, it is still everlasting wrong, and not Right.

Suppose in a given instance the old right has been repealed by one of your statutes, and the wrong enacted; what, then, is to be the conduct of the subject? Can there remain a doubt as to the real course of his action? " But he breaks the law of the land!" exclaims a pious patriot, with horror, " and all for such a flaw as conscience!" A word about that thing of breaking the "law of the land." How do you obey the law? Why, either by doing the things it enjoins, or submitting to the penalty it imposes. Both are equally obedience. Every citizen has this choice held out to him, by every penal statute, and you cannot proclaim a man a bad citizen when he acts conscientiously on his choice, nor say he disobeys your law when he submits to its requirements. Suppose such a man is wrong in his choice, he challenges respect and admiration, and is not amenable to the contumely of those who gibe and jeer him.

But if he is right, if the path of conscience in the onward progress of the race, is ultimately recognized as the way of truth and holiness, then, gentlemen, the dungeon to which you would send him becomes a luminous sanctuary, and the grave to which you would consign him, a star-crowned shrine, to which the feet of all coming generations will journey, to gather wisdom and inspiration! And hence the legal rule, while dealing with an alleged offender,

who, in the observance of one of those old great rights, has broken the contravening man enactment — the statute, as against him, shall receive the narrowest possible construction to exclude him from its penalty. Take the case before you as it would have existed in the absence of your statutes, and state it the most strongly for the Government. This boy John, so poor that he had no father to give him a name, and so abased that he could never be called a man, and in mature years could only graduate an uncle — was held to service to John G. Bacon, in Kentucky. Held how? by what contract? under what obligations, and for what benefit conferred on him? Because he was a slave, is replied. Because he was that thing which all the laws of God declare cannot exist. How came he a slave? What great crime had he committed, the adjudged penalty of which was this doom? The malignant genius of his race doomed him at birth — he was born a slave! He belonged not to the God who made him, the father who begot him, or the mother who bore him! but to John G. Bacon, of Mason county, Kentucky. He was a slave because his mother was a slave, and she because her mother was a slave. And *her* mother was ravished away from her demolished cabin, murdered husband, and slaughtered children, in the wilds of Africa, and did not perish in the horrors of the middle passage. And this felon right to this stolen woman, transmitted unimpaired through her descendants to this claimant, constituted his sole and exclusive title to the boy John, and he held him in Kentucky by just the same robber hand that the ancestor was held with in Africa, the hour of her capture. And this John, thus held, and under this obligation, with the wrongs of generations burning in his veins — with his face towards the North star, and, as if polarized, fled — fled in the night — frightened, as captives flee; over the snow-whitened earth, under the stars, and, at his approach, *the Ohio river congealed, that he might flee.*

The claimant pursued him, as the men-stealers pursued his ancestors, with shackles, six-shooters, and knives, and by the same right alone. Overtaking, they added the sneaking artifice of the thief to the violence of the robber, and seized him. As they thus held him in his agony, the defendant and his associates approached; and, knowing John was a slave in Kentucky, and how and by whom he was there held, that he had escaped, and how and for what purpose he was then seized and held; and knowing all this, they put forth their strong hands, and, wrenching John from the grasp of his captors, consigned him to the boundless realm of freedom! This is what they did, and all they did, and in so doing they obeyed the laws of God, as written in revelation, as written in the free creation, and stamped in the nature and instincts of man.

Don't be alarmed, your Honor; I know this case is to be adjudged by none of these principles here. I know that this highest embodied achievement of the Christian civilization of the nineteenth century — the fugitive slave act of September 18, 1850 — always to be named with profound gratitude and veneration, at one perpendicular sweep, attempts to clear the whole moral decalogue and scatter its divided fragments, and I know I may not ask you to set it aside, or the jury to disregard it. But, warring as it does upon every element of the common law and all primitive notions of right, I am authorized to demand of you as a court, the narrowest construction of this act — for Law I will not knowingly call it — for the very purpose of excluding this case from its straitened scope; and I may require at the hands of this jury, a liberal construction of all the conduct of the prisoner, so that his acts may fall outside of its penalty. In the defence of such acts, arraigned under such a statute, the arts and finesse of the bar, which, when exerted in favor of flagrant crime, approach chicanery, come to be a sacred host striking for beleaguered innocence; and that stale maxim, that "a man is presumed innocent till proven guilty," that floats an imponderable formula in the legal atmosphere of ordinary cases, arises around such a defendant, an impregnable fortress, until carried by overwhelming proof; and those intangible entities, called reasonable doubts, assume the form of robed angels bearing assurances of escape and safety. And if, over all, a conviction must take place, let the blow fall in the presence of averted faces; and when the convict stands up for sentence, he occupies a moral level above the tribunal that pronounces judgment, and the judge who dooms is abashed in the presence of the criminal he condemns.

Let not these defendants now or ever be denounced as fanatics, or bad citizens. If it shall ultimately be found that they violated this your statute, they come to suffer its penalties. They have not sought to place themselves beyond your jurisdiction. Your marshal had but to notify them, and lo! they are here, unresistingly to endure if they must.

Yet again, I repeat it, they must be reached only through "the strait and narrow way" of this act of Congress, unlike that other way, and leading to the other place. They are guarded by fiery cherubim, armed with the many-bladed sword of the common law, that flashes every way; and all are to be beaten down in this legal conflict ere they can be reached.

Let us now look directly at the case under the law and testimony. Mr. Riddle here made a point to the Court, on the sufficiency of the indictment. It was therein alleged that John was held to service in Kentucky, but did not state how he was holden, and hence the Court could not judge of the legality of that holding.

In Miller v. McQuerry, 5 McLean, 469, it was decided that the holding to service within the provisions of this slave act, must be by law alone; and hence this indictment should allege

that John was held to service in Kentucky by the laws thereof. It follows the language of the statute, but that is insufficient.

The Court: The Supreme Court in the U. S. v. Mills, 7 Peters, held, that for misdemeanors it is sufficient to set out the offence in the language of the statute.

Mr. Riddle: Very well, the Statute and Constitution must be taken together to form the law in this instance.

I have always understood the rule of good pleading to be, that where a statute creating a crime clearly defined it, you should follow its language in an indictment under it; but where it merely named the offence, the indictment in apt words must set up the acts and things going to make up the offence; and under that rule this indictment is wholly defective.

How can the Court learn from this indictment by what bond John was held to service, and short of that knowledge, how can it determine that he was holden as required by this statute?.

This is not the instance of good title defectively stated, but of title upon which they can alone recover not stated at all. If not necessary to allege that John was held to service, I am clearly certain that it is necessary to prove it by evidence to this jury, for it is a question of fact for them under instructions.

Does your honor, or can this jury be presumed to know what are the laws of Kentucky? Suppose, as a historic fact, you take it as true that Kentucky is a slaveholding State, can you go farther and say that certain classes and descriptions of persons are slaves? and that John is of that class and description? I know the U. S. Supreme Court and its judges, as such, will, ex-officio, take notice of all the laws of all the States, and for the amplest reasons. The rule and its reason, are thus stated by Judge McLean in the case just cited by me.

"The Supreme Court and its judges recognize without proof the laws of the several States, and territories. The jurisdiction of that Court and of its members extends throughout the Union. In the respective States they administer the local laws so that the laws of those States come under their special cognizance in acting upon individual rights."

The Supreme Court is bound to take notice of all laws within its territorial jurisdiction, because of that jurisdiction alone. A District Judge by the same rule takes notice of all the laws within its territorial jurisdiction only. How, then, can this Court take notice of the laws of Kentucky, any more than would or could any of the Courts of Ohio?

Suppose this Court will hold as matter of law that Kentucky is a Slave State, it will still, I presume, require proof of the status of this John. I know the witnesses swear John was a slave, but whether he is or not is mixed question of fact and law, not to be proven in that general way. By the witnesses the Government must prove a state of facts which under the Kentucky law, will constitute a slave. The facts as proven are, John's mother was a slave; and he labored, loafed, and lived in some sort without wages. If your Honor knows all the law of Kentucky, can you tell us whether a child born in that State follows the condition of the mother, contrary to the rule of the civilized world? and whether a person receiving no pay is a slave?

We are farther informed in this valuable document from the Grand Jury, that John was owned by John G. Bacon, an allegation to be proven as laid. John G. who appears before us a veritable Scriptural Patriarch, swears in set terms that John was in truth and fact his particular exclusive and unqualified John. He also says that he inherited John from his paternal Bacon, and has living a mother, and five brothers and sisters — which is every word he says about it. Mitchell whose especial mission to Ohio was to be a witness, goes farther and says, that John G. got John on the division of his father's estate, but frankly says he knows nothing of that division, or whether one ever took place, except by rumor. Thus it stands, then, Bacon the elder owned John, and died leaving a widow and six heirs at law, and then the proof stops. If the Court knows all the law of Kentucky, will your Honor have the goodness to inform me if by that law this particular John would fall to this particular John G.? If not, I beg to suggest, that in Kentucky as in Ohio, he fell to the six, who, for aught proven to the contrary, continue to own him as much as men may; and instead of his being the property of John G. as alleged, he owns the valuable interest of one sixth of him only.

This indictment farther says, that John being such slave, and so owing service — what an equitable debt — on the first day of January 1856, fled — the ungrateful infidel! He ran away, and good enough for him! On the whole proof I think that allegation true, and I congratulate all hands — the Court, the District-Attorney, and particularly this naughty John, that this is proven.

He went off with that "high-headed" Dinah, and "pop-eyed Frank," and it seems the infection reached the horses, for two of them went off at the same time. Yet whether John and Frank and Dinah went off with the horses, or whether the horses went off with Dinah, Frank, and John, does not quite appear, and may not be very material. It is very certain they all scampered off together, to the huge grief of John G., the detriment of religion South, the great danger of the Union, and the disgust of the American Eagle generally.

Court adjourned to Tuesday morning.

On resuming the next morning, after recapitulating, Mr. Riddle went on to say. John fled Jan. 1, 1856, and for two years and nine months his bereaved master lay in a trance of stupefied horror, at this act of ingratitude and treason, ere he fully awoke to the cries of mercy, and a bleeding Union; and kindly offered one half of John to whoever would catch and divide him. We are told that on the 4th of Sept. 1858, he duly executed the alleged power of attorney, under which the indictment says John was captured and held, to the redoubtable Anderson Jennings, of Mason County, Kentucky, which causes the elephantine proportions of that worthy, to loom ominously on the horizon; yet ere I turn my attention to him and his doings, I have a word to the Court as to the legality of this power of attorney. The 7th section of the Slave Statute provides, that the owner of any escaping slave "his, her, or their agent or attorney, duly authorized by power of attorney in writing, acknowledged and certified under the seal of some legal officer or court of the State or territory, in which the same may be executed; may pursue," and capture such slave, etc.

The power of attorney given in evidence which is alleged to have been acknowledged before Robert A. Cochran, Clerk of the Mason County Court, Kentucky, on its face purports to have been acknowledged before him by his deputy, one Richardson, which is clearly insufficient.

Does this Court know that by the laws of Kentucky, the deputy of the Mason County Court is a legal officer of that State? If so, the acknowledgment should have been before him as such officer in the exercise of such office.

Can it be performed before a legal officer, by his deputy? Clearly not. The laws of the State designate who are legal officers, and this statute designates them and no others, as having this peculiar virtue. In taking this acknowledgment they do not act by virtue of any State law, nor in discharge of any State duty, but wholly and purely by force of this statute, and a deputy under the State law can only act for his principal in the discharge of some State function; he as such deputy can do no act for his State principal under this act; the moment he steps out of the line of his duty as a State official, he ceases to be his deputy at all; and this act authorizes the appointment of no deputies.

Again, the taking of this acknowledgment is purely a judicial act, and cannot be performed by deputy. "The legal officers" of a State sustain the same relation to the statute of 1850, as did the justices of the peace, etc., to the old law of 1798, and, according to Prigg's case, might act under it or not, at their option. They must first decide whether they would train under it, and, having so decided, must then perform a judicial function. In the certificate under consideration it will be seen that the officer says he had personal knowledge, that the John G. Bacon is the veritable John G., etc. Now can it be claimed that the knowledge of the deputy is the knowledge of the principal; or that the chief, in profound ignorance of the fact, can have this vicarious knowledge through his subordinate?

And let it be borne in mind that this acknowledgment is an act before the clerk, and in no sense the action of the Court of which he is clerk, which could be certified to by a deputy only because it was the act of the Court.

It is, then, with entire confidence that we rely, that the ruling of this court will be, that this power of attorney for these reasons is wholly insufficient; which will dispose of the case.

It is further alleged, Gentlemen, that this Jennings, armed with this power of attorney, pursued this same John into Ohio, and there, by virtue of the same instrument and no other he captured and held this same John. Your closest attention to these propositions is required, because each must be proven as laid, and the Court will tell you if any other man than Jennings, by any authority, no matter what, captured and held this same John, this case must fail, no matter what the defendant may have done. Then with a desire only to arrive at the truth, and do justice between the parties, and remembering all the time that the Government must beyond doubt establish its side of the case; and not forgetting that it is seeking to enforce a statute made up of unmingled outrages, let us scan the proofs on these points.

Armed with this power of attorney, which, for the purpose of capture and the extradition of John, subrogates Jennings to the rights and powers of John G. Bacon, what does Jennings do? He finds himself on the 8th or 10th of September at Oberlin, with full authority. Mitchell, the witness to identify, is there, and dreaming, unsuspecting John is there. Does he want assistants? Is not Dayton, one of your deputy marshals, there also? Why under the heavens then, if John is to be taken under that power of attorney, is he not then and there seized? Why delay and give him a chance to become alarmed and so escape? Can any mortal tell?

Why, plainly enough, Gentlemen of the Jury, because *it was never intended to so act under that power of attorney.* He sneaks off to Columbus to one of these high and mighty commissioners, appointed to execute this Embodiment of all the Virtues of Christian Civilization in these Latter Days, and there uses his power of attorney for the only purpose for which it was ever given, namely, to *swear out a warrant* for the seizure of the negro; and this is all the use to which this power of attorney ever was put.

Why, what was Lowe there for? If Jennings could call Lowe to his assistance, exercising all the functions of the owner for the time being, he could just as well call any other man or number of men. The United States Marshal by virtue of his warrant has no more power to assist in the arrest of a slave than any other man. *He acts not by virtue, but in spite of* his high office. He forgets the dignity of his official position, and consents to play pimp and pander to this bawd of American Slavery.

Jennings passes by Marshal Dayton, goes to Columbus, arms a marshal there with a warrant, which is not needed to assist an owner or agent in the caption of his slave, and returns to the precincts of Oberlin. Keep it in mind, that this man Jennings is, for the time being, the owner, and *the only man who can capture;* and that *he sends Lowe* to take out the game after the trap has been sprung, himself the while sitting quietly at his ease, with the power of attorney safe in his inside coat-pocket, in his room at the celebrated Russia House. And will you mark it well, Gentlemen, that this man Jennings, being only an agent and not the actual owner, although clothed by his power of attorney with full authority to arrest the boy with his own hands, or by posse, in his immediate presence, *had no power to confer upon another, either by parol or writing, the authority vested in himself to seize and arrest this boy John.* The power to appoint is exhausted, so soon as it is transferred from the principal to an agent. It cannot be transferred from the agent to another. Jennings, then, Gentlemen of the Jury, not attempting himself to authorize Lowe to recapture this slave, but having discharged all the duty for which he came to the State of Ohio, in having sworn out the warrant, put it in Lowe's hands, and having pointed out the game, seats himself complacently in his chair at the Russia House, under the benignant administration of good Mr. Wack, having, as he himself tells us, his power of attorney safely bestowed in his revolver pocket, while Mr. *Lowe,* by virtue of his *useless warrant,* arrests the man, and establishes him in his custody.

I do not undertake to say that the agent may not call assistants; but I do say that they, if so called, must act either in his immediate presence, or so near that he, being constructively present, can direct and order their movements in any emergency: but he can never organize a posse, and send them away to make an arrest! any more than could the owner in Kentucky, by parol, organize a band and send them into Ohio and legally recapture an escaped slave.

I know, Gentlemen, that this man Mitchell, sent to Ohio for the express purpose of acting as a witness, says that the power of attorney was actually *shown to John!* A most gracious favor that, indeed, especially since he tells us in the next breath that he thinks John did n't read it, because he could n't, and had n't time if he could; and Mr. Jennings swears positively that, at the time Mitchell avers he showed it to John (when the arrest was made), it was in his own (Jennings') breast pocket, in the Russia House, at least two miles from the scene of the affecting interview between John and his old friend Mitchell.

But who seizes John?

It matters nothing in law, to be sure, since it is *not* Jennings, the only man who could seize him, or direct it to be done for him; but as illustrating the *animus* of the whole transaction, the question is one of some interest. The carriage containing the worthy trio, Lowe, his assistants Davis and Mitchell, overtakes and draws up along side of that in which the unsuspecting John is riding leisurely along with the little decoy Shakespeare. And now who seizes John? Mitchell, who may be said to be in the State of Ohio in some sort by the procurement of the owner, John G. Bacon? No. Lowe, the United States Deputy-Marshal, with a warrant in his pocket, under which he comes to act in behalf of the United States, and for the preservation of its essential "peace and dignity," — orders his *Davis*. Yes, *Davis* seizes John, as deputy-marshal Lowe's assistant, being the man farthest of all removed from the agent, Jennings, himself, who alone had any authority whatever to make the arrest under the power of attorney. *Davis* seizes John, and then Mitchell comes to his assistance, while *Lowe holds the horses!* And Mitchell says he then and there showed John the power of attorney. But his excellent confederate, Jennings, swears positively that he had it at that time in his own pocket, at the Russia House.

Rather an unfortunate difference of opinion! Mr. Mitchell may come up to the requisitions of a witness in the State of Kentucky, but for this latitude, is rather too pointedly contradicted by Jennings, — if Jennings may be permitted to contradict anybody, concerning which I grant that it is pushing legal impudence about as far as it will go.

But why hasn't Lowe and his man Davis been placed upon this stand to swear that Lowe sunk his high character as a deputy-marshal of the United States, and that he took some part of the authority vested in Jennings by the power of attorney, and by virtue of this fraction arrested the boy? and that he did not act as a marshal under his warrant if that is true. Can there be a particle of a reasonable doubt concerning the real capacity in which Lowe acted? He came as a marshal armed with a warrant to be served by a marshal, went out with his assistant and did serve it, and arrested John and held him as a marshal; which he cannot and dare not deny.

But, Gentlemen, when after that brief separation upon this benignant mission, the two streams of authority, one flowing from the owner and the other from the United States, united again at Wellington, is there, then, any giving up of the less to the greater, and Jennings assuming the control of John? Nothing of the kind. In the first place he couldn't do it, and in the second place you know absolutely and positively that he never did do it. It might just as well be said that a man who arms a sheriff with a writ of replevin, goes to a neighboring town, points out the property to

be taken, and pays the bills at the tavern — including of course the "smiles" — could say that the property taken by the officer was in *his* (the owner's) custody. Such a custody is the custody of the law and not of the owner. What sort of an arrangement was there between Lowe and Jennings — a joint possession? There can never be a joint possession. The officer captures the entire animal, holds the entire animal, returns the entire animal to the magistrate, who either gives up the entire animal to the owner, or entirely discharges him. I know, your Honor, that the very proposition shows its monstrous absurdity, and that the custody of the owner is completely, wholly, and entirely inconsistent with the custody of the law. The law tolerates no joint custody whatever. It takes the whole man, holds the whole man, and awards the whole man either to the claimant or to himself. Were it otherwise we might have the singular case of the commissioner discharging that part of the man arrested, and held by a marshal while the owner would retain his part.

But let us pursue the question of fact a little farther.

When they arrive at Wellington and the crowd gathers, and the inquiry is sent up — "Who holds this colored man, and by what authority?" — who is announced to the crowd? The best answer is found in the entire testimony itself upon this point. Permit me to read to you all there is of it bearing on this point. And first on the part of the Government, which may be condensed as follows.

J. G. Bacon. Made power of attorney to Anderson Jennings.

Anderson Jennings. Had power of attorney. Had it at Wellington, and showed it to the crowd. Fifteen or twenty of them looked at it inside the room. Sheriff came to arrest us; wanted to know by what authority we held John. Showed him the papers.

R. P. Mitchell. Power of attorney read to them [at Wellington]. Thinks a lawyer read it. Several asked by what authority we held John. Told them by power of attorney from Bacon to Jennings. Think Lowe showed John power of attorney at the time of arrest. Think John had it in his hand.

A. S. Halbert. Patton said that he had seen the papers, and that they were good.

Jacob Wheeler. Saw Jennings' power of attorney. *Lowe* called on all of us for help. *Lowe* would go anywhere and show his papers. Did go somewhere to read them to crowd.

Barnabas Meacham. Asked *Lowe* to go out and read his *warrant*, and I would see him back. We went. Stopped on steps a few rods from hotel. He began to read, and some one else finished. Went back. I told the crowd *he* had a *warrant*.

Isaac Bennett. Saw a *warrant* issued by United States Commissioner of the Southern District; also, a power of attorney. Told several that *Lowe* had a *warrant* to arrest John Price. *Warrant* was read. Think it was. The paper shown me by *Lowe* was a *warrant*, made by United States Commissioner, Southern District. Somebody put in my hands a power of attorney. When I spoke to crowd, told them of the *warrant*, and may have said "papers." Saw no other manifestation of the marshal's authority.

Chauncey Wack. Patton said the papers were right. Said nothing of any power of attorney.

Proof on this point by defence.

Joseph H. Dickson, lawyer at Wellington. Meacham, the constable, came for me and said they wanted to see me. Took me in. *Lowe* introduced himself to me as the *United States Marshal who held John.* Showed me the *warrant* under which he held him. I read it carefully. Noticed it had no seal. Lowe said it needed none. Saw no power of attorney, and heard not a word said about any. A man, whom I now recognize as Jennings, offered him (John) for fourteen hundred dollars. I told him he was not worth that in Kentucky. Said .he thought he knew the value of niggers. Another, a red-whiskered man, said he'd better take twelve hundred dollars. I supposed the man who offered to sell him was the owner. Said nothing to undeceive me; nothing about being agent, or having any power of attorney. Told crowd of the *warrant*. Never heard of power of attorney till I came here into Court.

James L. Patton. Went up. *Lowe* took me into adjoining room. Told me he was the marshal. Showed me the *warrant* issued by the United States Commissioner, Southern District. I read it. That was all the authority shown me, all the paper I saw or heard of. Never heard of power of attorney till after this trial began.

William Howk, Justice of the Peace at Wellington. William Sciples said the *marshal* wanted to see me. Went up. *Marshal* showed a paper understood to be a *warrant*. Had no glasses with me and couldn't read it. Think I saw the word "Columbus" on it. *Lowe* went out and read *it* to the crowd, as I understood. Said he was going to take the boy to Columbus. A committee might be appointed to go with him. Never heard of power of attorney till in the course of this trial. Talked with Bennett about the *warrant*.

L. S. Butler, law-student. Stood by *Lowe* and Patton when the *warrant* was read. Noticed there was no seal. No other papers were shown or spoken of. Asked some one, supposed to be of the party, if there were any other papers, and was answered, No. Heard nothing of any power of attorney.

Now, Gentlemen, can there be a particle of doubt as to who held that boy on that occasion, or by what authority he held him? Did *Jennings* come forward to show his *power of attorney?* Not a word of it. That power of attorney never transpired to that crowd outside in any form. LOWE came forward, and claimed that HE held the boy in HIS custody. And this Mr. Jennings all the while hid his ponderous proportions behind Lowe. He did so when Mr. Bennett went up and confronted him. Nobody but Lowe came forward, and if he showed any power of attorney, it was only to prove that the warrant was sworn out by one duly authorized. I know that Mitchell comes up here and swears that it was a power of attorney which was shown to Mr. Dickson, just as if Mr. Dickson, a lawyer of extensive practice there, and recently the District-Attorney of that county, couldn't tell a power of attorney from a warrant, after reading it through carefully, as he himself swears he did, and especially didn't know whether the power of attorney was properly executed, when if he saw it as it is here, he saw it in due form, and with the broad, staring seal of Mason county, Kentucky, upon it! And it is *altogether* probable that he said of a *power of attorney*, as Mitchell swears positively he did (and this Mr. Dickson corroborates as applied to the *warrant* of the United States Commissioner shown him), that he "*wasn't much conversant with that class of papers*, and could not consequently say positively whether it was accurately made out or not!"

And who told Dickson he was going to take John to Columbus? Jennings? Oh, no. But *Lowe*, the Marshal, says, "*I* am going to take him to Columbus before the U. S. Commissioner." And who went out at the call of the crowd, to exhibit the authority by whom and which John was held? The elegant and accomplished Mr. Jennings, who was himself three times as interesting an object to view, and who certainly could have been seen without placing himself upon any very elevated stand-point? No, not he; but Mr. Jacob K. Lowe, the redoubtable deputy U. S. Marshal of the Southern District of Ohio, who went out under the protection of Mr. Patton, a student from the infected district of Oberlin. This gentle Mr. Patton took the representative of the United States of North America patronizingly under his arm, and conducting him out into that dangerous crowd, read his warrant for him, under which alone it was claimed to that crowd that the negro was held, and then led him safely back again. *Not one word of a power of attorney;* not one glimpse of Jennings, who alone had power to hold the negro a single moment under it. I know that Mitchell swears that the power of attorney was shown to Patton and Howk; but I know farther that they both swear positively that they never so much as *heard of a power of attorney* until they heard of it with amazement first in this Court-Room. The warrant alone, which our less favored eyes are not permitted to see, was shown; the warrant —for withholding which the Prosecution have their own, and doubtless good and sufficient reasons, and without seeing which we must probably live out the remnant of our days, and die —

was only shown to them. If there was any thing ever shown in a Court of Justice under heaven, it has been shown in this Court, and in this case, that this negro, if arrested at all, was arrested by the warrant, was held by the warrant, and would have been carried off by the warrant, and by the warrant alone. And therefore if the law, as we see it, shall be recognized by his Honor, these facts will rise to Heaven like adamantine walls around the devoted defendant, outside of which the Prosecution may clamor as idly as did the worshippers of Moloch around the tabernacle of the living God.

Gentlemen of the Jury, whatever may be our private views and prejudices, I trust that by this time we have so far put them aside, that I may now look into your eyes with that confidence which springs always from the universal and instinctive love of Justice. But suppose — contrary, as I conceive it, to all possible fact — suppose that you should find that John was arrested and held by virtue of the power of attorney; — then there are a number of points which naturally range under other parts of the subject, still to be discussed.

Has it been shown that the John Price, arrested by Jennings or Lowe, is one and the same with the John that escaped from John G. Bacon in January, 1856; and that the defendant Bushnell knew he was not only an escaped slave, but that he had escaped from and belonged to this particular Bacon? For it is not sufficient that because John G. Bacon is a slaveholder, and has lost a John, he may send into Ohio a fishing process, and gather up with it any and every fugitive John, and then whoever shall dare to inquire whether he has got his own or the John of some one else, shall thereby make himself amenable to the penalties of this infamous Slave Act.

John escaped. Very singular, indeed, is n't it? There is some fault either in the law or in the theology of the Peculiar Institution. There is no doubt but that the whole race was doomed to slavery in Ham; that is not an open question. But somehow it is very strange that the Deity who thus doomed this nation did not make it, in its feelings and emotions, better adapted to its condition. Just think of John, careless of the fiat of his Maker, and still more careless of the interests of his owner, and the good of this Confederacy, lifting his huge, shapeless foot, with its enormous heel, and with the best part of the muscle of his leg on the wrong side, and driving it remorselessly through the priceless, precious porcelain of the Union. And all this because, contrary to the Act made and provided, he was smitten with the polar fever, to which persons of his class are so alarmingly subject. And then there is the Ohio river, which certainly ought to be indicted; for so chilly was its coolness toward the interests of the glorious Union, that it actually froze over, and the negro walked with impunity over its icy bosom, toward Oberlin! Was this escaping John the John arrested?

Jennings swears that the first time he saw John after his escape was at Wellington, on the 13th of September last, and that he sent to Kentucky for a witness to identify him; as he doubtless could not rely on his own knowledge of him; and now he comes up here to swear to the negro's identity! And Mitchell swears that during the seven days he was at Oberlin, prior to the 13th of September, he saw John but once, and that was when John chanced to be passing his window. Upon such testimony, up to the time of the capture, does the identity of the negro, upon the part of the Government rest. Bear in mind, too, that this Jennings had been at Oberlin before. And also that there existed at that time in that neighborhood, by reason of the overt acts of these and other parties, a feverish state of excitement with reference to certain colored persons being clandestinely seized and illegally carried off. Remember that Jennings had been one of the suspicious parties; a man who could by no means be hid in any one building in Oberlin; that Mitchell, who pretends to have been a very intimate companion of John's in Kentucky, had been in the place seven consecutive days; and then tell me whether, if John had been a fugitive, his instincts would not have been awakened to alarm, and had he been the John whilom a chattel of this Bacon, he must necessarily have known Jennings and Mitchell, and would certainly have fled while all the others were excited, he, who must have had the best means of knowledge, was not even alarmed. This goes far to show he could not have been the slave of Bacon. Remember too, that John escaped just at that period of life when youth is imperceptibly gliding into manhood; is gone two years and nine months, living meanwhile altogether a different life from that in which Mitchell knew him, acquiring entirely different habits and manners, and Mitchell after catching one glimpse of him through good Mr. Wack's window — I have no doubt it was perfectly transparent — at once pounces upon him. And then his owner comes up here and swears that when he left Kentucky at the age of eighteen, he was five feet eight or ten inches high, and would weigh 165 or 170 pounds, and was copper colored. At Oberlin they arrest a John, who is positively sworn by a number of unimpeachable witnesses, who had the best means of knowing, to have been not over five feet five or six inches tall, weighing from 135 to 140 pounds, and so black that he shone! Even Jennings swears the John they captured was black. Mr. Clay's laws of bleaching out seem to work the other way at Oberlin, whatever they do in Kentucky. If they say the Kentucky boy and the Oberlin boy were both Johns, they don't come any nearer. For the Kentucky boy was simply John, while the Oberlin boy was John Price. In no solitary point do the descriptions agree. Slaves never have more than one name. They are all boys till they get to be uncles. Do we then, Gentlemen of the Jury, claim too much in claiming that the boy captured at Oberlin by no means answers to the description of the boy who ran away from John G. Bacon in 1856? Certainly, if evidence is worth any thing, it has most clearly established a glaring discrepancy here.

But the Government rests strongly on the sayings and doings of John himself, after capture, to establish his identity. These rest wholly on the statements of Jennings and Mitchell, his so-claimed and newly-found old friends, who enforced their assertions of kindly interest with such mild persuasives as five-shooters, Arkansas tooth-picks, and substantial bracelets, as shown by their own testimony. Under such inspiring influences, and surrounded with such genial inducements to knowledge, it is said that he opened his mouth and spake wonderful things, — of his own freewill, of course. And what did the inspired property say? Why, the same things that all such property, similarly situated, always says; or, more accurately, is reported as saying. That he is the identical person sought for, guilty of the escape charged, truly penitent, tired of freedom, of course, and only anxious once more to behold the kindest of masters and the most angelic of mistresses, and have himself snugly and comfortably sold into a rice swamp, beyond the reach of temptation!

It is scarcely necessary to say, of all such yarns, that the circumstances of the speaker would utterly invalidate whatever he might say, while so situated, with any intelligent jury; and farther than that, his sayings, introduced here as they have been, have, of necessity, been ruled out by his Honor. Yet they are still pressed by the prosecution. But we are not left even to the plain inference, which would sweep away statements made in such durance. Mr. Mitchell himself tells us, that when they first met, John *denied any acquaintance with him !* Positively and pointedly *denied* it! Rather remarkable, was n't it? If this were the very John with whom Mitchell had been so intimate for eighteen years previous to 1856, with whom he had worked side by side so many months, and whom he had thus marked so well that after a separation of two years and nine months, during which John had undergone many and remarkable changes of stature, color, weight, manner, and dress, he instantly recognized him in a strange place, with no one to call his attention to him, and this through one of the immaculate magnifying windows of the Russia House.

John did not know Mitchell, and never saw him before. Oh, I know he knew him well when he arrived at Wellington. A duller than John would have profited by such suggestive lessons. Take an instance related by the graphic Mitchell. When he went up to John, in the wagon with Shakespeare, John had a knife in his hand, which Mitchell ordered him to give up. John declined. Mitchell's only reply was a significant movement of the right hand towards his revolver; and the knife fell; and, in the language of the immortal and ever-observing Shakespeare, in that serio-ludicro-comico-tragico farce of Measure for Measure, "the whites of John's eyes turned yellow!"

It was under such teachings, and so illustrated, that John rode into Wellington, and is even brought to such proficiency that he is made to say, that at some time he even left Oberlin and started back to Kentucky, and got as far as Columbus, when he was arrested and reluctantly forced back to Oberlin! And this wretched stuff, so forced from the very pores of this wretched negro in his extremity, in the grasp, under the pistols and knives of this gang of armed ruffians, is gravely and solemnly urged here by the gentlemen who observe the argument as proof; and we are tauntingly called upon to disprove it, or it is conclusive upon us. And this is to be listened to in a so-called court of justice, by a jury of freemen, citizens of a free State, in the trial of a freeman for his liberty!

The only pretence for any of John's sayings is, that they accompanied certain acts or things, and are given as part of the *res gestæ;* not to prove any fact, but merely as constituting part of a fact, or thing. But that miserable fiction of John's attempt to return, was not even coupled with any act or fact. Whatever John may say in the custody of his captors, and under their catechizing, is in durance, and would not be proof, even against himself; and one can but shudder at the measureless infamy of offering it for a moment against a third person, who was not even constructively present, and to whom nobody pretends a whisper of it was ever conveyed.

Follow this refreshing part of the case a little farther. At Wellington, after some hours of tuition, John was privately exhibited to a select few; among others Jake Wheeler, by his official position as Postmaster of Rochester, as well as from principle and instinct, enjoyed the high delectation of converse with him, since his regeneration, by the laying on of the hands of Marshal Lowe's posse.

Jake very properly indulged in philosophical speculations, of a naturally moral tendency, for John's benefit, explaining to him that he had not received at the hands of his master training more severe than certain wholesome exercises, which even white parents occasionally find it necessary to put their children through; and it is to be regretted that Jake's own education, in this particular, was so sadly neglected.

But these wonderful admissions of this negro boy in durance, prove even more yet. He is made, in Mr. Wheeler's own elegant phrase, to " on the whole, pretty much give him the impression that he was willin' to go back;" which another of the Government's witnesses explains by repeating what he said on the platform to the crowd, that "he supposed they had the papers for him, and he would *have* to go." And thereupon we are treated to a paroxystic parenthesis upon the attachment of slaves to their bonds. Why, Gentlemen of the Jury, if ever it should be my lot to have my loved ones wrenched from me, and carried by their captors to a distant land, and my government was not strong enough to wrest them back again, and I had not wealth enough to buy their freedom; and in after years some traveller should come from the far land where they were held in captivity under the hard hand of a tyrant, and should tell me that these my loved ones were sullen and moody and rebellious, I'd thank God with my full heart, for thus I'd know that my own blood still beat with its old pulse of freedom in their quivering veins. But should he say that they seemed gay and careless and glad — sang and made merry, and danced for their masters, I'd raise my hand to Him that liveth, and swear they were none of mine!

But what did the negro say upon the platform? He was sent out, after due training, to say certain things. What were they, and did he say them. The first query is satisfied by the answer to the next. What he did say, if he said any thing — which Jennings and Mitchell are loth to admit — was, that "they had the papers for him, and he supposed he *would have* to go back." In the presence of his captors and Wheeler, he *almost* said what they wanted him to, but upon the balcony, he could n't do even as well as that. I know that Mr. Wack testifies that "he thinks John was *just-a-going* to say he wanted to go back," when he got "skeered" and fled in, but I question whether even the Government is quite ready to claim to you, Gentlemen, that such supposition on the part of Mr. Wack is conclusive evidence of John's voluntary state of mind!

And now, on the whole proof, including John's statements upon this point of his identity, I claim the balance is with us. A copper-colored fled, an ebony black was captured; a youth of eighteen, weighing 165 or 175 pounds fled, a man weighing 135 or 140 was taken; a boy of the grenadier height of five feet eight or ten inches escaped, and one dwarfed to five feet five arrested! Can he be the same?

But there remain other and very important points to be noticed, waiving, for the purpose of considering them, even the question of John's identity.

If he was a fugitive slave, was this fact known, generally known? So generally known at Oberlin that this defendant can be charged with notice of it? If not thus generally known, it must appear either that it was brought to his notice personally, or to the notice of a crowd acting with unanimity and in concert, and of which he was a member.

It is not in proof at what time John arrived at Oberlin. The presumption in Ohio would be, not that he was a slave, but that he was a free man, so that whether he had resided any considerable time there or not, the legal presumption of every citizen would be that of the law in favor of his freedom, and there would be nothing in his color or his arrival to charge the defendant with notice that he was a fugitive, or to put him upon inquiry concerning his *status*. And he who would charge such notice upon the defendant is bound to prove it.

It is in proof here, perhaps, that to one or two citizens of Oberlin, privately, John said that he was an escaped slave; but, that that came to be a matter of general conversation and knowledge there is not a particle of proof. On the contrary, the proof is indubitable — there is not a particle of proof that looks otherwise — that on the early part of the afternoon of the day of the alleged rescue, on the hasty gathering of the people at Oberlin, it was said throughout the crowd that John had been *kidnapped*, the question of his having once been a slave not being raised. And upon this impression it is abundantly proven that the crowd acted both at Oberlin and Wellington. And so firmly fixed was this conviction in their minds, that when they got to Wellington they went and swore out a warrant, predicated upon the fact that the negro was certainly held in illegal custody. And one of the most important witnesses for the Government, Halbert, who claims to have been constantly in the crowd, both at Oberlin and Wellington, being asked why he spoke of John as a "fugitive," said, "*he did n't know!*" Nothing in the testimony favors the supposition that John was, or was regarded by the crowd that rescued him, as a fugitive. So far from it, every thing we can learn of his conduct and circumstances goes to show the contrary.

And now, what were the circumstances collateral with and immediately prior to the arrest of John, as bearing on this question of knowledge? I shall say little here of the means by which information was conveyed from Oberlin to Kentucky, of the residence at the former place of certain supposed fugitive slaves; it is an unpleasant subject. But I cannot conceive how any individual, born and grown — to say nothing of "bringing up" — here at the North, should have it in his heart to steal into that he might betray the confidence of a fugitive, be prejudiced as we may of his color and condition. And as to the condition of this crushed and smitten people, we should never forget that they are here always against their own will. The tribes of Africa never migrate. So many of them as are among us WE stole, and ironed, and forced here, and for this we at the North are as responsible as our brethren at the South. Our fathers were one with their fathers in this sad, sad work. Neither the men of to-day who hold slaves in Kentucky, nor we of Ohio, who to-day lift our voices against the institution, founded it, though we are all responsible for its continuance. There may be a difference in the responsibility of sanctioning and perpetuating it, and if there be, no words can express the greater guilt of him who here, untrammelled by education or prejudice, unfettered by public opinion, enlightened by the free and prevailing influences of Truth, *chooses* to sustain an institution in the presence of which all other crimes look pallid, stand blanched with horror into the pale semblance of innocence! I can in some degree understand and allow for the totally different sentiments of our Southern brethren on this great question. The first objects that meet the first opening of their eyes, are wrought and emblazoned forms and images of slavery. To the Southerner his first breath comes thick with its atmosphere and influence. All the sounds that steal upon his ear are its many-mingled voices, half joyous, all sad, at once a wail, a chant, a jubilee, and requiem. It is all around, over and under him, and becomes part and parcel of his being, and necessary to his existence. Wherever he goes, wherever he stops, lies down or rises up, it is everywhere with him, in Church and State, with all his memories of the past, his present surroundings, and hopes of the future. To him it is as if it always was, and must ever be — a present, permanent good.

To one of us, every breath, every mouthful of food, or shred of clothing thus enjoyed, is a larceny from the sinews, hearts, and souls of a whole race. I can also understand how, in the half-barbaric profusion and license of Southern slavery, these coarse, bloated, bullying, cowardly swaggerers, — great, hairy maggots warmed into life in the hot, seething carcase of rotten slavery, — can exist, and the needs for such existences, for I have seen them among us. But, I repeat it, I cannot comprehend how a mass of feculence can exist at the North, in which God can tolerate life, that outrages human nature by crawling into the human form, so abject and vile that it can prey upon and trade in the misfortunes of these wretched fugitives from slavery.

Take this John; without a father to protect, a mother to cherish, a sister to love, or a brother to sympathize with him, — a houseless, homeless, wandering vagabond, without money to buy friends, eloquence to charm, or beauty to seduce. Black, abject, ignorant, abased; unwashed, unfed, unclothed; infected with a disease that outlaws; a waif by the way-side of human life, whose presence offended even the eye of charity. And yet there was on this earth a being so abject that it could steal upon, and warming his brutal soul with the voice of affected kindness, for the only purpose of betraying into a captivity so abhorrent, that even John had the courage and energy to flee from it! Oh! this was a treason so measureless and profound, that the years of God's eternity will be strained to punish it!

And it is an everlasting answer to the charge of fanatical intolerance made against Oberlin, that such creatures are permitted to live and breathe there, and quietly pursue the only mission of their existences.

Let us look a little more into the detail of the facts of John's capture. That he was betrayed we already know, and in part the means of his capture. When we are told that a right of property in man is recognized and guaranteed at the South, we are bound to presume, in the absence of proof, that it is modified and held just like other rights of property. And now, gentlemen, if one of you owned a horse that had strayed into Lorain county, would you go to reclaim him wherever you could find him according to law, or would you hire somebody to steal him, and in such a way that you could only be thought to be a common horse thief, and in all human probability subject yourself to punishment as such? How did this Jennings seek to reclaim his principal's property, which for the purposes of arrest is considered to be his own? Does he come openly in the power and authority of the instrument which constitutes him an attorney to reclaim him? No. Or even with the mockery of an illegal and useless warrant? No. But he seeks out this little unfortunate Shakespeare Boynton, — for in my mind, Gentlemen of the Jury, I cannot conceive of a more melancholy sight than that alarmingly precocious little deceiver presents, himself the evil genius of this disgusting transaction, so far outrunning total depravity itself, that, halting behind, it soon strains its eyes in vain to see which way "he went." He seeks out this unfortunate boy, arranges with him to decoy John if possible to his father's, under the pretence of employment, where the residue of this wretched business might with security be accomplished. Jennings says he informed Shakespeare's father of the arrangement. I must hope that Jennings lied in this, and that this nameless crime had not the added infamy of paternal sanction. There is much in what we know of Jennings to warrant this hope. Bacon, for instance, swore that it was agreed that if Jennings returned John, he was to be sold, and the proceeds of his body, brains, and blood, honestly and piously divided between them. Jennings pointedly denies this, and in so doing unquestionably lies, deliberately, purposely, and unqualifiedly.

This arrangement completed, the Kentuckian returns to his quarters in Oberlin. The next morning Shakespeare, with a horse and buggy, makes an early appearance. The lie agreed on, it is found, will not work, for Frank has got his throat cut, and John must stay with him; but in an instant the little genius's fertile brain supplies another device. Jennings indorses it, doubles the promised hire, and the unsuspecting negro, trusting implicitly to the snakish generosity of his "young massa," accepts the extraordinary bounty of a ride into the country, and thus steps into the snare fitted for his feet. Shakespeare directs his horse to a secluded place in the highway, lags, is overtaken, and leaves the wretched, ignorant, helpless, unarmed, unfriended negro boy, whom he was hired to lie to and decoy, that he might be waylaid and stolen; in the hands of the miscreants who had the courage finally to steal him. I aver it was stealing, — the meanness of larceny with ruffian violence of the highway robber! And think by whom this outrage was perpetrated. The nation — the administration in the person of its official performed it. Hail Columbia! What a stride in a nation's glory! Ring down the curtain on every thing great and glorious in the old days! Spike and muzzle the old cannon that sunk the British breastworks at Yorktown, and the British fleet on Lake Erie! Roll up and lay away the old banner of freedom, that has flouted over a hundred red and rent fields! Ring up the curtain on this new era of fillibustering, reopening of the slave trade, and stealing negroes at the North! Let the shout ring through all the sunny South — "one more nigger catched, and the Union saved!"

We owe no grudge toward our brethren at the South, and least of all towards those of gallant Kentucky, to whom we are bound not only by ties of fraternity, but by an obligation of gratitude which we choose not to forget, for succor nobly given us in the hour of extremest peril. We remember that on Ohio soil there fought and died Kentucky heroes side by side with our fathers and brothers, all struggling together in the fervid heat of heroic patriotism in the common cause of our common country, when we yet had a country worth loving and dying for. And if to-morrow Kentucky should be invaded by a foe, to-morrow 150,000 bayonets would go sparkling across the Ohio, borne by arms as brave, and over hearts as true as ever faced an invader, and Kentucky should *feel* that Ohio was neither forgetful nor ungrateful. We remember, too, that Kentucky holds the grave of our Clay and the home of another. There, too, still lives Crittenden, in the effulgence of ripened honors, whom we love and venerate. But we will not tolerate this mode of reclaiming property of any kind, nor this mode of enforcing any law of Congress or otherwise. If the property of a Kentuckian strays into Ohio, let him come openly after it, like an honest man, and claim his own boldly. We will not tolerate that mode of approach which steals in like a thief, pounces upon its object of pursuit as upon prey, and flees away like a felon.

It is indeed to me a queer test of patriotism, that a man must not only swear by the Constitution, but also by the U. S. Statutes at Large, Story's Edition! Are we at that point, that no man can be a good citizen or a patriot, unless he believes not only in the Union, Star Spangled Banner, the American Eagle, and Bunker Hill, as we all now here do; but our faith must reach every Act of Congress, and every ruling of the Federal Court. You cannot and shall not so enforce this Slave Statute in Ohio. The united, concentrated, and condensed wisdom and power of the Union, cannot so enforce it here. If your slaves flee to Ohio, it is at least worth the while of trying to reclaim them by other means. Let their educated and gentlemanly proprietors come and seek them in as honorable a way as such a mission can be performed. But don't send your Jennings and Mitchells with revolvers and knives and manacles to rob and steal them away. If slavery is right, show it to us. If it is taught in the Bible send us your Doctors of Divinity to expound this gospel to us. We believe the Bible practically, every day and all the time. To us it is a present revelation for daily use. We do not thrust it by, never to be recurred to until it is wanted as a barricade to defend some hideous villany, under which the solid earth shudders.

A new test of fidelity to our country has indeed long obtained in political circles not to be here named by me, — but it was never until the gentleman's [Judge Bliss] argument yesterday, named in a Court — called of Justice — before. If this be the test, the last man in the Union to apply it on our brethren of the South. I need not to stop here to enumerate even a few of the many startling instances on record in which they have boldly risen up as individuals, conventions, communities, legislative bodies, and judicial tribunals, and whole States, and refused to obey edicts of the Federal Government, because they believed them oppressive, or unconstitutional. Why, the Democrats would never tolerate a United States Bank, notwithstanding the laws of Congress and decisions of the Supreme Court of the United States.

I have nothing to do with enticing slaves away, nor sympathy with those who do; but if a fugitive comes to me in his flight from slavery, and is in need of food and clothing and shelter and rest and comfort and protection and means of further flight, — if he needs any or all the gentle charities which a Christian man may render to any human being under any circumstances, so help me the great God in my extremest need, he shall have them all! [Great applause.]

[The District-Attorney hoped that if these disturbances were repeated, the disturbers would be taken into custody.

Judge SPALDING wished the gentleman to consider, before he urged such a motion, that such an order might include members of the bar.

The DISTRICT-ATTORNEY: "*What, sir!* do you mean that *you* sanction such manifestations?"

Judge SPALDING: "I do, sir."

The DISTRICT-ATTORNEY: "Well, sir, you will doubtless have an opportunity to leave with the rest then."

Mr. RIDDLE: "The Court will bear me witness that I have not provoked any disturbance, having strictly confined my address to the Court and the Jury."

The COURT: "Certainly, sir."]

Mr. RIDDLE resumed.

And if then the chivalry should seek out so unimportant an individual as myself for such conduct of mine, I can easily be found. If the Marshal of this or any other District were ordered to arrest me, it would only be necessary for him to leave word at my office or my house, and I should instantly wait on him. Never will I, or one under my influence, lift a finger against the regular and lawful administration of the laws of my country, think what I may of the justice of the laws themselves. But I say that no Government will long be able to administer any laws, which is not guided by those eternal laws of Justice which alone support the throne of the Almighty himself. And all this time John is in the hands of the Ishmaelites, and on his way to slavery. I know you are anxious to see the rescuers on his track but pardon a word or two more.

Many years ago, while Ohio was in the wilderness, there went another Pilgrim band into the woods of Lorain county, carrying with them the principles, but not the intolerance, of the Pilgrim Fathers. Cutting away the forests, draining the swamps, and with sweat and toil subduing a savage nature to the wants and wishes of a refined civilization. There in rapid process they laid the foundation of a school broadly on the principles of the Reformation, the deep throbbings of which, as wrought out in the State, had produced the American Revolution. Dealing in no dead and exfoliated dogmas, the teachings and inculcations of that school have been fully responsive to the hungry and naked needs and wants of our day, and of our country. Spite of early prejudice, misrepresentation, and a ribald intolerance, the claims of Oberlin are finally being recognized and acknowledged. From her teaching has gone forth an influence for good, and for good alone. From her class-rooms and recitations have gone forth strong, pure, earnest souled men and women, through all the ways of life, and a towering up of moral and political sentiment is already perceptible in the land.

In the fierce struggle through which our nation is passing, her professors have stood in the front, striking with us blow for blow for freedom. Already have we beaten a new window into the blind, dark side of our politics, through which we catch glimpses of the old Jerusalem of our fathers, and feel the air wafted to us from the plains of our first pilgrimage. Walled out from the heathen of the South by a power more relentless than the combined horrors of climate and the barbarism of a thousand ages, Oberlin has established her missions in the older and more teachable barbarous Africa, where her missionaries have illustrated with their deaths, the lives of mercy and devotion with which they enforced their ministry while living.

It is not true that the Oberlin leaders are, especially, champions of the negro race, over and above, or distinct from the white, or any other race. But it is true that at all hazards they will vindicate man's manhood, and woman's womanhood, no matter what complexion the all Wise One has stamped upon its outside. And if the abused of the black race seek that locality, it is because nowhere else is found a community that so practically recognizes the right of the Creator to fashion his creatures as seems good, without making that diversity a pretext to abase them, and this Christian element there produces its true result, a moral and intellectual elevation of this cast-off race, and a practical, absolute prohibition of the monstrous mixing of races, so necessarily the fruit of the degradation of the negro. Nor is it true that these people have any connection with any means or appliances to induce enslaved negroes to escape. They employ no agents, establish no missions, and furnish no funds for labor in such enterprises. And the presence of Prof. Peck in Kentucky, would be the signal of no servile insurrection — at any rate among the blacks — and would be followed by no unusual escapades. It is true, however, that the fleeing, the hunted, and the oppressed, do there find all the beautiful charities of benignant Christianity awaiting them with beckoning hands.

Situated as Oberlin is, hundreds of miles from the slave communities, if a single ray of her light, traversing the land of freedom, has reached and penetrated the hovels of slavery, lighting up an avenue and a hope in the bosom of the abject bondmen, that which is charged upon her as her crime, is her chiefest crown!

Nor is it true that Oberlin — her professors, students, and people — are the disciplined and armed horde here represented, turning her Colleges into fortresses against the Government and laws of the country. The transactions of the 13th of September, and the few days preceding, are an everlasting refutation of this idle tale. They show that, unfortunately, they had no leaders, no soldiers, no arms, no signals, no rendezvous, so that "when the drum beats at the dead of night," an armed host would spring in martial array to meet an invading gang of slave-hunters.

When the kidnappers invaded the home of the Wagoners, and the cry of murder rung out on the startled ear of midnight, it created unwonted alarm, but no signal-gun boomed on the night air. The presence of these foreign ruffians, from that night to the capture of John, though known, and their mission suspected, failed to suggest any organization, or prompt any means whatever for the safety of a single individual. And when on the return of Bartholomew and Lyman, in the afternoon of the 13th, a cry that John had been kidnapped, and was then being rapidly hurried away, was sounded through that peaceful village, it struck that quiet populace, all unused to arms, strife, and turmoil, with surprise, alarm, and intense indignation, as I trust it would strike the people of any free town in the Union. No leaders came forth, no rudiment of an organization was apparent; but hurryings and runnings to and fro, anxious questions, excited answers, hasty consultations, heat, excitement, and universal confusion, all mixed and mingled, prevailed.

The outline of all that is now known of that wretched foray, was, in a few moments, known to the people of Oberlin. That John Price, for years a resident there, whom they supposed — and by the laws of Ohio had a right to suppose — was a freeman, had, by a lying artifice, been decoyed from their midst, surrounded by a gang of Southern ruffians, and hurried off. And to this was added the old stock of feverish excitement that had kept the atmosphere in a glimmer since the outrage on the wagons. And so from their shops, their stores, their fields, their recitation-rooms, and their professors' chairs, they ran together for an instant consultation, followed by instantaneous action. It was supposed the gang with John would await the cars at Wellington, where he must be intercepted, and freed from the grasp of the kidnappers.

Then how do they go off? Scrambling into farm wagons, livery carriages, stages, private buggies, on foot, two by two, in companies of half a dozen or a dozen, just as each one can. Nothing that has the semblance of concert of action is apparent. Some go out of curiosity, some to "see the fun," and some led by the holiest promptings of a human heart "to deliver the oppressed and him that hath no helper." Nothing could be made plainer by evidence than this character of this crowd has been.

But it is said that the defendant was seen conversing with two men in a buggy, and that he said to one of them that he had no business in there without a gun. It is further said that he was found making arrangements for a buggy, and was heard to say that he thought he knew where he could get a gun. It does not appear where he wished to go, or for what purpose he wished a gun. But concede that he wished to go to Wellington, and wanted a gun to use in rescuing John. The question then is, under what impression did the defendant act? Why, according to the testimony, it must have been under the impression that John, being a free man, had been unlawfully seized and spirited away. For he was bound to presume him to be free until he was proven to be a slave, and there is no evidence that any information ever reached the defendant that would so much as lead him to suppose that John was a fugitive. What then? Why, if John, being a free man, had been thus summarily seized and hurried away, he had a right to rescue himself and had a *claim* on all the good people of Ohio for assistance in so doing, he and they using just so much force as, and no more than, was necessary to effect a rescue.

And suppose, then, that the testimony of the immaculate Bartholomew is not an error. Suppose that — as they all swear positively they were not — Peck, Plumb, and Fitch were together on the stoop of Fitch's store, and the defendant came up and asked if "they had got John," and one of them said "yes;" and then he asked what was best to be done about it; and one of them said, "Go and get 'em ready, and we'll come and tell you," and so he went to "get 'em ready;"—what then? Nothing is proved under the sun against any living man. Good heavens! Is it indeed so that there is such a sacredness in this especial institution of man-stealing, that when its minions are abroad upon their mission, a dozen decent men cannot assemble and talk about the occurrences in their midst, without every thing they may say being noted down and brought into this dignified Court, to implicate the group as violators of the Constitution and traitors to the Government?

But is it true that such a conversation was held? It matters nothing to the case at issue. But as a question of fact, and as a test of the truthfulness of the Government's witness, is it true? Bartholomew gives a minute detail of the group, the circumstances, and the conversation. In rapid succession, Prof. Peck, Mr. Plumb, and Mr. Fitch come upon the stand, and swear with the utmost positiveness that no such group, conversation, or circumstances ever existed. And then the Mayor, Ex-Mayor, and most prominent merchants and business men of the village testify that they have known Bartholomew from early boyhood, that he was a known thief and acknowledged liar, and not one tenth of the people of Oberlin would believe him under any circumstances, although Wack and the rest of his set in a way sustain him.

But I am entirely willing to place my client upon the issue made, granting that every word of Bartholomew's testimony is true.

Nothing is more evident than that the defendant was not prominent in the crowd, and that he was one of the last of the first party who left Oberlin. There is no indication of any rash words or actions. When he left Oberlin, no intelligence had yet been received as to the whereabouts of the kidnappers. He did not know that they were at Wellington, that they did or did not mean to take the cars, or that they might not pursue their journey in a land carriage, that the negro had not been already rescued, or any thing of the sort. He could not therefore have set out with any very definite purpose.

It is conceded on the part of the Government that it is essential to prove that this defendant had knowledge of the relation which John sustained to the individuals who had him in custody, and that, knowing that they held John in legal custody, he, with others, forcibly wrested him from such custody. This guilty knowledge alone can impart to the transaction that bad intent without which no crime can exist. So that the *felonious intent*, as we would apply the term in speaking of felonies, lurks under that expression of "knowingly" doing the act which forms the charge in the indictment. Ordinarily, no man can be guilty of a crime who is at the time unconscious of committing it. And if a party, in the pursuit of what is in itself lawful, unintentionally performs a thing which, if done intentionally, would amount to a crime ; of course, as there was no felonious intent, guilt is totally wanting.

One thing is a little singular about the manner of this prosecution. The crime charged here ranks in the statute under the mild name of a misdemeanor ; but if one might trust to the copious and strong language which was made use of by the gentleman who spoke yesterday for the Prosecution, it is something worse than a *felony*, and can be denominated nothing less than *heinous*,— a crime to be punished without benefit of clergy, in the popular or legal sense.

Now the people of Oberlin, with whom this defendant acted, if at all, are a highly cultivated people, and have the nicest appreciation of the obligations and sanctions of law. Among them you find the strongest, the extremest respect for law held and inculcated. But if this were forgotten, it would indeed seem not a little strange that these men, in the commission of a crime, should not have gone about it in such a way as to impart to it at least some of the characteristics which ordinarily mark a crime. Criminals do not ordinarily choose the broad daylight and the presence of a thousand witnesses for the commission of a felony. Why, they had those parties besieged there. Every mode and means of exit was cut off. Their numbers were an hundred to one. And yet what did they do ? Why — steady the tottering Union while I say it ! — they liberated, without even an attempt at violence, a KIDNAPPED fellow-citizen !! It seems that a cry had been sent up here to Cleveland for assistance. And it almost seems as though the authorities here must have known that this arrest was a flagitious outrage, and not the execution of a lawful process; otherwise I should have expected that some portion of that "*thousand*," who on some fitting occasion— which God and all good men conspire to put off — are to spring forth here and be reviewed by my military friend, Mr. District-Attorney, General of the Northern District, would have flown to the succor of their besieged brethren. Now if these parties had gathered at Wellington to rescue the man from competent authority—why, gentlemen, if there had been the least disposition to commit so grave an offence as to call forth an animadversion from the judiciary, why did they not wait an hour, and the thing would have accomplished itself, and it would have been impossible for my astute and learned friend to have made out a single case, or the semblance of a case, even before the Grand Jury.

But what did happen ?

Mr. Lowe and posse arrived at Wellington and took shelter and refreshment at the Wadsworth House. There had been, it seems, a large fire the same morning, which had attracted a great crowd, its exact size being variously estimated from two hundred to five hundred persons. Now the peculiar nature and extent of the excitement of a large crowd at a fire are perhaps as well known and understood in this city as in most populated regions. All the stirring emotions which go to make us excited humanely, are stimulated, and drawn out to their fullest extent. And if it were not a very extraordinary fire, *some* of the excited supported their flagging energies at the expense of a possible temperance pledge. And so far as we can judge from the testimony, if we include all who have in any way been named or referred to, the whole number who went from Oberlin to Wellington will fall within a score. The *crowd* was gathered in the forenoon by the fire. Nothing is plainer. And beside the large numbers still in the streets when the parties from Oberlin arrived, something like an hundred it is said were in the Town-House, attending the little trial there. A gentleman comes into this town-hall —so well satisfied that there had been an infraction of the laws of Ohio, that he goes forward and makes oath to such belief. And if he had knowledge of the facts as they have been testified to here by Jennings and Mitchell, he certainly was abundantly authorized to make such an oath. And it was upon such information, gentlemen, that that crowd acted. For at this time there is not the remotest particle of evidence that there had been any communication between these Southern gentlemen and any part of the crowd outside; this old crowd, the crowd that had assembled at the fire, and had had their feelings heated and excited and overwrought to the last extreme, by witnessing a fearfully destructive fire. There had been no advertisement at this time of the details of the kidnapping except as they advertised themselves, and were stated under oath by the gentleman who swore out the warrant for the arrest of the kidnappers. And the crowd arriving from Oberlin bring with them and find this solitary impression prevalent there, and act upon it.

They beleaguer the hotel, so that the Southern gentlemen themselves come to be advised that the natural consequences of their conduct are impending over them. And now what do they do ? Do they attempt to make known to the crowd that they (the crowd) are laboring under a misapprehension, and that the man is lawfully holden ? Not a word of it. They had taken him with a strong hand, and so they meant to hold him. Not a single effort to exhibit authority, remove an impression, or explain a circumstance. These men, not accustomed to violations of law and to bloodshed, not accustomed to arms, amenable, delicately amenable to every thing that has the show of authority, present no uninviting audience for such a representation of the legal status of the case. So far from attempting explanations ere the crowd was more excited, they take John, and tinker him up, and stuff him with a story, and put *him* forth to tell that tale to the crowd! Instead of this man Lowe — beg pardon, United States Deputy-Marshal Lowe, —or Jennings, or Mitchell, or Davis, or all four of them together, going out and proclaiming their legal authority, they take this miserable John, fill him with a *miserable lie*, and shove him forth to tell it. How sublime! the Chivalry, and the Executive of the United States pick up this miserable negro, and make *him* their orator! make *him* their mouth-piece connection between themselves and this excited and infuriated crowd! And when this scheme fails they all creep up into the little squat room away in the garret, and tie a rope to the latch — since the door unfortunately opens out — and the redoubtable General Jennings, takes hold of the rope's end, and getting round into a corner where he may be reasonably safe in case a deadly attack is made — holds on!

Oh, that boy could tell just exactly such a kind of story as they wanted him to tell, when alone with gentlemen occupying that "high Southern ground," which always means the latitude of the revolver and "tooth-pick." But when he came to be an oracle to the crowd, standing almost as near to it as to his kidnappers, the stimulus was not strong enough, and he made an utter failure; and the only thing they offer the justly excited crowd is this utter failure of John's to repeat, as bidden, that miserable, trumped up, lying tale.

Let me call your attention now, Gentlemen, to what did transpire on that marvellous platform — beside which all the platforms that I have yet been so fortunate as to learn something of are thrown far into the shade. First, let us hear *Jennings*:

"John went out on to the platform. Concluded to let him go out. I went out with him. Two or three rifles were put up to the nigger, and *skeered* him, and he went back, and did n't say what he was going to."

Mr. Mitchell. "John was taken out on to the platform, and said to the crowd that his master had sent for him, and he was going home. They had got papers for him, and were going to take him home."

Mr. Wood. "When John was first brought out on to the platform, the Southerners said if anybody wanted to ask John if he wanted to go home, they might. I asked him if he wanted to go back. He answered that they had got papers for him, and he supposed he would have to go. Don't know as he said any thing more."

Mr. Wack. "*Davis* brought John out on to the platform. *Did not see Jennings there.* Davis said he had brought the boy out to tell his own story for himself. John began to speak. He did not exactly say he wanted to go back. Said he was in the hands of the officers, and might as well go back. Was interrupted by the crowd. I think he was *just going to say* he wanted to go back, when the crowd interrupted him!"

Jennings says he did n't say any thing. Mitchell says he said one thing; Wood says he said quite a different thing, and did n't say any thing else; and then Mr. Wack, who is entitled to great consideration on several accounts, says he didn't exactly say he wanted to go back, but thinks he was *just going to say so*, and would have done it if the uncivil crowd had n't been so rude as to interrupt him!

Who will tell us, then, what John *did* say, or whether he said *any thing?*

Jennings says he himself was out there, but Wack swears positively that he did n't see him there. Now, gentlemen, could *Jennings* have been on that stoop, and not be seen! [Much laughter.] Why, you could see him all the way to Pike's Peak! and if Wack says he did n't see him, that is certainly conclusive that he was not there.

This remarkable disagreement of the Government's leading witnesses on so important a point, is worthy of serious consideration; and it would indeed be well for the prosecution if there were not many other equally grave differences between their witnesses. The witness, Jake Wheeler, differs from others in several very important particulars.

This transaction must have been near the time when the train was expected from Cleveland. And what next? About this time they sent for the magistrates and lawyer. For it would really seem that this was the first time that any honorable effort was made to give any information or to make any impression on the crowd. Lowe, afraid to face that justly incensed and outraged crowd, upon whom he had tried to play off that miserable lie, took some, whom he supposed to be influential men, into a private room, and tried to pursuade them to interfere for him with the excited throng outside. It is said that when you show a combination on the part of any number of individuals — so say the rules — whatever is shown to be the words or acts of any one of the party, is chargeable upon all. But it is altogether essential to show first that there is a combination; the *very opposite* of which — if the entire evidence may be trusted — was true in the case of this collection. The entire crowd, with the exception of a very unimportant minority, was called together solely by the fire; and, the minority excepted, hurriedly gathered in from all quarters, strangers to each other, moved only by spontaneous sympathy with the kidnapped or the kidnappers, as their hearts or politics dictated, without so much as speaking together, each with his individual purposes, views, and opinions, all agreeing to *differ*, perhaps, but agreeing in nothing else. The proof is, there were no leaders or followers, no organization, concert, or combination. And certainly it does not follow that because a man happens to be in SUCH a crowd, that he is chargeable with all the acts of all the people who constitute it. Until you prove the combination, each man is responsible for just what he himself actually says and does, and by no possibility for any thing more. That is the rule ; for it is the only rule which could work any thing else than the extremest confusion, mischief, and injustice. But what does Lowe do? Why, he shows his *warrant* to some of these principal men, *not one* of whom is charged with, or could be charged with, having any thing whatever to do with the taking away of the negro! Mark it well. *Lowe*, not Jennings, comes forward to meet the men sent for by the party. He takes them into a room *alone*, away from Jennings and the rest. He tells them solemnly that *he* is the U. S. Marshal, and that *he*, being so august an officer, holds this negro boy in his custody, by virtue of a *warrant* issued by a United States Commissioner, at Columbus, which he then condescends to exhibit for the first time for their inspection. They read it carefully, note the lack of a seal, express no opinion upon the merits of the case, and go down. The crowd, eager for information, ask what they have learned, and are truthfully told : that a man calling himself U. S. Marshal Lowe, of Columbus, claims to hold the negro in his custody by virtue of a warrant shown them, which purports to have been made and issued by a U. S. Commissioner, at Columbus, before whom the boy, when returned by the Marshal, is to be tried. This warrant has no seal, which the lawyer speaks of as a remarkable circumstance, and says he cannot tell whether, on such warrants, a seal is necessary. Not one of these men indorses the papers as sufficient. Not more than one claims to have seen a power of attorney, and he did not read it. The WARRANT was put forward in EVERY CASE as the paper under and by virtue of which the boy is held by this U. S. Marshal. A warrant which the Prosecution knew so well was utterly worthless that they dare not produce, and have not mentioned in this whole trial; but come and try by the oaths of these two scavengers of slavery, to overswear and impeach these dozen intelligent, educated, and utterly disinterested free citizens of Ohio, who had nothing to do with the alleged rescue, and were in the crowd only to make peace if possible between the kidnappers and the justly excited populace, and who swear to the facts as they exist. But Lowe finally comes down, under the protection of Mr. Patton and Constable Meacham. Does he go out like a man upon the balcony where John stood, and frankly stand there, where all could see if they could not all hear him ? Of course not. But he sneaks out of the back door, seeks a retired place, draws out a warrant which he cannot read, and must get his Oberlin protector to read for him, to the small portion of the people who

can get within seeing or hearing distance, and while this ridiculous little side show is going on, the mass of the crowd, who know nothing of it, and act under their first knowledge and belief, make a rush upon the beleaguered castle, take it by storm, and carry the boy off. And as an everlasting commentary upon that whole proceeding, and as showing its falsity and bad faith, the Government now repudiate Lowe, his warrant and authority, — say that was all a sham, and John was actually holden by Jennings, under his power of attorney, all the time ! Now it is altogether too late to talk about notice after this, to the defendant or anybody else.

The defendant Bushnell, during all this time, is not there. He has learned nothing, seen nothing, heard nothing of any show of authority, not even of the warrant. And the crowd is *not* one acting in concert, combination, or with any common understanding, however vague.

WHERE, THEN, IS THE PROOF that he "KNOWINGLY," — knowing that John was a slave; the slave of John G. Bacon, of Mason County, Kentucky; that he was lawfully arrested by Anderson Jennings, the legally constituted agent of John G. Bacon, and lawfully held by said Jennings under and by virtue of a legally executed power of attorney, — and having such knowledge, "FELONIOUSLY" assisted in rescuing said John from such legal custody, "contrary to the peace and dignity of the United States of America ?"

Of ALL such guilty knowledge, without which, Gentlemen of the Jury, his Honor will charge you there can be no crime in the eyes of the law, there is the most utter and absolute lack of proof. And it is further worthy of your especial notice, that not only does it appear that there was no sort of concert in the action of this crowd as a whole, but that this defendant is not known to have acted in concert with any single individual. And yet the Prosecution claim to you that he can be held chargeable with notice served in a private room in the third story of a building which he did not enter, upon persons who had no sort of connection with the Rescue, of a warrant which the Prosecution dare not name in this Court, by an officer whom they dare no sooner name, and that such notice, so charged, makes this defendant guilty of the crime alleged in the indictment, to wit, the *knowing* and *felonious* rescue of this boy John from the legal custody of Anderson Jennings! And that, too, when they now declare that John was not holden by that warrant at all !

Can you, then, Gentlemen of the Jury, looking through this case as we have reviewed it, by the indulgence of the Court, and with your remarkably kind attention, find that any John, the property of John G. Bacon, was any more than one sixth his property? Is there proof that he escaped, — that the power of attorney was properly executed, — that the boy who left Kentucky at eighteen years of age, five feet eight or ten inches high, weighing 160 to 175 pounds, and of a copper colored complexion, was the boy arrested at Oberlin nearly three years afterward, five feet five inches high or less, weighing 135 or 140 pounds, and so black as to *shine*, — that he was arrested by Anderson Jennings in person, or by his posse in his immediate presence, — that U. S. Deputy Marshal Lowe set up no claim to official authority or conduct, acting only as the humble servant of the overshadowing Jennings, — that the crowd at Wellington was a crowd gathered by mutual understanding and previous agreement or subsequent assent, acting in concert and obeying leaders, — and that after due and sufficient notice upon this concerted crowd, or else upon this defendant personally, that Anderson Jennings, the legally constituted attorney of John G. Bacon, had lawfully arrested and was then lawfully holding the veritable negro boy John named in his power of attorney, — this defendant, in defiance of the laws, the peace, and the dignity of the United States, helped to rescue the said negro boy John, from the custody of the said Anderson Jennings? It seems to me, Gentlemen, that to so plain a question you cannot be long in returning the only answer consistent with your oaths, or, as I doubt not, your wishes.

I know well that there are other questions connected with this case, such as are ever springing from that most perplexing fountain of difficulties, which, ignore as we will, is forever pressing itself upon our attention. But, Gentlemen, nothing could be more unnecessary than for me to remind you that with such questions you have nothing whatever to do; and last of all would we be to press them upon your attention. The right or the wrong of Human Slavery — "Sum of all Villanies" though it be — the constitutionality or the unconstitutionality of the Fugitive Slave Act, upon which the indictment before you is based, — and, last and least of all, political differences or personal or local prejudices, form no part of the testimony introduced in your hearing by either the Prosecution or the Defence. You have been here to listen to testimony; the Court will give you the law; and with nothing else have you to do, whatever expectations the Government may have of you.

And, in Heaven's name I ask you, Gentlemen, *is it not enough* that free citizens of Ohio must turn baying dogs at the bidding of Southern despots, or be lashed by the Federal Government for tardy slaves — that this unutterably loathsome, unconstitutional, and wicked Act of 1850 must be *obeyed?* Are men to suffer the infamy of its pains and penalties, on unsatisfactory proofs, and merely so that the present powers can say to their keepers, we have enforced the statute? If you find this defendant Guilty, it will be upon such grounds only. The testimony has gone to the great outside thinking, reflecting, and judging world, and that world is no less this man's jury than are you; and it is

more, for it will pronounce not only upon his guilt, but upon your verdict, upon you also, and forever hold you to account for that verdict, if it be not in accordance with the facts.

Standing here in this presence and upon these great elements of right, I may say to you, as a man speaking to men who are capable of rising to the serene atmosphere of truth and justice, that under the inequitable burden of this law there is no oversweeping evidence that binds upon you the inexorable necessity of subjecting this defendant to its weight. I fix it upon your understanding — I write it on your hearts — I sear it on your consciences — that the Government has failed to meet the wicked exactions of its wicked statute; and you may, you must, with your free breath syllabling your verdict, give relief to the tortured anxiety with which a whole people, with repressed breathing, look to the final result.

And should that result be averse to justice, I admonish you that such a verdict on such evidence will sow the whole North with Dragon's teeth — let him reap who may!

The tribunes of the people will go forth to mould and direct the impressible emotion into action. You shall hear their voices ring out —

"Ho, watchman on the tower! what of the time!"

And the answer —

"Stern silent men are wheeling into line,
Firm paced and slow a horrid front they form,
Still as the breeze, yet dreadful as the storm,
Low murmuring sounds along their banners fly,
Freedom or death the watchword and reply."

Oh! I know this thing is here held as law. That the decision of this Court is to add another scale to that great scab, that deforms and debauches American jurisprudence — that must remain till the increasing vitality of the body politic shall reclaim our jurisprudence to purity and justice. But it shall never be recognized and accepted by our people as law — never! never!!

Your fetters may bind our limbs, and your prisons may hold our bodies, for a day. You may lay your judicial fingers on our pulses and command them to cease beating, — you may attempt to roll the red tide back on the heart and adjudge it to stand still, — but it will throb, and beat, and bound on. Your manacles and dungeons can never still it. Prison it in the centre of the rock-ribbed earth, and it will beat on — the huge mountains cannot crush it — the deep sea cannot quench it — the everlasting fires cannot consume it, but, gathering its accumulated energies, the solid earth shall be driven asunder, that God may be vindicated in man!

I have sunk the lawyer, — I have sunk the advocate, that I might stand before you in my unsullied manhood, and appeal to you as men.

I have forgotten party prejudices, that I might remember and remind you of issues involving the common rights, franchises, and liberties of us all, as citizens of a great free State.

I have sunk the individual interests of the Defendant, that I might appeal to you to protect the interest of all living things, and vindicate the dignity and sovereignty of our glorious commonwealth, — all these are here embodied in the person of this Defendant. And if this appeal is heard in vain, let the consequences fall where they belong.

[The argument of MR. RIDDLE began in the latter part of the afternoon of the Seventh Day, and continued till near the close of the Eighth. Judge SPALDING occupied the remainder of the Eighth and the morning of the Ninth.]

Mr. RIDDLE was followed by his senior associate, Hon. RUFUS P. SPALDING, who said: —

May it please your Honor: —

It is now something near forty years since I took upon myself, on my entrance into my professional career, a solemn obligation to support the Constitution of the United States.

Since then, often, and under imposing circumstances, that oath has been renewed. And never, to my knowledge, have I departed one jot or one tittle from the responsibility thus gravely assumed.

But I took upon myself this obligation, as the once popular President, Andrew Jackson, said he did, promising to support the Constitution, indeed, but always reserving the right to interpret it for myself. And when President Jackson was appealed to for executive aid in a contest between the highest Federal Court in the nation, and the Supreme Court of a State, he answered promptly and like a true man, " I have sworn to support the Constitution of the United States, but not according to its interpretation by the Federal Court, and in this instance believing the State Court to be right and the Federal Court to be wrong, the power committed to me shall be used in behalf of the State Court and *the right, though it be against the Federal Court and its wrong.*"

If Andrew Jackson had done nothing else to insure his fame, so noble and patriotic a declaration would render his name illustrious so long as our country's history shall be read.

I stand here to-day as the advocate of a fellow-citizen who is in danger of losing his liberty ; — and *for what?*

For obeying the injunction of Jesus Christ! Nothing else.

" Whatsoever ye would men should do unto you," etc.

And now, forsooth, under the genial laws of this Republic, he stands in fear of the penitentiary. Aye, I say the *penitentiary*, sir, for it is not the least of the odious features of this outrageous law, that its provisions are so worded that they are no better than the laws of that Roman Emperor who hung his edicts so high

that no one could read their penalties, and then taught their import by summary vengeance upon every unconscious transgressor.

I read from Section 9 of the Act of September 18th, 1850.

" Any person who shall knowingly and willingly obstruct, hinder, or prevent such claimant, his agent or attorney, or any person or persons lawfully assisting him, her, or them from arresting such fugitive from service or labor, either with or without process as aforesaid, or shall rescue, or attempt to rescue, such fugitive from service or labor, from the custody of such claimant, his or her agent or attorney, or other person or persons lawfully assisting as aforesaid, when so arrested, pursuant to the authority herein given and declared; or shall aid, abet, or assist such person, so owing service or labor as aforesaid, directly or indirectly, to escape from such claimant, his agent or attorney, or other person or persons legally authorized as aforesaid; or shall harbor or conceal such fugitive so as to prevent the discovery or arrest of such person, after notice or knowledge of the fact that such person was a fugitive from service or labor as aforesaid, shall, for either of said offences, be subject to a fine not exceeding one thousand dollars, and *imprisonment* not exceeding six months, by indictment and conviction before the District Court," etc.

I have read the acts of Congress attentively, to find out what " *imprisonment* " meant. I was informed by the Executive of our own State that it meant the *penitentiary.* " Not so," said I. But, on recurring to the Statutes, I found that all the offences against the post-office and treasury, even the most flagrant, are thus worded, and the District-Attorney has informed me, this morning, that it lies in the breast of the presiding officer of this Court, on the verdict of the Jury, to decide whether the punishment shall be imprisonment in the county jail, or in " *the penitentiary.*"

Sir, I feel deeply the responsibility which rests upon me on this occasion, and I feel as sensibly my own weakness. I would that I had power to bring to the vindication of the true History of the Constitution of the United States, more ability than I possess. I would rescue it from the infamy cast upon it by the prosecution in this case. And now, sir, before I enter upon the argument which lies before me, I wish to be indulged in a remark personal to myself. I have plead in all the Courts of our country, but nowhere do I feel so fully at home as in this hall. Here I constantly associate with friends and acquaintances whom I love and respect. And here, I mean always to guard against " words and acts" that may seem disrespectful to the Court, or unkind to my brethren of the bar. But, sir, when I say this, I must say also, that my temperament is a mercurial one, and I see before me a train of argument, the only one to be pursued in this case productive of excitement in an unusual degree. I commend myself, sir, to your kind indulgence, trusting that you will do me the justice to believe, that I shall willingly be guilty of no discourtesy or rudeness. Whatever may seem to be undue warmth will, I hope, be overlooked for the sake of the great principles to be discussed, and their practical application to the most sacred rights of the traverser at the bar. For it is my first duty to defend those rights by the discussion of such principles to the best of my ability, faithfully and fully, be the consequences to others what they may.

Gentlemen of the Jury: —

I hear it intimated that every individual who speaks against this indictment or approvingly of the acts charged in this indictment; every counsellor who is called to the defence of the accused, must belong to some other party than to the old Democratic party, because none other is friendly to the Federal Government! But, Gentlemen of the Jury, I know a part of your number well enough to know that you cannot for a moment favor such a proposition. Why, Gentlemen, we are here assembled in the city of Cleveland, a city of sixty thousand souls, the pride of the Western Reserve, where, by thirty thousand majority, the electors have declared themselves opposed to the present administration of the Federal Government. Are these men of the Western Reserve all traitors? I, myself, for more years than the District-Attorney can boast of having lived, was a Democrat, and I am still a Democrat after the fashion of Thomas Jefferson. But I cannot do homage to the Moloch of Slavery by yielding obedience to this infamous Fugitive Slave Law.

We are told with especial and significant emphasis that this defendant is from the town of *Oberlin*, where all fugitives do congregate, and where the decrees of the Federal Court are set at defiance. Gentlemen of the Jury, are you to convict Simeon Bushnell because he comes from the town of *Oberlin*, where peculiar views are held on moral and political points; granting that these views *are peculiar*, which I shall presently show they by no means are?

You are told that you must not deal in abstractions. What are abstractions?

The doctrine of the Higher Law is said to be one — which is even at this moment met by the gentleman who represents the Federal Government with a smile of derision, such as is often coupled with a flippant mention of the phrase by pot-house politicians. Let me illustrate the abstract nature of the Higher Law dogma a little. When Napoleon the Great was about to enter upon his Russian Campaign, his uncle, the Cardinal Fesch, tried to persuade him to desist, saying, "Man proposes, but God disposes," Napoleon blasphemously replied, "Yes — but *I* propose, and *I* dispose!" He marched to the battle-field, and in a very few months was seen fleeing for his life, dethroned, disgraced, and worse than dead. Thomas Jeffer-

son, the Father of Democracy, speaking with reference to an apprehended insurrection of the slaves at the South, said: "Indeed I tremble for my country when I reflect that God is just, and that his justice cannot sleep for ever. *The Almighty has no attribute which can take sides with us* in such a contest."

Gentlemen of the Jury, Judge Bliss may scout the Higher Law, Judge Belden may scout the Higher Law; but we shall not one of us be the less presumptuous if we dare to say that any human enactments can overthrow the Divine and Higher Law. Is there a creature of the Almighty in existence who dare say to Him, who spins the world like a top on its intangible pivot, that *our* law is higher than His?

Although I am not so vain as to imagine that I can, in this Court, procure a reversal of those decisions which have been made in other Federal Courts of this Union, I hold it to be none the less my duty to argue with the same accuracy, fidelity, and fulness the questions involved, as though a sound argument would certainly influence the Court in coming to a correct decision. "Agitate! *agitate!* AGITATE!" is my motto, and my duty always, until the occasion for agitation is removed. The ingenious gentleman who opened on the part of the Prosecution took occasion to read at length from the opinion of Mr. Justice McLean, the claim of a compact in the Constitution to preserve the rights of slave-holders. I take issue with the learned Judge on this point. He is not the only learned man who has taken this view, in order to bolster up the legislation of Congress upon this subject. But I have an abundance of documentary history in my possession to prove the very contrary; that the *Constitution would never have been adopted* at all, if such a recognition of slavery had been made. It used to be called "*fugitives from service.*" It is now "fugitives from *slavery.*" The Convention that framed the Constitution would not allow the word "*slave*" to be placed anywhere in that instrument, for any consideration. And now we bring our school children into court, that they may hear District-Attorneys of the United States read indictments against free citizens of the State, for aiding the escape of "SLAVES." But, having some little knowledge of human nature, and understanding what moves the wills at Washington, I know perfectly well how offices and honors are dispensed; I know, very well, sir, that no man could obtain your place on the judgment seat, who was not known to be ready to send back a fugitive slave at the bidding of his master. I know that the same is true of the office of the District-Attorney. And so of all the other offices of this Court, to the very lowest. But I cannot forget that my friend, the District-Attorney here, has prepared himself for his place in a very short time; for it is only a few years since he pressed himself upon my notice as a candidate for the Governorship of Ohio. on the express ground that he was a thorough-going anti-slavery man, and as evidence thereof he declared that he voted for Martin Van Buren in 1848! But he was far ahead of me at that time, for I then adhered to the ranks of the old Democracy, and voted for Lewis Cass! [Laughter.] To illustrate still farther the fact that the people of Oberlin hold by no means peculiar views of the infamous Act of September 18, 1850, I will read, with the permission of the Court, from a slip which I hold in my hands, the proceedings of a meeting of the leading citizens of Cleveland, composed of men of all political creeds, and held, as it will be seen, directly after that unfortunate enactment was passed.

"On the 11th day of October, 1850, a large meeting of the most respectable citizens of Cleveland was called to express their sentiments upon the passage of the Fugitive Slave Law of September 18th preceding. The meeting was held in Empire Hall. John A. Foot was appointed Chairman, and M. C. Younglove and H. C. Brayton, Secretaries. A committee was appointed to present Resolutions upon the subject, composed as follows: —

"Joel Tiffany, Reuben Hitchcock, H. V. WILLSON, O. H. Knapp, and G. A. Benedict; which committee reported as follows: —

"1. Resolved, That the passage of the Fugitive Law was an act unauthorized by the constitution, hostile to every principle of justice and humanity, and, if persevered in, fatal to Human Freedom.

"2. Resolved, That that law strikes down some of the dearest principles upon which our fathers predicated their right to assert and maintain their independence, and is characterized by the most tyrannical exercise of power; and that it cannot be sustained without repudiating the doctrines of the Declaration of Independence, and the principles upon which all free governments rest.

"3. Resolved, That tyranny consists in the wilfully violating by those in power of man's natural right to personal security, personal liberty, and private property; and it matters not whether the act is exercised by one man or a million of men, it is equally unjust, unrighteous, and destructive of the ends of all just governments.

"4. Resolved, That regarding some portion of the Fugitive Law as unconstitutional, and the whole of it as oppressive, unjust, and unrighteous, we deem it the duty of EVERY GOOD CITIZEN to denounce, oppose and RESIST, by all proper means, the execution of said law, and we demand its immediate and unconditional repeal, and will not cease to agitate the question and use all our powers to secure that object, until it is accomplished.

"5. Resolved, That we recommend that a meeting of the citizens of this county be held at Cleveland on the 26th day of October, instant, to consider said law, and take such action thereon as may be expedient."

Gentlemen of the Jury, have you ever heard stronger denunciations of the Fugitive Slave Law from Oberlin? Unless you have, you will immediately divest yourselves of any prejudice against Oberlin, or against this defendant, because he comes from Oberlin, that may have been engendered in your minds. In Oberlin they don't believe in the Fugitive Slave Law; but neither do the best citizens of Cleveland, nor have they from the first day of its passage. I have not read the foregoing resolutions for the purpose of deriding them. I am with them heart and hand, in every sentence, word, and letter. I hold the Fugitive Slave Law to be unconstitutional. I believe that Congress had no right to legislate upon this subject at all.

The odious act which I shall now proceed to read and consider as a lawyer, reads, the first part of it, as follows. Brightly's Digest, 294.

"§ 1. When a person held to labor in any of the United States, or in either of the Territories on the north-west or south of the river Ohio, under the laws thereof, shall escape into any other of the said States or Territories, the person to whom such labor or service may be due, his agent or attorney, is hereby empowered to seize or arrest such fugitive from labor, and to take him or her before any Judge of the Circuit or District Courts of the United States, residing or being within the State, or before any magistrate of a county, city, or town corporate, wherein such seizure or arrest shall be made, and upon proof to the satisfaction of such judge or magistrate, either by oral testimony or affidavit taken before and certified by a magistrate of any such State or Territory, that the person so seized or arrested doth, under the laws of the State or Territory from which he or she fled, owe service or labor to the person claiming him or her, it shall be the duty of such judge or magistrate to give a certificate thereof to such claimant, his agent or attorney, which shall be sufficient warrant for removing the said fugitive from labor to the State or Territory from which he or she fled."

The eighth section of this statute, as found in Brightly's Digest, is inserted as an amendment to the law of 1793, p. 296, § 8. "When a person held to service or labor in any State or Territory of the United States has heretofore, or shall hereafter, escape into another State or Territory of the United States, the person or persons to whom such service or labor may be due, or his, her, or their agent or attorney, duly authorized by power of attorney in writing, acknowledged and certified under the seal of some legal officer or court of the State or Territory in which the same may be executed, may pursue and reclaim such fugitive person, either by procuring a warrant from some one of the courts, judges, or commissioners aforesaid of the proper circuit, district, or county, for the apprehension of such fugitive from service or labor, or by seizing and arresting such fugitive where the same can be done without process, and by taking or causing such person to be taken forthwith before such court, judge, or commissioner, whose duty it shall be to hear and determine the case of such claimant in a summary manner; and upon satisfactory proof being made by deposition or affidavit in writing, to be taken and certified by such court, judge, or commissioner, or by other satisfactory testimony duly taken and certified by some court, magistrate, justice of the peace, or other legal officer authorized to administer an oath and take depositions under the laws of the State or Territory from which such person owing service or labor may have escaped, with a certificate of such magistracy or other authority, as aforesaid, with the seal of the proper court or officer thereto attached, which seal shall be sufficient to establish the competency of the proof, and with proof also by affidavit of the identity of the person whose service or labor is claimed to be due as aforesaid, that the person arrested does in fact owe service or labor to the person or persons claiming him or her, in the State or Territory from which such fugitive may have escaped as aforesaid, and that said person escaped; to make out and deliver to such claimant, his or her agent or attorney, a certificate setting forth the substantial facts as to the service or labor due from the fugitive to such claimant, and of his or her escape from the State or Territory in which such service or labor was due, to the State or Territory in which he or she was arrested, with authority to such claimant, his or her agent or attorney, to use such reasonable force and restraint as may be necessary, under the circumstances of the case, to take and remove such fugitive person back to the State or Territory whence he or she may have escaped as aforesaid. In no trial or hearing under this act shall the testimony of such alleged fugitive be admitted in evidence; and the certificates in this and the first [fourth] section mentioned, shall be conclusive of the right of the person or persons in whose favor granted to remove such fugitive to the State or Territory from which he escaped, and shall prevent all molestation of such person or persons by any process issued by any court, judge, magistrate, or other person whomsoever."

Then in the 9th section is the interdiction against obstructing arrest, and rescuing the fugitive, the most of which I have already read.

I desire the Court to notice particularly the phraseology of these sections, because I shall comment upon them hereafter, and I do not like to be obliged to read them again. In the first section of the act of 1793, the constitutional expression "held to service or labor in any State or Territory under the laws thereof," is twice repeated, but in the 8th section, passed and approved September 18, 1850, the words "under the laws thereof," are wholly omitted.

My first point, sir, is that Congress had no more right to legislate upon this subject than I have, as an humble individual. And under what plausible — I cannot say substantial — pretexts do they claim such a right? Why first — and that which takes most hold on the hearts of the people — that the Act of 1793 was passed by a Congress composed in part of men who were in the Convention that framed the Constitution of the United States. But what if they were? The Supreme Court of the United States in the case of *Prigg* against *Pennsylvania*, declared that these men were all ignoramuses, because they gave power to the State Courts to interfere, to a certain extent, in carrying out the provisions of the Act. And if George Washington and John Adams and a score of such men might be mistaken as to the authority of State officers, might they not just as easily be mistaken upon any other equally debatable point? But, sir, we must never go to these men alone who framed the Constitution to learn its meaning. They can only shed light upon it. THE PEOPLE made the Constitution by adopting it, and we must take it as they adopted it, and ask how *they* understood it. It cannot be successfully argued here that the people were deceived and defrauded by the ingenious men who were sent to draft the Constitution. That they, without knowing what they did, adopted an instrument supposing it to be an instrument of freedom, which really consigned them and their posterity to slavery. But his Honor, the associate Justice who presides on this Circuit of the United States, tells us that the Constitution never would have been adopted without this *Fugitive* clause. I am thankful, sir, that I can read the English language as well as Chief Justice Taney — a little better now — and as well as any other Justice of the Supreme Court. And that is all that is necessary to enable me to understand the history of the Constitution — I set out with the proposition, that *this Fugitive servant clause never was looked upon as one of the compromises* between the North and the South, never was so regarded by the Southern States that ratified it, and never was so regarded anywhere else, until a very modern date.

[Judge BELDEN remarked that the Massachusetts Supreme Court had ruled with Justice McLean.]

Yes, and I know that Chancellor Walworth of New York, ruled the opposite, while Mr. Justice Nelson held with the Massachusetts Bench; *and that these two men being before the President as candidates for a vacancy in the Supreme Court of the United States, Walworth lost the prize and Nelson obtained it, just by this difference of ruling.* So true is it, Mr. Belden, that "*thrift follows fawning.*"

I do not stand here to claim that at that day, so soon after the seven years' struggle for freedom, the opinion that slavery was wrong in a free Government, was confined to any of the New England States. On the contrary, much to my own regret, I am warranted in saying, that, in the Convention, the delegates from Connecticut contributed more to the concessions to the Slave Power than did the delegates from Virginia.

In the Madison Papers, Vol. —, page —, I find that "Mr. SHERMAN disapproved of the slave-trade, yet as the States were now possessed of the right to import slaves, as the public good did not require it to be taken from them, and as it was best to have as few objections as possible to the proposed scheme of government, he thought it best to leave the matter as we find it. He observed that the abolition of slavery seemed to be going on in the United States, and that the good sense of the several States would probably by degrees complete it. He urged on the Convention the necessity of despatching its business."

On the other hand, it was said by Col. MASON : " This infernal traffic originated in the avarice of British merchants. The British Government constantly checked the attempts of Virginia to put a stop to it. The present question concerns not the importing States alone, but the whole Union. The evil of having slaves was experienced during the late war. Had slaves been treated as they might have been by the enemy, they would have proved dangerous instruments in their hands. But their folly dealt by the slaves as it did by the tories. He mentioned the dangerous insurrections of the slaves in Greece and Sicily ; and the instructions given by Cromwell to the Commissioners sent to Virginia, to arm the servants and slaves, in case other means of obtaining its submission should fail. Maryland and Virginia, he said, had already prohibited the importation of slaves expressly. North Carolina had done the same in substance. All this would be in vain if South Carolina and Georgia be at liberty to import. The Western people are already calling out for slaves for their new lands ; and will fill that country with slaves, if they can be got through South Carolina and Georgia. Slavery discourages arts and manufactures. The poor despise labor when performed by slaves. They prevent the immigration of whites, who really enrich and strengthen a country. They produce the most pernicious effect on manners. *Every master of slaves is born a petty tyrant.* They bring the judgment of Heaven on a country. As nations cannot be rewarded or punished in the next world, they must be in this. By an inevitable chain of causes and effects, Providence punishes national sins by national calamities. He lamented that some of our Eastern brethren had, from a lust of gain, embarked in this nefarious traffic. As to the States being in possession of the right to import, this was the case with many other rights, now to be properly given up. He held it essential in every point of view that the General Government should have power to prevent the increase of slavery." — *Madison Papers*, pp. 1390, 1391.

" Mr. SHERMAN said it was better to let the Southern States import slaves, than to part with them, if they made that a *sine qua non. He was opposed to a tax on slaves imported, as making the matter worse, because it implied they were* PROPERTY. He acknowledged that if the power of prohibiting the importation should be given to the General Government, it would be exercised. He thought it would be its duty to exercise the power." — *Ibid.*, 1396.

Mr. BALDWIN, in order to restrain and more explicitly define " the average duty," moved to strike out the second part of the words, " average of the duties laid on imports," and insert " common impost on articles not enumerated ;" which was agreed to, *nem. con.*

Mr. SHERMAN was *against this second part, as acknowledging men to be property* by taxing them as such under the character of slaves.

Mr. KING and Mr. LANGDON considered this was the price of the first part.

General PINCKNEY admitted that it was so.

Colonel MASON. Not to tax will be equivalent to a bounty on the importation of slaves.

Mr. GORHAM thought that Mr. SHERMAN should consider the duty, not as implying that slaves are property, but as a discouragement to the importation of them.

Mr. GOUVERNEUR MORRIS remarked, that, as the clause now stands, it implies that the Legislature may tax freemen imported.

Mr. SHERMAN, in answer to Mr. GORHAM, observed, that the smallness of the duty showed revenue to be the object, not the discouragement of the importation.

Mr. MADISON *thought it wrong to admit in the Constitution the idea that there could be property in men.* The reason of duties did not hold, as slaves are not like merchandise, consumed, etc. —*Ibid.*, 1429, 1430.

Mr. BUTLER and Mr. PINCKNEY moved to require " fugitive slaves and servants to be delivered up like criminals."

Mr. WILSON. This would oblige the Executive of the State to do it, at the public expense.

Mr. SHERMAN saw *no more propriety in the public seizing and surrendering a slave or servant than a horse.*

Mr. BUTLER withdrew his proposition in order that some particular provision might be made, apart from this article. — *Ibid.*, 1447, 1448.

Mr. BUTLER moved to insert after Article 15, " If any person bound to service or labor in any of the United States, shall escape into another State, he or she shall not be discharged from such service or labor, in consequence of any regulation subsisting in the State to which they escape, but shall be delivered up to the person justly claiming their service or labor," which was agreed to, *nem. con.—Ibid.*, 1456.

This was agreed to, nem. con. Now, is there any man within the sound of my voice who can suppose that such a proposition would have been thus unanimously agreed to, if those men could have looked forward and seen that such an act as that of Sept. 18, 1850 would be based upon it? *Never*, sir! I say again, sir, that no article which would have authorized the passage of such an Act as this infamous Fugitive Slave Law of 1850 could by any possibility have been put through that Convention; and if it had been inserted, before the *people* would have adopted it, they would have gone without a Constitution to this day! And this is as competent to be passed upon by any man who can understand the English language as if he had all the law-learning of Mr. Justice McLean. But we do not have the Constitution till we have another amendment.

Article 4, Section 2, of the report of the Committee, received on Wednesday, September 12, read : —

" No person *legally* held to service or labor in one State, escaping into another, shall, in consequence of regulations subsisting therein, be discharged from such service or labor; but shall be delivered up, on claim of the party to whom such service or labor may be due."

On Saturday, September 15th, Mr. Madison says in his diary (p. 1589):

" Article 4, Section 2 (the third paragraph), the term '*legally*' was struck out, and the words 'under the laws thereof' inserted after the word 'State,' in compliance with the wish of some who thought the term *legal* equivocal, *and favoring the idea that slavery was legal in a moral view.*"

So this paragraph, as finally adopted, reads:

" No person held to service or labor in one State under the laws thereof, escaping into another, shall, in consequence of any law or regulation therein, be discharged from such service or labor; but shall be delivered up on claim of the party to whom such service or labor may be due."

Such, then, is the history of this paragraph of the Constitution, and no one other has been so thoroughly misrepresented and misunderstood, and yet no one article or paragraph in that or any other document in the English language should be less liable to misconstruction. In and of itself, the words convey but one meaning; and, as if gifted with some dim foresight of the violence that might be done the compact by posterity, the members of the Convention guarded it by the use of the plainest language. " *Contracts of service made in one State, shall not be declared void by the laws of another State,*" is what this section says, and nothing else, more or less. And nothing can be more remarkable than the care taken that the words should be so chosen that they could, by no violence, be wrested to another meaning. Every equivocal word or phrase was jealously cut out. No tax should be laid on slaves, lest the Government *seem* to recognize property in them. The word " slave" must not appear in the Constitution, lest the Government seem to recognize slavery as a lawful institution. And the phrase " legally held" would never do, lest with apprentices and free laborers, fugitives from slavery being reckoned, the infamous institution might seem to be ranked with contracts for service sanctioned by the *Higher Law*, in strict accordance with which it was desired to frame this new Government. The States in Confederation had neither the power nor the right to abolish any institution existing by law in a part of the States, and upon no footing of equality could a union be effected, unless all existing local institutions were left to the care of the local authorities, and the different States were prevented from interfering with the internal policy of each other. To effect this essential condition of the Union, this paragraph was adopted. And here we are within three quarters of a century of the adoption of the Constitution, standing before a Federal tribunal, contending against the Federal Government, that it *is* necessary to aver in an indictment against a free citizen of a State, charged with rescuing a fugitive from service from his captors, that the fugitive *did owe service or labor in the State from which he is alleged to have fled, under the laws thereof!*

So fast, sir, have we degenerated; to such an " administration of justice" have we already come! Is it not time that we halt? Is it not important that we ask whether the time will not soon be upon us when *our* own children shall have the manacles now brought from Kentucky for African slaves, encircling their fair limbs? But we are told that there is no danger of mistaking Saxon children for African slaves. Gentlemen of the Jury, is there one of you who would not be proud to reckon that flaxen-haired little boy yonder among your children? His skin is whiter than the District-Attorney's, and his hair not half so curly! And yet, less than six months ago that child was set free in the Probate Court in this city, having been brought, a *slave*, from North Carolina! [Marked sensation.]

The Congress of the United States has the right to legislate upon such subjects only as are expressly assigned to it by the Constitution. But most certainly the Constitution gives them no power to legislate for the return of fugitive slaves, either expressly or by implication. But now the *Federal Court* — mark it, the *Federal Court* — helps Congress to the power, with THE TYRANT'S PLEA — "*It is* EXPEDIENT to legislate. It is *necessary for the Slave States*, in order to protect their property, that Congress should legislate; and whether the power was given by the Constitution or not, it is EXPE-DIENT that it should legislate, and legislate effectually. And if the Free North protests, its people shall be hung as *traitors*." This is where we stand to-day, while the whole civilized world is looking on, and a small part of it regarding us as FREEMEN!

I say the only intent of the last paragraph

of Section 2 of Article IV., was to prevent the free States from passing laws which would obstruct the capture of servants, should the master follow them, and insist on their return to service. No wider scope can possibly be given to it. And it is for this reason that I insist so strenuously that Congress had no power to legislate at all upon this subject. None whatever.

But here, however fully I might admit the right of the slave-owner to follow his fleeing slave into a free State and seize him, I differ from the gentleman widely, when he says that the slave-owner has the same *control* over his slave in Ohio that he has in Kentucky. He has the same privilege to reclaim his negro that he has to reclaim his horse, but he has no SLAVE in Ohio, for all that. He must, while in Ohio, treat the fugitive as *a man*. Not so, perhaps, in Kentucky.

I now proceed to my next proposition, which is, that the Act of 1850 is unconstitutional, because it provides pains and penalties for free citizens of Ohio, for acts concerning which they are not amenable to the Congress of the United States.

Before the Constitution was formed, the States were every one of them free and independent sovereignties. They fought together, shoulder to shoulder, through a seven years' war, to effect their independence of the dominion of Great Britain. Then each one for itself was a distinct, independent empire. Each one could make peace and war, levy duties upon commerce, make its criminal code, regulate its domestic police, or protect its frontier. Before and during the war, the States had entered into an alliance for common defence against the enemy. But after the peace it was found that these articles of Confederation were imperfect. And now I wish to call the special attention of your Honor to the fact, that the Convention which framed the instrument we now call the Constitution of the United States, was called together by the confederate Congress itself, to do a specific work. And that work was *not to frame a new Government*, but to *amend the old articles* of Confederation. For instance, before this Convention was called, there was no provision for a revenue for national purposes. It was therefore necessary that the foreign commerce of all the States should be put under the care of Congress, that a revenue might be raised upon it for the support of Government. There were a number of such important concessions made to the General Government. But certainly, it was never intended to frame, much less adopt, an instrument as a Constitution, which should eat up all State independence. And there was great sensitiveness on this point in the State Conventions which ratified the Constitution, from the proceedings of some of which I now proceed to read a few extracts. 4 Elliott's Debates, 285, I find that the principal topic of discussion in the State Con-

ventions, as well as in the General Convention, so far as slavery was concerned, was the stoppage of the foreign slave-trade, to which South Carolina was averse, even after the adoption of the Constitution. In the Convention of South Carolina (4 Elliott, 285), Gen. Pinckney said " he would make a few observations on the objections which the gentleman had thrown out on the restrictions that might be laid on the African slave-trade after the year 1808. On this point your delegates had to contend with the religious and political prejudices of the Eastern and Middle States, and with the interested and inconsistent opinion of Virginia, who was warmly opposed to our importing more slaves. I am of the same opinion now that I was two years ago, when I used the expressions the gentleman has quoted — that, while there remained one acre of swamp land uncleared of South Carolina, I would raise my voice against restricting the importation of negroes. I am as thoroughly convinced as that gentleman is, that the nature of our climate, and the flat, swampy situation of our country, obliges us to cultivate our lands with negroes, and that without them South Carolina would soon be a desert waste.

" You have so frequently heard my sentiments on this subject, that I need not now repeat them. It was alleged by some of the members who opposed an unlimited importation, that slaves increased the weakness of any State who admitted them; that they were a dangerous species of property, which an invading enemy would easily turn against ourselves and the neighboring States; and that, as we were allowed a representation for them in the House of Representatives, our influence in government would be increased in proportion as we were less able to defend ourselves. ' Show some period,' said the members from the Eastern States, ' when it may be in our power to put a stop, if we please, to the importation of this weakness, and we will endeavor, *for your convenience, to restrain the religious and political prejudices of our people on this subject.*' The Middle States and Virginia made us no such proposition; they were for an immediate and total prohibition. We endeavored to obviate the objections that were made in the best manner we could, and assigned reasons for our insisting on the importation, which there is no occasion to repeat, as they must occur to every gentleman in the house; a committee of the States was appointed in order to accommodate this matter, and after a great deal of difficulty it was settled on the footing recited in the Constitution.

" By this settlement we have secured an unlimited importation of negroes for twenty years. Nor is it declared that the importation shall then be stopped; it may be continued. We have a security that the General Government can never emancipate them, for no such authority is granted; *and it is admitted on all hands that the General Government has no powers but what are expressly granted by the Con-*

stitution, and that all rights not expressed were reserved by the several States. We have obtained a right to recover our slaves in whatever part of America they may take refuge, which is a right we had not before. In short, considering all circumstances, we have made the best terms for the security of this species of property it was in our power to make. We would have made better if we could; but on the whole, I do not think them bad."— 4 *Elliott's Debates*, 285, 286.

Now, may it please your Honor, if the statesmen of South Carolina would construe the Constitution in the paragraph which we have to deal with to-day, with the same *acumen* with which they would construe other articles, I should be safe, even with them in my reasoning. Indeed, one of them, Mr. Rhett, has done so in the Senate of the United States, and shown this act of 1850 to be wholly unconstitutional. But take the latitudinous construction now contended for in order to convict this man; where is the safety of slave property in any State? Congress has express power to legislate for the public welfare. Suppose a majority in Congress should say the public welfare required the abolition of slavery in the States;— may they not pass an act to that effect upon this loose assumption of power? And then where go their rights to their slaves? This argument of " expediency " is like the sword of the cherubim, — it turns every way, — and I warn the gentlemen against its incautious use.

In the making of this sacred instrument which was intended to be a " Charter of Freedom," it was supposed that a perfect system of checks and balances was introduced into the Federal Government. But alas! there was a great mistake made, for it now appears that in constituting a life Judiciary, they followed the example of Great Britain, without securing her " balance-wheel." The plea for a life Judiciary was, that the judges must be made independent of popular favor, or there was no security for the rights of the citizen. But the fact is, that our United States Supreme Court has greater power than any other judicial tribunal on the face of the globe! A power *absolutely unlimited*. It was forgotten that there was a check upon the courts in Great Britain, and that check was the Parliament. Every important decision of the Queen's Bench is subject to the revision of the Upper House of Parliament. And this has been found of the utmost consequence. But in our own free country we find a court which was constituted mainly for the purpose of carrying into effect the laws of Congress regulating the external concerns of the Confederacy, reaching out its Briarean arms and grasping every subject of jurisdiction until precious little of State Rights is left! Why, they have long ago determined that they have a right to take jurisdiction of cases in *State Courts*, by the removal of the cause under " an appeal " in the shape of a writ of error;

and by this miserable sham they have obtained control of *every thing* that can fall within the cognizance of our State court! It has come to this, that a State cannot regulate the levy and collection of its own taxes, in obedience to its own constitution, without being liable to a peremptory mandate from the Federal Court at Washington. There is scarcely any thing more of State sovereignty left us than the name, and the last vestige of judicial power in the States will soon be centred in the United States Supreme Bench. And, sir, it is because of this alarming state of things that I feel bound to animadvert upon the decisions of the Supreme Court of the United States. For they have now come to pronounce upon and affect to regulate the private conduct of free citizens of the States with reference even to the discharge of high moral duties. I say that this is a matter which cannot come within the province of Congress, and ought not to come within the jurisdiction of a Federal court. It belongs exclusively to State legislatures and State courts.

But again. The act of 1850 does violence to the constitution, for it overrides the writ of *habeas corpus*. The constitution says the writ of *habeas corpus* may be suspended only in times of rebellion, and of foreign invasion. But the escape of a negro slave is neither the one nor the other. Yet the Act of 1850 says: —

" And the certificates in this and the first [fourth] section mentioned, shall be conclusive of the right of the person or persons in whose favor granted, to remove such fugitive to the State or Territory from which he escaped, *and shall prevent all molestation of such person or persons by* ANY *process issued by* ANY *court, judge, magistrate, or other person whomsoever.*" In Blightly's Digest, from which I read, a note upon this latter clause says: —

" State tribunals and officers cannot, by the writ of *habeas corpus*, interfere with the Federal authorities when acting upon cases arising under this act. 1 Blatchford, 635, Sims's case, 7 Cush. 285."

The Attorney-General says it was never intended to override the writ of *habeas corpus*. And Judge Nelson, in his famous charge to the Grand Jury in New York, contained in the first of Blatchford's Reports, says, that a *Federal* court may *of course* issue a writ of *habeas corpus; the Act was intended only to prevent the interference of* STATE *courts!*

Has it come to this then ? May we no longer look to State courts for relief from oppression ? When our liberties are endangered, have we no protection at home ? Has the Federal Court already *all* the power ? If this is the doctrine, sir, you may just as well tell us frankly, that our State Governments are not worth a rush.

I turn again to the debates in the State conventions called to ratify the Constitution. In the North Carolina Convention, the Constitution being under consideration: —

" Article 4. The first section and first two clauses of the second section read without observation.

" The last clause being read,

" Mr. IREDELL begged leave to explain the reason of this clause. In some of the Northern States they have emancipated all their slaves. If any of our slaves, said he, go there and remain there a certain time, they would by the present laws be entitled to their freedom, so that their masters could not get them again. This would be extremely prejudicial to the inhabitants of the Southern States; and to prevent it, this clause is inserted in the Constitution. Though the word *slave* is not mentioned, this is the meaning of it. The Northern delegates, owing to their particular scruples on the subject of slavery, did not choose the word *slave* to be mentioned." — 4 *Elliott's Debates*, 176.

According to the statement of a North Carolinian, then, before this clause in the Constitution was adopted, slaves going into the free States would become free. But with this clause they might pursue and reclaim them. Yet not even here, and nowhere else in the history of these times, can it be found, that the right of Congress to legislate on the subject, and, above all, to make it the *duty of Federal officers* to capture and return fugitive slaves, was acknowledged or mentioned. Justice Mc Lean based his opinion upon the state of public sentiment in the South, at the time of which we speak: but even *that* does not bear him out in his assertions.

Gen. HEATH, a member of the Massachusetts Convention, declared, when this Constitution was under consideration in that Convention: —

" I apprehend that it is not in our power to do any thing for or against those who are in slavery in the Southern States. No gentleman within these walls detests every idea of slavery more than I do: it is generally detested by the people of this commonwealth; and I ardently hope that the time will soon come when our brethren in the Southern States will view it as we do, and put a stop to it; but to this we have no right to compel them. Two questions naturally arise: if we ratify the Constitution, shall we do any thing by our act to hold the blacks in slavery? or shall we become the partakers of other men's sins? I think neither of them. Each State is sovereign and independent to a certain degree, and the States have a right, and they will regulate their own internal affairs as to themselves appears proper; and shall we refuse to eat, or to drink, or to be united with those who do not think or act just as we do? Surely not. We are not, in this case, partakers of other men's sins; for in nothing do we voluntarily encourage the slavery of our fellow men. A restriction is laid on the Federal Government which could not be avoided and a union take place. The Federal Convention went as far as they could. The migration, or importation, etc., is confined to the *States now existing only; new States cannot claim it.* Congress, by their ordinance for erecting new States, some time since, declared that the new States shall be republican, and that there *shall be no Slavery in them.*" — 2 *Elliott's Debates*, 115.

The great Constitutional lawyer, Daniel Webster — he had his failings, but he was a great man, and a great Constitutional expounder — Mr. Webster held, among other positions which he never yielded, and from which he could never be driven, this one: that, so far as it regarded the provisions in the Constitution recognizing the existence of slavery at all, they were intended to affect the original thirteen States alone. " For," said he, " were slavery not thus geographically limited, by and by a few wealthy slaveholders would have the entire control of the Nation through the House of Representatives."

I read now a remark from Mr. ALEXANDER HAMILTON in the Convention of the State of New York. He has been extensively known as one of the great advocates of the Constitution. He was a member of the Convention which framed the Constitution itself; and also a member of the Convention of the State of New York which ratified it, and throughout the sessions of the latter authoritatively expounded the scope and meaning of each of the Articles. And it is to a remark of his that I wish to call the attention of your Honor, because it supports me in the position which I have taken, that the crime with which my client is charged is one of which the Federal Congress can take no cognizance. He says: —

" It has been asserted that the interests, habits, and manners of the thirteen States are different; and hence it is inferred that no general free government can suit them. This diversity of habits, etc., has been a favorite theme with those who are disposed for a division of our empire, and, like many other popular objections, seems to be founded on fallacy. I acknowledge that the local interests of the States are in some degree various, and that there is some difference in the manners and habits. But this I will presume to affirm, that, from New Hampshire to Georgia, the people of America are as uniform in their interests and manners as those of any established in Europe. This diversity, to the eye of a speculatist, may afford some marks of characteristic discrimination, but cannot form an impediment to the regular operation of those general powers which the Constitution gives to the united government. Were the laws of the Union to *new-model the internal police of any State;* were they to alter or abrogate at a blow the whole of its civil and criminal institutions; were they *to penetrate the recesses of domestic life,* and control in all respects *the private conduct of individuals,* —

there might be more force in the objection; and the same Constitution which was happily calculated for one State, might sacrifice the welfare of another." — 2 *Elliott's Debates*, 267, 268.

I read now farther — same book, 401 — from the remarks of Mr. TREDWELL in the same Convention, — that of New York. He was opposing the adoption of the Constitution, because of some of the provisions which Time has actually shown to be radical defects.

" In this Constitution, sir, we have departed widely from the principles and political faith of '76, when the spirit of liberty ran high, and danger put a curb on ambition. Here we find no security for the rights of individuals, no security for the existence of our State Governments; here is no bill of rights, no proper restriction of power; our lives, our property, and our consciences, are left wholly at the mercy of the legislature, *and the powers of the Judiciary may be extended to any degree short of Almighty.* Sir, in this Constitution we have not only neglected, — we have done worse, — we have openly violated our faith, — that is, our public faith."

On the next page he continues: —

" There is another clause in this Constitution, which, though there is no prospect of getting it amended, I think ought not to be passed over in silence, lest such a silence should be construed into a tacit approbation of it. I mean the clause which restricts the General Government from putting a stop, for a number of years, to a commerce which is a stain to the commerce of any civilized nation, and has already blackened half the plains of America with a race of wretches made so by our cruel policy and avarice, and which appears to me to be already repugnant to every principle of humanity, morality, religion, and good policy."

A little further on, page 405, he says: —

" A union with our sister States I as ardently desire as any man, and that upon the most generous principles; but a union under such a system as this, I think, is not a desirable thing. The design of a union is *safety*, but a union upon the proposed plan is certain *destruction to liberty*. In one sense, indeed, it may bring us to a state of safety; for it may reduce us to such a condition that we may be very sure that nothing worse can happen to us, and consequently we shall have nothing to fear.

" This, sir, is a dreadful kind of safety; but I confess it is the only kind of safety I can see in this union. There are no advantages that can possibly arise from a union which can compensate for the loss of freedom, *nor can any evils be apprehended from a disunion which are as much to be dreaded as tyranny*."

So much, may it please your Honor, and you, Gentlemen of the Jury, in vindication of the truth of history. I say, therefore, believing myself fully borne out in the affirmation by the history of the Constitution, that its adoption did not depend, wholly or in part, upon the adoption of the paragraph which provides that no State shall set at liberty a fugitive servant.

I say, that the sentiment throughout the States was such that no Constitution would ever have been ratified which was supposed to set up an uncontrolled despotism in the place of liberty.

May it please the Court, I know full well what have been the rulings of the Federal Courts on the subject under consideration, and that this is not the time, nor the place, to hope to stem the tide of despotism already moving with such alarming volume in our unhappy country; but I hold it to be none the less my right and duty to announce my own views as to the constitutionality of the act under which my client is arraigned.

The language of the Indictment is: —

" And the Jurors aforesaid do further present and find, that Simeon Bushnell, late of the District aforesaid, together with divers, to wit, 200 other persons, to the Jurors aforesaid unknown, heretofore, to wit, on the first day of October, in the year of our Lord one thousand eight hundred and fifty-eight, at the District aforesaid, and within the jurisdiction of this Court, with force and arms, unlawfully, knowingly, and willingly did rescue the said negro slave called John, then and there being pursued and reclaimed, seized and arrested, and in the custody and control aforesaid, he the said negro slave called John being then and there a fugitive from and held to service and labor, as aforesaid [to wit, held to service and labor in the State of Kentucky, one of the United States, the said John being the property of one John G. Bacon, of the said State of Kentucky, the person to whom such labor and service were then due], from the custody of the said Anderson Jennings, then and there the authorized agent of the said John G. Bacon, as aforesaid, and the said Jacob K. Lowe, then and there lawfully assisting him, the said Anderson Jennings, as aforesaid; he the said Simeon Bushnell then and there well knowing that the said negro slave called John was then and there a fugitive person held to service and labor, as aforesaid, and pursued and reclaimed, seized and arrested, and held in custody, as aforesaid, to the great damage of the said John G. Bacon, contrary to the form of the Act of Congress in such case made and provided, and against the peace and dignity of the United States."

I insist, may it please your Honor, and with great earnestness, upon the exception which has been already taken to the omission in the indictment of the averment that the slave owed service in Kentucky " under the laws thereof." I insist that the averment is necessary and material, and that without it the indictment is bad.

And I insist farther, that, a person entitled to service in the State of Kentucky " under the laws thereof," cannot come into the State of

Ohio for the purpose of reclaiming a fugitive. We have an instrument for our government made anterior to the Constitution of the United States or any act of Congress; I allude to the compact made between the States anterior to the framing of the Constitution.

In the Ordinance made for the government of the North-Western Territory, I read as follows: " *It is hereby ordained and declared, by the authority aforesaid,* that the following articles shall be considered as articles of compact between the original States and the people and States in the said territory, and forever remain unalterable, unless by common consent, to wit : —

"ART. 1. No person, demeaning himself in a peaceable and orderly manner, shall ever be molested on account of his mode of worship or religious sentiments in the said territory.

"ART. 2. The inhabitants of the said territory shall always be entitled to the benefits of the writ of *habeas corpus,* and of the trial by jury; of a proportionate representation of the people in the legislature, and of judicial proceedings according to the course of the common law. All persons shall be bailable, unless for capital offences, where the proof shall be evident or the presumption great. All fines shall be moderate, and no cruel or unusual punishments shall be inflicted. No MAN *shall be deprived of his liberty* or property, *but by the judgment of his peers,* etc."

I think there was no dissenting voice in the adoption of this Ordinance, or at most only a single dissenting vote.

" *Unless by common consent.*" Can there be any doubt of the import of this language?

"ART. 6. There shall be neither slavery nor involuntary servitude in the said territory, otherwise than in the punishment of crimes, whereof the party shall have been duly convicted ; provided always, that any person escaping into the same from whom labor or service is lawfully claimed *in any one of the original* States, such fugitive may be lawfully reclaimed, and conveyed to the person claiming his or her service as aforesaid. . . . . .

"Done by the United States, in Congress assembled, the 13th day of July, in the year of our Lord 1787, and of their sovereignty and independence the twelfth.

" CHARLES THOMSON, *Secretary.*"

I know that the Supreme Court of the United States has ruled that, notwithstanding this 6th article, the fugitive acts of 1793 and 1850 obtained over the North-Western Territory, but I believe this ruling to be erroneous; I do not consider myself a very learned man, but I do not claim to know much when I say I am the equal in knowledge of some of those Justices of the Supreme Court, whom I have seen upon the bench. I hold, that there can be no reclaiming of fugitive slaves escaping from the State of Kentucky into the State of Ohio, because it is expressly said that the escape must be from one of the " *original* States."

[Thursday Morning.]

A very pertinent inquiry was made of me by the Bench yesterday evening, and one which I ought to have answered, perhaps, a little more fully than I did.

The inquiry was, if I did not know that the U. S. Supreme Court had decided that the Constitution did away the force and effect of the ordinance of 1787 ? I do know it, sir, perfectly well; I know it was decided that the Ordinance of 1787 was no protection to a citizen of Ohio when charged with harboring a fugitive slave from Kentucky. And I said that though I had great respect for the Supreme Bench, I had no possible respect for such decisions, for I believed them to be totally wrong. It is claimed by the advocates of the Fugitive Slave Law that the Constitution should be interpreted by the acts of those who lived at the time it was framed and adopted. *The first Congress that assembled under the Constitution passed an Act ratifying the Ordinance of* 1787 as strongly as possible. It is found in 1 United States Statutes at Large, 50, and is entitled, ". An Act to provide for the government of the Territory North-west of the river Ohio." The purport of it is clearly set forth in the preamble : —

" *Whereas,* in order that the Ordinance of the United States in Congress assembled, for the government of the Territory North-west of the river Ohio *may continue to have full effect,* it is requisite that certain provisions should be made, so as to adapt the same to the present Constitution of the United States."

And that it may clearly appear that this additional statute has no bearing other than that of a recognition of this validity upon the quotations I have made from the original Ordinance, I will, with the permission of your Honor, read the entire Act.

" SECTION 1. *Be it enacted by the Senate and House of Representatives of the United States of America in Congress assembled,* That in all cases in which by the said Ordinance, any information is to be given, or communication made, by the Governor of the said Territory to the United States in Congress assembled, or to any of their officers, it shall be the duty of the said Governor to give such information and to make such communication to the President of the United States, and the President shall nominate, and by and with the advice and consent of the Senate, shall appoint, all officers which by the said Ordinance were to have been appointed by the United States in Congress assembled, and all officers so appointed shall be commissioned by him; and in all cases where the United States in Congress assembled, might, by the said Ordinance, revoke any commission or remove from any office, the President is hereby declared to have the same powers of revocation and removal.

"SEC. 2. *And be it further enacted*, That in the case of the death, removal, resignation, or necessary absence of the Governor of the said Territory, the Secretary thereof shall be, and he is hereby authorized and required to exercise all the powers and perform all the duties of the Governor, during the vacancy occasioned by the removal, resignation, or necessary absence of the said Governor.

"Approved, August 7, 1789."

With the alterations mentioned in this Act, the Ordinance is left in full force, and these alterations are made for the sole purpose of *continuing* it in force, as averred in the preamble.

Now if any single Judge or body of Judges, can overrule this Ordinance and put it down, and say that all the then Territory North-west of the river Ohio is not to-day covered and sheltered by this Ægis of Freedom, I beg to know, sir, what guaranty we have for any of our liberties!

I affirm that the sentiment of the people of the United States, at the time of the adoption of the Constitution, was *not* in favor of slavery, but decidedly opposed to it, and tolerating it only as a temporary evil, which must soon be done away. This has clearly appeared in my citations, few and hurried as they have been. Even the simple paragraph which closes Section 2, of Article 4, was not in the draft presented by Hamilton, nor in that of Randolph, nor in that of Pinckney, nor yet in that of Patterson, of New Jersey; but it was an afterthought, put in merely to quiet the fears of the Southern States that their slaves might be freed by touching Northern soil. How, then, it may be asked, were the rights of the Southern States to be protected? I answer, by simply forbidding the Northern States to interfere with them; by proclaiming the favorite doctrine of some modern politicians, the doctrine of " *non-intervention*." And this was all that was proposed to be done, or even desired by the Southern States themselves. Then, under the Constitution, what redress has a slaveholder *in one of the original thirteen States*, if his slave escapes into a free State? Why, the same that he would have if his horse had thus escaped, or that a citizen of a free State would have if his horse escaped into a slave State. He might pursue, overtake, and seize his horse by the halter wherever he could find him, and if no one interfered with his leading him away, well; but if some citizen of that State takes the halter away from him, and locks the horse up in his stable, claiming the horse as his, then let him bring an action of replevin or detinue for the *chattel*, trover or trespass for damage. And this is security enough. It was all that was ever dreamed of in the Convention which framed the Constitution. It is all the South thought of asking. It is entirely an after-

thought, this making extraordinary provision for this peculiar species of property. It is said that the Act of 1793 was passed by a Congress that understood the Constitution, inasmuch as some of its members were in the Convention of 1787, that framed it. Chief Justice Taney, with the concurrence of a majority of his associates, holds that in the Prigg case it did not understand the Constitution, because it gave, in that act, certain jurisdiction to State and local officers; and if they could commit a mistake on so important a point as that, I do not see why they might not on any other. We cannot be bound by any one error in that act more than another, that does violence to the Constitution. And, as a Reverend Doctor of Divinity said in the meeting, the resolutions of which I read here yesterday, "the Act of 1850 is to the Act of 1793 *as a dose of molten lead to a 'mint julep!'*" [Laughter.]

I have said that the Act of 1850 is unconstitutional, because it does away with the right of *habeas corpus*, and because it interferes with the internal police regulations of the State; and I now proceed to say that it is also unconstitutional, because it does not guarantee to the person arrested as a fugitive from service, the right of trial by jury. And why was not this guaranty given? Why did not the Congress which passed that bill of iniquity, give the right of trial by jury? It was stoutly and persistently contended for, but it was put down by *the tyrant's plea*, "IT IS NOT EXPEDIENT."

Mr. District-Attorney, you shake your head; but Mr. Mason, the father of that bill, in arguing this very point in the U. S. Senate, said: "If we commit such cases to a jury in the free States, they will inquire into the question whether the person really owed service or labor, and when *that* inquiry is raised, *we're gone, sir!* slaveholders have no longer any protection."

I was thought to be speaking lightly when I said there were none of us, however obtuse our moral sense might be, but respected irresistibly the Higher Law. If I change the term, and call it God's Law, perhaps it may not sound so very ridiculous in the ears of the gentlemen on the other side. Mr. Jefferson, though distinguished as a statesman, was not distinguished for the depth or fervor of his religious feelings; yet in his first message to Congress, he says: "All laws, in order to be respected by the governed, must be just, — must be founded on the principles of Eternal Justice." And in speaking of the partisan success which elected him, he adds: —

"Although we have triumphed by a signal majority, we must not forget that the minority have rights, and we must not pass laws which will infringe on the consciences or the rights of that minority."

It may be said that it is a dangerous doctrine to proclaim, that the people may judge whether a law ought or ought not to be obeyed. But without this doctrine displayed in practice, when should we have become an independent nation? Sir, governments are instituted for the benefit of the governed, and not for the convenience of the Administrators thereof. And if the people believe themselves outraged by their servants, and the " still small voice " of reproof is not heard, the thunder and the lightning of revolution will speedily follow. Gentlemen of the Jury, I remember, in the short course of my own experience, a case of quasi rebellion in this State. In 1848 I had the honor to be Chairman of what was called " the Dorr Convention," at Columbus. The Whig legislature had, with a high hand, divided the county of Hamilton for election purposes, so as to secure to their party a larger representation in the General Assembly. The Democracy of the State rallied in Convention under the very eaves of the Capitol; courageously denounced the law as unjust and outrageous, and pledged themselves under no circumstances to regard it. The Democratic voters of Hamilton, disregarding the new district limits, elected Representatives as before; secured them their seats in the House, and actually *compelled* the Legislature to repeal the odious act. In that struggle I took part as a *Democrat;* in this, with the same temper and spirit, I take part as a *Republican.*

Gentlemen of the Jury, this man Bacon from Kentucky says, that he owned the man JOHN. Now, gentlemen, I hope you will not be very astute to supply deficiencies in the evidence. If there is a link lacking in the chain, you will give the defendant the benefit of it; and watch against that infirmity which is common to us all; that pride of opinion and party prejudice, which would tempt you, being of a particular political cast, to work the conviction of a man because he comes from a locality which is said to be opposed to the enactment of the Fugitive Slave Law. None of us could go to sleep and sleep soundly after entailing fine and imprisonment upon a fellow-citizen, unless the law and the testimony imperiously required it.

Now, let us revert to the Constitution. It has been read to you upon the other side. We ought all to read it oftener than we do. "Article IV., Section 2. The Citizens of each State shall be entitled to all the Privileges and Immunities of Citizens in the several States."

Now this is all the protection that can constitutionally be granted or ought to be asked by any citizen North or South. But how often have we seen this clause infringed and violated and outraged in the port of Charleston, South Carolina, by the seizure and imprisonment of free men, because God made them men of color, and for no other pretended or alleged crime whatever. And more than that, when Massachusetts had been insulted and outraged in the persons of her citizens, until continued forbearance would be ineffaceable disgrace, and she sent one of her most venerable and upright Judges to inquire into the matter, according to

law, he was threatened, insulted, and mobbed, and but for the presence and protection of his poor sick *daughter,* would unquestionably have lost his life.

Oh! if I could live to see that proud day when no slave could set his foot upon our soil without feeling his shackles fall forever from his galled and bleeding limbs, I could say, Gentlemen, with all my heart, " Lord, now lettest thou thy servant depart in peace; for mine eyes have seen thy salvation ! " But all this is prevented by this Fugitive clause in the Constitution. The common law can say, " Slaves cannot breathe in England!!!" but alas, no act of the freemen of Ohio can enable us to say so here ! *Slaves may breathe in Ohio,* and they may be pursued, if escaping from any one of the original thirteen States, and with cords and whips and chains and bowie knives and revolvers be drawn back, and sold and doomed to the hopeless cotton fields and rice swamps of the South. But how can his recaption be made ? *Not* by an Act of Congress making all our citizens, *nolens volens,* a pack of bloodhounds to do the bidding of the man-hunter. Never, sir; never while our free Republic endures. But were even this possible, the traverser at the bar cannot be made amenable to the act of 1850 until the alleged title of property in the boy John is fully shown. Unless this claim of property is established beyond all cavil, the prosecution must fail. Mr. Bacon comes here and swears that John is his slave. That his father owned John and John's mother, and that he died intestate, leaving six children, who thus became his heirs. Here he stops. He neither alleges a release of the claim of the other five heirs, nor shows by evidence in any other way exclusive title in himself. This will never do. The six heirs inherited John, each inheriting *one sixth,* and no more. Until five had released to him their claim to five sixths of John, Mr. Bacon had not the sole control of him. And as he has not shown the release of the claim of a single heir, that power of attorney is wholly insufficient, because in it John G. Bacon assumes the exclusive control of joint property.

But does John owe service to either of them ? Why, Mr. Bacon swears that John is his slave. But is that sufficient proof in the free State of Ohio, where the presumption is always in favor of a man's freedom? What more is it than if you, Mr. Rhodes, should come forward and swear, " this man Spalding is my slave ? " And do the citizens of Ohio hold their liberties by a tenure *so* slight that the unsupported oath of any man within the bounds of the United States will at any instant sever it forever ?

Yet, Gentlemen, it is so claimed by the prosecuting officer of this Court; claimed seriously and positively, as the meaning of the phrase, " in a summary manner," in the Act of 1850. Gentlemen of the Jury, will you accept that construction ? Will you agree that your children, no whiter than tens of thousands of Southern slaves, shall be exposed to the loss of freedom by means of a false oath, on the part of any one inhabitant of the United States?

Such an oath is not enough. Even this law does not make it enough. And the Constitution is a great way from making it enough. It must be shown that the fugitive *owes* service in the State from which he fled, *under the laws thereof.* And here I am met by another vagary of Mr. Justice McLean, that the Court may take judicial notice of the fact that the State from which the fugitive is alleged to have escaped, is a slave State! Now, though this be a Federal decision, it is one against which I protest absolutely, as against one of those many judicial assumptions which are rapidly and fatally undermining our free institutions.

It is not pretended that the owner Bacon came in person, but that he sent Jennings, and authorized him in a joint power of attorney made by two individuals, and authorizing the arrest of three persons, to seize and arrest John, and return him to Kentucky. This is altogether too loose a practice. But I complain of the power of attorney more especially, because it is not acknowledged and certified as required by the Act of Congress. And this I hold to be a very important point for the consideration of the Court and Jury. The acknowledgment is as follows: —

State of Kentucky, }
 Mason County.   } sct.

I, Robert A. Cochran, Clerk of the County Court of the county aforesaid, do hereby certify that this power of attorney from Richard Loyd and John G. Bacon to Anderson Jennings, was this day produced to me and acknowledged by the said Richard Loyd and John G. Bacon to be their act and deed. The said parties are personally known to me, and the said acknowledgment is according to law.

Given under my hand and official seal, in the city of Maysville, this 4th day of September, 1858.   ROBERT A. COCHRAN, Clerk,
 by WILLIAM H. RICHARDSON, D. C.

Now, sir, this clerk of the county of Mason has been called to the stand by the District-Attorney, and he says that he was not present, and the instrument was *not* acknowledged before him. But what does he testify to? Why, he says that this young man who signs himself below as William H. Richardson, is his deputy, and this is his (the deputy's) handwriting. I ask, then, in the name of all the expounders of law that were ever congregated on the Bench, how can *this* be called an acknowledgment under the Act of 1850? For how can a deputy take an acknowledgment when the law requires the principal to do it?

The law says: —

" § 8.   When a person held to service or labor in any State or Territory of the United States, has heretofore or shall hereafter escape

into another State or Territory of the United States, the person or persons to whom such service or labor may be due, or his, her, or their agent or attorney, duly authorized by power of attorney in writing, *acknowledged and certified under the seal of some legal officer or Court* of the State or Territory in which the same may be executed, may pursue and reclaim such fugitive person, etc." — *Act of* 1850, *Brightly's Digest*, 294.

In the 6 McLean I find a decision upon a point bearing very much upon this: —

Weimer *v.* Sloane, 6 McLean, 259. " The Statute authorizes an arrest, either by the owner or his agent, with or without warrant; but, when made by an agent, he must be authorized by a written power of attorney, *executed and authenticated as required by the Statute.*"

Again, in Gibbons *v.* Sloane, p. 273, of the same volume, " The evidence was the same in both cases, except as to the manner of the execution of the power of attorney to Patton, who made the arrest as the agent of Gibbons; and by the consent of the counsel both cases were submitted to the jury at the same time. In this case it appeared that Gibbons had executed a power of attorney in the State of Kentucky, as required by the Act of Congress, in which either no name was inserted as the agent of the plaintiff, or, if any, that of some person other than Patton; and that afterwards and before the arrest of the fugitive by Patton, his name was inserted by the plaintiff or some other person, at Sandusky City, in the State of Ohio, without any acknowledgment of the instrument in that State. The Court instructed the jury, that, under the Act of 1850, this was not a valid power to Patton, and did not authorize him to make the arrest. The jury returned a verdict for the defendant."

These requirements of the law, therefore, must be lived up to. It won't answer to bring forward a power of attorney here without such an acknowledgment as the Statute prescribes.

I now refer to a case in the 3d of Barr's Pennsylvania State Reports, 495, Lothrop *v.* Blake, to show how the certificate of a deputy is regarded under the general law for the authentication of records.

" By the Constitution of the United States, Congress have the power to prescribe the manner in which the public acts, records, and judicial proceedings in the several States shall be proved in any other State; and by an Act of 1790 Congress has declared that the records and judicial proceedings of any State, shall be proved or admitted in any other Court of the United States, *by the attestation of the clerk*, and the seal of the Court annexed, if there be a seal, together with a certificate of the Judge, Chief Justice, or presiding magistrate, as the case may be, that the said attestation is in due form."

It cannot be admitted (as is justly said in Stephenson *v.* Banister, 3 Bibb, 370) that under this act any judge of any court may certify a record. It must be *the judge*, if there be but one ; or, if there be more, then by the chief justice, or presiding judge or magistrate of the court from whence the record comes; and he must possess that character at the time he gives the certificate. A certificate that he is the judge that presided at the time of the trial, or that he is the senior judge of the courts of law in the State, is deemed insufficient. The clerk also, who certifies the record, *must be the clerk himself*, or his successor : *the certificate of his under clerk, in his absence*, or of the clerk of any other tribunal, office, or body, *is held incompetent for the purpose.* See Sampson v. Overton, Bibb, 409 ; and Greenleaf's Evidence, sec. 506, and the authorities there cited. *Nor will the statute of Ohio, which enables deputies to perform the duties of the principal, make the authentication of the record by him, evidence ;* as this would enable the several States to alter and control an act of Congress. It must be construed by itself, independent of legislative enactments. This record is attested by the *deputy*, and is certified by N. C. Reed, Judge of the Supreme Court of Ohio, but by the record it appears that he is a member of the court of which the Honorable Ebenezer C. Lane is the Chief Justice. The record, therefore, is not certified as is directed by the act of Congress, and was on *both* grounds improperly admitted.

Gentlemen of the Jury, I have now concluded what I had to say upon the power of attorney. And the Court will tell you, I apprehend, that it is worthless, because not acknowledged before the Clerk in person.

What next ?

We find that on a certain day in September, 1858, the peaceful village of Oberlin was entered by three or four unusual visitors, and in rather an unusual manner. Oberlin has the character of being a moral town, much more than ordinarily moral, perhaps. And it has the character of containing very many minds utterly opposed to the infliction of involuntary servitude upon any human being, except as a punishment for crime. Now, if it be any benefit to the Prosecution to understand that this is the general feeling of that town, so be it. They may take the acknowledgment in welcome. I freely admit that Oberlin is an asylum for the oppressed of all God's creation, without distinction of color. So long as a man behaves well, they administer to him the common charities of life. There is no doubt about it. There is no doubt they are called sternly religious, and so have been very many men known to us in history, as the defenders of Freedom. The absolute character of the crown of Great Britain was effectually changed by such men as the men of Oberlin. The Roundheads of the days of Cromwell, who went into battle with a sabre in one hand and a Bible in the other, were such men. Their general orders were, " Trust in God, but keep your powder dry." By such men only could the liberties of England have

been successfully achieved. The Cavaliers or Royalists driven thence, unfortunately for us, during the Protectorate, took up their abode in our Southern provinces. They are there, in the persons of their offspring, to this day. But we have the spirit of the Roundheads in the North ; and God forbid that we should not speedily decide which shall have the supremacy here. For Slavery and Freedom cannot exist together; one must die that the other may live. And I say, with the patriots of '76, " Better that we do without the Union, than without our liberties."

The village of Oberlin was invaded by slave catchers. And I am glad that in this very first trial we have, within the precincts of this Connecticut Western Reserve, so fair a specimen of a Kentucky Slave Catcher. A man who would shine as the leader of a banditti : six feet four inches, and well proportioned : a short neck and bushy beard, a buffalo bull, from the prairies of Arkansas, with an Arkansas toothpick at his waist, and a brace of revolvers in his pocket. I say again, I am glad we have such an exhibition on this the first trial of a Rescuer on the Western Reserve : it may not need so frequent repetition. This man, together with as great a bully as himself, from Kentucky, a Deputy United States Marshal from the Southern District of Ohio, and the Columbus jailer, — the same who ironed the schoolmaster Lincoln, before his weeping scholars, and thrust him into the dungeon like a felon, among thieves and vermin, — made up the select party who descended upon Oberlin. Such men come for our chastening, no doubt, and are among the inscrutable dispensations of Divine Providence, which are manifested for our good if we would only lay it to heart. Such men come, it is said, to fulfil the law, not to break the peace ; armed with all necessary process, as they claim, and with the Marshal of the United States to execute the same. Why, then, did they not go to work openly and serve their process ? saying to the people of Oberlin, " we have a legal warrant for the apprehension of the negro John, and shall make lawful service of the same. Make resistance you may, but serve our papers we shall. Resistance, however, we do not anticipate : make way for the officer to execute his warrant peaceably, and we are away about our business." Now if they had done this, and the people of Oberlin had raised a mob, and thrown these ruffians into a " *horse pond,* " the law might have been violated, but I confess I should have been personally gratified !

But what do we find ?

This United States Marshal Lowe, and the tall gentleman from Kentucky, went, of a Saturday night to the dwelling of General Lewis D. Boynton ; — an old friend of mine, by the way : a man of large heart and generous impulses, but having curious notions about *politics* and *slavery.* The wife administered the rites of hospitality to these men in her husband's absence. The next morning they are introduced to the General, and make known their business. It would be interesting to have that conversation before us. But no matter. The bright, precocious little son of Boynton is put upon the stand, — and what a story does he tell! The most minute, disgusting details of this blood-betraying bargain. How readily he consented to play the Judas, and how well satisfied he was with the reward of his treason, — the twenty — it should have been *thirty* — pieces of silver!

[Judge BLISS: Twenty was enough for a boy.]

No, sir; it should have been "THIRTY." It is too sickening to go through again with the details of this loathsome transaction. You have heard it, Gentlemen of the Jury, from the lips of the witnesses, including this poor child himself, and my associate adverted to it at some length. But I do not wish you to pass it lightly. So foul a compact, in which the depravity of youth and the corruption of age are so nearly on a level, and that level so near the very "*pit*" itself, made in the sacred stillness of Sabbath hours, and that Sabbath shedding its holy light upon the free soil of our noble State, consecrated by a most solemn compact to perpetual freedom; that light disclosing to view at the same moment the church spire and the *man-hunter* — Gentlemen of the Jury, are you prepared upon your oaths to indorse, in the name and behalf of the Government of the United States, as a lawful and proper service of a just and lawful process that nefarious seizure, of which this unhallowed compact was the basis? Is there one of you who would wish his son to come upon the witness stand of this Court, and make oath to such confessions as you have heard recited with great glee by this most unfortunate child? Why, Gentlemen, what end will that boy come to, if he be so ripe for ruin already? A boy so young, and already an expert in the vilest and meanest passions that ever cursed a human heart! Ready to lie for hire to any extent, and even to crush the hopes of this poor, illiterate, honest-hearted, confiding negro, who, in common with us all, loves liberty better than every thing else, and would fight for it to the last gasp. He trusts Shakespeare because he knows him as a professed friend: he needs work to get his bread, and is exceedingly grateful for the kind offer of the boy, but in the house lies his friend disabled, and he cannot leave him to suffer. Very reluctantly he declines the needed charity, that he may be an almoner to one even more needy than himself. But to show something of his gratitude to Shakespeare, he volunteers to go with him to New Oberlin in search of a friend who will perhaps perform the stipulative labor. Before they get fairly out of town they meet the object of their search, but he cannot go. With surprising readiness of stratagem, the lit-

tle fiend exclaims, "Never mind then, John, you've been shut up in the house with Frank so long, let's have a good ride; I'll bring you back;" and the poor black man, unable to conceive of treachery coiled in such an exterior, again overflows with thanks to his young *massa*, and they drive on. A mile or two outside, in a lonely spot, with no one in sight or call, they are driving leisurely and chatting pleasantly, when poor trustful John wakes to the truth, as the hell-cats spring upon his back!!

And now they hurry him away towards Wellington, where they may take the train for Columbus. . . . . The inquiry now arises who made this capture of John? Was it Jennings, with his power of attorney? Why, Gentlemen, it was the man Lowe, the United States deputy-marshal from Columbus. Jennings was not there. He has told you that he had other business on hand. He lay back in Oberlin till the lad came to tell him that they had got John, and exhibited the card Lowe gave him with the address of some one with whom he should correspond if there occurred a chance to get Frank. Now, says the boy, "They've got him! I have done my part of the work, give me my pay!" *And Jennings pays him.*

But this is not all. There is said to be a rescue at Wellington. And it is found necessary by the District-Attorney of the United States to call the Grand Inquest of the nation, and institute a prosecution against the rescuers, and the father of the boy sits upon the Grand Jury and says "a true bill" as the indictments are severally presented against the rescuers — knowing all the while full well by what means and instrumentalities the negro was taken, and with what emotions and apprehensions the alarmed citizens came together.

The negro is taken to Wellington, where his captors dine at the hotel, and then take him to a room on the second floor, and thence, on the motion of Jennings, who comes soon after, to a more secure place in the attic. And now, when the sovereign people — the great originators of laws and governments — come to inquire concerning the boy and the character of the custody in which he is held, how are they answered? They were thirsting for information; anxious only to know the actual truth in the premises. They knew that the boy was last seen passing out of Oberlin with Shakespeare Boynton before he was met in the custody of his captors on the road to Wellington. No circumstances could be more suspicious. Well might they presume that foul means and not legal process had been employed. And in reply to their constant and importunate inquiries, what information was given them? What information, up to the very last moment of the Rescue, when the negro is alleged to have been driven rapidly away toward Lake Erie in a buggy with this defendant?

I will read to you certain parts of the testimony.

Jennings says: "The Sheriff came and wanted to see our authority for arresting the boy, and we showed it to him."

Now the " sheriff" proves to have been the constable, Meacham, for there was no "sheriff" about. The constable, who had a warrant for the apprehension of the kidnappers. You recollect how the warrant was obtained. Now Meacham had a peculiar interest in knowing by what authority they held the boy. Meacham says he did go up, as Jennings has averred, and inquired for their authority, and he says the *warrant* was shown him by *deputy-marshal Lowe*, and the *warrant alone*. Now do not mistake this, Gentlemen of the Jury; the *authority* was legally called for, and they produced the *warrant* from Commissioner Chittenden of Columbus, and the *warrant only*. It was exhibited as their authority for holding the negro in custody.

But we do not stop here: Joseph H. Dickson, the lawyer, and I believe the only lawyer in Wellington, formerly prosecuting attorney of Lorain County, went up, not of his own motion, but sent for by Lowe as a man learned in the law, to come to the room and see by what authority they held John there. This was the very object of his mission. Now is it to be supposed for one moment that this man was such an ignoramus that he did n't know a power of attorney from a warrant? Why, Gentlemen, Mr. Dickson swears to you without the least equivocation, that Mr. *Lowe took him into a side room alone*, and showed him the *warrant* as their authority for holding the negro, and *neither showed nor mentioned any other authority whatsoever*. That he saw no power of attorney, and never heard of a power of attorney till he heard of it in this Court-Room, after he had been summoned here as a witness. And after this exhibition of authority, Lowe asks Dickson to go out and proclaim what he has seen to the crowd, and use his influence to persuade them in view of *this authority* to disperse, and allow him to continue his journey.

But we don't stop here. Mr. Patton comes forward, a gentleman who has been so highly complimented by the counsel for the Government, as a man of extraordinary placidity of temper, a man of integrity and good manners, in short, a model for all the young men of Oberlin; and who behaved so wisely, that had his counsels been followed, there would have been no rescue, and no violation of law; one who can be relied on to protect the institutions and statutes of his country, in all times of danger, and I am very glad there is one man in Oberlin who can be depended upon besides Mr. Whack! [Laughter.] Mr. Patton comes forward and corroborates every word of Mr. Dickson's testimony. He says that *Lowe* took *him* aside and showed him his *warrant*, as the authority for holding the boy, and said *nothing of any other authority.* And farther he told Patton that he

would go down and read his authority to the crowd, if he could be protected; and if they were at all reasonable they would then, of course, disperse. Mr. Patton volunteered to be answerable for his safe return, and they went down. For what purpose? To show the power of attorney? Not a bit of it. To read the warrant, and the warrant only. They mounted the steps of the drug store, a little south of the hotel, and Patton, mark it, *Patton* read the *warrant* to the crowd, in Lowe's name, Lowe standing beside him and authorizing it to be read as *the authority* of the party for holding John. Now can this man Patton, who himself read that authority to the crowd, be mistaken? And yet he tells you that he read the warrant and the warrant only, and that he *never so much as heard* of a power of attorney until it was presented to the Court in the opening of this trial, by the District-Attorney. And while Mr. Patton was reading this warrant, the crowd made a rush at the front door, which, being speedily seconded by a rush at the back door, was successful, and the boy was brought down.

And now I put it to you, Gentlemen of the Jury, as the plainest possible question of fact, whether this defendant can be chargeable with a guilty knowledge that this arrest was made, and this custody sanctioned under and by virtue of the power of attorney, when in fact, no such authority was made known at any time during that day? With the facts before them as they are, I ask the Jury to say that the active instrumentality by which this boy was arrested and held, was the *warrant*, and not the power of attorney; and that the person arresting was not Anderson Jennings the agent, but Jacob K. Lowe, the Deputy United States Marshal. And I say to your Honor, that if there was a warrant there, and the arrest was made by it, and yet it has not been produced in this Court, the only presumption is that the warrant was defective, and the District-Attorney dare not let it see the light, *and so I charge it home upon him.* I say it was an infamous hoax, palmed off upon the people at Wellington. The names of Lowe and Davis were called among the witnesses, and Chittenden, the Commissioner himself, sat here in Court, and yet it has not been deemed advisable to make one solitary reference to the warrant, or to these witnesses, who are alleged to have issued and served it. The warrant being defective, the action of the officers under it was illegal, and makes them responsible to the law; and it strikes me that they are in a fair way to get their deserts.

The instant the authority by which the negro was arrested and held, proves to be a sham, the indictment falls to the ground. The individuals who effected the rescue, not only stand innocent of the charge of a violation of law, but challenge the plaudits of every human heart. For it is not claimed here that these men are to be punished for resisting *kidnappers*, who failed to observe even the easy conditions of the act of 1850! This defendant is charged in the indictment with a violation of the act of Congress, and must be acquitted by you, Gentlemen, unless you find him guilty according to the letter of the law. The courts have held, that a person is guilty of knowingly rescuing a fugitive, if they rescue him without availing themselves of whatever means may be within their reach for ascertaining his actual *status*. Well, for three entire hours this assemblage pressed their inquiries, sending by magistrates, lawyers, college students, citizens of age and respectability, and every one brought back the same answer: "*He is held by a United States Marshal, under and by virtue of a warrant issued by a United States Commissioner at Columbus.*" It is not shown that this defendant made in person such inquiries, or received directly or indirectly any information in answer to the inquiries made by others: we are willing to accept the worst the Prosecution charge, that he heard the answers brought to the crowd. We would be glad to claim it; for nothing could more effectually require his acquittal at your hands. And the Government have found themselves so pressed under the burden of this part of their own testimony, that they were fain to recall Jennings and Mitchell to bolster up a well-nigh hopeless case. Well, Jennings is a famous man by whom to bolster up a failing cause! The man who made two journeys from Kentucky to Oberlin to catch John, "just from a sense of *duty*, and a feeling of neighborly kindness, without the expectation of so much reward as the payment of his travelling expenses!" He was inquired of whether he contracted with Bacon for any pecuniary compensation for all this trouble, and swore positively that nothing was said by either of them about a money consideration. But Bacon testified differently, and on being asked the same question, swore — to the truth, undoubtedly; he seemed to be a very candid man in his testimony, and if any man was to have his slave restored to his possession, I should as soon it should be him as any man, judging from his appearance — Bacon swore positively that there *was* a contract, by which he became obligated to give Jennings $500, or one half the boy would sell for, provided he brought him back, and otherwise he was to have nothing. So Jennings is put upon the stand again to take back and correct his former explicit testimony, but will not do it after all. He says Bacon did remark something about his having offered in a general way to give half what the nigger would sell for to anybody that would catch him, but did *not* speak in a way that opened the offer to him, or make any other proposition whatever; that there positively *was no* such bargain as Bacon swore to. And so Mr. Jennings is an excellent witness to contradict the dozen disinterested witnesses from Wellington. Jennings says, "*he was present* at the conversation between Lowe and Dickson. They were not talking about the warrant, but about the *power*

of attorney! Dickson said he was not conversant with *that* sort of papers — (an ex-District-Attorney) — and did n't know whether it needed a seal or not — (there was the broad seal of Mason County before him) — and *Lowe* said it was *not* customary for such papers to have seals; and Dickson said he did n't know as it was!" Now, Gentlemen of the Jury, how many hundred men like Jennings need swear to so transparent a falsehood, before you would believe it? If Mr. Jennings was the most reputable man in the United States, you would n't believe him when he made such a statement as that. You would say, he must certainly be mistaken. And Jennings was but a third party, by his own testimony. Dickson talked with Lowe, not with Jennings, nor with Mitchell.

But they don't stop here. Mitchell is recalled. And he says, *he himself had the conversation with Dickson!* Dickson says, being sent for, as the messenger told him, by the parties having the negro in custody, went up; that *Lowe* came forward to meet him — as it seems he did whenever any one came in — and introduced himself by name as an United States marshal from Columbus; and that *Lowe* taking him alone into a private room, showed him the warrant directed to himself, and *Lowe* told him that he by virtue of that warrant had the negro in his custody and must return him before the commissioner, and that *Lowe* replied to his query about the lack of seal, that it was not customary for such papers to have a seal. But Mr. Mitchell steps quietly up here, and contradicts Mr. Dickson, asserting that *he*, Mitchell, is the individual with whom Mr. Dickson held the conversation, and not Lowe! Does Mitchell mean to say that he gave his name to Dickson as Lowe, and claimed to be the United States Marshal from the Southern District? If so, how is the case bettered by such a confession? But I may say, Dickson undoubtedly knew with whom he was conversing, and what paper he read. And I apprehend that the Government will find it difficult to induce you to give credit to the testimony offered to impeach him.

And now, Gentlemen, if it be true that this negro was apprehended and held in custody at Wellington under and by virtue of this warrant, which the District-Attorney cannot predicate his indictment upon, and which he dare not produce in Court, is there any reason why the vengeance of this odious law should be visited upon the head of this defendant?

Judge Leavitt says, in the case of Weimer against Sloane, 6 McLean, 267. "As already intimated, the jury must be satisfied that the defendant had . knowledge that the fugitives had been arrested and were in custody at the time of his alleged interference. If the plaintiff's agent held them without authority, they were illegally detained, and no one could have incurred liability by aiding them in their escape."

The act of Congress authorizes the owner to come into any county of Ohio, and arrest his runaway slave, and take him before any Commissioner or Federal judge in the District in which he apprehends him; or he may in the first place take out a warrant and arrest him; or the Commissioner may name some person to serve the warrant; or the agent, having a legal power of attorney may do the same thing. *But he must be governed by the one process or the other.* He cannot arrest by the warrant and hold by the power of attorney, or *vice versâ.* If he obeys the precept, in person or by the hands of an officer acting in his presence, under his direction, so far as to arrest in accordance with it, he cannot then draw back, but must hold the fugitive in obedience to its farther injunction, and release him before the Commissioner as it also enjoins; for, if he accepts its authority at all, he is bound by it until it is obeyed to the last letter, and he discharged from its control by the Commissioner who issued it. Now I say to the Court, that here was a gross mistake made by these parties, in the very inception of this proceeding. A warrant was issued by a Commissioner in the Southern District, while the fugitive was to be apprehended in the Northern District, of Ohio. The Deputy-Marshal, if he had power to proceed with that warrant into the Northern District, had no power, under the Act of 1850, to take his prisoner into the Southern District until he was taken before the officer in the Northern District, who should have issued the warrant. The law is imperative upon this point. There is no possible mistake about it. He must be taken before the Commissioner in the District where he is apprehended. We will read the law. The sixth Section is as follows. —

" The Commissioners above named shall have concurrent jurisdiction with the Judges of the Circuit and District Courts of the United States in their respective circuits and districts within the several States; and the Judges of the Superior Courts of the Territories, severally and collectively, in term time and vacation."

The eighth Section reads: —

" When a person held to service or labor in any State or Territory of the United States, has heretofore or shall hereafter escape into another State or Territory of the United States, the person or persons to whom such service or labor may be due, or his, her, or their agent or attorney, duly authorized by power of attorney in writing, acknowledged and certified under the seal of some legal officer or court of the State or Territory in which the same may be executed, may pursue and reclaim such fugitive person, either by procuring a warrant from some one of the Courts, Judges, or Commissioners aforesaid, of the *proper Circuit, District, or County,* for the apprehension of such fugitive from service or labor, or by seizing and arresting such fugitive, when the same can be done without process, and by taking or causing such person to be taken forthwith before *such* Court, Judge, or Commissioner, whose duty it shall be to hear and determine the case of such claimant," etc.

Well, that authority would be Judge McLean, of the Seventh Circuit, or his Honor, Judge Willson, of the Northern District, or some one of the Commissioners of the *Northern* District. So that if they had intended to make an arrest under the warrant, it was their duty to return him within the *Northern* District. They could not take him before the Commissioner at Columbus. They might with the same propriety take him before the Commissioner at Newport or Covington, Kentucky.

May it please your Honor, I am now drawing near the final discharge of the duty which has been cast upon me by the Defendant. It has been an unpleasant one from the outset. It is one which it will probably never fall to my lot to undertake again. I have availed myself of the indulgence of your Honor to express myself fearlessly, frankly, and fully. I am sorry that I am forced to differ so widely from many who are highly distinguished in all the learning of the law. I know that my own opinions have no official sanction, and can therefore weigh but little by the side of the authoritative decisions found in the books. But it is none the less my duty to speak as an advocate, and my right as a citizen, to give the results of my study and reflection.

I have said that slavery is like a canker, eating out the vitals of our liberties; and that the Supreme Court of the United States has become the impregnable fortress and bulwark of slavery: I now say that unless the knife or the cautery be applied to the speedy and entire removal of the diseased part, we shall soon lose the name of freedom, as we have already lost the substance, and be unable longer to avoid confessing that TYRANTS ARE OUR MASTERS. This man cannot be found guilty of the offence charged in the indictment upon the testimony that has been offered. I do not hesitate to say this. But had the testimony been sufficient to sustain the indictment, and he thus become amenable to this unconstitutional and infamous enactment, he would claim to have his name on the same page of history with those who have suffered for righteousness' sake.

And now, sir, as to the plain unconstitutionality of this odious act; I know full well, as I have already repeatedly said, what the decisions of the highest tribunal in the Nation have been with reference to it; and I know as well the deference which in all ordinary cases is due from tribunals of inferior jurisdiction to its rulings. But, sir, I hold that so glaringly unjust a decision as the affirmation of the constitutionality of this act *can bind no one ;* and had I the distinguished honor to occupy the seat which is so eminently filled by your Honor, full long should I hesitate before I pronounced that to be law, which so clearly contravenes the solemn compact of the Constitution, and the superior Ordinance of 1787, wantonly violates every personal right of the citizen, and stains with a foul blot the statute books of our country. I should feel bound to pronounce the Fugitive law of 1850 *utterly unconstitutional, without force, and void;* though in this doing, I should risk an impeachment before the Senate of my country; and, sir, should such an impeachment work my removal from office, I should proudly embrace it as a greater honor than has yet fallen to the lot of any Judicial officer of these United States!

NINTH DAY. — AFTERNOON SESSION.

District-Attorney's Argument.

Judge BELDEN did not know whether to address the court, the jury, or the audience. For three days has the crowd been addressed; not the court, not the jury. Are we in a dream? are we in a court of justice? or are we in a political hustings? If that is so, all counsel has to do is to ask the jury how they expect to vote. Here are the Saints of Oberlin, Peck, Plumb, Fitch, to which are to be added Saints Spalding and Riddle, and *sub-saint* Bushnell — all saints of the Higher Law. When it comes to pass that we take a cause from the jury and appeal to the crowd we had better disband. Sad will be our condition then.

The counsel commented very severely upon what he called the clap-trap argument of the white boy brought in to get up a scene. He pronounced the scene the most disgraceful he had seen in a court of justice. This was their constitutional argument! And their constitutional argument was continued by reading resolutions passed in this city in 1850 — and read for no purpose but to stab this Court; to stab his Honor upon the bench; read by a man who knew, or ought to have known that the resolutions were a libel on the opinions of the Judge, and were not his sentiments; such arguments will not weigh a feather, and such demagoguery must fail, though you had a thousand Probate or Crowbait Courts, and a boy to exhibit before you.

At the meeting referred to, Messrs. Hitchcock, Foote, and Bolton were appointed a committee to examine the law and report at a future meeting as to its constitutionality, and the chairman, after holding the resolutions some two months, came to the conclusion the law was constitutional, and no report was ever made. What the gentlemen and Saints of Oberlin called Higher Law he called Devil's Law.

Sam Johnson wrote that the Higher Law was the law of one's country. Your Higher Law, as interpreted by the Saints of Oberlin is just that law which makes every man's conscience and private opinion his guide. Such doctrine would make chaos, and until all men have the same conscience, same control of pas-

sion, don't talk of Higher Law as God's Law; it is Devil's Law, and it would make a Hell upon earth. Higher Law comes in and upturns government because there is slavery; it has piety and conscience for the black man, but devil take the white man.

Judge Belden then argued the question of the constitutional power to pass laws to enforce a Fugitive Law; the letter and spirit of the Constitution admit of such law. Counsel on other side forgot to say that Washington recommended the passage of the law of 1793, which is actually the law of 1850, and it was passed with only seven dissenting votes, and until abolition, Higher Law and Devil Law came in vogue to refuse the jails, to strike down officials, the law was enforced. Judge Belden entered into a review of the opinions of Mr. Webster upon the Fugitive Slave Law. That law was a peace-offering made by Clay, Webster, Fillmore, and others. In the midst of agitation and lawlessness this law was passed by the great lights of the country, signed by Mr. Fillmore, and sanctioned by Webster, the lover of law. Higher Law people run into the predicament of free love and infidelity. If St. Peck and St. Plumb "go off" on this law, he would advise them to go where some good man preaches the Bible and not politics. Do you teach the Bible at Oberlin, or do you point out the spires of the churches as hell poles? The counsel then went on to show what the state of the world was when Christ came; many were in bondage, and not a word was said against it; Christ denounced idolatry, polygamy, but not a word against slavery. He did not tell them of a Higher Law as against the laws of the land. He said, observe the law of the land, render to Cæsar the things that are Cæsar's, to woman and man, to slave and free. If these saints of Oberlin had half as much piety as the poor slaves, their masters and mistresses, it would be well as between them and their God. According to Higher Law we should turn our wives and children out of the house.

Counsel then argued that the slaves were not fit for freedom; and that there were very few white people fit for self-government, but the whites can be treated on an equality, although not equal in every respect. He argued the unfitness for freedom of the slaves, and contended that there was no perfection, and because there were cases of cruelty in slavery, these could not argue in favor of freeing the slaves. The Judge went into the history of West India emancipation, and argued from that emancipation that the white race must take charge of the blacks. He then referred to the introduction of slavery in this country, and argued that it was a creature of common law, and not of statute, in every colony of this country; and no law was passed in regard to it for fifty years after its introduction here. The whites must predominate over the blacks, they cannot exist on an equality.

The citizen who harbors fugitives from labor is a bad citizen; he don't deserve the blessings of this government.

The District-Attorney then read largely from Mr. Webster's opinion on the Fugitive Slave Law, and the effect of the law in its operation. He also read from the letter of some Englishman who wrote a letter to Mr. Webster upon the subject of slavery.

[The Court intimated to the counsel that there was no necessity of arguing the constitutionality of the law.]

Counsel proceeded on the facts.

The defendant is charged with rescuing the negro. Is he guilty of the act? Did he do it within the jurisdiction of this court? That's the question. Did John owe service to Bacon? We have been told that Bacon only owns one sixth; the proof is that the father of Bacon died without a will, and the slaves were divided by the heirs. The Court is bound to take notice *ex officio* of the laws of Kentucky. The ownership of John is complete, for in addition to Bacon's is the testimony of Mitchell and and Jennings.

The next question is, did John escape? Frank, Dinah, and John escaped in the night. Where did this negro go? He went to Oberlin; was there from spring of '58 to time of his rescue. Prof. Peck knew him, and some of the witnesses understood him to be a fugitive slave. If he had not been known to be a slave, there would have been no mob to rescue him. Was the man whom they rescued, John? Mitchell knew him to be the nigger John. When the Kentuckian met him, the negro went towards him and recognized him. John talked with a number, admitting he was a slave of Bacon. Was John in the custody of Jennings and Lowe? It matters not whether there was a warrant there or not. Jennings was the agent of the owner. The owner had a right to take his slave, and take him home. Judge B. then gave a history of the Prigg case in Pennsylvania.

Adjourned till 9 o'clock.

TENTH DAY. — MORNING SESSION.

District-Attorney BELDEN continued his argument by claiming that, according to the common law, a deputy could only act in the name of the principal, and this was incorporated in the Kentucky statute; therefore the power of attorney in the case was properly made out. He also claimed that it was not necessary for Jennings to have been present at the time of making the capture, as he could have legally directed the matter from any distance, and that Marshal Lowe was acting under such directions, and not under the warrant. In continuance of this argument, he gave notice that if the Lorain county authorities should attempt to arrest Lowe, Jennings, or Mitchell, for violation of the State law, he should claim, with

confidence of success, that they were not amenable to State law, because acting under the power of attorney which placed them beyond the reach of State jurisdiction in the matter.

He claimed that the jury should take no account of the quibbles and technicalities which might stand in the way of a conviction. He said that it was perfectly lawful and right for the gentleman from Kentucky to follow the negro to Oberlin with " Arkansas toothpicks," bowie knives, and revolvers, if he thought best for the purpose of the capture.

The District-Attorney claimed that full exhibition of the power of attorney was made; also that it was immaterial in what manner the negro was taken by the Kentuckians, in view of the fact that he was rescued from the immediate presence and control of Jennings.

The balance of the District-Attorney's speech was a recapitulation of the evidence in the case, liberally interspersed with attacks on the opposing counsel, imputations on the Press of the city, and abuse of the audience. The language and spirit of the address were in the worst possible taste, and evoked the indignation of the audience, evinced, in one instance, by unmistakable hisses. The speech was concluded at 11 o'clock, when the case was given to the Jury by Judge WILLSON, in the following charge: —

CHARGE OF THE COURT.

There is a preliminary matter in this case (and with which the Jury have nothing to do) that should be noticed before entering upon the consideration of the principles of law, which are applicable to the issue of fact to be tried by the Jury.

A motion was made by the defendant to quash the indictment, which motion (without argument of counsel, or reasons expressed by the Court) was overruled, with the understanding, however, that if at any time the grounds of the motion should be deemed to be well founded, the case would be withdrawn from the Jury.

In this motion to quash, the assigned causes are: —

1st. That the indictment is found and presented for an alleged violation of an Act of Congress, which Act is unconstitutional and void.

2d. That the pretended Grand Jury which found said indictment was not legally empanelled, but were selected and empanelled contrary to law.

3d. That said indictment is defective, informal, and insufficient in law.

4th. That it does not appear in said indictment, that said negro John was legally held to service, or that he was held to service under the laws of Kentucky or any other State or Territory.

5th. That it does not appear that the defendant knew him to be held under or by virtue of any law, nor that the defendant knew him to be lawfully held to service.

The 2d Section of the 4th Article of the Constitution of the United States declares, that " no person held to service or labor in any State under the laws thereof, escaping into another, shall in consequence of any law or regulation therein, be discharged from such service or labor; but shall be delivered up on claim of the party to whom such service or labor may be due."

This provision of the Constitution is a positive and unqualified recognition of the right of the owner in his slaves, unaffected by any State Constitution or any State laws whatever. It is a right of property, and like the ownership of any other species of property, it implies the right of seizure and recaption. In case of escape, the *status* of the slave in relation to his owner cannot be changed by, or in any way qualified, regulated, or controlled by the laws of the State to which the slave flees. Hence, all the incidents of the right of property in the owner attaches. Under and in virtue of the Constitution " he is clothed (said Judge Story) with entire authority, in every State in the Union, to seize and recapture his slave, whenever he can do it without any breach of the peace, or any illegal violence."

This clause of the Constitution does not stop with a mere declaration of the right in the owner. It also implies a guaranty, on the part of the national government, to provide the mode and secure the means to make the right available. It says : " The slave shall be delivered up on claim of the party to whom such service or labor may be due."

This imposes a specific duty upon the national government : and " when a duty is enjoined, the power and ability to perform it is contemplated to exist on the part of the functionaries to whom it is intrusted."

Accordingly in pursuance of the plain requirements of the national compact, Congress has passed two laws providing for the recaption of fugitives from labor. One is the act of February 12, 1793, and the other that of September 18, 1850.

Both of these laws have been the subject of judicial exposition and interpretation by the Supreme Court of the United States ; the former in the case of Prigg v. The Commonwealth of Pennsylvania, 16 Peters, R. 539, and the latter in the case of the United States v. Booth, decided at the late December Term of that Court.

In each of these cases the Supreme Court held both acts of Congress referred to, to be clearly constitutional in all their leading provisions, and free from reasonable doubt and difficulty.

It certainly does not become a Court of inferior jurisdiction to entertain a question upon the unconstitutionality of laws which have been fully considered and decided to be in strict accordance with the Constitution by the highest judicial tribunal of the country.

The objection that the Grand Jury that presented this indictment, was selected and empanelled contrary to law, has no foundation in fact.

The Grand Jury were qualified, selected, and empanelled as required by the 4th rule of the Circuit Court, which rule obtains in this Court. The legality of that rule is no longer an open question here. Both its legality and propriety were fully affirmed by the Circuit Court in the case of the United States v. Joseph S. Wilson, 6 McLean, 604.

Neither is there any foundation for the declared defect in the indictment, that the said negro John is not alleged to be legally held to service, or that he is held to service under the laws of Kentucky.

The indictment charges, that on the first day of March, 1857, a certain negro slave, called John, a person held to service and labor in the State of Kentucky, one of the United States, the said John being the property of one John G. Bacon, of the said State of Kentucky, the person to whom such service and labor were then due, and so being held to service, the said John did escape to the State of Ohio, etc.

This averment is almost in the precise language of the statute. It has been uniformly held by the Federal Courts, that in indictments for misdemeanors created by statute, it is sufficient to charge the offence in the language of the statute. There is not that technical nicety required as to *form*, which seems to have been adopted and sanctioned by long practice in cases of felony. United States v. Mills, 7 Peters, R. 142 ; United States v. Lancaster, 6 McLean, 431.

We are clearly of the opinion, that the exceptions to this indictment, both as to form and matters of substance, were not well taken, and that the motion to quash was properly overruled.

The case, then, Gentlemen of the Jury, goes to you for the determination of the issue of fact : — Is the defendant *guilty* or *not guilty* of the offence with which he stands charged in the indictment ?

The indictment contains but a single count. It charges that on the first day of March, in the year of our Lord one thousand eight hundred and fifty-seven, a certain negro slave called John, a person held to service and labor in the State of Kentucky, one of the United States, the said John being the property of one John G. Bacon, of the said State of Kentucky, the person to whom such service and labor were then due, and the said negro slave called John, to wit, on the day and year last aforesaid, so being held to service and labor as aforesaid, and said service and labor being due as aforesaid, did escape into another State of the United States, to wit, into the State of Ohio, from the said State of Kentucky ; that afterwards, to wit, on the first day of October in the year of our Lord one thousand eight hundred and fifty-eight, one Anderson Jennings, the agent and attorney of the said John G. Bacon, duly authorized for that purpose, by power of attorney, in writing, executed by the said John G. Bacon, to wit, on the 4th day of September, A. D. 1858, and acknowledged by him on said day, before Robert A. Cochran, Clerk of the County Court of the County of Mason, in said State of Kentucky, and on said day, certified by said Robert A. Cochran, Clerk as aforesaid, under the seal of said Mason County Court, the said Robert A. Cochran then being a legal officer, and the said Mason County Court then being a legal Court in the said State of Kentucky, in which said State said power of attorney was executed, did pursue and reclaim the said negro slave, called John, into, and in the said State of Ohio, and did, to wit, on the said first day of October, in the year last aforesaid, in said Northern District of Ohio, and within the jurisdiction of this Court, pursue and reclaim the said negro slave, called John, he then and there being a fugitive person as aforesaid, and still held to service and labor as aforesaid, by then and there, on the day and year last aforesaid at the District aforesaid, and within the jurisdiction of this Court, seizing and arresting him as a fugitive person from service and labor, from the said State of Kentucky, as aforesaid; and that the said negro slave called John, was then and there, to wit, on the day and year last aforesaid, in the said State of Ohio, at the District aforesaid, and within the jurisdiction of this Court, lawfully, pursuant to the authority of the statute of the United States, given and declared in such case made and provided, arrested in the custody and under the control of the said Anderson Jennings, as agent and attorney as aforesaid, of the said John G. Bacon, to whom the service and labor as aforesaid of the said negro slave called John, were then and still due as aforesaid, together with one Jacob K. Lowe, then and there, lawfully assisting him, the said Anderson Jennings, in the aforesaid arrest, custody, and control of the said negro slave called John. And the Jurors aforesaid do farther present and find that Simeon Bushnell, late of the District aforesaid, together with divers, to wit, two hundred other persons, to the Jurors aforesaid unknown heretofore, to wit, on the said first day of October, in the year of our Lord one thousand eight hundred and fifty-eight at the District aforesaid, and within the jurisdiction of this Court, with force and arms, unlawfully, knowingly, and willingly, did rescue the said negro slave called John, then and there being pursued and reclaimed, seized and arrested, and in the custody and control aforesaid, he, the said negro slave, called John, being then and there a fugitive from and held to service and labor as aforesaid, from the custody of the said Anderson Jennings, then and there the authorized agent and attorney of the said John

G. Bacon as aforesaid, and the said Jacob K. Lowe, then and there lawfully assisting the said Anderson Jennings as aforesaid; he, the said Simeon Bushnell, then and there, well knowing that the said negro slave called John, was then and there a fugitive person, held to service and labor as aforesaid, and pursued and reclaimed, seized and arrested, and held in custody as aforesaid; to the great damage of the said John G. Bacon."

The law on which this indictment is predicated is contained in the 6th and 7th sections of the Act of Congress of September 18, 1850.

In the first clause of section 6 it is provided, that, " when a person held to service or labor in any State or Territory of the United States, has heretofore or shall hereafter escape into another State or Territory of the United States, the person or persons to whom such service or labor may be due, or his, her, or their agent or attorney, duly authorized by power of attorney, in writing, acknowledged and certified under the seal of some legal officer or court of the State or Territory in which the same may be executed, may pursue and reclaim such fugitive person, either by procuring a warrant from some one of the Courts, Judges, or Commissioners aforesaid of the proper Circuit, District, or County, for the apprehension of such fugitive from service or labor, or by seizing and arresting such fugitive, when the same can be done without process, and by taking, or causing such person to be taken, forthwith before such Court, Judge, or Commissioner, whose duty it shall be to hear and determine the case of such claimant in a summary manner," etc.

Section 7 declares, " that any person who shall knowingly and willingly obstruct, hinder, or prevent such claimant, his agent or attorney, or any person or persons lawfully assisting him, her, or them, from arresting such fugitive from service or labor, either with or without process as aforesaid, or shall rescue, or attempt to rescue such fugitive from service or labor, from the custody of such claimant, his or her agent or attorney, or other person or persons lawfully assisting as aforesaid, when so arrested, pursuant to the authority herein given and declared " (shall be subject to fine and imprisonment, etc.)."

To effect a conviction of the defendant, the material allegations in the indictment must be established in proof, and the burden of proof rests on the Government.

These material allegations are, that the negro John was a slave, owing service to John G. Bacon in Kentucky; that said negro escaped from Kentucky to the State of Ohio, and was a fugitive from his master; that he was seized and held by Anderson Jennings, and his assistants, by virtue of a power of attorney, lawfully executed by said Bacon, authorizing the capture of the fugitive; and that the defendant, acting with others at Wellington, knowingly and willingly rescued the slave from the agent of the owner.

That slavery or involuntary servitude exists in Kentucky, under the sanction of law, is a matter of which the Federal Courts take judicial notice. The reciprocal relations between the National Government and the several States comprising the United States, are not foreign, but domestic. Hence the Courts of the United States take judicial notice of all the public laws of the respective States, when they are called upon to consider and apply them. It is not a question for the Jury to determine, from the evidence, whether or not slavery lawfully exists in Kentucky. That is an inquiry which belongs solely to the Court; and for the purposes of this trial, you will regard slavery as a municipal regulation, lawfully established in that State.

Was the negro John a slave, owing service to John G. Bacon in Kentucky? This is the first question of fact for your determination from the evidence.

On a question of this kind, the right of the alleged owner in his slave, is to be established by the same rules of evidence as in other contests about the right of property. Ordinarily, the fact of possession and notorious claim of ownership, in personal property, is sufficient to establish the *primâ facie* right of ownership. It was declared by the Court, in the case of Miller *v.* Dunnan, that the mere holding a person in involuntary servitude, and claiming ownership, is not sufficient *primâ facie* evidence of right to overcome the presumption arising from the marks of European descent. But that dark complexion, woolly head, and flat nose, with possession and claim of ownership, do afford *primâ facie* evidence of the slavery and ownership charged.

Here the prosecution claims to have shown, by the uncontradicted testimony of Bacon, Mitchell, and Jennings, that the negro John was held and treated as a slave by John G. Bacon and his father; that the mother of this negro was a slave all her lifetime, and bought and sold as such.

Further than this, the pedigree of the negro and the *status* of his ancestors were not attempted to be traced. Nor was it necessary. For, were it traced back to the maternal ancestor of 1785, no better evidence would or could be furnished. It then could only be proved that the ancestor was a slave, by showing that she had marks of African descent, and was bought and sold as a slave, and held as such. This is precisely the evidence and the only evidence necessary to show the slavery and service which this negro owed to his master.

It is like any other question of *status* of the relation of one person to another, which may be shown by the facts and circumstances attending that relation. This may be illustrated by the familiar case of heirship. To establish the fact that A. is the heir of B., it is necessary to prove that there was a lawful marriage and cohabitation, and B. the issue of that marriage. But it is competent and sufficient evidence of the heirship, that B. treated and recognized A. as his son.

Upon the principles of the common law, then, the testimony of Bacon, Mitchell, and Jennings is competent, and if uncontradicted, may be deemed sufficient to establish the fact, that the negro John was held to service as the slave of John G. Bacon, under the laws of Kentucky.

That this slave fled from his master and escaped from Kentucky into the State of Ohio, is an alleged fact, about which the testimony leaves but little room for controversy. Neither can it be seriously controverted, that Bacon executed to Jennings a valid power of attorney, duly acknowledged and certified, for the recaption of the slave.

The next question to be determined by the evidence is, did Jennings hold this fugitive by virtue of the power of attorney at the time of the rescue?

The statute provides that the owner or his agent authorized by power of attorney, "may pursue and reclaim such fugitive person, *either* by procuring a warrant from some one of the Courts, Judges, or Commissioners aforesaid, for the apprehension of such fugitive from service or labor, or by seizing and arresting such fugitive, when the same can be done without process, and by taking or causing such person to be taken forthwith before such Court, Judge, or Commissioner," etc., etc.

It is true, the language of the Act is in the alternative. The fugitive may be seized and arrested upon the warrant, or he may be seized and arrested by virtue of the power of attorney. Both modes of capture have the same object, to wit, to bring the fugitive before the Court or Commissioner. The person making the arrest is clothed with the same power and authority in the one case as in the other. He may at the same time provide the means of resorting to either or both modes of capture. Yet, when it is alleged in the indictment that the one or the other was adopted, the allegation being material, the proof must support the charge.

You will, therefore, determine from the evidence, whether or not Jennings held the negro John by virtue of the power of attorney from Bacon, at the time the rescue was made. If you find in the affirmative on this proposition, then the inquiry is, was the defendant implicated in the rescue?

If the persons who constituted the assemblage at Wellington on the 13th of September, 1858, had come together for the purpose, or when there, were engaged in rescuing a fugitive slave from those authorized to capture and hold him under the statute of 1850, they were engaged in an unlawful act, and whatever was then said and done by one, in the prosecution of the enterprise, were, to all intents and purposes in law, the declarations and acts of all. To implicate each and all, however, it must appear that there was a concert of action for the accomplishment of an unlawful purpose.

It is claimed by the prosecutor, that the evidence establishes the riotous and unlawful character of the assembly gathered in and about the hotel at Wellington, in which the negro was confined. And the implication of the defendant in the rescue is urged on the ground that the crowd in which he mingled threatened to demolish the building, unless the fugitive was surrendered — that the people assembled gave angry demonstrations of violence with firearms in their hands, and actually rescued the fugitive from his captors. And the further fact is urged, as showing concert of action on the part of the defendant and the crowd, that his buggy was stationed at a convenient distance to receive the negro, that the fugitive was tumultuously placed in it, and his escape effected by the defendant's driving rapidly away.

These are matters of evidence entirely for the consideration of the jury.

And yet, if these facts are as claimed by the Government prosecutor, the defendant is not guilty of the offence with which he stands charged in the indictment, unless it is proved that he acted *knowingly* and *willingly*. In other words, it must appear that he knew the negro was a fugitive from labor and was lawfully detained by the person or persons who held him captive; or that he acted under such circumstances as to show that he might have had such knowledge by exercising ordinary prudence.

Usually, a man is presumed to know and intend the legal consequences of his own acts. It will not answer to say that he can close his eyes and ears against the means of knowledge, and rush deaf and blindly into the performance of that which the law declares a crime. Were it otherwise, excesses against legal process in many cases might be indulged in with impunity. Criminals might be rescued from lawful caption, on the plea of mistake or misapprehension. The language of the statute should receive a reasonable interpretation.

Gentlemen of the Jury, I have, as briefly as possible, given you the rules of law which are deemed to be applicable to the case. The evidence submitted, I leave in your hands without any comment, as the questions of fact are for your determination.

This case, like every other which is tried in a court of justice, should be divested of every thing that is extraneous. It is to be determined according to the law and the testimony as delivered to you in Court.

Much has been eloquently said by learned counsel that would be entitled to great weight and consideration if addressed to the Congress of the United States, or to an ecclesiastical tribunal, where matters of casuistry are discussed and determined.

It is your duty to take the case and return a verdict according to the evidence.

After the above charge was delivered, Mr. BACKUS arose and said : —

The defendant asks the Court to charge the Jury,

1st. That in order to warrant a conviction in this case, the testimony must show beyond a reasonable doubt, that the defendant, as charged in said indictment, did " unlawfully, knowingly, and willingly " rescue, or assist in rescuing the negro John from the custody of the said Anderson Jennings, the said Jennings then and there having him in his custody as the agent of the said John G. Bacon; but that if the testimony shows that the custody was in Lowe by virtue of a legal warrant, or leaves it in doubt whether said John was, at the time of such rescue, in the custody of said Jennings, as such agent, or in that of said Lowe, then and there claiming to hold him by virtue of such legal process, then the defendant should be acquitted.

2d. That such custody could not, at the same time be in said Jennings *as such agent*, and in said Lowe, either *under and by virtue* of legal process, or by virtue of any other claim.

3d. That the power of attorney in question, in order to be valid, must be shown to have been acknowledged as alleged in said indictment, by said Bacon, before Robert A. Cochran, Clerk of the County Court of the county of Mason in said State of Kentucky; that the said Cochran certified, from his *own personal knowledge*, to the *identity* of said Bacon. But that if the acknowledgment was made in no other way than by the appearance of said Bacon before some other person, whether such person were or were not authorized by the laws of Kentucky, to do whatever the said Cochran, as such clerk, could legally do under the laws of Kentucky, then the power of attorney was not acknowledged before said Cochran, and this material averment in the indictment is not proved, and the defendant must be acquitted.

4th. That although the deputy clerk, who is shown to have been the person before whom the said Bacon in fact appeared for the purpose of making this acknowledgment, may by the laws of Kentucky, be a " legal officer," and therefore authorized by the Act of Congress to take such acknowledgment; yet the acknowledgment in this case neither purports to have been made before him, nor is it averred so to have been made in this indictment; and therefore such authority can add nothing to the validity of this acknowledgment.

5th. That the acknowledgment in this case is void, because it is not certified under the seal of the officer before whom it purports, through a deputy, to have been taken.

6th. That in order to find that John was a slave, and owed service to said Bacon, they must find from the testimony, that by the laws of Kentucky, a person in the condition of John at the time of his alleged escape, might be legally held to service as a slave; that John was, in fact, the slave of said Bacon at the time of such escape and of said alleged rescue; but that, if the testimony satisfies them that said John G. Bacon derived his title to said John by descent from his father, who died leaving five other children, all of whom are still living, the presumption is, in the absence of testimony showing that a division had taken place of the property of their father, that John was, at the time of his escape, and at the time of the alleged rescue, the joint property of all the children; and, therefore, that the averment of ownership is unproved, and the prosecution must fail.

7th. That before the defendant can be held liable for the acts and declarations of those constituting the assemblage of persons, who are claimed to have been instrumental in the rescue of John, the jury must be satisfied that all of that assemblage, whose acts were given in evidence, were there for the *common* purpose of illegally obstructing the claimant in the reclamation of John, and that the said defendant there and then was acting in concert with them.

8th. That if the defendant, in his connection with the rescue of John, was honestly of the opinion that John had been illegally seized upon, and was being carried away in violation of law; and the claim of right so to seize and carry him away, were given, by those who had him in custody, to be by virtue of a warrant in the hands of said Lowe, then the defendant cannot be convicted of the crime charged in the indictment.

In answer to the above, the Court gave the following special instructions: —

1st Request — The proof must show, as I have already said to you, that the fugitive was held by virtue of the power of attorney, and not by virtue of any other legal authority or process.

2d Request — In legal contemplation such custody could not be in Jennings, the attorney, and in the marshal, by virtue of *lawful* process, at the same moment. And it is proper and important for the jury to refer to all the testimony for the purpose of ascertaining whether any *legal process* was used in the arrest and detention of the negro. Because, unless the evidence clearly shows that a *legal process* was used, the fugitive cannot be considered as held by process at all, and although the slave might have been taken in the first instance upon a void warrant, it was nevertheless competent for the attorney, by virtue of his power, to take and control him at any time afterwards, and in Ohio no presumption exists that a man (black or white) is properly restrained of his freedom, except on clear proof of legal authority for that purpose.

3d Request — The power of attorney in order to be valid, must, unquestionably, be shown to be acknowledged as alleged in the indictment. It is a question of fact for the jury to determine, whether William H. Richardson was or was not a deputy clerk of Mason County Court. If he was, his official acts were the acts of Mr. Cochran who it is admitted, was the clerk of that Court. " *Qui facit per alium facit per se,*" is a maxim that obtains everywhere.

4th Request — Was complied with.

5th Request — Judge Willson refused to charge as requested.

6th and *7th Requests* — Judge Willson refused to give special instructions because the points were covered by the regular charge.

8th Request — Refused. Held that the defendant was bound to make inquiry as to whether John was legally held or not.

Court adjourned till 2 o'clock.

The record of the afternoon's occurrences is so accurately given by the Reporter of the Cleveland *Leader*, that we quote it entire, save the last two clauses, for which we substitute the account of the Evening *Herald*.

The Court convened in the afternoon at 2 o'clock, and a verdict having been agreed upon by the Jury, they came in and took their seats. The prisoner being present, the question was put by the Court —

" Gentlemen of the Jury, have you agreed upon a verdict?"

" We have, your Honor."

" What is your verdict, Mr. Foreman ?"

" GUILTY."

The room was filled with spectators, who heard and received the verdict with quietness. It had been expected until the last moment, but when the Judge charged the Jury in the forenoon, at the request of Mr. BACKUS that it was necessary to find it proven by the prosecution that the boy John was taken and held by virtue of the power of attorney and not by the warrant — then some hope was entertained that the decision would be for the defence. But the deed is done and the fiat has gone forth that Bushnell must submit to the penalties of the Fugitive Slave Act.

This case having been disposed of, the District-Attorney called the name of Charles Langston as the next case. The defence remarked that they were ready in none of the other cases except that of Prof. Peck. The District-Attorney insisting upon that of Mr. Langston, Mr. Spalding thought they might be ready with that case by the time the new Jury was ready to proceed.

Judge WILLSON said the present Jury was one struck and selected for the term, and it was proper that they should try all the cases.

Mr. BACKUS remarked that he was astonished to hear his Honor intimate that this Jury, who have sat through and upon this case — heard all the testimony, and who have now in the presence of the Court rendered a verdict, in which their minds are made up and fixed upon all the important points in the case, are to be held competent to try another case almost exactly similar ! The ownership of John — whether he owed service to Bacon — whether he was the same John — whether he was legally or illegally arrested by Jennings — and whether he was held by virtue of the power of attorney or by the warrant — all these points had been heard and determined by these men, and could it be pretended that they would come to another trial with no opinions formed in their own minds ? Why, it was an unheard of and a most villanous outrage on the sense of justice of the civilized world, and no one of the defendants would so stultify himself as to attempt a defence before such a jury. He had never known or heard of such a mockery of that justice which should prevail in every Court. It was a terrible, not to say a monstrous proceeding, the like of which had never been known since courts were first in existence.

The COURT remarked that the Jury would decide each case upon the evidence offered in that particular case, and there was no occasion for excitement or intemperate zeal to be exhibited, as the rule would be enforced.

Judge SPALDING then announced that if a Jury who had settled upon a decision upon every important point except identity, were expected to try every case, then the District-Attorney could call the accused up as fast as he pleased and try them, for neither would they call any witnesses for the defence nor appear by attorney before such a jury.

"Very well," replied Judge BELDEN, — "then I ask the Court to order these men all into the custody of the marshal."

The COURT then ordered the marshal to take the prisoners into custody, when Judge SPALDING requested that their recognizances might be cancelled. The COURT also ordered the marshal to send immediately for such of the indicted as were not in the Court-Room.

Court now adjourned to Monday morning at 10 o'clock, the counsel for the defence giving notice that they should consider it their duty to challenge the Jury at that time. Before the adjournment of Court, the DISTRICT-ATTORNEY moved that the defendants be released from the custody of the marshal on renewing their recognizances with sureties to the satisfaction of the clerk.

The COURT replied that the terms heretofore complied with would be sufficient, namely, personal recognizances in the sum of $1,000 each.

Immediately after the adjournment the room was cleared of all save the following persons, who had been called up by the marshal as the accused (a few had previously gone home on permission of the District-Attorney), their counsel, and the marshal : —

Charles Langston,   Wilson Evans,
John Watson,   David Watson,
Simeon Bushnell,   Eli Boies,

Loring Wadsworth,   James Bartlett,
Robert Winsor,   Matthew Gillett,
Jacob R. Shipherd,   O. S. B. Wall,
John H. Scott,   Daniel Williams,
Ansel W. Lyman,   Henry E. Peck,
W. E. Lincoln,   James M. Fitch,
Henry Evans,   Ralph Plumb.

These gentlemen being gathered together were requested by the marshal to enter their recognizance for their appearance on Monday morning. This being objected to, he, on his own authority and responsibility, offered to let them go home, if they would give him their parole of honor that they would return on Monday morning, with the exception of Mr. Bushnell, whom he would be obliged to retain. — Through Prof. Peck as their spokesman, and according to the advice of their counsel, they passed a resolution by which they agreed after due consultation to inform the marshal that, inasmuch as the District-Attorney had placed them in his custody they would remain there until relieved by due course of law. They would give no bail, enter no recognization, and make no promises to return to the Court.

They said this with hearty thanks to the marshal for his courtesy in the treatment of his prisoners.

This decision having been made known, the marshal informed them of the necessity of placing them in confinement, to which they made no objection. All this time the outside passage and halls (the doors having been kept locked) were filled with an eager crowd watching and waiting for an insight into the *Temple of Justice*, and waiting for the exodus of the prisoners. At length the door opened, and the marshal, arm in arm with the venerable and white haired Mr. Gillett, headed the procession, while after them came the culprits two by two, with their shawls, carpet-bags and valises, all arrayed and equipped for a few days' visit to Wightman's Castle.

On arriving at the jail they were kept waiting for some time in the rain, while Sheriff Wightman hesitated about receiving them as prisoners unless advised to do so by the County Commissioners, fearing that the county property might be endangered, and wishing some advice on the matter. Ultimately he received them as guests, until the decision of the Commissioners was made known. After a long and anxious session those gentlemen reluctantly consented to the use of the jail for the purpose, and the accused were received as prisoners. They are, however, well cared for, provided with apartments in that part of the jail kept as a private dwelling, are well fed, and treated with every kindness and courtesy.

So far are they from being cowed by their imprisonment, that they enjoy themselves as well as is possible under the circumstances. Last night most appropriate and affecting religious services were held in their apartments. They have been visited by large numbers of sympathizing friends from among the best of our citizens, and their residence in the jail confers disgrace on none but those whose malice sent them there.

> " Stone walls do not a prison make,
> Nor iron bars a cage;
> Minds innocent and quiet take
> That for an hermitage."

Last night they had beds made up in the upper range of cells, where they slept. To-day they are in the upper room of the jailer's residence, where newspapers and writing facilities have been furnished them.

Sheriff Wightman has treated them with kindness and courtesy; at the same time they are strictly confined within the walls, and no departure allowed from the regular discipline of persons in their condition.

We understand that this afternoon the prisoners will be visited by a large party of ladies from the congregation of the Prospect Street Church, accompanied by many other ladies residing in the city.

To-morrow afternoon, about half past two o'clock, Professor PECK will preach to his "brethren in bonds," and such of the citizens as can be accommodated, in the jail.

Perhaps no better idea could be given of the state of feeling inside the prison, than may be gathered from the two extracts next following, the first of which is cut from the Evening *Herald*, of Monday, April 18, and the second from the Morning *Leader* of the next day.

THE OBERLIN RESCUERS.

The Bond Preaching to the Free !

EXTRAORDINARY SCENE.

The jail on Saturday afternoon appeared more like a fashionable place of resort than a prison. Hundreds of ladies and gentlemen of the highest standing called on the Oberlin prisoners, and left them but few intervals during the day and evening for rest. On all sides they were greeted with assurances of sympathy and respect, mingled with severe comments on the extraordinary conduct of District-Attorney BELDEN, in ordering their arrest in violation of all precedent and in contempt of all decency and propriety.

On Sunday afternoon, according to previous notice, Professor PECK, one of the Oberlin Rescuers committed to jail to await trial, proceeded to address his brethren in bonds and such of the free as chose to come. The hour appointed was half past two o'clock, and at that time an immense crowd had gathered around the jail. The extensive jail yard was literally packed with human bodies, the space and street beyond filled, every roof and shed that afforded a prospect of the preacher, crowded, and the windows of the new Court House building occupied. A large number of ladies were in the crowd, in addition to those admitted by the Sheriff to the private apartments of the jail. The crowd was of the highest respectability, and numbered between three and four thousand persons.

Professor Peck stood just inside the doorway of the jail, and from that point conducted the exercises, which he opened with a short prayer. The immense congregation then united in singing the hymn

> " My soul be on thy guard,
> Ten thousand foes arise;
> The hosts of sin are pressing hard
> To draw us from the skies."

A portion of Scripture was then read, a prayer offered, and the congregation sung the hymn

> " Am I a soldier of the cross,
> A follower of the Lamb ?
> And shall I fear to own his cause,
> Or blush to speak his name ? "

Professor Peck then read his text from Matthew 9 : 9.

" And as Jesus passed forth from thence, he saw a man named Matthew, sitting at the receipt of custom; and saith unto him, Follow me."

It is of the utmost importance to men that they clearly apprehend *the great law of right.* Do they know that law; they are prepared to ascend from the knowledge to virtue and well-being. Are they ignorant of it; that ignorance sinks them to deepest sin and woe.

There are but few, however, who can apprehend the law if it is stated to them in a merely dogmatic form; and fewer still are those who, knowing the law, can reduce it to details; who can frame for themselves a logical system of ethics.

The infirmity of the human intelligence which prevents its comprehending *abstract* rightness has been kindly recognized and provided for by our Great Father. Making account of it, He sent here his Son in the form of a man, to embody in an apprehensible way the law which lays its precept upon us all. In the discharge of this errand, the Good Teacher seldom taught duty in an abstract way. He simply said to men, as he did to the tax-gatherer in our text, Follow me.

The doctrine thus taught was easily comprehended. Untutored "common people heard him gladly," and even children learned from his life the truth they had need to know.

When the Divine messenger left the world, he commissioned and inspired men to put on lasting record the life in which he had displayed the law. So Matthew, the business-man, and Mark, the plain, farmer-like man, and Luke, the cultivated man, and John, the susceptible man, wrote the story; each telling it in his own way. Thus the world got glad-evangels, which, written from different points of study, agreed in well presenting the common theme

— the life which showed the law. In this way, sage and savage, were provided with the means of knowing just what God would have them do. They had but *to follow Jesus* and the law would be fulfilled. And in following the blessed Christ *we* find *our* law. It will, therefore, be profitable for us to consider a few of those things in the life of Christ which have a bearing on or illustrate our duty.

We cannot but notice,

I. That the life we are studying was always pervaded by regard for the Father's will.

In infancy, he replied to the chidings of his mother, who sought him as he lingered in the temple, " Wist ye not that I must be about my Father's business ; " and when, on the last night before his crucifixion, a bitter cup was put to his lips, he only said, " Not my will but thine be done."

Nor could any thing ever divert him from accomplishing that will. When an arbitrary social law forbade his associating with publicans and sinners, he firmly kept on his own way, saying only, " I came not to call the righteous but sinners to repentance." And when civil law conflicted with the Divine will, by pronouncing the gospel he taught an illicit system, still did he not pause. He *would* preach, and his apology was declared in the comprehensive doctrine, " Render unto Cæsar the things which are Cæsar's, and *unto God the things which are God's.*"

Here, then, we get our first lesson. Divine will is to be paramount law with us. We must obey God always, and human law, social and civil, *when we can.*

Pursuing our study, we observe,

II. That the *Divine will was well expounded* in the life of Christ. It teaches us what that will is — that it is not an abstraction, but a living principle, looking to most practical results. Describe the life in one word, and that word is *love* — " He went about doing good " — such is the Evangelist's own summary of the career of Jesus. Visiting the poor, healing the sick, cheering the disconsolate, such were his occupations. So it was that Christ set forth his idea of the Divine will.

And we may well note here that it was from his understanding of his Father's will that Jesus took the gauge of his relations to men. Ordinary ties — those of consanguinity, for instance — did not bind him as they did other men. *The need* of men, was what inclined him to them. As they were poor, or despised, or sorrowing, so did he stand close to them, and the greater their want the closer was his relationship to them.

This, then, for we pause here for another lesson, is always the Divine will — that we love and do good to others, and that we fix our relationships and distribute our endeavors according not to inclination, but to the need of those for whose well-being we are called to act.

Passing on, we notice,

III. That the *spirit* with which Christ carried out his Father's will, illustrates *our* duty.

His was never a grudging nor a self-seeking service. He gave up himself to his work. He *assumed* that he could not accomplish the will, which was his law, without inconvenience and loss to himself. So he went his way, expecting sorrow and pain. And when sorrow overtook him, he cheerfully bore it. The indignities with which the ungrateful compensated his love, did not disturb him. The buffetings and mockings with which his persecutors assailed him, as they crowned him with thorns, clothed him with purple, and put a sceptre of reed in his hand, did not move him. Serenely did he bear that keenest grief which he suffered, when, looking from the judgment-hall, he saw his most beloved disciple hiding in the distance, and his boldest one openly giving himself up to treachery. And the last words which trembled upon his dying lips were, " Father, forgive them, they know not what they do."

It will be well for us to note here that it was the *spirit* which Christ exhibited which barred the mischief which had otherwise come of his refusal to obey human law, when that law contradicted the Divine will. His disobedience of Cæsar was not divisive. The State did not suffer from it. A spirit which is obviously benevolent and generous never divides. Selfishness divides society. The good-will, which Christ so well exhibited, unites men. It is when one follows Christ in this respect, that kindred and neighbors are gathered most closely to him, and that society about him becomes most compact. It is the God-obeying, loving spirit which Christ has communicated to those who follow him, which has given life to the social and political institutions under which we live, and are glad.

Let that spirit be ours. Let us be cheerful in doing our work. Let us, when we are wronged, give no place to vindictiveness, none to any desire but that of good will to all.

We find a *fourth* item of instruction with respect to our duty, in the manner of Christ, in looking for a reward for his labors and pains, not to any *personal* recompense, but *to the good to others* which was to follow that labor and pains. He never paused to ask whether his merit was recognized ; whether the honor due him was rendered ; whether he was to enjoy either present or posthumous fame. It was enough for him to know that the gospel he was preaching was in all time to be life to many souls ; that his beneficence, maintained through all the ages, by those who should follow him, would minister good to the needy ; that the poor and forlorn would be blessed by it ; that those " sick and in prison " would be cheered by it, and that it would strike the iron from countless wretches unjustly bound. This was sufficient recompense for him. And such should be the only reward for well doing, which *we* should seek. Is toil appointed to us ; are we called " to suffer for righteousness' sake ? " it is enough for us to know that what we do and bear will bless some child of want; that some poor wretch, who may never know our name or realize his obligation to us, will be cheered by the beneficent influence which we set on foot; that the ministry of love which we discharge, will, after we are gone hence, be to parched tongues a cooling drop.

We need pursue our subject no farther. It will surely leave with us these practical thoughts:

1. We are in all things to follow Christ. There is no position in which we shall need any other rule of life, than the example of the Lord who has gone before us. When duty is demanded, we need not look up an abstract law for our guidance; we have but to ask, "What would Christ do?" And when we can answer ourselves that Christ would do this thing or that, we need not hesitate to do it ourselves, even though human law or the customs of men should forbid.

2. We learn how and where we are to find Christ. It is not in the temple of worship only, or in the closet, that we are to seek our Lord. Do we go where the needy are, do we seek out, to bless, the wretch who is crunching his last crust, there shall we find Christ. Do we visit the sick-bed, from which fear of contagion has driven others, and there render needed offices, behold there will Christ present Himself. Do we take the panting fugitive from slavery by the hand, and help him on his weary way, pointing him to the Northern Star, so we shall presently find that "the Man of Sorrows" is also by his side. So let us seek our Lord, going as He always did, when He was here, where the neediest are.

And, finally, let us learn from our subject to be satisfied, in all our trials and labors, to be as our Master was. Must we submit to toil — did not He labor to utmost weariness? Are we paid for our self-sacrifices by the ingratitude of those we bless — was not He repulsed even by those He healed? Are we persecuted for righteousness' sake, and taunted and buffeted by those who are in power — has not He been in the judgment hall before us, and was not He crowned with thorns, and did not deriding persecutors mockingly rail at Him as the King of the Jews?

And when we have done all and suffered all, let us rejoice to know that we shall have our reward in the healing which shall come through us to some wounded spirit, and let us go cheerfully and joyously on our way, keeping in view Him who has trod the same weary way before us, assured that as His works followed Him so our works will follow us, and that the sons of sorrow will be gladdened by us even when our hands have long mouldered to dust.

At the conclusion of the sermon a prayer was offered, the doxology sung, and the congregation dispersed, very many previously passing through the jail and shaking hands with the prisoners.

The remark was general in the crowd, that were the prisoners in the custody of the U. S. officers and Southern slave catchers, instead of the friendly care of the County Sheriff, the jail walls would present but a frail barrier between a liberating crowd and the incarcerated prisoners. The numbers and the spirit for such an undertaking were both present, but under the circumstances it was well known such a measure was not necessary.

———

THE INCARCERATED.—The twenty Oberlin citizens who are incarcerated in the County Jail appear to enjoy life as well as they could be expected to do under the circumstances. On Saturday they had an almost ceaseless round of callers and friends, and President Buchanan hardly holds greater levees than did these men on Saturday afternoon. A large number of ladies made the "reception room" (12 feet by 18) cheerful and happy with their bright smiles and lively conversation. There was no lack of merriment and laughter, for even the "stern Oberlin saints" can enliven the routine of life with a hearty laugh when occasion calls for it. The spirits of the prisoners can be seen by the following correspondence which was written for the Plaindealer, but, being accidentally left out, was solicited by us : —

A VOICE FROM THE JUG. — My good friend Gray asked me to write this, and said he was going to head it

"Hark! from the tombs,"

so I shall save him the trouble, and add for *his* benefit the remainder of this solemn stanza; here is the whole : —

"Hark! from the tombs a doleful sound;
My ears attend the cry;
Ye living men come view the ground
Where *you* must shortly lie."

Apropos to this sacred quotation, some one in the farther part of the room is just now saying that Mr. Anderson Jennings, to whom we rascals are especially indebted for our comfortable quarters actually is, as Attorney Belden intimated, a distinguished member of a Hard Shell Baptist Church in the chivalrous State of Kentucky! Comments upon such a statement are quite unnecessary. Every man to his own inferences. But you are aching for items — sensation items. How came we in jail, and how do we feel here? Came we the defendants here by order of the Honorable U. S. District Court for the Northern District of Ohio, on motion of the U. S. District-Attorney. The immediate provocation of the imprisonment seemed to be the extraordinary position taken by the defendants in declining to accept as competent to decide upon their liberty the jury which had just rendered a verdict of guilty against one of their number. This Mr. Belden thought so impertinent as to destroy all his previous confidence in us. Hitherto we have come and gone upon our word. But now we are safe only within stone walls. Not feeling very guilty, we do feel very happy. We are in jail, and though treated with kindness, are none the less prisoners, for Sheriff Wightman is a faithful officer as well as a gentleman, and allows no personal feelings to interfere with the rigid discharge of his official duties; and here in jail, in the beautiful city of Cleveland, in the Free State of Ohio, we shall quietly lie, not for the crime of violating the act of 1850, not for the charge or suspicion of so doing, but for declining to intrust our liberty to the keeping of twelve men who had just announced under oath, their fixed opinion of the merits of our case. Now how do we look and feel?

The glass is passing freely around, backed by a huge pitcher. The contents are as good as the Cleveland Reservoir can furnish, but still a little behind Oberlin wells. The Deacon brought an armful of exchanges just after tea, and the genial Junior of the *Leader* came with as many more an hour later. Mr. Benedict had already supplied us the Evening *Herald*. The literarily inclined are therefore buried in news, and the rest chatter quietly between. A steady current of callers eddies through our room, leaving a cheerful sediment of anecdote, witticism, discussion, argument, querying, and comfort. Very respectable callers these are, too, without exception. Barristers, Editors, Legislators, Merchants, and Clergymen. And now comes our courteous Marshal Johnson to unite counsels with the Sheriff, the Jailer and the ladies, for the lodging of so unexpected and serious an addition to the number of the public guests. Next comes a friend with an armful of books. Then a gentleman and some ladies. Really, this is a lively evening. But, alas! every echo of our laughter rings with the hollow premonition of a sundering Union, a disaffected South, and an excited community. What shall be did? Something to quiet the distracted nerves, something to throw another hoop about the parting Union, something to make still more secure the slippery two-legged property of our unfortunate southern neighbors.

But they are laughing at me for writing for the *Plain-Pealer*, and your readers will laugh so much more yet to see such an abolitionist, incendiary, Freedom-shrieking, Kansas-humbug, Republican, Oberlin article in your columns, that I may as well stop off. If you feel infected, fumigate yourself with sulphur, dear reader, and be in Court on Monday.

DUNGEONER.

CUYAHOGA COUNTY JAIL, }
Friday Evening, April 15, 1859. }

As some individuals seem to have misapprehended the true grounds of the committal to prison, it has been thought best to insert in this connection an editorial which appeared in the Cleveland *Herald* of Saturday evening, April 16th. This article is selected as conveying precisely the impressions upon which THE TWENTY acted.

Thirty-Seven Free Citizens of Ohio consigned to a Jail because they Refused to be Tried by a Jury that had Prejudged their Cases.

The Wellington-Oberlin rescue case assumed a new phase on Friday, and we must occupy a brief space, although our columns have of late been filled with the details of the trial of Bushnell, in reviewing the history of this matter, and in calling attention to the unprecedented and unpardonable course of District-Attorney BELDEN. We do not know how to characterize the vindictiveness, the malice, the venom, with which the Prosecution calls for the vengeance of the law upon these men.

Let us go back to the finding of these indictments, merely to remind our readers that one of the men allowed by the Prosecution to sit on the Grand Jury, was Mr. Boynton, the father of the boy, who, for twenty pieces of silver, was hired to deceive and decoy a miserable, ignorant black man into the hands of his captors. Here was the first unblushing outrage upon propriety, — yes, upon decency.

The next step in this mockery of fair and honorable dealing, was the empanelling of a Petit Jury, *every man of whom was an adherent of the Democratic party, and one of them a Deputy United States Marshal.* We do not say law was violated by this, but we do say — and every right-minded person will agree with us — that this was ungenerous, unfair, and an utter violation of the dignity and magnanimity becoming the professional character and position of a high public prosecutor. It was fit only for a four-corner Justice's trial on a horse warranty question.

The trial was had on the case against Bushnell, and the jury, very summarily, found him guilty. We are not disposed to impugn the integrity of these jurors: they acted under the solemnity of an oath each had the intelligence to comprehend, and the responsibility of which they ought fully to feel. How those men could say — for by their verdict they have so said — that those two Kentucky slave-catchers told the truth about that power of attorney, while some half dozen of as good citizens as Lorain County contains were guilty of flat, deliberate, downright perjury, is a matter for them to settle with their own consciences. We do not arraign them for their opinion upon that subject, but proceed to the scene which ensued upon the rendition of their verdict.

The question came up as to the trial of the other cases, and the District-Attorney, in his vindictiveness, his malignity towards the remaining defendants, insisted that each of them should be tried by that same jury — a jury that under the solemnity of their oaths, had prejudged all these cases.

Let it be borne in mind that this jury, by its verdict, had found that there was concert of action at Wellington, on the part of the crowd of which these defendants were a component part. That, of course, prejudged *the vital point in the remaining cases.*

But the outrage upon judicial propriety and decency, can only be appreciated by adding this fact, that the jury which sat upon Bushnell's case, was a "*Struck Jury.*" What lawyer ever heard of a "Struck Jury" for an entire term of Court? We have it from the most experienced gentlemen of our bar, from those who for years have sat upon the Bench, who have grown gray in the profession, that a "Struck Jury" is always confined to the one case to try which it was empanelled. Ordinarily the term dockets do not embrace cases resting upon like facts, and in such case the claim of the District-Attorney that the "Struck Jury" is for the term, while it would be novel, would not, as a matter of course, be glaringly unjust; but in this instance it is monstrous.

When the defendants found that the District-Attorney, in his madness, was determined to put them through the wretched farce of a pretended trial, while the verdict of guilty had been already pronounced by the Jury before whom they were to be arraigned, they abandoned their defence, and Judge SPALDING said, in behalf of the defendants, that if compelled to go before this Jury, they would introduce no witnesses, and the trial would be solely on the part of the Government. The defence dismissed their Counsel, and refused to stultify themselves by appearing to accede to such a legal outrage upon their rights. Then it was the District-Attorney exultantly claimed his *privilege* of ordering Bushnell into the custody of the Marshal; and he *did more,* he moved that those persons who were at large, upon their own recognizances, be taken into custody. After their names were called, and they had entered the box assigned them by the U. S. Marshal, Judge SPALDING moved, in behalf of the defendants, that an entry be made on the Journal, showing the several recognizances cancelled. This was done, or ordered to be done by the Court. Subsequently, the District-Attorney applied for an order that these defendants be admitted to bail, at any time, by entering into recognizances, *with sureties to the satisfaction of the Clerk.* The Judge made the order, but distinctly said no bail or sureties would be required; that is, they might renew their own individual recognizances, if they saw fit. Then the vengeance of the District-Attorney seemed for a moment satisfied, and these men were marched to our jail, where they lie incarcerated. And for what? *Why, for refusing to be tried by a Jury that had prejudged their cases.*

That is the length and breadth of this matter, and we rest it here, begging the people of Ohio to ponder upon this outrage, and to answer to themselves this question: What is the trial by Jury worth in Ohio?

CHAPTER THIRD.

To gratify the reader, it is made a study, throughout this volume, to avoid repetitions. The testimony given on Mr. LANGSTON's trial will usually be introduced in this chapter only when it materially differs from that given on the trial of Mr. BUSHNELL. The compiler acknowledges his indebtedness to Mr. BACKUS and Mr. GRISWOLD, for the use of their notes of the testimony on this trial, from which his selections are mainly drawn. The indefatigable reporters of the *Leader* and of the *Herald* will occasionally recognize "familiar passages" in this as in other Chapters, for the privilege of using which, they need not be told he gladly makes grateful acknowledgments.

A chain of untoward circumstances, beginning with our incarceration, and ending with the foundation of this work itself, so interrupted the compiler's personal attendance upon Court during this trial, that he is mainly dependent upon the labors of others for its history. His deep personal regret that he cannot hold himself alone chargeable with any errors of omission or commission that may be detected herein, is however sensibly mitigated by the sincere pleasure the opportunity affords him to become the recipient of the numberless kind offices of friends.

So much of the testimony as is presented in this chapter may be received with every confidence in its accuracy; and it is believed that but little, if any, of importance has escaped selection.

TRIAL OF CHARLES LANGSTON.

FIRST DAY.— MONDAY, APRIL 18, 1859.

Court convened at 9 o'clock. On the reading of the Journal for Friday, in which it is stated that Charles Langston had appeared and given up his recognizance, on his own free will and pleasure, the Counsel for the defence objected, saying that it was on the motion of the District-Attorney, that the defendants, Langston being included, were ordered into custody, and that then after they had been taken into such custody, the defence requested that the recognizances be cancelled. The Journal entry is as follows: —

Friday, April 15th, 1859.

The United States ⎞ No. 71.
    v.   ⎬ Indictment for rescuing a
Charles Langston. ⎠ fugitive from service.

This day comes the said defendant and surrenders himself into the custody of the Court, in discharge of his recognizance heretofore entered into for his appearance at this term of the Court, to answer to the said indictment. Whereupon it is ordered by the Court that the said recognizance be and the same is hereby discharged and cancelled.

And it is further ordered, that the said Defendant enter into his own recognizance, without surety, before the Clerk of this Court, in the sum of one thousand dollars, for his appearance from day to day during the present term of this Court, to answer to said indictment pending against him for rescuing a fugitive from service, and, in default thereof, that he be committed to the custody of the Marshal of this District, to be by him conveyed to the jail of Cuyahoga county, there to remain until the further order of this Court.

Similar entries are made in the cases of all the others, except in that of Bushnell, in reference to whom the record is as follows: —

Friday, April 15, 1859.

The United States ⎞ No. 74.
    v.   ⎬ Indictment for rescuing a
Simeon Bushnell.   ⎠ fugitive from service.

This day come again the parties to this cause by their attorneys, the said Defendant, Simeon Bushnell, being present here at the bar of the Court, and also come again the jurors empanelled and sworn herein, on Tuesday, the fifth day of April, instant; and the testimony of arguments of counsel being concluded, the said jurors, after receiving the charge of the Court, retired to deliberate concerning their verdict, accompanied by a sworn officer of the Court.

And now having returned into Court here, the said jurors upon their oaths do say, that the said Defendant, Simeon Bushnell, is guilty in manner and form as he stands charged in said indictment.

And thereupon, on motion of the District-Attorney, it is ordered that the said Defendant be committed to the custody of the Marshal of this District, to await the further order of the Court.

Some discussion here ensued as to the correctness of the Journal entry. The COURT remarked that the entry was correct according to its recollection. The defence stated the case as it occurred. Judge BELDEN said that before he had expressed the hope that the defendants be ordered into custody, he had said that he hoped good security would be given in the sum of $500. This case having been freely discussed and stated, the Court still held that the entry was correct. Some sharp questions and statements being made, Judge WILLSON remarked that he would state, once for all, that no insolence would be allowed before the Court, and any counsel using such insolence would have his name stricken from the bar. Judge SPALDING replied that he had merely endeavored to assist the Court in a correct understanding of the case, and if for such statements and information, and for his efforts to shield and protect the right, the Court saw fit to strike his name from the roll it could be done at once. The COURT replied that it probably would be done.

The COURT remarked that this present Jury would be called, and any one of them could be challenged if there was an objection. There being a vacancy in the Jury, Harvey Rice and David J. Garrett were summoned by the Marshal to sit upon the case. Judge WILLSON further remarked that as it was impossible to prevent the Jury from reading the city papers, he should have a reporter authorized and sworn to report the testimony accurately and fully. Louis Feeser, the reporter for the Law College, was selected for this purpose. As no specific order was issued to prevent other reporters "taking notes," we took upon ourselves the authority to make our own report. All other reporters being left to find seats for themselves wherever they could about the room — and not being allowed to sit at the reporters' tables, in the area with the counsel and the bar, we must ask for indulgence as to any omissions and misapprehensions, as we were so far removed from the witness stand that we could not hear all that occurred.

On the question as to whether there was any objection to the Jury on the part of the defence, Judge SPALDING replied that there was. He challenged the array on the ground of its being a struck Jury, and although that struck Jury, after coming into Court, was adopted as the regular Jury of the term, that did not remove the objection. They had passed upon every important fact in the case except the sole fact of the identity of the particular defendant with the crowd who rescued the boy, and it would be a mere farce to go before them again for justice. Moreover it was a political Jury, selected and brought here for a specific purpose.

Judge BLISS replied that they were not disqualified for acting and deciding justly, on the ground of having already passed upon the facts in the case of Simeon Bushnell, for they must judge according to the evidence adduced. Such objections as had been raised had never been considered as sufficient grounds of disqualification.

Mr. RIDDLE referred to cases which he had known of in his capacity as public prosecutor, when three persons were severally and separately indicted, when the presiding Judge ordered the Sheriff to make up a new jury in each trial. And it had been the case in the Courts of Northern Ohio, to try before a new jury each case under the same or a similar indictment for the same offence, and in this case every one of the Jury had prejudged upon all the important points in the matter, and it could not be pretended for a moment that the juror who had fixed and passed a conviction in his mind upon these points, would go to a new trial with an unbiassed mind.

The COURT expressed its opinion to be quite clear, that if the allegation against Langston was throughout the same as that against Bushnell, with the mere substitution of one name for the other, then that would disqualify the jurors in the former case from sitting upon the trial of Langston. It then requested the former jury to vacate the jury box, and ordered the marshal to empanel a new jury.

Mr. BACKUS remarked that as objection had been raised to the former jury on the grounds of political proclivities, he hoped the Court would itself appoint the new jurors, that there might be no grounds for such complaint hereafter. The Court, however, considered that the Marshal would proceed with his duty fairly, and left it to him.

The Marshal wishing a little time to select his jury, a recess was taken until 2 o'clock.

AFTERNOON SESSION.

Court convened at 2 o'clock. The following jurors were called to the bar by the Marshal:—

Harvey Rice, Irvin K. Bishop,
David J. Garrett, Charles Howell,
John M. Hughes, Boliver Butts,
Andrew Cozad, Levi Johnson,
S. A. Case, William Burton,
Sturgis Lynes, Richard Hussey.

These gentlemen being severally questioned by the Counsel for the prosecution, replied that they had no objection to the enforcement of the Fugitive Slave Law, if the proof showed the defendants to be guilty of a violation of the same. Mr. Lynes was challenged by Judge BELDEN and withdrew. Mr. J. H. Crittenden was called in his place. Mr. BACKUS inquired of Mr. Bishop if he had been present at the trial. He had been present a part of the time. The question being asked if he had made up his mind upon the ownership of John by Bacon, it was objected to, but sustained by Mr. BACKUS by argument, that it was necessary to know as to their opinion upon the several averments of the indictment. Judge BLISS replied that this was contrary to all custom to inquire in respect

to every idea contained in the question at issue. This matter was discussed and argued by Mr. BACKUS, but the Court held that he might read the indictment to the jury, and make the general inquiry as to any opinion formed, but that they would not consume time by such particular inquiry. The indictment was then read to the jury by Mr. GRISWOLD, when Mr. Bishop was asked the questions: If he believed the boy escaped from his lawful master; if he had made up his mind whether this Jennings was a lawful agent of Bacon; if Bacon made acknowledgment of his ownership before the Clerk of the Court; whether Bacon made out this power of attorney to Jennings; whether the boy at the time of the rescue, was in the custody of Jennings; whether the defendant Langston, did rescue the negro boy John, from Jennings, who held the boy by virtue of power of attorney from Bacon, who (Bacon) was the lawful owner of the boy; and whether the defendant Langston, was aware at the time of the rescue that the boy was really a slave held by lawful authority. All of these questions were overruled by the Court as improper to be asked. Mr. BACKUS said he proposed asking all these questions of all the jurors, and supposed he was to understand that all were overruled. He then asked the juror what means he had for forming an opinion upon the case. Mr. Bishop said he had not read the papers, and had not formed an opinion. The same inquiry was made of Mr. Garrett. This juror confessed that he had not formed an opinion as to the guilt of Langston, but he believed the boy was a slave. This brought up a discussion as to challenging the juror upon this point. The defence asked to have the juror excused upon the ground of this opinion, but the Court declined to excuse him upon that ground. On being further questioned, the juror said that he supposed the slave did escape and was illegally rescued. He was allowed to stand aside, being quite too decided a character to act upon the jury. Mr. Daniel Cleveland was called in his place. In like manner Mr. Hussey was questioned, the counsel for the prosecution several times interrupting the questioning, but the Court held that it was competent to inquire on such points as would tend to bias a fair verdict.

All of the jurors were similarly questioned. Mr. Case, having formed too much of an opinion, was excused. S. T. Loomis was called in his place.

Mr. Howell being challenged, Mr. J. M. Armstrong took his place, but being challenged, Mr. B. Brownell was called in his place.

Mr. Loomis wished to be excused on account of business at home. Mr. H. B. Platt was called in his place.

Mr. Brownell being challenged by the defence, Mr. George A. Davis was called in his place.

Mr. Butts being challenged by the prosecution, Mr. J. W. Smith was called in his place.

Mr. Platt having formed an opinion, Mr. Wm. B. Hall was called in his place.

No further objection being raised, the following jurors were sworn : —

Harvey Rice,	Richard Hussey,
John M. Hughes,	J. H. Crittenden,
Andrew Cozad,	Daniel Cleveland,
John K. Bishop,	Geo. A. Davis,
Levi Johnson,	J. W. Smith,
William Burton,	Wm. B. Hall.

The politics of this Jury were too marked to escape notice. They stood : nine Administration men, two Fillmore Whigs, and one Republican, who had no objections to the Fugitive Slave Law. The preliminaries being arranged, the case of the United States *v.* Charles Langston, for rescuing the fugitive slave John, was opened by District-Attorney BELDEN, in remarks to the Jury, setting forth what was claimed by the prosecution, and reading from the law on the point of the recovery of fugitives. Also, what was charged and expected to be proved against the defendant. The indictment against Langston runs thus : —

United States of America, }
Northern District of Ohio, ss. }

In the District Court of the United States for the Northern District of Ohio, of the November Term, A. D. 1858.

The Grand Jurors of the United States of America, empanelled, sworn, and charged to inquire of crimes and offences within and for the body of the Northern District of Ohio, upon their oath present and find that heretofore, to wit, on the first day of March, in the year of our Lord one thousand eight hundred and fifty-seven, a certain negro slave called John, a person held to service and labor in the State of Kentucky, one of the United States, the said John being the property of one John G. Bacon, of the said State of Kentucky, the person to whom such service and labor were then due, and the said negro slave called John, to wit, on the day and year last aforesaid, so being held to service and labor as aforesaid, and said service and labor being due as aforesaid, did escape into another State of the United States, to wit, into the State of Ohio from the said State of Kentucky : — and that afterwards, to wit, on the first day of October, in the year of our Lord one thousand eight hundred and fifty-eight, one Anderson Jennings the agent and attorney of the said John G. Bacon duly authorized for that purpose by power of attorney in writing executed by the said John G. Bacon, to wit, on the 4th day of September, A. D. 1858, and by him on said day acknowledged before Robert A. Cochran, Clerk of the County Court of the County of Mason, in said State of Kentucky, and on said day certified by said Robert A. Cochran, Clerk as aforesaid, under the seal of the Mason County Court, the said Robert

A. Cochran then being a legal officer, and the said Mason County Court then being a legal Court, in the said State of Kentucky, in which said State said power of attorney was executed — did pursue and reclaim the said negro slave called John, into and in the said State of Ohio, and did, to wit, on the said first day of October, in the year one thousand eight hundred and fifty-eight, in the said Northern District of Ohio, and within the jurisdiction of this Court pursue and reclaim the said negro slave called John, he then and there being a fugitive person as aforesaid, and still held to service and labor as aforesaid, by then and there, to wit, on the day and year last aforesaid, at the District aforesaid, and within the jurisdiction of this Court, seizing and arresting him as a fugitive person from service and labor from said State of Kentucky as aforesaid ; — and that the said negro slave called John was then and there, to wit, on the day and year last aforesaid, in the said State of Ohio, at the District aforesaid and within the jurisdiction of this Court, lawfully pursuant to the statute of the United States given and declared, in such case made and provided, arrested, in the custody and under the control of the said Anderson Jennings as agent and attorney as aforesaid of the said John G. Bacon to whom the service and labor as aforesaid of the said negro slave called John, were then and still due as aforesaid together with one Jacob K. Lowe, then and there lawfully assisting him the said Anderson Jennings in the aforesaid arrest, custody, and control of the said negro slave called John. And the jurors aforesaid do farther present and find that Charles Langston, late of said District together with divers, to wit, two hundred other persons to the jurors aforesaid unknown, heretofore, to wit, on the said first day of October, in the year one thousand eight hundred and fifty-eight, at the District aforesaid and within the jurisdiction of this Court, with force and arms, unlawfully, knowingly, and willingly, did rescue the said negro slave called John, then and there being pursued and reclaimed, seized and arrested, and in the custody and control aforesaid, he, the said negro slave called John, being then and there a fugitive from and then still held to service and labor as aforesaid, from the custody of the said Anderson Jennings then and there the authorized agent and attorney of the said John G. Bacon as aforesaid, and the said Jacob K. Lowe, then and there lawfully assisting the said Anderson Jennings as aforesaid — he, the said Charles Langston then and there well knowing that the said negro slave called John, was then and there a fugitive person, held to service and labor as aforesaid, and pursued and reclaimed, seized and arrested, and held in custody as aforesaid ; — to the great damage of the said John G. Bacon contrary to the form of the Act of Congress, in such case made and provided, and against the peace and dignity of the United States.

And the Grand Jurors aforesaid, upon their oath further present and find, that heretofore, to wit, on the first day of March, in the year one thousand eight hundred and fifty-seven, a certain negro slave called John, a person held to service and labor in the State of Kentucky, one of the United States, the said John being the property of one John G. Bacon, of the said State of Kentucky, the person to whom such service and labor were then due, and the said negro slave called John, to wit, on the day and year last aforesaid, so being held to service and labor as aforesaid, and said service and labor being then due as aforesaid, did escape into another State of the United States, to wit, into the State of Ohio, from said State of Kentucky; — that afterwards, to wit, on the tenth day of September, in the year one thousand eight hundred and fifty-eight, one Anderson Jennings, the agent and attorney of the said John G. Bacon, duly authorized for that purpose by power of attorney in writing, executed by said John G. Bacon, to wit, on the 4th day of September, A. D. 1858, and by him acknowledged on said day before Robert A. Cochran, clerk of the County Court of the County of Mason, in said State of Kentucky, and on said day, certified by said Robert A. Cochran, clerk as aforesaid, under the seal of the said Mason County Court, the said Robert A. Cochran then being a legal officer, and said Mason County Court then being a legal court, in the said State of Kentucky, in which said State said power of attorney was executed, did pursue and reclaim the said negro slave called John, into and in the said State of Ohio; — and, to wit, on the said tenth day of September in the year last aforesaid did pursue and reclaim the said negro slave called John, by procuring, to wit, on the day and year last aforesaid, a warrant, to wit, at Columbus in said State of Ohio, from Sterne Chittenden, then and there a Commissioner of the United States Circuit Court for the Southern District of Ohio, duly appointed by said Court as such Commissioner, and who in consequence of such appointment was then and there authorized to exercise the powers that any Justice of the Peace or other magistrate of the United States could or might exercise in respect to offenders for any crime or offence against the United States, by arresting, imprisoning, or bailing the same, under and by virtue of the 33d section of the act of Congress of the United States of the 24th of September, 1789, entitled "An Act to establish the Judicial Courts of the United States," for the apprehension of the said negro slave called John, then and still a fugitive from and held to service and labor as aforesaid, which said warrant, bearing date the 10th day of September, A. D. 1858, was duly issued under the hand and seal of the said Sterne Chittenden, as Commissioner as aforesaid, and directed to the United States Marshal and to any Deputy United States Marshal of the Southern District of Ohio, and was then and there delivered to Jacob K. Lowe then and there being a Deputy United States Marshal for the Southern District of Ohio, and which said warrant commanded the said Jacob K. Lowe, Deputy-Marshal as aforesaid, to seize, arrest, and take the said fugitive negro slave called John, then and still held to service and labor as aforesaid, and who was escaped as aforesaid and him safely keep so that forthwith said Deputy-Marshal should have his body before some United States Commissioner within and for the Southern District of Ohio to answer the further command of the said warrant; — and the jurors aforesaid further present and find, that afterwards, to wit, on the first day of October, A. D. 1858, at the Northern District of Ohio, and within the jurisdiction of this Court, by virtue of the said warrant he, the said Jacob K. Lowe, Deputy-Marshal as aforesaid, and then and there lawfully assisting the said Anderson Jennings as agent and attorney as aforesaid, to seize and arrest the said negro slave called John, then and still a fugitive from and held to service and labor as aforesaid, did, then and there take, seize, and arrest the said negro slave called John, as a fugitive from and held to service and labor as aforesaid, and that the said negro slave called John was then and there on the day of the year last aforesaid, in the said State of Ohio at the District last aforesaid, and within the jurisdiction of this Court, lawfully arrested, in the custody, and under the control of the said Jacob K. Lowe, Deputy-Marshal as aforesaid, by virtue of the said warrant, he, the said Deputy-Marshal, then and there lawfully assisting the said Anderson Jennings, then and there the agent and attorney of the said John G. Bacon, as aforesaid: And the Jurors aforesaid do further present and find that Charles Langston, late of the Northern District of Ohio, together with divers, to wit, three hundred other persons to the said Jurors unknown, heretofore, to wit, on the said first day of October, in the year one thousand eight hundred and fifty-eight, at said Northern District, and within the jurisdiction of this Court, with force of arms, unlawfully, knowingly, and willingly, did rescue the said negro slave called John, then and there being pursued and reclaimed, seized and arrested, and in the custody and control aforesaid, he the said negro slave called John, being then and there a fugitive from and held to service and labor as aforesaid, from the custody of the said Jacob K. Lowe then and there being and acting as Deputy-Marshal as aforesaid, and then and there having the custody of the said negro slave called John as aforesaid, and then and there lawfully assisting the said Anderson Jennings, agent and attorney as aforesaid : he, the said Charles Langston, then and there well knowing that the said negro slave called John was then and there a fugitive person held to service and labor as aforesaid, and pursued and reclaimed, seized and arrested, and held in custody as aforesaid; — to the great damage of the said John G. Bacon ; — contrary to the form of the Act of Congress, in such case made and provided, and against the peace and dignity of the United States.

G. W. BELDEN, *U. S. Attorney.*

Mr. RIDDLE set forth the position of the defence, and some of the circumstances which would be shown by the testimony which they would bring forward.

Mr. John G. Bacon was first sworn. His testimony was substantially the same as it had been in the former case, and need not be repeated.

Just before adjournment, Mr. RIDDLE remarked that he understood the Court to intimate in remarks made in the morning, that the Journal entry relative to the cancelling of the recognizance of the accused, be struck out and they be released without entering any new recognizance, and be considered in the same position which they occupied prior to Friday last. The COURT replied that they could go out again upon signing new recognizances as before. Mr. RIDDLE remarked that they would do nothing of the kind, and so the matter stands. They will issue no new papers.

SECOND DAY.

Court convened at nine o'clock, Judge WILLSON presiding. Examination of John G. Bacon continued. Being in substance as heretofore reported.

Prof. Peck and Mr. Plumb are allowed to be in Court during its sessions, being accompanied to and from the jail by a bailiff.

Robert A. Cochran. Richardson was my deputy, and authorized (objected to and overruled) to act for me. They lay taxes on slaves in Kentucky, but whether John was ever listed I do not know. Under the laws of Kentucky, whatever the Clerk as principal may do, that his deputy using his (the principal's) name may do. The deputy is appointed by the court on motion of the Clerk. A power of attorney to convey personal property need not be acknowledged — for real estate it must be. Slave property in our State is a distinct class, part real, part personal. A married woman owning slaves cannot part with them unless her husband unites with her in making a *deed.* A man can part with slaves by giving a simple bill of sale. There is a mixture of habit about the signature of deputy clerks; some sign their own name, and some (more frequently so) the name of their principal. Know of no law fixing either mode.

SECOND DAY. — AFTERNOON.

I distinctly remember that I came in just as Bacon and Loyd were passing out, and had them come back and make the acknowledgment *over again* in my presence, as still appears on the paper, my deputy still doing the writing. I had him put in also the last two lines: " The said parties are personally known," etc. There is no statute prescribing the duties of a deputy. They take the same oath as the principals, and do the same things. On the previous trial I *did not* swear that I had no personal knowledge of this acknowledgment.

Anderson Jennings. Saw John last about a year before I heard he had gone away. First saw him in a room in Wadsworth's tavern at Wellington. Knew him at once. [The COURT ruled, in United States *v.* Bushnell, that neither the acts nor the words of the negro were evidence. On reflection, it was now prepared to rule that the *acts* but not the words were evidence.] Was administrator of James Jennings. Was in Oberlin first some five or six days previous to September 13, in search of a boy belonging to an uncle's estate. Staid a day and a half. Did not see John, but heard of him, and wrote to Bacon. (Bacon says the letter is lost.) Directed it to James Reynolds, because he would get it sooner than Bacon, and told him in the letter to send it on. Went from Oberlin to Sandusky, and thence home. Got home on Saturday and saw Bacon on Monday. May have been Sunday — was Sunday or Monday; can't tell which. Asked him if he had got my letter, and if he had sent the power of attorney and witness as requested, and he said he had. Had sent the power of attorney by Mitchell. I passed Mitchell on the river. Suppose I got home before Mitchell passed, but he didn't know it. Missed him. Didn't see him. I asked Bacon to come back. He said he couldn't. I asked if he thought Loyd would pay my expenses, or give me any thing if I brought my nigger back. He said he didn't know. I studied for some little time and told him as he had sent the power of attorney at some trouble at my suggestion, I would come back. Started back on Monday. Think I got to Oberlin on Wednesday night about 9 or 10 o'clock. Stopped at Wack's. Asked Mitchell if he had seen John. Got the power of attorney. Next morning sent for Warren. Had got acquainted with Warren on the first trip. He came. Asked him if he thought there would be any difficulty in trying to arrest Frank or John. He said he thought there would. Then asked him if he thought we could go and make the arrest after night and get out of town before we should be found out. He said he thought that would be a very dangerous operation. Might get shot and never know who done it. If we done it in the village at all, better do it by daylight by all means. But he thought the best way was to make some arrangements to get the boy out of town. I asked who would help us do this. He thought this young Boynton would. Went to Boynton's Saturday night. We was all sittin' in the room together, the General and family, and Lowe and me, and this little Shakespeare came in and went to asking his father about going to town early Monday morning, and looked so smart I thought I would try him. So I followed him out doors by the gate, and told him my business, and offered him ten dollars if he would get John out, and ten more for Frank. He said he would try. Then I thought I ought to speak to the old man about it and see if he approved. He (old man) said Shakespeare was capable to manage his own business, and he and me could fix it up between us.

Staid at the General's till dusk. Then went back to Wack's, and staid all night. This was Sunday. Don't remember whether I read the Bible much that day. Boy came down Monday and tried nigger, etc. Told him to tell John he had gone to the blacksmith's for his horse, and come up and tell me whether he had fixed up the second arrangement. When he come and told me the bargain was made, I told Lowe and Mitchell and Davis, that they had better fix up and go on. I had promised the boy $20, if he would get either John or Frank. They went, and the boy come back and told me they had got him. He was gone about three quarters of an hour. Paid him the $20, got dinner and went to Wellington, and there found John.

At Wellington told John I had a power of attorney for him. [The COURT ruled that unless it was shown that defendant Langston was present at this interview, or what passed in it was brought home to knowledge of defendant, it would be obliged to hold it incompetent. DISTRICT-ATTORNEY proposed to show this. The COURT said if he failed to show it, this part of the testimony would be ruled out.] Persons in upper room asked if John was a fugitive, and they were informed that he was. Asked if he was a fugitive servant from Kentucky. All persons in the room were thus informed. Showed the power of attorney. The lawyer and others read it, and I explained it to them. Told 'em they might talk to the nigger. They did.

Several came into the lower room. I don't recollect that I showed the power of attorney in the lower room. . . . Mr. Wheeler came in and asked questions. This was on the lower floor. He asked the nigger if he was a fugitive. Said he was. He then asked him to whom he belonged. He said to Bacon. Asked him if he wanted to go back. John said he did want to go back. Wheeler asked him if he knew us (me and Mitchell). He said he did.

He said Mitchell lived close neighbor to his master Bacon. Wheeler said he believed that, if he would make that statement on the platform, the crowd would let him go; he thought they certainly would let him off and not interfere. We took him out; this was from the lower room. This was about an hour, or an hour and a half after I arrived — about three o'clock, or half past three. I consented, and he got up and walked out. I went with him. The platform was over the front door. There was a big crowd; near one thousand. A good many men armed. I saw forty or fifty armed with guns, rifles, shot guns. Saw no revolvers. John commenced telling what he had said in the house; he mentioned that they had the papers for him, and he reckoned he would have to go back. Some one hollered from the crowd, "you will have to go back, will you? we'll see about that!" I did not know him. Just then, saw a negro point his gun. I stepped back, gave John a pull and came back into the house. The crowd had stopped him from saying that he wanted to back. They told him to jump down, they would protect him. I heard them say he shouldn't go back. I said nothing to the crowd. Mitchell and Lowe went out with me on the platform. Don't recollect that they said any thing. . . . The power of attorney and the warrant were shown. . . . Told them that come into the room, that I was going to take him to Columbus, to have him tried, and that they might send a committee, etc., and that if I could not show that I had a right to take him, we would let him go. Some of them said they couldn't let him go thar, it was too far South. Both the warrant and the power of attorney were shown in both rooms. I talked very freely about them; thought that was the way to succeed. I went further and told them I would sell the nigger. Some man asked me what I would take for him. This was the lawyer. I said $1,400. He said that was more than he would bring in Kentucky. He said that was too high. I told him I knew better. Mitchell suggested to let them have him for $1,200. They did not propose to pay the money. A man in the crowd said, "there's a chance now to buy the nigger." He said he would pay $5; another man said he would pay five cents. That's the last I heard of the purse.

They were working at the door for some time. I concluded at last that I would not let any more in. I held the door. The nigger was in the room, myself, and some others also. They undertook to get me away from the door. They struck through the stove-pipe hole; it went through my hat — hurt my head some. [Hat exhibited.] Should have fell had it not been for the rope. Don't know what they struck with. A short time after this Lowe came to me and told me it was not necessary to hold on any longer. They were putting up a ladder to the building. I looked around. The window was fastened. Patton came and spoke to me. . . . I directed the seizure of John at Oberlin. I had charge of him at Wellington. . . . Saw defendant in the upper room that evening. He had no arms. This was half an hour before the rescue. Don't recollect who he talked with, except with Lowe. The latter asked him to assist him in preventing them from taking John away. He refused to do it, and said we might just as well give him up, as they were determined to have him. He said, we are determined to have him. Don't think he staid in very long. Don't know whether any thing was said in his hearing about the authority by which John was held. Did n't hear all that passed between him and Lowe. . . . Eight or ten were in the room; Watson among them.

Cross-examined. Knew John, but did n't know whose son or grandson he was. He was some five feet six to eight inches. Was a thrifty boy. Never saw Prof. Peck till I saw him here. Heard of him before — he wrote me a letter in the newspaper. Have n't answered it yet. Don't know as I shall. Heard my boy Henry was at Elyria; got there, and heard he had gone to Painesville. Went there and found a worse place than Oberlin. Never see so many niggers and abolitionists in any one place in my life! Dayton was with me. They give us twenty minutes to leave, and then would n't allow us that! There was a crowd of fifty or sixty, armed. Might as well try to hunt the *devil* there as to hunt a nigger. Was glad to get away as fast as I could. Kept very close at Oberlin. Did n't tell my business to many. Dayton and Warren were at my room. Mc-Millen had a power of attorney to take John when I wrote for one. Don't know whether Bacon knew he had one or not. S'pose Mc-Millen went and got it for his own use, without Bacon's knowledge. Wrote for one for myself, because I had nothing to do with *his* power of attorney. Went to Columbus to get some help. Thought I'd need all the help I could get. Tried to get help from Dayton, but he refused. This was *before* we went to Painesville. Went to Columbus for Lowe because I knew him. Lowe told me I'd best get a warrant. So I did. Told Lowe I'd pay his expenses up to Oberlin, and if we got any of the niggers I would give him and Davis a hundred dollars. This was for both between 'em. I offered him this because I knew perfectly well that Bacon would pay all expenses. He never has paid me any thing. Made arrangement with Shakespeare on Sunday. Heard what Belden said about my piety. Don't often do business on Sunday. Did this on Sunday, for fear the nigger might be off. Did n't say a word to Boynton about my business till after I had made the arrangement with the boy. Never offered the old man any thing for his help. Watson and another yaller negro come tarin' up in their buggy, with a gun a-piece. Did n't see more than them two in the buggy. Did not say on the other trial that Watson was the only man I could identify that was there. Soon after we got there, Lowe come and told me he wanted me to take *charge* of the negro; he had had no charge of him on the road, though always acting under me. Everybody was shown the power of attorney and warrant both. Scrimgeour and another fellow come in and tried to get the nigger out while Lowe was in the crowd reading his warrant. Never said I was the owner of the nigger. Lowe did say to me that

we had better give him up, if they would agree not to hurt us. Lowe did command several persons to assist him, as United States Marshal, to execute his papers.

I had my power of attorney in my pocket when Lowe and Davis went to take John. I told Lowe of the arrangement I had made with the boy, and wanted him and Davis to go on and take him, and I would stay and settle the bills, and meet them at Oberlin. They did not take dinner before they left. I left, I judged, at about one o'clock in the afternoon. I did not suppose Shakespeare would tell. I drove along pretty free. Think I was an hour and a half on the road. Fifty people were there when I got there from Oberlin. The crowd collected mighty fast after I got there. I did swear that I had difficulty in getting up stairs when I first got there. Mr. Smith met me near the stable, and commenced talking to me. I dare not talk to him. Saw the crowd gathering, and I thought if I could get the negro out of the crowd, I would slip him off. I did not go to Smith. I stood several minutes, ten or fifteen minutes, before I went into the tavern. I stood there until the old man Watson came tearing along. He and another nigger; each had a gun. I then went into the house. Had difficulty in getting into the house. Do n't know that I heard the word "kidnappers" that day. Sheriff came then to arrest us. Did not say it was for kidnapping. Our own party were in the room, and a good many others — cannot state who. The door was shut. I called. Lowe came to the door. Do n't know whether he had to unfasten it. Saw John. He *riz* up and met me. Called my name first. I told him I had a power of attorney for him. Took it out of my pocket, and showed it to him. John could not read. Heard the boys say they had showed John the warrant on the road. I asked John if he was willing to go with us. He said he was. Did not tell John that he would be sold after he got home. Inquired of him after my nigger. Said he did not believe he had been to Oberlin. Then others kept coming in. They all saw the power of attorney and the warrant. There was not a man that came in there, but that knew of the warrant and the power of attorney, and understood all about it. I told them I was acting under my power of attorney. I did not hear Lowe say that he had the nigger by virtue of a warrant. He told Scrimgeour that we had him; then pointed to me and told him I had a power of attorney. He also said he had a warrant. Did not tell what he was doing with it. Dickson came in. Lowe told me he wanted to see our papers. I pulled out my power of attorney, and Lowe his warrant. Lowe took out his first. Cannot recollect what he said. Showed him his warrant, and then told him about me. We wanted him to know just how we held the nigger. I told him I had him by the power of attorney. Lowe did not tell how he had him. This was after John went on to the platform. Wheeler had been in and questioned him before going out on the platform. John said several words out there. I swore that John did not say what he went out to say. Wheeler said if John would go out and tell the crowd what he had told Wheeler, they would let him go. John said that his master had sent for him; that they had the papers for him, and he thought he would have to go. A nigger pointed a gun at him, and cocked it. I did not know but he was going to shoot me. I pulled him in. Patton was in before and after this too. I showed him my power of attorney. Don't remember about Squire Howk. I showed my power of attorney to a good many. To Bennett, to Patton, and to Dickson. Lowe went out with the papers — took the power of attorney and warrant both. Meacham told him the crowd wanted to see his papers. Lowe did not want to go. Patton and Meacham told him they would protect him.

THIRD DAY. — MORNING SESSION.

After Lowe started, two men came to the door and knocked. I asked how many were there. They said "two," and I let them in. One had spectacles on. They went back by the nigger and took hold of him and led him down by the door. I asked what they were going to do with him. They said they were going out. I told them "not with that nigger." Told them if *they* wanted to go out they could go. They then requested us to show our papers ; — by what authority we held the negro. I did not tell him at all that I held him by virtue of a warrant. I turned them round and told them "papers or no papers they could not take that nigger out o' that room." This was in the upper room. It was getting pretty well towards night. Lowe got back before the negro was taken away. I did not tell Scrimgeour any thing about the papers. He knew perfectly well that we had the power of attorney and the warrant. They did not ask me to go out. They asked Lowe to go out. I would not have gone. Patton came to the door and wanted to go out. I slacked the rope to the door and let him go out and then they made a rush. Would not have opened the door except to let Patton out. Eight or ten in all got into the window before the negro got away. I discovered the men getting in the window soon after the glass broke. They surrounded the nigger and hustled him out. Think Langston come in with the crowd by the door. I saw it was no use and let the door go. I did not tell Patton that I was the owner of the negro. Saw Langston there about half an hour before the rescue. Don't know as he was there more than once. The only time I saw him to notice him was when Lowe was there. Patton was in the most of the time. Lowe had sent for Langston. Don't know what he sent for him for. Lowe asked Langston if

he would assist us. He said he would n't do it; said we might as well give him up, as they were bound to have him. If Lowe said they might have John if they would let us alone, it was after John was gone. During the conversation Lowe and Langston were in the room where John was. Think Lowe did proclaim himself a United States Deputy-Marshal, that he had a warrant and ordered them to assist him in executing his papers. He showed them the power of attorney and the warrant. Don't remember who he called upon to help him execute the power of attorney. A brick-maker was called upon by the marshal to assist him in carrying out the law. Did not hear him say that he had a right as marshal to call for assistance. . . . All the conversation to which I have referred occurred in the room where John was. Won't state that Lowe did not take any of them into another room. Think he did not. Did not say to Scrimgeour that Lowe held John by virtue of a warrant. Had not been in the room a great while before I took him to the garret. Don't know how long. It strikes me that I saw defendant in the crowd that came in at the door at the time John was taken out. Would n't swear positively that Langston was there. Lowe called Langston in to see the papers. I thought he was a lawyer. Langston said, "you might as well give the negro up, as *they* are going to have him any way." He did not tell Lowe he would not interfere. I think me and Patton and Mitchell and Lowe and Davis were there. Think this was the *first* time that Langston was there. . . .

Richard P. Mitchell. . . . I was put in possession of a power of attorney for Jennings. This is the paper. I was along when this power of attorney was executed. Cochran had an addition made to it after it was made out. Bacon was there, and Loyd. The addition was put to it by the deputy, by the direction of the clerk, Cochran. John is a full blooded negro. I took the power of attorney to Oberlin and gave it to Jennings when he came. I arrived at Oberlin on the 6th of September. It was Monday night. Jennings got there Wednesday night, the 8th. I saw John there before Jennings arrived. Saw him pass Wack's house. I knew him. Was satisfied it was *him.* Had no conversation with him then. The next morning after Jennings arrived he left for Columbus. He got back Friday night. He staid until some time in the day, Saturday. Then he and Lowe went into the country. I staid at Wack's. They came back Sunday evening to Wack's, after dark. Don't know what time it was. I staid there until between eleven and one o'clock on Monday.

[The DISTRICT-ATTORNEY informed the Court that unless Prof. Peck desisted from suggesting questions to the opposite counsel he should order him back to jail. Mr. BACKUS begged the gentleman to quiet his fears, for Prof. Peck had suggested *no questions at all,* and if he had, the gentleman's sensitiveness seemed rather out of place.]

Found the boy a mile and a half, or a mile and three quarters from Oberlin. He was in a buggy with Shakespeare. Davis took hold of him first. Davis, Lowe, and I were along. We put him in the carriage in the back seat with me. Lowe drove. I knew John then. I talked with him about Kentucky.

[The COURT ruled that for the purposes of testimony, all persons whether black or white must be regarded as persons; and since the words of third parties were not evidence, the District-Attorney could not ask what John said.]

Took him to Wellington. Got there about two o'clock, P. M. Took dinner at Wadsworth's Hotel in Wellington.

THIRD DAY. — AFTERNOON SESSION.

Left Jennings at Oberlin. Saw him next at Wellington, after dinner, up in the room in the second story. He came into the room. John got up and shook hands with Jennings. Jennings had been there but a little while when he said, he did n't like that room — it was too open. He got one in the attic. . . . We were in the same room about half an hour after Jennings arrived. Then he took us to the upper room. A good many persons came into that room. Don't know whether they belonged to the crowd or not. Cannot say whether defendant was there or not. A man came into the upper room that was called Langston, but I don't recognize him. Don't know whether it was defendant or not. Don't know whether he saw the power of attorney or not. Heard no conversation between him and Lowe. We were in the upper room about two hours. John was taken out into the porch before going up. Jennings, Lowe, myself, and Davis went out with him. Said he was going home — that his master had sent for him, and that he was going home, that they had the papers for him, and he had got to go, or was going. There was a large crowd there. Cannot tell what they were saying. Some were excited. Nothing was done to John or the rest of us by the crowd. Saw no guns pointed. Some one called to John and asked him if he wanted to go home. John said, it did not make any difference whether he wanted to go or not, the law was against him. This was all. We then went back into the lower room, but soon went into the upper room. Was in the room when John was taken away. The railroad train had passed before. The door was pushed open. Cannot tell how. A considerable of a crowd rushed in and right out again. There were in the room, then, Mandeville and Sciples, I think. Jennings, Lowe, Davis, and myself, also. Think the window was broken — could not be positive. Think one or two came through the window which I heard was broken. This window is in front.

Saw a ladder put up to this window. The power of attorney was shown to a number of persons. I cannot say that any individual was asked to go out and inform the crowd. I was in the room all the time, from the time I first went in until the negro was rushed out. I thought Mr. Jennings had the management of John at Wellington.

[After the examination of Mitchell was finished, Deputy-Sheriff Whitney, of Lorain county, stepped forward and arrested Jennings and Mitchell on a warrant issued from Lorain Common Pleas against them, upon an indictment found in that County for kidnapping. The United States Deputy-Marshal then stepped forward and exhibited a Bench Warrant, by virtue of which the two were held in custody of the Marshal for the purpose of having them as witnesses on these trials.

Mr. Thayer, as counsel for the Lorain County officers, stated to the Court that the arrest was made subject to the claim of the Court, and he asked this Court to order, when the witnesses should be discharged, that they be delivered into the custody of the Lorain Sheriff. The Court said it would take the matter under advisement. The Lorain Deputy-Sheriff made the arrest and, with his assistants, took seat beside Jennings and Mitchell within the bar circle. There the matter rested, and the trial proceeded.]

Mr. Wack, the tavern-keeper at Oberlin, was then called.

Chauncey Wack. Live in Oberlin. Did in September last. Saw something of a gathering at Oberlin on the 13th of September. There were a hundred in the crowd; twelve or fifteen guns. This was at one o'clock. Know defendant. Did not see him in Oberlin at all. Did not see him start for Wellington. Saw eight or ten start for there. I went. Got there at half past two. A great many arrived at Wellington after I did — but few preceded me. Saw Langston at Wellington in the crowd before Wadsworth's Hotel. First saw him there, some time before the Rescue. Think about 4, P. M. Moving around in the crowd. Did not hear him say any thing. He was moving around like the rest of the crowd. When I first saw him he was on the ground. There were from three hundred to four hundred in the crowd, right about the building.

[During the examination of Wack, Marshal Johnson very suddenly appeared and removed Jennings and Mitchell from the vicinity of the deputy-sheriff of Lorain county, and placed them apart from said officer, and outside the bar circle, and at the left of the judge's seat. The Marshal then removed the Deputy-Sheriff of Lorain county, and the officers who were with him, from the bar circle to the right of the Judge's seat.

Mr. RIDDLE then asked if Mr. Lowe (who was within the circle) was a member of the bar. Marshal Johnson replied that Mr. Lowe was his deputy, appointed that afternoon, and had a right to remain within the bar circle.

The trial again proceeded.]

. . . This speech of Patton's was after the train had passed. It was but a little while after this that I saw the rush to take him out. Saw Langston on the balcony above. Did not see him in the rush. It was not five minutes after this that John came down stairs. The crowd cheered some — threw up their hats. Did not hear defendant say any thing. Saw him moving about in the crowd like the rest of them. Did not see him at the meeting after the rescue. . . .

Cross-examined. Knew Langston in 1844 and 1845. Knew him well. I could distinguish him at that distance. It was about 4, P. M. that I first saw Langston. John had made his speech before this. The speech was made soon after we got to Wellington. Saw defendant do nothing except move 'round. Saw defendant once on the balcony, but whether it was at the time Bennett was there I cannot say. Did not see defendant at either time the rush was made. Patton wanted them to go to Elyria to get a writ of *habeas corpus.* He was the only one I distinctly heard recommending this. Did not hear many others recommend going to Elyria for papers, but urging that the papers were right. Heard John Copeland and Jerry Fox say they did not care for papers, they'd have him any how. Heard similar threats from twenty. Don't know who said they had better wait to see whether the soldiers would come. Cannot state any other one person that made these threats. Did not see Lowe with Patton when he was on the stoop. The first rush was about 4, P. M. Some of the threats were about this time; some, at the time of the last rush. Don't know that I saw defendant before the first rush. Don't think I saw him on the balcony when Bennett was there. There were very few on the balcony with him. Defendant might have been there. I thought Davis came out with John when he made a speech on the balcony. Did not see Jennings there. I was in among the guns and could not see well. The crowd were excited. Some of them said John had come out to say he wanted to go home. I noticed Davis with John on the balcony, but no one else. Should n't think John had got through with his speech from his appearance. John Copeland called to John not to say any thing. I thought Davis put his hand on him and he went in. I got there at 2, P. M. Was moving 'round. Did not stay long in one place.

George W. Ells. Live in Oberlin. Have for eight or ten years. Remember the time John is said to have been rescued. Was at the meeting held that night. Think likely I saw the defendant there. Heard his voice. Various topics were spoken of. Don't know but I heard him say something about what had been done at Wellington. Said the slave was

brought back. Don't remember any thing else that was said. A remark was made that he should not call names. Was there but a short time. Think Langston was through before I left the meeting. I was there fifteen minutes or thereabouts. Saw some of the crowd that went to Wellington that day. Was there about 1 o'clock. Did not see defendant there. Some of the persons at Oberlin had arms. Don't know whether defendant lived in Oberlin then. The meeting was held on the corner of the square. There might have been thirty or forty there. Cannot tell what time in the evening, but it was a little after dark. Have not seen John since some time before he was captured.

Norris A. Wood. Live at Oberlin. Have for three or four years. Am acquainted with defendant. Have been a year or two. He has made it his home at his brother John's most of the time. Think he was in Oberlin on the 13th of last September. Saw him in Wellington that day; am not certain as to seeing him at Oberlin. It was the middle of the afternoon or after, that I saw him at Wellington. When I saw him the first time, it was between the buildings leading to the barn, in the alley — back of the main part of the house. I and another man (Marks, I think), were sitting on a box when he came up and shook hands. The crowd was all around the house. Guards were stationed at all the corners. Some were armed, some were not.

It was hard telling what was said in the crowd. The general cry was, to get the negro away from the Southerners. Some threats were made. . . . Don't know that I heard which held him. Some said they had papers — some that they were good for nothing — some that they kidnapped him. They had it at Oberlin and at Wellington, when we first got there, that he was kidnapped. Some contradicted it — some altered their minds. Did not hear any one come out and speak to the crowd. I was at the sides of the house, its front, and its rear. I was there when the general rush was made on the back side of the house. This was fifteen or thirty minutes before the rescue. I won't be certain whether Langston went in or not, but he was there on the platform. Willson Evans, John Copeland, etc., were there. *Fay,* I understand now, was the man that stood at the door. They were as thick as they could be on the stoop. Defendant was in the crowd. Won't say he went in. The crowd were urging the man at the door to let them go in. Some were coaxing, some said they would go in, some said they would shoot, some said they would shoot the *crowd.* These were those at the door. . . . Langston was with three or four persons back from the door. W. Evans, John Copeland, and Jerry Fox were right in the gangway. Defendant was back three or four persons from the door. Don't know as I can name any others. Evans took hold of the man that stood in the door, pushed him in, and then the crowd rushed in. Did not notice that defendant rushed in. He was on the platform. Did not see him again that day. I then went round in front. Fifteen or twenty were on the back platform. The biggest part of the crowd were in front. The platform is three or four feet wide — fifteen or twenty were on it. I left soon after; went round in front. I thought C. T. Marks was sitting on the box with me. Defendant came up and shook hands with me. I spoke to him. This was some fifteen or twenty feet from the platform. I said to him, " there is quite a crowd here." He said " yes; he thought they turned out well." Then I asked him what they were going to do. He said, " they have got the papers out to take those men — the Southerners." I told him the constable would n't act without bonds. He said, they would have him any way; "we will have him any way." Don't know that he said any thing about their papers. David Watson came up and asked him where his gun was. He opened his coat, and said "here's my gun." It looked like a pistol. Watson and defendant then went up to the corner of the house, at the end of the platform. It was half an hour after this that I saw him on the platform in the crowd. Don't know where defendant had been in the mean time.

[Just before the hour of adjournment the Court said the marshal had returned the writ by which he held Jennings and Mitchell in custody; that unless the witnesses could give bail for their appearance as such witnesses, the Court would be obliged to commit them. The witnesses, Jennings and Mitchell, said they could not give bail, and thereupon the Court ordered them into the custody of the marshal.

Mr. Thayer then renewed his request that the Court order those men to be held subject to the arrest as made by the Lorain County Sheriff, so that when these trials are over, they might not be spirited away, and thus escape the officers of Lorain County.

The Court remarked, that the arrest thus made was an unheard-of proceeding, and a contempt, for which the party making it was liable to arrest.

Mr. Thayer replied, that there was no intention of disturbing the Court, but that it was well known that Jennings and Mitchell had not been out of the building for two weeks, and no other opportunity was offered for their arrest on the indictment found against them in Lorain, and the intention was to make the arrest subject to the prior claim of this Court.

The Court remarked, that when it had got through with the witnesses, it would be time to argue that matter.

The marshal removed the two men into the Judge's room, and the Court adjourned.]

FOURTH DAY. — MORNING SESSION.

Heard nothing in the crowd as to the circumstances under which the Southerners held John. Butler came to me and wanted a horse to go to Elyria. He was then speaking about the papers the Southerners had. Said they were good. Said they could not get John without they went to Elyria to get a writ of *habeas corpus* to take John. Told him I had no horse — referred him to Marks. He went to him. Don't know what was said. Crowd were passing back and forth. Some were saying they would have him if they had to tear the house down. Some said they would get papers. The report was, that the Southerners had telegraphed for the Cleveland Grays. Some wanted to go into the house and take him before they came. They said if they did not they could not get him at all. This conversation was along at different times — not at any one time. It was after the train came in, I think, that I was sitting on the box. Don't know how defendant went to Wellington. The first I saw of him, was when I saw him sitting on the box there. I came along just as they were speaking at the meeting in the evening at Oberlin. Did not hear what was said. I just halted. Heard nothing said about " the law," except what I have testified. I knew John. He worked for me once in May, 1856. In June also, some, and in August. He was pretty dark. A dark negro. Think he was a full-blooded negro. He had a large leg. One that turned back when he stood up. I weighed him in 1856. He weighed 162 pounds. He was sick in 1858; was bloated. Saw him at Deacon Armstrong's. Know when he came from Kentucky, only from what he told me. When he was brought out on the platform, Jennings said any one had the privilege to ask him any thing. I was the first to ask him if he wanted to go back. He said he supposed he would have to go back. Then said they had got the papers for him. Then two or three or more men spoke up. Some said, " jump;" a good many hollered, "jump down," " jump off." John Copeland stood right beside me, drew his gun by my shoulder, and told John to jump, and he would shoot the damned old rascal. I stepped down. The gun was pointed by me at the man. Soon they turned round and went in, Jennings taking hold of John when they went in. This was before the occurrence in the rear, of which I have spoken. Cannot tell the time exactly. Was in the hall when John was rescued. There is a portico in front of the Hotel. The hall runs through the centre of the house. . . .

Cross-examined. About 1 o'clock in the afternoon I first heard of the capture.

Half an hour after this I left. Bartholomew came along and said they'd got John. I went down in front of Watson's. There were ten or fifteen there. Lyman was then telling that he had met John on his way to Wellington. Was considerable running. I did not run. I was excited. Did not go down to rescue John. Know that some did. Marks went with me. Suppose he went for the same purpose I did —

curiosity. Marks drove. Wack went with us. He went to inquire about a counterfeit bill the Southerners had passed on him. Wack thought the bill was good, but he said he had been to Kellogg's, and they told him the bill was not good. This was about two, P. M. Don't recollect who I heard say he was going to rescue John. John Watson said John was kidnapped, and he would have John, dead or alive. Cannot name any other one that said this. John Copeland was there. Don't know what he said. Some said they had papers for John there at Oberlin. Some said they were good, and some said they were good for nothing. It might have been the first time I was at Watson's that I heard about the papers. Stopped there perhaps five minutes. Some said they *might* have papers. *No one said they had papers.* Won't be certain that it was said that those that took John were the same that had tried to take the Waggoners. The understanding was that *Munson* was one of the men, *Dayton* one, and the Southerners. The cry was that he was *kidnapped.* That they had got Boynton's son to take him out of town. Watson had started before we went. We passed ten or fifteen teams. Did not pass Watson. . . . We got a ladder and put it up. Marks helped me. He was standing by me when the ladder was put up. I went up the ladder. Not to rescue John. Did not put up the ladder to help rescue John. Did it for *curiosity.* There were many others, I suppose, in the same situation as myself. A man threatened to shoot me. Marks followed me about half way up the ladder. I told the man at the top of the ladder who threatened to shoot me, "to *shoot and be d—d.*" I went into the hall on the second floor. John was passed down as I stood in the hall. Cannot say whether I was gone when John went off. Did not cheer. Don't know as I heard the cry, "fetch him down," before I went up the ladder.

Direct-examination, resumed. Langston, in his conversation with me, said, "we will have him (John) any way." I was owing John money. He came to me Sunday evening. Said he was going home.

FOURTH DAY.—AFTERNOON SESSION.

He had been talking of going home before. I paid him what I owed him. He shook hands with me and left. [There was a long discussion upon the admissibility of this evidence. The COURT, on reflection held with the Prosecution, and received it.] He had told me before, in the harvest-field, that as soon as he got money enough he was going home to his master in Kentucky. Did not say who his master was. He started to go in September.

Cross-examination resumed. Worked for me eleven days in August. Don't know what time in August. Gave John one dollar a day. Paid John five dollars then. This was in September, I think

Wm. B. Worden. Live in Oberlin. Have

for five or six years. Was there September 13, 1858. Saw some of the people go to Wellington. I saw some of the crowd before they started. Saw some near Watson's. Some were armed. I did not notice any other weapons but guns. They claimed that they had taken a fugitive slave away from there, and they were going after him. This was about two or half past two. I did not go to Wellington. Did not see defendant that day at Oberlin, until the evening. Did not see Jerry Fox in that crowd nor Richard Whitney. I am a carpenter and joiner. Saw defendant in the evening in the street and on the corner of the public square. There was some speaking there. Saw him at the meeting. He spoke there. There were quite a number there. Three or four spoke that evening. I was in the meeting half an hour or an hour, I should think. Heard what some of the speakers said in the meeting. Defendant was there ten or fifteen minutes of the time. Heard him speak. He said in substance (cannot give the words). It was a kind of a history of what had occurred at Wellington. Don't know how he came to give it. The principal thing he said was, that they had been to Wellington and brought John home, or rescued him. Think he stated how it was done, but I cannot tell how it was. Don't think I could state what he said he had done at Wellington. He said he was acquainted with Lowe, and had talked with him. Don't recollect what he said the conversation was between him and Lowe. Was there when he commenced speaking. Don't know what he stood on. Saw defendant when he first got up. Think he spoke ten or fifteen minutes. Cannot give the expressions he made.

Cross-examined. Sheppard made the first speech. John Langston the last.

Philip Kelly. . . . Was at the meeting in Oberlin in the evening, during part of the exercises. Defendant was there and spoke to the meeting. He came on the stand by request. The crowd hollered, "Charlie Langston." John Langston had been speaking just before. John Langston said he was not at Wellington himself,—but he would call on one who was there. Defendant then took the stand. He went on to state what had happened at Wellington while he was there. Said that when he got there, Lowe sent down for him. That he went up to see Mr. Lowe. That Lowe asked him to assist him in pacifying the crowd. Said he told him he would not assist,—would have nothing to do with it; that it was no use for them to try to keep John, for they would have him any way. I don't recollect any thing else that he said. Don't remember that I heard him say any thing else. Said they had got him and brought him back. Did not see John there that night.

Jacob Wheeler. . . . About the time I got my two last brothers in, three men came into the room, from the back way. These three were Wm. Sciples, Walter Soules, and John Mandeville. They begun to get up quite an excitement. Saw a buggy drive up before this. The men in it were swinging their hats. Not much excitement before this. The papers were handed out to Sciples, Soules, and Mandeville. They came in in an abrupt way. Lowe· called on them to assist him in keeping the slave, he held, and showed them the authority he had for taking him. . . . Told the crowd that Dickson said he had been in to see the Southerners and saw nothing wrong except he did not see the *seal* on the *warrant*. . . . Noticed defendant that afternoon several times.

FIFTH DAY.— MORNING SESSION.

As a general thing, when I saw defendant he seemed to be conversing with Patton and others on the best course and the proper course to be pursued to get the slave. Langston said the best way and only proper way to get him would be to take out a writ of *habeas corpus*. And he proposed if they would get a horse, to go himself to Elyria for one. I also heard him speak to others to keep cool. I saw him two or three times — three or four times, in the afternoon. He appeared to be excited, he and Patton were going in when his advice was to keep quiet and proceed legally. Have stated all that I heard defendant say.

Charles Wadsworth. Lived in Wellington in September last. Son of the landlord. Saw Defendant as I was standing on the top of the portico. I went away at five o'clock. This was about four. Langston came out from the hall into the porch. I asked him if the papers which the slaveholders had were all right. He said it made no difference whether they were right or not, they were bound to have John any way. Saw him walking up and down stairs three or four times. I went away a little after the train passed. Don't know that I saw defendant in the crowd. There might have been ten, fifteen, or twenty allowed to go up stairs to the room where John was, while I was there.

Edmund S. Lyman. Been five years in Oberlin. Know defendant. Know his brother John *well.* Don't know where John Langston was on the 13th of September. About the time the crowd left I saw it, but not defendant. I went to Wellington. Saw defendant there but not John. Noticed defendant a number of times. Saw him as I was round the hotel standing 'round. Was at the meeting at Oberlin that evening. Think most of the people that were at Wellington heard the speeches. Cannot tell who spoke first, nor how defendant was called out. Heard defendant say that they had been to Wellington and got the slave. Lincoln was mentioning names and some one said, " call no names." Heard at Wellington in the crowd that the papers were not right. Defendant was giving the particulars of what happened at Wellington.

Marshall T. Gaston. Have lived in Oberlin twelve years. Was there Sept. 13th. Did not go to Wellington. Saw the crowd that went, in front of Watson's store. Do *not* remember to have seen Langston then. Was there when the crowd returned. Saw defendant. Heard part of the speeches. Saw the crowd returning from Wellington. Shepherd spoke first.

[Here Mr. BACKUS arose, and with most determined manner pointed to Mr. Belden, and said this farce had gone far enough — he wanted Mr. Belden to say whether he expected to show the negro John was in that crowd or not. Mr. BELDEN thus pressed did not come to that point.

The COURT held that what that crowd said at Oberlin, in the evening after the rescue, was not admissible unless the negro John was with them, and therefore the assemblage was a continuous act with the doings at Wellington. What the defendant said in his speech was evidence, but that only.

Mr. BELDEN finally said he expected to prove the negro was there.]

Shepherd moved for three groans for Dayton and three cheers for the Rescue of John. Said that Winsor and Bushnell had brought John to Oberlin and he was there then. [Which of course " Shepherd" *never said.*] Langston was asked if they had got John. He said " we have." Said Dayton had gone off on the railroad his coat-tail flying behind.

As we are following the course of events chronologically, the spicy episode of the

KIDNAPPING OF A WHITE MAN

properly comes in here. We know that the charge of *kidnapping* is a grave one to bring against an U. S. officer, claiming to act under the sanction of his oath, and with the approval of his superiors. But if the facts do not support the charge to the reader's satisfaction, he may write any phrase that seems to him more accurately truthful.

The Court had committed Bushnell to the custody of the Marshal to await its further order. The remaining nineteen who were so summarily and causelessly imprisoned were ordered into the custody of the Marshal, to be by him conveyed to the jail of Cuyahoga county, *there* to await the further order of the Court. But the Marshal choosing to intrust his prisoner to the custody of the Sheriff also, made the same indorsement upon all the *mittimi,* commanding the Sheriff in each case to hold the prisoners subject to the order of the Honorable United States District and Circuit Court for the Northern District of Ohio, and thus parted with whatever control of his prisoner he might previously have had; the committal being precisely the same thing as a deposit of one's own money to the credit of another.

This being the state of the custody, about 10 o'clock on the morning of this day — Friday, April 22d — one of the Court House bailiffs called at the jail and said that Mr. Bushnell was wanted *in Court a few minutes.* As Prof. Peck, Mr. Plumb, and occasionally others had been wanted, either by their counsel or the Court for one purpose or another, and as perfect good faith had been maintained on both sides thus far, there seemed no reason why the Sheriff should insist upon forms, and he told Bushnell to get ready and go. During the preparation, the bailiff was careful to repeat that Mr. Bushnell was *only wanted in Court a few minutes,* and would be speedily and safely returned. Mrs. Bushnell standing by, was invited to accompany her husband, and together with the Sheriff did so. As they were passing the door of the Marshal's office, which is on the second floor, the bailiff said carelessly, "Mr. Bushnell, Marshal Johnson would like to see you barely a moment *before you go up to Court;*" and Bushnell, in his honest simplicity, with his wife upon his arm turned into the office, the bailiff and Sheriff Wightman passing on to the Court Room.

Mr. Bushnell tells us that, immediately on entering the Marshal's presence, he was — apart from his wife — invited into an adjoining room, and the next moment found himself *alone, and the* MARSHAL'S *prisoner!*

The Sheriff tells us that he had not reached his seat in the Court Room before Marshal Johnson caught his shoulder from behind, and in quite a fluster demanded the *mittimus* by which Bushnell was committed to his keeping! He was answered simply that it was not in his pocket. At once it flashed upon the Sheriff's mind that Johnson would doubtless send to the jail for it, and some one might thoughtlessly let it go. Hastening thither, he barely preceded — sure enough — another bailiff, who demanded "Bushnell's mittimus." Mr. Wightman then explained that a mittimus could never be surrendered, but must remain on perpetual file as the jailer's only protection against a suit from his prisoner for causeless detention; adding, that if Marshal Johnson wanted the custody of

Bushnell he had only to get an order from the *Court,* and all would be right. The bailiff urged that Mr. Johnson had sent for the mittimus, but was obliged to return empty-handed.

For this singular conduct, the Marshal gave at various times, and to various persons, very different and often contradictory reasons. At first he plead the relentless order of the *District-Attorney;* then confessed his own motion; then urged the *advice* of the District-Attorney, etc., etc. As to the deceit used by his deputy, he first denied that he knew any thing about it, then attempted to extenuate it, and finally explicitly refused to disown or condemn it. The underlying occasion of the whole transaction, however, he uniformly said was a rumor that a writ of *habeas corpus* had been issued by the Supreme Court of Ohio, in Bushnell's behalf, and he thought if he got Bushnell into his custody the writ would be served on him, and he should have the pleasure of obeying it! He earnestly declared that he had never once thought of doing otherwise than obeying it. When asked if he supposed the writ would be served upon any one except the person who *legally* had the relator in custody, his replies were seriously confused. Still he retained his man. For six days Mr. Bushnell was kept thus indungeoned in the Court House, with a guard at the outside door by day and by night. As his quarters were comfortable, so far as the mere necessities of the body were concerned, and there was no attempt to remove him elsewhere, the sheriff chose to indulge the marshal in his fancy rather than precipitate what might have proved a serious collision. No one could question the illegality of the marshal's conduct, and the sheriff was not accustomed to shrink from unpleasant duty; but his personal sympathies were known to be so strongly on the side of his prisoner, that he judged it best to permit the duress for the time being.

Mrs. Bushnell, with her little child, was her husband's constant companion in this solitary confinement.

We return now to resume the current of Mr. Langston's trial.

FIFTH DAY. — AFTERNOON SESSION.

Artemas S. Halbert. Live in Oberlin. Did in September last. Know defendant. Have for six months, perhaps eight. . . . It was not long before some started. Watson went first.

Scott went. Wilson and Henry Evans, Lincoln and Bushnell. Did not see defendant. I went to Wellington. Got there about 3, P. M. Saw defendant there. Saw him first in a lane that went from the street to the barn. There were quite a number, fifteen or twenty in the alley. They were talking about getting a paper to indemnify the constable against costs, if he served a warrant issued for the arrest of the slaveholders. Some one asked Evans if he would n't sign the paper. Don't remember who it was. It was some one that was in the alley. Evans said he would. Watson said he had or would sign it. Defendant was talking about signing it, or that he would sign. He was talking about the paper: either asking them to sign it, or said he had signed it, or would sign it. I saw a paper that was handed to Evans, and he stepped to the platform to sign it. I supposed it was this. Do not know what. Some said the constable and two or three men with him had gone up to arrest them. Think I heard afterward that the papers were served on them, but that they would not come down. The crowd said that those fellows that had the slave wanted to take him to Columbus and then have a trial. But they said they might as well have a trial *there*, or at Elyria. These remarks were common through the crowd where I was. It seemed to be understood by the crowd that they would have him any way. Don't remember to have seen Langston after I saw him in the alley. . . . When I got home and had put out my horse, I went to the square. Think Langston was speaking. Could not tell whether it was defendant or his brother John. Could not tell what was said.

At this juncture the DISTRICT ATTORNEY informed the Court that a notice had just been served upon him which would require his immediate official attention, and would possibly call him to Columbus before he could go on with this trial. He therefore asked a continuance of the case until Monday, which was granted, and at 3 o'clock the Court adjourned to Monday morning.

The nature and grounds of this notice appear in the following extract from the Cleveland *Leader* of the next (Saturday) morning : —

THE RESCUE CASE — HABEAS CORPUS. — In the Supreme Court yesterday, an application was made by Judge Spalding, in behalf of the citizens of Lorain County, now confined in the jail of Cuyahoga County, by order of the U. S. District Court for the Northern District of Ohio, for the writ of *habeas corpus*.

In making his application, Mr. S. remarked that, under this proceeding, he proposed to arraign the Congressional enactment of 1850 as an excess of Legislative power, and an innovation upon the sovereign prerogatives of the State, which alone had power to regulate, by pains and penalties, the internal police of the commonwealth.

He insisted that this tribunal was the constitutional guardian of the personal liberty of every citizen of Ohio, and, as such, it was peculiarly fit and proper that it should take cognizance of any infringement of this great right, whether by the Federal Court or any other power.

The Court entered a rule on the United States Marshal of the Northern District, and Sheriff of Cuyahoga County, as well as the United States District-Attorney for said Northern District, to show cause by ten o'clock on Saturday, the 23d inst., why the writ of *habeas corpus* should not issue according to the prayer of the applicants. — *State Journal*, 22d.

The following is a copy of the notice served on the Marshal, District-Attorney, and Sheriff. A similar notice was also served on them in the case of Bushnell : —

SUPREME COURT OF OHIO,)
December Term, A. D. 1858. >
To wit April 21, A. D. 1859.)

On motion of Charles Langston, John Watson, Lorin Wadsworth, Robert Winsor, James R. Shephard, John H. Scott, Ansel W. Lyman, William E. Lincoln, Henry E. Evans, Wilson Evans, David Watson, Eli Boyce, James Bartlett, Matthew Gillett, Oliver F. B. Wall, Daniel Williams, Henry E. Peck, Ralph E. Plumb, and James M. Fitch, citizens of the County of Lorain, in the State of Ohio, by Mr. Spalding, their Attorney, and it being made to appear that they are restrained of their liberty in the Jail of the County of Cuyahoga by Matthew Johnson, Marshal of the United States for the Northern District of Ohio, and David L. Wightman, Sheriff of said County of Cuyahoga, *it is considered* by the Court that notice of the pendency of this application be served on the said Matthew Johnson and David L. Wightman, and also upon George W. Belden, U. S. District-Attorney for said Northern District of Ohio, and they and each of them appear before this Court on Saturday, the twenty-third day of April, A. D. 1859, at ten o'clock, A. M. of said day, and show cause, if any they have, why a writ of *habeas corpus*, in this behalf, should not issue in accordance with the prayer of the applicants. Ordered, that a copy of this journal entry, properly certified by the clerk, be served on the parties as the notice of the pendency of the above application for a *habeas corpus*.

THE STATE OF OHIO, ss.

I, James H. Smith, Clerk of the Supreme Court of Ohio, do hereby certify that the foregoing entry is truly taken and copied from the Journals of said Court.

In testimony whereof, I hereunto subscribe my name, and affix the seal of said [L. S.] Court, at Columbus, this twenty-first day of April, A. D. 1859.

JAMES H. SMITH, Clerk S. C.
By H. S. MILLER, Dep.

District-Attorney Belden was not a little excited by the above notice. He was heard to threaten that the prisoners should not be taken to Columbus on a writ of *habeas corpus* from the Supreme Court of Ohio, and that they could not be taken to the cars save through the cannon's mouth! The bravado U. S. Officials evidently contemplate making the streets of our peaceful city bristle with U. S. bayonets! The U. S. District-Attorney cooled off enough however by evening to take the train to Columbus. Marshal Johnson remained to guard and wait upon his imprisoned witnesses, the kidnappers Jennings and Mitchell, and the convicted Bushnell, who was yesterday disgracefully decoyed from the county jail to the marshal's prison, *a-la*-fugitive John by the young villain Boynton.

The opening of the case was delayed at the request of the District-Attorney, from Saturday morning until Monday morning. We have been able to find no better report of the arguments than is contained in the next two articles, the first of which appeared in the *Daily Ohio State Journal* of Tuesday the 26th of April, and the second in the same paper of the 27th.

THE APPLICATION FOR HABEAS CORPUS IN THE RESCUE CASES. — The application to the Supreme Court of Ohio, for a writ of *habeas corpus* on behalf of the gentlemen now in prison in Cleveland for an alleged rescue of a fugitive slave at Oberlin, was argued yesterday. Rufus P. Spalding appeared for the prisoners, and the U. S. District-Attorney, Mr. Belden, of Canton, assisted by Noah H. Swayne of this city, for the United States Government.

Mr. Spalding opened the case, and consumed the whole of the forenoon and a large part of the afternoon session of the Court in a matured argument.

He contended that Congress had no power to enact either the fugitive slave law of 1793 or of 1850, but that if it was conceded or decided that the Federal Constitution gave Congress power to enact a law for the reclamation of fugitives from justice, then it transcended its power in the enactment of 1850.

Mr. Spalding traced the history of the formation of the Constitution, and claimed that the clause respecting "persons owing service" was understood then, and ought by any fair construction to be understood now, not as conferring on Congress power to enact fugitive slave laws, but simply as a compact between the States that they would not exercise their sovereign power to prevent the reclamation of fugitives from service.

He claimed, in view of all the responsibilities in the case, Congress had no more power to enact a law for the arrest and return of fugitive slaves than for the arrest and return of a runaway horse. Roger Sherman, asserted that doctrine in the convention which formed the Federal Constitution, and the clause which, it was claimed, authorized the law of 1850, would never have been adopted in that convention, if it had not been the general belief South as well as North, that slavery was a temporary evil. The people would not have ratified the Constitution containing that clause, if leading men had not insisted upon it that no difficulty grew out of the clause in question, because slavery was necessarily a temporary institution. So strong was the sentiment in the Constitutional Convention, that the phrase "legal service" was rejected, and in its place the words "service under the laws thereof" inserted.

The argument, against the position he urged, was that it was expedient Congress should legislate to reclaim fugitives from service; therefore, it must have the power — necessary that Congress should legislate, because citizens of the free States abhor Slavery, and are unwilling to return fugitives to their chains.

There was no difficulty in reasoning upon almost any other subject than this one of negro slavery. It would seem that men were blind on this infernal subject, but to him, it was clear that only a fair knowledge of the English language and ordinary common sense was required to understand that under the Constitution of the United States, Congress could exercise no power imposing pains and penalties on citizens of the States for doing what was neither in violation of the laws of those States, nor of the laws of God. Whatever power there was belonged to the States. They had never delegated any part of it to Congress.

He asked that the Supreme Court of Ohio should critically examine all the questions involved in the application now made to it. Let the whole responsibility be met. He planted himself, as counsel for the prisoners, on the Constitution of the United States, and of the State of Ohio, and there bid defiance to any constructionists. If citizens were to be confined for acts of benevolence, let it be done in a constitutional manner. It was important to the people of Ohio that they should know what rule of action was imperative upon them. Wisconsin had boldly taken its position. The U. S. Supreme Court had reversed the decision of the Wisconsin Supreme Court, but the Wisconsin Legislature had instructed the Court to maintain its position. He had no doubt of the final result. There was a growing sentiment that State rights must be maintained.

Mr. Spalding read numerous speeches and historical statements in support of the positions we have reported, and concluded by demanding that as the U. S. District Court was acting without jurisdiction, the citizens in its custody should be discharged.

Mr. Spalding was responded to by the District-Attorney, Mr. Belden. At the conclusion of his argument the Court adjourned till nine o'clock this morning, when Mr. Swayne will speak.

Mr. Belden understood that there was no question before the Court but the simple one of the constitutionality of the Fugitive Slave Law of 1850. If that law was constitutional, the prisoners were properly in custody.

Mr. Spalding said he rested the case on that point, but had designed to call the attention of the Court to the fact that the Ordinance of 1787 made a discrimination respecting fugitives from service, in one of the original thirteen States.

Mr. Belden said that the Ordinance of 1787 was superseded by the Constitution of the United States, and had no vitality but such as was given it by acts of Congress. He would not stop to argue that point. He would confine himself to the question — Will the Supreme Court of Ohio allow a writ of *habeas corpus* in favor of individuals held under a law of the United States? He would present authorities and argue that State courts cannot interfere with Federal officers, who held persons in custody under the fugitive slave law.

Against the position of the counsel for the prisoners, were authorities of State and National Courts, of Legislatures and of Executives. He had but one decision in his favor, and that was by a divided Court. History was against the argument of the opposing counsel as well as the authority of Courts. The Constitution of the United States was obligatory alike in all the States, and until modern agitations prevailed, the exclusive right of United States Courts in cases under examination, was not questioned. Mr. Belden deprecated earnestly a condition of things in which State Courts would conflict with each other and with the U. S. Courts in expounding the federal constitution.

He held that Congress had no power over slavery, and no power to enlarge or limit freedom — that the Scripture doctrine " do unto others as you would be done by," did not forbid slavery — that the demand of the opponents of the fugitive slave law for trial by jury was preposterous, and that when men turned up their noses and declared the law obnoxious, he had only to say it is the law. It is in the Constitution — let the laws be maintained.

The argument of Mr. Swayne will be heard this morning with much interest. We will give our readers the points presented in our next issue, but may thereafter publish more in detail the arguments of counsel on both sides of this important case.

THE APPLICATION FOR HABEAS CORPUS IN THE RESCUE CASES.

— The argument before the Supreme Court was concluded yesterday at noon, and the Court adjourned to Thursday morning. Noah H. Swayne, Esq., on the part of the U. S. Marshal, occupied the forenoon with an able, lawyer-like argument, citing the cases in which the fugitive slave law had been held to be constitutional by both federal and State Courts, and arguing that with so many decisions in its favor, and but one, the recent decision of Wisconsin, against its constitutionality, the question ought to be regarded as settled.

He argued also, the question of constitutionality, *de novo*, without regard to adjudications, and held that the constitutional provision, that fugitives should be given up, granted to Congress all the powers requisite to carry out the provision. While he claimed that the law was constitutional, he did not assume to defend the policy of enacting so stringent a law, nor deny that great wrongs might grow out of it; wrongs which would be insufferable. Such was not yet the case, and therefore there was no such case for this Court to consider. When that emergency arrived, the emergency itself, as was always the case, would beget the proper remedy; the right of revolution was the only resort of the people when their wrongs from this law become intolerable.

Judge Spalding, for the applicants, occupied but about fifteen minutes in a forcible and eloquent rejoinder. He referred to the importance of the case now before the Court, involving the liberties of thirty-seven citizens of Ohio, while all the cases cited by the opposite counsel were raised by the capture of some fugitive slave who was already far on his return South when the question of constitutionality of the law was adjudicated, and urged the Court to give it that consideration that its consequence demanded.

He argued with great force that if wrongs might grow out of the execution of the law that would justify the resort to the remedy of a revolution, it was of the most momentous importance that the resources of the Courts should be carefully investigated, and all legal remedies exhausted, before abandoning the case to so terrible a remedy as revolution.

He referred to the standing of the citizens now incarcerated in the jail of Cuyahoga county, including all classes, clergymen, professors of colleges, doctors, lawyers, merchants, and others, representing the best people of the State; that this was no case lightly to be disposed of by our prejudice or indifference towards an inferior race, but one involving the liberty of a large number of the first citizens of Ohio; and alluded to the announcement in the newspapers that the United States war-steamer Michigan had been ordered by the President to the port of

Cleveland to overawe the citizens with her guns, and provide a prison-ship for these captives, beyond the reach of process from the State Courts.

The case has assumed a momentous importance. The fundamental principle of the law, making a crime of an act which is an honor to humanity, and which in such circumstances as existed at Wellington can hardly be avoided without debasing human sentiment lower than brute instincts; the odious and tyrannical severity of the law; the star-chamber character of the indictment and the trial; the low partisanship of the Judge; his coarse and indecent stump speech charge to the Jury; the determination of the District-Attorney that none but a partisan Jury should try the case; the unmanly servility of the United States Marshal to the pleasure of a malignant President; packing juries to indict and try; not trying a man by a Jury of his peers, but by a Jury of known flunkies; his vanity, which leads him to aggravate the difficulty to magnify his own importance, and which endangers a collision between the citizens and the Federal officers; the offensive attempt to intimidate the citizens by a government war-vessel; all these, and many other circumstances and considerations have combined to excite an unprecedented feeling among the citizens of Northern Ohio, and make this question by far the most important ever brought before the Supreme Court of this, or perhaps any other State. Grave consequences hang on their decision. We are confident that the question will receive that consideration which its importance demands; that it will be decided strictly on legal principles, and that the Court will shrink from no responsibility which duty involves.

The Court took the case under advisement, and on Thursday, the 28th, rendered the following decision: —

SUPREME COURT OF OHIO.

Hon. Joseph R. Swan, Chief Justice, and Hon. Jacob Brinkerhoff, Hon. Josiah Scott, Hon. Milton Sutliff, and Hon. William V. Peck, Judges. L. J. Critchfield, Reporter.

TUESDAY, April 23, 1859.

In the matter of the applications of Simeon Bushnell, Charles Langston, and others, for a writ of *habeas corpus.*

PECK, J. It appears from the petitions filed in these cases, that all of the relators who ask for the allowance of the writ of *habeas corpus* are now in the custody of the United States Marshal for the Northern District of the State of Ohio; that they are thus in his custody under and by virtue of a mittimus regularly issued by the District Court of the United States for the Northern District of Ohio, on indictments preferred against them in said District Court,

for an alleged violation of a law of the Congress of the United States, respecting fugitives from service, passed September 18, 1850; that the relators are charged in said indictments with the rescue, and the aiding and abetting in the rescue of a fugitive from service; and that the proceedings under said indictments are still pending and undetermined before said District Court.

The separate application of Simeon Bushnell, indeed, shows that he has been tried upon said indictment and found guilty, and is now in custody, awaiting the final judgment and sentence of the Court. That on being arraigned upon said indictment before said District Court, he, by his counsel, moved the Court to quash the same for various reasons, one of which was, that the law of 1850, upon which it was based, is unconstitutional and void; which motion the District Court refused to grant. A motion to quash addresses itself to the sound discretion of a Court, and is never granted, except in very clear cases, but the defendant is left to raise the question in a more formal way, by demurrer or motion in arrest of judgment. The refusal to grant cannot be regarded as a *final decision* of the question raised by the motion, when the point is one which, if well taken, would be available on demurrer or in arrest of judgment; indeed, such motion should never be granted, if the question is, in any degree, doubtful, but should be reserved for hearing on motion to arrest the judgment. No judgment or sentence having been pronounced, and the question of jurisdiction being still an open one before that Court, we do not think the case of Simeon Bushnell, as to the question of jurisdiction, distinguishable, in principle, from that of the other relators.

Is it then legally competent for this Court, to withdraw the relators from the District Court, in the custody of which they now are, charged with the violation of an Act of Congress, while the proceedings against them are still pending and undetermined, and discharge them on the ground that the Act of Congress upon which the indictment is based, is unconstitutional and void?

The District Court now has possession of the case and the parties to it, and has the legal power and capacity to hear and determine for itself, the question of its own jurisdiction and right to act in the premises. The legal presumption in such cases always is, that a Court thus assuming to act, will determine the question of its own jurisdiction correctly, until it has acted finally upon it.

Hence it is a rule founded upon the comity which does, and for the prevention of unpleasant collision, should always subsist between judicial tribunals, that, where a court of general jurisdiction and legally competent to determine its own jurisdiction, has acquired prior jurisdiction *de facto* over person or subject-matter, no other Court will interfere with or seek to avert its action, while the case is still pending and undetermined. This rule is sustained and supported by all the analogies of the law. See Smith v. Iver, 9 Wheaton, 532; Hagan v. Lucas, 10 Peters, 400; Taylor v. Carryl, 20 How. 594; United States v. Morris, 2 Am. L. R., 351; Exparte Robinson, 6 McLean, 363; Keating v. Spink, 2 Ohio State R., 105. Hurd on Habeas Corpus, 199, et seq.

It is right in principle, and preventive of unpleasant collision between different tribunals. If another tribunal were thus to interfere with our action and withdraw from our custody a prisoner upon trial before us, and set him at large, we should resist such attempt to the uttermost. And shall we not extend to other tribunals the comity and the same confidence that we claim for ourselves?

In the recent cases in the State of Wisconsin, and which have attracted so much attention and remark, this point was expressly decided, and that, too, by the same Court which determined the fugitive slave law to be unconstitutional. Ex parte, Boothe, 3 Wis. Rep. 155.

The history of this case is as follows:—

Boothe had been arrested on warrants granted by a United States Commissioner, for aiding in the escape of a fugitive slave from service contrary to the law of 1850. One of the Judges of the Supreme Court of Wisconsin upon habeas corpus, discharged Boothe from the custody of the marshal, on the ground, that the law of 1850 as to fugitive slaves, was unconstitutional, among other things, in authorizing Commissioners so to act and issue warrants, and that a warrant issued by such officer was illegal and void, and a majority of the Supreme Court of that State on certiorari, affirmed the judgment. Boothe was subsequently indicted in the District Court of the U. S. for the State of Wisconsin, for the same offence, and arrested by the marshal on a warrant issued thereon. Boothe thereupon applied to the same Supreme Court then in session, for a writ of habeas corpus to be delivered from the custody of the marshal; but the writ was unanimously refused, on the ground that it appeared from the application, that he was under arrest upon indictment of a Court having jurisdiction of alleged offences against the United States, and that the case was still pending and undetermined. That Court decided that they had no legal right to interfere in his behalf while the prosecution was pending, even though the law of Congress under which he was indicted, was unconstitutional and void; recognizing, in its fullest extent, the principle and practice of judicial Courts to which I have adverted. They concede the privilege and right of the District Court to determine first and for itself, the question of its own jurisdiction, and in reply to the claim, that the law was unconstitutional and void, and that, therefore, the District Court could not have any jurisdiction, very aptly remarks, that that fact, if true, amounts, after all, to a question of

jurisdiction which they, in the first instance, must decide for themselves. Subsequently, the prosecution having terminated by a conviction and sentence of imprisonment, the same Court allowed a writ of habeas corpus, and discharged Boothe for alleged defects in the indictment, which did not bring the counts upon which he was convicted within the purview of the act of Congress of September 18, 1850.

We refer to these cases in Wisconsin with no design of expressing our assent or dissent to the decisions under the first and last writs of habeas corpus; but merely to show that a Court which had judicially decided the law to be unconstitutional, still held that in a case like that under consideration, they had no legal right or authority to interfere.

On the whole, we are unanimously of the opinion that the relators, upon their own showing, admitting the law in question to be unconstitutional and void, could not be discharged by us, if the writ had been issued, and they were now before us for deliverance. It would be an idle and expensive ceremony to award the writ to bring the parties here, and for the time, intercept the proceedings in said District Court, when our next duty would be to remand them into the custody of the officer who now holds them.

The application for writs of habeas corpus in behalf of the relators, is, for the reasons stated, refused.

This view of the case renders an examination of the other propositions mooted in the argument, as to the constitutionality of the Act of Congress adverted to, and the right of the State tribunals to interfere with the final action of the District Courts in that behalf, altogether unnecessary.

Swan, C. J., and Brinkerhoff, Scott, and Sutliff, JJ., concurred in the foregoing opinion.

We return again to the U. S. Court.

SIXTH DAY.—(MONDAY) MORNING SESSION.

On the coming in of Court, it was stated by Judge BLISS, associate Counsel for the Government, that District-Attorney Belden was in attendance upon the Supreme Court at Columbus, where was to-day to be argued the motion for a writ of habeas corpus. Thereupon the Court said a postponement of the case would be granted until Wednesday morning, the 27th inst., at 9 o'clock.

The Government then asked the Court to nolle the indictments found against Oliver S. B. Wall, and against James R. Shepard, for the reason that the Grand Jury had seriously misspelled the defendants' names. The nolle was entered on each indictment, and the defendants ordered to be released from jail.

It is but proper to remark here that the Marshal notified the Court, not only in the indorsement upon his warrant, but orally, and with explicit emphasis, upon the first appearance of the defendants, that these errors in the indictments were so serious as to be undoubtedly fatal; and farther, the counsel for the defence at once entered pleas of abatement for this cause. The defendants were, nevertheless, obliged to enter into recognizances for appearance and trial, and in all other respects put to the same inconvenience and expense, and treated in the same manner as their differently circumstanced associates. When the causeless order to prison was given, the attention of the District-Attorney was again called to these misnomers, to which the prompt and emphatic, if not so elegant, response was — "*Go 'long!*"

Eleven days afterward, no farther or other notice having been served by the defendants, but when it was expected on the one side and feared on the other, that the Supreme Court of the State were about to make an official investigation of the cases, a telegram came from Columbus to Judge BLISS, ordering the speedy discharge of the misnomered prisoners.

The Court met on Wednesday, the 27th, pursuant to adjournment. The counsel for the relators at Columbus having returned, every thing was ready for the continuance of the trial, until Judge BLISS informed the Court that the District-Attorney had not yet returned, and the Government found it therefore necessary to ask a farther adjournment; which was granted, and the Court took recess for twenty-four hours.

On Thursday morning, Judge BLISS presented a letter from District-Attorney Belden, asking a continuance of the case until the *following Monday.* No reason was assigned to the Court for so extraordinary a request; but as Mr. Belden spent the balance of the week in the bosom of his family at Canton, he doubtless desired a respite from his arduous official duties for social recreation and domestic enjoyment.

On Monday, May 2, the Government asking no farther postponement, the trial proceeded.

NINTH DAY. — MORNING SESSION.

Judge SPALDING asked that Bushnell's sen-

tence might be pronounced at the earliest convenience of the Court.

The COURT replied, that the matter would be taken into consideration, and that the time he had been in jail since his conviction would be taken into account.

George B. Barber. Live at Wellington. Did Sept. 13, 1858. Was at home on that day. Not far from two o'clock the crowd first commenced to assemble at the Hotel. I heard about this time, that there was a fugitive then in the hands of the Southerners. Some wanted to buy him. Some one said they brought him from Oberlin. Watson then came up the steps to the door of the Hotel. Saw defendant there, between three and four, P. M., in the lane. He was going up stairs, or going into the house. There were a good many in the passage. Some standing and looking on, some passing back and forwards. When I first saw defendant he was ten feet from back porch. Think he was handing a gun to another man near there, a man from Oberlin, when I first saw him. May be mistaken about his having a gun. He had his hand on a gun and another man had hold of it too. He may simply have put his hand on the other man's gun. Defendant then passed on to the porch towards the door. It may have been an hour from the time Watson came up, to this time. Saw defendant again in the passage-way. He then came out of the house, and another man with him, say half an hour after the first. The man with him as he came out wore a broad-brimmed hat. Heard that his name was Patton. The other man said he had seen the papers and believed they were legal. This was said in defendant's hearing, I think. He was very near. This man said he "believed the papers were all correct. That the only legal course now was to send to Elyria for a *habeas corpus* to take John." But he said he "understood they had sent to Cleveland for the military — for the Cleveland Grays; and now it is in your own hands." He said "it would take some time to go there and back, and it would then be too late." He then went out in front and addressed the crowd. Defendant was either ten or fifteen feet from this man. Thought he was talking with the crowd. Heard him say to them that they had better pursue a legal course if they could. Think this man was not so full in the face as Patton, but he might have been. Defendant was at this time twenty or thirty feet from the door. This I think was an hour and it may have been more before the Rescue. There was a good deal said by the crowd. Some said that he should never be taken back South — that they would tear the house down — that the "Hook and Ladder Company" of Oberlin were on the way there to pull down the house. A good deal of excitement. Saw John first through the window in the Bar Room. Saw a paper in De Wolf's hand. Don't know what it was.

William Sciples. Live at Wellington. Was there at the time of the Rescue. Saw defendant there then. Saw him round at the back door in the first place. About two o'clock, or between two and three, cannot tell the exact time. It was after we came from the Court at the Town Hall. This was not late in the afternoon. Saw defendant and several others. Cannot tell whom. I did not see defendant doing any thing out there. Saw as many as a half dozen 'round there then. They were marching back and forwards. He was then in the crowd. Next saw him pretty well towards night on the second floor, up one flight of stairs, in the hall. Watson, and two or three colored men were there, and some white men, five or six in all. One or two of the men with defendant had arms. I started to go down stairs.

NINTH DAY. — AFTERNOON SESSION.

Saw these men in the hall. They were talking about going to Elyria after a Writ. Some said they had sent to Cleveland for aid — for a force — that if the aid got there before they got him they would lose him. Defendant said "we will have him at any rate before he shall go South." There was considerable said, but I went right along. This was about half an hour before the Rescue. These were *mixed* men; three or four colored. I had been in the room where the negro was kept quite a while before this. Mr. Lowe had called on me for assistance. · Cannot tell when it was he called on me for assistance, but it was right after we came from the Lawsuit. I went to the room by order of Meacham, the *constable.* He said he had a warrant for Jennings, Lowe, and Mitchell. One of the justices of Wellington had issued it. Don't know what he was going to arrest him for. Soules and Mandeville were with me. Meacham told them he came to arrest them. Lowe told him he had no right to arrest them, as Jennings had the power of attorney that they had arrested the slave on, and that they were acting on. Jennings showed the power of attorney. I saw it. We then read it to all that were in the room. Lowe said he was acting as an agent, that he had a warrant — that he was a marshal; cannot say that Meacham examined the power of attorney. Jennings said it was a power of attorney, and they might read it. Soules and Mandeville were there. But Mandeville was in liquor, and I don't think he knew much about what was done there that day. I was there in the room all the afternoon, except once when I went for Watson, and twice when I went down to get people to examine papers. I went for Dickson. Did not find him. Then went down again for Squire Howk. Told him that Marshal Lowe wanted to see him. While I was in the room that afternoon, I should think twenty persons from the crowd went into that room. Might have been twelve or fifteen of these that talked about the slave. Mr. Jennings spoke to some one in the room, and told him he had better go out to the crowd and tell them that any of them could come up and see the papers. I was there when John made the speech to the crowd — just came up as he went out. I got out doors. He came out and commenced talking about going back. Said he would rather go back than have any fuss. Heard nothing about papers. Heard conversation in the room. There were in the room then, Doland, Doctor Wadsworth, W. Soules, J. Wheeler, Mr. Jennings, Lowe, Davis, Mitchell, and, I think, Barber. I sat down on the side of the bed. John said he was a slave; belonged in Kentucky; Bacon was his master; and he knew Jennings. Don't remember that he said any thing else. This was before I met Langston in the passage. There were two or three talking about getting the Writ at Elyria, and thought there would not be time, etc. Langston said, "we will have him any way before they come from Cleveland,— before he shall go South." (He used both the phrases.) I had gone to get water when John was rescued. I did not get it. Crowd at back door knocked down a man. Jake Wheeler threw his coat off and we would not let them go up stairs. I did not see the gun taken. It was not over three minutes after this before the negro came down. Ten or twelve rushed up at the first rush.

James Bonney. Was at Wellington at work at the Hotel on the 13th of last September. Saw defendant at 4 o'clock, P. M. He was in the hall up the first flight of stairs. Cummins was with him. No one else was with him. Cummins told me if I would get the key of the front door of the hall for this man (turning to defendant), he would give me five dollars. The door was locked. I told him I would not sell myself for five dollars. Nothing more was said. I was coming in from the barn.

R. E. Thayer. Was at Wellington September 13, 1858. Lived there. Was at the Hotel about three or half past three o'clock in the afternoon. The crowd were trying to get a colored man out of the hotel. Heard first that those who had him had no papers. Then heard they had. Should think there were about fifty guns in the crowd. Saw some pointed towards the house, and one towards me. I sent a man into the house to the Constable to see what the Constable's fees were in a certain case. The young man went up the ladder. I pulled him back. Another negro snapped his gun at me. I got the negro by the head, etc. Next I knew I was being carried on some men's shoulders. I then started to go to the back yard. Saw De Wolfe on the front steps. Some one by his side ; 600 or 700 in front of him. He had a paper in his hands, and said they had got a human being up there and we must get him. Heard it said that they had a paper to indemnify the Constable for taking the men. Did not hear him say any thing about the paper. The crowd said they could not get the slave. The Constable would not serve the papers on the Southern men, unless he was indemnified. This was what the crowd said the paper was for. I was not there when John was taken away.

N. H. Reynolds. Was at Wellington on September 13, 1858. Live there. Was up at the hotel the most part of the day. Got up before breakfast. The shop was on fire that I then worked in. Was there all day, in front and around the hotel. Saw Mr. Fay there. He and I stood in the back door, between 3 and 4 o'clock in the afternoon. I was tending the door. Had orders to keep the crowd out. Cannot state at what time Fay left, but he was driven away about half an hour before the rescue. He was borne back by the crowd, as was I. The crowd of black men said they would go in, law or no law. Saw defendant before this in the alley. He said they would have John. Did not exactly say John, but meant him. Said he wanted the man, or, he would have the man, law or no law. His language was, " we will have the man, law or no law." Saw a number of guns that day. This was about twenty minutes before I took my stand at the door with Fay. Saw defendant after that at the door. Did not see him do, or hear him say, any thing. Saw him last in the hall at the foot of the stairs. He apparently came in with the rush. He was fourteen or fifteen feet from the back door through which the crowd rushed in. There were a number of people with him, those who rushed in. Think their aim was to go up stairs. Did not observe them closely. Am troubled with cowardice. Think I heard Langston say something about the train coming from Cleveland, that they had got to have him before the train came in, or they would not succeed in getting him. This was a little after the other conversation.

Cross-examined. Am a shoemaker. Had kept the door twenty minutes when the rush was made. It was about fifteen minutes after the rush that John was taken out. His language was, " we will have him regardless of the law." What he said when I heard him the second time on the porch, was about the same; he said, " Yes, we will go in." I stated to Judge Bliss that he said what I have told you he said. There was something said about the train; that they must have him before the train came in, or they would get him away. Train was to come in at 5, P. M.

Jacob K. Lowe. Live at Columbus. Am United States Deputy Marshal. Was at Wellington at the time of the rescue, and at Oberlin shortly previous. Went there under the procurement of Anderson Jennings. First saw him at Columbus. There he secured my services. This was three or four days before the rescue — *four* days. I went with him to Oberlin. Davis was with us. No one else. Don't know that there was any agreed price

for my compensation with Jennings, but calculated I was to have two dollars a day. Arrived on Friday evening between sundown and dark. Found Mitchell there, standing on the porch of Wack's hotel, when we drove up. Remained there that night. Went there to get John. We staid there until Saturday evening. Could n't arrange to get him. Went to Boynton's Saturday evening. Jennings made the arrangement with Boynton's son, to have John come there to work. Got the negro in pursuance of that arrangement. Got him two and a half miles from Oberlin. Davis and Mitchell with me. This was about 12 o'clock, at noon. Took him to Wellington. Arrived at Wellington between 1 and 2 o'clock. Left Jennings at Wack's. Had n't paid our bills.

TENTH DAY.—MORNING SESSION.

Cannot tell at what time Jennings arrived at Wellington. Might have been 3, P. M., or a little after. We were in a room in the second story. Jennings appeared dissatisfied with the room. There was a crowd outside, and some excitement. Jennings said we must get a better room than that. He got another room in the attic. We went up there pretty soon. We remained there until the negro got away. I told Jennings, as soon as he came in, that I wanted him to take charge of the negro. I supposed that I had arrested the negro under the warrant. Was aware of the law making me liable for a rescue, and did not want him on my hands. I told Jennings I wanted him to take charge of the negro. He said he supposed he had charge of him all the time. He did take charge of him then in that room, and controlled things afterwards. Did so until the Rescue. I could not hear what was said by the crowd outside, when Jennings arrived. A good many there had guns. The only buggy I saw there from Oberlin was Watson's. Saw him just in the act of getting out of the buggy.

A good many came into the room where the negro was. They examined the papers we had. We showed all the papers we had, to most of those who came in. Cannot say they were shown to all. Those who came in were at liberty to talk to the negro. Recollect Patton, defendant, — have known him two or three years; knew him in Columbus, — Mr. Meacham, the constable, and the justice of the peace who issued the warrant for us. Think the papers were all shown to Bennett and to Patton. Don't know whether the papers were all shown to defendant. I told him that the negro was a fugitive, — was the one named, — that Jennings had a power of attorney, and I had a warrant, and that I had arrested him, or assisted in arresting him. Think I explained to him who the owner was, and where the negro was from. I had sent for defendant to come up. Had known him in Columbus. I explained the thing to him until he said he was satisfied. I sent for him. I told him that I would like to have him go down and explain to the crowd how things were. He expressed himself satisfied that the negro was legally held, and said he would go down and tell the people so.

While defendant and I were talking, the train passed by. I heard the train. Did not see it. This conversation was after we had gone up into the attic. Cannot say that defendant was up there more than twice. This was the first time. He went down and was gone some twenty minutes. He called me out of the room, to a little room. He said he had been down talking with the people below, and he could do nothing with them. Said they were determined, he believed, on having the boy. He asked me if I could get Jennings to give him up without any trouble. I remarked to him that there was no use to talk to them about that, for we were determined to keep him if we could. He said he did not like to see any trouble there. Would prefer to have it pass off quietly. There had been a proposition made before that, by one of us, or by some one, I don't know who, to Patton, to have a committee go to Columbus and see that John had a fair trial, and that if he was not held legally, he of course would be delivered up. He also talked of this plan, and he was very anxious to have that carried out. But the people below would not agree to it, or hear to it. We were sitting on the bed then. He got up, and just as he was about to go down stairs he said, " we will have him any how." He intimated no danger to me. Said some of us might get hurt, and that he was anxious to have it so disposed of as to avoid it. This conversation was about an hour and a half before the Rescue. Did not see defendant after this. I was in the room all the time after this. I went down to show the papers to the crowd. Patton and Meacham requested it, saying that they thought the crowd would be satisfied and leave. I told Jennings he had better go down. He said, " you don't *kitch* me down in that crowd." I took down the power of attorney and warrant. Patton and Meacham went down and around with me. We went to the steps south of the hotel. Patton said he would read the papers if they would keep silence and listen. He read all of one and part of the other. Don't know which one. There was a man at the back part of the house. I took the paper out of his hand and went to the house as fast as I could. It was probably ten minutes from this time, to that of the Rescue. I was out ten or fifteen minutes. I left in the room, I cannot tell whom. Saw a man there whom I have since found to be Scrimgeour. The attempt to lead the negro out was not in my presence. Don't remember that I said any thing to Patton as I took the paper from him. Not more than one-third of the crowd was in hearing of his voice. I think very little was said by the crowd. They kept quiet while the first paper was being read. As he commenced reading the second paper, some two or three said it made no difference about papers, they made their own laws in regard to such things, or something to that effect. When John was taken out to the platform he commenced saying that he had been sent for, and was going home, but he did not finish it. The crowd told him not to say any such thing. Some two or three had been in and suggested that if he would go out and state to the crowd, what he had said to them, they would be satisfied. I had conversed with defendant pretty freely. He had been to the crowd and talked to them, come back and told me that he could do nothing with them. Wanted us to give him up. Know that defendant said in the second conversation that "*we* will have him any how," because he had talked with me as if he was anxious for peace. He spoke as if he meant what he said. I was disappointed when he said so.

Cross-examined. Was Deputy U. S. Marshal. Had known Jennings. Knew him, say about two weeks before. Jennings was then after another negro. Don't know where the warrant is. It was given to Chittenden when the Grand Jury sat. Never seen it since. Made no return on it. Kept it till I sent it up to Chittenden. Got it in Commissioner's office. Jennings and I went together after it. Don't know which took it. I carried the warrant to Oberlin. Jennings took the power of attorney. Davis went with me from Columbus. He is jailer there, and also deputy-sheriff. I am deputy-sheriff. Don't know as there was any arrangement with Jennings as to compensation. Had before, on other occasions, charged $2 a day, and expenses. Jennings offered me $100, if we got the negro. I refused it. Was introduced to Mitchell. We four talked the matter over. Did not tell our business to Wack. Went to see Warren on Saturday. Also called on Dayton. Told them our errand. Never saw John till we took him. Spent Saturday round town. Jennings and Mitchell kept close. Davis went along to Warren's. I had been there only twice before. Both times on the same kind of business. Did not learn the location of many negroes. Went to Boynton's about three or four o'clock. Mrs. Boynton quizzed around Jennings. Told her we wanted to buy cows. She said the General would not be home till tea time. Saw Shakespeare that night, but said nothing to him about our plan till Sunday P. M. Had spoken to Boynton about it, Sunday A. M. I had not talked with Boynton about hiring the boy. Think I said to Jennings the boy would do as well as anybody. Jennings said he would see the boy; followed him as he went after the cows. Jennings told me he had let the old man know he had proposed to Shakespeare. Went back to Oberlin little after sundown. Got back little after dark. Did not leave our room after we got back that night — it was Sunday night — till we went away finally on Monday. None of our party went away Monday morning and came back to eat.

Found John about two and a half miles from Oberlin, in a wagon with Shakespeare. Drove up on the right hand side, Davis sitting on the left hand, and I driving. Jennings had the power of attorney. I had the warrant. John was seized about as soon as the buggy came to a stand-still. Mitchell took hold of John, I think. John first stepped on the ground. Mitchell got out and spoke to John, and shook hands with him. I had before told John he could get out of the buggy and get into my wagon; I would take charge of him. Did not tell him I had papers for him, till we were started for Wellington. Think John asked where we were taking him. We said, " to Elyria." John said, " All right." When we got where we turned off — say half a mile — John asked where we were turning to. I told him I had a warrant, and was going to take him back to his master. Read the warrant to him, and showed it to him.

Regarded John as arrested by virtue of the warrant, from the time I got into the buggy. Went to Wellington, washed. Had Wadsworth's buggy. Did not tell Wadsworth why I went to Oberlin. Arrived at Wellington between 1 and 2 o'clock. Started from Oberlin a little after 11 o'clock. Drove moderately to Wellington. Ordered dinner there. No trouble with crowd before dinner. Good many people in bar-room. Paid little attention to them. Acted before them as if travelling in company with John. Can't tell when I got through dinner. Saw first excitement after dinner — heard hollering. I looked out of the north door, saw Watson drive up to north-west corner. He was just in the act of getting out of the buggy. Did not know Watson then. Watson was calling to people to assist him, I concluded from his language. Did n't hear him use the word "kidnapper." He might have used it. Don't know as I heard it from anybody. Can't tell what word Watson used. Stepped right back. Mitchell and Davis then went up into the room. Jennings was not there then — came in half an hour. I staid in bar-room till Jennings came. Noticed persons came in and out before Jennings came — can't tell who. Watson came about an hour after I did. Others were in room up stairs when Jennings came — came to ask how and why we arrested John. We replied frankly — supposed we answered them correctly. Think I told them I had him under a warrant. Supposed myself to have him in custody. When Jennings came I told him he must take charge of John. I could not, under the circumstances, have the care of him any longer. Could not risk him any longer with such a crowd. As an officer I know I can take a fugitive before a commissioner, when I arrest him under a warrant. Don't know as it is my duty to do so. Supposed I had the privilege either to bring him before commissioner, or surrender him to the master. Jennings remarked in reply, " All right: I supposed I had charge of

him all the time." No more was said about custody. Did not stop to make return on the warrant, that I had delivered him to his master. My duties as deputy-marshal were now through. Acted afterwards as aid of Jennings. Did take the warrant down to read to the crowd, afterwards, at the request of Patton. Don't know whether it was read. Showed warrant to Bennett, to show by what authority I had made the arrest. Don't know as I told Bennett that I had surrendered the custody to Jennings. Think I did tell him. Think I showed both papers, and explained what we had done.

Did you say to Bennett that you arrested John by the warrant, but had handed John over to Jennings, who held him by power of attorney?

Don't know. Think I did.

Why did you show the warrant?

Because I wanted to show why I had arrested him.

Did you tell Dickson that you had only arrested John under warrant, but had afterward given the custody to Jennings, who had John under a power of attorney?

Think I did.

Are you sure?

I asked Dickson if he would assist us. Think I then explained to him the whole transaction. Have definite recollection that I or Jennings told Dickson that Jennings now held him under a power of attorney. I feel positive that I told this to Dickson. Don't know that I told Wheeler. I can't say that I told Patton. Can't say whether Patton was there when Dickson was. I recollect conversation with Bennett and Dickson. No recollection of a separate conversation with Patton. Told Meacham, Mandeville, Sciples, and some other men present. Can't tell whether Patton was there when Meacham came in to arrest. Think this was the second time that Meacham was there.

Was this on the upper or lower floor?

It was on the lower floor that I had given up custody to Jennings. Meacham said he had warrant for three men who had the negro. I told him that so far as I was concerned, I should not obey it. I referred him to Jennings, saying he had charge of the negro. I told him perhaps he had better not be too fast to take those men; if the negro was lost he would be liable; he'd better ask advice. He went away — came back and said he should not arrest unless indemnified.

Did you not take Meacham, Sciples, and Soules into your posse?

I called on them to help me. I did call on them to help, as deputy-marshal. Can't explain why I called for help as deputy-marshal when I had surrendered custody to Jennings. Did not know I had lost right of acting as deputy-marshal by surrendering custody to Jennings. Was advised that I had not, by Stanley Matthews.

[Mr. BACKUS: Stanley Matthews never gave such advice.]

Had not forgotten when I called for help that I had surrendered the custody to Jennings. Do you admit you cautioned these men against their course by referring to the Clarke County case, and thus showed the danger of resisting the marshal?

Don't recollect any such conversation with Patton.

Do you recollect the conversation referred to, well enough to say that you *did n't* make such reference?

Can only say I have no recollection of such conversation. Can remember part of such conversation. I think that in the part of the conversation which I do not remember. I did *not* refer to the Clarke County case. Do not recollect conversation with Squire Howk. Can't say but what I had conversation with another magistrate beside Howk. Think it was half an hour from the time I showed the paper to Meacham, till I went down with Patton to read papers. Went at the request of Patton and Meacham. Had not before this offered to go to the Town House to read the warrant. Did n't so offer any time in the day. Did n't say any thing to any of them about going to the Town House to show papers.

When Meacham was in the act of arresting you, did n't you say, "you can't arrest a United States officer discharging his duty?"

Think not — nothing to that effect. Refused to go only because I thought he had no right to arrest, because I was a deputy-marshal. May have told him so. That was the reason in my own mind why I refused to go. When I proposed to Jennings to go down, I proposed he should go and read the papers. Think Patton read the papers. I might have started to read them, and Patton took them out of my hands. Patton said to the crowd " be silent and I will read the papers." Don't know that there was any explanation to the crowd that I was a deputy-marshal arresting under warrant, etc. Warrant, if read, was read as a paper under which the custody then was. Am *sure* Patton read more than one paper; read one wholly, can't tell whether it was the power of attorney or the warrant. Hearing a noise, I made for the house, taking the papers from Patton's hand. Had no conversation with Patton, Dickson or Bennett, or any one that afternoon with regard to a seal being wanting to a paper.

Did not Dickson say, " I see no defect except it wants a seal?

No recollection. Think I can swear no such thing occurred. Don't recollect of any thing being said to the crowd between reading the papers. Took two minutes to get back to the room. It was getting dusk. As I passed through, the hall was partially dark. It was immediately upon hearing the noise at the back door that I went. At the head of the second pair of stairs. I could n't tell a white man from a black. In lower stories not quite so dark. Think I first saw Langston in front of

the house. Sent for him 'cause I supposed he was a reasonable man.

Did n't you tell him that you arrested John on a warrant and was going to take him before Chittenden, a commissioner at Columbus, where he should have a fair hearing?

Might have said so. Don't recollect showing him any warrant. Before this there had been a proposition to have a committee go to Columbus. Don't recollect whether Patton, Dickson, or Howk were there when I had first conversation. Some of the folks said Langston was doing all he could to pacify the crowd, but they would n't hear. Some of the time he talked as if he was willing to have the boy taken to Columbus, and see if the examination was fair. Said he'd rather not see any trouble there or any of us get into trouble. I replied, "no use of talking, we are going to hold him as long as we can."

Did n't he say "I won't interfere any way?"

He did not — am *sure*. .... As Langston rose from the bed he said, "*we* will have him any how." I was surprised. I asked no explanation. I was not excited, at any time during the day. I felt disappointed when Langston said what he did. Mitchell and Jennings were in the other room while this conversation was going on.

Direct examination resumed.

[Warrants shown witness by District-Attorney.] This is the warrant I had.

Cross resumed. Don't know whether I read the warrant very carefully or not; don't know whether the quirk at the end was made into an L. S. Did not hear the warrant objected to because it had no seal.

[The warrant was now filed in evidence subject to exceptions. We introduce it with a copy of the affidavit upon which it was based.]

United States of America, {
Southern District of Ohio. {

Before me, S. Chittenden. Am United States Commissioner within and for said District, personally came this September 10th, A. D. 1858, Anderson Jennings, who, being duly sworn to tell the whole truth and nothing but the truth, deposeth and saith; that on or about January 15th, 1857, the negro slave John, being the property of one John G. Bacon of Mason County, Kentucky, did escape from the service and possession of his said owner, and is now a fugitive within the State of Ohio; and that the said John is a person held to labor in the State of Kentucky (U. S.) under the laws of said State; and that he is a person owing service to his said owner; and that he has escaped into and is now a fugitive slave as aforesaid in the State of Ohio, and therefore, subject to arrest under the Act of Congress in such case provided; — and further this deponent saith not.

ANDERSON JENNINGS.

Sworn and subscribed by Anderson ⎫
Jennings before me this 10th day ⎬
    September, A. D. 1858.   ⎭
    S. CHITTENDEN,
        U. S. Commissioner, S. Dist. Ohio.

United States of America, Southern ⎱
District of the State of Ohio, ss.   ⎰
To the United States Marshal and to any
    Deputy United States Marshal of said Dis-
    trict: Greeting:

    Whereas complaint has been made before
me, an United States Commissioner within and
for the Southern District of Ohio, upon the
oath of Anderson Jennings, that the negro
slave John, late of the County of Mason and
State of Kentucky, and the property of John
G. Bacon, resident in said County, did on or
about January 15th, 1857, escape from the
service and possession of his said owner, and is
now a fugitive within the State of Ohio; and
that the said John is a person held to labor in
the State of Kentucky, one of the United
States, under the laws of said State; and that
he is a person owing service to his said owner;
and that he has escaped into and is now a
fugitive slave as aforesaid in the State of Ohio,
and therefore subject to arrest under the law
of Congress in such cases provided: —
    These are therefore to command you and
each of you to take the said John, a fugitive
and person escaped from service by him owed
to John G. Bacon as aforesaid, and one held
to labor under the laws of Kentucky, as aforesaid, if he be found within the limits of the
State of Ohio, and him, the said John, safely to
keep, so that forthwith you have his body
before some United States Commissioner,
within and for the Southern District of Ohio
aforesaid, there to answer the said complaint,
and be further dealt with according to law.
    Given under my hand and seal at Columbus
this 10th day September, A. D. 1858.
        S. CHITTENDEN,   [L. S.]
            U. S. Commissioner for
                Southern District of Ohio.

Sterne Chittenden. Was acting Commissioner. Had never issued a warrant before. Supposed I had power to issue this warrant. I put
the scroll there. Put it there for a seal. I
called it a seal. Do not remember any thing
being said about the discrepancy.

Anderson Jennings being recalled swore to
the genuineness of the warrant and of the affidavit.

Samuel Davis. Live at Columbus. Have,
off and on, for eight years. Was along at the
time of the arrest, also when John was taken out
on the platform. Saw defendant in the room two
or three times that afternoon. Talked to the
crowd in there. He wanted us to release John,
to let him go. This was but a few minutes before the rescue. We told him we would not.
We were going to hold on to him. This was

in the upper room, in the room where the negro
was. He turned round and said, " We will
have him any how." John, Lowe, myself,
Mitchell and Jennings were presented. I don't
know that Lowe was there. He went out once
or twice; I know that defendant was in the
room two or three times. He came in there
and appeared to me to be excited. This was
about sun-down. Jennings had charge of John
during the afternoon.

TENTH DAY. — AFTERNOON SESSION.

Cross-Examination. Jennings got me to go.
It was the Friday before the Rescue that we
left. I told him that I did not know that I
could get off. Jennings was to give me $2 a
day and expenses. No other bargain. I was
deputy-sheriff and jailer. Not deputy-marshal.
Had had no business connection with him before. Never saw him before. Lowe introduced
me to him. Asked me if I would go to Oberlin with him to get John and Frank.

Was there any arrangement between you,
Jennings, Mitchell, and Lowe about keeping
the nature of your business private?

    Objected to.

    Objection overruled.

Don't know. No arrangement before we got
there. Not a word. After we got there somebody said we couldn't get the negro — think it
was on Sunday this was said — think it was on
the steps of Wack's hotel. The remark was
addressed to the party standing about. Left
Oberlin about 11 o'clock, to arrest John.
Lowe, Mitchell, and I went.

At whose instance did you go to arrest
John?

    Don't know.

    To aid whom did you go?

    To aid Jennings in executing his power of
attorney.

Didn't know whether Jennings was to go or
not. Think Jennings was to meet us at Wellington. Jennings was to stay behind to pay
the bills. Supposed I was aiding Jennings in
the arrest. Believe I first found out at Wellington that Lowe had a warrant.

What had Lowe said about the custody of
John?

Not any thing. In the room in the third
story something was said about the nigger's being put into the custody of Jennings.

What makes you think he was taken into
Jennings's custody up there?

    Can't tell.

Prosecution Rested.

Witnesses for the Defence.

E. S. Kinney. . . . I went to Wellington for
the same purpose that others did, to release a
man that had been kidnapped. I did not get to
Wellington until after John was rescued. We
left Oberlin about 5, P. M.

Cross-examined. Winsor was in the wagon

with Bushnell, swinging a gun, and saying, "All is well." A majority of the crowd went towards Oberlin, after John went away. The cry in the crowd was, that some one had been *kidnapped.* It was with the understanding that John had been kidnapped that I went.

Joseph H. Dickson. Live at Wellington. Am a lawyer. Was in Wellington the 13th of Sept. last. . . . Was at the Town Hall. Watson came and made affidavit and got out a warrant for three persons by fictitious names. Did not know who it was that was in custody. Bennett issued the warrant. Howk sat with him. Next, Meacham came for me with a message. Said the defendant in that warrant wished to see me. He went with me. Was admitted to the room where the negro was, by Lowe. This was in the attic, and at about three in the afternoon. Don't remember about Meacham's going in with me. Lowe said, "My name is Lowe." I said, "Lowe the marshal?" He said, "Yes." Said I, "Are you the man that has this man in custody?" He replied, "I am." I asked him by what authority. He said he had a warrant. Took it from his pocket and showed it to me. I sat down on the bed and read the warrant. I said to Lowe, I saw nothing irregular about it, except that there was no seal on it. Lowe said it was not customary for such papers to have a seal. That it was issued by a Commissioner who was a very good lawyer. Afterward I talked with Jennings about buying John. He asked fourteen hundred dollars. Mitchell advised him to take less. Nothing said about Jennings being an agent for the owner on a power of attorney. . . . No other paper was shown me then, nor was any thing said about any other paper under which he was held. I asked Lowe for his authority, and he showed me his warrant. Heard nothing about a power of attorney until the indictment was found. *Know* that nothing was said about a power of attorney to me, or in my hearing, that day. . . .

Cross-examined. I was sent for to go to the room. Meacham came for me. Said he was sent by Lowe. I swear that no power of attorney was shown me. I drew the affidavit on which the warrant was issued. I said to the crowd that the warrant appeared all right except that it had no seal. I referred to a *stamp seal.* But my recollection is, that no *scroll seal* was observed by me. After leaving the room, I went to a drug store and drew an indemnifying bond for the constable. Distance to Elyria, sixteen miles. I advised them to abstain from all interference. I advised those who talked with me about the bond, not to sign it. Think Lowe said to me he wanted I should communicate what I had heard as to the authority by which John was held. The object in getting out the warrant for the arrest of Jennings, etc., was to arrest them for kidnapping. Watson alleged that John was a freeman.

Direct examination resumed. I did not ad-vise against resorting to a writ of *habeas corpus.*

Cross-resumed. I did not advise about getting a writ of *habeas corpus.* Said that the Probate Judge was the only one that had the power to issue that writ. I then understood so, and do now, that the Probate Judge had such power.

Direct resumed. Had no conversation with Jennings in which Mason County seal was spoken of.

Isaac Bennett. Live at Wellington. Am a Justice of the Peace. Between two and three in the afternoon, Watson came into the Town House. Said a man had been kidknapped, — made affidavit. I questioned him as to his being free. He said he supposed they were taking him without any authority whatever. I issued the warrant. Next, I heard that John had been arrested on a warrant.

ELEVENTH DAY. —MORNING SESSION.
Thursday, May 5.

[The Court was not in session yesterday, being in attendance upon the festivities connected with the marriage of its only daughter. This morning the trial proceeds.]

Loring Wadsworth, Daniel Williams, and Eli Boies have been released from jail on $500 bail each.

Court convened at 9 o'clock. Before proceeding with the trial of Charles Langston, Judge SPALDING presented a motion of the counsel for the defence, 'for the immediate sentence of Simeon Bushnell, who has been convicted by the jury, the special cause for this motion being that the said Bushnell desires and intends to apply to the Judges of the Supreme Court for a writ of *habeas corpus* that he may be set at liberty, that Court having decided upon the petition lately presented that the cases had not proceeded far enough to have the writ granted, the defendants not having been sentenced." The Court received the motion, but remarked that it was evident that when he was sentenced there would be another interruption of the proceedings of this Court, for which reason it would be better to conclude this case before passing sentence upon Bushnell.

Isaac Bennett. — Examination-in-chief continued. The constable said they had a warrant. Asked me about it. I told him not to send the warrant, if they had papers. Heard of the indemnifying bond. Advised against signing it. Was gone a part of the afternoon. It was about a half hour or an hour before the Rescue when I went to the room where John was. Lowe, I think in the ante-room, showed me the warrant. I read it. Made the same observation in regard to it that Dickson did. I expected to see an official seal, but saw none. Did see the small scroll seal. Lowe said he was a Deputy United States Marshal, and had John under arrest. After this, I went into the room where John was. There were there Lowe, Mitchell, Jennings, Mandeville, I think Soules, and perhaps Sciples. Think Mr. Meacham was with me at the entrance in the ante-room with Lowe. Don't recollect what was said in the room with John except that Jennings took a paper out of his pocket and handed it to me, saying it was a power of attorney. I took it — did not read it. Handed it back, and nothing more was said about it. I think this was said, — that they would go down and show their paper, or papers, to the crowd. Don't know but he said (Lowe) that he would go to the Town House. He said so at one time, and I think it might have been then. Don't recollect who proposed it. Lowe said nothing to me of any other paper, nor did he say that there was any thing but a warrant, and he said it was that under which he held him. Not a word was said about the boy having been arrested under the power of attorney, nor about his having been arrested under a warrant and then turned over to Jennings to hold under his power of attorney. Never heard of this until to-day in Court.

Lowe went below and commenced reading a paper, which Patton took and finished reading. I was about six feet from them, at the left. He had one paper only. I understood that the paper read was the warrant. Saw nothing and heard nothing of another paper then. I never heard the claim there that the boy was held by virtue of the power of attorney. I dissuaded from violence, etc. A good many — the most of our Wellington folks coincided with me in this. There were four hundred or five hundred in the crowd in the afternoon; the most at the last. At this time about two thirds or three fourths of them were made up of Wellington people, and people from its vicinity. All there then that I talked with, agreed with me. I don't recollect of conversing with any one but our people there. Saw defendant towards sun-down, on the platform south of the tavern. There was quite a crowd there, discussing the propriety of serving the Justice's warrant. Langston said it was best to take legal measures if any, and not do any thing by force. I think he expressed that opinion generally. I had some talk with defendant about serving this warrant. I thought it better not be served. He thought it had. I said I thought the constable had better not interfere with the authority of the United States if they had a commissioner's warrant. I think that Langston said that a constable, if he had a process put into his hands was under obligation to serve it. That a constable couldn't judge of any thing outside of his warrant. It was somewhere in connection with that, that he said was best to pursue legal measures and avoid violence. This is the only time that I saw him that day.

William Howk. I spoke to defendant Langston. Asked him if he was brother of J. M. Langston. He said he was. He (Langston) thought it best to have a public examination. Said that he didn't mean to have any thing

illegal done. He told a man to keep quiet, This conversation took place shortly before the rescue. Just at the time of this conversation, Lowe came down to read his warrant. . . .

. . . *Cross-examined.* Langston said he did not want any thing illegal done. But he thought it was due to the people that there should be a trial on the magistrate's warrant. Did not hear him say that the negro ought to be rescued whether the papers were right or wrong. Don't know what the man or men that defendant advised to be quiet was or were doing. . . . I have given all, in substance, that I heard Langston say.

Direct resumed. The great majority of the crowd stood looking on. There was talking and laughing. I was there myself to keep the people quiet. Heard Doctor Boies advising to quiet. Saw no appearance of any taking the lead. . . .

Direct resumed. I was on the ground all the time, from the time I left the Town House until the boy was taken. Saw what was going on.

B. Meacham, Constable at Wellington. I was there all day. Crowd there attracted by the fire at 2, P. M. A man from Oberlin (Watson) came in the Town House not far from three in the afternoon. Got a warrant for arrest of the Southerners. I went immediately to the attic. Went alone, I think, at first. There was quite a crowd around the house when I first went there. They were then keeping people out. Wadsworth told me, on telling my business, that I could go in. Think the door of the room the boy was in was fastened. Think a man by the name of Phelps went up with me. Found Lowe, Jennings, and Mitchell there. Wadsworth also was in the room. May have been more there. Don't remember whether Jacob Wheeler was there. I applied to Lowe. Told him I had a warrant. Commenced reading it to him. He said I had no authority to arrest him. That he had a warrant that he had got at Columbus, signed by one of the Commissioners. Showed me the warrant. Claimed to hold the man under that warrant. No claim to hold him under any other paper. None shown. Nothing said about a power of attorney, nor about an agent. Jennings was lying on the bed. Took no part in the conversation. Lowe said he was marshal, and held the boy in custody under the warrant. Had been in the room but a few minutes when I went out. Went to see Esq. Dickson or Bennett on my own motion. Saw Dickson. Returned with him to the room. Lowe read the warrant to us. Dickson read it. Said he saw no defect in the warrant except the want of a seal. Lowe said none was necessary. Dickson advised me not to arrest. Lowe showed me his authority — his warrant. Nothing but the warrant showed to me and Dickson. Jennings staid on the bed. Took no part in the conversation. Nothing said then by any one about a power of attorney, nor about his being held under any. Lowe did not say that he had arrested him under the warrant, and had turned him over to Jennings to be held under a power of attorney, nor any thing of the kind. I kept before Dickson. Heard nothing said then about the purchase of the negro. I returned again pretty late in the afternoon. I had refused to make the arrest. A good many were urging that I ought to make the arrest. As I went in the third time, either Soules, Mandeville, or Sciples asked me to go in with them, or I asked them to go. I went this time to get Lowe to exhibit his papers to the crowd. My impression is that three men stood at the back door below and volunteered to go. Lowe hesitated, but finally agreed to go out and read his warrant. Nothing was said at that time by any one about a power of attorney. None showed. Jennings said nothing then, nor to me that day. Patton read the warrant below. It was then I saw him for the first time. I told the people before I went up, that I would go up and get Lowe to come down and show his warrant. When we came down, I think I said to the crowd, if they would listen, Lowe would read his authority. He commenced, but Patton took it and read it. Lowe was not able to read it well. But one paper shown then. Never heard any thing said about a power of attorney until the first trial. Warrant was read to the crowd. Saw Langston two or three times in the afternoon. He spoke to me about serving the warrant I had. Did not see him after I went to the room the last time. Defendant said it was my duty to serve the warrant.

Cross-examined. Defendant did advise me to serve the warrant several times. I was round in the crowd. I was trying to get signers on the bond. Some signed the bond, I think, but it did not come into my hand after it was signed. Told defendant of this. Defendant, and perhaps fifty or a hundred others, urged me to sign it. . . . . Don't know what passed after I left the room with Dickson. Lowe did not refer me to Jennings, as the person who had John under a power of attorney. The warrant was all he claimed under. Lowe said he would take the negro to Columbus or to Cleveland, and have an examination, and if he was not legally held, he should be given up.

John G. W. Cowles. Was at Wellington and at Oberlin on the 13th. Arrived at a little after one in the afternoon at Oberlin. No excitement then. Went to my home, three fourths of a mile. Learned first of the arrest of John about two in the afternoon. Had walked home and taken dinner. Was in my room, when Patton and Scrimgeour came to my room in haste, and told me a boy had been kidnapped. Asked me to get up my horse and go in pursuit. Did get it up. We then started for Wellington. Saw a crowd at Watson's store. Went right by. If it were half past one that the team arrived, it must have been late that we started. It took me fifteen minutes to walk home, twenty minutes to eat dinner, was in my room five minutes, took five minutes to harness up. We passed some parties on the road. Watson got there first. Met a boy coming back on horseback. Said John was there. Said there was a crowd about the hotel then. There was not two hundred then — think 150 scattered all about the square. Mostly away from the hotel. There seemed to be men standing all around the hotel. Noticed none at the time I arrived. Saw nothing like organization, or any one giving directions. It was at first said that he was a boy who had been at work on the railroad, and that he had been taken while the others were at dinner. This was afterwards corrected by the true statement. First I heard that it was claimed that there was any authority for holding him. I heard it from Patton. This was an hour or more after our arrival. He said that he knew the man who had him; it was Lowe, of Columbus, a Deputy-Marshal — had him under a warrant. Nothing more was said during the whole time, as to any other paper than a warrant. Saw John Watson on the porch above, some time after our arrival. He came out of the house, gesticulated, and said the boy had been kidnapped. Told the crowd to keep quiet, to wait. As soon as they could have the men arrested, it would all be right. That they would have them arrested. This was before I had heard from Patton that there was a warrant. Saw Bennett on the platform after this. Among the first things that I heard, after my arrival, was, that John had been brought out. Mr. Marks told me that the boy had been out, and said he wanted to go back. I told him that amounted to nothing; that under different circumstances, he would tell a different story — that he could say nothing else, with them at his back. Intimated that he had told John to come out. Said they would have had John, if the guns had not been pointed and scared him. Said *we* (Democrats) want John as much as you do.

ELEVENTH DAY. — AFTERNOON SESSION.

It was the smaller portion of the crowd who had weapons. Some of them that seemed to be excited, a third or a quarter of the crowd. I heard a number of persons say that what they wanted was some one to take the lead. I replied, "keep quiet" — that things were going well enough as it was — that Patton had gone up stairs, and would learn how the thing was. Some feared the train would come in, etc. I was not in the attic room. Saw Lowe on the steps; Patton by his side. I heard they had come down, and were reading a warrant. This I learned on asking for Patton, of the landlord. He said he had gone out, and was reading the warrant. Went to him. He was reading it. I looked over his shoulder, and read it. There was no other paper read there, or begun to be read. I know there was no other paper there. This was but a few minutes, not more than from ten to fifteen, before the rescue. Lowe said something — that it was not customary to have a seal, in reply to Patton's remark, after he had finished reading the warrant, that he noticed the warrant lacked a seal. He said it was not the custom to have one. Lowe then appealed to the crowd that, as they saw he had the proper papers, they should let him go on in the discharge of his duty. Did not see Mr. Langston there, to my knowledge.

Cross-examined. Mr. Patton began to tell the crowd, after he had read it, that the warrant had no seal. The portion of the warrant relating to the power of attorney had been read before I got there. From one hundred to two hundred persons near the place where the warrant was read. *Did not* hear the reply to the reading of the warrant, that they "did not care for the papers, they would have the boy any way." Patton and Scrimgeour went with me. The first intimation that I had that there was any warrant or legal authority for holding John, was from Mr. Patton, about an hour after we got there. He had been up stairs and returned. The first information I had was derived from Mr. Patton. Afterwards it was talked of in the crowd. Understood that there was a marshal there. This was after 4 o'clock, P. M., at least an hour and a half before the rescue. I heard it said that it was claimed that John was a negro slave. Do not recollect of hearing any one remark that he was a fugitive; but some said he should not go South, at any rate. The front door was locked. I applied at the back door for admission to go up stairs, but was refused. Marks and Wood said they knew John. Said nothing as to his being a fugitive. These were the Democrats, who said they were as anxious as we to have John get away. Don't recollect but these two, who knew John.

James L. Patton. . . . The first I heard when I got into the crowd was, that John had been out on the platform. I set myself to work to inquire into the real state of things. Learned but little, for some time. Three quarters of an hour after I came there, John Watson came out on to the platform. Said he had been in — seen the boy — talked with him; that the boy had been kidnapped. He first asked the crowd to wait and keep quiet; that a warrant was being got out for those who had him in custody, and as soon as this could be done, and they had been taken before the magistrate the boy would be set at liberty. This was not far from 4 o'clock in the afternoon. Don't remember that any thing was said in reply to this. . . . Lowe said nothing to me about there being an agent or power of attorney, or that he had arrested him and turned him over to the agent, or any thing of this kind. . . . Lowe complained to me that the 5 P. M. train was gone, and he now would have to wait till 8, P. M. We had a con-

versation about his going to the Town Hall, or obeying the warrant, so as to go and show his papers. He urged that he should not go, because he was a United States Marshal; that they had no right to serve the warrant on him for that reason. . . . He objected to going down, on excuse of personal safety. I assured him he should be safe. He then went down with me. The constable was ahead of us. Lowe wanted to stop at the back door. Took him to front side, south of it. I or the marshal called the crowd. Lowe took the warrant out of his pocket and handed it to me. I read it. I objected to it for its want of an official seal. Lowe said it was not customary to have one. He then said they had seen his authority, and now he wanted them to let him go. A man whom I did not know, stepped up and said that he was a stranger, and what he could say would have no influence on the crowd, but that he thought the crowd would pay no attention to the papers. This address was in a tone not calculated to reach the crowd. There was no other reply. As this gentleman was yet talking with Lowe, we heard a noise at the back door. Lowe said advantage had been taken of his absence. We then went to the room, and the stranger with us. When we got to the door, Lowe spoke. Said he wanted myself and the stranger to come in. We went in. After we got in, the stranger, Lowe, and myself, went to the other side of the room. Jennings, Mitchell, and Davis were in the room. Do not remember Sciples, Mandeville, etc. We urged upon Lowe the policy of letting the boy go. The stranger said, "You had better let the boy go than to lose your life." Lowe said, *No* — that he knew what the law was — that he could not let the boy go without being liable for the boy. Just then there was a rush — the window was broken in. There was a number in the hall as we passed in. Negotiated about letting the boy go. Appealed to Jennings — no response. Lowe finally asked if we would protect him if he let the boy go. We said we would. He said to Jennings he did not want the house torn down — these people had befriended them.

Jennings then let the door go gradually open. I had shouted to the persons outside the door, and asked if they would stand by me in protecting the men if they gave up the boy. They said they would. As the door opened I asked where the boy was. Just then he passed by me with some one with him. He passed down. It was getting dark then, but I could see so as to recognize persons in the room, but not on the outside. The boy went out with one who was there when I went in. Only one was with him. No one came in. This was the third time I was there. I heard nothing said about a power of attorney. I never heard of that power of attorney except as it is recited in the warrant until the former trial. It was not read or commenced to be read when Lowe was below reading or having his papers read. There was but one paper read there or then. Jennings told me at the second visit to the room that he owned the boy. At the time of John's escape, the persons in that room were Lowe, Jennings, Mitchell, Davis, Mandeville, Winsor, I think, and this stranger, Griffin. There were others, but I did not know their names. Langston was not in the room to my knowledge. I know him. Did not see Langston when I went up, nor in the inside of the building at all.

Cross-examined. Saw defendant on the porch that afternoon. The negro got away just as I have stated. I did not describe in my testimony before the manner in which the negro was taken out of the room. I did say that I saw the negro put into the wagon. I did not go out of the door, until some time after the negro went out. He went out with that one man alone. He did not go out by the order of Lowe, Jennings, Mitchell, or myself. Did not know of Jennings getting the punch in his head. There was a good deal of noise come up to the room from below. No one went out of that room to my knowledge before John did. After my arrival in the crowd I heard it reported that there was a warrant, but heard it contradicted. I saw the warrant in the room, but did not read it. The first I read it was at the time I read it to the crowd. Between half-past four and five I communicated to the crowd the proposition about a committee, made by Lowe. I may have said to them that the marshal held him there by virtue of a warrant issued by a court of the United States — that I thought the marshal's papers or authority were right. I told them that he had told me that he had telegraphed to Cleveland for aid — that if they wished to proceed legally they would have to send to Elyria — that if they waited to do that it would be too late. No reply. As to the Committee, some said Columbus was too far south. The marshal did not request me to assist him. I could not swear positively that no one came into the window, because my back was turned to it for about a minute. I never spoke to John in my life. The name of the stranger is Charles C. Griffin. I heard the remark from some one the first time I went that they did n't care any thing about the papers, they would have the negro at any rate. I supposed the man that went out with John to be Winsor, but could not swear to it. Thought so because I had seen him and John walking together.

R. H. Stevens. Reside at Oberlin. Did in September last. Was there when the young men were getting together to go to Wellington. I was at work. Saw men moving back and forward. Asked what was up. It was replied that John had been kidnapped. That he was taken by some suspicious characters who were hanging 'round Wack's tavern. That they had no legal authority, but had kidnapped John. This was about two in the afternoon. I saw no common design on the part of the people then. Not more than fifty went from Oberlin that I saw. Heard no other statement except that John was kidnapped. Never heard defendant's character as a peaceable, law-abiding citizen called in question.

Cross-examined. Character is estimated in Oberlin somewhat as elsewhere. The people of Oberlin would not call it a case of kidnapping if a slave was arrested under papers in legal form. It was said that the crowd were going to rescue John from the kidnappers. I heard afterwards that the suspicious-looking men, who were hanging about Wack's, were Kentuckians.

John Watson was called to contradict the testimony of Sciples. He swore positively that he was not upon the second floor of Wadsworth's tavern with Langston a second time, nor did he there have any such conversation with him as was averred by Sciples. He went after Langston at Lowe's request, when Lowe and Langston had their first interview, and they went up to the attic without stopping. And they did not go up together or meet up there under any circumstances afterwards.

Mr. BACKUS here remarked that the defence had but one more witness, who had been tele-graphed for, but, owing to a mistake in the name telegraphed, he had not reached the city as yet. He then recalled Mr. Cowles to inquire on one or two points. He testified emphatically that no one passed up the ladder which was put up to the attic window for some time before John was rescued. The ladder was lifted up by several men, and pushed against the window by which the window was broken. No one passed up the ladder at that time.

TWELFTH DAY. — MORNING SESSION.

On the opening of Court, District-Attorney BELDEN called the attention of the Court to the following cases: —

United States *v.* John Mandeville.
Same *v.* Henry D. Niles.
Same *v.* Daniel Williams.
Same *v.* Robert L. Cummings.

The DISTRICT-ATTORNEY stated to the Court that the defendants in the above cases wished to withdraw their plea of Not Guilty, and enter that of *nolle contendere.* He said he had carefully examined into the facts bearing upon the cases of these men, and that although a breach of the law had probably been committed, he was satisfied the defendants acted from impulse. He viewed the cases of these men in a different light from those who came ten miles for the purpose of rescuing John. The defendants were poor men, had voluntarily*
come forward to answer to this indictment, had

---

* A tough story; the District-Attorney's agents had been "at them" for a number of days, giving them absolutely no rest till they *consented* to this arrangement.

borrowed money to get here with, and wished to save expense of counsel [a truly funny idea], and would therefore throw themselves upon the Court. The District-Attorney hoped that in consideration of these facts the Court would make their punishment as light as possible.

The Court called upon the defendants to rise. It then asked them if they had any thing further to say with respect to their cases. They replied that Judge Belden had substantially expressed their feelings and wishes.

The Court then said that in consideration of the arguments offered by the District-Attorney, it would make the punishment light, and would name as the penalty twenty dollars fine, and the costs of the prosecution, and imprisonment in Cuyahoga County Jail for 24 hours.

The Marshal chose to consider Bennett's Forest City House the rendezvous, and the *city limits* the bounds of " Cuyahoga County Jail," and enforced the sentence accordingly.

[As the precise nature of the plea of *nolle contendere* has been made a matter of considerable dispute, we append here the Journal entry of the Court in respect to these defendants. The first case will serve as the text; the entry being similar in each case.

Friday, May 6th, 1859.

The United States ⎞   No. 79.
           v.   ⎬ Indictment for rescuing a
John Mandeville. ⎠   fugitive from service.

This day came the District-Attorney on the part of the United States, and the said defendant being present at the bar of the Court here, on his motion the said defendant has leave to withdraw the plea of Not Guilty before entered to the said indictment, and thereupon the said indictment being again read to him, he protesting that he is not guilty in manner and form as he is charged in said indictment, — for plea says that he will not farther contend with the said United States, with which plea the Attorney for the United States is content.

It is farther considered by the Court that the said defendant, John Mandeville, be imprisoned in the jail of Cuyahoga County, for the term of twenty-four hours, and pay a fine of twenty dollars and the costs of this prosecution.

And thereupon the said defendant is committed to the custody of the marshal of this District, to be by him forthwith conveyed to the jail of Cuyahoga County, in pursuance of the sentence of the Court.]

—— The examination of witnesses then proceeded.

Nelson Sexton. On the morning of Sept. 13th, heard it said that a boy had been kidnapped and taken off. Shortly after, a boy came from Wellington on horseback and reported that the kidnappers had the boy at Wellington. I spoke to him several words. Said he came to inform the people of Oberlin.

Cross-examined. I live at La Grange. I was in Oberlin that day to make arrangements to study — am studying there now. First saw the excitement at Watson's store about one or two o'clock. Don't recollect seeing Langston in the crowd. Think the remark to which I have testified was made by Mr. Lyman.

Clark Elliot. Live in Oberlin. Was there Sept. 13th, 1858. Was among the crowd at Oberlin. It was said in the crowd that John Price had been *kidnapped.* Heard no other representation as to the manner in which he was taken away. Nearly two o'clock in the afternoon when my attention was first attracted to the crowd. Cannot say how many people left that afternoon.

Isaac M. Johnson. Live at Oberlin. About 2, P. M., Sept. 13, 1858, persons came up to a buggy in the street, and inquired " whose wagon that was?" The owner said, " What's up?" " Why, a man has been kidnapped and we want to go after him." They took the wagon and started after him. Bartholomew and Lyman it was said, had seen John in the hands of the Southerners.

Henry Evans. Was in Wadsworth's Hotel at the time of the Rescue, in the third story of the building. There was a door leading out of the entry into the room in which he was, swinging *out* towards me. I had been in this anteroom twenty minutes. Was then at the door on the side it opened. There was no handle to the door on the side towards me. There was no person went out of the ante-room in which I was into that in which John was, except Lowe and Patton, and perhaps another. As soon as the door opened John passed out, and only one man with him. Langston was not there.

Cross-examined. There were eight in the ante-room. Lincoln, Scott, Butler, Fox, Copeland, Rutledge, Nevins, and self. There was but one man armed that I have knowledge of.

(On the question as to whether the witness was armed, the defence urged that he should not be forced to give in any evidence that might tend to criminate himself or be used by the District-Attorney when the witness was put on his own trial. After some discussion by counsel the Court ruled that the witness could refuse to answer if he chose, but if he did his whole testimony would be ruled out.)

Witness had a small rifle. When John came out, Winsor came out with him and partly carried him.

J. L. Wadsworth. Was at Wellington on the day of excitement; saw the negro come down the stairs; witness was at the head of the first flight of stairs; had been there a short time; went into the house at the rear; when the Marshal went out to read the papers, witness had a conversation with Langston — he thinks it was at that time — at the front door right against the door post; this conversation was either when the Marshal came out to read the papers, or it was after the boy escaped. Was present only about half an hour.

Wm. Bryce. Lives in Cleveland; is a lawyer; was in during trial of Bushnell, and heard R. A. Cochran give his testimony in that; heard him also in this. In the Bushnell case Cochran testified that he was not present at the time the acknowledgment was made; think he said the first time he saw that acknowledgment was after he came here.

Cross-examination. Witness has no doubt that Cochran, in the Bushnell case, swore he was not present when the acknowledgment was taken; and in this case he testified that before the parties left his office he came in and suggested some alterations, which were made; this difference in his testimony surprised the witness when he heard it.

Direct resumed. Mr. Cochran, in the first case, said he had no personal knowledge of the acknowledgment.

Mr. Patton being recalled, testified to the above discrepancy in the testimony of Robert A. Cochran in the two trials.

Mr. Cowles, being recalled, testified as to Cochran's testimony in the first trial, that he had no personal knowledge of the acknowledgment.

Here the defence rested, with the exception of several witnesses upon this point of the impeachment of Cochran, which should afterwards be brought in.

Prosecution in rebuttal.

William Sciples, recalled. I was at the foot of the stairs in the lower story at the time John was taken out, at the front door. As John came down there were two had hold of him, one on each side. Langston and Watson came up to where I and Jacob Wheeler were standing, and went up stairs, and three or four minutes after that, John came down. I was standing at the foot of the stairs at the request of Wadsworth.

Cross-examined. Had been down but a few minutes, not ten minutes. Came down from the room where John was with Jennings, Mitchell, Doland, and Dr. D. Wadsworth. What I said was, that John Watson was the only man in the crowd in the hall above, who, a short time before had been talking about going to Elyria after a Writ. I did not say before, that Watson was the only man in the crowd that went up in the first rush, that I knew.

Jacob Wheeler, recalled. I was in the front of the house when John passed out. Sciples and I had, a few minutes before, been standing at the foot of the stairs to prevent the crowd from going up stairs. About the time we were standing there the defendant and Watson and another colored man came there and wanted to go up and we let them go up. It might have been five minutes before the boy came down.

Cross-examined. The trouble about the gun happened after Watson and Langston went up first. I was not standing at the stairway with Sciples guarding the door there. Think this was after Lowe went down, but am not sure.

Jacob K. Lowe, recalled. Was in the room when John was taken out. Cannot state that I saw any one come into the room just before John left. From eight to twelve were in the room when John went out. Patton did not talk through the door of the room, nor say that if we would give up the negro we should be protected, nor any thing of the sort.

Cross-examined. Witness recollects no conversation about letting the boy go for fear they would injure Mr. Wadsworth's house; pretty positive that witness had conversation with Patton after returning to the room; don't know that Patton returned to the room with witness; the remarks made to witness by the stranger to the effect that the people would not regard the warrant, was made before the time Patton says it was.

Mr. Jennings, recalled by prosecution. There was no conversation between witness and Patton about letting John go; Mr. Patton hallooed to the crowd outside that he would have the nigger soon; he asked witness to let John go, and he, witness, slacked up; the crowd came in and John was taken out and Patton backed out with them; Langston came in to the door with the crowd when John was taken out.

Mr. Bennett, recalled by defence. Witness is acquainted with William Sciples and has been for six or seven years; the character of Sciples for truth and veracity is not as good as men's in general. Would believe him under oath *in some cases.*

Mr. Meacham, recalled by defence. Witness has known Sciples for seven years; his reputation for truth and veracity is not as good as men's in general; should not believe him on oath.

Mr. Watson, recalled by defence. Witness went up stairs but once during the afternoon with Langston, this was before any paper was read at all. (This contradicts Sciples).

Mr. Gillet, sworn. Lives in Wellington; have known Sciples six or seven years; it is generally believed he is not a man of truth; it is not as good as men's in general. Would not believe him under oath if he were interested.

(This witness is one of the indicted and has the snows of seventy-four winters upon his head. The sensation in Court, as this old man, one of the most respectable citizens of Lorain County, and of the State, came from the jail, was very decided and deep.)

Loring Wadsworth, has known Sciples for ten years. Would not believe him under oath if he were interested.

Here the testimony closed, and the argument for the prosecution was opened by District-Attorney BELDEN. As in the former case we can find no better reports of the arguments for the Government than those given in the city dailies. The report of Judge BELDEN's speech is cut from the *Herald*, and that of Judge BLISS from the *Leader*.

District-Attorney BELDEN opened for the Government. After introductory remarks he took up the testimony in the case under the several heads.

1st. The District-Attorney assumed that it is proved that John was a slave of Bacon's, and escaped into Ohio, and was pursued by Bacon's agent, and seized as alleged in the indictment. Those facts are so plain that he would not spend time upon them. That John was rescued, he argued, was equally plain, unless it be true that, as Patton says, Jennings let him go. The District-Attorney argued that, even if the negro was given up by fear of destruction of property, etc., was just as much a rescue as if actually forced from them.

Counsel then commented upon the power of the master to take his slave either by himself or agent, and claimed that the power of attorney was properly executed and was good; he characterized the attempt to impeach Mr. Cochran as impotent and miserable. Counsel then passed on to the manner in which John was captured at Oberlin, arguing that the course pursued by Jennings was the proper one, owing to the state of feeling at Oberlin.

Counsel then passed on to the agency Langston used in the rescue, characterizing his conduct as very cunning and very hypocritical, very shrewd, but very deceiving. Counsel then argued as to the evidence showing the exhibition at Wellington of the power of attorney, claiming that it was well known to Langston that there was such power in the hands of Jennings; that the crowd knew as well about the existence of the power of attorney as they did of the warrant.

The District-Attorney then said he would read some law to the jury. Here Mr. Backus, counsel for the defence, arose and asked if he understood the counsel for the prosecution was about to follow the case of the *Wanderer*, in South Carolina, where counsel claimed that the jury were the judges of the law as well as the facts; and where the Federal Court held that the jury were the judges of the law. Mr. Belden thereupon became very much excited, and pronounced Mr. Backus a demagogue, — said the Court of South Carolina did not hold any such thing. Mr. Backus said such was the newspaper report. And thereupon Mr. Belden grew as black in the face as the Devil is painted, and yelled out, "*Yes, newspaper reports, they are pretty authority, when the very atmosphere we breathe is blackened with their lies.*" The District-Attorney evidently hates newspapers.

The District-Attorney cooled down and came back to the case, arguing that the proof showed a common intent, and therefore notice to one of the crowd was notice to all. He argued, also, that Langston was in the crowd not to keep the peace, not to punish kidnappers, but to rescue the negro. Counsel claimed that the negro was in the custody of Jennings from the time Jennings arrived in Wellington; the expressions used by Langston were pointed out and commented upon as proving his agency in the rescue.

THIRTEENTH DAY. — MORNING SESSION.

District-Attorney BELDEN continued his argument, and made the following proposition which he claimed to be law, to wit, That if a party interfere with a Federal officer, who is discharging his duty, by arresting him under legal process issued by State authority, the interference is as unlawful as the interposition of violence would have been, and the fact that interference was made under cover of legal process can be plead not in justification of the act, but merely for mitigation of sentence after conviction. The proposition was sustained by a citation from a newspaper (whether one "blackened with lie," the District-Attorney did not say), of a recent decision in the United States Supreme Court in the Booth case. This decision was pronounced by Chief Justice Taney, and the point referred to is as follows: —

"And although, as we have said, it is the duty of the marshal or other person holding him to make known by a proper return the authority under which he detains him, it is at the same time imperatively his duty to obey the process of the United States; to hold the prisoner in custody under it, *and to refuse obedience to the mandate or process of any other government.* And consequently it is his duty not to take the prisoner, nor suffer him to be taken, before a State Judge or Court upon a *habeas corpus* issued under State authority. No State Judge or Court, after they are judicially informed that the party is imprisoned under the authority of the United States, has any right to interfere with him, or to require him to be brought before them. And if the authority of a State, in the form of judicial process or otherwise, should attempt to control the marshal or other authorized agent of the United States in any respect, in the custody of his prisoner, it would be his duty to resist it, and to call to his aid any force that may be necessary to maintain the authority of the law against illegal interference. No judicial process, whatever form it may assume, can have any lawful authority outside of the limits of the jurisdiction of the Court or Judge by whom it is issued; and an attempt to enforce it beyond these boundaries is nothing less than lawless violence."

[If the above is good law, our State Courts have no right to inquire into the validity of any process purporting to issue from the United States Courts. Even if all the papers were totally irregular, the fact they were issued by a

Federal official is sufficient, and the State Court has no authority to interfere. That places the United States Commissioner above the Supreme Court of Ohio; under the warrant of the former, even if he entirely transcends the plain letter of the Fugitive Law, and sends his warrant out of his own District, even, the State Court cannot interfere. According to this doctrine, Lowe could — had he seen fit — have held John under a warrant admitted to be void, and the State writ of *habeas corpus* would be powerless. The doctrine is as monstrous as that of the Dred Scott decision.]

The argument of the government this morning was only upon legal points involved in the case.

The District-Attorney claimed that the rescue was made from Jennings, the agent of the owner of the slave, aided and assisted by Lowe, the Marshal.

Mr. GRISWOLD opened the argument for the defence.

May it please the Court, and Gentlemen of the Jury: I quite agree with the District-Attorney in the desire expressed by him, that this case should be tried upon its own merits, and without reference to any outside influences. It is manifest, however, that this is a case of peculiar interest, — that considerable excitement has attended this prosecution, and that this case has become and still is a matter of much public remark and comment. I doubt not that the novelty of this prosecution has in part contributed to this; for although we live in a District containing over a million of inhabitants, and not a day's journey distant from a large extent of Slave Territory, yet this is the second case which has ever occurred of a prosecution for the violation of the provisions of the Act of 1850, or of that of 1793. Of the other causes out of which the public interest and excitement have arisen, I need not speak, for I cordially unite with the District-Attorney in urging you to judge of this case impartially and without bias for or against the prisoner at the bar. Yet when I heard the learned gentleman urging you to give this case a fair and candid hearing, I could not shut my eyes to the fact, that you, gentlemen, had been selected as jurors from the ranks of one political party. I mention this to impugn no man's motives, or to impeach the integrity of any officer of this Court. Notwithstanding your political associations and affinities, from my personal acquaintance with you, and my knowledge of your characters, I have confidence to believe that while acting as jurors, you will lay aside all political bias or prejudice, and in nowise be influenced in your decision by any such consideration. For I see among your number men who have filled with credit to themselves and satisfaction to the public, high offices of trust, both in our Municipal and State Government, and others, who, by long lives of industry and integrity, have won the confidence and esteem

of community, and certainly, in any ordinary case, I have no hesitation in saying I would as soon intrust the interests of a client to your keeping as to that of any twelve men I ever saw empanelled in the jury-box. And I have adverted to this matter of your being selected in view of your political associations only the more earnestly to ask of you to judge and decide upon this case regardless of any such influence or prejudice. Again, gentlemen, there is another consideration I feel bound for my client to call to your attention, and to press upon your notice. You know that this right of the jury trial is one of the earliest institutions of the Anglo-Saxon race. Upon this foundation — upon its fairness and equity — has the superstructure of all our liberties been erected. To be tried by a jury of his peers was the right of the humblest man. So deeply was this principle of fair play impressed into the mind of the race (except in the case of Treason), this privilege, from the early days, was extended to all aliens and denizens within the realm. An alien or denizen was entitled to be tried by a jury, one half of whom were of his own race or people, in the language of the law, by a *jury de medietate linguae.* I am aware that in the time of Philip and Mary this right was abolished as to people called Egyptians. It was owing, perhaps, to the then Spanish Alliance, and not to the color of those people. But this harsh provision, as Mr. Chitty calls it, was repealed, and the right restored in the reign of George III., and so far as I know, still exists in England. I am aware that this provision has not become a part of American law, for all men in this land were supposed to be equals.

This may have been theory, but my client can have no jury of his race or color, or of those who are his peers. Not only is he an alien, but in the view of the law which governs this Court, he is an outcast. He has no equality, no rights, except in being amenable to the penal statutes. His condition is described, in the vulgar language of the Kentucky witnesses, to whom in every attribute of manhood he is incomparably superior, as being "only a nigger." In view, therefore, of this misfortune of his birth, — of his color and condition, — that he is one of this outcast race, — that he has no other right but that of being punished, I ask you the more carefully to consider his case, and give him a fair and impartial hearing. I ask you to forget his race and color, and try his case as though he were one of your equals; as though he were, as he is, a man, and had rights; to try him in accordance with your oaths, and the well-established maxims of the law, — that he must be held innocent until his guilt is proven, and that guilt established beyond a reasonable doubt.

With these preliminary remarks I proceed to call your attention to the charges in the indictment and the testimony bearing upon them. The issues presented by the indictment and plea have been properly stated by the District-

17

Attorney. And first, as to the alleged status of John in the State of Kentucky: according to the rules of evidence prevailing in our State Courts, he has not been proved to be the slave of Bacon; mere possession or control establishes no property in man. I do not deny, however, that according to the rulings which obtain in this tribunal, the status of John, as alleged, has been sufficiently proven; and so as to his escape, though we have no direct proof on that subject.

The next point to be considered is the execution of the power of attorney. That John G. Bacon signed the power of attorney I do not propose to controvert; but that it was a legal power of attorney, or that it was legally executed, it seems to me cannot be claimed, and I address myself to your Honor, by any rule of law that obtains in Kentucky or elsewhere. It is shown in proof here that the acknowledgment was taken by a deputy; and yet he has signed to it the name of his principal. I do not deny that if he were authorized to acknowledge instruments of that class, and in doing so had used his own name instead of his principal's, it might have been legal enough; but it seems to me beyond question, that, under no circumstances whatever could he certify with the name of his principal to the *knowledge* of that principal! Certainly, your Honor, no rule of law can authorize one man to certify to *another's knowledge!* There is no question here as to the maxim referred to by your Honor, that what one *does* by another he does by himself; but can it be said that what one *knows* by another, he knows by himself? And if not, how could this deputy certify that his principal knew the persons named in this paper to be the identical persons alleged? And, Gentlemen, if the Court shall thus hold, as it seems to me it certainly must, then, of course, the prosecution must utterly fail. For although Mr. Cochran testifies on this trial that he came in to his office just as Bacon, Mitchell, and Loyd were passing out, having finished the acknowledgment, and that they showed him the paper, and he said he would have an addition made to it, and so took it back to the deputy and had him add two lines in his presence, — yet there is no pretence that this was any *re-acknowledgment;* and it is not denied that the acknowledgment had been fully made before Mr. Cochran came in; and this addition was only an amendment to the *deputy's certificate.* The acknowledgment is alleged to have been made before Cochran; and on the former trial he swore positively that the acknowledgment was not made before him, and that he had no other certain knowledge that it was ever made, than the recognition of the handwriting of his deputy furnished him. But if the Court hold the acknowledgment legal, the next question is, by whom was this arrest made, and from whose custody was John rescued? The District-Attorney has claimed that it makes no difference whether the arrest was made by the Marshal or by the agent. But it seems to me that on this point he has misconceived the law. For it is one matter whether the Fugitive is arrested without process by the agent or his servants, in which case the custody is in the agent only; and quite another matter when he is arrested by virtue of a warrant, issued by a United States Commissioner or Court, in which latter case the custody is in the officer under the warrant, by the terms of which he *cannot* deliver him up to any person whatsoever until he is returned before the commissioner by whom the warrant was issued. The marshal is commanded by the commissioner to bring the alleged slave before him for trial. And these cases are, therefore, infinitely wide apart. If however the marshal is the mere servant of the agent, it is true, as the District-Attorney has said, that it makes no difference whether the agent is at Columbus or at Oberlin. But it is a different matter if the marshal acts under the warrant in his official capacity. And I claim, therefore, that if the arrest be made by the marshal, under, by virtue of, and in obedience to the warrant of the commissioner or court, he cannot part with the custody of the person arrested, without showing contempt of that officer's mandate, and violating his official duty. For the jurisdiction of a commissioner in these cases is precisely that of a district or circuit judge. And would your Honor say, that if your Honor had issued a warrant for the apprehension of a person, that warrant being in the usual form, and commanding the return of the person to be apprehended before your Honor, to answer to the complaint of the person who sued out the warrant; will your Honor say that the officer could make the arrest and then deliver the person out of and away from his own custody into the hands of some other person, before he had returned him before your Honor, as the warrant commanded, without disobeying the precept of the warrant, and treating with contempt the authority under which he made the arrest? Is an agent thus authorized to override all courts and processes? Will your Honor so rule? Unless your Honor does, which of course we cannot believe you will; then, since, according to Mr. Lowe's own testimony, he made the arrest, under and by virtue of the warrant, the custody was in him, and could not be alienated by him, until the boy had been returned before the commissioner. And if the custody was in him, the rescue was from him, and *not* from the agent. But this defendant is charged in the indictment with rescuing the boy from the *agent*, — the District-Attorney has totally abandoned the second count of the indictment, — and the Court will tell you, Gentlemen of the Jury, that unless the testimony proves the indictment, the defendant must be discharged. How, then, can you find this defendant guilty? How can you avoid acquitting him, if you must find the custody in the agent Jennings?

But I understand the ingenious District-Attorney to claim, that if the marshal makes the arrest by virtue of the warrant, while the agent is an hundred miles away, the agent may at any time intercept the marshal before he has returned his prisoner to the commissioner, and overriding the authority of the process, take the alleged fugitive into his own custody; take him wherever he pleases, and even SELL him on the spot!! Will your Honor *so* hold? And the District-Attorney claims further, that, while the fugitive is thus held by the agent, whoever shall *advise* a legal inquiry into his authority for so doing, is guilty of nothing less than TREASON against the Government of the United States!!! What does the gentleman mean? Does he soberly claim such to be the *law?* I hope your Honor will not fail to observe the gentleman's position. He bases his claim on the ground of joint custody; that the agent after having taken control of the prisoner, takes further control of the marshal, retaining him as his assistant, and thus invests *himself* with the authority of the United States; and the marshal, retaining his official character and functions, thenceforth has with him a joint control of the person of the prisoner, though the authority of the agent is absolute; resistance to either is resistance to both, and resistance to them is "LEVYING WAR AGAINST THE UNITED STATES." Does the gentleman propose to *hang* my client? No; he says it would be perfectly proper, but unfortunately the indictment is for rescuing under the Act of 1850, and not for treason. But if resistance or rescuing a fugitive from an agent was Treason, I fear the District-Attorney would be no better off, for the custody still remains with the marshal. If the marshal have any power under the law, he must retain the custody of the person whom he has apprehended in obedience to a warrant, until the officer issuing the warrant so commands him. But how can the custody be said to be joint? If the marshal act under the law, then the fugitive is in the custody of the law, and that custody is exclusive. But, again, this joint custody is not alleged in the indictment. The charge is, that the alleged fugitive was in the custody of Jennings, assisted by Lowe. And this new claim of joint custody is something different from the allegations in the indictment. It is a variance to claim that the custody was joint. We are called on to answer for rescuing a person alleged to be a slave, from the custody of one Anderson Jennings, the agent of Bacon, and not from Jacob K. Lowe, a Deputy United States Marshal. What relevance, then, has the decision quoted at such length by the District-Attorney with reference to resisting the process of the United States in the hands of a marshal? Does he seriously claim that the custody of an agent stands upon the same footing with the custody of a marshal? If he does, I should like to have him cite authorities to that effect! But

the gentleman would not for one moment claim that the custody of an *agent* could not be inquired into!

I desire now to call your attention, Gentlemen of the Jury, to the inquiry as to the custody of the alleged fugitive, by whom he was held. Let us first look at the serious contradictions and differences that exist between the leading witnesses on the part of the Government, as to the facts of the arrest and custody.

Lowe swears that he made the arrest, but the District-Attorney urged, and Davis and Mitchell both swear that *they* made the arrest, and that Lowe sat and had the horses; and so the District-Attorney avows flatly that "*Lowe had nothing to do with it.*" Now, doubtless, Mr. Lowe is incorrect; and verily, the District-Attorney cannot be mistaken!

Again, Lowe says that he gave up his custody to Jennings, soon after they arrived at Wellington. But no one supports him. Jennings says he "supposed that he had the control of the nigger all the time;" "but if there was any custody in Lowe, he *probably* gave it up when he, Jennings, joined him." But neither Davis nor Mitchell know any thing about it; they neither saw nor heard of any surrender of authority or change of custody, and pretend not to have had any clear idea of what authority their superiors were claiming to act under; they contented themselves with obeying orders. All they can say about the authority or the custody is, that they think — they won't swear positively — that the power of attorney was shown to Howk, Patton, Dickson, and Bennett. But here they are contradicted, point blank, by every one of these men, who all swear positively and explicitly that not one word was said about a power of attorney, or a solitary reference made to it, except that it was handed at one time to Esquire Bennett, in a way that led him to believe it was shown simply as the basis of the warrant: — which was undoubtedly the case, since it is the only hypothesis consistent with the whole course of the transaction. And whereas the witnesses for the Government deal altogether in vague generalities, and probabilities, and suppositions, and beliefs, any of which they will swear positively to when it seems necessary to make a point, reckless of absurdity, or mutual, or even self-contradiction, the witnesses for the defence impeach them boldly, unqualifiedly, definitely; and in a frank, candid, reasonable, straightforward way, that irresistibly challenges confidence. In the midst of these conflicting statements, you are left to make your own decision. I do not stand here to question or deny that there was a rescue under the provisions of the act of 1850, *provided* the power of attorney was valid, the arrest legal, and the custody as charged in the indictment; but I do claim, and I am justified by the testimony in claiming, that no authority for holding *John* was shown or mentioned, except the warrant; that no one but Lowe pretended to have him in custody, and that the actual custody was in, and the rescue was from Lowe, acting as a Deputy U. States Marshal, and not from Anderson Jennings, as charged in the indictment. The only witnesses upon whom the Government relies to establish the custody are Lowe and Jennings themselves. But Lowe and Jennings are contradicted in almost every material statement by Howk, Dickson, Patton, Bennett, and Cowles. Take their statement as to what occurred in the interview with Dickson. They sent for Dickson to consult with, as a legal adviser, and, of course, as they claim, made known to him the authority under which they were acting. They pretend that the power of attorney was shown, and that Jennings was the chief actor. But Dickson swears positively that nothing whatever was said about any power of attorney; that Lowe was the principal; that he showed the warrant, and claimed that he, as United States Deputy Marshal, had arrested, and then held the alleged fugitive under said warrant.

Again, look at the circumstances connected with the reading of the warrant by Lowe, in front of the building. Lowe swears he had both the power of attorney and the warrant; that one was read, he don't remember which; that the reading of the other was commenced; that when the arrest was made, he seized the paper out of Patton's hands, and hurried back into the hotel. But Patton, Howk, and Cowles contradict and impeach him in the most positive manner.

These witnesses are intelligent, they testify in a fair and candid manner, and there is nothing to impeach their truthfulness. I know the District-Attorney is severe upon Patton, but he can say nothing against Howk, and is forced to respect Cowles, and I feel free to say that in point of intellect, in distinctness of recollection and clearness of statement, I never heard Mr. Cowles surpassed upon the witness stand. He and the others all swear that the warrant alone was read, and that all which Mr. Lowe states as to the power of attorney is absolutely false. The purpose of the reading was to notify the crowd of the authority for holding the alleged fugitive; Cowles and Howk were desirous of ascertaining the truth of the matter. It seems to me that this must be convincing to show that the custody was in Lowe, and not in the agent Jennings. Jennings is no more to be relied upon than Lowe. Why, Jennings swears positively that he saw eight or ten, and he thinks fifteen men come in at that "attic window," and he swears to it over and over again, yet every other witness, including Lowe, Mitchell, and Davis swears that not a soul entered at the window. So as to the number of the crowd and armed men he is equally at fault. I have no doubt Jennings imagined he saw legions, and that to his excited fears a shadow was an armed man. Seeing sights that never happened, hearing sounds that were never made, he the chief witness of the prosecution stands before you self-impeached.

It seems to me, therefore, that the government have failed to establish the custody in Jennings, while, on the other hand, we have abundantly proved it to have been in the marshal under the warrant.

I have briefly adverted to these legal points, and the testimony bearing upon them as they will be fully discussed by my learned associate. But I feel authorized in saying that if the Court shall charge you as we claim, as to the custody of the fugitive, you cannot hesitate for a moment in finding that he was held by the marshal and not by the agent, and that the defendant is clearly entitled to an acquittal.

But if we are wrong in our view of the law, if the power of attorney was legal, if the custody could be joint, we then come to the farther inquiry, whether this defendant was in any manner identified with the rescue of John. Is this charge of the indictment sustained by the proof? and it is upon this part of the case I propose chiefly to direct your attention.

I propose to show from the testimony, that there is no proof that this defendant, Charles Langston, was in any way identified with the crowd who effected the rescue at Wellington, so as to become responsible in the eye of the law, either as actively or passively a participant in its acts. And in order to enter upon this investigation, I lay aside for the time being all questions in regard to the nature of the custody and the guilt of the parties effecting the rescue. Assuming that the custody was legal, and the rescue criminal, I propose to set my client before you in such a light, by the testimony alone, that your oaths will not only warrant, but require of you his acquittal. It is claimed by the prosecution, that he was a member of the crowd, came there for an unlawful purpose, and acted, no matter how quietly, with the unlawful crowd, and is therefore guilty. The fundamental principle of common law, that a man must be held to be innocent until he is proven to be guilty, seems to be reversed by the District-Attorney. He starts out with the presumption that the defendant is of course guilty, and in the light of this assumption he goes at work to set forth portions of the testimony bearing against the defendant, in the strongest possible colors, and endeavors, if possible, to reconcile that in his favor, with this hypothesis of guilt.

But you, Gentlemen, I trust, will not be misled by such logic. You will remember that the law guarantees to the defendant the presumption of innocence, that the entire burden of the proof is upon the prosecution, and that to proceed in this investigation with an assumption that the defendant is, or may be, guilty, is to reverse the law, and disregard his dearest rights. Not only is the defendant entitled to the presumption of innocence, but the proof must not only be consistent with, and establish the guilt, but it must be so strong as to exclude the possibility of innocence, before you should find him guilty. If any act or deed of his is consistent with either guilt or innocence, you are bound to presume against the guilt. Again, the proof must not be a mere preponderance of probability against probability, as to the question of guilt, but must amount to such certainty that not a reasonable doubt can remain; and so long as a reasonable doubt may remain, the defendant *must* be acquitted. It is not optional with the jury. This is the law, as the Court will lay it down for your guidance. And, as I have no doubt you will be governed by it, I am confident that you will find a verdict of Not Guilty. For, starting out, as we are bound to do, with the presumption of innocence, it seems to me there can nothing be found in the proof to change this presumption. And I feel confident that, were the defendant accused with any other charge, and were the testimony no stronger against him, you, Gentlemen, would not leave your seats, to pronounce him innocent. The District-Attorney, however, would have you assume that the gathering at Oberlin was an unlawful gathering, a gathering for an unlawful purpose; that the gathering at Wellington, or at least 300 of the persons in it, were assembled presumptively for a like unlawful purpose, that the crowd were presumptively assured and notified that John was a slave, and in the custody of Jennings; and that this defendant, being in some part of the whole crowd of 500, was, necessarily, one of those seeking to effect a rescue, and presumptively active in the use of unlawful means!

Now was there ever before such a perversion of law witnessed in a court of justice? Is *that* the way in which the Federal Government would have its prosecuting attorneys *attack* every man suspected of crime? Why, Gentlemen of the Jury, I venture to say that this gentleman himself never took such a position before, and that he cannot seriously intend it now. But how are these things when viewed in the light of the testimony before you?

The report went out at Oberlin, that a man had been unlawfully seized and carried off by persons who were identified as those that had been skulking in close hiding-places, or abroad under cover of night, evidently enough with no honest purpose in view, for some days or weeks previous. No combination of circumstances could warrant stronger suspicions that a foul deed, and not a lawful one, had been committed. The people hastily ran together, and, being able to learn nothing more than the fact of the abduction, and that the seizure had been made through the vilest deceit, and the parties had been met hurrying toward Wellington, set off thither at once, without consultation or concert, other than the spontaneous unanimity of the desire to ascertain the facts, and, if not too late, prevent an outrage. Surely nothing could be more honorable to the people of a vir-

tuous community, than such a response to such tidings. But the skilful District-Attorney would be glad to dodge all this, if he could, by urging that the people of Oberlin are fanatics, and call any seizure of a colored man, "kidnapping." But, unfortunately, the witnesses unanimously disagree with him. They none of them know of the phrase "kidnapping" being applied in Oberlin, more than elsewhere, to the seizure of a man according to *any* law. What right, then, has the District-Attorney to claim to you that, because such an alarm induced a man to travel nine miles,— that an inhabitant of *Oberlin* should travel nine miles upon any alarm, he intimates is proof presumptive of a guilty purpose! — to look after a man's liberty, which is much dearer to any man than life, he may be safely presumed to have gone about the inquiry with no good intent! And yet the gentleman does gravely urge all this! When an Oberlinite drives out of town nine miles on an ostensibly benevolent mission, you may be sure he has mischief in his heart! This the gentleman urges with no little assurance, as a self-evident proposition; and thereupon the gentleman indulged himself in an harangue against Oberlin generally.

It is worthy of your notice, Gentlemen of the Jury, that this defendant does not appear to have been at any time in the crowd at Oberlin, before their departure to Wellington. Nor does it appear that the defendant is a resident of Oberlin; on the contrary, it is shown he was only there on a visit; that he was a fellow-citizen of Marshal Lowe; that he has resided in Columbus, and is now an inhabitant of Cleveland. I suggest, therefore, to the District-Attorney, that his diatribe upon Oberlin was entirely uncalled for and out of place. The gentleman's denunciations of the unlawful gathering at Oberlin fall harmless at the feet of my client. It does not even appear that the defendant went from Oberlin to Wellington. He was first seen at Wellington, and when or how he came there, we are not informed. And were it shown that he went from Oberlin, which it is not — it should still be remembered that as there were a number who went thus from Oberlin, with no purpose to assist in the rescue, although with more or less interest in, and sympathy for John, this man has the same claim that they have upon the presumption of the law that his purpose was no guilty one, until it is so distinctly proven.

And as to the excitement of the crowd, concerning which so much is said, it will be well for you to call to mind the testimony of the witness Wood, who, although taking great care to make all he could for the government, thoughtlessly allowed it to leak out how the excitement was kept up: that he and others like himself were there, not to participate in the rescue, but to have "*fun generally*," and that they had it by raising such cries as, "Here he goes!" "This way," "Look out, there,' and so kept the crowd rushing from one place to another with much noise and confusion. So, therefore, it is shown a man might go from Oberlin, mingle with the crowd, aid in keeping up the excitement, and still have no part in the rescue. But the District-Attorney claims that going there and remaining, no matter how short a time, in the crowd, was clearly unlawful, and that, having once entered upon an unlawful undertaking, the defendant could not abandon it. I have simply to say, that no authority is shown to sustain so absurd or monstrous a doctrine. But whether law or not, it has no application to this defendant. The point for the government to establish is, Did he entertain any guilty purpose? That he went from Oberlin is no proof of such intent. Nor is it proved by his mere presence in the crowd. For it is abundantly shown, and the Government admits, that a large portion of the crowd had no sympathy with the rescuers, and that numbers went from Oberlin, were there from first to last, and yet took no part in the rescue, nor had any intention of committing any unlawful act, and cannot be charged with any unlawful combination. The mere suspicion of the District-Attorney that this defendant was there to commit an unlawful act, I am sure will not convince you, Gentlemen, that was the fact. The District-Attorney is forced to admit that the conduct of the defendant was peaceful, that he committed no overt act of violence; but he claims the defendant was "a snake in the grass," that, in a secret and underhanded manner, he was inciting others to violence, and was, in fact, one of the instigators of the whole affair. But, in my view, Gentlemen, there is no proof to warrant any such conclusion; but, on the contrary, his whole conduct, so far as the testimony shows, instead of contributing to the excitement, inciting others to perform acts of violence, he was counseling peace and a resort to legal measures. If such be the result of your convictions, I do not doubt he will receive at your hands an honorable acquittal.

Were this an ordinary case, and had it been tried in an ordinary period, I should not longer detain you. But it is something like three weeks since some of the witnesses testified, and the District-Attorney has so confidently claimed a conviction at your hands, I feel it my duty somewhat carefully to review the testimony of the witnesses of the Government bearing upon the conduct of the defendant. And I feel confident that, weighing the evidence and considering the facts in the light of those rules of law, to the benefit of which every man is entitled, you cannot but agree with me in the conclusion I have formed. The first witness was Jennings.

Jennings says, Defendant came into the room and talked with Lowe;—I have taken great pains to give this testimony accurately. Lowe asked him to assist him. He refused, and said we might as well give him up, for "*we* are de-

termined to have him any way." On cross-examination, the same witness says the defendant said, "for *they* are determined to have him." You all recollect the difficulty we had with this witness in fastening him to any tolerable degree of accuracy in his statements, and that, in his grammar, there is no such thing as the first person.

Mr. *Lowe* stated that while he was talking with Langston the train passed Wellington. That this was their *first* interview. And by other witnesses it was ascertained that the train passed at 5:13, P. M. Lowe further says that he, seeing Langston in the crowd, and having known him well at Columbus as a prudent, discreet, and well-disposed person, sent for him to come up, believing he could be persuaded to intercede with the crowd to regard the law and disperse. There is no proof that Langston was in this room — the room where John was — with Lowe either before or after this interview, during which the train passed. It is proved that he was in that room only then. And that when any one testifies that he thinks he was seen going up and down that house at other times, such testimony is altogether unsupported. And Jennings would be least of all reliable upon such a point. He has been proved to have made already too many glaring mistakes and exaggerations. In the matter of the language Langston used, for instance, he shows well enough to you that he is utterly unable to state any material point with accuracy and certainty. At what time this talk was he isn't able to tell you, but thinks it was but a short time before the rescue, not more than half an hour or so; while Lowe swears positively that it was while the train was passing, an hour and a half or two hours before. So he tries to locate it upon Langston at a time and place when Langston could not have been there at all, and when Lowe himself swears he was not there. So that in all this confused and worthless testimony of Jennings, there is nothing to implicate Langston at all. Again, Lowe, who knew Langston well, swears he didn't come into the room at the time of the rescue; others swear positively that no one came in; and yet Jennings is quite sure he saw Langston come in! Doubtless he was one of the immortal *fifteen* that came in through that *window!* What confidence can any one place in such a witness? He soberly believes, he tells us, that ten or fifteen came in through that attic window, when the ladder was put up and every other witness from outside and inside swears positively that no one went in at that window. And so he thinks a crowd came in at the door, — and I believe Mitchell does too, — and hustled John out, while Lowe and all the rest say they saw no one come in; but that the two or three who were in the room all the time went out with him! That "lick" on the head seems to have very dangerously affected his optic nerves!

Mitchell says Langston was there, thinks he

was there more than once; is n't certain about it, and can't tell any thing that was said.

Wack saw Langston about in the crowd, but does n't remember any thing that he (Langston) did. He was acquainted with Langston; testifies to the detail of what was said and done by others, but can remember nothing that Langston said or did, and is quite unable to charge him with doing any thing to favor the rescue. And that nothing could give this Mr. Wack so much pleasure as to testify to any thing that would seem to implicate any of these defendants, we all knew long ago. The relation which he sustains to the people of Oberlin is too peculiar to allow him any other feeling. He is an important witness for the Government; he was one of the first at Wellington; was there from the beginning to the end; saw the whole transaction; knew Langston perfectly well; and yet *even he dare not say* that he saw any thing in his conduct that would implicate him with the rescuing part of the crowd. A willing witness for the Government — none could be more willing — saw Langston often through the afternoon, — watched him closely, — and cannot lisp a syllable against him! Is n't there something significant in such a state of things, Gentlemen of the Jury? And Mr. Wack says, as all the others do, that the crowd was a very promiscuous one, made up of all extremes of sympathies; that there was no concert of action even among the rescuers, but every man was acting for himself.

Wood testifies that he saw Langston some time in the afternoon sitting on a box, and that accosting him, he asked him how things were getting along, and he replied, "They 've turned out well." Then witness told defendant that "there were papers got out for the Southerners, but the constable would not serve them without indemnity bonds," to which Langston replied that "they would have him any way." Now who did he mean by *him?* John the negro, about whom nothing had been said, or Lowe the Marshal for whose arrest the warrant had been issued? It is for you to infer, Gentlemen; and you will say that the latter inference is the only natural one. Nothing could be more violent than the other.

And now I understand the District-Attorney to claim, that, if a person learning that some one has been arrested and seized in a suspicious manner, and so firmly believing that the seizure is contrary to the laws of the State as well as unauthorized by any law whatever, as to be ready to affirm such belief upon oath, calls for or *advises to* a legal inquiry into the facts of the seizure, by state process, before a state magistrate, no matter who the magistrate be or how suspicious the circumstances of the arrest, if the claimant *professes* to act under United States authority, — such call for or advisement of such legal inquiry by such State Tribunal is nothing short of TREASON, being constructively levying war against the United States!!! This is

not for you to decide upon as jurors, but for the Court. But it must go to you, Gentlemen, to show you to what straits the prosecution are driven! And, your Honor, if that has come to be the doctrine of the Courts, I apprehend that it is something totally new in law. For it is not claimed that the boy was in the custody of the Marshal, but the charge of the indictment is that he was in the custody of Jennings as agent, and of Lowe as his assistant. Not in the custody of Lowe as marshal. And if for calling for the legal investigation of *such* a custody, a man is to be held guilty of Treason, I undertake to say that it is worse than any constructive Treason that was ever known in the darkest ages of English tyranny. I will not argue so monstrous a proposition, but leave it for you to decide, Gentlemen of the Jury, so far as it is for you to pass upon it, under what I am sure must be the instructions of the Court.

Wood further says that he saw Langston near the back door shortly before the rush was made, but that he was neither saying or doing any thing, and can't say whether Langston went in or not. Now Wood is evidently mistaken as to the time he saw Langston, if he saw him at all, in the crowd who were trying to enter. Now the rush was made while Lowe was reading the warrant. When Lowe came down with Patton and Meacham to read the warrant they passed out at this back door. But Wood, you remember, saw nothing of that transaction, neither Lowe's coming down nor the reading. It is clear he must have been absent at the time of the rush, or at least for some time previous thereto. Again, Howk and Bennett both saw Langston about the time Lowe came down, and he was then in front of the Hotel, so that Wood cannot be correct as to the time. He undoubtedly saw Langston, for he was perfectly ubiquitous on that occasion; but even Wood can lay nothing to Langston's charge. For the purpose of testing the logic of the prosecution, let us suppose that this fellow Wood was on trial instead of my client — I am doing injustice to my client, I know, by supposing that such a man as this Wood capable of filling his place for a moment — but grant the supposition for the sake of the argument. In the first place, if arraigned here, he certainly would n't have much to brag of in the way of *color.* And I speak of this, because in the eyes of the District-Attorney the fact that a *colored* man, — no matter if, as in the case of my client, the tinge in his skin is scarcely perceptible, — was in the crowd at Wellington, is proof conclusive that he was there with an unlawful purpose. But it is not claimed that Wood went there with any unlawful purpose, — the very contrary is boldly asserted. And yet this man Wood went to Wellington in great haste — among the very first — swears he was greatly excited, — cannot give any good reason for going, — bustled about there wonderfully, — spoke to John on the platform, — made more noise than any other man in the crowd, — at the time the rush was made and John rescued, ran across the road for another ladder after one had been forcibly thrown down, — says it was a very heavy one, but it seemed light because he was very much excited, — set it up against the balcony and sprang on to go up, — a man, pointing his pistol, threatened to shoot him dead if he did n't stop, — told him to shoot and be d——d, — rushed right on up, — and so on all the afternoon; helping the crowd and intensifying the excitement by every means in his power; and yet he swears here himself that he knew all the time that John was a slave, and wanted to go back to his master; for John had worked a good deal for him and told him all about it!

And now I ask, if this man Wood was on trial at the bar, charged with participating in that rescue, would not an infinitely stronger case be made out against him than against the defendant? Could not the District-Attorney triumphantly claim that Wood was a man of color, — that he resides in Oberlin, that he went nine miles to look after a *fellow-citizen*, that he mingled with the unlawful crowd both at Oberlin and Wellington, that he moved about in the crowd, contributed to the excitement and helped in the rescue, well knowing that John was a fugitive and held in lawful custody? It is clear, however, that Wood took no part, either in thought or deed in the rescue. His despicable brain conceived no such laudable act as that. I state the case simply to show that all the acts which the District-Attorney claims as proving guilt, are consistent with perfect innocence of the charge in the indictment.

The next witness was *Wheeler*. He says he saw Langston, heard him advise the crowd to keep quiet and use no violence, but resort to legal measures, and that the only legal way to release John was to obtain a writ of *habeas corpus*. And so impressed was Wheeler with Langston's conduct that he says he testified in the former trial that if every one had acted like Langston there would have been no unlawful proceedings. Now, Gentlemen of the Court, I shall charge you, that if you find this defendant in thus advising a legal investigation as to the custody of the alleged fugitive, was guilty of an unlawful interference, as claimed by the District-Attorney, then, indeed, are the labors of this defence at an end.

But no authority has been shown for such a monstrous doctrine, and I have no fear that such will be the instruction given you. You are to look at this conduct of the defendant as upon his other acts, for the purpose of determining his purposes, and whether or not he was identifying himself with those who were there for an unlawful object. We claim that this conduct of the defendant shows beyond doubt that he was in no manner connected with the unlawful crowd, nor in any manner identified with

them, but that he came there with a lawful purpose and sought, so far as he was able, to carry it out. Remember, Gentlemen, this witness is one on the part of the Government and, that when they prove his peaceful acts, the defendant should have the whole benefit thereof.

The next witness was *Charles Wadsworth*. He says that he met defendant in the building up stairs and asked him if the papers were all right; that Langston replied, that it made no difference whether the papers were right or not, that they were bound to have him any way; and he says he thinks Langston went up and down stairs three or four times. But this witness says he left when the train came in. You will remember that the interview between Lowe and Langston occurred while the train was passing, and that that was the first time Langston went into the hotel. It is therefore doubtful if this witness saw Langston at all, but if he did, what does the expression he claims to have heard prove? He does not state whether this was a determination of Langston's or simply an expression of opinion by him as to the feelings of the crowd, just such a declaration as Lowe or Jennings or Davis or Wheeler might have made without any imputation. Why not Langston as well? Is it because he is a nigger? The District-Attorney does n't claim that Langston was openly aiding the rescue, but was "engineering it from behind." Only by assuming the defendant is guilty, and that he was lying when he advised resort to legal measures. Only by misinterpreting his every word and look can you by possibility find him guilty of any participation in the rescue. I have no fear that when a man's conduct appears fair and honest, you will torture it into lying and deceitfulness.

Marks saw Langston at Wellington, but always found him quiet and still; neither doing nor saying any thing. Now Marks, too, is an Oberlin witness for the Government, — knew Langston well, — was by when Wood had his conversation with Langston, but it made so little impression on his mind that he cannot tell any thing that was said. He came with Wood and Wack, among the first, — was there constantly till the rescue was over, — saw Langston frequently, — has no more sympathy for niggers or Republicans than Mr. Wack or Mr. Wood, — and yet cannot say that he saw any thing in Langston's conduct that favored the rescue.

Halbert saw Langston at Wellington, and thinks he heard him talking about a paper to secure the constable. He understood that the object of the warrant in the hands of the constable was to secure an investigation merely, to ascertain whether or not the custody was a legal custody, and that Langston was advising to the serving of the warrant for that purpose. This young gentleman is also a Government witness, brought here by no means thus to exculpate, but to convict the defendant. The Government, therefore, find themselves forced to abandon the case, or else to claim that this advice as to the service of the warrant was a mere cover or subterfuge, or was illegal and revolutionary; — but we apprehend that the Court will, in due time, relieve them from this latter position, and instruct you more in accordance with reason and law.

Barber saw Langston at Wellington advising only legal measures, and doing nothing whatever to excite the crowd to a forcible rescue. He thinks he saw him stand at one time with his hand upon a gun, but has no reason to believe that it was Langston's gun, nor does he know that it was not. It is said that when sent for to go up to Lowe, he left the gun with, or handed it back to some one, and went up unarmed, and at no other time during the afternoon did any one see any arms in his possession. And I take it that the testimony of this witness, Barber — called by the Government — a candid and fair witness, whose testimony is straightforward and clear, should have great weight with you; and that since he swears positively that Langston acted constantly as a peacemaker when he acted at all, you should well consider the remarkable concurrence of his testimony with that of the other Government witnesses already mentioned.

Sciples swears that he heard Langston talking with Watson, up stairs, about a *habeas corpus*, and saying that it was too late to send for it, because troops from Cleveland had been sent for, and would arrive by the 5 o'clock train. Now can you believe Sciples, when Watson swears positively that he had no conversation with Langston upon any subject whatsoever, in any part of that building during that day? I need say nothing about Sciples' character, when he has already, in your presence upon the stand, acknowledged himself to be a liar, and has been impeached here by half a dozen of the best citizens of Wellington, who declare him to be notoriously untruthful and unreliable. And as to what he says about seeing Langston go up stairs with Watson, just before the rescue, he is as positively contradicted again by Watson, and is entitled to no sort of credit.

Bonny says that Cummings said to him, that if he would open that door — the front door — Langston would give him five dollars. But he does n't claim that Cummings was authorized to make any such statement, or that it was any thing more than an expression of private opinion, and what the grounds of that opinion were he does not pretend to know; nor does he say that Langston knew or heard of the offer.

Reynolds' appearance alone is abundant impeachment of his credibility. Full of conceit, overflowing with airs, and anxious only to display his wonderful self. He swears that, at a certain time, he was guarding the back-door, when it was shown that, at that time, Fay and Davis were guarding it, and he was not. And he undertakes to make us believe that Langston said, half an hour after the train had passed, that they must have him soon, or the train

would come with the soldiers! And every other statement he makes is equally absurd and incredible. He claims that Langston came at the time the rush was made. We have previously shown that, at that time, Langston was in front of the hotel.

THIRTEENTH DAY. — AFTERNOON SESSION.

Mr. GRISWOLD continued: I was proceeding with the testimony touching the conduct of Langston at Wellington. The next witness was *Davis*. What was his testimony? Why, he thinks that Langston was the man that was with Patton, when Patton had a conversation with Lowe, which Lowe thinks was before the reading of the warrant, and which Patton swears, positively, was afterward; but Lowe and Patton agree in contradicting Davis, that Langston was not with them, but it was a man by the name of Griffin, whom neither of them knew, and who claimed to be a stranger passing through the place on his journey.

We now come to the only remaining witness who testifies as to what Langston said, and, as I take it, must be almost the only witness the Government will undertake to rely upon. And, as I view it, without his testimony — I refer to Mr. *Lowe* — there is no evidence that would weigh a feather against the defendant if this were even a *civil* instead of a criminal suit. I do not deny that, if Mr. Lowe's testimony were correct, well supported by collateral evidence, and consistent with itself, it would tend strongly to connect the defendant with those engaged in the rescue of John. But Mr. Lowe has been proven to be so uncertain a witness, his memory shown to be so utterly at fault, that, when he undertakes to charge this defendant by a single expression, and that expression being at variance with the defendant's whole conduct, when the whole thing rests on the accuracy of Mr. Lowe's recollection of a particular word, it seems to me great caution should be used in taking the statement as true, and that the defendant's liberty ought not to be taken away from him on such testimony. Mr. Lowe says, " I sent word for Langston to come up; think I explained to him all about the matter. Langston expressed himself satisfied. I told him I wanted him to go down to the crowd (this was the only conversation we had when others were present) and inform them of what I had told him. Langston said he would go down and do so. Think this was about 5 o'clock. The train passed while we were talking, — remember this distinctly, — it passed nearly two hours before the rescue. He went down and was gone some twenty minutes or more; came up and called me out into the little room, — we two were there alone, — said he had talked to the crowd, but could do nothing with them, — they were bound to have him any how, — asked me if I could n't get Jennings to give him up peaceably. I told him it was no use to talk about that; we should hold him as long as we could. Langston said he was anxious to have a committee go to Columbus with us, but the people below would n't hear to it, and so he wanted me to get Jennings to give him up peaceably, because he did n't want to see any trouble. When I told Langston that we should hold on to John as long as we could, he rose up, and turned to go away; as he rose up, he said, 'we will have him any how.' I was surprised at this, because, up to this moment, I confidently believed he was working for us." Now this is the chief testimony upon which the Government relies to show that the defendant was identified with the rescuers.

It all turns upon a single word. The prosecution claim that he here showed "his cloven foot," and expressed his own determination, that all his words of peace and fairness were lies, that failing to deceive he was ready to use violence. If, however, Mr. Lowe is mistaken as to a single word it changes the whole face of the matter. If he simply said "they 'll" have him any how, as he had before stated to Lowe, it would have been duly an expression of opinion and not a determination. Is a man's liberty to be taken away on merely the accuracy of Mr. Lowe's recollection of exact words a man uttered at a particular time? Did Mr. Lowe stand before you as a perfectly candid and trustworthy witness, it would be going a great ways to stake a whole case on his recollection of a particular statement.

Even in a civil case his testimony should be received with great caution, for you all know that verbal admissions are most doubtful testimony. With the permission of the Court let me read to you what Mr. Greenleaf says on this subject. I read from Greenleaf's Evidence, I. 258, § 200, "with respect to all verbal admissions it may be observed, that they ought to be received with great caution. The evidence, consisting as it does in the mere repetition of oral statements is subject to much imperfection and mistake, the party himself either being misinformed, or not having clearly expressed his own meaning, in the witness having misunderstood him. It frequently happens also that the witness by unintentionally altering a few expressions really used, gives an effect to the statement completely at variance with what the party actually did say." Now the change unintentionally of a single word, instead of a few expressions by Mr. Lowe, gives his testimony an entirely different character. The rule I have read is applicable in civil cases, how much more should that caution be exercised in a criminal case. This is the rule given when the witness is perfectly honest, unimpeached, and endeavors to the best of his ability to tell the truth. But where a man's liberty is staked upon the recollection by a witness of a single word, when that word is inconsistent with the whole conduct of the defendant, when that witness has been contradicted by numerous other witnesses, on other material points, when his memory is proved to be uncertain and inaccurate as to transactions much more prominent, it seems to me that this caution mentioned by the writers on evidence should by all means give way to prompt *rejection;* and I cannot doubt that your verdict will prove that you do not differ with me here.

Why, there is not a single occurrence which Lowe has undertaken to state here in which he has not made positive statements which were contradicted by the most reliable witnesses, on material points, and these have as often been witnesses for the Government as witnesses for the defence. He says he was all the while perfectly cool and collected, and ought therefore to be believed. This does but make matters seriously worse. For if he were excited, as other witnesses confess they were, and everybody was, there might be some sort of apology for him; but if as he claims in the midst of all this crowd and excitement and imminent peril — as the prosecution have labored so hard to show there was — he alone was cool and collected, and yet can tell nothing straighter than he has done, he fatally impeaches himself as having the most unveracious of memories, to say the least. To say that a witness making such pretensions, who is contradicted on the plainest points by the united testimony of such men as Howk and Bennett and Patton and Cowles and Dickson, — I say when the Government undertake to put such a witness forward as so reliable that the liberty of the defendant may safely turn upon his accuracy of memory about a *single word,* — they are going, as your verdict, I take it, will teach them, considerably too far.

I believe I have now gone through with the Government's testimony in this case as to what occurred prior to the rescue. They call the witness *Ells* to show that the defendant took part in a meeting at Oberlin, after the rescue had been effected. Mr. Ells says he heard Langston say something there, but he can't recollect what it was, only that he said something about the affair at Wellington. And because he does n't give down to suit the Government, he meets with not the most gentle treatment at their hands. It *is* a little odd for counsel to abuse their own witnesses, but we must remember that the District-Attorney is in a very tight place.

Warden heard Langston in the evening. He says Langston gave a statement of what took place at Wellington. He heard him make no reference to himself that would implicate himself as having had any hand in the rescue. He says further that there were other men there who took no part in the rescue, who could give as clear a statement as he did.

Philip Kelley. (And in connection with this testimony of Kelley, I would have you refer again to the testimony of Lowe.) *Kelley* says Lowe sent for Langston and asked him to assist him to pacify the crowd, but Langston refused and said he would n't interfere in any way; the crowd would have him any how. But Lowe says he expressed himself satisfied with the authority shown him, and promised to go down and see if he could n't persuade the crowd to regard it; so that Lowe believed up to the last moment of the second interview, when he heard the word "*we*," as he thinks he did, that Langston was working for him, as against the rescuers. "So neither do these witnesses agree together."

Lyman says that Langston made a speech at Oberlin, and recited what had been done at Wellington, without in any way referring to himself. I think it is Lyman, also, who testifies that while Langston was speaking, some one said, "Mention no names;" but another witness says that this was while Lincoln was speaking.

The other witness, and the one upon whom the Government place great reliance, is this man

Gaston. Now it is some time since he testified, but you remember how confused he was in every thing. He said Shipherd called for certain groans and cheers, and then Langston began to speak at once. But, on cross-examination, it appeared that, between Shipherd's calling for groans and cheers, and Langston's beginning to speak, half an hour had escaped, during which the witness went to the post-office and back, and when he came back he found Langston speaking on the other side of the street, in an entirely different place. And he says that some time during Langston's speech some one asked, "Have you got John?" and he said, "We have." But no one who heard Gaston's testimony, confused, mixed up, disconnected, uncertain, self-contradictory as it was, but felt sure that the witness neither knew what he had heard at the meeting, nor what he was testifying to here on the stand. Indeed, this was evident in what the witness said in regard to what he heard about Marshal Dayton at that meeting. He would have you believe that Langston spoke of Dayton's "putting down the railroad track, his coat-tail sailing in the wind," to use the elegant phraseology of the learned District-Attorney, "like a stub-tailed bull in fly-time." It is clear that Dayton was in no way connected with the doings at Wellington; that Langston at this meeting only gave a detail of what had happened, not identifying himself in any manner, but simply stating what he had witnessed.

According to the testimony, then, this defendant was at Wellington; but whence he came there, or how, or for what purposes, the Government do not show.

Therefore, according to the law, we presume them to have been altogether lawful. He found, on arriving there, that John was in custody, and embraced the earliest opportunity to inquire by what authority. Getting answer, he advised strenuously against the use of force,

counselling rather a resort to legal measures; and, when called upon by Lowe for advice, told him frankly that the crowd were excited and seemed bound to rescue the boy at all hazards. And then at Oberlin, in response to a call of the community, he gave an impartial statement of the occurrences which he had witnessed at Wellington.

Gentlemen of the Jury, will you for one moment think of saying that *such* conduct makes him amenable to the pains and penalties of the Fugitive Slave Law?

In the case of Giltner v. Gorham *et al.*, reported in 4 McLean, 402 seq., and cited by the District-Attorney, where the testimony against Gorham was vastly stronger than in this case it has been against Langston, the Court laid down the law thus, p. 423: "If from the whole evidence it shall appear that Gorham and Comstock and Herd, the other defendant, went upon the ground with a view to preserve the peace, and they, nor either of them, while on the ground, said nor did any thing to excite the crowd to oppose the seizure of the fugitives for the purpose avowed; and especially if the tendency of their acts was to allay the excitement without encouraging the rescue of the fugitives, they are not guilty as charged in the declaration."

And this, your Honor, I take to be the law applicable to this case.

The jury in that case disagreed, although it was in a *civil* case, where it is not required that the proof shall be "beyond a reasonable doubt," but simply a "preponderance."

It certainly cannot be claimed, then, that this defendant was there using violence, or encouraging others to use violence. But he most certainly — with whatever motive he came, and concerning that we know nothing — while there expended all his influence to allay excitement and prevent violence, according to every one of the Government's witnesses. There is another matter out of which they seek to charge him; to wit, that he implicated himself by expressing joy that John had escaped, — was carried off from the custody of the Kentuckians. Now, as I consider it, Gentlemen, the bare statement of the District-Attorney that Langston "gloried over the rescue," can hardly go to you as testimony; because the learned counsel for the Government is not a witness in the case. *He* says that Langston gloried over it, but his witnesses have not said so. That there were such expressions in the crowd, is altogether likely; but I believe none of them have yet been attributed to Langston individually. The District-Attorney's favorite "common responsibility" doctrine can hardly be stretched to cover as much ground as this. And even if he had expressed himself gratified at John's escape, forgetting for the moment the "awful wrongs done to a violated law," he would only have done as the District-Attorney himself, and your Honor, and every one of you, Gentlemen of the Jury, would have done too, if there had been a spark of humanity left in your bosoms. I take it, that the impulses of our better natures are such, that, because a man rejoices over the escape of a brother man from that bondage to which no higher power nor greater right than brute force has bound him, even if the law has been violated, he cannot safely be set down as necessarily an anarchist and a traitor. Laws, to claim the respect of good men, must be good; as must the men that make and the men that execute them, so long as nothing of human creation is infallible. And let us thank God if the noblest impulses of the human heart are so strong that no cruelty of law itself can chain them down.

I believe these are all the testimony brought forward by the Government. Their chief reliance is upon declarations which they claim go to identify this defendant with the rescuers, and yet these are almost without exception cases in which he was advising a resort to legal measures. And in no case have the witnesses been willing to hold themselves responsible for the exact language.

Let us look back for a moment — to show the remarkable harmony among the leading witnesses for the Government — to the speech of John from the balcony. That John went or was taken out there, seems to be agreed. But beyond that nothing. For Jennings don't know as the boy really said any thing, or if he did, what it was. The rest agree that he said something, but differ the poles apart as to what it was. Mitchell, Davis, Lowe, and Wack, each undertake to give a version of the distinguished gentleman's remarks, and yet no one hearing them separately would in the end believe either, so utterly diverse are their remembrances. Somewhere I have collated and compared these different versions, but cannot lay my hand upon the paper now. And yet, all of these undertake to give very nearly or precisely John's words, though they differ almost as widely with themselves on cross-examination as they do with each other on the examination-in-chief. And now the prosecution will ask you, Gentlemen, I suppose, incredible as it would seem in any ordinary case, to convict this man upon such testimony, and the confidence they expect you to exercise in the absolute integrity and infallibility of Mr. Lowe's memory of *a single word*, in a conversation where no one can differ with him except the defendant — who is debarred from testifying — because no one else heard it; the only instance in which he has not been impeached. It seems to me, Gentlemen, but I may be mistaken, that this is a manifestation of zeal required of the gentleman neither as a lawyer nor as a prosecuting officer. I cannot account for such an anxiety to convict. It is not his business to convict every person merely suspected of crime. Courts were never instituted merely to punish,

but to see that justice was done alike to the law and the prisoner. In one sense, every person charged at the bar is to be considered as part of the nation, which is represented by the District-Attorney, and I trust he will not forget that persecution is not laudable zeal in the performance of duty.

I have gone through with the testimony on the part of the prosecution, and I need not refer to the testimony of the defendant's witnesses which is fresh in your recollections. From first to last it appears that Mr. Langston was laboring to promote peace, to prevent violence, urging the crowd not to use force but to confine themselves strictly to lawful measures. The attempts to prove the statements of defendant contrary to this, and identifying himself with those using force, are absurd and abortive, the alleged statements being inconsistent in themselves, and the witnesses either contradicted or impeached. With great pleasure, therefore, Gentlemen of the Jury, I commit the interests of my client to your keeping, confidently believing that you will lay aside all prejudice to his color, that you will give the testimony a fair and candid examination, and that the defendant will receive at your hands a prompt and honorable acquittal.

[It being already three o'clock, and the afternoon of a Saturday, the Court adjourned until Monday morning, May 9th, at nine o'clock.]

FOURTEENTH DAY. — MORNING SESSION.

Mr. BACKUS opened his argument for the defence.

[He begged the indulgence of the Court and the Jury, as he was laboring under severe indisposition, and must speak under great disadvantage.]

Gentlemen of the Jury: —

The disposition of the issue now before you will depend upon the facts which have been brought out in the long examination to which you have listened. Much of the evidence in the case has been ably analyzed and commented upon by my associate; and so far as my own judgment is concerned, I should be willing to submit the case to you, and with confidence await at your hands a verdict of acquittal. But I know that my client would not be satisfied; that those who are with him, and whose interests in this case are similar to his own, would not be satisfied without a still further examination in accordance with the usual practice of the facts in evidence. I only wish that I were in a condition, in regard to health, that would better enable me to discharge the service which they expect at my hands.

It need not be said that this case is new; that around it are clustered circumstances which are not usually connected with cases at this bar. It need not be said that it is a peculiar case, and that political considerations enter largely into its facts; — not the considerations of common partisan politics, but political questions that affect the nation at large.

The charge against the defendant is based upon the statute which is claimed to have been passed to make effective the Constitutional provision for the reclamation of fugitives from service. The offence here charged, then, is a political offence. The defendant is charged, not with the breach of a moral, but of a legal rule. He is not charged with the commission of one of those crimes at which Humanity revolts. He is not charged with one of those acts upon which the whole world has always looked as immoral and infamous. He does not stand before you accused of the commission of a ny thing which is in itself a crime, but with an act which is only a crime, because the law declares it is. And if he be found guilty as charged, his character will not be affected as is his who has been convicted of theft, of arson, or of murder. There is not one of you, Gentlemen of the Jury, who would look upon him after conviction as you would look upon a *thief*, or one convicted of a *moral wrong*.

The motives which lead to the commission of these two classes of crimes are widely different. That of the one is selfish and base, and usually impels to action the low and degraded; and subserves ends base in themselves. The other is good — acts upon the good — and leads only to deeds good in themselves. In one case the transgressor is indeed a criminal, and became so with that accompanying malice which you all know constitutes the very virus of crime. The other may be a transgressor, but can never be a criminal, for he is inspired by the noblest of motives, such as all good men approve. I do not regard the duty of a jury as the same in both classes of cases. In the one, the effect of the transgression is the mere breach of a statutory provision, the punishment of which is justifiable solely on the ground that the general good requires the maintenance of the prescribed rule of action. In the other, a law of our moral nature is trampled upon, at the same time that the civil law is violated. In the former case, a jury will convict with reluctance, although satisfied of the truth of the charge; in the latter, if in their judgment the proof is sufficient, their moral duty will cordially unite with the convictions of their judgment. The act charged here, Gentlemen, is not one which, even should you be compelled by the obligations of your oath to find the defendant guilty, would lessen him in the estimation of any good man. You would trust him as an honest man just as readily after conviction of such a crime — for the law calls it, technically, *a crime* — as you would before. If you find him obnoxious to the provisions of the statute, you will return him "Guilty." We use that odious word for want of another, and in its bare technical sense. Guilt means turpitude, baseness. But I must not be understood as applying any such epithet as *baseness* to the act with which Charles Langston stands charged before you!

Now I say, that, in the case before you, the statute must clearly have declared the offence, and the proof brought to sustain the charge must be plain. The assembled wisdom of this country, in the Convention which framed the Constitution, could never have intended to say that it was morally wrong for a citizen of this free country — a country whose liberties that Convention had met to secure forever — to extend a helping hand to a mortal who had been suffering life-long the most cruel and galling oppression, or to aid him in escaping from such bondage. They cannot have looked upon such an act as wrong in the absolute sense, because that would have been utterly at war with the fundamental principles of the government they sought to establish. But the political exigencies which were upon them, and which they were compelled to consider, obliged them to make some provision for the pursuit and reclamation of persons "owing service," who might escape from States where municipal regulations made such service legally due. That Convention did not advocate the justice of such a measure, in its discussions upon the subject. It simply provided that if in any State there were laws subjecting any one class to another class, though such laws rested not upon any moral right, but only upon physical force, no other State should so legislate as to impair the effect of such laws. For, as the States were all to remain sovereign and independent in matters not delegated to the General Government, without such a provision in the Federal Compact, such laws would have no validity beyond the limits of the State that enacted them. The question was one of Union upon this footing, or no Union at all. The "peculiar institution" had at that time no existence in England, and was wholly inconsistent with the theory of her laws; yet the mother country did not protect us against the evil; — and I may be permitted to say, in the language of the illustrious Jefferson, that she in truth *forced it upon us*, in opposition to the remonstrances of the colonies themselves.

But why was it necessary for a government that had thrown off the yoke of foreign oppression, and through a long and bloody war had waded to National Liberty, and thus set an example of heroism and love of justice to all mankind for all future generations, — a government composed of a body of men whose every pulse beat for liberty, — to make this hard provision concerning those who might escape from another and a more cruel despotism? Why? It was, I repeat, because the question of national freedom, and even of nationality itself hung upon that provision. Trusting too largely to the love of justice, intelligence, and good sense of the people, they confidently believed that an institution so intrinsically and plainly evil, and even a greater curse to the free than to the enslaved, would soon be voluntarily abandoned by the slaveholding States themselves; and with such motives and such hopes, and under the pressure of such emergencies and necessities, the clause in question was reluctantly inserted.

In 1793 Congress saw fit to pass an act for the purpose of carrying out this provision of the Constitution, as well as another clause of the same instrument for securing the recaption of fugitives from justice. That act stood for a long time unaltered, and was considered amply sufficient, even by the South itself, for the purposes it was intended to accomplish, until, in the turbulent times just prior to 1850, it began to be claimed that there was a defect in this legislation, and, after long and heated debates, the amendatory Act of September 18, 1850, was passed. Upon this amendatory act the indictment against my client is based.

Now it is not the place here to discuss the propriety of that legislation. Congress has been declared by the Supreme Court of the United States to have possessed the power to pass this law. Unquestionably, if Congress had jurisdiction over the subject-matter, it was alone for it to judge what form its legislation should take. If it have adopted an unfortunate mode, the way is open for its legitimate rectification. The people of the United States have it in their power, whenever they will, to rectify any legislation of their representatives, and I trust in God the day is not far distant when that rectification with respect to this act shall take place, in the legitimate mode; — the mode appointed by the Constitution. It is not for me to say whether Congress was or was not authorized by the Constitution to pass the Act of 1793, or the more questionable Act of 1850. The Supreme Court, within whose province such questions legitimately fall, has passed upon this point; and so long as we remain under this Constitution; so long as we are content to abide by the Government, as it was formed by the adoption of that Constitution; — so long, it seems to me, we are bound by the decisions in the premises of this constitutionally appointed tribunal. So far, then, as I myself am concerned; — and when I say this I am speaking for no man but myself; — whatever my own opinion may be as to the original question in regard to the constitutionality of that provision, I feel myself bound to recognize the authority of the Supreme Court of the United States, to say whether this act of Congress be law or not. And they having pronounced it law, I must obey it.

There is a right other than the one to which I have referred. There is a mode of redress other than that which I have already indicated, to which, of course, we have a right to resort at any time, when the terms upon which we can enjoy the blessings — or endure the curses — of this union — whatever they may be — shall seem too onerous longer to be borne. We — the people of the North — have the right to overturn, if we can, this government, and to adopt a new one, acting, not *under* that Constitution, but upon those principles which underlie all Constitutions. I refer to the right of revolution, the ultimate and legitimate resort of people who find their government too oppressive longer to be borne. I shall then, in the discussion of this question before you, gentlemen, look to the issues that are made here under that law as that law has been construed by the Supreme Court of the United States. And, looking thus at these issues, I shall ask you to do that which you would do in every other case where an individual is charged with crime — no matter whether that charge be for the commission of an act that is a crime in itself, or whether it is criminal only because prohibited by the statute — I shall ask you to see to it that the prosecution brings itself within the limits of the provisions of the statute. And I know, Gentlemen, that there is not a man upon that Jury who would not prefer to find, if warranted by the testimony, that the evidence before you does make a case against the defendant. I know that there is not a man on that Jury but would prefer, so far as personal preferences could go, — I know that the Court itself would prefer that this man, who is brought here for the commission of no act that is in itself wrong, — of no act that would tarnish the fair fame of the best of men; — but for the commission only of that which is prohibited by a statute of questionable character, inspired to such transgression — if he ever did transgress it — by the noblest impulses of a manly heart, — I know, I say, that you all would prefer that he should be found not to have been proved guilty. You can have no desire that a man should be convicted of a crime of which he is not guilty; and although you may be compelled, after mature deliberation, to return a verdict against him — which I am confident you never will, whatever your political biases may be, if you have regard to the testimony — I am sure it would be with the utmost reluctance that you would find yourselves thus compelled to return. Why, it cannot be that there is a man in that box who has a "political end" to answer by finding a verdict against this defendant! — That there is a man *there* so debased, so utterly prostituted, as to render a verdict against this defendant, subjecting him to the penalties of *such* a law, for the purpose of being able to say to his brother *Democrat*, the party leaders, or to the South, that he had firmness enough, that he had backbone enough, to stand up in this case, and on this Reserve, and render a verdict in favor of Slavery and against Freedom. You, gentlemen, can be actuated by no such desire as this! You are no such crawling hounds, such lickspittles, such craven wretches as that! I have known you too long to believe this of you.

You have lived too long upon this free Reserve, to wish to inflict the pains and penalties of this statute upon any man who may have allowed his own feelings so much sway as to render him obnoxious merely to *suspicion*, that he has been violating its provisions. I take it, therefore, that you will look at this case as at any other, and if you are compelled to find that the defendant is guilty, you will so find with the utmost reluctance. And I know, too, that this Court, if compelled to pass sentence upon my client, in obedience to the oath administered upon assuming the judicial ermine, and in obedience to the law as it is found upon the statute-book, and construed by the Supreme Court, will with no feelings of pleasure perform that official act. From my acquaintance with this Court, and with you, Gentlemen of the Jury, I know that nothing could be more grateful to the feelings of both the Court and the Jury, than to feel warranted in the conclusion that the charge contained in this indictment is not sustained by the testimony introduced. And I think I may say the same of even the District-Attorney himself. For I cannot believe that this man whose whole life thus far has been characterized by an uncompromising love of Freedom, can have become so changed within a few short months as to rejoice at the conviction of a morally innocent man; nor can I think that the petty triumph it might afford him to be able to report to the authorities at Washington that the *penalties of this law* had been enforced against individuals of certain political connections in this neighborhood, would compensate for the upbraidings of his conscience consequent upon an unjust conviction. I know it is his business, as the prosecuting officer, to press the case against the defendant, and that it is no part of his duty to look after the defendant's interests. That duty belongs to the counsel for the defence. But still I have faith to believe that he would not wish to go beyond his duty in the matter, and bring extraordinary and unwarrantable means to bear for the purpose of securing a conviction. And I believe that I may say the same thing is true of his learned associate. And though you who are not fully initiated into the language and manners of the bar, may have thought the bearing of these learned gentlemen at times severe, you must not construe too closely or too literally the expressions they may have inadvertently dropped.

If it be true, then, that the Court, the Jury, the District-Attorney and his associate, would rejoice in an acquittal of this defendant, unless his guilt be proven beyond a reasonable doubt, even if he were by law entitled to all the rights, immunities, and privileges of an American citizen; then, certainly, as he is not so privileged, but is, without reason, deprived of the rights asserted by the Declaration of American Independence to belong to all men, the anxiety must be tenfold greater on the part of all of you, that the penalty of this statute should be added to the burden that is already crushing him to the earth, only in case of the most conclusive proof of guilt.

For this defendant, who can count a long line of ancestry on the one side *not* of African blood, but wealthy and respectable Anglo-Saxon sires, was brought here by his father to enjoy the freedom of our State. But though personally moral, honorable, talented, and every way qualified for the privileges of citizenship, by the rigor of your law, those privileges have been wrested from him.

And therefore it is that I say, if you would reluctantly return a verdict against any, even the meanest citizen of Anglo-Saxon blood, your reluctance must be tenfold greater by your verdict to shut out this man — emphatically a MAN — from the few privileges yet allowed him in this " land of the free."

Did any of you ever travel abroad, and there meet with an American citizen, stranger though he were to you personally? and if so, was not your heart irresistibly drawn to him by the knowledge that he was from your country, and was attached like you to her institutions? At such a meeting did not your heart go out toward your brother countryman, and did you not lay it open in unrestrained sympathy with him? and would you not do for him and claim of him what you would *never* do or claim at the hands of one of another race?

It may be permitted to me to suppose a case applicable to one of our own blood.

Suppose, then, that there were a State here at the South, or at the West, or at some other place, not included in the boundary of our own Union, but a neighboring State, with whom we had a treaty, by the terms of which that State was to deliver up to us fugitives from service, and we in turn were obliged to seize and send them back their slaves. And suppose it were true that by some law of that State unknown, perhaps, to the makers of that treaty, every man of Anglo-Saxon blood were subject there to be reduced to slavery; that every American citizen, finding his way into that territory under certain circumstances, were subjected to be reduced to bondage for life, — and that such an Anglo-Saxon, such an American citizen — one who had been a citizen and had expatriated himself — had been thus seized and reduced to servitude in this neighboring State, — that after being thus reduced, and suffering wrong and oppression till it was no longer tolerable, he had fled hither into our midst, taken an asylum among us; suppose farther the officers of that State, by virtue of the treaty had pursued after, and captured him; and it were noised abroad that one of Anglo-Saxon blood had thus been pursued and overtaken, and the right were claimed, by virtue of this treaty, to return that American citizen to hopeless and unending bondage; — what would your feelings be, if the marshal, in the discharge of his duty in such a case, should summon you as his posse?

Would you obey that summons? It might be provided by statute that you should be subject to penalties if you refused. Would you consult even, whether you would obey or not?

And suppose you and your neighbors had arisen in your might to resist the execution and return of the marshal's process, and had rescued your fellow man from the officer who had seized him; — would you not justify yourselves on the ground that it was a case appealing *irresistibly* to your sympathies and to the noblest impulses of your manhood? A case appealing much more strongly to you than as though the prisoner had been a man belonging to another race? Would you not expect yourselves to be influenced much more powerfully in such circumstances than in those which are now from time to time occurring in our midst in which the negro is the victim?

Why, we have seen that recently in Italy there has been a capture of a young boy by an ecclesiastical society, under circumstances that render it an outrage of great enormity. That boy belonged to a particular race. Now there can be but one reason why one class of the people of the United States should feel themselves more outraged by this occurrence than another; and that is, that the former and the captive are of one race, and bound together by kindred ancestral blood. It is for this reason, that while the capture of this young MORTARA is known and spoken of by every JEW in the United States, and while, probably, there is not one of that class of our citizens that is ignorant of this occurrence; yet such is not the case with regard to the great body of the American people. You and I condemn the act in the abstract as heartily as can any one belonging to the outraged race, yet at the same time we well know that it does not *take hold of us* as it does — and naturally does — of them; and hence petition after petition has gone up to the President, with the name of nearly every Jew in the land attached, imploring his interference. Why? Because of this bond of kindred. Well then, when one thus allied to this *defendant*, a man belonging to the same race with himself, has made *his* escape from this eternity of bondage to which he was doomed by the local law of Kentucky — has succeeded in escaping from his oppressors, and has come here into the State of Ohio, is pursued, decoyed, and seized, and is about to be hurried back to a deeper and more hopeless bondage than that from which he fled; — do you not know, do you not understand that the feelings of this defendant would naturally be affected to a degree to which you would not expect those of one of the dominant race here to be stirred? Why, Gentlemen, you know it is in human nature that it should be thus! God has made us so; we can't help ourselves. And you will regard the conduct of a man thus situated, moved by such sympathies, with a greater degree of tolerance, — you will find far more excuses for his conduct, growing out of this sympathy of blood, and this mutual outlawry, than for one of an-

other race. And there can be nothing wrong in your so doing.

Now I do not call your attention to these considerations for the purpose of asking you to disregard your oaths, to disregard the law, and to lay aside the testimony in the case; but I refer to them for the purpose of enjoining upon you that which the law enjoins upon you, that you shall regard this man as innocent of the crime charged, until he shall have been proved to you to be guilty; and proved beyond the existence of a reasonable doubt. And I shall ask you to give effect to that principle of the law recognized by all the writers and all the courts, that where there is conflicting testimony as to acts and motives necessary to constitute a crime, before you can be satisfied of his guilt, you must be satisfied that the facts in the case are reconcilable with no other hypothesis than that of guilt. For if this defendant was at Wellington for any other purpose than that of illegally wresting the alleged fugitive from the possession of those who had him legally in custody; if the facts, I say, are reconcilable with any hypothesis of innocence, or with any other hypothesis than that of guilt, and you are in doubt which has the preponderance of probability, judging from the evidence, it will be your duty, as the Court will charge you, and as you doubtless already know, to adopt without hesitation the supposition of innocence, and find a verdict of acquittal.

And now, Gentlemen, I wish to call your attention for a few moments to the issues which are involved in this case.

In the first place, it is charged in this indictment, that a certain person, termed here "the negro slave called John," "was heretofore, to wit, in March, 1857" — though the proof says January, 1856 — the slave of John G. Bacon, in the State of Kentucky. That he owed service to John G. Bacon in the State of Kentucky; and that so owing service to Bacon, he escaped from that service, and fled into the State of Ohio.

That is the first statement of the indictment.

Well, now, may it please the Court, there is no averment in this indictment expressly declaring that *under and by virtue of the laws of the State of Kentucky*, this individual could be held to slavery there. But it is claimed that the Court will take judicial notice as a matter of history that this John could there be held to service by virtue of such laws. Now it seems to me that an averment is necessary in the indictment to that effect; for it certainly cannot be claimed that every man with African blood in his veins, is in such a condition that he can be held to service in the State of Kentucky. *That* proposition can be deduced neither from history nor from law; for as I understand the law of slavery, it is, that the child follows the condition of its mother, and certainly it is a clear proposition that a child with African blood in his veins may have for parents a white mother and an African father. Now the fact that the father of an individual in Kentucky may be a pure African, and he — the son — a mulatto, half African and half Anglo-Saxon, does not constitute the condition upon which he may be held in bonds.

There is no general law that this Court can take notice of which would authorize the holding to servitude of an individual thus born and of such parentage.

Now it seems to me that before the Court can take notice of the fact that slavery or the involuntary servitude of a certain class can exist in Kentucky, there should be an averment that this individual was, under the laws of Kentucky, in such a condition that he could be held to service or labor as claimed. I concede that if there be an averment that he was of African descent on the mother's side, and then the additional averment that he was in fact held to service, then you have got a case upon which this rule may operate, for the Court will take notice that an individual of such parentage may be held to service; and then it is for the proof to show that he was so held to service. But, upon the supposition that I have already made to you, that he were a person partly of African and partly of white blood, and the African blood were derived from the father, and not from the mother, the Court certainly could *not* then take notice that such a person might be a slave.

How, then, can the Court assume that the law of Kentucky is applicable to this case? Now it is necessary that the law should be averred in the indictment, slavery existing only by special and not by general law. It is not sufficient to state it as in the case of the United States *v.* Stowell, referred to by the District-Attorney. The question in that case came up upon the warrant. Now the proof would have shown that Loring was a Commissioner authorized to issue such a warrant, if the averment had been made in the indictment. The Court there held that it was not enough to leave this to the proof. It must not only be shown, but it must be averred in the indictment. So we say with regard to this averment with reference to the owing of service in the State of Kentucky. It is not sufficient to prove that such laws exist. It must be averred that they exist, and then leave it to the proof to sustain the averment, and also to show that this person claimed to have been a slave was held to service under and by virtue of those laws.

I know not, Gentlemen of the Jury, whether John was legally held to service in the State of Kentucky or not. You have the testimony before you. You have the testimony of Bacon that he owned John, and that his father held him, and that he came to him by division of property, on the decease of his father, among his children. He says, also, that he knew the mother of John, and that she was a slave also. Now I shall not ask you to require such proof

of title as old Judge Payne, of Vermont, required. He said he would be governed by the law, and remand the slave upon the making out of the title; but nothing short of a deed from *God Almighty* himself would satisfy him!

I shall not go as far as that; but I shall hold you to such proof as is required by the decisions of the Supreme Court.

Bacon says that all he knows of the relation which John's mother sustained to his (Bacon's) father is, that she lived on the plantation with the other slaves, obeyed her master's orders, and worked without pay. And that all he knows of his father's title to John is, that John lived and obeyed and worked in the same way.

John went off in his absence, he says. He don't know what directions were given to John by the Irishman during this absence, or what else happened; but at all events when he came home he didn't find John, and a couple of horses were missing besides. The horses he afterwards found in Brown County, near Ripley, in this State, but John he never found, and has n't seen him to this day. I shall spend no time upon this; take the question of ownership as it is, and you must find as you please; and the proof of his escape, though equivocal, is, perhaps, as good as they could make it. And then as to the identity of John, — we have gone into no proof on that point. And I don't know as I could ask you to raise any question upon the identity of the boy John in Kentucky, with the boy John rescued at Wellington. But the next point at which we arrive, gentlemen, is one about which there is a difference of opinion between the prosecution and the defence, and that is as to the authority furnished to Jennings.

And, Gentlemen, with regard to the fact that this Mr. Bacon signed the paper which has been shown to you, there is no dispute. The only question is whether that paper has been acknowledged in such form as is required by the statute of the United States; for if it has not been thus properly acknowledged, then it gave no authority to Mr. Jennings, under the statute, and no offence could have been committed by the defendant in rescuing the boy John from Mr. Jennings's custody.

May it please the Court, the provision of the statute upon this subject is as follows. It is found in Section 8, as the act is arranged in Brightly's Digest : —

"When a person held to service or labor in any State or Territory of the United States has heretofore or shall hereafter escape into another State or Territory of the United States, the person or persons to whom such service or labor may be due, or his, her, or their agent or attorney, duly authorized by power of attorney in writing, acknowledged and certified under the seal of some legal officer or court, of the State or Territory in which the same may be executed, may pursue and reclaim such fugitive person," etc.

Now who are empowered to take the acknowledgment and to certify to it?

Why, any "legal officer" or Court of the State or Territory" from which the fugitive made his escape, is authorized by the terms of this act, your Honor, to take the acknowledgment and certify to it. But certainly when it says "any legal officer," it don't mean a *pathmaster*, it don't mean a *constable*, although these may be as "legal" officers as any in the State. There must be some limitation, and it seems to me a fair construction, that *any officer authorized by the laws of the State or Territory to do a similar act*, is intended by this Act. For it would certainly be too broad to say that *any* legal officer — a school-commissioner, or any other one of ten thousand "legal" officers in the State of Kentucky, might take this acknowledgment, according to the terms of the statute. And it would seem to be not only a fair construction, but the only fair one, that the authority extends to any officer who, under the laws of the State, is authorized to take such or similar acknowledgments for use within the same State, as well as to any Court of the State. Now, then, if this acknowledgment be a valid acknowledgment, it must be so because it was taken by such an officer as is referred to in this statute, or by such a Court as is referred to in this statute. It is not pretended that it was taken before any Court, and hence Courts may be laid out of the question. It was indeed competent for Bacon to have gone before a Court, as he might go before this Court to-day, and have that acknowledgment taken in open Court; and the acknowledgment would then be properly attested by the seal of the Court, and would prove itself, for it would be an act of the Court, and the attestation of the seal, as we have it here, would be sufficient proof of its genuineness. But there is no pretence that it was taken before a Court; it must, then, in order to be valid, have been taken before some such "legal officer" as is referred to in this statute. The claim is, that it was taken before a certain legal officer, to wit, the Clerk of the County Court of Mason County, Kentucky. It is averred, it is true, in the indictment, that the County Court of Mason County is a legal Court; but that is mere surplusage, it is not of a moment's consequence, except to show, perhaps, that Cochran was a legal officer, by showing that he was an officer of a legal Court. On this supposition, that averment may be well enough. Now, then, if I am right in the position I take as to what is a reasonable construction of this statute, none but a person authorized by the laws of Kentucky to take such acknowledgment, would be such a legal officer as is referred to and intended by the statute. Suppose, then, that that person had fled from Ohio, Ohio being a slave State, and the acknowledgment had been taken here before the

Clerk of a Court of Common Pleas, would it come within the requirements of this Act? No; because the Clerk of a Court of Common Pleas is authorized to do only certain specified things, administer certain oaths, etc.; but it is no part of his duties or prerogatives, as such clerk, at common law, to take acknowledgments of powers of attorney, or of deeds or conveyances, of any sort whatever. If the Clerk of the Court of Common Pleas, then, have any authority to take the acknowledgment of powers of attorney, that power is not derived by virtue of, or as incident to, the office, but by special statute, and we have no such statute. And therefore the Clerk of such a Court has no power to take such an acknowledgment, and if he should take it, it would, of course, be worthless. If the broad construction of the letter of the statute is to be followed, and any man who is a "legal" officer may take and certify to these acknowledgments, then a watchman here in the street, the Clerk in the Court of Common Pleas, a pathmaster, a jailer, may do it; for they are all "legal" officers in the strict sense, but this construction of the statute cannot be the right one.

It seems to me, therefore, that the clerk of a court of common pleas in Ohio, if it were a slave State, from which such escape could be made, would have no power to take such an acknowledgment; but for the purpose of such acknowledgment it would be necessary to go before a justice of the peace, a judge, or some similar officer, who by the laws of Ohio is authorized to take such acknowledgments.

Now, then, where is the authority for the County Clerk of Mason County to take any such acknowledgment as that of this power of attorney? There is no testimony to show that the clerk of the county court of Mason County or of any other county in Kentucky is authorized by the laws of the State of Kentucky to take acknowledgments similar to this. And will this Court say that it knows the law of Kentucky to authorize it? Does this Court know the law that will authorize it? Do the gentlemen know any such law? At common law this officer has no such power. And it seems to me that this Court, unless there be a special statute, or the common law as construed in Kentucky, will authorize it, cannot, of its own mere motion, in the absence of any testimony, by parole from an expert, or in writing from the State Statutes, or from the decisions of the courts of that State, — I say, in the absence of all proof, it seems to me that this Court cannot assume to lay it down that the law is so, and instruct this jury that the clerk of the county court of Mason County was an officer authorized to take acknowledgments under and by virtue of the laws of Kentucky. If, then, he was not thus authorized by the laws of Kentucky to take such acknowledgments, and the restricted construction which I claim ought to obtain, shall be held to be the correct one, then I say, that, if this acknowledgment had been taken personally before Robert A. Cochran, it would have been taken before a person having no authority under the statute to take it.

Again, this statute not only requires that the acknowledgment should be taken before some legal officer or court, but that it shall be certified to under the *seal* of some legal officer or court. Now, then, admitting that Robert A. Cochran was authorized to take the acknowledgment of this power of attorney, it clearly appears that he should have certified to it under *his* seal, — not under the seal of the *court*, which certainly can never in the absence of express legislative provision be used to certify any action of his which is not an act pertaining to him as an officer of the court. Here is the seal of *court*, attesting his act apart from the court! Now if the *court* had taken the acknowledgment, then it would have been necessary to certify to it with the seal of the court; but if the *officer* takes the acknowledgment, by virtue of power vested in him, it must be certified to by his own seal, — not by the seal of some one else. Why, your Honor, what better right has Robert A. Cochran to certify to his personal acts with the seal of Mason County Court than with the seal of this Court? What right has any one except the court to use the seal of the court? What are seals good for, if they may be passed around so, and half a dozen or fifty different officers or courts use one seal, or exchange seals as it may happen? But, aside from the absurdity of the thing, the statute expressly forbids it. The statute *will not allow* the clerk to borrow the seal of the court to authenticate his individual action with. He must certify always to his own acts with his own seal. Now, then, if he were such an officer as has power to take acknowledgments of this kind of instruments, he would, in some instances, have an official seal, and in some he would not. Justices of the Peace have no official seal; but Notaries Public have. A Judge has none of his own, and a clerk may or may not have. And where the statute which appoints an officer furnishes him with no seal, and another statute devolves upon him duties which require the use of a seal, he must use his own private seal. If Mr. Cochran, then, had an official seal of his own — as the seal of *the clerk* of the County Court of Mason County, he should have used it: but there undoubtedly was no such seal; and he should, therefore, have employed his own private seal. But the seal that he has employed is the seal, not of the clerk, but of the Mason County Court, and he has employed it to authenticate his individual acts independent of the Court.

The District-Attorney, then, cannot claim that this Mr. Cochran had authority under the laws of Kentucky, or under any other laws, to take this acknowledgment; and if he had, he certainly will not claim that it is properly authenticated by the use of the seal of Mason County *Court!*

No one will deny that in Kentucky, as here and elsewhere, such acknowledgments may be taken before Justices of the Peace. Suppose, then, that this acknowledgment had been so taken — had been taken before a Justice of the Peace. Now a Justice of the Peace has no official seal. Suppose, therefore, that he had taken this acknowledgment, and then, like Mr. Cochran, instead of attaching his own private seal to it, had assumed the use of the seal of the Mason County Court, and attested the acknowledgment with it! Would any one call *that* a proper attestation? But what better right has Mr. Cochran to use the seal of the Mason County Court for private purposes, than a Justice of the Peace, or any other man? Certainly, none at all. If the application had been made to a Notary Public, he, having an official seal, would, of course, have used it. And a Justice of the Peace would have used his private seal.

Now, has this statute been complied with? Has this Robert A. Cochran attempted to certify to this acknowledgment under his seal? Not at all. He has employed the seal of the County Court of Mason County, and has thus destroyed the efficacy of the acknowledgment, granting that he had a right to take it and to certify to it at all. By virtue of his office, as Clerk of the Mason Court, it may be, and undoubtedly is, both his right and his duty to make use of the seal of the Court in authenticating the acts of the Court, or his acts as an officer of the Court; but to use it for such purposes as this, even if he had a right to take the acknowledgment, is just as absurd and illegitimate as it would be for any Justice of the Peace in that State to use it to attest the acknowledgment of instruments taken before him. The acknowledgment of this paper is ambiguous. It does not purport to have been acknowledged before the Court, and yet comes attested with the seal of the Court. It does purport to have been acknowledged before Robert A. Cochran; but his seal, official or private, is sought for in vain! Can it be claimed for one moment, then, that the requirements of the statute have been met, granting — what is also unproven — that Robert A. Cochran had any authority to take and attest acknowledgments of this kind?

I think it safe enough to say, therefore, your Honor, that this power of attorney, upon which this whole prosecution rests, is worthless, because, in the first place, Robert A. Cochran, although as "legal" an officer as any pathmaster for ought I know, is no more qualified than such a pathmaster to acknowledge such instruments, not being such an officer as was intended by the statute. And, in the second place, if he were fully authorized, being altogether such an officer as the statute intended, the acknowledgment is defective, and not according to law, because he has not certified to it under his own seal, as the law requires, but has unwarrantably made use of entirely another seal.

But this is not all. I have another objection,

lying still nearer, and if possible more fatal than either, to the manner of the acknowledgment of this paper; and that is that this acknowledgment was not made before Cochran personally. I know that I have an issue here for the jury on a question of fact; but I claim that it appears from the instrument itself, as well as from the testimony, that the acknowledgment was made before the *deputy* and before the deputy only, and not before the principal clerk himself; and if the Jury shall so find, then I claim that the instrument is worthless and void.

I know that Cochran testified that Richardson was his deputy, and that, by the laws of Kentucky, the deputy is authorized to perform all the duties of the principal clerk. I am not sure that the testimony went quite so far, but I am willing to concede that it did. Granting all this, the deputy could not take the acknowledgment, because, may it please the Court, when you have admitted all this, *neither of them*, according to the laws of Kentucky have power to take this acknowledgment. The principal clerk gets his power, if he has any, to take that acknowledgment from the United States statute from which I have already read to you; the laws of Kentucky never gave him that power. Conceding that the deputy may do, under the laws of Kentucky, any thing that the principal may do, you have n't advanced one step toward proving that the instrument is good, for you have n't shown, and you can't show that the principal has any power to take acknowledgments himself. And it is just as necessary that the power should be given to the deputy by the act of Congress — before he is authorized to use it — as that it should be given to the principal clerk. If the deputy can do any thing the principal may do, under the laws of Kentucky, this can confer no power upon him to take an acknowledgment under the statute of the United States, when the taking of such acknowledgment is authorized only to the principal clerk himself. I have already said that the laws of Kentucky could be referred to for no other purpose than to determine what officers are embraced in this clause, by showing what officers are authorized and empowered to take similar acknowledgments under the State laws.

The authority conferred is special and personal in its very nature, and such as cannot be delegated to an agent or deputy. Why, how can my friend Mr. Cleveland (a deputy clerk of this Court) take my acknowledgment of a fact here to-day in the name of his principal, Mr. Green, and certify to the personal knowledge of Mr. Green! Why the *personal knowledge* of Mr. Green is his own, and no other person under heaven can certify to it. If Mr. Cleveland were one of the officers specified in the statute, then he could certify to *his* personal knowledge and sign *his own name*, as deputy, to show that he was one of the officers referred to in the statute; but he can *never* certify to Mr. Green's knowledge, and sign Mr. Green's name to it — *never!*

I say, therefore, that whatever may be the authority of the clerk to take an acknowledgment, the deputy cannot take the acknowledgment in the name of his principal, and certify to the knowledge of the principal. He has no power to act, except only in his own name, and can certify to no one's knowledge but his own; and if the proof shall satisfy this Jury that no acknowledgment was taken other than that taken before the deputy, then the instrument must be held by them to be null and void. I have already conceded, that, if the deputy had power under that statute, as well as his principal, to take acknowledgments, then he could take and certify them over his own name; but never over the name of any other person whatsoever. But this acknowledgment purports to have been taken by Cochran "by his deputy." Now I 'am ready farther to admit that if the acknowledgment were taken in the presence of Cochran, and the deputy simply acted the part of an *amanuensis* in signing the name of his principal, in the presence of his principal, by the command of his principal, then the objection to the deputy's part in the acknowledgment falls. But if he acted in the absence of the principal, of his own mere motion, and still professed to act for his principal, then the acknowledgment on this ground, if on none other, is void.

And now, Gentlemen of the Jury, I wish to call your attention for a few moments to the testimony as to the manner in which that acknowledgment was made. The first witness that is called by the Prosecution, to establish the fact of the acknowledgment, is the owner Bacon.

Here is the acknowledgment of the power of attorney : —

" STATE OF KENTUCKY, }
        Mason County, ss. }

I, Robert A. Cochran, Clerk of the County Court of the county aforesaid, do hereby certify that this power of attorney from Richard Loyd and John G. Bacon," etc.

Bacon said in reference to this instrument when it was handed him : —

I executed it, and sent it to Mr. Jennings at Oberlin by Richard P. Mitchell. He was a close neighbor to me. He left — my recollection is n't distinct when. The instrument was executed on the day of its date. Again he says : —

Saw Jennings after I had forwarded the power of attorney, at Col. Mitchell's, a neighbor's, the next day after Mitchell had left. Mitchell started with the power of attorney the same day it was executed.

Then comes Mr. *Cochran*, who says : —

The certificate to the acknowledgment of the power of attorney exhibited is in the handwriting of Wm. H. Richardson, and signed by him. My name was signed to it by him. He was acting for me as clerk when the certificate was made. I was absent at the time the acknowledgment was made. Came to my office on my return just as Bacon, Loyd, and Mitchell were coming out. They showed me the paper; I took it, and went in, and directed the deputy to put in the words that appear in the last two lines, and he did so in my presence.

On cross-examination he says: —

They were at the door, just passing out as I came up. Bacon showed me the paper, and I went in and had the last two lines added.

And in reply to the interrogatory whether he did or did not swear on the previous trial — that of Bushnell—that he had no personal knowledge of this acknowledgment, he said: —

" I did *not* so swear ! "

Mitchell, on cross-examination, says, " We went from the book-store to the clerk's office. Found Richardson. He took the acknowledgment. We started out and met Cochran at the door coming in. Bacon showed him the paper; he said he would have a little addition made ; took it to his deputy, and had the addition made ; he gave it to Bacon, and Bacon gave it to me. I have stated all that took place."

It seems, then, Gentlemen, that they went to Richardson, the deputy; *he* took the acknowledgment; they left the office: and just as they were going out the door, they met the principal clerk, Cochran, coming in ; the power was shown Cochran, according to this statement on the present trial, and he went back and directed the deputy to write an addition ; and he points to that (Mr. Backus held the paper in his hand) as the portion which he had put in, commencing after the word " deed," and reading, " The said parties are personally known to me ; and the said acknowledgment is according to law ;" and he says this was put in by his direction. It is said that there is a difference in the handwriting that shows it was put in. I am myself unable to see any such difference ; perhaps my eyes are not as good as those of the District-Attorney. But, admitting all this, what is shown ? What but that the acknowledgment was taken by the deputy in the absence of the principal clerk ; and that, on his return, the principal clerk directed an addition to be made, and that the deputy-clerk made that addition by such direction ? Now Mitchell says that this is *all* that was done. All that is claimed by Cochran is, that he did meet them on the steps there, did take them back into the room, and did direct the clerk to make this addition. This is all the District-Attorney has yet claimed. Whether it will by and by be claimed that a new acknowledgment was gone into by the gentleman who will close for the Government, I do not know. But there is nothing at all to show this ; nothing to show that there was any acknowledgment made except that taken by the deputy in the absence of Cochran, and finished before his return. For not only was the certificate completed to the satisfaction of those who made the acknowledgment, and they were already leaving the office when they met Cochran, but the acknowledgment itself, which was the presentation of the paper to the deputy by the parties who had made it with the profession that they had made it voluntarily, deliberately, and in good faith, and that it was their true act and deed for the purposes therein named, must necessarily have been concluded before the deputy began to make out the certificate, or, in any event, before he signed it. To the completed certificate of this by-gone acknowledgment the clerk proposed an amendment. For, I take it for granted, Gentlemen, that the ordinary and only proper course was pursued in this case ; that they acknowledged the instrument to be their true act and deed for the purposes therein named, and that the clerk then made out and signed a certificate to the fact of such acknowledgment. And I fancy the gentlemen upon the other side will not controvert this supposition, — will not think it would be to their credit to claim that, in Kentucky, public officers certify to acknowledgments first, and have them made afterwards. I apprehend, however, no difficulty on this point.

The certificate being made out, then, *after* the acknowledgment had been taken, Bacon, Loyd, and Mitchell started to leave the office, and passed out of the door ; but just as they were going down the steps, they met this Mr. Cochran : Bacon handed him the paper ; he looked at it, and said he would have a little ADDITION made to the CERTIFICATE, and by his direction the deputy made the addition : — " The said parties are personally known to me and the said acknowledgment is according to law." Nothing can be plainer, then, than the character of this worthless acknowledgment. No one claims that the acknowledgment was made before Cochran. All agree in swearing that it *was not ;* that it was before the deputy and the deputy alone. On the first trial the veracious Mr. Cochran swears that he has no knowledge of it beyond the recognition of his deputy's handwriting ; now he swears he didn't swear so — although we all know he did — and with the help of the District-Attorney tries to make a great parade about a certain *addition* to the *certificate* which he says he directed, but which, if all true, you all see amounts to nothing at all. Now, Gentlemen, I cross-examined this witness myself. I had in mind this very point. I did n't believe then, as I do not believe now, that the deputy had any power to take the acknowledgment, even if his principal had. With the full conviction of this principle of law in my mind as applicable to this case, I examined the witness on this very point. I did propound to him the question, as has been shown in testimony here, " whether he had any personal knowledge of this acknowledgment or not ? " and he did just as unequivocally and positively state as he ever stated any thing in his life, that he had *none;* and my notes and memory upon this point have been corroborated by the oaths of several witnesses who had such means of knowing that their memories cannot be at fault. Therefore, Gentlemen, as good-looking as Mr. Cochran was, and as gentlemanly as he was, I was taken very much by surprise at this addition and amendment to his first positive statement, this important — to his veracity — revision of the narrative; and I have reasons for noting the significance of this new vamping of the story, such as have not been brought into evidence here, and it is not therefore proper for me to comment upon. And although this gentleman was the Clerk of the County Court of Mason County, and therefore had a right to a seat in the clerk's desk here, and thus exhibited his good looks to us pretty much all the time the testimony in this case was being given, — I was none the less, but all the more surprised, and you know I had good reason to be. And I took it upon me to introduce several unimpeachable witnesses to show that he testified to one thing on the former trial, and then, after hearing the arguments which attacked the validity of the acknowledgment on the ground that it was taken by the deputy alone, he came forward and amended and contradicted and denied his first assertions in an effort to patch up and improve this case for the Government. And this impeachment, Gentlemen, I take it, ought very seriously to shake your confidence in Mr. Cochran's credibility. You can have no doubt that he testified as we have proved, upon the former trial. And he knows perfectly well that he so testified. I say therefore that the Government have no right to place reliance upon any part of this witness's testimony. Mitchell corroborates him so far as to say that they met him at the door, went back, and the deputy made the addition. But I do not understand the District-Attorney to claim that this was any thing more than the witnesses declare it — an addition to the certificate, but no new acknowledgment. [Mr. Backus addressed this in the tone of an inquiry to the District-Attorney personally, without interruption or reply.] Of course, nothing else could be claimed.

It seems, then, that the only acknowledgment taken was that made before Richardson, and not certified to by him, but with the name of the principal clerk in Richardson's handwriting; and of all this, as Cochran still swears, he was entirely ignorant until it was finished; and the certificate is attested by the seal of neither Richardson nor Cochran, but by the seal of the *Mason County Court.*

Now, if this Court will accept an instrument *thus* acknowledged as a legal instrument, I have nothing more to say about it. But if the Court shall, on any or all of these grounds, hold and charge with me — as it seems to me it cannot avoid doing — then you will find that in the rescue of John no offence such as is mentioned in the statute was committed; and the defendant, whether implicated as an active or passive participant in that rescue or not, must be acquitted.

AFTERNOON SESSION, 2 O'CLOCK.

Mr. BACKUS continued: —
Gentlemen of the Jury:

The testimony shows that Mr. Jennings, after having received this paper which he counts upon as a power of attorney, came to this State in pursuit of the boy John. You well remember the testimony, of course. He had been here, skulking about, after some runaways of his own. Not finding them in Oberlin, he got track of them, as he supposed, at Elyria. Not finding them there either, he went to Painesville, and tried his hand, but met with very poor success in Painesville, I believe [laughter]; so he left [renewed laughter], he left there and went to Sandusky; and from Sandusky I think he headed himself for Kentucky. After he had reached home, and found that the power of attorney had been sent forward by Mitchell to him at Oberlin, he returned thither again. I shall say something by and by about the conflicting memories of himself and Bacon in regard to the arrangement under which he returned; but for the present we'll follow him to Oberlin. He got back there at the old stamping ground, and put up with his old friend Wack. Says he arrived Wednesday night at Oberlin; staid all night; and the next day went to Columbus for a warrant. Says he reached Columbus; applied to Lowe, and also to Mr. Chittenden, the United States Commissioner; procured a warrant; made an arrangement with Lowe and with Davis; with Lowe to go to serve the warrant, and with Davis to go along to assist. Here is another remarkable discrepancy between the recollection of Jennings and that of the men Lowe and Davis, but I pass that. He procured his warrant, and he and Lowe and Davis repaired together to Oberlin, arriving there on Friday evening just at dusk. They staid all night there; spent the day on Saturday in cogitating, seeing in what way they'd go to work; found Mitchell on their arrival, and Mitchell told them that he had had the happiness to see John — (Jennings you know had n't had that pleasure; he had n't seen any thing of him since he saw him hauling sand to build his master's house with, in Kentucky, some time before he ran away). Mitchell says he did get sight of him. The difficulty then was, to know how to find John, or to get hold of him. They spent most of the day on Saturday about the town; Lowe and Davis perhaps going at large, but Mitchell and Jennings keeping in pretty tolerably close. It seems that the people of Oberlin had been put in a state of alarm by an attempt a few days before to run off a family by the name of Waggoner.

Judge BLISS. That is not in evidence in this case.

Mr. GRISWOLD. Two witnesses swear to it.

Mr. BACKUS. It is of no particular consequence excepting in connection with one view of this case. Well, for reasons that were satisfactory to themselves, these gentlemen adopted a peculiar course, as it seems to me, in the arrest of John. They came here, they claim, armed with a regular power of attorney from Bacon to Jennings, who (Bacon) claimed to be the owner of the boy John, granting full authority to arrest and take him back to Kentucky. To make assurance doubly sure, Jennings had gone to Columbus and procured a warrant, together with the services of a United States Marshal and his assistant. Here, then, according to their claim, they stood upon high legal and moral ground, having the power of attorney, and the warrant, and the marshal, and his assistant, and authority to summon the posse of the county — all to aid and support them in making the arrest. Well, now, one way would have been to have found John and arrested him. And that would have been the legal and respectable way. But instead of this, by going about the town and its vicinity, and under one pretence and another, getting ladies to keep them over night, alleging that they wanted to "*buy cows*," they took such a course as necessarily to awaken the fears of the people that unlawful designs were entertained and about to be executed against some of the colored people of that place. I know that if a police officer or a sheriff has a warrant for a man who is skulking about and keeping out of the way, it may be proper that he should use secrecy — and for what purpose? Only to enable the officer to get his hands upon the rogue; but for no other purpose. But there could be no such pretence or excuse in this case, for John was always within sight and reach at any time of day or night. There is no intimation that he took the slightest pains to keep himself out of the way, or supposed himself in any more danger than any of the rest of the people of his color in that place. On the contrary, the very opposite appears from testimony, and more clearly still in the very circumstances of his arrest, and the *ease* by which he was decoyed into the trap. And with such assistants as Wack and Warren and Dayton, surely these gentlemen could have no difficulty in finding out the whereabouts of any "nigger" in that town! Why, then, should they act as though they were going to do a mean and shameful thing, and thus necessarily awaken the suspicions of the good people of Oberlin that foul play was brewing?

But, taking their own course, they went over to Boynton's, and there cooked up a plan on Sunday — I suppose that was n't *communion day* with friend Jennings, or that Christian worthy would not have been absent from his accustomed seat at the Sacred Table: — but I believe this is not in evidence in this case either; so I will refrain from any comments upon it; it was on the other trial that the District-Attorney testified to Jennings's devout piety, and could wish Oberlin nothing better than that its piety was half as sanctified as his; so we 'll let that pass: — This little Shakespeare Boynton was employed to go and decoy the boy out of town, under pretence of hiring him to dig potatoes, or something of that kind. So the next day he went and found John; but he was nursing Frank, who had got cut in some way; either in a fuss with Jennings trying to get him off, or perhaps in some little domestic difficulty. And John, true to the instincts of his affectionate nature, preferred to stay and care for the wants of his disabled friend, rather than to embrace the opportunity of earning the money he so much needed. But he told Shakespeare that he knew another negro who would perhaps go and dig the potatoes. So the idea straightway took possession of Shakespeare that this offer might be turned to advantage, and he, receiving John's assurance that he would go with him if desired, in search of the other man, put out for Wack's to consult with Jennings. Jennings scratched his head [laughter] and concluded the game would do to try at any rate, and Shakespeare returned to John. They proposed to drive to New Oberlin, where this other colored man resided, but were only fairly out of town when they met or overtook him, and he, pleading previous engagements, and declining the overtures, there was another standstill. But only for an instant, for Shakespeare, never at a loss, quickly urged, "Well, John, you've been cooped up there so long, the fresh air must feel good to you; and you may as well have a good ride while you 're about it; I'll bring you back again," and John being nothing loth to accept so flattering an offer, they drove on. Some two miles out, the kidnappers, Lowe, Davis, and Mitchell, overtook and drew up with them, and Davis, springing first out, seized John; Mitchell helped get him in, while Lowe held the horses, and, whirling about, they headed for Wellington, with their helpless victim. Shakespeare, returning to Wack's, found the faithful Jennings awaiting him; got his twenty dollars, and went home to boast of the exploit; and Jennings, getting a hasty dinner, set out to join his cronies at Wellington. This is the statement of the arrest briefly, as given by the four worthies themselves, and entirely corroborated by Shakespeare. I believe these five all tell the story, so far, alike.

Now I understand from the District-Attorney, that this indictment charges a rescue, not from the custody of the marshal, nor from the custody of Mitchell, nor from the custody of Davis, nor from the custody of any person whatsoever, except the custody of Mr. *Anderson Jennings*. This is the first count. The second count, the District-Attorney tells us, has a great deal of surplusage and immaterial matter in it, which, sifted out, leaves it in substance the same as the first. I shall, therefore, as in duty bound, accept his construction of the two counts, and argue upon the one charge, that the rescue was from the custody of Jennings, the alleged agent of Bacon, the alleged owner.

Now then, Gentlemen, you have heard the testimony with regard to the issue of this warrant, and with regard to the presence of Lowe there with the warrant. You will remember that Jennings remained back at the tavern, with the understanding that he should stay and pay their bill, and pay Shakespeare, and join them at Wellington, having of course the power of attorney all the while in his possession. Lowe, who had the warrant, and Mitchell and Davis proceeded to the spot where John was. The vehicle in which John was riding, in accordance with the arrangement between them and Shakespeare, slacked its pace, that they might overtake him, and then stopped, that they might seize and carry him off. You remember Mitchell's testimony as to how John was ordered to change conveyances, and how they finally transferred him from one carriage to the other, with the use of such physical force as was necessary, Lowe holding the horses, and Mitchell helping Davis manage John. It is said that the authority under which he was arrested was not shown him, until they had got so far on the way as to reach the spot where the Elyria road branched from the one they were travelling; and then since they had thus far told him they were going to take him to Elyria, it became necessary to explain away such a representation, which they did by frankly telling him, as Lowe says he himself did, that he was under arrest as a runaway slave, by virtue of the warrant of a United States Commissioner, and would be taken back to his master forthwith. There can be no doubt, then, in the mind of any living being, that, so far as Lowe was capable of making an arrest under that warrant, this arrest was complete. It cannot be claimed, except by very fine-spun logic, that, although Lowe was there under the Ægis of the United States, for the execution of the warrant then in his hands, when he took John into his possession by virtue of that warrant, he then had not John in *his* custody, but that John was in the custody of *Jennings*, who was back there in Oberlin, playing " hob nob " with his friend Wack. I know that Lowe was set in motion by Jennings, directed in some of his movements by Jennings, and all that: but it seems to me that John was just as much in Lowe's custody, as though he had acted upon a letter from Bacon alone. Why, of course, he had Jennings's advice. Scarcely any one is arrested unless at the instance of some private citizen : the party who sues out the writ, as a general thing advises and directs the officer. It sometimes happens that under some circumstances a warrant is sworn out for a crime of such a character, that the officer will go on and serve the writ without re-

gard to the person who swears it out. But ordinarily, in nine cases out of ten, the officer follows the advice and direction of the party getting out the writ, to a very great extent; and who ever supposed a defendant, a party charged with crime, to be in the *custody of the complaining witness*, because the officer in making the arrest had followed the direction of the complaining witness, and because the warrant was placed by him in the hands of the officer.

Again, whenever a process in a civil case is placed in the hands of an officer to be served — in the case of a levy upon property, for instance — why, the officer is under the direction, of course, of the party for whom or in whose behalf the writ issues; he levies in pursuance to the direction of the party getting out the writ; and in case of replevy the same is true; — now, then, after the levy or replevy is made, and the property taken into possession, it is undoubtedly in one sense under the control of the plaintiff in execution or replevin; and if at any time after the levy or replevy, and before bail given, has been made, this party shall say to the officer, " I want you to release that levy or replevy," he will be most likely to do as requested, taking care to indorse this direction upon his writ; but who ever thought that in such cases the property was in the *custody* of the plaintiff in execution! Who ever heard it said that, while that property yet remained in the hands of the officer, it was nevertheless in the *custody* of the party in whose behalf the writ of replevy or execution was issued! Who ever dreamed, when indicting a man for stealing property thus held, of alleging that it was stolen from the *plaintiff in execution!* Why, an indictment would not lie still a minute containing such an averment of ownership of property alleged to have been stolen from such custody! Undoubtedly the case is the same here. Lowe followed the directions of Jennings, but he had a warrant in his hands, and it was under and by virtue of that warrant, if at all, that he had the custody of this negro boy John. And it seems to me to be idle to talk about the negro boy John's being then in the custody of *Jennings*, after he had thus been arrested, and before the officer had relinquished control of him. I am not going to deny that it was in the power — however improper it might have been — of Lowe to have refused to obey the mandate of that writ. The writ commanded him to arrest this slave John, and to bring him before the commissioner who issued the writ, that he might then and there receive all and singular those things which should then and there be considered of him in that behalf, and it gave him no authority whatever to surrender him after arrest and before return, to the agent, the owner, or any person whomsoever. And whenever the officer under such circumstances should discharge the person named in the warrant, after arrest and before return, or deliver him into the custody and control of another, he would thereby disobey the writ, and do what he had no right to do; although as there might be no one to complain except the person who sued out the writ, he might be held harmless. But so long as that officer of the law continued to control the person arrested by virtue of that warrant, and down to the time when he should deliver him over to the control of some third party, it seems to me to be idle to talk about his being in the custody of anybody else than the officer.

Now I say, Gentleman of the Jury, that this boy John was arrested by Lowe, was taken into his custody, and remained so, under and by virtue of that warrant, from the time of the arrest down to the time when he says he delivered him over to Jennings, on his entrance into that room there on the second floor of the tavern.

There can be no sort of question, there can be no sort of doubt, that, during all this time at least, John was in the custody of this Marshal Lowe, and any rescue made during that time must necessarily have been alleged to have been made, not from the custody of Bacon or of Jennings, but from the custody of the marshal having him in custody under the law.

The question of fact then arises here, as to whether the custody that was taken of this boy John by Lowe, under and by order of his warrant, did cease upon the arrival of Jennings at that tavern, where he found John in the second story, by arrangement between Lowe and Jennings; or whether that custody did continue down to the time that he was in fact rescued? And I shall claim, may it please the Court, that if that jury shall find, that the testimony does not establish the proposition that there was a change in the custody of John, between the time of the arrival of Lowe with the negro in his custody at Wellington, and the time when John was rescued, then the allegation in this indictment being that the rescue was from the custody — not of the officer of the law, not of Lowe — but from the custody of Jennings; whether there were a rescue or not, this prosecution must fail, because the testimony proves one thing and the indictment alleges another.

How is the fact, then, with regard to any change of custody? I claim without hesitation and without doubt, that you will agree with me, that, down to the time of the arrival of Jennings at the public house at Wellington, Jennings finding them on that second floor, John was in the custody of Lowe as a United States Marshal. Now, Lowe says, that, fearing his liability under the statute, he transferred the custody of John to Mitchell, the agent of the owner, immediately upon his arrival — to Jennings, I would say. And from that time he was no longer acting as a Deputy United States Marshal, was no longer acting under and by virtue of that warrant, but was acting merely as an assistant of Jennings, the agent of the owner. Now, Gentlemen, is that true? Why, who swears to it? Who heard any thing of that kind at the time Lowe alleges it transpired? Lowe himself swears that such was the fact. He *does not state so in his direct testimony;* but on being asked in the course of the cross-examination, if he ever parted with the custody of the boy, he sees what is needed to make out a case, and immediately "remembers" that he *did!*

Jennings goes on to give a detail of what happened. Says he arrived there; went up into that room; thought the room insecure; gave directions, or made arrangements for another room; saw the landlord; procured another room in the third story, that he regarded as more safe; and so on. Jennings don't tell you any thing about a transfer of the custody of the boy to him by Lowe. But in the end, when he was finally questioned as to whether there was any transfer, he says that *he thought he had the custody of the boy all the time!* He thought that John was in his custody all the time that he and his captors were on their way from the place of arrest to Wellington! But Jennings certainly has no very luminous ideas on any phase of the subject. But if it be true, as Lowe swears, that he transferred the custody to Jennings, then the custody must have been in Lowe down to that time, which contradicts the shadowy impression that seems to have brooded on Mr. Jennings's mind, that the boy was from the first, and all the time, in his custody; and it is, therefore, farther evident that the stupid Mr. Jennings and the sagacious Mr. Lowe were at that time acting upon entirely different views of the case. Now, Gentlemen, you have the testimony of Lowe, and he is the only man who swears to any such transfer. If Jennings comes to this at all, it is by a very vague and general and undefined notion that he has, away up somewhere in his head, that the custody was in him *all the time.* If there was such a transfer of custody, why did n't Jennings know of it, or Mitchell, or Davis, not one of whom knows any thing about it now? Lowe alone swears to it, and he alone professes to know any thing about it. I have heard it said that it takes two to make a bargain, but here is an arrangement of vast importance between two, and made only by one! A very extraordinary kind of a bargain, it seems to me!

If you are bound to take every thing as true to which Mr. Lowe may choose to swear, then there need be no farther investigation upon any point. But if you are bound to take his testimony in connection with the testimony of others, then let us go over the ground and see what was the conduct of Lowe and Mitchell and Jennings and Davis on that afternoon. By whom was it claimed to the crowd; by whom was it represented to those who came in to inquire, that the boy was held? Why, they tell you that the "*papers*" were shown; and when you ask them, What papers? they tell you that the warrant was shown, and are painfully fearful lest they forget to add, "and the power of attorney too."

Well, now, we have an issue as to whether that power of attorney was or was not shown. The witnesses for the prosecution — some of them — say it was, others think it was, and others don't know; while the witnesses for the defence, a most formidable and unimpeachable array, swear positively that it *was not.* But there is no controversy between the witnesses for the prosecution and the witnesses for the defence, as to whether the *warrant* was shown, on any and every possible occasion, as authority, *among* the papers, at least. The Government witnesses say the warrant and the power of attorney were both shown. They might very properly both be shown, although they all understood very well that John was arrested, and was then held by the warrant alone. Why, that warrant asserts that it was issued upon the oath of Anderson Jennings; but it does n't say that Anderson Jennings was the *agent* of anybody. Who Anderson Jennings was, or what power, or what right he had to go and make an affidavit, nowhere appears outside the power of attorney itself. It was, therefore, in the highest degree proper, that at the same time the warrant was exhibited the power of attorney should be exhibited too, for the purpose of showing that not only had the officer a proper warrant, but, going behind it, there was a proper affidavit, and authority to make such affidavit was conferred in the power of attorney. But I want you to observe, Gentlemen, that in every instance, when Wheeler went there — and he is apparently one of the friends of these claimants — made their acquaintance immediately, and sympathized with them to no inconsiderable extent, having himself a brother down there who might some day be in as bad a fix, and with whom at least one of these Kentuckians was acquainted: — what papers were shown him? Why, the *warrant* at any rate, and I believe also the power of attorney. And you remember that when Watson came from Oberlin, on the alarm that a man had been kidnapped, and, knowing their previous suspicious conduct, had gone before Esquire Bennett, and made an affidavit, charging that these persons had kidnapped John, and got a warrant issued for their arrest, and the constable Meacham, an intelligent and respectable man, at least so far as appearance goes, and in fact, having the warrant in his hands, went up and informed Jennings, and informed Lowe, and informed Mitchell, and informed Davis for what purpose he had come, — they replied to him, — and what was the reply? Why *Lowe* came forward in behalf of all — and this was in the room in the third story, a considerable time after the transfer of custody had taken place, according to Lowe — and *Lowe* says, "you can't arrest *me;* you have no power to take *me* into your custody on a warrant from a State magistrate; I am an officer of the United States; I have a warrant here, regularly issued by a United States Commissioner, *under which I am acting;* I have this boy John in *my* custody, by virtue of that warrant; and now, sir, if you proceed one step towards the execution of this magistrate's warrant of yours, you proceed at your peril." Now if Lowe had in fact, a little time previous to that, not to exceed perhaps half an hour, divested himself of all authority and control over the negro boy John, and changed positions, from that of a United States officer, executing a warrant, and having the negro in custody under and by virtue of that warrant, to the position of a private citizen, assisting Jennings the agent, can you credit for a moment that he would have said to Meacham, " Why, sir, I am a United States Deputy-Marshal, *acting under and by virtue of this warrant,* which I show to you — there it is — read it for yourself, and *it is under and by virtue of this warrant that I have* this negro in custody: now, sir, you must not interfere with me?" Can it be possible that he would have used that language, if he had already made such a transfer? Can it be said that for the purpose of magnifying his position he would tell this downright lie? If so, then of what consequence is it to what he swears? But I tell you nay, Gentlemen; he told the truth, the exact truth, and utterly omitted to count upon any authority of Jennings. That power of attorney was not shown to Meacham; no reliance was placed upon it by Lowe; none by Jennings, who was there threatened momentarily with arrest by this State officer; no reference was made to it by this man Mitchell, who was imported here to do the business of swearing. They stood — all stood — upon the warrant and upon the warrant alone. By virtue of the power of that warrant they warned the State officer off. Now it seems to me, that, if that man Lowe should stand upon that stand and swear until doomsday, that he had, a little while before this interview with Meacham, transferred the custody of John from himself to Jennings, not one man of you would believe one word of it. You know that *it cannot be* true, in the very nature of things. If such a transfer had been made, *Jennings* would have said to Meacham, " Why, my dear sir, *I* have that boy in custody, as the agent of John G. Bacon, his owner, and here is the power of attorney by which I am authorized to hold him, and do you let that boy alone, or *I'll* make you smart for it, for I am protected by this power of attorney;" and Mitchell, who is most of the time under oath without the ceremony of administering it, would have come forward and testified to the accuracy of the instrument and the identity of the boy; and that man would not have been allowed to go below stairs without being fully notified of the authority by which the boy was held; and he did not go below without such a notification, for Lowe gave it to him in the most explicit terms. But go farther; Esquire Bennett was sent for, — the magistrate who issued the warrant for the arrest of Lowe and his party. He went up; he saw the papers; they were freely exhibited to him. What did he see? what was exhibited to him? what were the papers? He went up for the purpose of seeing whether the warrant that he himself had issued should be executed and enforced or not. He calls for the papers, and they are shown;—what papers are shown? Why, that *warrant*, and that warrant alone, was shown as authority. The power of attorney was handed him for the purpose of showing that the commissioner's warrant had a legal basis, and was legally issued, and for this purpose only, as Bennett himself testifies; solely for the purpose of showing that that commissioner's warrant had been regularly issued. I know that with regard to Meacham, Jennings and Lowe and Mitchell all swear that the power of attorney was exhibited to him; but, Gentlemen, you will believe that man Meacham, taking into consideration the circumstances and probabilities, against a great many more such as Mitchell and his cronies.

Then again, Dickson, who is a lawyer, was sent for; a lawyer living there at Wellington; he too a man taking no part in this disturbance, if any disturbance there were. He inquires, the first thing, for their authority. The warrant was shown him too, and the warrant alone. You will remember, then, that to Meacham, the constable, threatening them with instant arrest, the warrant alone was put forward as their authority and protection; to Bennett, the magistrate who issued the warrant for their arrest, and who came up to see if he should not enforce the service of his process, the commissioner's warrant alone was put forward as their authority and protection, with a casual reference to the power of attorney as its basis; to Dickson, the lawyer who was called in by them, and sought to be employed as their legal adviser, the warrant alone is spread out as the broad platform upon which he is invited to stand with them. Dickson read it carefully through; observed that there was no seal; he didn't observe that little quirk there, which the District-Attorney said had escaped his notice, until his attention was particularly called to it the other day, and would have escaped the notice of almost any one. Dickson remarked, that every thing seemed to be regular about the warrant except the lack of a seal. Lowe replied that it was not customary or necessary to have seals to this kind of papers. He, being an officer accustomed to the service of such kind of writs, might naturally be supposed to know what was necessary to their validity. And now when Mr. Dickson came, thus sent for to be employed as their counsel, how came Lowe and Jennings to exhibit to him this warrant alone, if it be true that such a transfer of custody had taken place as Lowe alleges?

Other parties came up too. Patton was there. You saw him on the stand; an intelligent man, a man likely to have influence in the crowd. They saw this, and were desirous to satisfy him of the legality of their process, and of their right to hold John. And for the purpose of doing this, what paper did they exhibit to him? Why, this *warrant*, and this warrant alone! In reading the warrant, he noticed that it purported to have been sworn out by Anderson Jennings, without stating what relation the said Jennings claimed to sustain to the fugitive; and when, on Patton's asking him if he was the owner of the boy, he replied that *he was*, without giving his name; and before Patton had learned his name from any source, Patton was necessarily left to infer that Anderson Jennings was the owner. And as he did not—he says so upon his oath—so much as hear of a power of attorney at any time during that day, nor at any time subsequent or previous, till he heard of it and saw it presented on the first of these trials, there was no supposition left him but that, as Lowe said, *he* held the boy, and had the owner along as one of his assistants, instead of acting himself as the assistant of this man Jennings, who claims at one time to be owner, at another to be the agent, and at another to act only irresponsibly, out of pure neighborly regard, just as he thinks he can best carry his points. No attempt was made to exhibit to Patton any authority beside the warrant, or any person as the custodian other than Lowe. Now, how can anybody reconcile this with Lowe's story of a transfer of custody? Again, as the affair progressed, and as night approached, these men growing anxious to get away, it was proposed to them to go below and show their authority—to read it—to the crowd, for the purpose of making the crowd see that if they made any resistance, or interfered in any way to interrupt the return of the process, they would be acting illegally. The proposition was finally accepted, and then who went? *Jennings*,—to whom Lowe swears he had long ago surrendered all his authority, and in whose custody alone the boy now was? Oh, no; but Mr. *Lowe*, the pompous Deputy-Marshal of the United States of North America! And what paper did he take with him to read? The power of attorney? Of course not; but the identical *warrant* which had been kept in such industrious activity throughout the entire afternoon. They passed out the back door—Patton and Meacham had promised to see him safely out and back—to the south of the tavern, on to the steps of the drug-store [Mr. BACKUS here exhibited a diagram to the jury], and the paper was read to the crowd. What paper was read? Why, if Jacob K. Lowe tells you the truth when he says that on Jennings's arrival he transferred the entire custody and control of John to him—to Jennings—and after that Jennings alone held him, and held him, of course, only by virtue of the power of attorney, no paper but the power of attorney could have been read, unless the intention was to perpetrate a solemn hoax upon the crowd. Now Lowe says he can't remember which was read; that he had both papers with him, and that Patton read one, and began to read the other, and then he saw the rush into the house, and knew that foul play would be used, and so snatched the second paper away from Patton, and ran into the house and up to the room. Now Patton, the man that read whatever was read to the crowd, swears most unequivocally and positively that the warrant was handed to him to read, and that he read it and handed it back again; and that he saw no other paper in Lowe's possession; that none other was handed or offered to him to be read, and that he neither read, nor began to read, nor thought of reading any other. Cowles stood next to Patton, and looked over his shoulder while he read; and he says that it was the warrant that was read, and the warrant only, and that no other paper was offered or shown, and this Mr. Cowles is a gentleman who certainly has intelligence enough to know what he is testifying to, and integrity enough to tell the whole truth, as any one would be satisfied at a glance; which, as I have already said, is equally true of Mr. Patton. And Patton commented on the lack of a seal in the hearing of the crowd, and Bennett was near by and understood what was read, and says it was the warrant and the warrant only. Can you then have any doubt, Gentlemen, that Lowe was mistaken about that transfer—to use the mildest phrase—and that John continued to be in his custody down to the very moment of the rescue? You cannot doubt which paper was read to the crowd, or that it was the paper under and by virtue of which the boy was held; and that when Lowe, at the close of the reading, commanded the crowd, in the name of the United States, to disperse, and allow him to complete the return of his process, he did so, not as a private citizen, and the assistant of Anderson Jennings, but as a Deputy-Marshal of the United States, acting — as he claimed — under and by virtue of that Commissioner's warrant which had just been read. And if, at the close of the reading of this warrant, the custody was still in Lowe, it certainly was at the time of the rescue, which was only five or ten minutes later, during which Patton was constantly with Lowe, and no transfer in the mean time is claimed to have been made. Whatever, then, was true as to the party in whose custody John was at the time of the reading of that paper down there in the crowd in front of that drug shop, was equally true at the time John passed out of the house, ten minutes or less afterwards. And I say to you, Gentlemen, that you cannot hesitate one moment in coming to the conclusion — and I care not where your political biases are, or what your inclinations are — your intellect will *force* you to come to the conclusion that John was rescued, if rescued at all, *not* from the custody of Anderson Jennings, but from the custody of Jacob K. Lowe; and if that be so, the allega-

tion of the indictment is not met; the rescue was a different one from that alleged, and the prosecution must of necessity fail.

But, Gentlemen, there still remains to be considered another phase of this case, and that has reference to the agency of the defendant in the rescue, be it what it may have been. Now the proof shows that there was a crowd there at Wellington surrounding that house, commencing a comparatively small crowd, called together many of them by the fire on the opposite side of the street by which the interests of many in that place had suffered severely — you see by the diagram where it was — but when the rumor became prevalent that there was a negro there in the hands of Southerners, on his way to the South, and that rumor was reiterated by the parties coming in from Oberlin, and the word went out through the crowd that it was a case of *kidnapping*, and that a warrant had been issued for the arrest of the parties having the boy in custody as kidnappers, the crowd began to gather about the hotel, and kept increasing till I think Jennings was able to count a thousand — though that is some five hundred more than any one else estimated it at. It is undoubtedly true that the indications were such as to inspire the men who had John in custody with the apprehension that there might be a rescue. I am not disposed to question this. And these men were thus kept there from dinner-time till six and a half or seven o'clock. Now whether John may have been forcibly withdrawn from the custody of these Southerners, headed by Lowe the marshal, or whether such intimidations were brought to bear upon them as to induce them to let John go, — in a legal view matters nothing. Unquestionably it would be a rescue in either case. It may be conceded, then, on this testimony here, that so far as a rescue could take place from the custody of the marshal, under the circumstances of the case, a rescue did take place there. But whether such a rescue could have any effect upon this defendant would depend first upon the question as to whether the rescue proved was the rescue charged in the indictment. If the rescue proved was from a custody other than that charged, the defendant must go acquit so far as this trial is concerned. But I propose to discuss the question whether he took part in the rescue of John from the custody of any human being there that day. And I say without hesitation, that you must agree with me, that the prosecution has utterly failed to prove the case as it must be proved on a criminal trial. I know there has been testimony here such as might lead a shrewd Yankee to *guess* that Langston might have had something more to do with the rescue than he ought to have had; but while he was guessing so, five others would guess that if Langston's counsels had been followed, there would have been no rescue there that day, and only legal measures attempted. And although an " African sun may have burned upon him" or upon some of his ancestors, thank God, the defendant has at least one remnant of a right yet left him, and that is the same right to justice in this trial before this Anglo-Saxon jury that any one of their own color would have. And the jury must find him proven guilty beyond a reasonable doubt, and that his action can be accounted for upon no other hypothesis than that of guilt, or else they must acquit him. If there is any other possible hypothesis, you must accept it in preference to that of his guilt, and acquit him; and they need not be evenly balanced to demand this at your hands; there must be a preponderance; and not only that, but the proof must be so clear that *not a reasonable doubt can remain.*

Now there are two hypotheses here, either of which will account for his presence in that crowd. First, that he was there to effect the rescue, law or no law; and second, that he was attracted there as hundreds of others were, by the cry of kidnapping, having known the suspicious conduct of these parties in and about Oberlin for some time immediately previous. You know well, Gentlemen, that numbers of men went from Oberlin to Wellington, actuated by this understanding of the case; and that others went out of mere curiosity; and whether they hindered or not, had no sort of purpose of aiding the rescue; and the Government has been compelled to put witness after witness upon the stand, who swear that they were such persons, and were as much in the crowd as this defendant, and, so far as their acts went, several of them are vastly more open to the charge of aiding in the rescue than he. Now we say to you, that the same motives which took them took this defendant — curiosity; some sympathy perhaps — much more I should hope than some of these had. I say that this defendant, my client, went there out of curiosity, interest, sympathy, and I hope, too, with a determination that, if this man had been spirited away unlawfully, he would bare his arm and *strike* if need, and employ physical force to any necessary extent, but that the outrage should be averted. There is no proof, however, that he used or advised any degree of physical force whatever, illegal as it has been proven here the arrest and custody were. But it would seem that he supposed the custody to have the sanction of law. There is no proof as to what his motives or his intentions were, but I hope, and believe they were those of an honest MAN, and that he meant to prevent an outrage if he found one threatened, at any cost, and by the most effective means within his reach. I should be ashamed of him if it were not so. You would be ashamed of him. You would be ashamed of yourselves if, in a like emergency, this were not true of you. But certainly there is no proof that he meant to break any law, and we say his course was marked out

by a determination to adhere strictly to legal measures. His object was to ascertain whether these men had seized John legally — with a legal process. And we say that you will find him, if you will follow him step by step from the time he left Oberlin, or is supposed to have left there — there is no evidence to show that he came from there at all — you will find his course characterized all the way it is traceable, by advice for the pursuit of legal means for the purpose of ascertaining by what authority John was held. What he wanted all the way, and what he determined to have, was light upon the subject, that he might know under what circumstances and by what means John had been borne so suspiciously away. I say, then, here are two hypotheses; the one that of the Government, that he went there for the purpose of rescuing John whether he was held rightfully or wrongfully, — I must not use these terms lest they may seem to have a *moral* bearing, and in this case there is a very wide difference between the *legal* and the *moral* view. I will say, then, *legally* or *illegally.* And the other is, that he only sought to ascertain the character of the custody; and we say, that his whole endeavor was to ascertain whether these men, who had John in custody, held him by legal or illegal authority. You are to say which is the true hypothesis. If the testimony leaves any reasonable doubt on your mind as to whether he was actuated by the one motive or the other; if you should find even, upon the whole, that the testimony going to establish the proposition of the Government were the stronger, but you could still see that there was reason to some extent for doubt; that it might be after all that what Langston professed over and over again was true, that he wished only legal measures to be pursued; — why, then, you are bound by your oaths to bring in a verdict of acquittal. Yes, and much more firmly bound than by that other obligation of your oath, which will compel you under this statute — objectionable as this statute is, outraging the feelings of every man who cares an iota for the rights of his fellows — this statute which has begotten and can beget nothing but trouble and turmoil and disturbance; — I say your obligation to bring in a verdict of acquittal, is tenfold stronger than that to bring in one of condemnation; for the one will have only the approbation of the judgment, and the other has superadded to this, the gratification that must prevail in the breast of every man of you that you are not forced to bring in a verdict of guilty against that man who has been guilty of no moral crime, who has been guilty of no selfishness, who has sinned not against his conscience or his God, but against the provisions of a law only, which denies to men of his color the rights of manhood. Well, Gentlemen, what is the testimony upon which the prosecution relies to establish the guilt of the defendant Langston? Why, you must have seen that a large portion of the testimony — perhaps it is the "nine tenths" to which Mr. District-Attorney alluded, and which he himself characterized as "utterly useless," in which I heartily concur with him — has been of no service to the Government, but your time has been mostly occupied in giving attention to what the crowd at Oberlin said and did; what the crowd on the way to Wellington said and did; and what the crowd at Wellington said and did, which is of no pertinence to the issue, and has no competency here unless to show that what the crowd said and did, Langston said and did. This might be done by first showing that there was concert of action in the crowd, or in that part of the crowd with which Langston unmistakably identified himself; but you must find the connection, you must find the combination, you must see that they had confederated together for a common and definite purpose. I do not claim, and it is idle for any one to claim, that to show such a combination it must be shown that they had an organization, a formal meeting, with a moderator and secretary, or adopted any special rules or resolutions. But what I do claim is, that before you can charge one man with the acts of others, you must show that that man, whom you seek to affect, has united in purpose with the other men whose conduct is given in evidence; for short of that it would be an outrage on his rights to say that he was to be affected by any thing that was said or done by individuals chancing to stand within a given number of feet of where he stood. This testimony, then, Gentlemen, that has been permitted to go to you by the Court, under the pledge of the District-Attorney that, before he closed his case, he would show such combination as would charge upon Langston all the acts of the crowd, — which indulgence of the Court was right, of course, upon the conditions made, but not otherwise, — this testimony, I say, if you will scan it closely, it seems to me, can produce in the mind of no man of you the conviction that this crowd, including the defendant, did confederate by words or communication of thoughts for the accomplishment of an unlawful purpose. And, again, I say, the Government has placed witness after witness on that stand, who were in the crowd, who acted with the crowd, but who were in no combination with that part of the crowd that may have had unlawful purposes in view. If, then, Gentlemen of the Jury, it be true that Bennett was there in that crowd for a lawful purpose, that Meacham was there in that crowd for a lawful purpose, that Howk was there in that crowd for a· lawful purpose, that Marks was there in that crowd for a lawful purpose, that Wack was there in that crowd for a lawful purpose, that E. S. Lyman, Halbert, Barber, and even *Norris A. Wood*, and dozens of others, all apparently more or less active participants in some, at least, of the actions of the crowd, beside the two hundred or three

hundred, brought there by the fire, were all there for lawful purposes, taking no voluntary part in any unlawful proceedings, — then I submit that this defendant cannot possibly be implicated by the evidence with the rescue made by a part of that crowd. While he stood dumb and inactive, Wood and Marks and Wack were laboring in all possible ways to increase the excitement of the populace, by putting up ladders, by shouting, "Here he goes!" "This way!" "Keep a sharp look-out!" etc., doing much more to disturb the peace and promote such excitement as would prompt to the rescue, each one of them, than a score of men like this defendant. The testimony on this point is clear, unanimous, and unmistakable. I say, then, if these were all there, thus active, and actuated only by lawful motives, then, to say the least, this defendant *may* have been in the same crowd and actuated with an equally lawful purpose; and, more than that, I say the testimony abundantly shows that he was so. I say, therefore, proof of what was done in the crowd cannot affect this defendant, Langston, without additional proof that he was connected with that part of that crowd which had an illegal purpose in view, and that illegal purpose, the rescue of John from lawful custody. Now what portion of that crowd, Gentlemen, did participate in any illegal purpose with regard to the rescue of John from lawful custody, as it is claimed? I am not going into any detailed examination of the testimony on this point, for, if I did, — I — should — wake up — my old friend there (one of the jurors), [laughter] which I do not wish to do! But I wish to say, in brief, that, so far as the evidence shows, all the persons in that whole crowd who purposed to rescue John, in violation of law, would not exceed *fifty*. Now, then, upon what testimony does the Government rely for the purpose of showing that Langston was connected in purpose and intent with this insignificant minority of that crowd; — the *few* who were bent upon doing what they had no legal right to do? Why, you have heard the testimony; it has been detailed and presented to you by my friend and associate, Mr. GRISWOLD, in a very clear and able manner; and it is not necessary for me to go into it at length again.

Jennings is the first witness called. What is his testimony? I want you to scan his testimony closely, and notice how poor his memory is on some points, and how confusedly stubborn it is on others. How is it that Langston is first seen in that crowd between four and five o'clock? Where he came from or for what purpose he came, the testimony does not show. Now if there is any witness who has sworn that he saw Langston at Oberlin that day prior to the rescue, it has escaped my notice. If any one has so sworn, if it should turn out so, all there is of it is that he was at Oberlin in the forenoon, and at Wellington at some three, four, or five o'clock in the afternoon; but how he got to Wellington, or for what purpose he came, does not appear. But what did he do after he got there? I don't know but I may as well take Lowe for my text. He says that after he and his party got into the upper story, he looked out of the window and saw Langston in the crowd, and as he had known him for years in Columbus, and knew that he was a well disposed, law-abiding, and reasonable man, and just such a man as he wanted at such a time — *just such a man, Gentlemen, Lowe swears he had for years known him to be, as we now claim him to be* — he sent for him, or said in some one's hearing that he wished he could see him; and so John Watson — not our worthy member of the Legislature to be sure — though I thought it was he that was indicted until I was introduced to this other gentleman, — by no means a less respectable one, although happening to have a deeper colored skin, — Watson went down to find Langston. Barber says when Watson found Langston, Langston had his hand on a gun. He can't say whether the gun belonged to Langston or to some one else; but Langston took his hand off from it, and went up without it. He may have handed it to some one else to keep for him, or he may have returned it to its owner. The Court will tell you, Gentlemen, that you are here — as everywhere — bound to infer that the defendant's connection with that gun was innocent, in the absence of sufficient proof to establish without reasonable doubt that it was criminal. And as this is the only occasion during the entire day when arms of any sort were seen at all in his possession, the balance of probability alone will oblige you to believe that this was not his gun, and that he was only temporarily leaning or resting his hand upon it. Watson goes back and Langston goes with him, up to the room where Lowe was. Lowe tells you that when Langston came up they talked together about matters generally. Lowe says he explained to him how things were, and *explained* the papers to him — can't remember that he *showed* him any papers; it is no matter whether they were shown or not. Lowe says Langston expressed himself satisfied; the papers were either shown or " explained " to him; and Lowe, counting upon the knowledge that he had of the defendant by means of a long-standing acquaintance, asked him to use his influence with the crowd for peace; and he says he promised he would, and expressed himself in favor of legal measures. At the instance, then, of Lowe, as Lowe says, Langston went down to the crowd, and after having been gone some twenty minutes, returned. Now this first conversation was in the room where John was.

Whether there were any persons present and listening I do not now know. It is very probable there were; but thus much is perfectly evident, that the whole tenor of that conversation, so far as John was concerned, was to the effect that he (Langston) was satisfied with the state of the case as shown by Lowe. Lowe

requested him to give his aid in quieting the crowd and to help them get away with their prisoner, and *Lowe* swears — whatever Jennings or Davis or Wheeler may have dreamed — that he said he *would*, and appeared to speak candidly and honestly. And I wish you to observe, therefore, that in *this* conversation, neither Mr. Jennings nor any other man could have heard Langston say to Lowe, that he would *not* assist him, but *would have John*, papers or no papers; for if he had so told Lowe, most certainly his ears are not so short that he would have been left with the conviction that Langston was acting in good faith in going down to the crowd for the professed purpose of using his influence in Lowe's behalf; I wish you also to notice that Lowe swears that Langston was up stairs, to his knowledge, only twice on that afternoon; that the first time, when their conversation was held in the room where John and others were, the tenor of the conversation was such as to leave on Lowe's mind the most favorable impression of Langston's disposition to assist him in retaining the custody of the negro, and that therefore no such thing could possibly have been said during this conversation by Langston as has been attributed to him by Jennings and Davis, and perhaps others. Lowe swears that in pursuance of his own request and Langston's promise, Langston did go down to the crowd, and that in about twenty minutes he returned, and taking Lowe aside into the little room adjoining, where they two were *alone* together, and no one else was present or in hearing, Langston told him that he had been using his influence with the crowd to dissuade them from attempting any force or other illegal measures. Did Langston tell the truth when he said this? Do not Bennett and Howk and Wheeler, all Government witnesses, tell you that about this time — and to locate it, it is only necessary to refer to the passage of the train, which Lowe says passed during their first interview, and its regular time at that station is said to have been 5:13 — do not these Government witnesses all tell you frankly and explicitly that about this time they found Langston in the crowd, recommending peaceable measures, and urging that there should be no appeal to force; saying that he had been up stairs and had learned by what authority the negro was held? And do they not further swear that he expressed his belief that the papers were legal, and that the only proper course was for them, if they wanted to test the question whether John was or was not legally held, to go to Elyria and procure a writ of *habeas corpus;* that he proposed himself, if they would furnish a horse and buggy, to go and procure that writ? And now it is attempted to be established that he said it was *too late* to go to Elyria, for troops had been sent for, and before they could get back from Elyria, the troops would be there by the train; — *when the train had already passed*, while he was holding that *first* conversation with Lowe! You see, then, how utterly unjust it is to claim that he was serving a double purpose; that he was communicating the information that he had derived up stairs from Lowe, and at the same time covertly advising the crowd not to follow those peaceful means, which he had himself all along recommended.

Now, it is said that he and Patton came out about the same time — or Barber, who swears to it, says he saw them coming from the direction of the back yard; that he, standing in the lane (see diagram), saw them coming along there, approaching him from the direction of the door leading up stairs; did n't know whether they came out of the door together; did n't know, in fact, as they came out of the door, either of them, at all at that time. What he does know, is that he saw them approaching him, moving outward toward the crowd in the street, Patton some fifteen feet ahead of Langston, and that Patton, addressing himself to the crowd, said, that the only legal way to inquire into the custody was by a writ of *habeas corpus* from Elyria, but it was too late then to go for one, and they must do as they pleased. He says that Langston had nothing to do with this proclamation; does n't know as he even heard it, or was near enough to hear it. That Langston stopped some fifteen or eighteen feet back of Patton, and went to talking with persons there, advising the use of peaceable and legal measures. I shall not attempt to allude to all the testimony on this point. Here you have Bennett and Howk and Wheeler and Barber perhaps, and others who all swear to the unvaried tenor of Langston's conversation and conduct, as not only passively, but actually and positively law-abiding. After having been absent some twenty minutes, he returned and called Lowe out into the little room at the head of the stairs. They went into that room and sat down on the bed together, and there they talked, no one beside themselves being present. There was no conversation on this occasion in the room where the negro was, but all that was said was said while they were alone together in the little room adjoining the stairway, and beyond the reach of the ears of those who were in the room with John. Well, Mr. Lowe himself tells you what transpired in this second (and besides the one already alluded to, during which the train passed, the only) conversation they had together that day. He tells you that Langston said to him, " I have been below, talking to the crowd, endeavoring to influence them to take a legal course, but without success. They are determined to take their own course." Was he then playing false to Lowe? Not unless Bennett and Howk — and you all saw in Mr. Howk's honest face, at any rate, that he was a man that did n't *know how* to lie — unless Jacob Wheeler swears false, he told Lowe the truth. Now, Lowe tells you that he saw Langston but twice that day; that the first interview broke up

twenty minutes before the second, and that down to the last moment of the second, he believed that Langston was acting in good faith in his behalf, endeavoring to still the crowd and persuade them to the use of peaceable measures. And that he was induced to suspect Langston's honesty only by the observation he made as he was passing out of the room at the close of this second interview. He says that when Langston had urged him, in view of all the circumstances, to get himself out of what then seemed to be a dangerous position, by using his influence with Jennings — who had declared himself to be the *owner* — to give up the negro, and Lowe had peremptorily declined making any such attempt, Langston rose up and passed out rapidly, and as he passed out, said, " Well, we 'll have him, any way." Now I want you to compare this testimony of Lowe with that of Jennings and Davis. (Of Davis I know very little; but having been privileged with a longer acquaintance with Mr. Jennings, I think *he* could bring himself to believe almost any thing, particularly since he got that "*jabble*" on his head!)

Now, because *Jennings* testifies to a thing, I know there is no man on that Jury simple enough to suppose that it must necessarily be true. Not that Jennings, in telling his absurdities, would always know that he was *lying*; he might have some indistinct idea that he was doing something not quite in keeping with the *Code of Honor* down in Kentucky, but as to *lying*, nothing is surer than that they never taught him what that was in that Church of which he is such an exemplary member, down there! [Laughter.] What possible plausibility is there for believing that Jennings and Davis heard Langston say to Lowe in the first interview — and at no other conversation were they present — "I *won't* help you; but we 'll have him any how?" Mitchell won't swear to any such thing; he was brought here for the express purpose of swearing, but you can't fetch him quite up to *that!* So that either Jennings and Davis testify to what was not true, or else Lowe testifies to what is not true. And Lowe gives you the best reason in the world for believing him, for he declares that up to the time Langston left the room, at the close of that second private interview, he had entire confidence that he was faithfully working for him. And how is it possible to suppose, for a moment, that he could have retained such an impression if Langston had met his overtures in the first interview with such unqualified refusal and repugnance as Jennings and Davis represent? But I know very well how these good easy souls, and especially my old friend Jennings, after hearing Lowe tell of this remark of Langston in the second interview, might actually imagine that they heard it too; and Lowe, unfortunately, not having taken pains to impress upon them that it would n't do for them to swear to it, since he would have to swear that it was made in the second and private interview, at which neither of them was present, nor near enough to be within possible earshot, they out with it before it could be stopped, and then there was nothing but the "jewel of consistency" left to them; — so they stick to it. And now with so strong a reason for believing Lowe rather than Jennings and Davis, is n't your course a plain one, Gentlemen ?

There are other witnesses upon whom the prosecution rely to implicate Langston. In this confusion of testimony it is next to impossible to fix the time of the occurrences which are testified to. But it seems to be clear, that, during the earlier part of the time Langston was there, busied about the arrest of these men for kidnapping, in order that their authority might be subjected to official inspection, he was getting up or helping to get up a bond of indemnity for the constable, who, it seems, was a little tender-footed about serving the warrant that had been issued by Mr. Justice Bennett. It is said that Dickson drew up the bond, and Langston circulated it. This was *before* Lowe sent for him, it is important to remember; *before* he had any reliable intimation of the authority under and by virtue of which they claimed to hold John. It was not Langston who swore out the warrant. The warrant had been sworn out, and the constable had attempted to serve it long before Langston was seen anywhere in that crowd. On his arrival, he heard a dispute about the legality of the custody. Patton, or others, may have expressed, in his hearing, a belief that the custody was legal ; but here was a warrant already issued, and in the hands of the constable, the service of which would insure a satisfactory examination. Making use, therefore, of that common sense, which, I take it upon me to say, he showed himself to be possessed of in an enviable degree, he thought it on all accounts best to have a legal investigation, that John might neither be rescued nor carried off without any one knowing what sanction there might be for either course. He very properly told the constable, "You have no right to go behind the warrant in your hands, and inquire into the legality of its issue ; your sole business is to serve it." Bring the men before these magistrates, candid, honorable men as they are, and it will then appear whether the custody of John is legal or not, and the decision of these magistrates will or ought to satisfy the crowd. Suppose he did hear something about a warrant, and perhaps even something of a power of attorney ; — he none the less justly demanded a legal, official investigation. Why, some of you must have heard of the case in Akron, where, a short time since, a colored man was seized by certain scoundrels, under the pretence that they were arresting him for passing counterfeit money ; they exhibited a forged warrant, which purported to have been issued by Minor, the Clerk of the U. S. Court; but some one happening to look at it, who knew Minor's handwriting, detected the fraud, and

the villains were forced to release their prey. There was reason enough, then, why this defendant should say, that that investigation before the magistrates ought to proceed, and that the crowd should be satisfied with nothing short of it. And even, Gentlemen, if, hearing that Lowe had a warrant — I am talking now about his action in reference to the service of this warrant, which, you will not forget, was immediately after his arrival in the crowd, and *before* Lowe had sent for him to hold the first conversation — if, I say, hearing that Lowe had a warrant, he was satisfied in his own mind ; still, and none the less, for the satisfaction of the crowd, and because he might be deceived himself, and because the man's *liberties* were all at stake, was it not his unquestionable duty — did he not owe it to humanity and justice to do by that boy as you would have demanded of him to do by you in like peril — to press that official investigation, and to rest satisfied with nothing short of it ? I know the District-Attorney has said, and his associate may reiterate it, that it was not proper for the constable to obey the mandate of any such warrant, or to attempt any such arrest. But suppose Langston honestly thought the law authorized it, and acted upon such honest belief, solely for the purpose of securing the rights of *all* parties, and paving the way for the escape of the officer from the difficulties that environed him, if his papers were found to be right ; — and if they were not right, the District-Attorney would not be seen standing up here to claim that that crowd ought to have *allowed* a case of *kidnapping* in their midst ! — shall a man for *such* conduct be branded by this Court as a violator of the public peace and the rights of citizens ? A man intending only a lawful course, and advising it only to prevent an outrage which was equally liable to be perpetrated by either or both parties ; coming between them as a peacemaker to adjust their difficulties according to *law* — shall he be branded a *felon*, I say, and punished with the enormities of the provisions of this Fugitive Slave Act ?

But this attempt to get the constable to arrest failing, afterward you hear of him in that alley stating that a *habeas corpus* from Elyria might be obtained, and was, therefore, the next best legal and peaceable resort, and offering, if a horse and buggy were furnished him, to go for it. And is it not probable then, are you not bound to believe, that he was anxious that a legal course should be pursued; if not for his own satisfaction, at least for the satisfaction of the more turbulent portion of the crowd ?

As I have already said, I shall not attempt to go over in detail all the testimony that has been given as to what he said and what he did in connection with this transaction. It has been accurately done by my associate, and must be fresh in your recollection. But I wish to call your attention now to the conflict between the testimony of the Government witnesses upon several important points, for the purpose of reminding you that it must be with a great degree of caution that you give credit to what they say; that their testimony is such as plainly to show that they have either forgotten what occurred, or else their inclination is such as to debar them from credit at your hands. For instance, you have had the testimony of Jennings and Bacon as to the arrangement under which Jennings came out here in pursuit of John. I frankly confess that I see nothing in the appearance of this man Bacon, to authorize me to asperse his character for truth and veracity, though I cannot but regret that he could not employ his valuable time to better advantage than in hiring some wretch to recapture the boy John, so ardently loving his own freedom; or in being here to carry on this prosecution against a man who sought only to keep and not to break the law. I know that it may be said that he is here as a witness under process; but I know, too, that if he be, as is alleged, the owner of the boy John, a wave of his hand would doubtless have prevented the indictment being found.

Bacon swears that he promised Jennings, as the consideration for attempting the capture of the "nigger," $500, or one half what the "nigger" would sell for, provided he brought him safely back; and otherwise he was to have nothing. He says that this was an explicit agreement. Jennings swears that there was no arrangement whatever about compensation; that he undertook the return of this wayward youth as a neighborly duty, an act of pure benevolence; expected that his actual expenses would probably be paid—though for some reason they never have been yet—but had no idea of ever getting any thing more. Now why is it that these men, at the very threshold of the first trial, cross each other's path in this way? Do they not impeach each other, or, at least, one impeach the other? What credit can they expect you to give them? I verily believe Bacon, for he appears truthful, and testifies to what is reasonable; but I am inclined as strongly to distrust Jennings, because he appears any thing but truthful, and talks any thing but common sense. Why does Jennings disclaim the influence of any definite number of pieces of silver upon his pious and neighborly heart? Can it be that *that gun* penetrated so far into his head as to awaken to activity some latent moral perceptions of the reputableness of "nigger hunting" as compared with other walks of Christian usefulness? It is of course of no pertinence to the issue on trial what the terms of Mr. Jennings's engagements were; but it is of some importance to the government and to you, Gentlemen of the Jury, whether the chief witnesses for the Government can tell the truth when there is no possible inducement to lie!

On this trial Mr. Jennings swears that his bargain with Lowe was that he was to give Lowe one hundred dollars, if he got the "nigger," and pay his expenses from Columbus to Oberlin at any rate; that he made the same agreement with Davis; which latter statement he afterwards explained by saying that it was to be one hundred dollars for both. But Lowe comes up and swears roundly that there was no pecuniary arrangement whatever made; but that he expected to charge his usual price, which is $2 a day and expenses; that Jennings indeed offered him a hundred dollars, but his incorruptible integrity spurned the bribe, and so there was no definite arrangement made. Davis says he never heard of the hundred dollars, and made no bargain; expected to charge his usual fees as deputy-sheriff. Isn't it rather unfortunate that there should be such a difference of opinion among these gentlemen, and especially that Mr. Jennings can't get *any* of his stories to *jibe* with anybody's else?

Now there is another witness for the government, one Sciples, who testifies that he saw the defendant twice on the afternoon of that day, and that the second time he saw him was on the floor of the second story with Watson, some time about the middle of the afternoon. Saw him only twice, and the second time he was with Watson on the second floor of the hotel, and this was about the middle of the afternoon. But when recalled to patch up a lame case, he swears that he saw him going up the stairs with Watson when the rush was made, immediately—only a few moments—before the rescue. An important addition to his reminiscences, and a little remarkable that he could'nt think of it before. So much for his consistency. And so with a large portion of all the witnesses for the Government.

But some one of them testifies that while Langston was circulating a bond of indemnity for the constable, he was told that the constable would n't serve the writ, that he had refused to do so, and he replied, "I do'nt care; we'll have him, any how." And of this the learned counsel for the Government are disposed to make much handle. But is it fair to do so? How impossible for any one hearing so equivocal and isolated a remark to fix positively upon its meaning; to say absolutely whether he meant that they would have Lowe, whose arrest was the sole object of his immediate attention, and who might be taken with this warrant by any one of numerous constables, other than Meacham, within a few minutes, call; or whether he meant John, whom he had as yet promised no relief, directly or indirectly, except by the hands of the proper officers of the law and through the operations of strictly legal processes? And it is really remarkable how this single phrase seems to have been heard by every one of a certain class of the Government's witnesses, up stairs, down stairs, out of doors, and everywhere,—the echo seems to haunt them all; and yet nothing can be more flimsy than the statements in connection with which this phrase is quoted by every one of them. Even Lowe gives the whole weight of his testimony against the probability of its use in his presence; and the others are either flatly contradicted or impeach themselves.

And now notice this remark and its connection, as Lowe says it was made to him alone, at the close of that second private interview, in the little room up at the head of the stairs. Until this moment, every word, look, and act of Langston had inspired Lowe with confidence that he had in Langston a friend who would, at least, labor against a forcible rescue. Even Langston's kind endeavors to get Lowe out of the scrape, by advising him to urge upon Jennings the expediency of parting with John voluntarily, rather than risk a defence against the excited and stubborn crowd, did not shake his confidence. He trusted him confidently until, at the last moment, when it became plain, as he says, that negotiations were wellnigh at an end, Langston rose, and striding rapidly out, said, " I don't care," or " well," or something of that sort—" we 'll have him any how." I need not dwell on this point, since my associate has done so; but you would be surprised if I passed over so important a point, without calling your attention urgently to it. The statement was not repeated; Lowe asked for no explanation; Langston went off, and did not return; Lowe says he did not come up with those who took John off; he neither saw nor heard any thing afterwards on that day, that would implicate him with the rescuers, any more than he did before this fatal word was let slip; so that the whole of his conduct that day, except in the use of this ONE WORD, was peaceful. Mr. Lowe, of course, though he can hardly tell day from night on any other point, could not have misunderstood Langston, and thought he said " WE," when in fact he repeated what he had already said with impunity, " THEY!" No; it suits the purposes of the prosecution, Gentlemen, that you believe in Mr. Lowe's infallibility on this point, since his testimony in other points does but help the defence, and on this point there is no one to contradict him but the defendant. So that it appears, I say, that the whole of the defendant's conduct on that day, except that ONE WORD, was that of a peacemaker and law-conservator. But Lowe comes here into Court, and the anxious witnesses all seeing what a ghostly chance the Government has left, and hearing Lowe fix up that little pronoun so nicely, scratch their heads and swear that they heard him say it too, and that he was saying it on all manner of impossible and improbable occasions. Now, Gentlemen of the Jury, can you lay your hands on your hearts and say there is NO ROOM FOR A REASONABLE DOUBT as to whether the word used by Langston was " we," or " they ? "

One word more about Sciples's testimony, or that part of it in which he avers that he saw Langston passing up those stairs with Watson, but a moment before the rescue took place. He says he saw that. Watson is brought to the stand, and swears straight out, with the emphasis and boldness of an intelligent and honest man, that he was only in that hall— that he only passed up those stairs—in company with Langston, once on that day, and that that was when he was sent by Lowe after Langston, and returned with him, which was immediately prior to the first interview between Lowe and Langston, during the continuance of which Lowe distinctly remembers that the train passed; and this, he says, was at least two hours before the rescue, and that the testimony of Sciples in reference to his going up with Langston immediately prior to the rescue, is utterly false.

It is said that Wheeler swears he also saw him pass up some time before the rescue, though he can't tell exactly when. But he also swears that he saw him going up those stairs with Watson only once, and Watson very clearly fixes the time and adds that they went up together only once. So Wheeler only corroborates Watson without particularly helping the Government. And as to Sciples, — you, Gentlemen, heard the testimony that was given here as to his life-long reputation for truth and veracity, and it was of such a character that I need make no comments upon it—you cannot feel yourselves authorized to give his testimony the slightest weight.

I believe then, Gentlemen ——

[Mr. GRISWOLD called off Mr. BACKUS's attention for a few moments.]

—— I am reminded, Gentlemen of the Jury, may it please the Court, that before I close I should not pass over without comment a position taken by the District-Attorney in his opening remarks; and that was that any interference with the parties having John in custody whether by way of legal proceedings or otherwise was unwarrantable and inexcusable resistance to the authority of the United States; that it was not in the power of any magistrate to order an examination of them by arrest, or in the power of a constable to serve a warrant if it were placed in his hands; and that whoever advised such proceedings was equally criminal, guilty, and chargeable with unlawfully participating in attempts to rescue, with those who appealed only to intimidation and force. It seems to me that nothing farther need be said upon this point than was said by my associate. I cannot for one moment believe that any one will stand up here and say that a person thus acting in good faith to secure merely a legal investigation of the tenure — going behind no paper presented — by which a presumptively free person is claimed to be held in close custody, under circumstances which not only justify but oblige the darkest suspicions, makes himself liable to, and is to be held primâ facie, as worthy of condign punishment as one who appeals only to physical violence ! Certainly, I say, it cannot be that any gentleman who makes the slightest pretensions to a knowledge of *law* will stand up here and risk his professional reputation upon so reckless a statement as *that!* The gentleman cannot be serious. The indictment alleges no such resistance to authority, but resistance with "force and arms," and therefore if it be resistance, and be proven, it cannot come before you, Gentlemen, who sit here only to ascertain whether the allegations of the indictment are proven. And I take it, therefore, that the discussion of this point — if a *discussion* could be seriously maintained! — must fall altogether outside the limits of this case.

But if it were involved in the case, I should take it upon myself to say, as my associate has said, that if a person should procure such an investigation, not for the purpose of honest and impartial investigation, but as a cover for other and illegal proceedings, then the parties criminally and deceitfully acting under such cover might be amenable to this statute. But even then, the movers in the matter acting with dishonest and criminal motives, if any other person in good faith should promote such issue and service of process for the sole purpose of lawful inquiry, in good faith and for the promotion of justice, and in ignorance of the true character of the power under which the parties sought to be arrested held their prisoner, can this Court lay down such a rule of law as it is requested to by the District-Attorney? that my client, thus acting in good faith, for the sole purpose of ascertaining the truth, that he might govern himself by it, is amenable to the penalties of a criminal statute, and chargeable with "*unlawfully, willingly,* and *knowingly*," resisting competent legal authority? I know that the gentleman read an authority from McLean's Reports, in a civil case for the recovery of the value of a slave, that it can make no difference what are the motives to interference so long as the injury to the plaintiff is the same; but where has it been laid down as a rule of law that a man can be guilty of *crime* when his motives are innocent and absolutely submissive to Law? I utterly repudiate the existence of such a doctrine, and I shall most assuredly take it for granted that no such rule will be laid down by *this* Court, till my own ears bring me the incredible proof. Why, who ever heard of an individual being convicted of *larceny* for going into your house and taking an article under the *honest* impression that it was his own, while in fact it was yours and not his all the time? Though an action for *trespass* undoubtedly would lie for the full value of the article thus abstracted. I know that it may be necessary to invoke such a rule of law for the purpose of procuring a conviction in this case, for certainly without its aid this Jury can never on their oaths find a verdict of guilty; but I think I can risk nothing in saying that I know this Court will never lay down *such* a rule as law, and that you will not take the talk of the District-Attorney as a part of the Charge of the Court.

And now, Gentlemen of the Jury, I know that there is a mass of testimony, which it has taken us some two weeks or more to draw out, that I have left untouched, even after so lengthy remarks as I have already made. But we will let all of that pass. I feel sure that you will not lay stress upon isolated scraps or garbled words and phrases in the testimony, especially such as run utterly counter to the entire drift of the whole. And that you will not do this is all I could wish to ask at your hands; for, unless you should do it, you must render the verdict most grateful to your own feelings, and which I am sure could not be unpleasant to my client or his counsel.

Under the instructions of the Court, you will find, if those instructions shall be as I anticipate, that the power of attorney was fatally defective, and that all proceedings under it were incapable of laying a foundation for this charge. But if the Court shall differ with me here, and you travel down to the next point, I am certainly unable to see from what portion of the evidence you are to discover that the rescue was, as the indictment alleges, from the custody of *Anderson Jennings!* But if, contrary to all my most confident expectations, under the ruling of the Court, you are forbidden to investigate this point, and are forced on to the next, then I know that, on this question of fact — from the investigation of which you cannot be driven, — I say, then, I know that you can never find — in my humble estimation — that the purpose of this defendant, in his connection with that crowd, was to make a breach of the peace and to encourage an illegal rescue. You must find — unless you throw away all this testimony and manufacture for yourselves — that he labored for peace and for peace only, — for legal measures, and for legal measures only. And I know, too, that there is not a man among you who can lay his hand upon his heart and say that there *is not ground for one reasonable doubt* whether the allegations of the prosecution in this indictment are proven or not; so that, in the case of this defendant, let the character of the rescue itself be what it may have been, you will be *forced* to find a verdict of Not Guilty.

And now, Gentlemen, I believe I have said all that I am warranted in saying upon this subject. I have endeavored to meet the issues presented fairly and squarely. Whatever may be my own views of the constitutionality and propriety of the statute upon which this prosecution is founded, I must, for the purposes of this trial, regard it *as* constitutional and of full force. But I do not wish to be misapprehended, and to seem to occupy a position that I do not occupy. And, therefore, I wish to say of that threat of the District-Attorney, that he hoped the counsel for the defence would not be allowed unrebuked by your Honor to comment upon the enormity of the statute itself, that I hope you will do me the justice to believe that

I have said what I have as to the binding force of this statute without the remotest regard to this miserable menace, but with sole reference to the interests of my client and the maintenance of my own self-respect.

With these remarks, Gentlemen, I leave that man in your hands, standing here and appealing to you to deal out to him, at least, in this *one* instance, equal justice, as you would to a man whose complexion was of another hue. It is, as I have already said, almost the only case where, under the rulings of our Courts, and under the laws of the land, he is entitled to demand equal justice with a white man at the hands of his fellow men; but your oath obligates you to deal impartially by him, and your inclinations, I have no doubt, sanction that oath; and I leave him in your hands, therefore, with the utmost confidence, that upon neither of the issues made, and especially upon all of them, will you ever be able, under your oaths, to find a verdict of Guilty against him.

FIFTEENTH DAY. — MORNING SESSION.

CLEVELAND, May 10, 1859.

Court convened at 9 o'clock. Judge BLISS commenced the closing argument for the Government.

Whether the offence charged upon the defendant, Charles Langston, was one against the moral ideas or simply against the civil statute, it was immaterial in the consideration of this case, and if he was guilty of this offence, he as truly merited punishment as if it was wrong in itself, for this laxity in respect to the laws of the land will lead to perilling if not subverting the privileges and rights which the laws grant to every citizen. In cases like this, where the crime is not prompted by feelings of momentary revenge, an offence is as truly committed as if such was the case.

It was known by the defendant and his associates that this negro was satisfied with his relations with his master, for it was so said by the boy himself. It was not, then, a feeling of sympathy for John, that prompted Langston and his associates to rescue him from the hands of the party which was taking him back to the South. No, his purpose, fixed and determined, was to violate and set at defiance one of the laws of the land — a law which they were determined should never be executed, and their end and aim was to show that that law could be successfully opposed by force. This spirit which would tear down and annihilate the Government of these United States, and which would prostrate the civil fabric of this country, was the spirit which actuated the defendant and his associates on that day. The students who attend that Oberlin College are taught sedition and treason in connection with science and literature, and they graduate from that institution to go forth and preach opposition and treason. The right of a portion of our inhabitants to hold property in slaves may be an unpleasant one to contemplate, and we may regret that such an institution exists, but it is not our sin, and the people of Ohio are not guilty of its commission, and so long as it is recognized as an institution of one portion of the country by the laws of the country, so long must we respect the right of those who hold property in slaves. The right of the residents of Kentucky can no more be broken down by such men as Charles Langston than can the institution in the Island of Cuba, and why, then, should they take up arms and follow the man who seeks upon our soil to exercise his own proprietary right to secure his own property?

The reasons of the adoption of the original resolution for the rendition of fugitive slaves, were shown and dilated upon by the Counsel, and the history of the "peculiar institution" briefly passed over.

In 1802 the people of Ohio deliberated upon taking upon themselves the Constitution with all its provisions and clauses, including this one which distinctly provides that fugitive slaves shall be rendered up to their owners, and having deliberated upon it, applied for admission into the Union and were admitted, thereby binding themselves to support and abide by all the provisions of that Constitution. How, then, can they stand up to-day and repudiate and impugn this same Constitution?

Passing then to the evidence, the Counsel considered the testimony brought to bear against Langston for rescuing the slave John. The prosecution had no possible malice against the defendant, and assuredly did not desire to have him wrongfully convicted, but if it was conclusively proved that he was guilty of the crime for which he was indicted, then the agents of the Government asked for a punishment as a warning to those who wilfully violate the laws of the land.

Judge BLISS then discussed the nature of the crowd which assembled at Wellington, setting forth that Jennings, Mitchell, and Lowe, had gone to Oberlin for this slave — had obtained possession of him by some little *finesse* — had taken him to Wellington — that the Oberlin people pursued them, determined to have him whether he had been taken with or without authority, and whether he was or was not a slave. He then went on to show by the testimony that it was generally known in that crowd at Wellington that the boy was a slave, but that they "did not care for the law," that they "made their own laws."

If Langston was in that crowd that was determined "to have him any how," without doing some act or making some protestation against the evident design of the rest, then he was guilty; and it has been shown that he was circulating in that crowd and actively engaged. He expressed himself at one time satisfied with the papers which Lowe and Jennings held. With the scheme of the warrant which Meacham held, and which John Watson had caused to be made out for the arrest of the keepers of the slave, Langston was so connected by his advice to Meacham to serve it, as to make him one of the rescuing party, for the statute prohibits taking away a slave from the officers of the law.

Recess taken until two o'clock.

AFTERNOON SESSION.

Court convened at one o'clock. Judge BLISS continued his argument for the Government, reviewing the course of Langston at Wellington, where he pretended friendship to Lowe, but at the same time urged the execution of the writ for his arrest. He claimed that from the very commencement the defendant had had one steady aim to set the slave at liberty, and that he encouraged and sympathized with the rescuing crowd. He told Lowe that he could do nothing with the crowd, that they were determined to have the boy, and afterwards made the proposition to let the boy go peaceably. Lowe refused, when Langston said, "we will have him any way," and from this moment he showed his true purpose and design.

Here reviewed the evidence of witnesses, showing that Langston had said in answer to a remark that there was a large crowd, "Yes, they have turned out well." Yes, they had turned out well, for that old buzzard's nest of Oberlin, where the negroes who arrive over the underground railroad are regarded as dear children — that nest had been broken into, and one of the brood had escaped. And these Oberlin men, who had been taught to set at defiance the laws of the United States, rushed off to rescue the boy who had been taken. That was an army that old General Satan himself might have selected from the chief spirits of Hell to fight against the power of Earth and Heaven. Langston said, after returning to Oberlin, "We got the boy and brought him home." Now, Gentlemen, has it not been clearly and unquestionably shown that the defendant was actively engaged in the rescue?

Leaving the question of the evidence, the counsel then spoke upon the legal questions which give the right of process to owners or agents to pursue and recover their fugitive slaves, holding that the rescue was made from Jennings assisted by Lowe. But even if from Lowe, then the second count of the indictment charges that the rescue was made from Lowe.

The counsel closed with remarks upon the interest which Charles Langston had in the purpose of the rescue, being determined that at all events and all hazards, John should be rescued and should never be taken South, and leaving the case for the Jury to decide upon.

The Court then gave the case to the Jury in the following charge:—

The United States,
     v.
Charles Langston,

WILLSON, Judge.

The defendant, Charles Langston, is indicted for rescuing a fugitive slave, alleged to be the property of John G. Bacon, of Kentucky. His plea is not guilty, and it is upon the issue made by this plea that you are sworn to return a verdict according to the evidence.

There is, perhaps, no severer test to a juror's integrity, or a greater demand upon his impartial judgment, than when called upon to act in a case where political partialities or prejudices are invoked to sway his conduct. The very nature of our Federal system is such, that all men become more or less interested in the legislative policy of the Government. This has resulted in political organizations, in which, at different periods, the great masses of the people have been arrayed in parties, antagonistic to each other, and often characterized by strong prejudices and bitter animosities. Hence, congressional legislation often becomes distasteful to a portion of the people of the country. It is so at the South with reference to laws enacted to suppress the slave-trade, and peculiarly so at the North, with reference to the fugitive slave law of 1850. Yet ours is a representative Government, where the people themselves control its legislation. It is indispensable to good order and to the well-being of society, that acts of Congress, placed upon the statute book, should command obedience, and that partisan feeling should cease and prejudice be forgotten, in the observance of the law. Courts and juries especially are bound to impartially administer and enforce the laws, and this sacred obligation is imposed with the most solemn sanctions.

It is the first duty of a juror, who is sworn to determine the guilt or innocence of one charged with crime, to divest himself of any and all prejudices he may have against the law itself, or of any partiality or ill-will he may have towards the accused. It is enough to know that the law alleged to be broken is the law of the land, and that the accused is presumed to be innocent until his guilt is proved. A jury that yields to any other influences than those legitimately produced by the law and the testimony, is recreant to its trust, and unworthy of occupying the seats of twelve honest men.

This caution is given, Gentlemen, not because it is feared that you will *intentionally* swerve from a true and just line of duty, but simply that you may guard and brace yourselves against any undue influences, while considering and weighing the evidence in the case.

What, then, is the case you are sworn to try, and what are the material facts necessary for the Government to establish in order to work a conviction of the defendant?

The indictment is predicated upon the 6th and 7th sections of the Act of Congress, approved Sept. 18, 1850. You have already become familiar with the provisions of this statute, and a more minute reference to this law is unnecessary.

This indictment contains two counts. The second having been substantially abandoned by the prosecutor, it is only necessary to call your attention to the first.

The first count charges that the negro in question was a slave owing service to John G. Bacon, in Kentucky. That said negro escaped from Kentucky into the State of Ohio, and was a fugitive from his owner, — that he was seized and held by Anderson Jennings and his assistants in Ohio, by virtue of a power of attorney lawfully executed and acknowledged by said Bacon, authorizing the capture of the fugitive; and that the defendant acting with others at Wellington in this District, unlawfully, knowingly, and willingly rescued the slave from Bacon's agent and attorney.

You will call to mind the evidence pertinent to the first of these allegations.

Is it proved that the negro John owed service to John G. Bacon in Kentucky?

The existence of slavery in Kentucky as a municipal regulation, is a question of law, which belongs solely for the consideration of the Court; and for the purposes of this trial you will regard slavery or involuntary servitude as recognized and lawfully established in that State.

Whether the relation of master and slave existed between Bacon and the negro John, is a question of fact to be ascertained by the jury, from the testimony; and this may be established by the Government according to the same rule of evidence that obtains in other contests about the right in personal property.

The general rule of law is that the proof of the actual possession of such property, accompanied with the claim of ownership, is sufficient to establish the *primâ facie* right of ownership. It is like any other question of status of the relation of one person to another, which may be shown by the facts and circumstances attending that relation, — as for instance that of husband and wife, parent and child, etc. It is not necessary to trace the pedigree of this negro through a maternal ancestry of slaves, nor is it necessary to prove that he was held by deed or contract of purchase, or that the ownership was acquired by inheritance.

If Bacon exercised that control over him which is ordinarily done in Kentucky by a master over his slave, and if the negro had the usual marks of African descent, and was held as a slave and treated as such by his alleged master, the proof of these facts, if uncontradicted, establishes the allegation in the indictment, that the negro John was held to service as the slave

of John G. Bacon, under the laws of the State of Kentucky.

That this negro escaped into Ohio and was a fugitive from Kentucky is not seriously questioned.

But it is objected by the counsel for the defendant that there is a fatal variance in the proof from the allegation in the indictment; as to the time of the escape, the allegation being that he left his master on the first of March, 1857, and the proof showing his departure from Kentucky to have been early in January, 1856.

This is not a descriptive averment, nor is the date an essential ingredient in the crime charged to have been committed, to wit, the unlawful rescue. If the precise day of a fact be a necessary ingredient in the offence, it unquestionably must be truly stated. But when the fact is mere inducement to the offence, the time is immaterial. Such is the case here. And hence it is sufficient to prove the escape at any time previous to the actual commission of the offence charged in the indictment.

It is also objected that the power of attorney, under which Jennings acted, was defective in its execution and acknowledgment, and that it is consequently void.

If the power of attorney, which has been produced in evidence, was lawfully executed and acknowledged in Kentucky, where it was made, it is valid and effectual in Ohio to accomplish the purpose for which it was given.

It is not essential to the validity of a power of attorney in Kentucky that it should be sealed by the party giving it, unless it was executed for the purpose of authorizing the conveyance or incumbrance of real estate, or of mixed property.

We are also satisfied that the acknowledgment was valid in law. It is sufficient that the acknowledgment appears to be taken before a legal officer of the Mason County Court, certified to be in due form of law and authenticated by the seal of that Court. The Clerk Cochran was a legal officer of that Court. By virtue of his office he was authorized to take this acknowledgment, and as it was by virtue of the powers conferred on him by the Mason County Court, that he was authorized to do the act, the seal of that court was, by legal implication, *his* seal to authenticate such official act. It is not competent to go behind this authenticated act of an officer of a court of record. The language of the statute is, " acknowledged and certified under the *seal* of some legal officer or court." The objection that the signature of the clerk was made by his deputy is not deemed to be important. *It is the seal of the Court which authenticates the act of acknowledgment;* and hence the point is not involved as to the authority of the clerk to delegate to a deputy the power of doing an official act which devolves upon him personally. This is the doctrine of the case of Smith *v.* U. S. 5 Peters, 302.

You will, therefore, regard this power of

attorney, if executed by Bacon, as valid in law, and effectual to accomplish the purpose for which it was given.

This brings you, Gentlemen of the Jury, to the consideration of an important question of fact, namely, did Jennings hold the fugitive, at the time of the rescue, by virtue of the power of attorney?

When the agent acts under this law by power of attorney, the statute provides that he "may pursue and reclaim the fugitive, either by procuring a warrant from some one of the courts, judges, or commissioners (named in the act), for the apprehension of such fugitive from service or labor, or by seizing and arresting such fugitive, when the same can be done without process, and by taking or *causing* such person to be taken forthwith before such court, judge," etc.

The fugitive may be seized and held upon the warrant, or by virtue of the power of attorney. Both modes of capture and detention have but the single purpose of bringing the fugitive before the judge or commissioner. The person making the arrest, has the same power and authority in the one case as in the other. And yet the agent may, at the same time, resort to both modes of capture and detention. The agent may himself take the fugitive before the judge or commissioner, or he may *cause* him to be taken before such officer by virtue of the warrant. The authority of the agent holding the power of attorney is paramount to that of the officer holding the warrant. The warrant, if obtained, is procured at the instance of the agent, and when used is merely auxiliary to the authority conferred upon the agent by virtue of the power of attorney. The Marshal, in executing the warrant, may act under the direction of the agent, and in the matter of holding the fugitive when so arrested, the agent has complete control over the whole subject, and may unquestionably set the fugitive at liberty before the return of the writ.

It is not the case of the execution of process, emanating from different and conflicting jurisdictions. In such a case, the officer first making the seizure has, by virtue of his process, exclusive control and possession of the thing seized. Under this statute, it is clear that the warrant is auxiliary to the power of attorney.

If, then, the proof shows that at the time of the rescue at Wellington, Jennings and Lowe had a joint control over the fugitive, the former in virtue of a good and sufficient power of attorney for his reclamation, and the latter assisting him as the agent of the owner of the slave, by means of a warrant or otherwise, such proof sustains the allegation in the indictment, that said negro was in the custody and under the control of Anderson Jennings, as agent and attorney of John G. Bacon, together with one Jacob K. Lowe, then and there lawfully assisting him in the custody and control of the said negro slave called John.

I have been thus explicit upon this point, because it is one that has been the subject of much discussion by counsel, and because it was proper that the instructions given to you upon it should be the result of careful consideration.

Should you find from the testimony, that Jennings held the fugitive by virtue of the power of attorney, and that the negro was the identical slave that escaped from Bacon, there still remains the all-important inquiry in the case, did the defendant unlawfully, knowingly, and willingly *rescue* the fugitive from his lawful captors?

The rescue could not be obnoxious to the provisions of the statute, unless it implicated the defendant as acting knowingly and willingly in the matter. That is to say, it must appear in proof that he knew the negro was a fugitive from labor, and was lawfully held by those who had possession and control over him at the time of the rescue, or that the defendant acted under such circumstances as to show that he might have had such knowledge by exercising ordinary prudence.

It is claimed by the prosecutor that this knowledge, on the part of the defendant, is established by the positive testimony of Jennings, Lowe, and others, and that, upon this point, the proof permits of no doubtful inference or conjecture.

It is asserted (and whether truly or not is for you to determine from the evidence) that Lowe, as Deputy-Marshal, acting under the direction of Jennings and in virtue of a Commissioner's warrant, seized and arrested the fugitive near the village of Oberlin; that he conveyed the slave to Wellington and there surrendered the principal control over him to the authorized agent of the owner, and thereafter acted in subordination to, and as an assistant of, that agent; that the defendant was fully informed by Lowe, at two several interviews, of the relation which the negro bore to Bacon, and of the authority by which he was captured and held.

But the defendant contends that, notwithstanding the proof may show his knowledge of the servitude due from the negro to Bacon, his master, and of the authority by which he was held, that yet, it fails to establish the defendant's guilt as a participator in the *rescue* charged in the indictment. And it is further insisted, in view of all the evidence in the case, that, on acquiring the knowledge that the negro was a slave and lawfully held, the defendant not only abstained from the commission of any unlawful act himself, but was, in fact, really active and sincere in persuading others to a peaceful course of conduct, and to a faithful observance of the law.

In regard to the legal implication of the defendant's guilt and his complicity in the *rescue* of the fugitive charged in the indictment, the instructions of the Court, given on a former occasion, may properly be repeated here, as they enunciate the principle of law which is deemed to be applicable to this branch of the case.

If the persons who constituted the assemblage at Wellington on the 13th of September, 1858, had come together for the purpose, or when there were engaged in rescuing a fugitive slave from those authorized to capture and hold him, under the laws of 1850, they were engaged in an unlawful act, and whatever was said and done by one in the prosecution of the enterprise, were, to all intents and purposes, the declarations and acts of all. But to charge one, against whom there is no specific proof, of things done by him, with what was done and said by others in the prosecution of the unlawful enterprise, *concert* of action, between him and those others, for the unlawful purpose, must be shown. And for this purpose it was competent for the prosecutor to give in evidence the defendant's declarations to others, encouraging the rescue before it was accomplished, and of his statements in the meeting at Oberlin, immediately upon his return after the rescue. What was said by others that were engaged in the unlawful act, after the assemblage at Wellington had broken up and dispersed, is not evidence against the defendant. Accordingly what Shephard and others said at the meeting at Oberlin on the evening of the 13th of September, is excluded from your consideration, on the ground that it is incompetent testimony.

The inquiry, then, becomes important, Was there concert of action between the defendant and those actually engaged in the rescue of the fugitive? If there was, the defendant is guilty, and as much so as if he had rendered manual service in the act.

The rule of law is, that every one who enters into a common purpose or design, is deemed a party to every act which had before been done by the others, without regard to the time in which he entered into the combination, and, also, a party to every act which may afterwards be done by any of the others, in furtherance of such common design. This concert of action, on the part of the defendant with the rescuers, if it existed at all, is to be determined by his declarations and conduct. If he advised and urged others into the commission of the unlawful act, he made their conduct his own in effecting the rescue. He thereby acted in concert with them in the common design, to wit, the rescue of the slave.

It is contended by the counsel for the Government, that the defendant, by his words and conduct, evinced a determined (though cautious) purpose of effecting the escape of the fugitive in violation of law. That his pretensions for suggesting a resort to the forms of law, was but another more subtle and effectual mode of accomplishing the rescue; and his urging the constable to serve the State warrant against Jennings and his assistants for kidnapping the negro, after being informed of his lawful capture, is claimed as conclusive of the defendant's complicity in the rescue.

In a free State like Ohio, every human being in it, whether white or black, is presumed to be free until a different status is shown. And hence when one is restrained of his freedom by another, a resort to the ordinary forms of proceeding under the State laws, to inquire into the cause of such restraint or imprisonment implies no wrong. But when a fugitive from labor is captured and held in any of the modes and under the authority designated by the Act of Congress of 1850, any interference by the State authorities has no justification, nor can those be justified who invoke their interference, when they know the fugitive is thus held.

If Jennings seized and held the fugitive by virtue of a good and sufficient power of attorney executed for that purpose and was lawfully assisted by Lowe, the Justice of the Peace at Wellington, who issued a State warrant against them for kidnapping such fugitive, was acting in a matter over which he had no jurisdiction. And if the defendant was informed and had knowledge of this condition of things, and afterwards urged the execution of the warrant for the purpose of liberating the fugitive, his conduct in this particular implicated him as much in the common design of the mob, as if he had given his aid to the rescue by physical force.

What the defendant said and what he did, in relation to the rescue, has been detailed in the testimony of various witnesses, and this testimony has been so minutely brought to your attention by the counsel on both sides, as to require no further recapitulation.

I have throughout regarded it as an acknowledged fact (and as conceded by the defendant's counsel) that an unlawful rescue of the negro was made. For, in legal contemplation, it matters not whether he was released from capture by the manual force of the mob, or whether that release was effected by threats and demonstrations of violence. It would be an unlawful rescue as much in the one case as in the other.

With these rules of law for your government, Gentlemen, the case is now committed to your hands. Treat it as you would any other case involving the question of the guilt or innocence of a man charged with a criminal violation of the law. All matters of fact in this controversy are exclusively for your consideration. And if from a careful and impartial review of the proofs, you come to the conclusion, beyond a reasonable doubt, that the defendant is guilty of the offence charged, you will say so by your verdict. But if the proof fails to produce that conviction upon your minds, you will return a verdict of acquittal.

The Jury after being out about half an hour returned to their seats and rendered a verdict of

"GUILTY!"

CHAPTER FOURTH

CLEVELAND, WEDNESDAY, May 11, 1859.

Court convened at 9 o'clock. The fact that sentence was to be passed upon Bushnell, and probably Langston, caused the court room to be densely crowded with eager listeners and watchers of the proceedings. A large proportion of the audience was composed of ladies.

Judge SPALDING announced that he had a motion to make before the Court, that the next case of those indicted, that of John Watson, be immediately taken up and proceeded with. This matter was, however, deferred until after sentence should have been passed upon Bushnell.

Mr. Bushnell, who, with his wife and child, occupied seats near the bench, was told to stand up. The COURT asked the prisoner if he had any thing to say why sentence should not be pronounced. Mr. Bushnell intimated that he had not. The COURT then asked if he had *any regrets* to express for the offence of which he stood convicted. Receiving another negative, it proceeded to pronounce sentence from *manuscript*, as follows:—

"It is at all times a disagreeable and painful duty for the Court to pronounce the sentence and impose the penalty which the law demands for its violation. The discharge of this duty is peculiarly painful in dealing with the class of offenders to which you belong, who deem it a praiseworthy virtue to violate the law, and then seek its penalties with exultation and defiance.

"A man of your intelligence must know, that the enjoyment of a rational liberty ceases the moment the laws are allowed to be broken with impunity, and thereby fail to afford any protection to society, — that if the standard of right is placed above and against the laws of the land, those who act up to it are any thing else than good citizens or good Christians. You must know that when a man acts upon any system of morals or theology which teaches him to disregard and violate the laws of the Government that protects him in life and property, his conduct is as criminal as his example is dangerous.

"The good order and well-being of society demand an exemplary penalty in your case. You have broken the law, — you express no regret for the act done, but are exultant in the wrong. It is therefore the sentence of the Court, that you pay a fine of six hundred dollars, and be imprisoned in the county jail of Cuyahoga County for sixty days from date, and pay the costs of this prosecution. It is made the duty of the marshal to see this sentence executed; and in case any casualty should interfere with the security of your confinement in the jail named, it is made the duty of the mar-

shal to enforce the confinement in some other county jail within this District.

"Mr. Marshal, you will take the prisoner into custody."

This sentence was received with quietness by the prisoner and his friends.

The COURT then asked for any farther motion.

Mr. RIDDLE moved to proceed with the case of John Watson.

The COURT inquired if the District-Attorney was ready in that case. No, he replied, he was not ready. He had learned that the Sheriff of Lorain County had that morning arrested Jennings, Lowe, and Mitchell, on a charge of kidnapping, and that they were now in the custody of that officer. He believed, and could say he knew, that all this machinery of arresting these men and confining them on that charge, thereby delaying and hindering the business of the Court, was the work of the defendants who thus endeavored to put a stop to farther proceedings against the indicted. He had also taken notice that a writ of *habeas corpus* in the case of Bushnell would be applied for, which would perhaps interrupt the proceedings of the Court.

He also stated that he had been appointed by the Government to defend these witnesses in the Lorain County Court in his official capacity. Under these circumstances it would be impossible for him to proceed at present with the case of Watson.

Judge SPALDING replied that the District-Attorney knew, as well as the Court and every lawyer at the bar, that if the Court needed these witnesses, a writ of *habeas corpus ad testificandum* would bring them at any moment from any jail in the State, and keep them at the convenience of the Court. The plea that they were carried off was a mere sham, as anybody could see.

The next case upon the list, John Watson, had a right to an immediate trial, and the convenience of no District-Attorney in the land was to be consulted. If the prosecution wanted the case postponed he asked that the motion be submitted in writing and sworn to.

Judge BELDEN remarked that his official character would give power enough to the bare motion to postpone.

Judge S. "Your official character can add nothing to the statement."

"Nor your blackguardism."

"And your private character still less."

The District-Attorney then moved to the Court that the bail of the prisoners be reduced to $500. Considering that this has been the amount of secured bail which has been required from the first, the magnanimity of the affair can be properly appreciated. He also stated that he had been told that Mr. Plumb on Tuesday night abused the Sheriff of Lorain county for not having before executed his writ. This Mr. Plumb denied *in toto*, Marshal Johnson also showing that it was not true.

A recess was at length taken until 2 o'clock for the preparing of affidavits on both sides.

AFTEROON SESSION.

Court convened at 2 o'clock.

In accordance with notice given in the morning, Judge BELDEN presented to the Court a motion for continuing the rest of the cases of those indicted, the motion being in substance as follows:—

Grounds for Continuance.—1st. That Anderson Jennings, Jacob K. Lowe, Richard P. Mitchell, and Samuel Davis, necessary witnesses, had this morning been arrested by the Sheriff of Lorain county by a warrant issued on an indictment for "kidnapping" in Lorain county Court of Common Pleas, and had been, or would be, during the day, taken away, so that their testimony could not be had.

2d. That the next term of the Lorain county Court of Common Pleas would commence on Tuesday next, and that the District-Attorney had been appointed by the Government for their defence.

3d. That the offence charged against these men was based solely upon the facts that these defendants were engaged in seizing and arresting, by virtue of the laws of the United States, the very fugitive from service, mentioned in the indictment for rescue; and that the indictments for kidnapping were found on testimony of some of the rescuers, or on testimony procured by them.

4th. That Lowe was arrested on his way here and compelled to enter into recognizance with surety for his appearance in the Lorain county Court, on Tuesday next, which recognizance would be forfeited unless he appeared, and if he appeared, he might be detained two or three weeks.

5th. Cochran and Bacon were absent without the consent of the District-Attorney, and their testimony was indispensable.

6th. That writs of *habeas corpus* would be applied for in the Bushnell and Langston cases, which would require the immediate attention of the District-Attorney.

7th. That no trial could be had in any of the remaining cases, in all probability, without a most unreasonable delay, which would be caused by the action of the defendants, or their confederates, or by advice of their counsel.

The Court read the 50th and 51st Rules, and under them adjudged itself bound to allow the motion of the District-Attorney. The Rules are the same as obtain in the State Courts.

"RULE 50. Motions for continuance for reasons known to the party at the commencement of the term, shall be filed on or before the second day thereof; and the facts on which such motions are founded, shall be verified by oath, or statement of counsel, unless they appear of record; and such motions shall be submitted without argument.

"RULE 51. On such motion, the affidavit or official statement will be taken as true; and no contradictory, supplemental, or amended affidavit or statement will be permitted."

It consented to receive, however, an independent motion from the counsel for the defence, which was presented by Judge TILDEN, and reads as follows:—

United States of America,   } U. States District Court.
Northern District of Ohio, ss.

United States,   }   No. 72.
    v.   } Indict. for Rescue, etc.
John Watson.   }

The defendant, John Watson, moves the Court that he may be put on his trial to the Jury, on the plea of "not guilty," without further delay.

In support of said motion the said John Watson upon his oath says:—

1st. That he was arraigned before this tribunal on the 8th of December, A. D. 1858, and plead "not guilty," to said indictment, and demanded an immediate trial. At the instance of the U. S. District-Attorney the trial was at that time postponed, and this defendant entered into a recognizance in the sum of one thousand dollars for his appearance in this Court on the 2nd Tuesday in March, 1859. Before that day arrived, however, at the instance of the U. S. District-Attorney, and for his special accommodation, a further postponement of the trial of defendant was had, by consent of defendant's Counsel, until the 5th day of April, 1859, when defendant duly appeared in Court, and thereafter regularly appeared from day to day until the 15th day of April, 1859, when, on motion of the U. S. District-Attorney, he was ordered into the custody of the U. S. Marshal for said Northern District of Ohio, and was on the same day last mentioned, by him committed to close confinement in the county Jail of the county of Cuyahoga, in the State of Ohio, where he has ever since been, and is now, restrained of his liberty, and awaiting his trial, upon no other charge than that contained in said indictment of rescuing a fugitive from service.

2d. This affiant says it is not true that, anterior to the time when he was placed in close confinement in the jail of Cuyahoga county as aforesaid, he had ever contemplated a breach of his recognizance, voluntarily entered into as aforesaid, and it is not true that he, at any time, surrendered himself in discharge of his said recognizance; nor yet is it true that his counsel proposed to surrender him in discharge of his recognizance; on the contrary, this affiant says that he should, undoubtedly, at this moment be at large upon his said recognizance, if he had not been ordered into custody as aforesaid on the 15th day of April aforesaid, upon the motion of the U. S. District-Attorney as aforesaid.

3d. This affiant further says, that the journal entry of this Court, made on the 15th day of April, aforesaid, so far as the same purports to show that this defendant, in connection with other individuals resting under similar charge, surrendered himself in discharge of his recognizance, was made under a mistaken conception of the facts as they transpired, and, so long as said journal entry is permitted to stand in force, this defendant will be unable, consistently with the preservation of his own self-respect, to renew his individual recognizance, or to give bail for his appearance at a subsequent term of this Court. He must, therefore, continue to lie in jail unless he can have the benefit of a speedy trial.

4th. This affiant says further, that in addition to the injury likely to be sustained by defendant in his bodily health, by a long-continued imprisonment in warm weather, he has reason to believe that a farther postponement of his trial will lose him the benefit of a very material witness in the person of William D. Scrimgeour, who is fast wasting away by means of a consumption, and is by his friends expected to live but a short time. Said W. D. Scrimgeour resides at Oberlin, in the county of Lorain, and can be brought into Court, as this affiant is advised, during any day of the present or the next coming week. He has hitherto, since the commencement of this class of trials, been too unwell to be brought so far from his home.

J. WATSON.

State of Ohio, Cuyahoga County, ss.

Sworn to before me by the said John Watson, and subscribed by him in my presence, the 11th day of May, 1859.

JOSEPH S. GRANNIS,
Notary Public for said County.

Spalding, Tilden, and Riddle, Att'ys for Defendant.

The counsel upon both sides endeavored to make some remarks upon these two motions, but the Court remarked that no explanation or comment was necessary, as the first motion, filed by the District-Attorney was sufficient, and would, for the reasons set forth, be granted.

The Court announced that the remainder of the cases, John Watson's included, would be continued.

Mr. RIDDLE then arose and remarked:—

Mr. RIDDLE. With the indulgence of the Court I will call its attention to a matter to which I have already incidentally referred, and that is in reference to the circumstances under which these defendants are in the custody of the jailer.

Now, it makes no matter who these parties are, no sort of difference what the offence with which they stand charged, nor where they reside — of course — nor how much or how little may be known to your Honor of their possible

or probable guilt through the medium of the trial just closed. They are at present in the custody of the jailer under an order of this Court. I think your Honor must be satisfied that that order was made and embodied in the Journal under a misapprehension of the facts.

They are simply these. These parties were in attendance upon this Court regularly and constantly, in obedience to the order of the Court, bound by their own recognizances in the sum of one thousand dollars each; and were in faithful observance of all the conditions of those recognizances. Now I need not stop here to discuss the rights of these defendants on the one side, and the rights of the government upon the other. Ordinarily a recognizance is ample protection against custody or arrest, so long as its conditions are not infracted. But I do not say — no lawyer will attempt to sustain — that when persons at large upon their recognizances are here at the bar of the Court in its presence on actual trial, it is not competent for the Court to order them into custody, when it becomes absolutely necessary to retain their persons beyond the possibility of escape. But I do undertake to say here, in deference to the decision of the Court and to the profound learning of the gentleman who appears in behalf of the Government, that *never before, anywhere* was a motion ever made to order a man into custody who was on bail, and constantly in the most submissive obedience to every condition of his bond, and to every order of the Court: or such an order given, unless it was in such exigencies of *trial* as have been referred to. I know — we all know — that it is customary to order, on good cause shown, an increase of the amount, or the sureties of bail, even when there has been no infraction of that already given. But certainly, with respect to actual *arrest*, they have this right, that while they are in the full discharge of the condition of their recognizances, they have a right to expect that the Government will respect, and that every one else will respect, their rights under it, and if that bail is insufficient, an order for its increase can be made, but an arrest *never*.

Now it is said on the part of the Government that these parties surrendered their recognizances, and hence were taken into custody. I wish to avoid any question of veracity, comparative or unqualified.

But that these parties did *not* either intend to surrender their recognizances, or as a matter of fact did not surrender them, whatever may have been the understanding of the Government officials in the hurry and perhaps the excitement of the occasion, I take it, your Honor, must be true. And what followed? Why, after they were taken into custody, that was followed by an order of the Court to remit these parties back on their own personal recognizances to *the very position which they occupied before;* which would seem to imply that in the judicial mind, after ordering them into custody the question had been raised whether after all there was any good reason for such an order, and it had been decided negatively.: — for if there were such a reason it must have been a discovery of some infraction of the conditions of the bond, or an insufficiency in the amount or in its sureties. And in deciding that these parties be remitted to their former standing, it would seem that the Court became satisfied that there neither was an infraction of the conditions of the recognizance, nor a deficiency in the amount of the sureties. And now, your Honor, these defendants, knowing perfectly well the circumstances under which they were ordered into custody; I say knowing *perfectly well, and beyond the possibility of a mistake*, all the circumstances under which they were ordered into custody, — that it was done without any show of cause or pretext, — they cannot with self-respect comply with that order of the Court discharging them on their own recognizances; for that is a conclusive admission that they were in the wrong — an admission they cannot make, and it is an outrage to attempt thus to force them to make it.

A question now arises upon the propriety of their course ; and I do not now refer to any outside discussions; we have nothing to do with opinions or occurrences outside the Court Room — I refer to this question and its bearings upon the position these parties occupy before this Court. And now we ask, will your Honor, while always remembering, as we always will, that you are a Court, also remember that you are a *man!* That this presumption of the law, that these parties must be presumed to be innocent until they are proven to be guilty, is not a mere idle worthless formula ?

What can these parties do ? They are perfectly unconscious of having at any time entertained any intention to infract the conditions of their recognizances or the orders of the Court, and no less perfectly unconscious of having ever voluntarily surrendered their recognizances. Much more than that — they KNOW that they never did so surrender them; and they KNOW that they *did* ask to have them cancelled *after* they had been taken into custody. Now, is it not plain, looking at this matter fairly, that these parties cannot come forward into Court, and enter into recognizance again without tacitly conceding, not only to the compromising of their own self-respect, but in the face of the universal world, that they were *wrong*, when they *know* as this Court must now know that they are *right;* I now speak of course with reference to the manner in which they came into custody. And now certainly your Honor cannot fail to see the precise position in which they are placed, and wholly through the misunderstanding of the officers of the Court. They most assuredly have never coveted imprisonment. There is nothing in such a mode of life to gratify their refined and sensitive tastes, nor have they any morbid relish for self-inflicted martyrdom. But they do value their self-respect; they do prize the dignity of manhood, and they call upon your Honor as a man, as well as a Court, to judicially correct a judicial misapprehension which has subjected them to this gross injustice, and not require them to regain their freedom at the price of their manhood. Am I asking too much then when I ask, as I now do, that the Court will direct a correction of the Journal, so that it will appear that as these parties were placed in custody by a mistake, that that mistake is corrected, and they can go forth honorably. It seems to me that I am not asking too much. It seems to me that the Court will not hesitate to grant such a request. That it will gladly direct such a correction of the Journal, to be made, that it may no longer prevent the truth and work gross injustice. This is not asking any action on the part of the Court that will reflect upon the veracity or dignity of any officer of the Court, and least of all upon the Court itself. It is asking simply the correction of a judicial misapprehension by judicial direction. It is asking on behalf of these defendants what the Court will always grant to every one else, that if a misapprehension has inadvertently crept into the record, it may be set right to their advantage, and to the advantage of truth and justice, objects that Courts have generally pretended to have in view.

Judge BELDEN replied.

I wish to say a very few words with reference to the extraordinary request the gentleman has just preferred.

He professes to have asked nothing that would, if granted, compromise the dignity of the Court, and yet in the same breath we have the declaration that his clients stand and have stood for three weeks upon the merest technicality, upon which they are at issue with the Court. Why, where else do your clients stand? Where else have they stood ever since they have been in prison ? if what you say is said sincerely. Now here are two or three things about which my friend on the other side will not differ with me. And I refer now to the circumstances preceding the commitment of these individuals. He knows, I know, your Honor knows, and he admits now, that when the motion was made to change the relative position of these parties to this Court, it was the very motion which he says here would be appropriate, and that was, that individuals, who, by unparalleled leniency on the part of your Honor, had been permitted to go at large upon their own personal recognizances for so many months after they were indicted for crime, that these individuals, thus long and largely privileged, when a " stage in the trial" *had* been reached, by the conviction of one of their number, after a full and impartial hearing of testimony and argument, in which it became my duty to look more particularly after the certainty of their presence; and when they had already surrendered themselves into custody by surrendering their recognizances, that I made the motion that the security be raised from recognizances to bail with sureties. And this is the very motion which the gentleman has just admitted to be a proper one.

But the gentleman was not satisfied with this, but wished to go two or three steps in the rear. He states that upon my application the cases were delayed —— .

[Mr. RIDDLE corrected the gentleman; the statements of which this last was the first were made in the affidavit just read by Judge Tilden.]

—— that the cases were delayed till the 7th of March. I say this was not so. Not to impugn him; I charge nothing beyond a mistake. I wished to take up the cases as soon as ten or twelve days from the time of their appearance. The Grand Jury had adjourned some two weeks before the bills were properly returned, without my being three minutes in the Grand Jury Room while the testimony was being given before them, and I could not keep the witnesses here at the expense of the Government. I was willing and anxious to take up the cases so soon as I could send for witnesses, which would not be longer than ten or twelve days; it would have been much more convenient for me to have gone on then, but the learned counsel who then appeared for the defence, suggested the 8th of March, to which the Court acceded. The postponement from the 8th of March to the 5th of April was made by my request, and greatly to my own accommodation, for which kindness and indulgence on the part of the counsel for the defence I desire to express my sincere thanks.

But now to the other matter. When Bushnell was convicted it became my duty, in behalf of the United States, which I represent, to put him in custody. And when the verdict of the jury was brought in there was a good deal of confusion, and here our difference of understanding occurred. The confusion arose out of the question whether the jury could sit on the second case. I simply objected to the challenge of the array. I never intimated but that the jury could be challenged for cause. I believed they would nearly all excuse themselves. Your Honor overruled me. I thought I was right, and think so still, but submitted to the ruling without a complaint or a murmur. In the midst of this confusion and excitement the learned counsel for these defendants had their clients called and surrendered into custody.

Mr. RIDDLE. — That's false, utterly false.

Judge SPALDING. — That's a lie.

Judge BELDEN. Well, Gentlemen, I cannot believe you mean to seriously insult me; but if you do, I have only to retort upon you. I say it is true as I have stated it. They had their clients called and surrendered of their own motion into the custody of the Marshal, and then notified the Court that they themselves would back out, your Honor, that they'd have nothing farther to do with the defence of these men. And when this excitement had passed away and the Court was about adjourning, I did think that in the discharge of my duty as counsel for the Government, it might be proper for me to make a motion, that by giving some reasonable security they might be released from custody again. Again, your Honor overruled me, and said they could go out as before upon their personal recognizances. And again, I submitted without complaint.

But I do say that when these gentlemen, beseeching a favor, stand here and put the question of grace upon the ground that your Honor is wrong, that the Clerk is wrong, and that I am always wrong and they're always right, that they do not exactly occupy the suppliant and respectful attitude which they claim to your Honor that they do. And I do think that it is my duty and my right to object, to protest, and to claim that these men now occupy a position where they ought to be required to give security, and I think the amount I stated was a reasonable amount. I have no disposition to ask your Honor to demand of them unreasonable bail; but I do feel it my imperious duty to ask and to *demand* that these persons occupy the position of other persons indicted for crime, and a portion of them already convicted upon fair and impartial trial. And I do this in no bad spirit. Much as I have been abused and charged with all manner of unworthy motives, I have not taken any one step which I thought in my own mind would *even look* like unkindness, severity, or unfairness; and if any word or look or tone or manner of mine has conveyed to any of you a different impression, I beg that I may be excused here, by these Gentlemen, and by your Honor. Now I do hope that these gentlemen will not, here, without a motion, ask your Honor that these defendants may go upon their own recognizances. And whether the record be true or false, no harm is done by it to the defendants.

Mr. RIDDLE. I do not wish to press my motion, your Honor, but I wish to set myself right on a point raised by the gentleman.

The COURT. Mr. Riddle, there is no motion before the Court, and further remarks are quite unnecessary.

Mr. RIDDLE. May I not correct the error of the gentleman, by which I am placed in a false position?

The COURT. There is no motion before the Court, Mr. Riddle; further remarks are unnecessary.

Mr. RIDDLE. I understand your Honor, then, to deny me the privilege of making an explanation.

The COURT. Further remarks are quite unnecessary, sir.

So far as regards the correction of the Journal entry, I certainly would not allow it to stand for a moment, if I did not believe it to be correct; and until I am satisfied that it is not correct, I certainly shall direct no amendment of it. My own recollection accords with it, and differs from that of the counsel. There has been no disposition on the part of the Court to oppress or give pain to these defendants. Nothing could be further from our wishes, or more repugnant to our feelings; and until some of them were convicted, we were willing they should go at large on their own recognizances, and if there is any misapprehension upon either side, it is a mere matter of *punctilio* to adhere to it.

Mr. RIDDLE. There is another matter that I wish to speak of, your Honor. It was intimated to your Honor this morning, that the counsel for the defence might be disposed, after some consultation, to make a motion in the case of Langston. I have to say to your Honor that no motion will be made; Mr. Langston is prepared to receive his sentence at the earliest convenience of the Court.

Judge SPALDING. Until when will the other cases be continued, your Honor?

The COURT. Until the July term, sir. The Court has now been in session some two months, and I apprehend that the defendants will not be particularly incommoded by so brief a delay.

Mr. RIDDLE. I shall take the liberty of saying, your Honor, if permitted to say nothing else, that the counsel for these defendants do not yet stand before this Court in the attitude of *beggars!*

Judge BELDEN and the COURT at once. By no means; certainly not, sir.

Mr. RIDDLE. The District-Attorney took pains so to represent it.

Judge BELDEN. Oh, no, sir; I meant no such thing.

Court adjourned to meet next morning at 9 o'clock.

CLEVELAND, May 12, 1859.

Court convened at 10 o'clock. The usual opening being passed and the crowded house stilled, the Court asked: —

Mr. Marshal, is the defendant Bushnell in the house?

Mr. RIDDLE. Mr. Bushnell has been sentenced, your Honor; perhaps your Honor refers to Mr. Langston.

The COURT. An exchange of names only; yes, sir, Mr. Langston was meant. Mr. Langston, you will stand up, sir.

Mr. LANGSTON rose.

The COURT. You also have been tried, Mr. Langston, by a jury, and convicted of a violation of the criminal laws of the United States. Have you or your counsel any thing to say why the sentence of the law should not now be pronounced upon you?

Mr. LANGSTON. I am for the first time in my life before a court of Justice, charged with the violation of law, and am now about to be sentenced. But before receiving that sentence I propose to say one or two words in regard to the mitigation of that sentence, if it may be so construed. I cannot, of course, and do not expect that any thing which I may say will in any way change your predetermined line of action. I ask no such favor at your hands.

I know that the courts of this country, that the laws of this country, that the governmental machinery of this country, are so constituted as to oppress and outrage colored men, men of my complexion. I cannot, then, of course, expect, judging from the past history of the country, any mercy from the laws, from the constitution, or from the courts of the country.

Some days prior to the 13th of September, 1858, happening to be in Oberlin on a visit, I found the country round about there, and the village itself, filled with alarming rumors as to the fact that slave-catchers, kidnappers, negro-stealers, were lying hidden and skulking about, waiting some opportunity to get their bloody hands on some helpless creature to drag him back — or for the first time — into helpless and life-long bondage. These reports becoming current all over that neighborhood, old men, and women and innocent children became exceedingly alarmed for their safety. It was not uncommon to hear mothers say that they dare not send their children to school, for fear they would be caught up and carried off by the way. Some of these people had become free by long and patient toil at night, after working the long, long day for cruel masters, and thus at length getting money enough to buy their liberty. Others had become free by means of the good-will of their masters. And there were others who had become free — to their everlasting honor I say it — by the exercise of their own God-given powers; — by escaping from the plantations of their masters, eluding the blood-thirsty patrols and sentinels so thickly scattered all along their path, outrunning blood-hounds and horses, swimming rivers and fording swamps, and reaching at last, through incredible difficulties, what they, in their delusion, supposed to be free soil. These three classes were in Oberlin, trembling alike for their safety, because they well knew their fate should those men-hunters get their hands on them.

In the midst of such excitement, the 13th day of September was ushered in — a day ever to be remembered in the history of that place, and I presume no less in the history of this Court — on which those men, by lying devices, decoyed into a place where they could get their hands on him — I will not say a slave, for I do not know that — but a *man*, a *brother*, who had a right to his liberty under the laws of God, under the laws of Nature, and under the Declaration of American Independence.

Many of us had believed that there would not be courage to make a seizure; but in the midst of all this excitement, the news came to us like a flash of lightning that an actual seizure by means of fraudulent pretences had been made!

Being identified with that man, by color, by race, by manhood, by sympathies, such as God has implanted in us all, I felt it my duty to go and do what I could toward liberating him. I had been taught by my Revolutionary father — and I say this with all due respect to him — and by his honored associates, that the fundamental doctrine of this government was that *all* men have a right to life and liberty, and coming from the Old Dominion, I brought into Ohio these sentiments, deeply impressed upon my heart. I went to Wellington, and hearing from the parties themselves by what authority the boy was held in custody, I conceived, from what little knowledge I had of law, that they had no right to hold him. And as your Honor has repeatedly laid down the law in this Court, that in the State of Ohio a man is presumed to be free until he is proven to be legally restrained of his liberty, I believed that upon that principle of law those men were bound to take their prisoner before the very first magistrate they found, and there establish the facts set forth in their warrant, and that until they did this every man had a right to presume that their claim was unfounded, and to institute such proceedings for the purpose of securing an investigation as he might find warranted by the laws of this State. Now, sir, if that is not the plain, common sense and correct view of the law, then I have been misled both by your Honor, and by the prevalent received opinion.

It is said that they had a warrant. Why then should they not establish its validity before the proper officers? And I stand here to-day, sir, to say, that, with an exception, of which I shall soon speak, *to procure such a lawful investigation of the authority under which they claimed to act, was the part I took in that day's proceedings, and the only part.* I supposed it to be my duty as a citizen of Ohio — excuse me for saying that, sir — as an *outlaw of the United States* [much sensation], to do what I could to secure at least this form of Justice to my brother whose liberty was in peril. — *Whatever more than that has been sworn to on this trial, as an act of mine, is false, ridiculously false.* When I found these men refusing to go, according to the law, as I apprehended it, and subject their claim to an official inspection, and that nothing short of a *habeas corpus* would oblige such an inspection, I was willing to go even thus far, supposing in that county a sheriff might, perhaps, be found with nerve enough to serve it. In this again I failed. Nothing then was left to me, nothing to the boy in custody, but the confirmation of my first belief that the pretended authority was worthless, and the employment of those means of liberation which belong to us all. With regard to the part I took in the forcible rescue, which

followed, I have nothing to say, farther than I have already said. The evidence is before you. It is alleged that I said, "*we* will have him any how." *This I* NEVER *said.* I did say to Mr. Lowe, what I honestly believed to be the truth, that the crowd were very much excited, many of them averse to longer delay and bent upon a rescue at all hazards; and that he being an old acquaintance and friend of mine, I was anxious to extricate him from the dangerous position he occupied, and therefore advised that he urge Jennings to give the boy up. Further than this I did not say, either to him or to any one else.

The law under which I am arraigned is an unjust one, one made to crush the colored man, and one that outrages every feeling of Humanity, as well as every rule of Right. I have nothing to do with its constitutionality; and about it I care a great deal less. I have often heard it said by learned and good men that it was unconstitutional; I remember the excitement that prevailed throughout all the free States when it was passed; and I remember how often it has been said by individuals, conventions, communities, and legislatures, that it never could be, never should be, and never was meant to be enforced. I had always believed, until the contrary appeared in the actual institution of proceedings, that the provisions of this odious statute would never be enforced within the bounds of this State.

But I have another reason to offer why I should not be sentenced, and one that I think pertinent to the case. I have not had a trial before a jury of my peers. The common law of England — and you will excuse me for referring to that, since I am but a private citizen and not a lawyer — was that every man should be tried before a jury of men occupying the same position in the social scale with himself. That lords should be tried before a jury of lords; that peers of the realm should be tried before peers of the realm; that vassals before vassals, and *aliens before aliens*, and they must not come from the district where the crime was committed, lest the prejudices of either personal friends or foes should affect the accused. The Constitution of the United States guarantees — not merely to its citizens — but *to all persons* a trial before an *impartial* jury. I have had no such trial.

The colored man is oppressed by certain universal and deeply fixed *prejudices*. Those jurors are well known to have shared largely in these prejudices, and I therefore consider that they were neither impartial, nor were they a jury of my peers. And the prejudices which white people have against colored men, grow out of this fact: that we have, as a people, *consented* for two hundred years to be *slaves* of the whites. We have been scourged, crushed, and cruelly oppressed, and have submitted to it all tamely, meekly, peaceably; I mean as a people, and with rare individual exceptions;

and to-day you see us thus, meekly submitting to the penalties of an infamous law. Now the Americans have this feeling, and it is an honorable one, that they will respect those who will rebel at oppression, but despise those who tamely submit to outrage and wrong; and while our people as a people submit, they will as a people be despised. Why, they will hardly meet on terms of equality with us in a whiskey shop, in a car, at a table, or even at the altar of God. So thorough and hearty a contempt have they for those who will meekly *lie still* under the heel of the oppressor. The jury came into the box with that feeling. They knew they had that feeling, and so the Court knows now, and knew then. The gentlemen who prosecuted me have that feeling, the Court itself has that feeling, and even the counsel who defended me have that feeling.

I was tried by a jury who were prejudiced; before a Court that was prejudiced; prosecuted by an officer who was prejudiced, and defended, though ably, by counsel that were prejudiced. And therefore it is, your Honor, that I urge by all that is good and great in manhood, that I should not be subjected to the pains and penalties of this oppressive law, when I have *not* been tried, either by a jury of my peers, or by a jury that were impartial.

One more word, sir, and I have done. I went to Wellington, knowing that colored men have no rights in the United States which white men are bound to respect; that the courts had so decided; that Congress had so enacted; that the people had so decreed.

There is not a spot in this wide country, not even by the altars of God, nor in the shadow of the shafts that tell the imperishable fame and glory of the heroes of the Revolution; no, nor in the old Philadelphia Hall, where any colored man may dare to ask a mercy of a white man. Let me stand in that Hall, and tell a United States Marshal that my father was a Revolutionary soldier; that he served under Lafayette, and fought through the whole war; and that he always told me that he fought for *my* freedom as much as for his own; and he would sneer at me, and clutch me with his bloody fingers, and say he had a *right* to make me a slave! And when I appeal to Congress, they say he has a right to make me a slave; when I appeal to the people, they say he has a right to make me a slave, and when I appeal to your Honor, *your Honor* says he has a right to make me a slave, and if any man, white or black, seeks an investigation of that claim, they make themselves amenable to the pains and penalties of the Fugitive Slave Act, for BLACK MEN HAVE NO RIGHTS WHICH WHITE MEN ARE BOUND TO RESPECT. [Great applause.] I, going to Wellington with the full knowledge of all this, knew that if that man was taken to Columbus, he was hopelessly gone, no matter whether he had ever been in slavery before or not. I knew that I was in the same situation

myself, and that by the decision of your Honor, if any man whatever were to claim me as his slave and seize me, and my brother, being a lawyer, should seek to get out a writ of *habeas corpus* to expose the falsity of the claim, he would be thrust into prison under one provision of the Fugitive Slave Law, for interfering with the man claiming to be in pursuit of a fugitive, and I, by the perjury of a solitary wretch, would, by another of its provisions, be helplessly doomed to life-long bondage, without the possibility of escape.

Some persons may say that there is no danger of free persons being seized and carried off as slaves. No one need labor under such a delusion. Sir, *four* of the eight persons who were first carried back under the act of 1850, were afterwards proved to be *free men*. The pretended owner declared that they were not his, after his agent had "*satisfied the Commissioner*" that they were, by his oath. They were free persons, but wholly at the mercy of the oath of one man. And but last Sabbath afternoon a letter came to me from a gentleman in St. Louis, informing me that a young lady, who was formerly under my instruction at Columbus, a free person, is now lying in the jail at that place, claimed as the slave of some wretch who never saw her before, and waiting for testimony from relatives at Columbus to establish her freedom. I could stand here by the hour and relate such instances. In the very nature of the case they must be constantly occurring. A letter was not long since found upon the person of a counterfeiter when arrested, addressed to him by some Southern gentleman, in which the writer says:—

"*Go among the niggers; find out their marks and scars; make good descriptions and send to me, and I'll find masters for 'em.*"

That is the way men are carried "back" to slavery.

But in view of all the facts I say, that if ever again a man is seized near me, and is about to be carried Southward as a slave, before any legal investigation has been had, I shall hold it to be my duty, as I held it that day, to secure for him, if possible, a legal inquiry into the character of the claim by which he is held. And I go farther; I say that if it is adjudged illegal to procure even such an investigation, then we are thrown back upon those last defences of our rights, which cannot be taken from us, and which God gave us that we need not be slaves. I ask your Honor, while I say this, to place yourself in my situation, and you will say with me, that if your brother, if your friend, if your wife, if your child, had been seized by men who claimed them as fugitives, and the law of the land forbade you to ask any investigation, and precluded the possibility of any legal protection or redress,—then you will say with me, that you would not only demand the protection of the law, but you would call in your neighbors and your friends, and would ask them to say with you, that these your friends *could not* be taken into slavery.

And now I thank you for this leniency, this indulgence, in giving a man unjustly condemned, by a tribunal before which he is declared to have no rights, the privilege of speaking in his own behalf. I know that it will do nothing toward mitigating your sentence, but it is a privilege to be allowed to speak, and I thank you for it. I shall submit to the penalty, be it what it may. But I stand up here to say, that if for doing what I did on that day at Wellington, I am to go in jail six months, and pay a fine of a thousand dollars, according to the Fugitive Slave Law, and such is the protection the laws of this country afford me, I must take upon myself the responsibility of self-protection; and when I come to be claimed by some perjured wretch as his slave, I shall never be taken into slavery. And as in that trying hour I would have others do to me, as I would call upon my friends to help me; as I would call upon you, your Honor, to help me; as I would call upon you [to the District-Attorney], to help me; and upon you [to Judge Bliss], and upon you [to his counsel], *so help me* GOD! I stand here to say that I will do all I can, for any man thus seized and held, though the inevitable penalty of six months imprisonment and one thousand dollars fine for each offence hangs over me! We have a common humanity. You would do so; your manhood would require it; and no matter what the laws might be, you would honor yourself for doing it; your friends would honor you for doing it; your children to all generations would honor you for doing it; and every good and honest man would say, you had done *right!* [Great and prolonged applause, in spite of the efforts of the Court and the Marshal.]

The COURT. These manifestations cannot be allowed here. The Marshal has orders to clear the room if they are repeated.

You have done injustice to the Court, Mr. Langston, in thinking that nothing you might say could effect a mitigation of your sentence. You have presented considerations to which I shall attach much weight.

I am fully aware of the evidence that was given to the jury; of the circumstances that were related; of your action in relation to the investigation of the cause of the detention of the fugitive, and of your advice to others to pursue a legal course; and although I am not disposed to question the integrity of the jury, still I see mitigating circumstances in the transaction which should not require, in my opinion, the extreme penalty of the law. This Court does not make laws; that belongs to another tribunal. We sit here under the obligations of an oath to execute them, and whether they be bad or whether they be good, it is not for us to say. We appreciate fully your condition, and while it excites the cordial sympathies of our better natures, still the law must be vindicated. On reflection, I am constrained to say that the

penalty in your case should be comparatively light. It is, therefore, the sentence of the Court, that you pay a fine of one hundred dollars; that you be confined in the jail at Cuyahoga County, under the direction of the Marshal, for a period of twenty days from date; and that you pay the costs of this prosecution: and that in case any casualty or other occurrence should render your confinement there insecure, that the Marshal see the sentence executed in any other county jail within this District.

Judge SHERLOCK J. ANDREWS then informed the Court that Matthew De Wolfe, Abner Loveland, and Loring Wadsworth, citizens of Wellington, indicted for participating in the rescue case, wished him to enter a plea of *nolle contendere*, and were ready to submit themselves to the judgment of the Court.

Judge ANDREWS said, that he had been informed by the defendants that they were not represented by Counsel, and he had been desired to bring their case to the attention of the Court. He said they were among the oldest citizens of Lorain county, and law-abiding men, enjoying in a high degree the respect and confidence of their fellow-citizens, and that they were unwilling any longer to occupy a position in which they were charged with a wilful violation of the law. Their connection with this rescue was entirely incidental, and they had assembled with other citizens to arrest the progress of a fire which had broken out in their village, and had been hard at work in saving property, and while thus engaged, were informed that one of their magistrates had issued a warrant for the apprehension of two men charged with an attempt to kidnap a citizen of the State. The feelings of the people were strongly roused before, and when this new element was added to the other cause of excitement, the defendants admit that they yielded to the impulse that moved others, and that they did at first give encouragment to the officer in his attempt to execute the process in his hands, but they say, and are abundantly able to show, that from the time they became satisfied that the negro was held by lawful authority, they abstained from all participation in the proceedings.

Mr. Andrews said that, whether under the rulings of the Court in relation to the responsibilities of men engaged in the execution of a common unlawful purpose, or in relation to the prudence and vigilance which should be exercised in these cases, to ascertain the authority under which the fugitive is held, whether under these rulings (which he believed to be law) these men had undesignedly been guilty of a technical violation of the statute, whether, in the tumult and confusion of the hour, they were as careful in their inquiries, as guarded in their conversation and conduct as they ought to have been, he would not pretend to say; but this he would say, that they never for a moment cherished a purpose to resist the law, that they never did, in fact, knowingly and intentionally, resist it; and that, if they were betrayed into conduct which amounted to a punishable offence, it was attributable solely to a misapprehension, on their part, of what their rights and obligations were. They were desirous that their position should be perfectly understood; they did not invoke sympathy because they had violated the law; the agitation connected with these trials has brought to the surface a variety of opinions in relation to the course that should be pursued when attempts are made to enforce this law. Good men among us differ in opinion as to what the duty of a citizen is in such emergencies. Some counsel a disregard of the law altogether. Some think that the unanimous decision of the Supreme Court of the United States, affirming its constitutionality, carries with it no authority and imposes no obligation to obedience; and some, impelled by stronger sympathies, and to more intense hatred of the law, think that, when the owner of a slave comes into this State, and asserts his right under the Constitution and laws of the United States to the person and services of a fugitive, he should be resisted, *even to the shedding of blood ! ! !*

Now these defendants have no controversy with those who hold these opinions, but they wish the Court to understand that they are the sentiments of a later school than that in which they were trained. They have no conception of a worse government than that would be, which the Constitution and laws should set aside, and every man should become a law unto himself. They believe it is the duty of every good citizen to submit to the laws of the land; that, when the constitutionality of a national law has been judicially determined by the Supreme Court of the United States (the tribunal created for the very purpose of deciding such questions), its decisions, while they stand, are to be followed by respect and obedience, and they sympathize with no effort that can be made to bring the State Government in conflict with the National Government, or to cause to be deprecated or undervalued the Constitution of the United States. With all its imperfections — with all its compromises — even with the stain of slavery upon it, they still esteem it a privilege to live under such a Constitution, and believe that, while the people of a State acknowledge its authority and enjoy its benefits, they ought, in good faith, to carry out even its obnoxious provisions. These gentlemen are utterly opposed to slavery and to the provisions of the Fugitive Slave Law; but they think that bad laws, under our system of government, can be better encountered in a constitutional way than by an armed resistance. These are, in substance, the remarks which I have been requested by the defendants to submit in their behalf; and while they deny that they have knowingly violated the law, while they insist

upon having their protest recorded that they are not guilty, as they stand charged in the indictment, they still instruct me to say that they will no longer contend with the Government in these prosecutions.

Judge Andrews concluded with saying, that he thought the Court would concur with him in the opinion that the course now pursued by the defendants was one not unbecoming good citizens, that it would go farther than any pains or penalties to sustain the supremacy of law, and that as against such men, under such circumstances, the public justice could be adequately vindicated by the infliction of the mildest punishment.

The COURT inquired of the District-Attorney if he had any remarks to make.

Judge BELDEN. Nothing, may it please the Court, but to add my voice to that of Judge Andrews that a light punishment may be inflicted.

After Judge BELDEN had concluded, the Court proceeded to pass sentence upon them. In consideration of the facts stated, he sentenced them to pay a fine of $20 each, to pay the costs of prosecution, and to be committed to jail for twenty-four hours.

Court then adjourned until Saturday morning.

The record of the Court is the same in these cases as in the cases of the four sentenced a few days previous on a similar plea, with the following remarkable exception: —

"*And the District-Attorney stipulating that the record in this cause shall not be used to his prejudice in any civil action.*"

The following editorial, cut from the Morning *Leader*, conveys the sentiment which seemed to be general among the friends of the defendants, at the time of these sentences; and so far as it ventures upon a rehearsal of facts, it is believed to make only reliable statements.

SUB-SAINTISM. — HOW IT WAS DONE.

Messrs. Loveland, Wadsworth, and DeWolfe, the "old friends" of Judge Andrews, humiliated as they have been by their volunteer advocate, deserved better treatment and a better fate. They are substantial men of Lorain, belong to the class of hardy pioneers who broke up the wilderness, built the dwellings, schoolhouses, and churches of the county, and have ever sustained irreproachable characters as good men and good citizens. No fugitive from slavery ever went unfed from their hospitable homes, and their hatred for the Fugitive Slave Act is just as deep seated as their hatred of the accursed institution which Dred Scott Courts and pro-slavery Administrations are laboring with true Algerine ferocity to force upon the Free States and Territories of the Republic. They have homesteads, hard earned and dear to them, have reached the down-hill side of life, and in acting out the noblest sympathies of nature and religion towards a fellow man, unwittingly found themselves in the tender mercies of a Federal Court despotism. The relentless Government pursuers held them and their homes in their grasp. The vindictive charge of the modern Jeffreys in the convictions had left them no hope. Fines and costs — the latter oppressively enormous in the U. S. District Court — would leave them in their old age homeless and penniless. These considerations pressed heavily upon them. They sought legal advice of an " old friend " in whom they placed implicit confidence. The result, preconcerted between the Court and counsel no doubt, was as humiliating to them, as the speech preceding it was uncalled for, and astounding to the public. If the self-abasement of the Advocate to the Slave power and its Government officials was voluntary, the " old friends," who have not a pulsation in sympathy with either, should have been spared the pain and disgrace of a like, but on their part, an involuntary degradation.

The way the thing was done is a subject of much inquiry by the public. A portion of the *modus operandi* is stated as follows : — The Wellingtonites were assured by the U. S. District-Attorney that he did not consider them in reality responsible for the Rescue. The Oberlinites are the ones the Government wishes to punish ; and he would advise them to trust themselves to the mercy of the Court, and give their influence towards maintaining the law of the land.

The Wellington men replied that the Fugitive Slave Law outraged all the principles of right, and that they never could obey it, or admit that they had done wrong in the case of John.

District-Attorney Belden becomes a " *subsaint*," and urges, it is true, that law is an outrageous law, and I am frank to confess that even I would not obey it under certain circumstances. If a fugitive slave should come to me for money I would give it to him and tell him to go on his way. Now you were on the ground, and if you go to trial you will certainly be convicted. We shall convict all the Oberlinites. Patton and Cowles will be indicted.

The Wellingtonites encouraged by the District-Attorney's " *sub-saintism*," conclude that he is ready to meet them half way, and they consent to throw themselves on the Court, some of them, at least, understanding that they were not to withdraw their plea of " not guilty ; " and that their counsel should only protest that they were innocent, and that they had in no wise changed their minds upon that law.

Pilate *kissed* them, and Andrew(s) *crucified* them. How crucified, let the following card proclaim from the house-tops : —

MR. LOVELAND'S STATEMENT.

The card below is inserted on personal request made by Mr. Loveland : — *Herald.*

MESSRS. EDITORS : — After reading your remarks in last evening's *Herald*, in reference to me, I deem it due to myself to ask you to state that I did not intend to authorize my counsel yesterday to give my views on government, to the Court ; and disclaim holding to many of the doctrines expressed by him. I simply authorized him to enter for me the plea of *nolle contendere*, protesting at the same time that I am not guilty of violating any law, and requiring the protest to be entered on the records of the Court.   ABNER LOVELAND.

About this time the following manifesto was published. It will explain itself.

STATEMENT OF THE OBERLIN PRISONERS NOW IN JAIL.

CUYAHOGA COUNTY JAIL, }
May 12, 1859.   }

To the People of the Western Reserve :

The undersigned, citizens of Lorain county, now confined in this prison, under indictment for alleged violation of the Fugitive Slave Act, have reason to know that the history of their incarceration is quite generally misapprehended, and that this misapprehension is greatly prejudicing their cause with the public.

It is to state the facts pertaining to the imprisonment, clearly and correctly, and to define the present position of the imprisoned, that this article is offered to your consideration.

To make the statement proposed intelligible and complete, the narration must begin with the arrest which brought us before the U. S. Court. At the rising of the Grand Jury in December last, Marshal Johnson visited Oberlin, and notified the indicted, who lived there, that he had warrants for their arrest, and that he should expect to meet them in Cleveland at a given hour on the next day. The parties on whom the notice was served proved their appreciation of the politeness of the Marshal, in dispensing with the usual forms of arrest, and their disposition to give prompt answer to whatever charges the law might bring against them, by appearing in Court at the time appointed. Being brought to the bar, they declared themselves ready and anxious for immediate trial. The District-Attorney, evidently taken by surprise at the unexpected promptness of the defence, asked delay. The defence earnestly protested against an adjournment of their cases. The Court, however, granted the motion of the District-Attorney ; but, in consideration of the fact that the defendants had made prompt appearance, and that they had been refused trial, discharged them on their personal recognizance, instead of putting them under bail as the prosecutor had asked them to do. The cases were set for trial on the second Tuesday of March. At the approach of that time the District-Attorney asked for a farther continuance of the cases to the fifth of April. The delay, although it put the defence to great inconvenience, was conceded by its counsel. When the appointed time at length came, all the indicted who had been arrested, except one gentleman who was very ill, presented themselves at the bar of the Court, nor did any of them fail of daily attendance during the Bushnell trial without the express permission of the District-Attorney.

In the course of the Bushnell trial it was made clear to the defence that there was a desire on the part of the Court to secure the conviction, and a determination on the part of the District-Attorney to bring about the humiliation of all the indicted. The proofs of a purpose to make a judicial and personal war upon them were so plain, that the defendants could not shut their eyes to them. They felt constrained, therefore, to be on their guard and to be watchful against emergencies which might involve them in lasting injury and reproach. This purpose, however, did not prevent their continuing the full compliance with the rules of the Court, and with the terms of their recognizances, which they had before rendered.

Affairs being in this posture, the Government evidently seeking opportunities for assault, and the defence looking well to its means for parrying the assault, the Bushnell trial came to an end. On the rendition of the verdict, conversation arose between counsel on the two sides as to what case was to be tried next. It was finally determined by the Government that Langston's case should be called on, and counsel for the defence, which had previously said that it was not ready to go on with that case, signified that it would be ready by the time the jury was drawn. What was the surprise of counsel at hearing the Court declare that the same jury was to try all the "rescue" cases — all of them, be it noted, involving the same material points. How then could a jury just having risen from the consideration of one of them, *impartially* address itself to the consideration of another? Against this remarkable order of Court, the counsel for the defence made earnest protest, and finally declared that "under such a ruling, the Court might go on with the cases as fast as it pleased, the defendants would not stultify themselves by either offering evidence or appearing by counsel." With this, the District-Attorney moved that the defendants be ordered into custody. The Court replied, — "The District-Attorney is entitled to the order. Let the accused be called."

The Clerk then read the names of the indicted, and those present were directed to put themselves under the control of the marshal, who cleared seats for them. While this was going on, Mr. Ralph Plumb, one of the indicted, whose case had previously been put over to the November term, went to Judge Spalding, and asked if his recognizance would not be taken up, so that he could cast in his lot with his now imprisoned brethren. The Judge replied affirmatively, and moved the Court in Mr. Plumb's behalf to cancel his recognizance, and allow him to join those who had been put in custody. The motion was granted. This occurrence called the attention of counsel to the recognizances of those who were now in the Marshal's keeping, and Judge Spalding arose and said, "Your Honor will, of course, direct the Clerk to cancel the recognizances of *all* the gentlemen who have been put into custody. It would be improper that their recognizances should stand while they are in prison." "Certainly," replied Judge Willson, "it will be done of course."

The Court and some of its officers seemed to realize, at once, that injustice had been done to the parties in custody, and that some means for escape from the odium which would be incurred by the order for imprisonment, should be found. Accordingly, the Marshal soon came to the party in duress, and proposed that the whole party should go home, giving its promise to return on the next Monday morning. (The proposition was accompanied, however, with the distinct statement, repeated at least once, that "Bushnell was not to be included in the category.") The Court, also, in reply to a proposition from the District-Attorney, that ample security should be required of the persons in custody, before they should be permitted to go at large, replied that if they chose, they should go out on the same terms on which they had had liberty since their arrest, viz., by giving personal recognizance. This ruling plainly implied that the procedure which had resulted in the commitment had originated with the District-Attorney and Court (otherwise it would have been rebuked by a change of the terms of bail), or in short, that it was warranted by no wrong-doing coming on the part of the persons committed, and that it was regarded by the Court itself as being legally unjust.

Confident that the commitment had proceeded from personal malice and a determination to humble them, on the part of the District-Attorney, and at least a willingness to have them driven to the wall, on the part of the Court, and feeling that they would enter most emphatic protest against the insult and legal injustice which they had suffered, by remaining in custody of the Marshal until the Court should amend the wrong or the law should relieve them, and that while the question as to the jury was yet open, it would be politic to let the responsibility of the commitment rest with the Court, the defendants for the time refused the offers both of the Court and Marshal. They were further prompted to this course by the consideration that it would permit them to share Bushnell's fortunes as long as possible. They did, however, say to the Marshal that "they were under his orders, and should do, to the letter, what he directed." He replied by sending them to jail.

It was, therefore, because the Court, without being justified by wrong-doing of any kind on their part, had ordered them into custody, and thus grossly insulted and wronged them, and because they were unwilling to be made the scape-goats of the judicial outrage (as they would have been, had they, by making concessions or accepting favors, relieved the Court of the burden of the indignity which it had forced upon them) that the committed "rescuers" came to jail on the afternoon of Friday, April 15th.

But it was expected by the imprisoned company that when Court was called on Monday morning it would, by recalling its order respecting the Jury, if not otherwise, open the way for their restoration to liberty upon the same footing which they had occupied before their commitment. They were not disappointed in their expectations that the Court would recede from its (as its seemed to them) exceedingly unjust ruling as to the Jury. But they were disappointed in finding that their way to an honorable release was hedged by an entry on the Journal of the Court, which averred that the defendants were taken into custody because they had surrendered themselves in discharge of their recognizances. They at once saw that this entry either grew out of a misapprehension of facts, or resulted from a determination to compel them to remain in custody, or to regain liberty at the expense of a plain acknowledgment that they had been guilty of folly and indiscretion which well deserved punishment. Hoping that the first was the correct view, they made, through counsel, a statement of the facts, and asked that if the Journal could not be so corrected as to correspond with the truth, it should be either vacated or made to present, in a new entry, the fact that they differed with the Court in their understanding of the matter. The Court kept the request under advisement through the day, and then announced that it had determined to let the record stand as it was. This announcement compelled the imprisoned to believe that their humiliation was determined by the Court. Under such circumstances self-respect forbade their entering into new bonds.

Knowing that the matter they had in hand was an important one, and that either remaining in custody or giving new recognizances involved great issues to themselves and others, the imprisoned took time to consider both their position and their duty. While they were pursuing their inquiries, they entertained the hope that the Supreme Court would release them from the duress by granting them *habeas corpus.* Their hope in this direction was presently blighted by the refusal of the Court to grant the writ, and then they found the way to honorable escape from custody more effectually closed than it had ever before been. If they had entered into recognizances or given bail upon the heels of their defeat at Columbus, they would

have encouraged the Prosecution in the belief that they were effectually humbled, and that they had forsaken their cause as being lost. That they were justified in believing that their entering into recognizances or giving bail at this time would have been regarded in this light, is proved by the despatch which Marshal Johnson sent to the President of the United States on the afternoon of the 27th, the substance of which was stated in the Washington *Constitution* as follows: —

"The President last evening received a telegraphic despatch, dated at Cleveland, from the Marshal of the Northern District of Ohio, stating that the Supreme Court of that State had unanimously refused the writ of *habeas corpus* in the case of the persons in his custody, under the fugitive slave law, and that three of the most respectable of them had given bail for their appearance to stand their trial before the District Court of the United States. Every thing was quiet."

The obvious implication of this despatch was twofold; first, that Northern repugnance to the fugitive slave act had received a decided blow from the decision of the Supreme Court, and secondly, that the hearts of those who had entertained this repugnance and had actively expressed it, were fainting under the blow. The imprisoned felt that they could not, in honor or in duty, justify the second intimation of this singular despatch, and that if they were ever to yield it must be when the cause they loved was not going backward, and when their yielding would not accelerate its decline. So they waited for a better day, all the time longing to be at home and about the business which sorely needed their presence, and suffering under the irksome constraint of prison life, they eagerly sought the place for honorable escape. They thought they would perhaps find that place at the close of the Langston trial. They assured themselves that the developments of that trial would prove to the Court that if the testimony for the Government was justly weighed and the evidence for the defence was measured as it should be, no one of the rescuers could fairly be convicted, and that the prosecution would be dropped. But the end only showed a judicial bias stronger than before, and a partisan feeling on the part of the Jury, which could not rest short of a verdict of guilty.

Thus was the prospect for making honorable escape, which the imprisoned sought, made darker than it had yet been.

But that they might leave no stone unturned, the imprisoned presented, on Wednesday last, as from John Watson, one of their number, an affidavit setting forth the facts respecting their imprisonment, and followed it with an appeal from Mr. Riddle, in which, reciting again their story and asserting their rights, they demanded either speedy trial, discharge from process, or such a correction of, or entry upon the journal as would permit them to occupy, without discredit to themselves, the position they formerly held before the Court. But the appeal was in vain. A bland intimation that there was no barrier to the liberty of the imprisoned but "*punctilio*," and a positive refusal to do what was asked, was the only reply which the Court saw fit to give. And so the incarcerated company finds itself effectually shut out from all relief except such as it cannot but scorn.

To sum up the points involved in the above history, the imprisoned are here because an order of the Court put them here; they stay here because a judicial wrong under which they suffer is unredressed, and because a journal entry of the Court will not allow them to go out without personal disgrace — the disgrace they would suffer in virtually acknowledging that they had been guilty of a most foolish action, and that they were ready to sneak away from the dilemma in which that action had placed them. The self-respect of the imprisoned, the sense of honor which Heaven planted in their souls, and which revered parents carefully nursed, will not permit them to involve themselves in such disgrace. It could *never* be with them a matter of mere "*punctilio*" to avoid the dishonor to which their only chance of escape exposes them, and *now* the circumstances in which they are placed and the relation which they sustain to a good cause, beset and imperilled by oppressive power, make what might, in another case, be an inconsiderable affair, rise into a duty of the greatest magnitude. The imprisoned cannot allow it to be said that when Freedom was assailed on her last field, they ingloriously dropped their banner to save themselves inconvenience and suffering. They are not willing to have even *an appearance of submission* to tyrannical power on their part, become a pledge that the diabolical Fugitive Slave Act is hereafter to work its own on the Western Reserve.

It will be observed that in both the historical sketch, and the summary above presented, we (for we will here drop the third person) have laid special stress on the necessity for maintaining a protest against what we regard as judicial tyranny, and the point of honor which prevents our liberating ourselves by giving bail. Nothing has been said with respect to the *policy* of our course. This, however, is a matter which has been constantly kept in view. We have thought, and still think, that in various ways, a manly and straightforward course on our part, would promote our cause. Precisely how the maintaining of our determined protests against what we have regarded as injustice and falsehood, would advance our interests in the defence of our cases, it would not be politic for us to say. In due time we shall give to the public a full disclosure of the motives which have acted on us in this direction, and we believe that such a disclosure will fully satisfy all who have doubted the propriety of our course, that it has been wisely taken.

We must not close without saying, that in all that we have done, we have cautiously inquired what is right, and what expedient? Nor have we trusted to our judgments only. We have invited the counsel of as wise and judicious men as we could reach, and our conclusions have been those to which we have been conducted by what has seemed to us the decidedly preponderating opinion of the seven or eight eminent lawyers with whom we have been in constant consultation.

And, withal, we have constantly looked for direction to that Superior Intelligence, which gives " wisdom to all who seek it and upbraideth not." At every step, what we have regarded as manifest, Providence has pointed the way. We still look to our Divine Guide for direction. We know that if earthly tribunals deny the relief we ask, the higher Court to which we look will, in due time, send it. We assure ourselves that the Great Arbiter will not be pleased with conduct on our part, which will degrade ourselves, or betray a good cause; and we are equally confident that if we stand to our integrity, he will appoint an issue to our troubles, which will honor Him and fully satisfy us. We cheerfully wait the opening of the " door which no man can shut ! "

H. E. PECK,	DAVID L. WATSON,
RALPH PLUMB,	WILSON B. EVANS,
CHAS. H. LANGSTON,	HENRY EVANS,
A. W. LYMAN,	RICHARD WINSOR,
J. H. SCOTT,	W. E. LINCOLN,
JAMES BARTLETT,	J. M. FITCH,
JOHN WATSON.	

STATEMENT OF COUNSEL.

Messrs. Peck and Others, Prisoners, etc.,

GENTLEMEN: — The following we believe to be an accurate statement of what transpired in the U. S. District Court on the 15th ult., in connection with the order made by the Court, that you be taken into custody by the marshal: —

Upon the announcement of the verdict of the Jury in the case against Bushnell, the case of Langston was called by the Court, and inquiry was made as to whether the parties were ready. The District-Attorney stated that the Government was ready. Defendant's counsel replied that they were not ready in that case, but were in the case against Peck. The District-Attorney insisted upon taking up the cases in the order in which they stood on the Docket. The Court said the Government had the right so to insist; and again asked if the defence was ready in the case of Langston. His counsel replied that they probably should be by the time a Jury should be empanelled. The District-Attorney and the Court both said that the Jury then in the box (being the one that had just returned the verdict against Bushnell), were the regular Jury for the trial of all the cases. The counsel for the defendants strongly protested against being compelled to go to trial in the remaining cases before a Jury that must have already made up its mind against them on all the principal questions, except one, involved in the cases. The Court observed that the mere fact that the Jury had tried Bushnell, would constitute no good reason why they should not try the other defendants, — intimating, at the same time, that it would be competent for the defendants to challenge them for cause, if they had made up their mind as to the guilt of those about to be tried. The defendant's counsel then notified the Court that if it was determined to try the remaining defendants by that Jury, no one of them would make any defence whatever, but that the Court might proceed with them as it saw fit. The District-Attorney thereupon instantly arose, and with a great deal of petulance in his manner, moved the Court that all the remaining defendants, with the exception of Loveland, De Wolfe, and some others, whom he had permitted to go home for the time being, be ordered into custody. To this Judge Spalding, still occupying his seat, said, sharply, "I second the motion." The Court observed that the District-Attorney had the right to require the order to be made, and directed the clerk to call the names of the defendants, with the exception named in the motion; which was accordingly done, and those of them then in the court room were taken into custody by the marshal. As this was being done, Judge Spalding asked that their recognizances might be cancelled; to which the Court replied, "Of course," — and directed the proper entry to be made for that purpose by the clerk. Judge Spalding also moved the Court that the continuance in the case of Mr. Plumb, which had before then been entered, might be cancelled, and he be permitted to surrender himself in discharge of his recognizance, which was accordingly done.

We cannot be mistaken in the fact that you were *ordered* into custody, as above stated, and that you *did not surrender* yourselves, as alleged in the Journal entry.

R. P. SPALDING,
A. G. RIDDLE,
S. O. GRISWOLD,
F. T. BACKUS,
as Counsel for Defendants.

Cleveland, May 14, 1859.

—— Great efforts had been made to rid the docket of the indicted from Wellington, as may already have been inferred. The prosecution was fast becoming so emphatically a "pursuit of" — no matter what — "under difficulties," that "retrenchment" somewhere grew to be a necessity too urgent for neglect, and the Wellington defendants were considered on several accounts the more proper to be first dropped. Finding it not so easy to "drop" them by simply opening the hand, there was no choice but to retreat, bolt, or plead. The Court preferred pleading. A number of individuals were employed to approach them from various quarters, and with various inducements. The total success of these combined forces has already appeared. Our venerable FATHER GILLETT still represented Wellington in prison. Nothing could move him. An endless series of inducements were presented, pressed, argued, urged — but to no purpose. They had, indeed, met a rock in the strait, and there was no getting farther. He was finally besought to leave the Jail at least, and offered release upon his personal recognizance, just after three of his neighbors had been inflexibly held to bail with sureties. The quiet answer was: " I was ordered to jail when you had my recognizance inviolately observed: *I never give you another!*"

Down on the other knee then.

" Will you give us your *word* to return when we send for you?"

"*Never*, gentlemen. You have treated me like cowards, insulting my honor when it was pledged. I shall not allow you an opportunity to repeat the outrage."

What was to be done? The testimony against the old gentleman would be next to nothing; the indictment was only to harass; the game with him was out, and they found themselves in decidedly the worst of it; — the old man MUST be shaken off at any cost.

All along on their faces!

" *Will you go home if you are turned out of jail?*"

" If the choice were to sleep in the streets or go home, I think I should *go home!*" said the good-humored old gentleman, shaking his sides with quiet merriment.

" And come back when *your counsel* advise it?"

" I shall be likely to follow the advice of my counsel so long as I employ them."

" *Well, then, go!*"

So FATHER GILLETT went.

Fourteen Oberlin men now remained in prison, twelve of them yet to be tried. The Court gave out — by the Court is meant, in this connection, not only the Judge, but the District-Attorney, the Marshal, the Clerk, and all their attachées as well, since they acted in perfect unison and with a common understanding in these cases — in every direction, and almost under the ears of the prisoners, that if they would only knuckle handsomely and "acknowledge the corn," they would get off almost as easily as the Wellington men; *but if they did n't*, they should every one be *pinned to the wall;* for it "*was high time that* OBERLIN, *the strong-hold and hotbed of Abolitionism and* REPUBLICANISM was SUBDUED.*" If this had not come time after time direct from the authorities themselves, it would indeed be unpardonable to publish it.

THE SECOND APPLICATION FOR HABEAS CORPUS was made in behalf of the two who had been sentenced, to Judge SCOTT, of the Supreme Bench, on the 17th of May. As in duty bound, he immediately issued the writ, returnable before the Full Bench, and then telegraphed to his brethren who were just dispersed to their several circuits, requesting them to sit with him in Special Session. As the recent assaults made upon this great bulwark of Freedom have awakened much inquiry in regard to it, we are sure of gratifying the reader by presenting him the form of the writ.

The State of Ohio: —
To David L. Wightman, Sheriff of Cuyahoga
County : —
We command you that the body of Charles Langston, — in your custody detained, as it is said, together with the day and cause of his caption and detention; by whatsoever name the said Charles Langston may be known or called, — you safely have before the Judges of our Supreme Court, at their court room in the City of Columbus, on Wednesday, the 25th day of May, instant, at ten o'clock in the morning, to do and receive all and singular those things which the said Judges shall then and there consider of him, in this behalf; and have you then there this writ.

Witness James H. Smith, Clerk of
(Seal.) our said Supreme Court, at the City of Columbus, this 17th day of May, A. D. 1859.
JAS. H. SMITH, Clerk S. C.
By H. S. Miller, Dep.

Many threats had been made that the Marshal would adhere to the plain path of his duty as marked out in the Booth decision, and repeated by special autograph instructions from Attorney-General Black, and see that *under no circumstances* was the order of the Supreme Court obeyed in the production of the bodies of the relators before its bar. The Marshal's

own salaried editor thundered it morning after morning, and the penitent Douglas print echoed it every evening; till all the country round about, as well as every dweller in the town, was aware that MARSHAL MATTHEW JOHNSON WOULD DO HIS DUTY! So the anxious grew calm; half-cleaned weapons were thrown aside, and nobody was surprised to learn that the Marshal had "compromised" by threatening to serve a "WRITTEN NOTICE" on the Sheriff not to move the men out of jail; and added that, *if he did,* — let the reader be calm and ready for the worst, — he, Marshal Matthew Johnson, *should positively* — let the reader take breath and compose himself — *should positively* — so he said — do what? — why, he should POSITIVELY *take the same train to Columbus!*

Did he ?

Of course not.

He went the night before!

And so the Union was once more saved.

Here is the notice: —

U. S. MARSHAL'S OFFICE, Northern Dist. of }
    Ohio, Cleveland, May 24, 1859. }
To DAVID L. WIGHTMAN, Esq., Sheriff of Cuyahoga
Co. : —

SIR, — I am in receipt of your letter of the 19th instant, in which you state you have writs of *habeas corpus* commanding you to have Simeon Bushnell and Charles Langston before the Judges of the Supreme Court of Ohio, at their court room in Columbus, on Wednesday, the 25th day of May, 1859, at 10 o'clock, A. M., with the cause of their imprisonment, and you also state that you will obey said writs of *habeas corpus.*

The Supreme Court of the United States having decided that the State Courts have no power to discharge persons imprisoned under process of the United States Courts, for violation of the laws of Congress, and it being clearly your duty to return in answer to the writs, the cause of the detention of the prisoners, without producing their persons, I hereby protest against your removing or permitting to be removed from the Jail of Cuyahoga Co., the said Simeon Bushnell and Charles Langston until the expiration of the sentence for which they are respectively imprisoned.

Yours, respectfully,
M. JOHNSON,
U. S. Marshal of the Northern Dist. of Ohio.

Supreme Court of Ohio,
Columbus, May 25th, 1859, 10 A. M.
Simeon Bushnell, and }
Charles Langston, }
    v. } Habeas Corpus.
David L. Wightman, }

Present: — Full Bench.

ARGUMENT FOR THE RELATORS.

MR. A. G. RIDDLE: —

May it please the Court: —

This is a proceeding before the Judges of the Supreme Court at Chambers, yet I recognize the presence of the Court.

The relators by affidavit informed the Court that at the date of their application they were imprisoned in the jail of Cuyahoga County, by the Sheriff of said County, without legal authority; and thereupon one of your Honors issued the writ of *habeas corpus,* commanding the sheriff to produce the bodies of the applicants before you to-day, and show why he detained them. The sheriff returns these writs with the persons of the applicants, and appends to his return as a part of it, and in addition to the statement that he held them under the mittimus of the U. S. District and Circuit Court, a certified copy of the Journal entry and an exemplification of the records, by which it appears that they were imprisoned by that sheriff, pursuant to an alleged final judgment, — awarding that as punishment of the U. S. District Court for the Northern District of Ohio.

In the face of that record and directly meeting that exemplification as it is witnessed by that seal, we still stand here, with the permission of the Court, to say that that imprisonment is illegal; that that judgment is a nullity; that there is no such crime as the act alleged in that record; that the law by virtue of which and under which it is said that these proceedings were had, is no law. We say that that alleged law is not law: —

First; because the Congress of the United States under the Constitution thereof had no power to legislate upon that subject-matter.

Second; that the Congress of the United States under that Constitution had no power to pass *such* a law — or such an act, as the one upon which these proceedings were based.

Third; that under that law this record charges no crime.

Fourth; that that claimed law is in contravention of the provisions of the Ordinance of 1787, which is of antecedent and paramount authority.

It was not the fortune of either the Attorney-General with whom it is my good fortune to be associated in this case, or of myself, to hear the arguments recently submitted to your Honors, upon a prior application by these relators for relief, while the proceedings in the U. S. Court were still pending. For myself, I wish merely to add, that if it shall be found that I do not follow the same course of argument, it is not because I seek in the slightest degree to waive the positions then taken; and if I should chance to offer some of the same arguments, I hope not to be altogether amenable to the charge of tautology. I am perfectly aware,

your Honors, that in approaching this grave question of Constitutional authority, that it is claimed, that we are completely hedged in, or walled out, from the consideration of it by the adjudications of the Supreme Court of the United States.

But, your Honors, with all due respect to that high tribunal, I suppose it will not be contended that a decision of the Supreme Court of the United States can impart any Constitutional vitality to an act of Congress which that act intrinsically, and in the first instance, does not possess. In other words, such a decision cannot make an unconstitutional act a constitutional law. The utmost that can be claimed is that it precludes parties from farther inquiry — acts as a sort of judicial estoppel, concluding the question. It will not be my purpose in the few remarks in the way of the opening argument which I shall have occasion to submit to your Honors, to enter to any considerable extent into any criticism or analysis of these decisions. That duty will fall more properly within the labors of my associate. I shall barely refer to them, and possibly make a passing remark in reference to one or two of them. I believe the leading one of them referred to and relied on as essentially such, is the case of Prigg *v.* Pennsylvania, 16 Peters, 611. There are also as repeaters, reëchoers, the cases of Jones *v.* Van Zandt, 5 Howard, 215; Moore *v.* Sill, 14 Howard, 13, and the famous Simms case, in 7 Cushing, 285, as also others.

I do not know, but it will be sought to add to these, what is known as the Boothe case, recently said to have been decided by the Supreme Court of the United States, on a writ of error to the Supreme Court of Wisconsin. But I do not know as that has been given to the courts in such a form that it can be treated by the Courts as authority. I think the Supreme Court of Ohio will hardly find itself called upon to resort to the columns of *newspapers,* however veracious they may be, for authority. *Res adjudicata* can hardly be claimed to reside there.

And first of the Prigg case. And while I would approach this with due respect, I would yield it no more deference than I would any of the decisions of this high tribunal in whose presence I stand.

This is the case cited as settling the question of the power of Congress to legislate upon the reclamation of fugitive slaves; but it will be found when this case is fairly analyzed, it covers no such ground.

It is difficult for the legal mind to see how that question could have been properly before that Court, so that its passing upon it is to be taken as an adjudication, in the judicial sense of that expression. A party — Prigg — was prosecuted under the State law of Pennsylvania for kidnapping, convicted, and sentenced to the penitentiary. The case was taken to the

Supreme Court of the U. S., and the main question upon which that Court was called to pass, was solely and exclusively the constitutionality of the act of the State of Pennsylvania. The Supreme Court of the U. S. decided that that act was unconstitutional, and unconstitutional because they settled a certain other question, namely, that the Constitution guarantees to the master the right of recaption, and by virtue of this bare guarantee the master, or owner of the slave who escapes in another State, may pursue and make manual recaption of him; and return him to the State from which he escaped; and because this is so and not otherwise, the law of Pennsylvania, which contravenes this constitutional right of recaption is necessarily unconstitutional. That disposes of the case. And therefore, as I have already intimated, it is difficult to see how the power of *Congress* to legislate in aid of the master was at all before that tribunal. It was not before them, and all they say of it and other points, is the purest *obiter dicta.*

And, if not irreverent, it seems to me that that case is amenable to just criticisms of quite another sort. That court commences — with all veneration be it said — by establishing new rules of interpreting the Constitution, and it winds up that singular process by saying that no uniform rule will apply to the whole instrument, but that each provision must dictate its special rule of construction!

It is alarming, indeed, when we find that court in such a case recasting old definitions, or reconstructing old — or manufacturing new rules! It would certainly challenge fair criticism when we should find that no uniform rule could be applied for the construction of the Constitution of the U. S. ! It would also seem that that Court, or rather its judges, were obliged to ward singly and alone the various and devious processes of argumentation by which a majority scatteringly arrived at the conclusions to which they finally gathered in. It is not necessary now to inquire, whether any two of them came to the same result by the same process; — but it is shown that there was no place upon the legal earth to be found where those venerable pilgrims could all finally reunite, except the point from which they started. I remark, then, in reference to this celebrated case, that it does not involve the question to which I now invite the attention of the Court, to wit ; the power of Congress to legislate in aid of the reclamation of fugitives from service or labor. And I wish to say that even if it shall be found in the riper and better conclusions of this Court to cover that ground, that by a single decision of these questions we are not bound. For I say, in the second place, that, passing as it does upon these great questions, under which lie great, original principles, the utmost which ought to be claimed for it, is that that decision furnishes a rule for that case before that Court ; but not that it furnishes the

law of the land; and I submit that the Supreme Court of the United States can give no sanction, that shall make its adjudications the law of the land.

May I be permitted, in the third place, to say, that in my humble judgment there is nothing in that decision by which this Court, representing the judicial sovereignty of this State can be estopped ? I need not detain your Honors with any pedantic schedule of the elements of sovereignty which necessarily enter into the combination of that definition as applied to States and nations; but among them I take it that the most important will be found to be *the protection of the rights of the citizen ;* while he lives in strict observance of this golden rule of the civil law; and "lives honestly, hurts nobody, and gives to every man his due ;" — and that it is going far to say that the right on his part to demand protection, and the duty of the State to render it is not so imperative as to be a question involving the sovereignty of the State. And it seems to me that it is a part and parcel of the nature of *such* things as States, that when the question of State sovereignty, as between itself and its citizens, is broached, this tribunal is the exclusive court of the last resort and is *not* bound, and *cannot be* bound by the decisions of any other tribunal whatsoever; unless you lay the whole sovereignty of State at the foot of that foreign jurisdiction.

I press this with modesty. Now we may say of States as we say of individuals, that they have certain inalienable rights, with which they cannot part. That they have duties which they owe to themselves, to their subjects, and to surrounding States ; that to the discharge of these duties it is absolutely essential that they should have, to a certain extent, inalienable rights. I am not here to say but that they may have parted with some of these rights; if the people of the State have consented ; but the presumption must be that they are all retained intact, until it is proven otherwise. It is not true, your Honor, that the States have grown up under the iron and inflexible rule of the Constitution, and have only by sufferance been allowed to crop out in one direction, or grow out in another, and have been choked and checked, whenever the Constitution did not permit them to shoot upward. The States are older than the Constitution, and in contemplation of law were all present at its formation, without reference to chronology ; and if they have parted with any rights it has been of their own choice, by their own freewill, in express grants ; their people assenting thereto ; and against them no presumptions or implications can prevail. But approaching more directly the Constitution itself, both for the purpose of ascertaining incidentally what the State of Ohio has to concede to it so far as its own sovereignty is concerned ; and more particularly to inquire whether the State of Ohio, with other States, has given power to Congress to legislate in regard to fugitives from service.

Now, may I be permitted to say here, that the Constitution is not made up entirely of compromises, as the modern notion seems to be? I certainly shall not attempt to seem to be learned, and undertake to make any new schedule of the provisions of the Constitution. All this is old and hard-beaten ground. But with reference to the compromises themselves we find that there was a compromise between the larger and the smaller States, resulting in equality in the Senate; and also a compromise with reference to slave representation; and another with reference to the African slave trade; — but beyond these, will some learned man tell us of another? As to the much talked of third clause of the second section of the fourth Article, that it is not, and that it never was intended to be a compromise — judicial falsification of history to the contrary notwithstanding — I undertake to say. That the clause contains a *compact*, as do other clauses of the same section, and other sections of the same article, I not only admit, but insist; but that there is any grant of power necessarily implied in the nature of the compact, I emphatically deny. In this instrument the grants of power to the new Government must necessarily occupy a prominent place, and as among them the power to make treaties is also conferred, it was eminently proper that the same instrument which conferred it should also provide for all such treaties or compacts, among the States, as a far-seeing sagacity could then provide. And hence the compacts, and the fact that they are contained in the Constitution, no more confers on Congress a power to legislate in reference to them, to enforce them; or otherwise, than as if the States had assembled prior to the formation of that instrument, and had formally agreed upon and entered into them, and had made them perpetual.

In addition and as adjuncts to the grants enumerated, there are prohibitions, standing out in just as bold and broad relief all the way along these grants, limiting their exercise on the one side; or prohibiting it altogether on the other. Guarantees, no less important, perhaps, than the others, occupy just as prominent a position; which provide for certain rights, and certain privileges, of paramount importance — standing pledges that they shall be protected.

Equal to all, yet occupying less space, your Honors, are found in this Constitution *reservations*. Thus wherever a grant of power is made, you find it surrounded and hedged in with prohibitions, guarantees, and reservations, all of which are to be beaten down and annihilated, before an usurpation can find place and toleration. With this outline, I am to approach this instrument for the purpose of searching for a power, not only to legislate upon the subject of fugitive slaves, but to legislate in its favor. For it cannot be contended that a power authorizing the enactment of a law, which provides for, and authorizes, and furnishes the means of recapturing fugitive slaves, is not a law directly sustaining slavery. Before entering upon this investigation I beg leave to call to mind two or three so well-established propositions, that they have become inflexible rules. And first, Slavery is not national, but local. In the face of solemn platforms, and in the teeth of national politicians, I undertake to say, that slavery is not legally or constitutionally a national institution; and hence, certainly the fostering protection of it, would not naturally fall within the sphere of the duties of the General Government. That it is a purely State local institution, and therefore all regulation of it, must fall outside of the powers delegated to the General Government, and be left entirely to individual States and lesser localities.

I remark, second, — that slavery — I need not refer your Honors to authorities in support of this proposition — in the United States exists wholly and exclusively, by virtue of positive law. Farther, that all presumptions are, necessarily and essentially, adverse to its existence. It follows, then, that if slavery is to exist only by express authority, it cannot exist by implied authority; and if the presumptions are against slavery, the presumptions are just as conclusively against the existence of a law by virtue of which slavery would exist. If it cannot exist by implication, you cannot imply the law, or the power to enact the law; and as a converse of all this, all the presumptions are not only against slavery, but in favor of Freedom. Then, your Honors, if slavery can only exist by positive law, and not by implication; and if we must presume against the existence of slavery, and against the existence of any law authorizing it; and of course against the existence of any power by which such a law could be enacted. We unroll the Constitution, with an absolute presumption that it does not contain such a power, a presumption that can yield only to an express grant of it. We are to inquire, then, whether there is in the Constitution an express grant of power to Congress, to legislate in favor of slavery; or whether there is an express grant for some necessary object or purpose; such that for its accomplishment, such a grant in reference to slavery must necessarily be carried with it.

In considering this instrument, much valuable information may be gleaned from the history of those times; as to what was the object and purpose of the framers of it. But the historical argument I leave entire to the Attorney-General.

In contemplating the Constitution itself, we find inscribed upon its portal the very objects of its creation, to which alone it is solemnly dedicated; and under it is subscribed the names of its framers, the time, place, and date of its erection.

Hear that solemn inscription and ordination: "We, the people of the United States, in order to form a more perfect union, *establish justice*, insure domestic tranquillity, provide for the common defence, promote the general welfare, and *secure the blessings of liberty to ourselves and our posterity*, do ordain and establish this Constitution for the United States of America."

When we ponder upon this inscription, which not only makes the purposes of the creation of the instrument itself known, and also makes this solemn dedication of it to these purposes, and when we find named among the very first of these objects, — "to establish justice" and "secure the blessings of liberty to ourselves and our posterity," — it seems perfectly hopeless to expect to find any thing within authorizing and protecting an institution annihilating liberty and rendering justice impossible.

Having passed within the Constitution, and bringing with us the rules already mentioned, and in the strong light that flashes all over it from the preamble, I wish to add the solemn weight of the tenth amendment — "The powers not delegated to the United States by the Constitution, nor prohibited by it to the States, are reserved to the States respectively, or to the people."

Thus, then, under these conditions, and with these lights, we must find an express grant of power or a grant of a subject-matter, carrying with it the grant of power; and that without the aid of any implication. Now I take it that no one has ever yet found this power in any portion of the first article of the Constitution. In all those special grants it nowhere exists, openly or covertly. It neither lurks under one, nor is appended to the skirts of another. And if your Honors will turn your attention to the last clause of the eighth section, which is a general grant of such powers as are contained in it, to wit, "to make all laws which shall be necessary and proper for carrying into execution the foregoing powers and all other powers" — not compacts, guaranties, injunctions, or reservations — "vested by this Constitution in the Government of the United States, or any department or officer thereof" — it is no more to be found there. Certainly it never has been contended, except in a single instance, and, I trust, never will be again, that there has been conferred upon any department of the General Government, any power over or in reference to slavery, and we have already seen that no power not specially granted can be held to exist. But it is said in the Prigg case, that the warrant for legislation on this subject arises from the *necessity* which results from a certain combination of circumstances. I understand Mr. Justice Story to say that the power is found in a just construction of all the bearings of this much talked of second section of the fourth article. It is established so far as it can be by the opinion of that Court, that the claim

of a master upon his fugitive slave, is a judicial claim under the Constitution of the United States; and that being such, it necessarily called to its aid and for the purpose of its enforcement the legislative power latently vested in Congress. Is that true, your Honors? With all deference to this famous decision, if it be true that the legislative power of Congress is coextensive with the judicial power of the Federal Courts, then I ask what becomes of State authority, legislative or judicial? For, in various ways, all conceivable questions of right can be brought before the Federal judiciary, and has Congress so boundless a range of legislative power as that?

Otherwise, I submit that the proposition is not true. If the legislative power granted to Congress, be coextensive with the power vested in the national judiciary, then it must follow, that every matter, which falls within the jurisdiction of the Courts, by necessity falls within the legislative power of Congress, which absolutely cannot be true! For then if a party in Kentucky brings a suit upon a promissory note for $500, against a citizen of Ohio, in the Federal Courts as he may do, Congress would necessarily have the power to legislate upon it, as upon all other possible matters which might constitute "a judicial claim under the Constitution," which is an annihilation of the States. Yet this is the doctrine which the Court in that case unqualifiedly and in express terms lays down. And thus I do not find — a thing which I certainly was not very anxiously looking for — I cannot find in these grants of power, that either directly or indirectly, by express grants of power or by grants of subject-matter, that this instrument thus far conveys any power to Congress to legislate in reference to fugitive slaves. I pass to the fourth article.

This article seems to contain provisions with reference to certain compacts between the States as individual States; guarantees them certain rights, and provides for the government of the territories, etc.

Section first is as follows: —

"Full faith and credit shall be given in each State to the public acts, records, and judicial proceedings of every other State. And Congress may, by general laws, prescribe the manner in which such acts, records, and proceedings shall be proved, and the effect thereof."

If your Honors will turn back to the articles of Confederation, you will find the first part of this, which is a compact merely, to be almost a literal transcript of the last clause of the fourth article of the Confederation.

As it existed there it was taken to be and was a naked compact, conferring no particle of power to legislate for its enforcement, and was never supposed to confer any. This last clause of the fourth article of the articles of Confederation, now makes the first section of the fourth article of the Constitution. Ten years it stood, the last clause of the fourth of the Confede-ration, uncoupled with any power; whence it was taken, and promoted to the first section of the fourth article of the Constitution. And not only that, but when it is transferred *there is coupled with it an express grant of power*, because the framers of the Constitution knew — as everybody knows, that without an ex-press grant, there could be no power; and the experience under the Confederation, had demonstrated the necessity for a proper en-forcement of this provision, and hence the power was granted.

The second clause, of the second section, of article fourth, is a condensed form of the pro-visions of the first clause, of the fourth article, of the articles of Confederation, which read, " The better to secure a perpetual friendship," etc. (See 4th Art. Const.)

Standing in that place in the fourth article, when the framers of the Constitution came to " make up their jewels," and incorporated it into their structure, they gave it the place of the first clause, in the second section, of the fourth article. But there is no grant of power attach-ed to it, in the transfer, as in the case of the first section of this article. And I claim that since, as a matter of historical verity, the neces-sities arising under the provisions of that clause are sufficient to have invoked that power into life, if it is supposed to have slumbered within the folds of that purview. And yet no one has contended, that I am aware of, that there is any power in Congress to legislate for the purpose of enforcing that solemn compact, — it stands in remarkable contrast with its fellow section, which had long remained without a grant of power, but when transferred into the Constitu-tion had such a grant appended to it, while this remains without.

The second clause, of that second section, of the fourth article, is the one in reference to the extradition of fugitives from justice. This is followed by the third and sorely contested clause, which treats of the return of fugitives from service, or labor.

" No person held to service or labor in one State, under the laws thereof, escaping into an-other, shall, in consequence of any law or reg-ulation therein, be discharged from such service or labor, but shall be delivered up on claim of the party to whom such service or labor may be due."

In some respects, standing together and treat-ing of the extradition of certain classes of per-sons — in each case spoken of as *persons* — these second and third clauses, of this second section, of the fourth article, are proper to be compared, to see how far they may be taken to-gether. As the third clause was taken from the Ordinance of 1787, so was the second from the articles of Confederation; and as the third is not materially changed, neither is the second: both preserve the same thoughts and the same meaning, in the Constitution, that they several-ly had in the articles of Confederation and the Ordinance of '87, and both alike, in both places, are uncoupled with any grant of power what-ever. This Ordinance of '87 was, I believe, the first declaration of law or compact, in which the people of the United States, as a nation, had embodied and set forth a provision for the rendition of fugitives from service, and this clause there stood uncoupled with any grant of power to Congress. It is true, that the lapse of time between that Ordinance and the Constitu-tion was not so great as to afford the States any considerable experience of its workings, but it is none the less true that it was transferred without the expression of any serious desire for its amendment, or the addition of a grant of power; it was transferred to the Constitution, and there embodied without material change, to the entire satisfaction of all the members of the Convention, and the people of the States, where it reposes in its own original force; and not im-plying, because not expressly declaring, the power of Congress to enforce its provisions by legislation.

Transferring it, then, as they did, and leav-ing it uncoupled with any grant of power, the conclusion is irresistible that it — like its two predecessors in the same section — is to be treated as a simple compact, conferring no more power upon Congress, and calling Federal leg-islation no more to its aid, than any compact outside the Constitution. And when it is re-membered that the first section of this fourth article has an express power appended, and when we see that the succeeding third section also contains a grant of power, which is omit-ted from all the clauses of section second, the conclusion is perfectly irresistible that it was in-tended that no power should attend any of the clauses of that second section.

I do not mean to contend, your Honors, that the contemporaneous construction of that ar-ticle is not manifest, to some extent, perhaps, in the legislation which was ventured upon under it, by a Congress composed in part of the fram-ers of the Constitution itself; nor yet that such construction is wholly valueless, but I am not aware that the presumption drawn from the fact that a law was enacted, is any stronger in reference to the action of the national legisla-ture, than in reference to the acts of the legis-latures of the several States upon the same sub-ject. But if this be taken as a guide, the legis-lation of the several States neutralizes, and more than neutralizes any legislation of Con-gress. Take the act of Pennsylvania alone, and then group about it the dozen others, in-cluding the States of Ohio, Indiana, Illinois. It is known as an historical fact that the enact-ment of 1793 did not arise out of the necessi-ties of any case which sprung up under this clause of the Constitution. But a question arose between the executives of Pennsylvania and Virginia, in reference to the return of a fu-gitive from justice, who had fled from Pennsylvania to Virginia; and it is said that, in the course of that debate, the Governor of Virginia doubted his power to deliver up the fugitive, and the matter being communicated to President Washington, and by him transmitted to Congress in a message; for the purpose of settling *this* controversy, the legislative power of Congress was invoked, and the Act of 1793 passed. It is certainly true, as I think, that both sections of this Act are equally unconstitutional, for I see no more authority conferred upon Congress to legislate in reference to fugitives from justice than in reference to fugitives from service.

These two matters stand, in my judgment, as mere naked compacts. There certainly is not, in either case, any grant of power, as I submit to your Honors, by the provisions of this instrument itself. None, whatever! I submit, so far as these two clauses are concerned, — and, pre-eminently, so far as the third is concerned, — that the text nowhere, in any form, invests Congress with any power. It is not necessary here to inquire what the purpose and object of its creation, so far as the means are concerned were. It is sufficient for my purpose, and for the purpose for which we stand before this Court, to say that if we go back to the original right meaning of this instrument — to which we all shall go when we have the grace and courage — no one will contend, for a solitary moment, that there lurks in it, anywhere, any grant of power to Congress to legislate upon the subject. None, — absolutely none. By the very nature of it, such a grant is impossible. The main force of this clause is spent in the prohibition.

"No person held to service or labor in one State, under the laws thereof, escaping into another, shall, in consequence of any law or regulation therein, be discharged from such service or labor, but shall be delivered up on claim of the party to whom such service or labor may be due." It declares that the States shall *not* legislate adversely; and that, in my humble judgment, is the whole force of it, and the latter part of it seems to explain the degree of the prohibition: — so far are they prohibited from legislating adversely, that the fugitive not only shall not be discharged from the obligation to serve, but he shall be delivered up. This is said to impose a duty upon the Federal judiciary; and the sweeping argument in the Prigg case is, that whatever falls within the jurisdiction of the Federal judiciary is within the legislative purview of Congress, which I have already disposed of. But it is clear enough that this enjoins a duty upon the States alone, and upon no department of the General Government. I am perfectly frank to say — if I may be permitted so far to depart from the argument — that, as a citizen, I accept the Constitution with all its compacts and injunctions, and I stand here only for the purpose of contending for the Constitution in its purity, and protesting against un-

warranted and unwarrantable perversions of it.

This brings me to my second proposition.

We claim that if your Honors shall find, either looking at this instrument as it invites your attention; or through the decisions of other Courts, whose decisions you accept as binding; that Congress has power delegated to it by the Constitution to legislate upon the subject in question; we still claim that *Congress had no power to enact this particular law.*

And first, they had not this power because this act violates the otherwise inviolable right of persons to personal liberty. It subjects a person to the actual manual caption of whoever pretends to be his master. I need not stop here to detain, much less to attempt to entertain this Court with that part of the legal argument which pertains to this point; nor to call the attention of the Court to the fact that slaves as slaves, are excluded from the Constitution by name. Nor need I read to you the debates in reference to this matter, which took place in the Convention where the Constitution was framed, as well as those which sprang up in the various State Conventions which were called to discuss and pass upon the Constitution as it was offered to the people. That the Constitution, if it treats of slaves at all, treats of them as *persons,* and hence confuses them — if such a term may be used — with the great mass of other persons within the States, I think cannot be disputed. I do not now recollect that there are more than three allusions in the Constitution which are supposed to have reference to slaves. The first is in the third clause of the second section of article first, which relates to the apportionment of representation. The second is found in section ninth of article first, in reference to slave trade. The third, and I think the only remaining one claimed, is found in this third clause of the second section of article 4th.

This matter has been passed upon by the Supreme Court, in the case of Grous *v.* Slaughter, 15 Peters, where the Court, Judge McLean, giving the opinion, expressly decides that the Constitution treats slaves as persons exclusively.

If this be so, then not only is there nothing in the Constitution which intimates what portion of the people shall be treated as slaves, but no Act of Congress might distinguish between the persons who might be so classed under it, and the great mass of other persons. That is not attempted on the part of this statute. It provides that PERSONS — all persons — owing service or labor, in one State and escaping into another, may be seized by manual caption; and in this, we submit, it completely violates the provisions of the Constitution itself. This cannot be tolerated. There is nothing which designates the persons who may be seized, but it arms every man who may choose to assume to be the owner of another man, with power by mere brute force, to seize him and drag him away from the protection of law. Can it be claimed for a moment that the Constitution confers power to enact such a law? In a free State the presumption is that every man is a freeman. Does this presumption cease with the approach of one who *claims* to be the owner of a citizen? Does it not go on up to the ultimate point where he is legally *proven* to be a fugitive, owing service or labor, as claimed? Now it is true that third parties are to take notice from acts and claims; the claim may be notice to them; but it does not destroy the presumption of the law, that the man claimed is a freeman. I know that in this same Prigg case, the Court undertake to say that the title of the master to his slave, as it existed in Kentucky, is preserved intact in Ohio; but I submit with all deference, that this is not and cannot be true. The decision of no court can carry the municipal laws of one State into another, and say that when a slave runs away, he wrenches from the statute book a portion of the law of the State from which he flees, and carries it with him, as a sort of legal halter upon which the master may seize, and lead him back whence he came. Will it be claimed that a man can *sell* and *transfer* his slave in Ohio? or that he may whip him for insubordination to subdue him? Then slavery is actually an institution of Ohio! I say that the instant a slave touches Ohio soil, he casts his chains — the whole *exuviæ* of the slave from him, and becomes a freeman, but still owing service — not morally, not by virtue of any contract, but by this curiously worded phrase of the Constitution — "owing service or labor;". he brings with him this obligation as a dark stain, a horrid contingency, and through it may be seized as a PERSON — but *never as a slave* — and BY "DUE PROCESS OF LAW," this obligation being proven, may be delivered up to his master, and again resubjugated to slavery in the State from whence he escaped, but not in Ohio. While here, for every other conceivable purpose, he is wholly within the protection of our laws. This is the whole extent and force that this article of the Constitution permits. A slave cannot be claimed as *property*, because nowhere in the Constitution of the United States, any more than in the Constitution of Ohio, is any property in man recognized. The instant, therefore, that a master in Ohio undertakes to deal with a fugitive from his service as property, he is without color of constitutional right, and should be dealt with as a criminal. A fugitive from service cannot be held as property, not only because property in man is not recognized in the Constitution, but because with property, and its incidents as such, the Federal Government has nothing to do, save in the very limited manner specified. Congress can, under any circumstances, legislate upon slaves only as persons, even if it had full power to legislate in aid of the provisions of this clause. I know

the decision in the Prigg case claims to settle the rule to the contrary, but your Honors are aware that I do not recognize that decision as conclusive of these questions. I say, then, that this statute reduces persons to things, and is therefore no law.

I claim further that this statute directly violates the fourth article of the Amendments to the Constitution, which provides that, —

"The right of the people to be secure in their *persons*, houses, papers, and effects, against *unreasonable* searches *and seizures, shall not be violated*, and no warrants shall issue but upon probable cause, supported by oath or affirmation, and particularly describing the place to be searched, and the person or things to be seized."

Again it is in express violation of article five. "No person shall be held to answer for a capital, or otherwise infamous crime, unless on a presentment or indictment of a grand jury, except in cases arising in the land or naval forces, or in the militia, when in actual service in time of war or public danger; nor shall any person be subject for the same offence to be put twice in jeopardy of life or limb; nor shall be compelled in any criminal case, to be witness against himself; *nor be deprived of life, liberty, or property, without due process of law; nor shall private property be taken for public use without just compensation."

Now am I forced, your Honors, to stand here and claim that a man cannot, by virtue of a mere power of attorney, or of his own unsupported claim of ownership, come here, and having already decided that a certain citizen of Ohio is his slave — no matter what may be his color, lineage, or condition — be his own bailiff, magistrate, jury, and sheriff, and that such a deprivation of a man of his liberty is not "DUE PROCESS OF LAW?" If so, there is no constitutional guaranty for the personal security of a man, woman, or child in Ohio.

As to what is due process of law, see 2 Kent's Com. p. 3.

I claim, in the second place, your Honors, that this act is void because it vests judicial powers in certain commissioners, who are neither created, appointed, nor paid in accordance with the requirements of that part of the Constitution which defines the conditions upon which Federal officers may exercise judicial functions. See article third. This question will arise in the second count of the indictment set forth in the record of Langston's case. The Government therein count upon a seizure of the alleged fugitive John, by virtue of a process issued by one of these U. S. Commissioners.

I claim, in the third instance, that this statute is void because it not only authorizes the recaption of a person by an alleged owner with or without one of these unconstitutional commissioner's warrants, but authorizes the master to fix his *status* as being a slave and to return him to endless bondage in violation of the seventh

Amendment of the Constitution, which guarantees a trial by jury in all cases where the value of the matter in controversy amounts to twenty dollars or upwards; and here we are not estopped by the Prigg case. For the question was not there made. Judge Story himself since declared that that question was not passed upon. (See his memoirs by his son, W. W. Story.)

Then we ask the discharge of these relators on the ground that the act, upon which all the proceedings against them are based, is unconstitutional and void; and we claim that it is unconstitutional because Congress had no power to enact any law upon the subject; and because most emphatically it had no power to enact a law like this; which in its several provisions so flagitiously tramples upon the fundamental rights of the citizen as guaranteed by the Constitution in explicit terms.

And now I wish to call your Honor's attention to one point more — my third general proposition.

I claim that even if your Honors should adjudge my previous positions unsound, and should hold that Congress not only had power to legislate in regard to fugitive slaves, and in aid of the master, but that it had power to enact this particular law — so glaringly unjust and unwarranted, as we have been accustomed to believe it to be; — still, in looking into this record your Honors will find *no crime charged under that law.* The District Court of the United States for the Northern District of Ohio, from which this record comes, being a court of limited jurisdiction, we have nothing to suppose in its favor, and if no crime under the act upon which the proceedings are claimed to be based is charged; that Court had no jurisdiction of the case. Briefly on this point. First. It does not appear from that record, that the alleged fugitive John, was held to service in the State of Kentucky, "*under the laws thereof;*" and if he were not held to service in accordance with the laws of the State from which he escaped, then he had a right to escape, and no one had a right to recapture him, and if any one did recapture him, no offence could be committed in rescuing him from such custody. For the *presumption* will not be that he was so held to service, in the absence of such averment, but always the contrary, because presumptions are always in favor of liberty. I claim that the allegation that he was held to service in the State of Kentucky, "under the laws thereof," is material, and its omission fatal. 5 McLean, 460–469.

Second. It is decided in the Prigg case, if that is to be taken as law, that in the absence of any legislation whatever, the owner of a slave has a right, without the color of any process, to pursue, recapture, and return him to the domicil of his master. That is a judicial construction of the provision of the Constitution. And indeed the Fugitive Slave Act of 1850 provides also, following that construction, that the owner, or his substituted agent, may in like manner pursue and recapture; — but for what purpose? To return him? No:— for the sole and solitary purpose of taking him before a U. S. Commissioner, to have in a qualified manner his status judicially determined; — so that outside of that law the owner may seize and return him; but if he acts under that law, neither he nor his agent can restore him to his domicil, but he shall take him before a U. S. Commissioner, who shall first settle the question of status, and authorize the return. When your Honors come to examine this record, you will find that the alleged fugitive John was sought to be seized, not outside of the law, but by virtue of a power of attorney under the law, — and there it stops. Now it is not sufficient for this indictment to allege that the fugitive was recaptured and held; it must go farther, and allege that he was to be taken before a commissioner, which it does not. Hence from such a holding it was no crime to rescue him. And therefore I repeat my claim, that these indictments are fatally defective under this law, because they do not allege that the fugitive said to have been rescued, was held to service in the State of Kentucky, "under the laws thereof," nor that he had been seized for the purpose of taking him before a commissioner, to establish his status.

And lastly, I further claim that in the State of Ohio, and in reference to all slaves escaping from the State of Kentucky, that law is inoperative. I claim this under the preëxisting, and the still existing, and the paramount authority of the Ordinance of 1787. I need not stop here to detail the provisions of that ordinance. But I remark that that Congress of the Confederation, representing the sovereignty of the nation, in whom the title of the North-west Territory vested, had the power to make that ordinance. I claim that it was, as it alleges to be, a compact for all time to come. I am not here to claim that by the full consent of all possible parties concerned, it might not be changed; but I do claim that no such change, repeal, modification, or amendment has been made. It was not repealed by the adoption of the Federal Constitution, nor by the admission of the State of Kentucky in 1792, for the people of the North-west Territory were not parties to those acts, nor by the Act of Congress authorizing Ohio to form a constitution, for that required the new State to come in pursuant to the ordinance. And certainly the adoption of the State Constitution did not repeal it, for that embodies the provisions of the ordinance in itself. When, where, how, and by whom have the terms of this grand old charter been set aside?

I need not remind this Court, that in a solemn adjudication by this Court, it was decided that the provisions of that ordinance were in force. See 5 Ohio, 419, and also in the case of Spooner *v.* McNeil, 1 McLean, 349, this doctrine is solemnly reaffirmed, and his Honor, Judge McLean, takes judicial pains to dwell upon the perpetual and inviolable freedom thus pledged to this soil, declaring that nothing short of revolution can ever plant upon it *in any form* the accursed institution of slavery. I do, therefore, stand here solemnly to contend, that, under that ordinance, which limits in its very terms the capture of slaves to those *who escape from some one of the original thirteen States,*— Congress had no power to authorize the recaption in Ohio of fugitives from service in Kentucky.

And now, with this brief presentation of the points to which I have called attention, and leaving whole regions of argument untouched, and leaving also all the grave and great considerations which gather about this case, and strongly press for strong speech unuttered, I submit this weighty matter with all interests and consequences, to the decision of this High Tribunal.

The Court took a recess until half past 2, P. M.

FIRST DAY. — AFTERNOON SESSION.

Mr. SWAYNE, in behalf of the respondent, declined making oral argument, for the reason that he thought the authorities presented in his printed brief must, without elaboration, more than satisfy the Court of the soundness of the positions therein taken, and also because but recently he had argued before the Court similar points at considerable length.

His printed brief is this : —

Supreme Court of Ohio,
Special Session — May 25, 1859.
Simeon Bushnell ⎤
v. ⎬ Habeas Corpus.
D. L. Wightman, Sheriff of ⎨
Cuyahoga County, Ohio. ⎦

Statement, Points, and Authorities under Rule II. (for Oral Argument).

STATEMENT.

The relator has been indicted and convicted, before the District Court of the United States for the Northern District of Ohio, of offences under the Act of Congress, upon the subject of fugitives from labor, passed September 18, 1850. He has been sentenced, and is in confinement accordingly. The object of this writ of *habeas corpus* is to set him at liberty. The respondent's return shows these facts.

POINTS AND AUTHORITIES.

I. The statute of Ohio, in regard to writs of *habeas corpus*, expressly excepts and excludes from its operation " *persons convicted of some crime or offence for which they stand committed.*" This is a case of that kind. 3 Howard 103, Ex parte Dorr; 3 Pet. 193 ; 7 Wheat. 38.

II. Where a Court has acquired prior jurisdiction or possession of a subject of litigation, a coördinate tribunal will in nowise interfere with the action of such court touching such subject. The tribunal which first acquires jurisdiction holds it to the end, and it is exclusive. 3 Ohio St. Rep. 105, Keating *v.* Spink ; 16 Ohio Rep. 405, Merril *v.* Lake, et al.; 9 Wheaton 532, Smith *v.* McIver; 20 Howard 594, Taylor et al. *v.* Carrol; 10 Peters 400, Hagan *v.* Lucas; 3 Peters 304, Harris *v.* Dennie; 7 Howard 471, Peck *v.* Jennis; 8 Howard 107, Williams *v.* Benedict; 17 Howard 475, Pullian *v.* Osborne ; 6 McLean 365, Ex parte Robinson ; 4 East 523 ; 25 Eng. Ch. Rep. 474; 3 Paige 199; 5 Id. 489; 7 Idem 514; 9 Vesey 335 ; 1 Jacobs 572; 2 Sch. & Lef. 229.

III. The judgment of the District Court is conclusive. It cannot be collaterally questioned. 1 Ohio St. Rep. 233, Bank of Wooster *v.* Stevens; 3 Id. 494, Sheldon's Lessee *v.* Newton.

" The power to hear and determine a cause is jurisdiction ; and it is *coram judice* whenever a case is presented which brings this power into action." Ibid.; case last cited.

See also 2 Smith's Leading Cases — *Duchess of Kingston's case* — and the authorities there cited.

IV. The validity of a judgment cannot be collaterally questioned in this way. A writ of *habeas corpus* cannot be made to perform the functions of a writ of error. If the process under which the relator is held be regular on its face, this Court will not interfere in this mode of procedure. 1 Barb. 341, In the matter of Prime ; 51 Eng. Com. Law Rep. 648, 655, Ex parte Partington ; 57 Idem, 215, In re Richard Dunn ; 57 Idem, 416, Ex parte Cobbet; 68 Idem, 564, 567, Dimes case ; 2 Greene 312, Peltier *v.* Pennington ; 4 McCord 233, Ex parte Gilchrist ; 1 Watts 66, Comm. *v.* Leakey; 5 Ind. 290, Wright *v.* The State ; 6 McLean 355, Ex parte Robinson ; 2 Paine 348, In the matter of Martin ; 3 Pet. 193 ; 7 Wheat. 38.

V. When it appears, in proceedings upon a *habeas corpus*, issued by a State Judge, that the relator is held under authority emanating from the laws of the United States, the Judge can proceed no farther, but must remand the prisoner. 21 How. —, United States *v.* Booth; 5 McLean, 199, Morris *v.* Newton; 9 Johnson, 239, Ferguson's case ; Hurd's Hab. Cor. 198, Mr. Justice Nelson's charge.

VI. The adjudications of the Supreme Court of the United States, upon all questions within its jurisdiction, are binding upon the State Courts, and conclusive.

(2.) The Constitution of the United States provides : —

Art. 6. " This constitution, and the laws which shall be made in pursuance thereof, and all treaties made, or which shall be made, under the authority of the United States, shall be the supreme law of the land; and the judges in every state shall be bound thereby, any thing in the constitution or laws of any State to the contrary, notwithstanding."

(3.) Art. 3, sec. 1. "The judicial power of the United States shall be vested in one Supreme Court, and in such inferior courts as the Congress may, from time to time, ordain and establish."

Sec. 2. " The judicial power shall extend to all cases, in law and equity, arising under this constitution; the laws of the United States, and treaties made, or which shall be made under their authority; to all cases affecting embassadors, other public ministers and consuls; to all cases of admiralty and maritime jurisdiction; to controversies to which the United States shall be a party; TO CONTROVERSIES BETWEEN TWO OR MORE STATES; between a state and citizens of another state; between citizens of different states; between citizens of the same state, claiming lands under grants of different states; and between a state, or the citizens thereof, and foreign states, citizens, or subjects."

(4.) The last clause of Art. 6, provides that " all executive and judicial officers, both of the United States and of the several States, shall be bound by oath or affirmation to support this constitution."

(5.) The 25th section of the judiciary act of Congress, of 1789, gives to the Supreme Court of the United States appellate jurisdiction over the adjudications of the highest State courts, in the numerous class of cases therein specified.

(6.) The proposition contended for on the other side, involves these consequences: —

It would make the subordinate equal or superior to the appellate tribunal. There would be thirty-two independent judicatories besides the courts of the Union, with equal authority to expound the constitution and laws of the United States.

The same property, real or personal, recovered in a court of the United States, might be recovered back in a State court.

If a party be convicted of treason, piracy, murder, counterfeiting, robbery of the mail, the importation of slaves from Africa, or any other offence against the laws of the United States, any State Judge or Commissioner, authorized to issue writs of habeas corpus, may issue such writ, and set the prisoner free. Vide 7 Cush. 300; 12 Wend. 314, 326; 3 Cow. 753; 5 Cranch, 136; 21 How. United States v. Booth; 1 Serg. & R. 352, Com. v. Robinson; Hurd's Hab. Corp. 204; 16 How. 369, State Bank v. Knoop; 18 Id. 331, Dodge v. Woolsey.

VII. The Act of 1850 is constitutional and valid. See Const. U. S., Art. 4, Sec. 2; for the Act, see Brightley's Digest, 294.

(1.) The question of constitutionality is the same under this Act as under the Act of 1793. " The law of 1850 stands, in this respect, precisely on the same ground with the Act of

1793; and the same grounds of argument which show the unconstitutionality of one, apply with equal force to the other; and the same answer must be made to them." 7 Cushing, 285, Sim's case; Hurd on Hab. Corp. 196.

(2.) The Act of 1793 was held to be constitutional and valid in the following cases: — 9 Johnson, 67, Glenn v. Hodges, 1812 (Supreme Court of New York — Kent, Spencer, Thompson, Varness, and Yates); 5 Sergeant & R. 64, Wright v. Deacon, 1819; 2 Pick. 11, Com. v. Griffith, 1823; 12 Wend. 314, Jack v. Martin, 1834; 16 Peters, 539, Prigg v. Pennsylvania, 1842; 10 Barr, 517, Kaufman v. Oliver, 1848; 5 How. 229, Jones v. Van Zandt, 1847. The Act of 1850 has been held to be valid in —7 Cushing, 294, Sim's case; 16 Barbour, 268, Henry v. Lowell; 21 Howard, United States v. Booth.

The case last cited was decided by the Supreme Court of the United States, last winter. The Court was unanimous. They have been so upon all occasions, when the constitutionality of the Act of 1793 was before them. It is deemed unnecessary to refer particularly to the numerous decisions of the Circuit Courts of the United States, in regard to both acts. They all agree with the cases above cited.

VIII. No court will hold a law to be unconstitutional, unless its unconstitutionality be clear beyond doubt. 1 Ohio State Rep. 82, 83, 84, C., W. & Z. Railroad Co. v. Clinton County; 7 Idem, 548, State v. Kennon et al.; 3 Dallas, 171; 4 Dallas, 14; 8 Cranch, 87; 14 Mass. 345; 16 Pick. 95; 11 Penn. 70; 2 Monroe, 178; 9 Dana, 514; 2 Yerger, 623.

With such a body of adjudications, and the judgment of jurists of such learning and ability, sustaining the constitutionality of the law, who can say that its unconstitutionality is clear beyond a doubt?

GEO. W. BELDEN, and
N. H. SWAYNE,
of Counsel for the Respondent.

It is but proper to say that Messrs. Belden and Swayne were never employed by the Respondent, but acted either in behalf of the U. States, or of their own motion.

The State of Ohio, ex rel. Simeon Bushnell et alius v. David L. Wightman, Sheriff of the County of Cuyahoga. } In the Supreme Court of the State of Ohio. Habeas Corpus.

ARGUMENT ON BEHALF OF THE STATE, BY MR. ATTORNEY-GENERAL WOLCOTT.

MAY IT PLEASE YOUR HONORS: — It is to be regretted that the learned counsel, who on this occasion represent the Government of the United States, have (as one of their number has just announced to your Honors) concluded not to argue this cause in open court, because that conclusion deprives us of all those advantages which grow out of an orderly oral discussion, where voice responds to voice, and eye looks into eye, the best mode which the wit of man has yet 'devised for eliciting the truth as between contending parties. But while I regret, I have no right to complain of their decision. It is their undoubted prerogative to conduct the case on their part in such way as to them shall seem best, even though the result is, as here, to leave us utterly in the dark as to the grounds on which they rest their resistance to this application, except so far as the same may be gathered from the skeleton " brief of points," which was only a few moments since placed in the hands of your Honors and myself.

And now, what is the case before your Honors ? The State of Ohio, in the exercise of one of its most unquestionable attributes of sovereignty, and proceeding upon the representation of two of its citizens, presented, in the appropriate mode, that they were unlawfully restrained of their liberty by David L. Wightman, Sheriff of Cuyahoga county, has sent forth its great prerogative writ to that individual, commanding him to produce before your Honors, as the repositories of the Supreme Judicial Power of the State, the bodies of its citizens, and to certify to you the authority by which he so restrains them.

Responding to this writ, the sheriff has here and now produced their bodies, and for answer as to the cause thereof; returns that he holds them in custody by virtue of a warrant issued to him by the Marshal of the United States for the Northern District of Ohio; which warrant is predicated upon certain proceedings had in the District Court of the United States for that same District; an authenticated transcript of which is incorporated into his return. From this transcript it appears that the relators have been convicted of a violation of the act of Congress known as the Fugitive Slave Act, approved on the 18th of September, 1850, and were thereupon sentenced to imprisonment in the jail of Cuyahoga county.

This conviction and sentence being the cause of the relators' detention, the Court are here called upon to inquire into the validity thereof. That validity is now challenged alike by the relators, and the State of Ohio, which latter alone I represent — on the ground that the act of Congress under which the conviction was had and the sentence pronounced, is incompatible with the Constitution of the United States, and therefore void.

But at the very threshold of the proceeding I am met with a claim of power on the part of the Federal Government, which, if well founded, is an insurmountable objection to any further inquiry, but which, I must add, strikes one almost dumb with its audacity. It is insisted that, whenever, by a return to its writ of *habeas corpus*, the tribunal of a State is advised that the relator is detained in custody under *color* of Federal authority, whether the exercise of that au-

thority be assumed by any court, judge, or ministerial officer of the Federal Government, the State of which the relator is a citizen, and within which he is detained, is powerless, to inquire into the validity of that detention. In other words, it is said — for the claim presupposes and admits all this — that however unwarrantable may be the exercise of the assumed authority, however tyrannical, arbitrary, and unlawful the detention, however directly prohibited in the particular instance, by the plain words of the Constitution ; yet the State tribunals are powerless to redress the acknowledged wrong; the victim has no appeal but to the usurper himself. Now I submit to your Honors, that the bare statement of this claim is its own most conclusive answer. For, in effect, the proposition as narrowed down to this particular case, is that Federal judges may, by asserting in the form of an adjudication, power to do an act unconstitutional in itself, bind all persons whatever, and preclude them from inquiring either into the validity of the act done or the existence of the power to do it.

But, may it please your Honors, if a Judge, by declaring that he has power to imprison, can estop all inquiry into the existence of that power, he may equally, by insisting that he has power over property or life, estop all inquiry into the existence of that power. And what is this power but that absolute, arbitrary dominion over all things and persons, which constitutes the very essence of despotism ? Now, whatever power these Judges may legitimately exercise, is derived from the Government of the United States. That Government is one of limited and delegated powers. The authority of its judicial, and all other departments, is defined by specific metes and bounds; and that there may be no mistaking these limits, they are written down in what is called the Constitution ; and to make assurance doubly sure, the same instrument declares that all powers not comprehended within these limits do not belong to it. But to what purpose is it that this power is thus specifically bounded in, if the power so intended to be restrained may at any time overleap these limits ? The distinction (said Chief Justice Marshall, in Marbury v. Madison) between a government of limited and of absolute power is utterly gone, if the defined restrictions do not in fact restrain the power, and acts authorized and acts prohibited are to be taken as of equal obligation. Now it is plain beyond all argument that any adjudication of a Federal Judge repugnant to the Constitution is void, or if not void, that such Judge may, by his own decision, alter the Constitution. From one or the other of these alternatives there is no escape. It is either an absolute nullity to be everywhere treated as void, or else instead of a republican government exercising only specially delegated powers, we have one whose sway is bounded only by its own will, and have vainly attempted to limit a power which, in its very nature, is illimitable. Again I ask, then, does a judgment of a court repugnant to the Constitution, and therefore void, notwithstanding its invalidity, bind all persons and things within its apparent scope? To ask that question is to answer it. In this case the judicial action of this court is invoked to liberate these applicants. Upon the one hand the Constitution which you are sworn to support, prohibits these men from being imprisoned for the cause alleged. While on the other hand, the Federal Judge in Cleveland says they shall be imprisoned. Which of these two is to command the obedience of the Court? Is the Constitution superior to the ruling of that Judge, where the two conflict, or is the *ipse dixit* of that Judge to override the Constitution? That is the simple question. If the latter is to control, then an act which, upon the very theory of the government, is entirely void, is yet in practice completely obligatory, an act which the Constitution expressly forbids to be done is, notwithstanding the prohibition, entirely effectual. To what purpose, then, does the Constitution itself declare that it is obligatory upon you as judges, and why require you to swear to support it, if, at the same time, you are obliged to violate it at the will of any Federal Judge?

But then it is said that the courts of the United States are supreme within their sphere; all agree to that; but what then? So also are the State Courts supreme within their sphere; and the same argument which proves that the Federal Courts have a right to determine the extent of their jurisdiction and impose that determination on State Courts, proves equally that the State Courts have also the right to determine the extent of their jurisdiction and conclude the Federal Courts by that determination. But the question here is not of the supremacy of the Federal Government within its sphere, but whether it is supreme beyond it; for the proposition implies that the adjudication in the case supposed, was an usurpation of power. And, may it please your Honors, the dogma of the supremacy of the Federal Courts within their sphere, and their utter impotence beyond it, suggests the true rule; for it is only the statement, in another form, of the maxim that the judgment of a court of competent jurisdiction is everywhere conclusive, save on proceedings directly instituted to review it; while the judgment of a court which has not jurisdiction, is, in law, no judgment at all. By competent jurisdiction is meant, that the court has constitutional and legal capacity to determine the subject-matter of the litigation, and that the parties interested in that subject-matter, and whose rights therein are to be determined, have been properly brought before it. When these two conditions exist, it has jurisdiction. The right to adjudicate the case is vested in the court; and, whether that right is exercised regularly or irregularly, erroneously or otherwise, its judgment binds all persons and things which fall within its legitimate scope.

But this immunity from collateral question depends solely upon the presence of these two conditions, for if it has not the constitutional capacity to hear the cause, or if the party sought to be affected has not been duly brought into court, then its judgment concludes nothing. If it has this jurisdiction, its proceedings import absolute verity; if it has not, its judgment is an absolute nullity. When, therefore, in any proceeding in any Court, the judgment of another tribunal, whether as between the same parties or otherwise, is interposed, either to establish or defeat some right then in litigation, the very first inquiry always is: Had the tribunal, rendering this judgment, jurisdiction? If it had, it concludes in the then litigation of all rights which were within its scope; if it had not, it is treated as mere waste paper, and the rights which it sought to adjudicate still remain open for discussion and judgment. No judgments, civil or criminal, are exempt from this rule. It is of absolutely universal application; from the court of a justice of the peace up to the highest tribunals. Each one, when called on to recognize the judgment of another power, whether state or national, home or foreign, first inquires and first determines whether it had jurisdiction. Nor until now, and in these cases under the fugitive act, has it ever been hinted, that any court was concluded from making this inquiry because the other tribunal which rendered the judgment asserted itself to have competent jurisdiction. Now if the learned counsel who represents the Federal Government (Col. Swayne), should bring his action against me in a State Court, upon a judgment which he claimed to have recovered against me in the Circuit Court of the United States, and upon the production of the record of that Court it should appear affirmatively, either that in that Court he had sued me to recover a penalty given only by a statute of this State; or that — the subject-matter being within its jurisdiction — I had never been served with process or otherwise brought into Court — does any lawyer within the sound of my voice, does even the learned counsel himself, suppose that the State Court would hold itself or me concluded by that judgment? Surely not. Every tyro in the law knows better. In the one case the judgment would be void for want of constitutional capacity to adjudge any such penalty; in the other for want of jurisdiction over the person of myself. Nobody doubts that. But, may it please your Honors, if in an action touching the rights of property, you may in a State Court impeach the judgment of a Federal Court for the want of jurisdiction, *a fortiori*, may you do the same thing in every proceeding which concerns the rights of personal freedom.

If in an action pending before it, a State Court may inquire whether a Federal Court had power to dispose of an ox or an ass, how much more upon this great writ of *habeas corpus*, may it not inquire whether that same court has power to dispose of the liberty of the citizen? When, therefore, in response to Bushnell's challenge, made in the prescribed legal mode, — Marshal Johnson says he restrains him of his liberty under a sentence pronounced by Hiram V. Willson, Judge of the District Court, it is a sufficient reply to say either generally that Mr. Willson was no judge at all, or that his judicial power did not extend to the case in which Bushnell was sentenced. For if, as to the particular case he had no power to render judgment, it is precisely the same as if he were not judge at all. Now suppose he had undertaken to try Bushnell without a jury, or the offence charged was that of selling game out of season, are we to be told that simply because in doing this the Judge claimed to act under Federal authority — we are bound to shut our eyes to this usurpation of power; that the sentence is an estoppel concluding all inquiry save on a writ of error to review it? Looking, then, only at the general principle applied daily to the most solemn adjudications of every tribunal, this Court must inquire and determine for itself whether Judge Willson had jurisdiction to award the judgment under which these two citizens are held in custody.

But again; the right of the State to inquire into the validity of any authority imposing restraint upon its citizens as against every power, be it State, national, or foreign, stands on an even firmer basis, for it results from the very nature of sovereignty itself. The first and chief characteristic of all sovereignty is its right to the allegiance and service of its citizens; a right fundamental to all other rights of a State, for on this its very existence in war or peace continually depends. Correlative to, or rather comprehended in this right, is the power to remove any unlawful restraint enforced against its citizens, to the twofold end that the State may not be improperly deprived of his services, and that it may efficiently discharge that supreme and imprescriptible duty of protection, which, as a return for his allegiance every State owes to its citizens. On these two principles, allegiance to the State, protection to the citizen, rests not merely all sovereignty, but the very social compact itself. Any nation which has wholly surrendered the allegiance of its citizens or its correlative incidental right to protect them while within its territorial limits, has in that very act abnegated every attribute of sovereignty and become the mere local dependency of the power to which that allegiance and right has been surrendered. But Ohio, thank God, is still a sovereign State, and has therefore never yielded this right, as she never could yield it, and still preserve her sovereignty, to the Federal, or any other government. In all the Constitution, I find no such grant. I find nothing prohibiting its continued residence with the States. In a few carefully guarded, and specifically enumerated instances, the State has delegated to the Federal Government power to punish; and has

renounced the right to prevent that punishment; but in even these instances, she has retained the power to inquire whether this limited authority for punishing is kept within its narrow bounds. In all else, save these special instances, the State reserved the power to prevent all punishment not imposed by itself; and in all cases, including even these, she reserved the right to inquire into the nature of every authority which sought to deprive any citizen of his liberty. For it will not be questioned that the general guardianship of the citizen is confided, not to the Federal Government, but to the State alone. It follows that the power to which this guardianship is intrusted, must, as an indispensable condition of its exercise, have the right to inquire into and determine for itself the validity of any authority which assumes within its limits to deprive the citizen of that natural right of freedom, for the security of which it has pledged its most solemn faith. Chief, and most efficient of all the instrumentalities by which the State asserts its sovereignty, and exercises this duty of protection, is the great writ of *habeas corpus*, universally called the great bulwark of freedom, which has come down to us through many ages, and which, issuing always in the name of the sovereign, was specially designed to inquire by what authority any person was restrained of his liberty, and to deliver from all unlawful imprisonment. This was the sole office of the writ when the Constitution was framed, and when its makers — as if apprehensive that possibly authority to suspend it might be inferred from some grant of power to the Federal Government — commandingly declared that its privileges should never be suspended except in cases of rebellion or invasion. This emphatic prohibition speaks alike to every department of that Government — judicial as well as legislative and executive. Not only this, but the Constitution of this State has thrown around this writ in like terms the same absolute immunity.

Since, then, the power to inquire into all imprisonments belonged originally and necessarily to the States; since it has never been and never could be surrendered; since the constitutions, State and Federal, alike declare that it shall not be suspended, I submit to your Honors that there is no power in either Government to abridge the right of the State to inquire into the validity of every authority, Federal, State, or Foreign, which assumes to restrain its citizens.

Again, if it please your Honors, the right of the States to inquire into the validity of every imprisonment of persons held under Federal authority has been constantly asserted and exercised by every State since the organization of the Government. Persons arrested for alleged offences against the United States have been frequently discharged, and you can hardly open a New York paper without finding cases where the State Courts have discharged soldiers or mariners, held in custody by virtue of an enlistment under Federal laws. Metzger, though arrested under a warrant of extradition, issued by the President in supposed conformity with treaty stipulations, and though a Judge of the Federal Courts (Betts) had held the warrant to be valid, was discharged by the State Courts of New York; and still more recently this Court, in the case of Collier, has affirmed its undoubted power to discharge persons held under color of Federal authority.

The right, then, of the State to issue this writ, stands on grounds as firm as the earth itself. When it goes forth, let all men know that it is the State, exercising the highest of all its attributes, which sends out its great prerogative writ,—inquiring into the condition and restraint of its citizens, that no man to whom it is directed, be he Marshal or Chief Justice, King, Kaiser, or President, may omit to give heed to its peremptory behest, that no power on earth can absolve him from obedience to it, or shield him from the consequences of disobedience.

Taking it, then, as established that your Honors—exercising the SUPREME JUDICIAL POWER of the State, have the right to inquire into and determine the validity of every pretext under which the citizen is held in custody—I next proceed to ascertain the nature and authority of that adjudication upon which the sheriff of Cuyahoga county assumes to restrain these two citizens of their freedom.

Bushnell's conviction rests upon an indictment containing a single count, which, in substance, charges him with obstructing the master of the alleged fugitive, without any process or color of process in the exercise of the right alleged to belong to the master by the Federal Constitution, of seizing his runaway slave wherever he may find him, and taking him back by force to the State from which he escaped. Langston's conviction rests on an indictment containing two counts, the first of which is precisely similar to the single count in Bushnell's indictment; while the second charges, in substance, that Langston had obstructed a Deputy-Marshal of the United States, in the execution of a Commissioner's warrant, issued to him and held by him, commanding the arrest of John, an alleged fugitive from service.

These indictments are each founded on the Act of Congress known as the Fugitive Slave Act; the provisions of which, it is therefore necessary now briefly to examine.

[Mr. Wolcott here stated the effect of each of the sections of the act, which being generally known, are here omitted, and then proceeded.]

From this analysis of the provisions of the Act, as it has been construed by the decisions hereafter to be adverted to, it results that any man may come into one of the free States, and upon his mere claim that one of its apparently undoubted citizens, resident here during many years, is his slave, or owes him service or labor,

drag that citizen beyond the limits of the State of his residence, and that no one may interfere with this forcible capture, even to ascertain the validity of the claim so made, except on pain of fine and imprisonment, if it shall ultimately turn out that the captured citizen, though born in a free State, and originally free, was once arrested in a slave State upon suspicion of being a slave, and finally, no claimant appearing for him, was sold into perpetual slavery to pay the costs of that very arrest and detention. Bad as this is, it is not all. This Act has a depth of atrocity which no plummet shall ever sound. It provides a safer remedy for the man-stealer. If he do not choose to risk the private caption, he may obtain a warrant of arrest from a Federal Commissioner, seize the alleged fugitive, take him before the Commissioner, who is to hear the case in a summary manner, on such *ex parte* affidavits or depositions as may be produced, and if these satisfy him of the existence of the claim made against the fugitive, he is to issue his certificate thereof, which is made conclusive evidence of the claimant's right to remove, and confers upon him absolute authority to make that removal; and upon his mere oath that he fears a rescue, the Marshal himself is to return the alleged fugitive, and may, if needful to accomplish that end, call to his aid the whole naval and military force of the United States. But even this is not the worst. The intending kidnapper may go before some Judge of the most distant State, and upon *ex parte* evidence, perhaps his own alone, obtain a record reciting the fact of some alleged slave's escape—a record which shall absolutely foreclose the questions of slavery and of escape therefrom,—"with a general description, of such convenient certainty as may be," of the alleged fugitive, and, under it, seize any man who corresponds to this description, drag him before any Circuit Judge of that circuit, though resident in another State, and then upon mere proof of the captive's identity with this "general description of convenient certainty," obtain a warrant for the removal of the free citizen to the State from which the *ex parte* record asserts he escaped (to be enforced with the whole power of the Federal Government), and there retain him in perpetual bondage. Not only may no man, even by a resort to judicial process, attempt to inquire into the lawfulness of the taking, but no tribunal, State or Federal, may, either by the writ of *habeas corpus* or otherwise, molest the claimant in the exercise of this power, for the prohibition of the eighth section is without limitation, and includes all officers and courts, State and Federal. Indeed, the Supreme Court of the United States, in its recent opinion in the Booth case, has declared that the allowance of the writ in such a case would be an act of "lawless violence." The citizen is thus not only without the means of protecting himself, but any endeavor to detain him long enough to ascertain the validity of his caption, is made a criminal act. This enactment, under pretence of preventing the escape of bondmen, strikes down every safeguard of the liberty of the citizen. Does the citizen hold his liberty by this frail tenure? Yes! if your Honors do not here and now interpose. Other refuge on all this earth, there is none. You or I, or the Governor who sits here, or our Senator in Congress (Mr. Pugh), who also sits here, or any other citizen, may, at any moment, be seized and rapt away to another State, under the provisions of this Act, for all alike are subject to its operation. Does any say that the supposition is improbable? I reply, first, No. Under its provisions, freemen have not unfrequently been adjudged to be slaves, and surrendered to that condition. Second, that since the Act itself, by its very terms, authorizes seizures in the very instances just mentioned, these instances may fairly be supposed to test its validity, and their probability or improbability is beside the question. But, beyond this, if this very fate does not befall one of your Honors or myself, it is not because of any exception or qualification in the Act itself, excluding its application to you, or me, or any free citizen, but because no scoundrel has either the baseness or the audacity to attempt its application, so that we enjoy our exemption from its operation against us, not because we are freemen; not because the law protects us any more than it does the negro against this arbitrary seizure; but merely for the reason that no one sees fit, from whatever motive, to assert dominion over us.

But this awful power is one not exercised by this State under its own control as against its own citizens, for the State had disabled itself from that; but authority to assert it within the territorial limits of this State is claimed by another distinct and independent government. The asserters of this power, therefore, maintain not merely that the liberty of the citizen is absolutely at the control of every villain who may, by *ex parte* and perjured evidence, swear away his freedom, in a proceeding of which he has no notice, in which he has no voice, which he cannot impeach, but that the State to which the citizen owes allegiance, and to whom it owes the correlative duty of protection, has not simply, of its own voluntary choice, submitted to the exercise of this power within its limits, but that it has disabled both itself and the government to whom it is said to have delegated this absolute dominion, from any right to inquire into the propriety of its exercise in any given instance, and has also delegated authority to the government assuming this power to punish as criminal any one who shall invoke the process of law, applicable to all other cases of imprisonment, to inquire into that proceeding. For under the recent ruling of the Supreme Court of the United States, the great writ of *habeas corpus* itself is virtually declared to be unconstitutional, and your Honors for allowing it — where you are advised that the person is

detained under a commissioner's warrant — though such allowance be made in the plain and imperative discharge of your judicial functions — for the same authority which made you judges absolutely requires this writ at your hands — are liable for this judicial act to fine and imprisonment. These and not less than these are the proportions of the doctrine on which the claim of the Federal Government is now urged.

This doctrine it is my duty, as most assuredly it is my pleasure, to resist here and now, with all my mind and will and strength. In the name of the STATE, the sovereignty of which is thus assailed in its most vital part; on behalf of its citizens, all of whose liberties are thus imperilled, I am here to maintain that the power now claimed on behalf of the Federal Government has no existence, and that its exercise under color of the authority of that Government is a gross usurpation of the powers retained by the States, and a flagrant violation of the natural and guaranteed rights of the citizen.

The grounds upon which the claim of this power in the Federal Government is founded are twofold, namely, first, that the States have in and by the Constitution delegated to the master of every escaping slave, authority to pursue him in any State to which he may flee, and there without process and by force seize him, again reduce him to the condition of slavery, and retake him to the domicil of the master; and second, that the States have also by the same Constitution, delegated to the Congress of the United States power to legislate in aid of this right of reclaiming fugitive slaves.

Now if this right of recaption be not given by the Constitution itself to the master; and if this power to legislate for the reclamation of fugitive slaves be not conferred on the Congress; very obviously the act under which Bushnell and Langston have been convicted, the one of obstructing this right, the other not only of that but of resisting process issued under legislative provision in aid of that right, is unconstitutional and void. Being void, it could confer no jurisdiction upon the District Court, and the sentence against the relators under which they are now detained in custody, would be a nullity.

The great question, then, may it please your Honors, is: Does the Constitution delegate to the master this right of recaption, and to the Congress this power to legislate in aid or for the enforcement of this right? To determine this it is necessary to examine the provisions of that instrument. But before entering directly into this examination it will not be amiss to advert to certain established principles in the light of which this examination must be conducted.

1. In discussing the powers of the General Government it must be always borne in mind that the Constitution was not formed by a people who were then living without a Government, but by the people of several distinct and

Independent States, each of which had a full and thoroughly organized government in operation therein, each having full power to declare war, make peace, contract alliances, establish commerce, and do every other act which free and independent States may of right do. These States, independent in themselves, had entered into a confederation under which they had formed a union for the purpose of maintaining their independence, then the subject of perilous and deadly struggle. After this was achieved, and the outward pressure of a common danger which had largely contributed to preserve harmony of relations was removed, the articles of confederation were found wholly inadequate for their continued government as a nation. Under the influence of this reason, these independent States again resolved to attempt the formation of a more perfect union, and accordingly sent delegates to a convention assembled for the purpose of framing a Constitution which should secure that end. Meeting thus as sovereigns, this object could be accomplished in no other mode than the surrender by each of some portion of the power which had hitherto pertained to it in virtue of this sovereignty, while still retaining all those attributes not necessary to the efficiency of the common government it was designed to found. The Convention thus assembled, did, in process of time, agree upon a constitution to be submitted to the several distinct sovereignties for their ratification; and these sovereignties did, after prolonged and critical examination of its provisions, and with more or less reluctance in each instance, yield its final assent to the new frame of government created by that Constitution. This Government, therefore, consists simply of powers theretofore pertaining to the States, but delegated by them to the new governments. But, then, it was necessary to do something more than simply confer active powers upon the new Government. Powers not at all necessary to that would still remain with the States — the exercise of which might violate the fundamental principles of justice and freedom, or be inconsistent with the exercise of the powers given to the General Government — and this condition would be met by simply disabling the States from the exercise of these powers. But then there would still remain a class of subjects, which, not being of national concern, called for the exercise of no national power, and therefore required the delegation of none to the General Government; and which, on the other hand, required more or less of regulation by the respective States themselves, so that they could not properly or safely renounce their power over them; and yet which at the same time so far concerned the maintenance of harmonious relations between the States, or the people thereof, as to render some common understanding necessary concerning the extent to which each should exercise its undelegated and unrenounced powers upon these subjects of common interest. This exi-

gency would be fully provided for by a simple agreement between the States not to press the exercise of their reserved powers upon the subjects indicated, beyond a certain defined limit. From the very necessity of things, then, we might, *a priori*, have determined that the Constitution would consist, first, of grants of power to the Government created by its provisions; second, of prohibitions upon powers not delegated; and third, clauses of compact, by which each State covenants with the other, so to exercise or forbear the exercise of powers, neither delegated nor prohibited, and, therefore, still retained, as not to affect, in certain defined ways, subjects which, though not of national concern, were yet of importance as affecting the exterior relations of the States to each other. All of the constitutional provisions do accordingly range themselves under the one or the other of these three great and natural divisions. Now, very evidently, no one of the constitutional provisions operates to give any power to the Government, unless it range itself under the head of grants, so that no power as to any given subject is to be imputed to the Government simply because that subject has been made a matter of regulation, for that regulation may consist either of a total prohibition of power to the States over it, or of a simple compact between the States to do, or omit to do some particular thing, the execution of which rests with the States alone. But again, the government created by this constitution consists not merely of delegated and limited powers. The States, as if to guard against the known tendency of all power to overpass prescribed limits, have made no general grants and then undertaken to hedge it in by metes and bounds, but has specifically expressed the subjects and objects to which the power of that government should extend. Thus, whenever it was designed to confer power over any subject, that subject has been selected, and calling it by its proper and ordinary name, the States said, " The Congress shall have power to borrow money, declare war, to establish post-offices, to punish piracy on the high seas, etc." The Federal Government is, therefore, one of enumerated as well as limited and delegated powers.

Still again, the powers granted, being granted by independent sovereignties, it not only follows as the result of all just reasoning that all powers not granted are withheld, but the Constitution, not content to rest upon a mere logical result, however irresistible, has itself declared that, the " powers not delegated by it to the United States, or prohibited to the States, are reserved to the States respectively, or to the people."

From this undeniably correct view of the nature of the Constitution, it follows, First, that as the Government is one of limited and enumerated powers, and as every grant is in derogation of State sovereignty, it has no authority save such as is expressly granted, or as is merely subsidiary to the execution of the expressly granted powers; or, in other words, no substantive, independent power, the exercise of which is one of the ends of government, can be implied. Such a power has no existence, save as it is founded in express grant. This rule necessarily results from the Constitution, and with a single exception, hereafter to be noticed, has been uniformly sanctioned and acted upon by the Supreme Court of the United States.

2. That as to all powers not thus expressly delegated to the United States, or expressly prohibited to the States, or* the exercise of which has not been regulated by any of the clauses of compact, each State has the complete, exclusive, unlimited, and undeniable jurisdiction and power over all persons and things within its limits, to the same supreme extent which has ever pertained to any nation in any age. As to these powers, the States stand to each other and to the Federal Government as absolutely foreign nations.

With these two general principles, applicable alike to all discussions of the powers of the Federal Government, kept constantly in view, there still remain two other established rules of special application to the particular subject now under discussion; which subject, be it remembered, is the power of the master to recapture by force in the free States his escaping slave, and of Congress to legislate in aid of this right, or, more generally speaking, of the General Government to protect the relation of master and slave within the limits of those States which forbid its existence.

" The state of slavery," said Lord Mansfield, pronouncing judgment in the great case of Somerset, " is of such a nature that it is incapable of being introduced on any reasons, moral or political, but only by positive law. It is so odious, that nothing can be suffered to support it but positive law ;" and every court of every State, slave and free, has echoed and reëchoed these immortal words! And when one pauses a moment to reflect on it, no wonder that even the slaveholder himself acquiesces in this statement of the sole condition upon which it can found its existence. Looking at its bad eminence, well may the jurist, no less than the moralist and statesman, declare that this wrong can have no existence in any system of government except by positive and express sanction. It can found itself on no inference, however strong ; it can derive no support from phrases of ambiguous meaning ; but he who claims its existence or recognition in any form, however qualified, must be able to show some clear affirmative enactment, which will admit of no other sense or interpretation.

But a second principle of the common law, applying to the judicial resolution of all questions touching the personal rights of man, is also to be kept constantly in view. By a rule older than the Constitution, — older than the Declaration of Independence, — older than

Magna Charta, — older even than the common law itself, — wherever the right of man to his liberty is the subject of question, every doubt is to be resolved in favor of liberty. Alike in the bond of the apprentice, — in the laws relating to serfdom and villanage, — in the statutes and judicial proceedings, which deprive a person of his liberty as the punishment of crime,— every word is to be constructed strictly as against the power to deprive him of freedom. Even as against the acknowledged criminal the law permits no inference or intendment or presumption, but every thing is to be construed in favor of freedom. Still more, then, must this be so in a constitution framed by a people who had just emerged from a seven years' war, to establish the self-evident truth, that all men are born free and equal, and which the Constitution avowed upon its very front in words of fire, that it was ordained to secure the blessings of liberty to the people of the United States, and their posterity. Now we have these four great rules, which are to guide us in discussing this question of Constitutional power, — First, that the General Government has no power save that which is expressly delegated by the Constitution. Second, that all powers, not expressly delegated, or restrained by absolute prohibition or qualified by compact, belong to the States in all their original supremacy. Third, that slavery is of so odious a nature that the power to recognize its existence can be derived only from an affirmative, positive grant, permitting no other interpretation ; and lastly, that honored maxim which requires every doubtful phrase to be construed in favor of liberty. These four rules, all converging to one result, enable me to declare, and I speak with the united authority which has established these rules — an authority greater and more decisive than can be found to sustain any other juridical proposition — that if the power has not been given to the master to recapture and resubjugate his slave in a free State, and to Congress to legislate in aid of this recaption and resubjugation ; if, I say, this power has not been delegated in express and affirmative terms — terms of the most unequivocal and imperative import — then the power has absolutely no existence ; and this cruel act, which, though aimed at one race, strikes down all, is as vain as it is wicked and cruel. This leads me directly to the one question to be decided : Has the Constitution, by an express grant, vested in the master power to make a raid into every State in pursuit of a runaway slave, and finding him, to drag him back without process ; or has it given Congress power to enforce his surrender ? This question is to be decided, not upon argument, not on the weight of reasoning — for it neither requires or admits of reasoning — but simply upon inspection, and by the use of the eyes. Does the Constitution say, in so many words, Congress may do this thing? Let us see. I look first at the eighth section of the first article, which contains the general enumeration of powers granted to Congress, and I do not find it there; nay, no one pretends that it is there. I pursue my search through the other parts of the Constitution, reading it article by article and section by section, but I do not find it there. In all the Constitution the word slave or slavery is not there; nor is there any other equivalent word or phrase which aptly defines that relation, and nothing else. Even those words which may, by construction, perhaps, be deemed to include slaves, equally express the condition of freemen who owe service or labor in virtue of voluntary contract obligation. Nor is this omission accidental. All the world now knows, and I shall hereafter show, that every word and syllable which meant slave or slavery, and nothing else, was carefully and anxiously excluded from the Constitution, for the very reason avowed by Madison, who uttered the general sentiment of the Convention, "that it would be wrong to admit into the Constitution the idea that there could be property in man." But even in those clauses of doubtful phraseology, which in one sense may be construed to include slave, not, be it remarked, as property, but as persons; even in those, I say, I find no mention of the rights of recaption; no mention of the master, or of Congress, or of any other department of the Federal Government; still less do you find any grant of power to either over this subject. Vainly do you read the whole instrument in search of any such express grant. It is not there; and nobody pretends to say it is there. Still less does anybody pretend that this power to reclaim fugitive slaves, either by the master or by the Congress, is subsidiary to any expressly granted power. But this being ascertained, the examination of the question ends. By each and all the rules of interpretation I have invoked, and their correctness, no one will doubt, if the power is not expressly granted — if it do not stand out from the text of the Constitution in characters so unmistakable that he who runs may read — the power has no existence. Since, then, it is not expressly granted, — since it does not so stand out, there is nothing left to discuss, nothing to be done, but to declare the result which the settled rules inexorably affix to this absence of express grant, namely: that the power claimed does not exist, and the act is therefore VOID. That is the conclusion, and it is as irresistible as Omnipotence itself. The wit of man cannot get over or around it, and here this argument ought to close. Why should one truth be demonstrated more than once? Upon this ground alone I might well claim that the applicants are wrongfully detained in custody, and here rest their right to an immediate and unconditional discharge. But as the question now under discussion is one which so nearly concerns, not only the sovereignty of the States, but the personal rights of the citizen, it may not be wholly unprofitable to show still farther the immovable stability of the base upon which that sovereignty rests, and the impregnable safeguards with which the liberty of the citizen has been hedged about. Now let it be supposed, though the supposition seems quite impossible, that I am utterly mistaken as to each and all of the four principles upon which I have asserted that the power of Congress over this subject is to be ascertained and determined, — let it be granted that powers may be imputed to Congress by implication, that slavery may exist in virtue of doubtful phrases or equivocal enactments, and that in construing the Constitution no intendment is to be made in favor of freedom, then I have to say that even if you apply to the Constitution the same rules of interpretation by which you would ascertain the sense of a mere huckstering bargain between two traders, forgetting all narrow prejudices in favor of freedom, it is still easy to show that even upon that mode of interpretation you can find no warrant for the exercise of this power. All who insist upon the existence of this power derive it from the last clause of the second section of the fourth article, which provides as follows:—

"No person held to service or labor in one State, under the laws thereof, escaping into another, shall, in consequence of any law or regulation therein, be discharged from such service or labor, but shall be delivered up on claim of the party to whom such service or labor may be due."

Now, upon looking at the sections of the constitution which immediately precede and follow this clause, I find various provisions in which power is expressly given to Congress over various subjects, but in this clause not only is Congress not mentioned, but there is no grant of power to any one. Upon the maxim of *expressio unus*, etc., the ordinary rules of interpretation, and the laws of common sense infer, that since power is given in relation to other subjects provided for in the clauses immediately before and after this, and none is given as to this, none was intended to be given. If they intended to give the power in this instance why not say so, as they said in all other cases? *Si non dixit non voluit.* But again, upon looking at those subjects in respect to which power is affirmatively given, I find them all to be either of national concern, that is, affecting the General Government and necessary to its efficiency, or subjects in which the citizens of all the States have a common interest. But here the subject is neither of national concern, nor is it one in which the citizens of all the States have a common interest. On the contrary, this subject was one of purely domestic policy — it was entirely a local affair; the institution which is thought to be intended by its circuitous phraseology, was one to which a portion of the States were utterly hostile, and this feeling was growing stronger daily — and it was therefore one in respect to which it was not proper to confer any power. Hence no power was given.

Still again, upon looking at the language of the clause itself alone, it is seen that it contemplates : —

First. That in some of the States persons are held to labor or service under the laws thereof. So far, of course, the clause has plain reference to *States* alone.

Second. That persons so held under the laws of one *State* may escape into another *State*. Still again, having reference to *States* only,

Third. That in the *State* to which the person thus held to service under the laws of another *State* has escaped, there may be laws or regulations which would operate to discharge him from that labor or service ; still, again, having reference to *States* and *State* laws or regulations.

Fourth. Then providing that such *State* laws or regulations shall not have the effect or consequence to discharge the escaping person from the labor to which he is held in another *State* under its laws; still having reference to *States* and nothing else. Now if the section stopped here no' one would pretend that the least iota of power was intended to be conferred upon Congress. It does not, however, stop here, but without break or pause proceeds in the same sentence to add by way of antithesis, " but shall be delivered up," etc. To whom is this addressed? Obviously to the same object which had before been addressed, for no new one is introduced as the subject of the command. " Shall be delivered up." By whom? No one is specified, but by the laws of well-speaking, not less than by the laws of the structure of language, the clause has necessary reference to some power which has been named before; and that power is the *States* alone. Somebody "shall not discharge;" somebody " shall deliver up," and the body addressed in the one case is the body addressed in the other. Now who " shall not discharge ? " The States, for so says the clause in terms. Then, who shall deliver up ? The States plainly. But how many of the States ? Not all, nor any two or more of them at any one time, any one fugitive, but the solitary State whichever it be, into which at any time, any given fugitive may escape, from any other State.

Have I not then established my position that even if you may resort to inferences to attribute a power to Congress, if you may ignore the great rules which apply to all questions of personal freedom, and if you may interpret this instrument by the same rules which you apply to any commercial compact, a contract of copartnership, a constitution of agency, that the result is still the same, and on no rule of construction can you find here any power in Congress. For what can be plainer than that here is a compact between the States upon a mere matter of comity and good neighborhood, providing a rule for the adjustment of certain relations which might be sustained by any two States at a given time, and *nothing more or less !* Congress is not once mentioned ; no matter of national interest is mooted, and least and last of all, is there the slightest hint from which by any process of torture Congressional or Federal jurisdiction can be implied of the relations here adjusted. Just before and immediately following this section, three times in the same article, Congress has delegated to it certain powers, — but not a mention of power here, except individual State power. What could be more conclusive upon this question ?

And then, when I go back to the true rules by which this great instrument is to be interpreted, and find the result to be the same as by the most ordinary rules, then I may say, not untruly, that this result is absolutely impregnable, — that this clause is one of compact merely, which the States alone can execute; and that the Congress has no more power to provide for the caption of fugitives from service within the States, than the Parliament of Great Britain, or a " Pow Wow " of the Camanche Indians.

Conclusive as this is, this is by no means all. The history of this clause confirms, with irresistible certainty and force, the result arrived at from an examination of its language alone. This provision, and the other three which precede it in this article, are, as the Court well know, by no means new in the Constitution. That which relates to the effect of records, except as to the grant of power, — that which relates to the privileges of citizens, and that which relates to the extradition of fugitives from justice, were taken from the old articles of confederation, while that which relates to the surrender of fugitives from service is taken from the Ordinance of 1787. What did these clauses mean originally, in the places from which they came ? Were they compacts or grants of power ? Let us see, and first of those contained in the articles of confederation.

The first article of the confederation establishes the style of the confederacy, the " United States of America." The second article is the key to the whole, and deserves special attention. It declares that, " Each State retains its sovereignty, freedom, and independence, and every power, right, and jurisdiction, which is not by this confederation *expressly* delegated to the United States in Congress assembled." No implied powers here ? Jealous of the Government they were about to create, — limited as it was, and weak as it proved to be, — the States insert this limitation as the first, fundamental condition of the confederacy, and by it sternly and explicitly forbid the assumption of any function or power save that expressly delegated, and carefully retain to the States every scintilla that is not in terms granted. There can, then, be no difficulty in ascertaining what powers belonged to the Congress of the old confederation. They are carefully enumerated; we have only to read the schedule; none others exist. Let us go on. In the third article, " The States severally enter into a firm league of friendship with each other" for their common defence, and "bind themselves to assist each other against all force," etc., — a simple treaty, compact, or obligation, but no grant of power to Congress.

By the first clause of the fourth article, the free inhabitants of each State, except paupers, vagabonds, and fugitives from justice, are entitled to all privileges and immunities of free citizens in the several States; still a clause of compact, but no grant of power.

The second clause of the same article is in these words : —

"If any person guilty of or charged with treason, felony, or other legal misdemeanor in any State shall flee from justice, and be found in any of the United States, he shall, upon demand of the Governor or executive power of the State from which he fled, be delivered up, and removed to the State having jurisdiction of his offence."

No power is here delegated expressly or otherwise, to the Congress to deliver up the person guilty or charged; but, under the second article, each State retains that power as entire, unquestionable, as if the confederation had never existed. This clause was also simple compact, and I desire special attention to be given to this.

The third and last clause of this article provided that "full faith and credit shall be given in each of these States to the records, acts, etc., of the Courts and Magistrates of every other State." No grant of power here, and Congress therefore could not enforce or regulate this clause of compact. Each State retained in all its fulness and vigor "every power, jurisdiction, and right" over the manner in which this agreement should be performed. So much for the force and effect of these clauses as they stood in the articles of Confederation — compacts all — no power over them in the Congress — full and absolute power over them in the States and in them alone. And how was it with the provision relating to "fugitives from service," as that stood in the Ordinance of 1787 ? That Ordinance was passed on the 13th of July, 1787, while the Convention that framed the Constitution was still in session, and in the midst of its labors. Its first provisions are devoted entirely to framing a temporary government which should suffice during the condition of territorial pupilage. Having by a few carefully drawn provisions accomplished this object, the Congress, casting its eyes into the distant future, proceeded with a wise and provident forecast, to establish certain great principles which should forever secure to the millions who were thereafter to inherit it, the rights of personal liberty, the security of property, the freedom of conscience, the blessings of education, and the right to self-government. In order that these principles might not be deemed either to partake of the character, or be subject to the incidents of ordinary legislative enactment, the Congress, after a brief preamble, reciting that for extending "the fundamental principles of the civil and religious liberty, which form the basis whereon these republics, their laws and constitutions are erected; to fix and establish those principles as the basis of all laws, constitutions, and governments which shall forever be formed " in said territory," — proceeded, not to enact an ordinary statute, but to ordain and declare that the following articles shall be considered as articles of COMPACT between the original States and the States and people of said territory, and forever remain unalterable, except by common consent. The first five articles of compact define, in a few brief words, the great principles which underlie all free government, and then last and greatest of all comes the sixth article of compact, containing, first, the memorable ordinance which consecrated the soil of the North-west to freedom forever; and second, this proviso, " that when any person escaping into the territory, from whom labor or service is lawfully claimed in any one of the original States, such fugitive may be lawfully reclaimed, and conveyed to the person claiming his or her labor as aforesaid." Now, this was undeniably a mere compact, and it is so distinctly named; conferring no power on the Congress of the Confederation, not only because simply a compact, but because the United States is not even a party to it. This clause was copied from an old New England compact, made in 1642, between Massachusetts Bay and some of her neighbors. But it granted no power, being simply an agreement to return each other's runaway servants. Dane copied a familiar provision of New England policy. In all its mutations it was simply compact. Now the substance of each of these four articles of the compact, which we have been considering, three of which existed in the Confederation, and one in the Ordinance of '87, found its way into the Constitution, forming the first and second sections of the fourth article, as we have already seen. How came these agreements of the old compacts of '77 and '87, into the Federal Constitution? What change did they undergo in passing there ? Have they in any way been transformed from mutual covenants between contracting parties, into grants of power by parties surrendering what they had retained to themselves for ten years, to a new government, then for the first time created ? If so, how, when, by what apt words were these mutual stipulations transformed into grants of power ? Let us trace the history of the progress of these covenant obligations until they became incorporated into the present Constitution. But before doing this it may be well to premise that during the whole ten years of the old Confederation, no complaint was made of the non-performance by any of the

States of the clauses of this compact contained in the articles, or any apprehension expressed of such non-performance in the future, or any charge as to the terms or effects of them suggested as desirable from any quarter, save in a single instance. On the 25th June, '78, South Carolina moved to insert the word "white" after the word "free," in the clause stipulating for the immunities of the free inhabitants of one State in all the other States, so as to limit the operation of the compact to free *white* inhabitants, on which proposition the States voted — ayes two, noes eight, divided one, and so the motion was decisively rejected. Nor during this whole period of ten years was any desire expressed to add to these stipulations any agreement for the reclamation of fugitives from service, though in many other respects the articles of Confederation were the subject of vehement disputes among the States, approaching at times to the very verge of arbitrament by battle. In this condition of entire satisfaction as to these causes of compact now under discussion, the convention first met at Philadelphia on the 14th of May, 1787, and on the 25th of that month organized by the election of George Washington as its President, and commenced its labors. On the 29th of May, Charles Pinckney, of South Carolina, submitted the first draft of a Constitution, which became the basis of the further action of the Convention, of which the twelfth and thirteenth articles were as follows: —

XII. — " The citizens of each State shall be entitled to all privileges and immunities of citizens of the several States. Any person charged with crimes in any State, fleeing from justice to another, shall, on demand of the Executive of the State from which he fled, be delivered up, and removed to the State having jurisdiction of the offence."

XIII. — " Full faith shall be given in each State to the acts of the Legislature, and to the records and judicial proceedings of the courts and magistrates of every State."

Except that the words free inhabitants in the first clause was changed to " citizens," and some merely verbal alteration in other respects of the same clause, not at all changing its effect, these clauses are identical in all particulars with the provisions in the articles of confederation. As to the two relating to fugitives from justice, and the effect of records, there is absolutely no difference. They are, therefore, still clauses of compact, — nothing else ; and no intimation yet of an intent to transform them to grants of power, nor any suggestion yet made from any quarter, to provide in any form, either by grants of power or simple stipulation, for the surrender of fugitives from service. For, as yet, no such provision existed anywhere, the Ordinance of '87 not yet having been adopted. But let us look still farther. Six other plans were submitted to the Convention, but in no one of these other six was the subject either of

the faith due to records, the immunities of citizens, or the surrender, either of fugitives from service or justice, once alluded to, and this, though the very object of all these different drafts was to bring before the Convention the views of their authors in respect to the matters upon which provision should be made in the Constitution. These plans were : —

Edmund Randolph, 29th May.
Mr. Patterson (N. J.), 1th5 June.
Hamilton, 18th June.
Randolph's amended, 19th June.
Committee of detail, 1 Rep. 26th July.
"   "   "   2 Rep. 4th September.

All of these plans were discussed and referred to the appropriate committee, and on the 6th of August, a month after, what are called the compromises, were settled, and all difficulties overcome. This committee of five — of which John Rutledge, of South Carolina, was chairman — reported a constitution entire, of which the fourteenth, fifteenth, and sixteenth articles were as follows: —

Art. XIV. — " The citizens of each State shall be entitled to all privileges and immunities of citizens in the several States."

Art. XV. — " Any person charged with treason, felony, or high misdemeanor in any State, who shall flee from justice, and shall be found in any other State, shall, on demand of the executive power of the State from which he fled, be delivered up and removed to the State having jurisdiction of the offence."

Art. XVI. — " Full faith shall be given in each State to the acts of the legislature, and to the records and judicial proceedings of the courts and magistrates of every other State."

These articles are the same as the articles of confederation, except as to immunities of citizens, and are in every respect identical with Pinckney's draft, except that one of his articles is here divided into two. Still, as before, clauses of compact; still no grant of power asked for; still no hint from any source that the reclamation of fugitives from service should be provided for in any form. This report was referred to committee of the whole, and, August 28th, these articles came up in their order for discussion, and here is what transpired : —

I read from the third volume of Madison Papers, page 1447, every word that transpired : —

" Article fourteen (which related to the immunities of citizens) was then taken up. General Pinckney (Charles Cotesworth) was not satisfied with it. He seemed to wish some provision should be included in favor of property in slaves."

Did any one second this suggestion ? No. It was received with silent contempt; for, without the utterance of another word from any quarter, the Convention proceeded to vote on the article, and adopted it as it stood, — nine States voting aye, South Carolina uttering a solitary no, and Georgia being divided. What next? Still reading the Madison Papers, we shall see: —

"Article fifteen being then taken up, the words, 'high misdemeanor' were stricken out, and the words, 'other crime' inserted, in order to comprehend all proper cases; it being doubtful whether 'high misdemeanor' had not a technical meaning too limited.

"Mr. Butler and Mr. Pinckney moved to require 'fugitive slaves and servants to be delivered up like criminals.'"

"Mr. Wilson. This would oblige the Executive of the State to do it, at the public expense.

"Mr. Sherman saw no more propriety in the public seizing and surrendering a slave or servant, than a horse.

"Mr. Butler withdrew his proposition, in order that some particular provision might be made, apart from this article.

"Article 15, as amended, was then agreed to, *nemine contradicente.*"

Here is every word that transpired on that subject, but still no hint that the clause should be changed from compact to grant of power.

The next morning (Aug. 29), "Art. 16," (that which relates to the effect of records, etc., and I still read from the Madison Papers) being taken up,

"Mr. Williamson moved to substitute, in place of it, the words of the articles of confederation on the same subject. He did not understand precisely the meaning of the article.

"Mr. Wilson and Doctor Johnson supposed the meaning to be, that judgments in one State should be the ground of actions in other States, and that acts of the Legislatures should be cluded, for the sake of acts of insolvency, etc.

"Mr. Pinckney moved to connect article 16 with the following proposition: 'To establish uniform laws upon the subject of bankruptcies, and respecting the damages arising on the protest of foreign bills of exchange.'

"Mr. Gorham was for agreeing to the article, and committing the proposition.

"Mr. Madison was for committing both. He wished THE LEGISLATURE MIGHT BE AUTHORIZED to provide for the *execution* of judgments in other States, under such regulations as might be expedient. He thought that this might be safely done, and was justified by the value of the Union.

"Mr. Randolph said there was no instance of one nation executing judgments of the Courts of another nation. He moved the following proposition: —

"'Whenever the act of any State, whether legislative, executive, or judiciary, shall be attested and exemplified under the seal thereof, such attestation and exemplification shall be deemed in other States as full proof of the existence of that act; and its operation shall be binding in every other State, in all cases to which it may relate, and which are within the cognizance and jurisdiction of the State wherein the said act was done.'

"On the question for committing article 16, with Mr. Pinckney's motion, nine States voted aye. New Hampshire and Massachusetts alone voted no.

"The motion of Mr. Randolph was also committed, *nemine contradicente.*

"Mr. Gouverneur Morris moved to commit also the following proposition on the same subject: —

"'Full faith ought to be given in each State to the public acts, records, and judicial proceedings of every other State; and the Legislature shall, by general law, determine the proof and effect of such acts, records, and proceedings;' and it was committed, *nemine contradicente.*"

Here, then, we see that Madison wanted a grant of power over the subject of judgments and records, and so did the majority. No one intimated that it was there already; but the clause was recommitted, for the very purpose of giving it. This committee afterwards reported back a clause substantially like that proposed by Gouverneur Morris, which was the same, in effect, with the clause as it now stands; and then all three of these articles were sent to the committee of "style and arrangement," where, for the present, I now leave them.

Now, how did the compact relating to the delivery of fugitives from service, which was taken from the Ordinance of '87, find its way into the Constitution? The Madison papers shall tell us. On the same 29th of August, the record says: —

"Mr. Butler moved to insert after article 15th, 'If any person bound to service or labor in any of the United States, shall escape into another State, he or she shall not be discharged from such service or labor in consequence of any regulations subsisting in the State to which they escape, but shall be delivered up to the person justly claiming their service or labor,' which was agreed to, *nemine contradicente.*"

And this is every word that was uttered in relation to this clause, either on this or on any other occasion during the entire convention, with a single pregnant exception, shortly to be stated. A bare reading of the clause, and an immediate, unanimous assent to its provisions. That is the whole record.

This provision of Butler's, the Court has, of course, noticed, is substantially like that contained in the ordinance, and was undoubtedly taken by Butler from that instrument which had been adopted by the Congress of the Confederation, then also in session, only forty-seven days before he introduced it into the convention. It was then still compact, and nothing else. No mention of Federal Government, much less any grant of power. Having been thus agreed to, this clause was also sent to the committee of "style and arrangement," to which, as we have already seen, the other three clauses taken from the old articles of confed-

eration had also been committed. The function of this committee (of which Benjamin
Franklin was chairman) was precisely what its
name imports. Its sole duty was to see that the
various provisions which had been adopted by
the convention should, without any change of
meaning or effect, be expressed in apt language, " style," and then " arranged " in a natural and orderly manner. What did this committee do with these four clauses ? After settling the style, but still preserving the effect,
they proceed to " arrange " the order in which
they shall be placed, and this is how they did
that : They took the clause relating to records,
which, until then, had stood last in order of the
four; but to which a grant of power had, in
the mean time, been added ; and put that at
the head of the list as a distinct section. They
then took up the clause relating to fugitives
from service. Add that clause to the one relating to fugitives from justice, and to that
again add the stipulation relating to the immunities of citizens; and these three stipulations
they constituted as the second section of that
article ; thus grouping together all those clauses
which constituted merely articles of compact
into one section, but separating into a distinct
section, and placing at the head of the list
what, though originally a compact, had been
purposely transformed by express words of
grant into a delegation of power.

But from this mere order of arrangement,
one sees at a glance that the committee of style
and arrangement thought there was something
in the first section, independent of its subject-
matter, which distinguished it from the other
three which they grouped into a section by
themselves. What was that ? *The one had a
grant of power in it; the others had none.* A
very obvious and conclusive ground for distinction.

In this order, the order in which they now
stand — these sections were reported back to
the Convention. What did the Convention do
with them ? The clause relating to fugitives
from service, as reported back, read : " No person legally held to service or labor in one
State, escaping," etc. ; but the Convention
struck out the word " legally," and inserted
after the word " State " the phraseology, " under the laws thereof," as it now reads, for the
reason, says Madison, that " some thought the
' legally ' equivocal, and favoring the idea that
slavery was legal in a moral point of view."
With this single change — one by the way of
the deepest significance in its bearing on other
questions yet to be discussed, — the Convention
adopted these clauses just as they were reported
back, and just as they now stand in the Constitution. This is the veritable history of each of
the provisions which constitute the first and
second sections of the fourth article; and the
lesson which it teaches cannot be mistaken or
forgotten.

But before leaving this subject, I desire to

advert briefly to some considerations which that
history suggests.

If either of the clauses which now constitute
the second section, contains any grant of power
to the Congress, so did the first section before
any grant was added to it. Congress already
had the power to prescribe the effect of records
as the article stood originally, if it has it now —
power either over fugitives from justice or service, or the immunities of citizens. But so
thought not Madison, who desired a grant;
Pinckney, who first brought it before the Convention, and the Convention which ordered
the article recommitted, that the grant might
be added. All these clauses were originally
articles of compact in confederation or ordinance ; as first reported to the Convention they
were still articles of compact; but on reflection,
the Convention agreed to add to one of them a
grant of power, and not to the other three ;
and this one clause which then stood last they
then make the first, and say that Congress shall
have the power to determine the mode of proving and the effect of the public records of the
States. Now why was power given them in
express language in that one clause, if they had
it already in all the clauses ? and they had it
in all, if they had it in either. Did n't Madison
and Randolph and Franklin, and the rest of
these men, have sense enough to know if it
was there already ? And if there already,
would Pinckney and Butler and Randolph,
the chiefs of the slave-holding interest, have
consented to the addition of the express grant
as to one of these clauses, unimportant to the
slave-holding States as such ; and by this very
fact of express grant in one clause have cast
doubt as to the existence of the power in
another clause, important to them alone ? No!
nobody understood there was any power there,
and if the Convention had wanted it there, it
would have done as it did with the first clause
— said in terms : and " the Congress shall have
power to prescribe the manner in which such
delivery shall be made." They wasted no
words, but they never omitted any when they
meant to give power to Congress.

And there was no reason why they should
ask the power. Judge McLean tells us in his
opinion in the Prigg case (page 660) that from
a very early period, fugitives from labor were
claimed and delivered up by the colonies under
a spirit of comity or conventional law. And
this statement is confirmed by the fact that no
complaints upon this subject were made in the
convention — that the topic was never alluded
to but twice during its session (28th and 29th
August) when the convention had arrived
within less than twenty days of the close of
its labors, and that the whole discussion thereon
on both occasions could not have occupied ten
minutes in all. The South, therefore, might
well have been content to secure, by compact stipulation, a continuance of the same
spirit of comity which had worked so satis-

factorily for them in the past, and the northern delegates with all their determination not to foster slavery or recognize it as a matter of national concern, might well be equally content to stipulate that they would continue to do precisely what they had been voluntarily and habitually doing from a very early period of their history, the manner of delivery being still as theretofore, left to their own exclusive regulation. That is the reason why this provision was adopted *nemine contradicente*. If it had been supposed that this clause gave any power to Congress, it would have been kicked out of the Convention. Does not all this make a clear case? If not, will somebody tell me how — the language remaining substantially the same — this clause did *not* convey power in July, '87, and *did* grant it in September, '87, two months later? At the same time, I would like to know how Roger Sherman and Elbridge Gerry were induced to put that power there? Why, six days later, when the clause apportioning taxes and representation came up again for discussion, the word " servitude," which originally stood there, was unanimously stricken out, and the word " service" unanimously inserted, on the motion of Randolph, a Virginia slaveholder, for the avowed reason that the former phrase was " thought to express the condition of slaves, and the latter the obligations of free persons;" while, at other times, Madison and Mason and other Southern men had declared their purpose not to recognize the existence of slavery in the National Constitution; and is it to be supposed that these men, and this convention, intended to give, or thought they were giving, power to this Government to keep up a continual raid and foray through all the States for fugitive slaves? Is it conceivable that they meant to constitute the catching of negroes as the first function of this free Government, and that that Government should be broken up the moment it failed to discharge that duty? Are we to believe that one half of the convention, just out of the blood and fire of the Revolution, with the smell of its gunpowder and the marks of its shot upon their garments — a Revolution begun, continued, and achieved to establish the inalienable rights of personal liberty, would have so far belied their principles, their instincts and professions, as without any cause, without any inducement, for no one asked or desired that this power should be given to Congress, as to make themselves and all their posterity voluntary parties to an eternal national slave hunt? Where is the evidence for this? Not a jot or tittle can be found anywhere. Why, from all the debates in all the State conventions, down through all the discussions before the people, through all the letters written or journals kept by the public or private men of that day, no single word or letter has ever been produced from which it can be inferred that any man, large or small, slaveholder or non-slaveholder, sane or insane,

in or out of the convention, supposed in 1787, that this clause contained any grant of power. Had the Northern States imagined that by assenting to this constitution they were thereby conferring upon the Federal Government the power to enter their territory in pursuit of a runaway negro; to employ the whole military and naval power of the United States in that pursuit; to subject their houses to search; to override their own municipal laws and regulations; to strike powerless the writ of *habeas corpus;* to deny the right of trial by jury; does any one believe that it would have received the assent of a single State, nay even of a single freeman in all those States? Why, to speak of no other names, Samuel Adams, thundering out from Massachusetts, and Patrick Henry, Virginian as he was, responding from Virginia, would have rocked this continent from end to end, till, of this elaborately contrived structure, not one stone should have been left upon another. And here I leave the history of this clause; but, before doing so, I desire to express my obligations for the strongest points which it furnishes to the literally exhaustive argument of the lamented Rantoul on the same topic. If there is any truth in history, any force in reason, this clause is to-day what it was on the day in which it first saw light, a compact stipulation, and not a grant of power. Now, if to the result already attained from a consideration of the text of the Constitution under any rule of interpretation known to the law, I add the coincident result attained from the history of the clause itself, the conclusion that Congress has no power over this subject, and its corollary that the applicant is unlawfully detained in custody, is established with all the completeness and certainty of a mathematical demonstration.

But then I am told that, however absolute and irresistible the demonstration may be, it comes too late. Some of the State Courts, and the Supreme Court of the United States, it is said, have ruled the other way. So much the worse then, be it said with due respect, for the State Courts, and even the Supreme Court of the United States. If the result at which I have arrived be the true one, and I submit this to the judgment of the Court, then it is absolutely of no importance to the success or stability of that demonstration what any Court has said or ruled about it. If they have decided contrary, their decisions, of course, are erroneous, and they beat in vain against its steadfast base. There are such cases. But is this Court to override the CONSTITUTION, because other courts, no matter of what rank or how many, have done so? If a wrong adjudication is made in one case, must every other like case, therefore, be also wrongly determined? If one man starts upon the downward road, is every other man in the universe to follow till the precipice yawns sheer? When and how, in this blind adherence to acknowledged error, is the right ever to be established? Settled? *Why, no question which concerns constitutional freedom can ever be settled till it is settled absolutely right.* You may pile decision on decision till from the summit of the mass you can scale the heavens, but it will avail nothing against the inherent, irrepressible power of the Constitution to vindicate even against judicial chicane the guarantees with which it has fortified the liberties of the citizen. At some time — I know not when, perhaps it may be now — there will be found some Judge, some Court — oh! may it be this Court! — which shall, by a few fit words so fitly spoken, as to carry conviction to all hearts and heads — establish the RIGHT at once and for all coming ages.

Let us see, however, precisely what the cases cited are, and what it is that they are said to have "settled." The cases referred to by the counsel for the Federal Government as having been decided by the State Court, are four in number: Wright v. Deacon, 5 Serg. & Rawl. 62, in Pennsylvania; Commonwealth v. Griffith, 2 Massachusetts Rep. 11; Jack v. Martin, 12 Wend. Rep. 314; and 14 Wend. Rep. in New York, and lastly, the Simms case, 7 Cushing, again in Massachusetts. These are all in which so far as my researches have extended, the question of the power of Congress to legislate upon this matter, has been the subject of discussion by any State Court of the last resort. Other cases there are in which the Fugitive Act of 1793, has been acted upon; but none other, I think, in which the question now made was discussed. Of these cases, the first three arose under the act of '93; the last under the act of 1850, and this last case I shall leave for consideration to a later period of the argument.

Before, however, examining these cases, it will not be amiss to state the history of the act and the effect of its provisions.

In 1790, some Virginian kidnapped three free negroes from the State of Pennsylvania, and carried them into Virginia. He was indicted for the offence in the proper court in Pennsylvania, and thereupon the Governor of that State made a requisition in due form, on the Governor of Virginia for the surrender of the kidnapper. The Governor of the latter State affecting to have scruples about his power to surrender, consulted the Attorney-General of that State, and finally, upon his written opinion, declined to make the surrender, on the ground that he had no power, under the Constitution, till Congress should prescribe the manner of its exercise. The Governor of Pennsylvania forwarded the correspondence to President Washington, who laid it before Congress. A bill covering this subject, originated in the Senate; but by whom it was introduced, favored or opposed, what was the original form, what were the changes by amendment, what the discussions upon it, we know not, since the Senate

then sat with closed doors, and no journal of its debates, if any were kept, has ever been published. But at length it came down to the House in the simple form of an act to provide for the extradition of fugitives from justice. Some astute slaveholder seeing the opportunity for a valuable "compromise," added a second section, providing for the extradition of fugitives from service, and the North were coolly presented with this alternative: —

"We, the South, will protec from punishment all your runaway criminals, unless you give up all our runaway slaves."

Under this pressure, I am sorry to say, the act in both sections passed into the forms of law. Thus this famous (or why not infamous?) act found its way on the Statute Book. This history of its passage suggests a reflection not irrelevant to the case.

Though the clause in the Constitution stood precisely the same in 1791 that it had been during the ten years of the confederation, and though during these ten years no State had before objected or could object to its want of power to surrender, yet we here find it made for the first time. Looking at the offence which the fugitives had committed, there can be no doubt of the cause of the refusal. He had kidnapped a negro, and it is no strained inference to add, had reduced him to slavery; and thus Virginia, in order to protect the man-stealer against the consequences of an act done in the interests of slavery, committed a direct aggression upon the Constitution, and this first aggression was cunningly made the pretext of another aggression, still in the interests of slavery, by inducing Congress to usurp the power of providing for the reclamation of fugitive slaves. And here, and then commenced the first of those assaults upon the integrity of the Constitntion, which have been constantly renewed with fresh vigor every day, until what with Prigg decisions, and Dred Scott decisions, all of its ramparts have been breached, and that instrument, designed to be the great charter of freedom, has been converted into an immense machine, which operates chiefly in two ways; one in the catching of runaway negroes, the other in planting this "abomination of desolation" in "fresh fields and pastures new." But to recur to the act of '93. The third section of the act in substance, authorizes the owner of a fugitive from service to seize the fugitive and take him before any Federal judge residing within the State, or before any magistrate of any county, city, or town corporate in which arrest is made; and on proof being made to the magistrate that the person seized doth owe service to the claimant, it is his duty to give certificate thereof, to claimant; which shall be sufficient warrant for removal of fugitive to the State. The last section visits with a penalty of five hundred dollars, for the benefit of claimant, any one who shall obstruct or hinder him in so seizing fugitive, or rescue fugitive from him, or conceal or harbor fugitive after notice. As before stated, all the State adjudications cited save one, arose under this act which, be it noted, depends for its efficiency, wholly upon the action of State authorities, for in most of the free States you can only find a single Federal judge, and in the great proportion of the cases, it would be quite impracticable to take fugitive before Federal judge.

Now, let us look at the cases decided under this act. [Mr. Wolcott here subjected each of these cases to a rigid analysis, showing the precise facts, and questions involved, and then proceeded.] Thus, may it please your Honors, it is seen, that in none of these cases had any Federal functionary undertaken to execute this act, and that each of these cases, if they "settle" any thing as to the power of Congress, settle only the one point, *that Congress has power to devolve the duty of delivering up fugitive slaves upon State magistrates and State officers.* Let this result of the cases be especially kept in mind.

Next in the order of time, we come to the famous Prigg case, 16 Peters' Rep. 650, decided by the Supreme Court of the United States, and which it has also said, "settles" the question. So much stress has been everywhere laid on this case that it must be thoroughly examined; and, by the blessing of God, I mean to do it justice.

Let us first see the precise question it involved. Pennsylvania, in 1826, at the request of the State of Maryland, passed an act providing for the extradition of fugitive slaves, through the action of its own State, judges, and officers, of which it is now sufficient to the present purpose to state, that it punished, by the most severe penalties of fine and imprisonment, any person who should — except in accordance with the provisions of that act, or of the Fugitive act passed by Congress in '93 — carry any colored person out of the State with the intent to reduce him to the condition of a slave.

Prigg and his co-defendants were indicted before the proper courts of York county for forcibly taking away Margaret Morgan, a colored woman with intent to reduce her to the condition of a slave, contrary to this act. The jury returned a special verdict, finding, among other things, that Margaret was formerly a slave in Maryland; that five years before the seizure she had escaped into Pennsylvania; that the defendants, as the constituted agents of her former master, had seized Margaret and children — one of whom was born more than a year after the mother had escaped — took them by force into the State of Maryland, and there delivered the mother and her children as slaves to her former master. Upon this verdict the court below rendered judgment against defendant, *pro forma,* under special legislative act, and, after some intermediate proceedings, not necessary to be stated, a writ of error was prosecuted out of the Supreme Court of the United States to re-

view this judgment. This is the whole case; and upon this simple statement it is obvious that the only question before the Court was the validity of this act of Pennsylvania. Accordingly, the very first question considered by the Court, was as to the effect of the constitutional provision upon the rights of the owner of an escaping slave; and the Court unanimously held that this provision of the compact so far executed itself as to confer upon the owner the right of recaption; and, consequently, that the act of Pennsylvania, which attempted to prohibit and punish the exercise of this right, was void. Now, when the Court had held this, the case was decided; and no question could possibly be made in that case as to the power of Congress. No matter whether it had or had not power, when it was once held that Prigg had, under the Constitution, without any legislation, State or Federal; nay, in spite of legislation, the right to seize Margaret, that case was ended; all other questions were *coram non judice;* and every thing that is said about the power of Congress is the purest *obiter;* which, however forcible as a mere argument, carries with it no weight as authority whatever.

This case, then, "settled" nothing as to the power of Congress, but leaves that question just as open as before the case was decided. It still remains, however, to examine the *obiter* opinion expressed by the Court, not because authority, but as presumably the strongest presentation that can be made of the argument in favor of the existence of the power.

At the very outset of the case, it is openly confessed that, in order " to free the case from difficulty," it is necessary to resort to a new rule of construction, exclusively applicable to this clause, without reference to those which generally apply to all of its other parts and provisions. But what authority had the Court thus to ignore all the rules previously established by its own uniformly concurring decisions, as those alone applicable to the interpretation of constitutional provisions? and why is it that the rules which lead to right conclusions in all other cases, are to be openly repudiated here? The truth is, and it is right to speak it boldly, that the Court well knew that any rule heretofore recognized would absolutely exclude the idea of any power in Congress, and as it had predetermined to come to the opposite conclusion, it began its work by throwing these rules to the winds. Having thus liberated itself from all allegiance to the rules of reason, the law of logic and its own declared canon of interpretation, the Court proceed directly to the oft-cited provision of the fourth article.

Its first proposition, and one that underlies its whole reasoning is, that, " Historically, it is well known that the object of this clause was to secure to the slaveholder the complete right and title to their slaves as property in every State into which they might escape," — " and that the full recognition of this right was so vital to the slaveholding States, that it constituted a fundamental article, without the adoption of which the Union could not have been formed."

It is quite difficult to speak of these two paragraphs respectfully, and yet with that fidelity to truth from the obligation of which no one can absolve himself, — that fidelity requires me to say, that no greater mistake, as to undeniable historical fact, was ever committed, than is embodied in those two assertions.

All the world now knows, and I have already shown, with what painful and anxious care the framers of the Convention — slaveholders and all — Madison and Mason, and even Randolph, the special and ablest advocate of the slaveholding interest — excluded from the Constitution the idea that there could be property in man.

But, again, so far is it from being true that this clause was deemed vital to the slaveholding interest, that it was not even named in the Convention till it had been in session more than three months, and within less than sixteen days of the time when the Constitution was reported complete; that the subject was never mentioned save by two slaveholders — Butler and Pinckney; — that it never came before the Convention except on two succeeding days; that the whole discussion on it could not have occupied ten minutes; that no complaint was made that any State had hitherto refused to surrender fugitives; and that it was agreed to *nem. con.* for the obvious reason that it only embodied a stipulation to continue that spirit of comity which the States had theretofore voluntarily observed in respect to the same matter. This matter was in no sense one of the compromises of the Constitution, and was never hinted at till long after all those compromises had been definitely settled; and not, indeed, until after all the provisions deemed essential to be incorporated in the Constitution had been agreed on, and referred to a committee to report back in due form. The compromises were five: —

1. Power to regulate commerce.
2. Prohibition of duties upon exports.
3. Weight to be assigned to the States.
4. Basis of taxation and representation.
5. Power to prohibit African slave-trade.

And this subject had nothing to do with either. Founding myself on these undeniable facts, I am justified in affirming that the assertion, that the adoption of this clause was a fundamental condition of the Union, has no foundation whatever.

THE CHIEF JUSTICE — Mr. Wolcott, I think you have omitted one statement that was made in the Convention.

THE ATTORNEY-GENERAL — By sheer inadvertence, then, if your Honor please!

CHIEF JUSTICE — Of course, sir; but there is a statement which I think you will find has escaped your attention.

THE ATTORNEY-GENERAL — Possibly; will your Honor please mention it?

THE CHIEF JUSTICE — Mr. Pinckney, of South Carolina, said he would not vote for any Constitution unless it protected property in slaves.

THE ATTORNEY-GENERAL — This statement of Pinckney did escape my attention. But the fact that no one went with Pinckney, is of the last significance. I do not understand your Honor to say that there was any one save Pinckney took this ground, and this solitary remark of a solitary man upon a solitary occasion, certainly furnishes no justification for the broad assertion of Mr. Justice Story, that the adoption of such a provision was fundamental to the formation of the Union.

But to proceed. Upon this twofold mistake of fact, the Court assume that this clause must be so constructed as to effect the object erroneously imputed to the convention in adopting it, and so they affirm " that it manifestly contemplates the existence of a positive unqualified right on the part of the owner of the slave, which no State can in any way restrain, qualify, or control," and that any State law or State regulation, which interrupts, limits, delays, or postpones the right of the owner to the immediate possession of the slave, and the immediate command of his service and labor, operates, *pro tanto*, a discharge of the slave therefrom. The question can never be how much the slave is discharged from; but whether he is discharged from any, by the natural or necessary operation of State laws or State regulations. The question is not one of quantity or degree, but of withholding or controlling the incidents of a positive and absolute right.

Just consider this proposition for a moment. If a State, undertaking to discharge the obligations of this compact, arrest one supposed to be a fugitive, gives notice to the supposed master, and when he comes, says to him, " Sir! we have arrested this man as your fugitive slave, and now you have only to satisfy us that he *is* your slave, and we will deliver him over to you; but we can't give him till you do show that." This condition of delivery, it is said, " operates *pro tanto* a discharge," because it detains him from the "immediate possession of his master." You cannot, it is said, detain a man claimed as a fugitive slave, even to inquire whether he is a slave or not; for if it shall turn out that he is such slave, then you have been discharging him *pro tanto* from the service and labor he owes his master! Shall I stand here and beat the air? Shall I waste my strength and your Honors' patience over such a proposition as this? But this is the foundation of the conclusion that the States have no right to legislate.

But again, this argument, if good for any thing, cuts up by the roots the power of Congress to legislate. No one will pretend or admit that Congress has any more power to discharge, absolutely or *pro tanto*, the claim of the master, than have the States. But if the power to legislate, when vested in the States, implies the power to regulate, that is, to prescribe conditions, so also does the like power when vested in Congress; and if the provisions of a State enactment, requiring the master to prove his claim before a local magistrate, are, *pro tanto*, a discharge, so also are the provisions requiring like proof before a commissioner *pro tanto* a discharge; and if the one is for that reason incompatible with the Constitution, so equally is the other.

Having in this way arrived at the conclusion that the States have no power to legislate, the Court next proceed once more to affirm " that the clause puts the right to the service of labor upon the same ground and to the same extent in every other State as in the State from which the slave escaped, and in which he was held to the service or labor. If this be so, then all the incidents to that right attach also; the owner must therefore have the right to seize and repossess the slave, which the local laws of his own State confer upon him, as property; and we all know that this right of seizure and recaption is universally acknowledged in all the slave-holding States. Indeed, this is no more than a mere affirmance of the principles of the common law applicable to this very subject."

Then, after quoting Blackstone, he proceeds: " Upon this ground we have not the slightest hesitation in holding, that, under and in virtue of the Constitution, the owner of a slave is clothed with entire authority, in every State in the Union, to seize and recapture his slave whenever he can do it without any breach of the peace, or any illegal violence. In this sense, and to this extent, this clause of the Constitution may properly be said to exclude itself, and to require no aid from legislation, State or National."

Now of this monstrous proposition I have to say again, not only what everybody now knows to be true — that the Constitution nowhere recognizes property in man, and therefore nowhere recognizes the right of private recaption, which is incident only to property — but that this very clause affirmatively excludes all possible idea of such recognition. For upon whom does this clause, by its very terms, operate? " Persons," not property — MEN, not chattels. Why, if this man whom Bushnell undertook to rescue, and whom Langston undertook to rescue, was not a *man*, a " PERSON," within the ordinary meaning of that phrase, then he is not comprehended by this clause; and how is it that they have been indicted, tried, and convicted of an attempt to violate this clause by rescuing a " person " — so the indictment calls the fugitive " John " — within its operation? I know, that according to the Dred Scott case, and still more emphatically by this very Prigg case, John is not a " person," but a " thing," — for this Prigg case declares his *status* in the free States to be precisely what it was in the slave States. But in the slave States, John was not a " person," he was an article of prop-

erty, a chattel, and nothing else. In Ohio, then, by this decision, John was not a person; it was therefore no offence to rescue him, for the fugitive act speaks of " persons " only, and these applicants having committed no crime, must be discharged. Thus, this Prigg case, in its holding that an escaping slave is still a slave, as he was in the slave States, falls into the inevitable absurdity of withdrawing such slaves from the operation of this clause, which applies to " persons " only. Such is its suicidal construction. But to proceed.

This decision to the contrary, I affirm that John was a " person " *here* — still owing service, if you please, to his former master in Kentucky, but yet a *person* and nothing else. The Federal Constitution calls him a " person," the fugitive act calls him a " person," the indictments now before your Honors call him a " person," the conviction under which these applicants are confined is void if he is not a " person," and most of all, God made him erect and stamped on him every attribute and characteristic of manhood. The laws of Kentucky may deny his personality, and treat him as property, but these laws have no extra-territorial operation. When, therefore, John left Kentucky he left that local *status* which the local laws alone gave him while there. The laws of Kentucky were left in Kentucky, for certainly they could not cross the Ohio river. The moment, then, John touched Ohio he became invested with the characteristics which the Constitution of this State and the Federal Constitution impressed upon him, with these and none other, since these alone bear sway on the soil of Ohio.

How do these regard him? The Constitution of Ohio pronounces him a man, and, save as to the single right of suffrage (and even that he may acquire by residence, if he be less than half black), he stands here on an equality with the Governor of your State. Subject to the clause in question, which I will presently consider — he has all the rights and is entitled to all the protection which our laws extend to any of our citizens. He may sue and be sued; contract and be contracted with; acquire, hold and enjoy property which even his master may not touch; give and be given in marriage, and rear up children which, thank God, are all his own. How does the Federal Constitution regard him? Still as a man, a " person " but as a person owing labor and service *in* Kentucky, and under *its* local laws, to his former master. All that the Constitution of the United States requires is that Ohio shall not discharge this person from the obligation of labor and service which he owed in Kentucky under its laws, and shall, on " claim " of the party to whom, by those laws, his labor is due, deliver up this " person " — this man. It does not recognize the fugitive as bound to labor *here* in Ohio for his master, but as still owing it in Kentucky, not elsewhere, and it requires Ohio to deliver him up, that he may be returned to Kentucky, and *there*, in that State — render the service which he owes *there and there alone*.

Like Archilles, he is invulnerable, save in a single spot. Subordinate only to the single, but awful contingency of a claim properly proven by the very party — no one else — to whom in Kentucky he owed service; and of his return to the condition of a slave, when he shall again come within the territorial limits of that State; subject, I say, to this one awful hazard, John, in Ohio, was, to all intent and purpose, a freeman. Thus, this right of recaption, which has no existence, save as against *slaves in the slave States*, cannot be asserted in the free States. Here this point might be left, but let us look a little farther at this proposition of the Prigg case.

The master, it is said, has, as against his escaping slave in the free States, "the same right," to the "same extent," and with "*all* the incidents" which he had under the local laws of the State from which the slave escaped. So, then, all the local laws of all the slave States, with all their hideous enginery of cruelty and torture, follow a slave fleeing into Ohio; and upon its FREE soil do all these slave codes bear supreme sway? The *same* right? *All* the incidents? Never, never! The very first incident of that right, nay, the very essence of that right, is to constrain by force the labor of the slave! May the master erect the whipping-post before your capitol, and use the lash upon his fugitive woman slave in Ohio, if she refuse here to work for him? Another incident of that right is, to brand the slave or slit his ears to mark him as his property! May *that* be done in Ohio by the owner of a runaway negro? Another incident is, that on the rule of *partus sequitur ventrum*, the offspring of a slave mother is also a slave, though the father be free. But may the slave-owner claim as his property the issue of a fugitive slave woman who was here intermarried with a freeman? Still another incident is the right of the master to sell him! Can he open a slave auction here for the fugitive?

Another incident is the right by the law of the slave States, to kill the slave if he resist by force the master's attempt to punish him? May *that* be done here? Is the right guaranteed by the Constitution to the master to MURDER in Ohio his fugitive slave? Don't let it be said that this is exaggeration. For by precisely the same process by which you establish here the right of recaption, you equally establish here every other incident of this system. No matter how hideous it may be. Indeed, that is the very major proposition, for, say the Court, the master has here "the same right" as to a runaway slave, which he had in the slave States, "with all the incidents" which the local law gave, that local law (such is the deduction) confers the right of recaption, therefore that right exists in the State to which the slave has fled. If one incident given by the

local law follows the fugitive here, so do all. What some of these incidents are, we have seen. Again, I say, NEVER! We *won't* have the whipping-post in Ohio. We won't have the knife, and the branding-iron, or the revolver here. We won't have the barracoon here. We won't legalize murder here. If a slaveholder whip his fugitive slave in Ohio, it is a battery, and he shall go to jail for it. If he slit his ears, it is maiming, and he shall go to the Penitentiary for it. If he kill the slave for resisting the lash or the branding-iron, it *is* murder, and he shall hang for it, though there were a thousand Prigg cases, as Georgia hung Graves and Tassells over the writ of error of this same Supreme Court. God bless Georgia for that valiant and beneficent example!

And here I leave to the just contempt and just indignation of all freemen this hideous dogma of the asserted power of recaption. It has no existence; and this point is of vital importance, for Bushnell is convicted only of obstructing an attempt at a mere private recaption, and if this power has no constitutional warrants, then Bushnell is unconstitutionally restrained of his liberty, and must be discharged.

The next proposition of the Prigg case is, that the simple right of recaption must, in many instances, prove unavailing; the owner may not be able to lay his hands on the slave; persons may secrete him; local legislation may limit him as to the proofs of ownership; or the Courts in which he shall sue or the process he may resort to, or fail to aid him in any way, so that it is said if the Constitution gave nothing but the power of simple recaption, it would prove a delusion and a snare; and the inference is that the Congress must have power to legislate. Now, all this supposes that the States would wantonly refuse to fulfil their solemn compact. But what right had the Court thus to insult the whole community of free States? What, in their past history, justified this calumniation? On the contrary, I say that, in spite of the odious nature of the duty which this compact imposed upon the free States, they fulfilled it with too much alacrity, too much fidelity — too few safeguards to protect the citizen, until this very Prigg case withdrew the subject from their control; and Congress, following its lead, endeavored to give the force of law to an act which not merely humbled the sovereignty of the States, but struck down, by a single blow, all the constitutional guaranties of the liberty of the white citizen; an act which no man can read without the utmost indignation.

But, again. If that was the theory — if the Convention did not mean to trust to the legislation of the States, just as little would they have trusted to the legislation of Congress, controlled as that has always been, in one branch, at least, by the Northern States; and the Constitution itself would have prescribed the specific mode, and leaving nothing to the States either in or out of Congress.

But still, again, when, before, was the falsely imputed infidelity of the States made the grounds for implying in Congress power to remedy such assumed possible or probable neglects?

And how, and where, in the Constitution, do you find any power in the Congress to assume a duty belonging to the States, because the States refuse to discharge it? Nowhere!

The Court next proceed to assume that this clause " implies at once a guaranty, and enjoins a duty, that it contemplates" some remedial measure "beyond the rights of recaption; that many questions arise as to the nature of this contemplated remedy; that legislation alone could determine these questions; that where a duty is enjoined, the ability to execute it is implied; that the " clause is found in a National Constitution, not that of a State;" that "it does not point out any State functionaries who shall execute it," and that " the natural, if not the necessary conclusion " is, that in the absence of all express provision to the contrary, the General Government is charged with the execution of the duty, and has therefore power to execute it.

It will be found quite difficult to find, elsewhere, a course of reasoning which violates so many canons of constitutional interpretation.

It not only starts out with a pure assumption, (for where is the foundation? the assertion implies a *guaranty?* and *who* is the guarantor, who is the guarantee? and where are any words of guaranty?) but even with the aid of this assumption, can it derive power of legislation in Congress, only by a series of implication of not less than four successive gradations, in utter contempt of its own settled rule that the Congress had no *implied* power, save that which is purely auxiliary to those expressly granted. For see, it is just said that a guaranty and a duty is implied (implication 1); next, that the nature of the duty implies the necessity of legislation to its effective discharge (implication 2); that, as the States are not specially named, and the clause is found in the National Constitution, it is to be implied that the duty is enjoined upon the Federal Government (implication 3); that a duty enjoined implies the power to execute it (implication 4); and hence the Congress has power to legislate upon this subject. Need I stop here to argue that this process can never be resorted to in order to create a power in the Federal Government, or that if this piling of implication on implication is permitted, that the Federal Government may be proved to have power over every conceivable object? But again, the great step in this reasoning, by which the Court attempts to show that Congress has the power, consists in the assertion that because the clause does not specially devolve the duty on the States, and designate State functionaries for its discharge, it

is, therefore, to be *intended* that the duty is to be enjoined upon and the power given to Congress. The bare fact that it is found in the Constitution is of no significance, for there are many provisions there which do not grant power to Congress, and the rule is, that if power be not given in terms, it is not given at all. Still less important, that it does not point out State functionaries; for if the States themselves were to execute the clause, the selection of means to execute must, of necessity, be left to the States themselves. But neither, on the other hand, does it point out Federal functionaries; and this very omission *is* of stern significance, and conclusively proves that it is the States who are to execute it; for the rule of the Constitution itself is, that all agencies and powers not granted to the Federal Government, are reserved to the States and the people. And for the Court to assume that wherever State authority is not specially mentioned, Federal authority is to be implied, is not only a flagrant violation of all the principles heretofore asserted by itself, but a plain NULLIFICATION — I mean just what that word imports — of the tenth amendment, which declares all powers not delegated, to be reserved — that amendment which Jefferson so emphatically and so truly said was the "foundation corner stone of the Constitution." This reasoning of the Court I also leave to the judgment and common sense of this Court. But next: —

The Court next proceeded to say that the " claim " mentioned in this clause contemplated a demand "made by the owner of possession for the delivery of his slave," and must of course be made against some person (I add parenthetically that it must be against the slave himself, since usually he is in our possession), that this claim involves " a right of property capable of assertion in a Court of justice between adverse parties;" so that it "constitutes in the strictest sense a controversy between the parties, and a ' case ' arising under the Constitution of the United States, within the express delegation of judicial power given by that instrument." " Congress then may call that power into activity" so as to "give effect to that right," and " if so may prescribe the mode and extent to which it may be applied, and how and under what circumstances the proceedings shall afford a complete protection and guaranty to the right." Still, again, implication on implication.

Now I agree, nay I insist (and I mean to prove it before I close), that the claim mentioned in this clause constitutes a controversy between adverse parties — not as to a right of property, but a right of liberty — the master being one party, the alleged fugitive the other, and therefore that it is a suit, a suit at law, to be determined by some judicial power. Let this point in the Prigg case *not* be forgotten. But I stop here. I do not agree that this suit is to be determined by the Federal judiciary, for in all the Constitution I find no power over this subject granted expressly to that judiciary; none even by necessary implication. But without stopping now to controvert this at length, I have to say that this position proceeds upon the theory, for that is the argument of the Court, that a grant of power to the Federal Courts to determine certain cases implies a co-extensive power in the Congress to legislate upon the subject-matter of all these cases. Surely, surely this cannot be. By precisely the same process of reasoning, heaping inferred power on inferred power, the Federal Government would soon absorb all the powers of all the States.

Thus jurisdiction is given to the Federal Courts over suits, and appellate jurisdiction over the State Courts in certain cases between citizens of different States. The subjects of these suits are as various as litigation itself, land titles, notes, bills, policies of insurance, trespasses, frauds, matters of copartnership, and if a power of legislation over these subjects can be grafted by implication upon a judicial power, Congress may assume the whole power of regulating these matters within the States, and accomplish at a blow the overthrow of State sovereignty.

Whatever power the Federal Judiciary may have over this subject is preventive, not active — to restrain, not compel. If a State should by legislation attempt to emancipate all fugitive slaves within its limits, perhaps the Supreme Court of the United States, exercising its appellate jurisdiction, might declare such hostile legislation void, so far as respected the rights of the parties to the case then before it for adjudication. But this is the utmost scope of its power, — and, as for Congress, that I have shown has none. The truth is that whatever power the Federal Government has in this class of cases, if indeed it have any, is just the power of the judiciary of determining any case in which the question of the validity of unfriendly State legislation may be involved; and, second, power in Congress to provide an avenue by which such a case may reach the Federal tribunals; but not all power to legislate upon the subject-matter of the litigation.

In fine, of this whole opinion, it may be said that all of its reasoning consists either in an unfounded and pure assumption of the very question to be decided; or if the premise does not, in every instance, go to quite the length of begging the entire question, it does in every instance assume as its predicate some position false in fact or false in logic, and even upon this unstable basis is driven to the accumulation of implication on implication, in order to show power in Congress.

The argument of the Court next becomes again historical, and a most unfortunate attempt is made to show that contemporary construction and continued usage have practically settled the question in the same way.

And, first, the Act of 1793 is cited, which, it is said, was passed immediately after the adoption of the Constitution by Congress, composed in part at least of its framers, has since been uniformly acquiesced in and executed by the States.

But of this I have just to remark, first, that this act did little more than organize the States themselves to execute their constitutional duties under this compact, that the cases which arose were only few in number, that though objectionable in some of its features, it was not oppressively enforced, that it had none of the infamous provisions which characterize the Draconian Act of 1850, so that public attention was not roused, and that since the execution of the act was thus mainly left to the States themselves they might well acquiesce in it, not as having any binding force, but as furnishing a convenient mode of performing a duty which they had stipulated to discharge.

Again, however, this contemporaneous construction and long usage prove entirely too much, for so far were the States from supposing that they had no power over this subject, that most of them legislated upon this very point.

If the fact that Congress passed the Act of '93 is of any weight as touching the construction of the Constitution, surely the contemporaneous action of State Legislatures is entitled to no less weight. Now every slave State, at an early period, passed laws providing for the surrender of slaves escaping from other States into our limits.

Nor were the free States themselves unmindful of this obligation; nor odious as was the duty, did they seek to shelter themselves from its performance behind the miserable pretence that they had no power.

Thus Connecticut enacted an extradition law upon this subject. New York, New Jersey, Pennsylvania, Indiana, and Illinois each passed one, and perhaps each of the other States, though as to them I have no knowledge. Ohio, too, responding to the request of Kentucky, presented in a most imposing form, enacted a most stringent statute in fulfilment of this compact. The contemporaneous construction and usage of the States then prove that the power belonged, not to the Federal Government, but to the States.

But still more, the Supreme Court of the United States has again and again ruled that no part of the power of the Federal Government, judicial, legislative, or executive, could be devolved on State legislators, State judges, or State ministerial officers. Nay, in this very Prigg case it was established, if any thing was, that Congress had no power to compel State authorities to execute the duties imposed on them by the Act of '93, and if no power to compel, then it has no authority to devolve the duty on them; for authority to prescribe a duty implies power to enforce its discharge. Now the only feature of the Act of '93 which had any efficiency, the only one, therefore, which was generally called into action, was that which devolved its execution on State judges and State officers. The only usage under, and acquiescence in its provisions, was in that provision which enjoined powers on State authorities. But in this respect, say the Court in this identical case, the Act of '93, the contemporaneous exposition, the usage and long acquiescence prove nothing. In spite of all these, we now affirm that Congress had no authority to devolve the execution of this power on State authorities. If contemporaneous construction and usage can't prove that a supposed power has been rightfully exercised, still less, I submit, can this judicially condemned exposition and acquiescence be used to prove the very existence of the power. Here, then, the argument drawn from this source is shattered to fragments by this very Prigg case, though in the same breath cited by it as authority, and is buried beyond the reach of resurrection. Let no one who respects that tribunal, or who respects the dead seek again to invoke its false and ghastly presence. But the decisions of the State courts which I have already criticized, are next cited by the Court to fortify its conclusion. But as we have seen, the question in each of these cases was solely as to the authority of Congress to confer this power and impose this duty on State authorities, and the one point decided by them was that Congress had that very power.

These very cases are overruled, therefore, distinctly by this same Court, not only in Martin's Lessee v. Hunter, but in this identical Prigg case, and yet the Court, while in the very act of so overruling them upon the only point affirmed by them, cites them as authority for its own opinions. Let these cases, slain by the same relentless hand — be buried, too, in the same grave where their kindred — "contemporaneous exposition and long usage," now sleep their last sleep.

I have thus considered every position upon which the *obiter dicta* in the Prigg case are founded. As authority it has no weight whatever. How far will your Honors deem it prudent voluntarily to commit yourselves to its opinions; for you must do it voluntarily if at all? Let the result answer.

With a few more words which seem needful to its just appreciation, I take leave of that case forever.

While all the judges concurred in reversing the judgment of the Court below, yet Baldwin, J., did so only on the ground that the verdict found Margaret to have been a slave; and the owner could not be punished as a kidnapper in reclaiming her. He dissented from the *obiter* that the States had no power, or that Congress had any to legislate upon this subject. This left only eight judges, of whom five held that the power was vested exclusively in Congress; while three (Taney, Thompson, and McLean,) held that it was concurrent in the

States. But of the four who held it was exclusive, three delivered separate opinions, each stating that he could not concur in the reasoning by which his brethren had arrived at that result; of the three who held that the States had concurrent power, each delivered separate opinions, differing from his brethren in its reasoning; while of the eight who thought Congress had power, either exclusive or concurrent, six delivered distinct opinions, each one demonstrating that the principles upon which the others place their opinion are altogether wrong. Thus five arrive, each in his own separate way, at the result that this clause enjoins a duty on Congress, and then upon the principle that where duty exists, power to execute is implied — and that is their main argument — hold that the power is in Congress; while the other three, each in his own mode, arrive at the opposite result, namely, that the Constitution enjoins this precise duty on the States. These latter three thus demolish the position on which the other five erect their argument; while the logic of the five applied to the premise of the three — that this duty is enjoined on the States — destroys utterly the common conclusion of the whole eight, by demonstrating that the power belongs exclusively to the States. And this *obiter* opinion, which, beginning with a gross mistake as to the facts of history, without persisting in which its conclusion cannot be sustained, and proceeding on this mistake to erect a fabric of reasoning which utterly overthrows every rule of constitutional interpretation hitherto declared to be unalterable; which ignores the maxims that every presumption is to be made in favor of liberty; which not only overrules the authorities on which it assumes to rely for support, but in which each judge who aided in declaring it, is pronounced by his brethren to have been wholly wrong in his reasons for so declaring it, thus literally devouring itself — this extra-judicial opinion, it is now said, has "settled" the rights of thirty-three States, and grave questions touching the liberties of twenty-three millions of people. HAS IT? But I am reminded that the Prigg case has since been twice affirmed by this same Court in the Jones and Van Zandt, and the Booth case. Of course it has. Did anybody knowing *how* that Court is constituted (and I must allude to that presently) expect them to do ought but affirm it? Did n't they decide the Dred Scott case too? Now how did they affirm it? When these two subsequent cases came before them and in one of them the obiter of the Prigg case was utterly demolished by counsel, did the Court again consider the question according to the invariable custom, where a question depends on a single decision, which is assailed? No! but seizing hold of the extra-judicial opinions in the Prigg case, they say adroitly, if not truly; that *decides* the question; thus giving their own simple obiter the force of an absolutely conclusive adjudication! This is *res adjudicata* with a vengeance.

These, may it please your Honors, are the cases in which this question has been considered by the highest Federal Court. Before, however, taking leave of that Court, there is one consideration affecting the weight which ought to be given to its opinions, on this class of questions. It pains me that the fact to which I am about to allude is so; but my sense of duty will not allow me entirely to suppress it.

When the extra-judicial opinion of any Court is passed upon me as foreclosing by its simple assertion any question which concerns the sovereignty of the State, or the natural and constitutional right of the citizen, I cannot refrain from considering the claim to confidence which the dictum of its individual members might possess. My inquiry would not be limited to their learning and ability, but I should ask of the school of government, in which they had been trained; of their personal independence; of their freedom from bias or extra-judicial influences; and of their general fidelity to the great principles which underlie all *free* governments. Let me, then, barely, and with as much reserve as the truth will permit, allude to the manner in which this Court is constituted; giving voice only to what is in every man's head, and on every man's tongue, when the relations of this Court to any question connected with slavery are mentioned. How, then, is this Court constituted? Five of the nine Judges who compose it are themselves slaveholders, and therefore, directly and personally interested in all these questions. The other four are selected from the Free States, but upon what motives and by what influences are these selections governed? Let one or two well known facts answer.

During the administration of President Tyler, Mr. Justice Thompson, then resident in New York, a very able and learned Judge of that Court, died. As his successor, the President first nominated John C. Spencer, also of New York, one of the most learned, able, and eminent jurists in this or any other country. The Senate did not confirm the nomination of Spencer. Why? The President next sent in the name of that accomplished judge, Chancellor Walworth, the man, be it remembered, who, as Chancellor of the State of New York, had, many years before, when the case of Jack against Martin was before the Court of Errors of that State, declared that the Congress had no power to provide for the reclamation of fugitive slaves.

Of Walworth's fitness, there could be no manner of question. The Senate did not confirm the nomination of Walworth. Again, why? President Tyler then nominated Mr. Justice Nelson, who, when this same case of Jack against Martin, was before the Supreme Court of New York, had, as one of the judges thereof, delivered an elaborate opinion in which he affirmed that Congress had exclusive power to legislate for the delivery of fugitives from service. Of Mr. Justice Nelson, it is no disrespect to say that in none of the qualities which go to make up the great judge, would either Spencer or Walworth suffer by any comparison with him. *The Senate did confirm Justice Nelson.* Still again, *why?*

These undeniable facts warrant me in declaring, as I do here and now emphatically declare, that this Supreme Court of the United States is a sectional court, composed of sectional men, judging sectional questions upon sectional influences. And here I take leave of the Supreme Court of the United States and its opinions on the question.

Still again, however, it is said that some of the State Courts have, since the Prigg decision, declared their adherence to it. This is true, but every one has so adhered on the assumption that the questions discussed in that case were *res adjudicata.* How unfounded that assumption was we have seen. These cases all revolve about the Prigg case, leaning on that for support, *not* fortifying it; and if that can't stand alone, these *must* fall with it.

Let us sum up, now, the authority relied on to support the power of Congress. Three or four cases in the State Courts prior to the Prigg case, and virtually overruled by that; then the case of Prigg; then the cases of Van Zandt and Booth, and a few cases in the State Courts; but every case standing on the pretended authority of Prigg alone.

Now, if, instead of these few scattering cases, resting on a single extra-judicial assertion, — mistaken in its facts and erroneous in its law, — and on an intermittent usage pronounced to be wholly wrong, I had found a thousand cases, and the continuous, unbroken usage of centuries, I should still insist that the question was not settled; if, upon examining the settlement, it was clearly proved to be wrong. I repeat, again, that no question which concerns the liberties of the citizen can be settled till it is settled exactly right. The pathway of judicial history is strewn with wreck upon wreck of decisions, and with the broken fragments of usage on usage, by which Power has attempted — and though successful for a time — vainly attempted to fetter or undermine the rights of property, liberty, and life.

In adverting to this subject, I cannot forget that the raising of ship-money was practised for years, and the validity of that practice recognized time and again by Courts, till the days of Hampden, when its illegality was so strongly demonstrated that the same Courts, composed of different judges, were obliged to decide that, in spite of usage and precedent, the power was an usurpation of the ancient and undoubted privileges of Parliament. I remember, too, that General Warrants, though plainly prohibited by *Magna Charta*, had been constantly resorted to in every reign of every king for centuries;

that, upon elaborate argument and consideration, all the English Courts had, by a series of decisions, which you can almost count by the score, judicially affirmed their lawfulness, until Sir John Pratt, afterwards Lord Camden, by his great judgment in the case of Wilkes, overturned from its foundations this usage, hoary with the age of centuries, entrenched behind almost countless precedents, and in a single moment, forever established for the Anglo-Saxon race an unalterable exemption from the exercise of this arbitrary power. More, and most of all, I remember that, though the Congress of the United States had, from the very foundation of the government, and for an uninterrupted period of sixty years, asserted and exercised the power of legislating for the territories; though every President, from Washington to and including Polk, had officially approved its exercise; though the Supreme Court of the United States had by a solemn and unanimous judgment, pronounced by the revered Marshall, affirmed the undoubted existence of this power, and though, during all this time, no man had hinted a doubt as to its validity, yet we all saw in this same Supreme Court the temple of freedom, which, by the exercise of this power, we had been almost twice forty years in building, torn down in a single day! No, — I am wrong. It was *not* torn down, but only not, because of the impotence of these judges to shake its stable base. And now, when I am pressed with any decision of that court as concluding any right of the citizen, I reply simply and only, — " Dred Scott ! " Shall that Court extort more respect for its decisions than itself yields to them ? If so much usage and precedent may be overturned in the interest of slavery, surely, surely, an extra-judicial opinion may be well disregarded in the interest of constitutional liberty.

If, then, your Honors, looking to the text of the Constitution, shall be clearly, decisively satisfied that the Congress has no power to legislate in aid of the reclamation of fugitives from service — and that, I submit, has been demonstrated — then, in the name and by the authority of that Constitution, the SUPREME LAW, binding alike Judges and Presidents and Congresses by its absolute power, I invoke of your Honors — nay, I might not improperly demand — the restoration of these applicants to that liberty of which they are now restrained only by a flagrant usurpation, on the part of the Federal Government, of the undelegated power distinctly reserved to the States.

And here, if my own personal convenience alone was consulted, I should leave this case. Perhaps it ought to be left here; but the application involves other questions of the gravest moment, which it seems to be my duty yet to consider.

My next proposition is, that if — against, as it seems to me, all human probability and reason — your Honors shall be of opinion that Congress has some power to legislate upon this matter, still, the act of 1850 is in its essence and structure, a violation of the Constitution. And now I go back again to the clause itself, which provides "that the fugitive *person* who owes labor or service, shall be delivered up on claim of the party to whom such labor or service is *due*." By the preceding section, a fugitive person who is simply *charged* with crime is to be delivered up. Here, the person who is to be delivered up is not a person who is *charged* with owing labor or service, but only one who *in very fact*, owes it. The first condition of delivery then, is, that he owes labor and service; the second, that he has escaped. When is he to be delivered up? Of course, not until it is shown that he owes that labor or service. How is the delivery to be made ? On claim of the party to whom that labor or service is due. Here, then, are three questions of fact to be determined before the obligation to deliver becomes operative. 1st. That the person owes labor and service. 2d. That he has escaped; and 3d. That he owes such labor or service to the very person who demands his delivery. But how is the existence of these conditions to be ascertained ? Why a claim that such service or labor is due must be first made, and the claimant is denominated by the Constitution itself a "party." But the claim — and I here quote from the Wisconsin case — must be made of some one, and ordinarily can be made only of the fugitive himself, who, if he resists, becomes the other party. If he really owes labor and service to the party and has escaped, he must be delivered. If this claim is unfounded, or he has not escaped, he cannot be delivered up. Now, what can be plainer than that here is suspended a legal right, upon issues of fact and law ? That the determination of these issues involves the exercise of judicial power, and that consequently here is a suit or action to be tried ? The Constitution itself has arranged the issue and made up the parties. The Supreme Court of the United States has itself passed upon this very point twice. In Cohens *v.* Virginia, 6 Wheat. 407, they define a suit " to be the prosecution of some claim, demand, or request " — and in this very Prigg case, as we have seen, they rule that this " claim," whenever made, constitutes " in the strictest sense, a controversy between the parties, and a case within the judicial power."

The power, therefore, to adjudicate upon this " claim," to decide this " case " is — the Supreme Court itself being witness — an exercise of the judicial power — and if exercised under the Federal Government, of the judicial power of the United States. But the Constitution in terms, ordains that the whole judicial power of the United States shall be vested in one Supreme Court and in such inferior courts as the Congress may from time to time ordain and establish — that the judges of the Supreme and inferior courts shall hold their offices during good behavior, and shall at stated times receive for their services a compensation which shall not be diminished during their continuance in office." And in Martin's Lessee *v.* Hunter, the Supreme Court held that the power here given was the whole judicial power, and that Congress had no authority to vest any part of it elsewhere than in courts constituted of judges holding their offices by this tenure. The act of 1850, however, attempts to vest some portion of this very judicial power (so held to be by the Supreme Court), in certain officers called commissioners. But these commissioners are undeniably not "judges," within the language and plain meaning of the Constitution. A commissioner does not hold his office during good behavior, but at the will of the circuit court which appointed him, and he does not at stated times receive a fixed compensation, but is paid by fees, getting (O shame!) thrice as much from the claimant if he decides for him as if he decides against him. To this extent, then, the act of '50 is a clear violation of the Constitution. This point is fairly before the court, if it shall fail to recognize the power of private recaption; (and who can doubt that?) for then the only offence charged against Langston is that of resisting the process of a commissioner.

But I proceed to a still more serious objection. The Constitution by one of its amendments declares that "no person (mark that word 'person'), shall be deprived of life, liberty, or property without due process of law." What do these words, "due process of law," mean? What did they mean, when they were incorporated into the Constitution? They meant the trial of any right asserted against a man's liberty, life, or property, by a regularly constituted judicial tribunal, sitting in the light of day, proceeding after established rules, confronting the man with the witnesses against him, securing to him the right of cross-examination, and due opportunity to produce evidence in his own behalf.

That is what the words, "due process of law," mean. It was what they meant in Magna Charta, for there they were first used. But in spite of Magna Charta, it was the practice of English sovereigns, backed up by the servility of English Judges, down to the revolution of 1688, to seize men and try them before irregular tribunals, unknown to the common law, such as the Star Chamber, and which proceeded in secret, and in the absence of the accused. Or not unfrequently, when a man became obnoxious to the Crown, it would appoint commissioners, constituting irregular courts, not the regular courts of the common law, with stated terms, but often commissioned to try a specifically-named person, and they went down and tried the case in secret, without a jury, without confronting witnesses, without the presence of the accused, and upon ex parte evidence would take away his property, liberty, and life, and

attaint his blood. Right here let me ask, Will some one tell how the function of the commissioners and their manner of proceeding differs in kind or degree from that of the commissioners under the Fugitive Act?

It was in consequence of these arbitrary proceedings, by which this great barrier of the subject against the usurpations of the sovereign had been broken down, that it was again declared in the Petition of Right during the time of the first Charles, and still again affirmed in the "Bill of Rights" at the revolution in 1688. This great provision was obviously intended to protect Englishmen against such arbitrary secret ex parte proceedings; and it was put into the Constitution, by way of amendment, to protect all men against the same thing here. "Due process of law," then, means that careful, guarded, precise, and strict proceeding known to the English law, which is had in open and regularly constituted Courts, and which secures to every person due means and opportunity of defending his life, liberty, and property. But we are not without judicial authority on this point.

"The better and larger definition of *due process of law*," says Kent, " is, that it means law in its regular course of administration, through courts of justice."

"The *law of the land*"— (which is always held equivalent to *due process of law*)—"in bills of right," says Chief Justice Ruffin, of North Carolina, in the elaborate opinion delivered in Hoke *v.* Henderson, 4 Dev. N. C. Rep. 15 (and one replete with sound Constitutional doctrines), "does not mean merely an act of the legislature, for that construction would abrogate all restrictions on legislative authority. The clause means, that statutes which would deprive a citizen"—(in the Federal Constitution the word is "person")—"of the rights of person or property, without a regular trial, according to the course and usage of the common law, would not be the law of the land in the sense of the Constitution."

The Constitution, then, intended to secure to every "person" a regular trial in due course of law, before regularly constituted courts of justice, the party being allowed to be present, confront his witnesses, cross-examine them, and due time and opportunity of making his defence. But in all these respects the act of 1850 violates this provision of the Constitution. Now suppose you seize a man here in Columbus to-day, upon claim that he is a slave. When seized he is at liberty. The very first question is, shall this man, then at liberty, be deprived of this liberty? Whether he is white or black, you start out with the presumption in his favor, that he is free; a presumption older than the Constitution, older than the common law, older even than Christianity itself, for it was a maxim of the Roman law before Christ was born, and it is to-day a maxim engrafted on the laws of every civilized country, all the world over, except the slave States of this Christian Republic.

The question then is, shall he be deprived of his liberty ? *How* shall this question be determined ? The Constitution says, " Only by due process of law." It says that you shall not deprive him of that liberty in which you found him — that liberty to which the law presumes him entitled — you shall not hold him as a slave unless you first establish that he *is* your slave, by the judgment of a regular judicial tribunal, in a proceeding regularly instituted and duly conducted in open court, confronting him with the witnesses against him, or yielding him the opportunity to cross-examine them, and giving him reasonable time and opportunity to produce the evidence, if he have such, of his freedom. *This* is what the Constitution says you shall do before you shall take him away as a slave. But how does the act of 1850 say you may do this ? Let its provisions answer. By its very terms the judge or commissioner is specially enjoined to determine the case in a summary manner, and he is specially authorized and required to receive as evidence, *ex parte* affidavits taken in a distant State. Or by still another provision, upon the production of a record, made upon *ex parte* proof, in a distant State, perhaps years before, which certifies that the fugitive owes labor and service and has escaped — containing a general description of the person with such convenient certainty as may be — upon the bare production of this *ex parte* record, coupled with simple evidence of "identity," the judge or commissioner is required imperatively to adjudge him a slave and deliver him up to the claimant. And now I desire the court, by their judgment, to say, whether *this* is the "DUE PROCESS OF LAW," without which no man's liberty can be taken away — whether *this* is the tenure by which we all hold our property, liberties, and lives. But the safeguards for the liberty of the person do not stop here.

Another provision ordains that "in suits at common law, where the value in controversy exceeded twenty dollars, the right of trial by jury shall be preserved." This provision has been repeatedly discussed and passed on by the Supreme Court of the United States, so that its effect is no longer the subject of question. To the operative effect of this provision three conditions must co-exist: 1, a suit; 2, at common law; and 3, the value of the matter in litigation must exceed twenty dollars. Now, as we have already seen, the Supreme Court in Cohens v. Virginia (6 Wheat. 407), hold that the prosecution of a claim was a suit, and that in the Prigg case, that the claim for the surrender of a fugitive slave constituted in the strictest sense a "case," that is a "suit," "for the exercise of the judicial power." The proceeding then under the act of 1850 is a suit beyond all doubt or cavil. But next this suit is a suit at common law, and here again, fortu-

nately, not simply general principles but the Supreme Court itself has illuminated this particular question so as to exclude all possibility of mistake. To determine what is a suit at common law, we have only to look at the proceedings authorized and conducted under its own rules as distinguished from cases in equity or admiralty. Now looking back to very remote period at common law, we find that there existed a system of slavery known under the apt name of villanage, the slave belonging to the lord of the soil. This relation, with all its incidents and the mutual remedies given to master and servant, was duly regulated by the common law. Slaves then as now escaped from their masters. What was the remedy of the lord ? Without undertaking here to enumerate them or the precise nature of each, I may say generally that the lord could not seize and retain his slave, except in virtue of some common law proceeding which involved a trial by jury before one of the Superior Courts. Your honor will find the various proceedings enumerated and explained in Hargrave's notes to the case of "Somerset," 20 Howell's State Trials, 38.

Thus, as determined by that law itself, the remedy of the lord for a fugitive slave, was a suit at common law, a suit to be tried by a jury; and the forms of the writs, counts, pleadings, verdicts and judgments, in these suits are still to be found among the precedents of the common law. But this is not all. I come back again to the Supreme Court of the United States, and fortify myself with its authority. In Parsons v. Bedford (3 Peters, 456), considering this very constitutional provision, that Court says : —

" By ' common law,' the framers of the Constitution of the United States meant what the Constitution denominated in the Third Article, ' law,' not merely suits which the common law recognized among its old and settled proceedings, but suits in which legal rights were to be ascertained and determined in contradistinction to those where equitable rights alone were regarded, and equitable remedies were administered ; or where, as in the admiralty, a mixture of public law and of maritime law and equity was often found in the same suit.

" The amendment to the Constitution of the United States, by which the trial by jury was secured, may, in a just sense, be well construed to embrace all suits which are not of equity or admiralty jurisdiction, whatever may be the peculiar form which they may assume to settle legal rights."

Now, since the proceeding to recover a fugitive slave is not a suit in equity or admiralty, but is a suit to settle the legal right of the master to his custody and possession, it must be a suit at common law, within the meaning of this provision. Here, then, whether we look back to the common law itself to see what suits it embraced or to this exposition of the Constitution, the proceeding to reclaim a fugitive is a suit at common law. This point is "settled."

If, now, the value of a man's freedom is worth more than twenty dollars; or if, supposing him to be a slave, he is worth more than twenty dollars, he is entitled as of right and under the express sanction of the Constitution, to a trial by jury. And here again we have an exposition of the clause in this respect, by the Supreme Court of the United States. In the case of Lee *v.* Lee (8 Peters, 44), which was a petition for freedom, instituted by the appellants in the Court below, and there decided against them, objection was made that the value in controversy was not one thousand dollars; and therefore the appellants were not, under the statute of the United States, entitled to appeal the case to the Supreme Court. Now what did the Court hold on this question? I read from the report : —

"By the Court — The matter in dispute in this case is the freedom of the petitioners. The judgment of the Court below is against their claims to freedom; the matter in dispute is, therefore, to the plaintiffs in error, the value of their freedom, and this is not susceptible of a pecuniary valuation. Had the judgment been in favor of the petitioners, and the writ of error brought by the party claiming to be the owner, the value of the slaves as property would have been the matter in dispute, and affidavits might be admitted to ascertain such value. But affidavits, estimating the value of freedom, are entirely inadmissible; and no doubt is entertained of the jurisdiction of the Court."

This case, then, founding itself on principles of universal justice and humanity, affirms that the right of a man to his freedom is worth, not merely one thousand dollars, but is above all pecuniary valuation.

Summing up these results, what are they? Mark: I appeal now to no "new-fangled radical" doctrine; to no wild utterance of some fanatic, "crazy" on the subject of freedom; but to *res adjudicata;* to the Supreme Court of the United States, whose decisions are claimed by the other side to "conclude" every question within their scope. That Court first declares that the "claim" for a fugitive slave is a "suit." The same Court next declare that it is a "suit at common law." The same Court next declare that "the value in controversy in any such suit exceeds twenty dollars;" exceeds all valuation. All these results are "concluded" by the Supreme Court of the United States, if that Court can conclude any thing. The Constitution, then, as construed by the tribunal — here asserted to be its final expositor — ordains that upon every claim for the reclamation of a fugitive slave, he shall have the right of trial by jury. How do the learned counsel for the Federal Government like *this res adjudicata?* and how, upon their own reasoning, do they escape its force? If the decisions of the Supreme Court

have the effect here attributed to them, then the learned counsel for the Government cannot deny — this Court cannot deny — that the Fugitive act of 1850 is void.

The act of 1850 is also void on the further ground that it protects or assumes to protect the asserted right of private recaption — for an alleged obstruction of which Bushnell is now restrained of his liberty. The absolute non-existence of this pretended right has, I think, been already demonstrated, and might, perhaps, be left there. But I am yet to show that the exercise of any such power is not simply not authorized, but explicitly and affirmatively prohibited by three distinct constitutional guarantees. Now if, as I take it to have been already established, the master may not, by virtue of the adjudication of a commissioner which preserves some semblance of trial, seize and carry off this alleged fugitive slave, because that adjudication is the exercise of a judicial power, which cannot be vested in a commissioner; still less may a private person assume the exercise of that power and determine for himself his own rights. If the master cannot retake under the summary adjudication of a judge, because though it has the form of legal proceedings, it is not due process of law; and because it deprives the alleged fugitive of a jury trial; still less may he do it constituting himself judge, jury, and ministerial officer, without the intervention of any process, without the color of any adjudication. Still more, even than such an adjudication, is this infamous doctrine of recaption incompatible with the two constitutional provisions which secure the trial by jury and protect liberty against every thing but due process of law.

This doctrine is also pointedly prohibited by that other amendment which declares that "the right of the people to be secure in their persons, houses, papers, and effects, against unreasonable searches and seizures, shall not be violated."

Now I beg to know whether the seizure of a person, white or black, on the mere claim that he belongs to you, unsupported by oath, affirmation or evidence, without the color of process or pretence of trial, and the transportation of him to another State, where he is presumed to be a slave if he have a taint of negro blood in his veins, though no trace of it in his skin, I beg to know whether this is not just such a seizure as this clause meant to prohibit; and if it does not forbid this, what, in the name of freedom, *does* it forbid? In answer to these objections, it is sometimes said that neither the power of recaption, or the adjudication of a commissioner, deprives him of his liberty without due process, or of the right of trial by jury, but that when he has been taken into a slave State all these rights shall be accorded to him. I reply, First, that the very act of caption deprives him of his liberty. Second, that the adjudication of the commissioners not only in terms, pronounces him to be a slave, and delivers him as such to the absolute control of the claimant, but that adjudication, though rendered on an *ex parte* record, or *ex parte* evidence, is, by the act of 1850 itself, declared to be everywhere conclusive, in the slave as well as free States. I reply, thirdly, that the moment the master gets his fugitive, even without process, into a slave State, the maxim which presumed him free, is changed, and he is from thence intended in law to be a slave; and possession of him is *primâ facie* evidence of slavery; and, lastly, of those who babble about his instituting there a suit for his freedom, I desire to know how a freeman, sent as a slave to the rice swamps of South Carolina, in the custody of one who, in virtue of that very possession, is his presumed master, and who, as such, holds by law the power of life and death over him, — I desire to know how, under this absolute duress and with all these artificial and cruel presumptions against him, this free man is to assert his title to freedom? and if this is not depriving a man of his liberty, what act of forcible seizure can be defined as such? This paltry subterfuge is an insult not less offensive to common sense than to common humanity.

Finally, then, if the Court please, I arraign this ACT of 1850 as a FLAGRANT USURPATION BY CONGRESS OF WHOLLY UNDELEGATED POWERS.

1. Upon the argument drawn from the history of the Constitution, the truth of which history no man can gainsay, and the strength of which argument no man can resist.

2. Upon the authority of the Supreme Court of the United States itself, which, times without number, and everywhere, save in the Prigg case, in the Booth case, and in the Van Zandt case, has declared the great principle that Congress has no powers save those expressly granted, and such as are purely subsidiary to the expressly granted powers, so that obedience to the Supreme Court in the Prigg case, is disobedience to its judgments in a thousand other cases.

3. Upon the TEXT of the Constitution itself, which not only confers no power on Congress over the subject; but leaves all power with the States, in language too plain to be mistaken, too clear to admit of misinterpretation.

But if, notwithstanding these seemingly irresistible grounds for that impeachment, the Court shall nevertheless be of opinion that Congress has some power to legislate upon that subject — then I arraign this act as transcending those prohibitions of the Constitution which circumscribe and limit all Federal power, whether executive, legislative, or judicial, within impassable bounds.

1. It vests a vital portion of the judicial power of the United States in tribunals not known to, and inhibited by, the Constitution.

2. In a suit at common law, where the value in controversy exceeds twenty dollars, where it is beyond all price, it takes away the trial by jury.

3. It deprives all persons subject to its operation — and every person, white or black, is so subject — of their liberties, without due process of law.

4. It openly contravenes that right of the people to be secure in their persons against unreasonable searches and seizures.

Against this arraignment what do you find interposed? Denial of its truth? No What *is* the answer? Still and only still *res adjudicata*. But what is meant by this *resadjudicata?* Has any Court, Federal, or otherwise, ever passed upon the application now before your Honors? No such thing is pretended. Assuming the Fugitive act to be unconstitutional — and this plea virtually admits that — has any competent tribunal ever passed upon the rights of Langston and Bushnell in this behalf? No, for the proceedings in the District Court are a nullity. Will it be claimed that the judgment in the Prigg case, or the Booth case, operated by its own force to bind these applicants, that it estops them? Surely not. How then can the Prigg case or any other be set up here against them? Why, say the counsel, that case "settled" or "declared" as the law of the land, a certain rule which applies to these cases, and by which the rights of the relators must be determined. With deference I beg leave to say that Courts don't and can't settle or 'declare' the law of the land. In a constitutional government that function belongs to the law-making power, the legislature, alone. If Courts can usurp that function, it would be wise economy to abolish the Legislature and get that useless machine out of the way. What then *do* Courts settle? The rights of the parties litigant in each case, nothing more, nothing less, nothing else. In discharging this vitally important duty Courts endeavor to ascertain the principle of law which applies to the particular state of fact then before them, and ascertaining that or supposing themselves to have ascertained it, they decide the rights of the parties to that particular suit, accordingly. Obviously the only thing which has been adjudicated, is that one or the other of these parties shall have such judgment in his favor as the Court deems it proper to render, and that judgment becomes a law to *those parties* and the law of *that case.* Now a single decision or a series of decisions settling the rights of parties litigant, according to some supposed general rule, are *evidence* more or less strong, depending entirely on the strength of the reasoning, and the justice of the conclusion, that the rule acted upon in those cases is the right rule, and ought to be applied to all cases similarly circumstanced. But still such adjudications are only evidence, and the weight of their testimony, in favor of any supposed rule, must be determined for itself by every Court when called on to apply that rule to the resolution of any case pending before it. Every day's practice in every Court illustrates this. Judges sometimes err as to the correctness of a rule by which they decide a particular case, sometimes the error becomes inveterate, but finally it is found to be erroneous. Do even the same Courts, therefore, persist in deciding all future cases, by this wrong rule? Not at all. If the error involve any important question, touching property, liberty, or life, the Court applies the right rule, or what it conceives to be such, to the very next similar case that depends before it. Every Court, this Court, the Supreme Court of the United States, habitually disregards any rule affecting important interests by which they have decided previous cases, whenever satisfied that the rule is not the right one. On no other condition is improvement in the law possible. But how* could Courts disregard any such previously accepted rule, if it became the law of the land? For it is a mere truism to say that Courts are as much bound by the law of the land; have no more power to change or disregard it than the humblest citizen.

Your Honors, then, are not bound to follow the rule on which the Prigg, or the Booth, or any other case was decided, if, on careful examination and reflection, that rule is, in your judgment, wrong. Especially are you bound by your solemn oaths to disregard it if exercising your best judgment — and it is *your* judgment alone that must be exercised — you conscientiously believe it to be repugnant to the Constitution. To that you owe your first and last and chief allegiance; and if any case conflicts with it, you must throw that case to the winds. Why, to what end were the limitations and prohibitions of the Constitution to which I have adverted, and upon which I claim the discharge of these applicants — to what end, I say, were they made? For the very purpose of securing the natural birthright of man to his freedom, a right in itself a very sacred thing, by the most explicit and absolute recognition of its inviolability, so that — I quote from Burke — to the inherent sacredness of the right itself, is added the sanctity of that solemn public faith so formally pledged for its security. Against whom were these limitations and prohibitions directed? Undeniably against every department of the Federal Government, since they are operative only against that Government.

They were meant to secure this great natural, sacred right, not only against usurpations by the Executive and Legislative Departments, but especially as their subject-matter indicates, to protect them against the chicane of the judicial power of that Government. But can your Honors be made to believe that these very inhibitions, designed expressly to hedge in this judicial power, may be overpassed by it at its own pleasure; and that if in one or more cases, it has asserted its right to transcend these limits, this Court, and all other courts are forthwith bound,

by the very Constitution which has been thus violated, to acknowledge the existence of this asserted right? On the contrary, these formal recognitions and guarantees by the Constitution, of an original action of man, cannot be subverted, by even the judicial power, without uprooting "the holding, radical principles" of the Government, nay, even of the SOCIAL COMPACT ITSELF.

But then, I am asked, where is this to end? If the State courts refuse to recognize the general principles of constitutional interpretation declared by the highest Federal Court, which of the diverse interpretations, which, it is said, must then ensue, shall prevail? The question, though not pertinent, admits of several answers, but one shall suffice. Every court must, from the necessity of things, determine every case before it, upon its own view of law. If the given case be not within the appellate jurisdiction of the Supreme Court of the United States, the decision of the State Court is final, and there the matter ends. If, on the contrary, the case be within the appellate jurisdiction of that Court, it will decide that case on its own notions of the law, and as that decision will be final as to the case, there the case will end. This is the rule of the Constitution, and while it leads to no conflict of jurisdiction, it yet devolves on each system of courts its own proper rights and duties, and holds it to its own due responsibility.

Before leaving this topic, I desire to ask of those who insist so strongly on res adjudicata, which of two differing res adjudicata shall the Court obey? Shall it follow Martin's Lessee against Hunter, Cohens against Virginia, and that long bead-roll of cases in which the Supreme Court has declared that Congress has none but expressly delegated powers, — or the Prigg, and Booth, and Van Zandt cases, three by tale, in which it has declared an exactly opposite conclusion? And again, by the four cases which I cited when considering that subject, the Supreme Court declare in effect that no fugitive slave shall be delivered up until the master has established his right by the verdict of a jury. On the contrary, by the Booth case, that same court declares that he may be delivered up without such verdict. You cannot follow all of these cases. Pulled in opposite ways by these contending forces, to which shall your Honors yield? GO BACK, I SAY, TO THE TEXT OF THE CONSTITUTION, PLANT YOURSELVES ON ITS PRIMAL GRANITE, AND FOLLOW THE RULE WHICH YOU SHALL FIND SO PLAINLY AND INDELIBLY GRAVEN THERE. That rule needs no authority other than its own, for it is supreme. But if you still desire the authority of adjudged cases, I have shown them to you. I ask the Court to tread no new path. Let it stand *super antiquas vias*. Let it follow the ancient maxim upon which I have insisted, coming as it does from Pagandom down to

Christendom, surviving, by its inherent vitality of justice, the overthrow of empires and the wreck of civilization, — let it follow the track blazed out for it by the Supreme Court of the United States itself in the earlier — and it may not unfitly be added — the better days of the Republic.

There still remains a single topic of which it is difficult to determine how much or how little ought to be said. No man has dared to breathe it in this presence, and yet the Federal functionaries have filled the air with it, so that I hear and you hear it openly said, that if this court — following these ancient landmarks, following the track of the Supreme Court before it became a sectional court — shall, in the exercise of its highest and most imperative function, enlarge these relators, there will be a collision between the State and the Federal Government. WHAT THEN? Are we children; are we old women, that we shall be frightened from duty by this menace? Are the court, coerced by these threats, to pronounce a decision which shall stultify their judgments and blast their consciences? Has it come to this, that the Federal authorities, instead of invoking the appellate power of the Supreme Court to review your proceeding, are to trample your judgments under foot in your very presence? And are you, therefore, to remand these applicants to an unlawful imprisonment? If these be the only alternatives — if collision can be avoided only by striking down every safeguard with which the Constitution has hedged about the liberty of the citizen, LET COLLISION COME — COME NOW. Let the question be settled while I live. I don't want to leave the alternative of collision or of the absolute despotism of the Federal Government as a legacy to my children. But, do not misunderstand me. It is not in a judicial tribunal that one should hold the law as naught, or undervalue the inestimable blessings of order and peace. LAW I reverence; but not the "law of King Bomba." ORDER, I stand by that, but not the "order" which "reigned in Warsaw." PEACE — that I would preserve at almost any cost — but not that peace which is only the quiet of the grave.

But there will be no collision. These threats and fears are alike idle. If this court shall by its judgment discharge the relators, the Federal Government will acquiesce in that judgment until it shall have been reviewed in the mode contemplated by the Constitution. Whenever another like case shall again arise, the State Court will again discharge, and this process must be continued until the Federal Government, listening to reason, shall voluntarily return again to the sphere of its legitimate functions and duties; or until the PEOPLE, roused to action, and exercising the constitutional remedy, shall constrain its return by a will only less sovereign; and with reverence be it said — only less divine than the WILL OF GOD.

And here, I leave with your Honors, this case and all the great interests which it involves. Weightier consequences never hung on the arbitrament of any tribunal. The strain of the Federative System has come, and your Honors are to determine, at least for the citizens of Ohio, whether under that system there can be any adequate protection, for the reserved Rights of the States, or any efficient safeguards for the Liberty of the citizens. THE CAUSE OF CONSTITUTIONAL GOVERNMENT IS HERE, AND NOW, ON TRIAL. GOD SEND IT A SAFE DELIVERANCE.

SECOND DAY. — MORNING SESSION.

The masterly argument of the · Attorney-General occupied the entire afternoon of yesterday, and the morning of to-day. The Court adjourned till afternoon to hear argument in another and somewhat similar case.

SECOND DAY. — AFTERNOON SESSION.

After hearing argument in the case of the relator from Cincinnati, the Court took recess until Saturday morning, to make up its opinion.

THIRD DAY. — SATURDAY.

The Chief Justice, opening the Court, announced that as the case was one of much importance, and the authorities cited by counsel were numerous, the recess had been consumed in industrious labor, without finishing the work as thoroughly as it seemed to the Court desirable, and, doubtless, would also to all parties interested. The Court would, therefore, take further adjournment until Monday afternoon, at 3 o'clock, when it was hoped the decision would be rendered.

FOURTH DAY. — MONDAY, MAY 30.

At 3:24 the Judges took their seats. The opinion of the majority was read by Chief Justice SWAN, only a syllabus of which his Honor was willing to furnish for publication :—

JUDGE SWAN'S OPINION.

Judges SWAN, SCOTT, and PECK held : —

I. That the provisions of Article 4, Section 2, of the Constitution of the United States, "No person held to service or labor in one State under the laws thereof, escaping into another, shall, in consequence of any law or regulation therein, be discharged from such service or labor, but shall be delivered up on claim of the party to whom such service or labor may be due," guarantees to the owner of an escaped slave the right of reclamation.

II. That a citizen, who, knowingly and intentionally, interferes with, for the purpose of rescue, or rescues from the owner an escaped slave, is guilty of a violation of the Constitution of the United States, whether the Acts of 1793 and 1850, commonly called the fugitive slave laws, are constitutional or not.

III. That the question in this case, is not

whether the Fugitive Act of 1850 is unconstitutional in respect to the appointment and powers of Commissioners, the allowance of a writ of *habeas corpus*, the mode of reclamation, etc., but whether Congress has any power to pass any law whatever, however just and proper in its provisions, for the reclamation of slaves, or to protect the owner of an escaped slave from interference, when duly asserting his constitutional rights of reclamation.

IV That Congress, from the earliest period of the government has, by legislative penalties, vindicated the constitutional right of the owner of slaves against unlawful interference.

V. That such legislation was adopted in 1793, by the second Congress elected under the Constitution, composed of many of the members of the Convention who framed the Constitution, has, from that day to this, been in active operation, and has been acquiesced in by all departments of the Government, National and State; and the legislative power of Congress on this subject has been *recognized* by the General Assembly of the State of Ohio in their statutes; by the Supreme Court of the United States, and by the Supreme Courts of Massachusetts, New York, Pennsylvania, Indiana, Illinois, California, by the Supreme Court of Ohio on the circuit, and, indeed, by the Supreme Courts of every State in the Union, where the question has been made, and has never been denied by the Supreme Court of any State — the Courts of Wisconsin, notwithstanding the popular impression, not forming an exception.

VI. The right to rescue escaped slaves from their owners being denied to all citizens of the United States by the Constitution; Congress having prohibited it and enforced the prohibition by penalties; the Supreme Court of the United States and Courts of the free States having recognized and acquiesced in such legislative prohibition and punishment, if the question is not thus put beyond the reach of the private personal views of Judges, and if they possess judicial discretion or power to overrule on the authority of their individual opinions, this unbroken current of decisions and this acquiescence of the States of the Union, and change the settled interpretation of the Constitution of the United States; then there is no limit, and no restraint upon Judges at any time and under any circumstances, their own individual opinions, the arbitrary interpreters of the Constitution.

VII. Whatever differences of opinion may now exist in the public mind, as to the power of Congress to punish rescuers as provided in the acts of 1793 and 1850, no such vital blow is given either to constitutional rights or State sovereignty by Congress, thus enacting a law to punish a violation of the Constitution of the United States, as to demand of this Court the organization of resistance. If, after more than sixty years of acquiescence by all departments

of the national and State governments, in the power of Congress to provide for the punishment of rescuers of escaped slaves, that power is to be disregarded, and all laws which may be passed by Congress on this subject from henceforth, are to be persistently resisted and nullified, the work of revolution should not be begun by the conservators of the public peace.

Judge SCOTT orally assented to the foregoing, saying that he agreed with its logic in the main, and with its conclusions altogether. He might or might not write out his opinion hereafter.

Judge PECK delivered an elaborate written opinion, coinciding with Judges Swan and Scott, comprising a review of the decisions of the courts, and particularly of the State courts, upon the questions involved in the case, and treating the whole matter as a *res adjudicata*. We were not able to procure either the opinion or a synopsis of it. It was mainly an elaboration of the brief of Mr. SWAYNE.

JUDGE BRINKERHOFF'S OPINION.

BRINKERHOFF, J., said:—

Since the close of the argument of these cases — Sunday and a visit to my family intervening — I have not had time to do more than hastily to sketch a brief outline of my opinion on the questions they present. This I give; and I may and may not, as leisure or inclination may prompt, commit them to paper, with the reasons on which they rest more fully and in detail hereafter.

I. Under the advice of the District-Attorney of the United States, the indictments under which the relators were convicted, are appended to, and form a part of the return to these writs. The question whether they charge a crime or not, is therefore before us. Both indictments are fatally defective in this, to wit, that neither of them aver, that John was held to service or labor in the State of Kentucky "*under the laws thereof.*" 2d section, 4th article, Constitution United States.

1. This defect is not a mere error or irregularity. If it were, so far as this point is concerned, we should be obliged to remand the prisoners; for the writ of *habeas corpus* cannot be made to perform the functions of a writ of error. But, 2d. This defect is an illegality. The averment omitted is of the essence of the crime; without the fact omitted to be averred, there is no crime; for it is no crime to rescue from custody a person held to service or labor in another State *otherwise* than "under the laws thereof." If there was no crime charged in the indictment, the judgment of the District Court of the United States under which the relators are held is *coram non judice* and void;

they are illegally restrained of their liberty, and they ought to be discharged.

II. 1. The indictment against Bushnell contains but one count, which charges the rescue of John from the custody of an agent of the claimant of his labor and service in Kentucky — John having been arrested and held in custody without warrant or any color of legal process.

It appears, then, on the face of the record which is made a part of the return to this writ, that here was a person domiciled or sojourning in Ohio, a free State, and therefore presumed in law to be a free man, " unreasonably seized " and " deprived of his liberty," not only " without due process of law," but without the pretence or color of any process whatever. This arrest and custody was in direct contravention of the fourth and fifth articles of the amendments to the Constitution of the United States. The rescue of a person thus " unreasonably seized " and " deprived of his liberty without due process of law," cannot be a crime; and any statute or judicial procedure which attempts to make or treat it as a crime, is unconstitutional and void.

2. The indictment against Langston has two counts; the first of which is entirely similar to that against Bushnell; and the second of which alleges a similar rescue of John while arrested and held in custody under a warrant issued by a Commissioner of the Circuit Court of the United States, authorized by act of Congress to issue such warrant, and, under the authority thereof, to arrest, hold, and remove the person described therein to a foreign jurisdiction as a slave.

The acts of Congress referred to clearly attempt to confer on these commissioners the powers and functions of a court; to hear and determine questions of law and of fact; and to clothe their findings and determinations with that conclusive authority which belongs only to judicial action. And the issue of the warrant mentioned in the indictment was a judicial act.

These provisions of the acts of Congress referred to, and all warrants issued under them, are unconstitutional and void, for the following reasons: —

These commissioners are appointed by the Circuit Courts of the United States only; hold their office at the will of such courts; and are paid by fees. Whereas, by the express provisions of the Constitution of the United States (Art. 2, Sec. 2, and Art. 3, Sec. 1), the judicial functionaries of the United States must be appointed by the President, by and with the advice and consent of the Senate, hold their offices during good behavior, and receive a fixed compensation which may not be diminished or increased during their continuance in office.

The warrant of such a commissioner, therefore, is a nullity; it could afford no authority to hold John in custody; and to rescue him from such illegal custody could not, by the law of the land, be a crime; and therefore the imprisonment of Langston by way of punishment of such pretended crime, is an illegal restraint of his liberty, and he, too, ought therefore to be discharged.

III. These relators ought to be discharged, because they have been indicted and convicted under an act of Congress upon a subject-matter in reference to which Congress has, under the Constitution of the United States, no legislative power whatever.

As to the correctness of this proposition, there does not rest on my mind the shadow or glimmer of a doubt.

The federal government is one of limited powers; and all powers not expressly granted to it, or necessary to carry into effect such as are expressly granted to it by the terms of the Constitution, are reserved to the States or the people. Amendments, Art. 10.

" No person held to service or labor in one State, under the laws thereof, escaping into another, shall, in consequence of any law or regulation therein, be discharged from such service or labor, but shall be delivered up on claim of the party to whom such service or labor may be due." Art. 4, Sec. 2.

This is the only clause of the Constitution from which anybody pretends to divine, or in which anybody pretends to find a grant of power to Congress to legislate on the subject of the rendition of fugitives from labor. I can find in it no such grant. The first part of it simply prohibits State legislation hostile to the rendition of fugitives from labor. Such fugitive shall not be discharged " in consequence of any law or regulation " of the State into which he shall escape. " But shall be delivered up." By whom? By Congress? By the Federal authorities? *There are no such words;* and no such idea is hinted at. This is evident from an inspection of the whole of the preceding portion of this article.

Art. 4, Sec. 1: " Full faith and credit shall be given in each State to the public acts, records, and judicial proceedings of every other State. *And the Congress may by general laws prescribe the manner in which such acts, records, and proceedings shall be proved, and the effect thereof."* Here, in the first place, is a compact between the States respectively — an agreement of the several States to and with each other, that the " public acts, records, and judicial proceedings " of each shall have " full faith and credit " given to them in all. Had this section closed here, would any one claim that it embraced any grant of legislative power to Congress? I think not. But the framers of the Constitution thought that Congress ought to have the power " to prescribe the manner in which such acts, records, and proceedings, should be proved, and the effect thereof; " and hence they gave the power in express terms. When they intended a grant of power to Congress, and not a mere contract stipulation by, or injunction of duty upon the States, *they say so*, and leave us no room for cavil on the subject. But let us go on —

Sec. 2. "The citizens of each State shall be entitled to all privileges and immunities of citizens in the several States."

"A person charged in any State with treason, felony, or other crime, who shall flee from justice, and be found in another State, shall, on demand of the executive authority of the State from which he fled, be delivered up, to be removed to the State having jurisdiction of the crime."

That these clauses of section two are mere articles of compact between the States, dependent on the good faith of the States alone for their fulfilment, I suppose no one will dispute. They do not confer upon Congress any power whatsoever to enforce their observance. Then follows the last clause of section two, in respect to fugitives from labor or service, first quoted. And this, like all the other preceding clauses of this article, except the first, is destitute of any grant of power, or even allusion to Congress or the Federal Government. Now, if a grant of power to Congress was here intended, why this silence? If the framers of the Constitution intended a grant of power to Congress in this clause, why did they not say so, as they did say in the first section, in respect to "public acts, records, and judicial proceedings?"

It seems to me that no rational answer can be given to this question, except by a denial of such intentions. *Expressio unius exclusio alterius*, is a legal maxim as old as the common law. The express mention of one thing implies the exclusion of things not mentioned. It is the dictate of reason and common sense. It is a maxim which applies alike in the interpretation of contracts, statutes, and constitutions. Its application was never more obviously proper than to the question before us; and when applied, it seems to me to bring with it a force little short of mathematical demonstration.

Thus far I have reasoned as if we were ignorant of the history of the Constitution. But a glance at that history confirms the conclusions to which we are brought by the ordinary rules of interpretation, and makes "assurance doubly sure."

The Articles of Confederation, under which the struggle for Independence was carried through, and for which the present Constitution of the United States is a substitute contained *nothing but* articles of compact. The fulfilment of its obligations was dependent upon the faith of the States alone. The Congress could make requisitions, but had no power to enforce them.

Again: Certain provisions of the ordinance of 1787, for the government of the territory North-west of the Ohio River, were in express terms declared to be "Articles of Compact."

Now, every one of the clauses of the fourth article of the Constitution above quoted, was borrowed and transferred, with but slight verbal alterations, from the articles of confederation and the ordinance of 1787 — the first three from the former, and the last from the latter — with this exception only, that to the first of these clauses was added a grant of power to Congress to prescribe the manner of proof and effect of public acts, records, and judicial proceedings. Here, then, we have certain articles of compact — admitted or declared to be such, and nothing more — borrowed and transferred from one instrument to another, with no intimation of any change of their character as articles of compact, except in a single instance where the change is expressly declared. The inference seems to me to be irresistible, that, except so far as the change is expressly declared, they remained, after the transfer, the same as they were before — articles of compact, and nothing else.

I conclude, therefore, that the States are bound, in fulfilment of their plighted faith, and through the medium of *their* laws, legislation, and functionaries, to deliver up the fugitive from service or labor, on claim of the party to whom such service or labor may be due under the laws of another State from which the fugitive has fled. But the Federal government has nothing to do with the subject, and its interference is sheer usurpation of a power not granted, but reserved.

But, it is said, the question is settled, and our argument comes too late. I deny that it is settled.

The federal legislature has usurped a power not granted by the Constitution, and a federal judiciary has, through the medium of reasonings lame, halting, contradictory, and of far-fetched implications, derived from unwarranted assumptions and false history, sanctioned the usurpation. I deny that the decisions of a usurping party in favor of the validity of its own assumptions, can settle any thing. It is true that the courts and legislatures of several of the States have decided in the same way; but they have been decisions of acquiescence rather than of original and independent inquiry. The fact that such jurists as Hornblower, Walworth, and Webster thought on this subject as I think, shows that the question is not settled. The fact that a majority of my brethren, as I understand them, admit that if this were a new question they would be with me, and that they yield the strong leanings of their own minds to the force of the rule of *res adjudicata* alone, proves that this question is not settled. The truth is, it is not until recently that the mass of intelligent and inquiring mind in this country has been brought to bear upon this question. It required the enactment and enforcement of the fugitive slave act of 1850, overriding the most sacred and fundamental guaranties of the Constitution, and disregarding in its provisions even the decencies of legislation, as if for the very purpose of irritation and humiliation, and the fine and imprisonment under it of *white* men for the exercise of the instinctive virtues of humanity, to awaken general inquiry. That inquiry is now going forward. And so surely as the matured convictions of the mass of intelligent mind in this country must ultimately control the operations of government in all its departments, so surely is this question not settled. When it is settled right, then it will be settled, and not till then.

But contemporaneous construction is appealed to. I admit its weight, and its title to respectful consideration. But contemporaneous construction speaks with a divided voice. It is true, Congress as early as 1793 legislated for the return of fugitives from labor. But nearly if not quite every one of the old States had also legislated on the same subject in fulfilment of what they deemed a matter of constitutional obligation resting on them. And such legislation on the part of the States, old and new, continued until the Supreme Court of the United States, in the Prigg case, so late as 1842 (16 Peters, 539), assumed for the federal government exclusive authority over the subject. And those who appealed to contemporaneous construction should themselves respect it. From the foundation of the government until within the last ten years, Congress claimed and exercised without question, full and complete legislative power over the territories of the United States; and as early as 1828, in American Insurance Company v. Canters (1 Peters, 546), the Supreme Court of the United States, Chief Justice Marshall delivering its opinion, unanimously decided that in the territories Congress rightfully exercises the "combined powers of the general and of a State government." Yet, in the recent case of Dred Scott v. Sanford (19 Howard, 393), all this is overturned and disregarded, and the whole past theory and practice of the government in this respect attempted to be revolutionized by force of a judicial *ipse dixit*. We are thus invited by that Court back to the consideration of first principles; and neither it nor those who rely on its authority have a right to complain if we accept the invitation.

I know of no way, other than through the action of the State governments, in which the reserved rights and powers of the States can be preserved, and the guaranties of individual liberty be vindicated. The history of this country, brief as it is, already shows that the federal judiciary is never behind the other departments of that government, and often foremost, in the assumption of non-granted powers. And let it be finally yielded, that the federal government is, in the last resort, the authoritative judge of the extent of its own powers, and the reservations and limitations of the Constitution, which the framers of that instrument so jealously endeavored firmly to fix and guard, will soon be, if they are not already, obliterated; and that govern-

ment, the sole possessor of the only means of revenue, in the employment of which the people can be kept ignorant of the extent of their own burdens, and with its overshadowing patronage, attracting to its support the ambitious by means of its honors, and the mercenary through the medium of its emoluments, will speedily become, if it be not already, practically omnipotent.

These were my opinions, freely declared, for years before I had the honor of a seat on this bench; and, having learned nothing during the pendency of these cases to change, but much to confirm them, I know no reason why I should hesitate to avow them now.

I give my voice in favor of the discharge of the relators.

Judge SUTLIFF agreed with Judge BRINKERHOFF in dissenting from the opinion of the majority. His opinion was very elaborate and full, but professional duties forbade his preparing it for press in season for this work, and he therefore favored us with the following syllabus:—

JUDGE SUTLIFF'S OPINION.

SUTLIFF, J., held:—

That the return to the writs, necessarily presented for consideration the constitutionality of the Act of Congress of 1850, called the Fugitive Law. He thought that if the Court were satisfied beyond reasonable doubt, that Congress had no power to legislate for the extradition of fugitives from service; or even, if having such power, the law under which the prisoners were held was clearly repugnant to express provisions of the Constitution. In either case the return to the writ was insufficient.

After a careful examination of the whole subject, he could not say that he had any reasonable doubt that this Act of Congress was unconstitutional upon both grounds.

Upon the first ground he insisted upon the consideration that the legislative power being in the States respectively prior to the adoption of the Constitution, the reasonable presumption, as well as the express provision of the tenth amendment of the Constitution, showed that power still remains with the States, unless delegated under the Constitution to the Federal Government. And if the power claimed by the Federal Government to legislate, it is incumbent to show title thereto, by pointing out the clause under which the same had been ceded by the States.

He then referred to the rules given by commentators, which were applicable to the construction of the Constitution. 1st. That the meaning of the instrument was to be sought for according to the sense of the terms and understanding of the parties; that where the terms are clear and the sense distinct from the language, recourse to other means is not admissible to ascertain the meaning. 2d. Where the words are not plain and clear, but the meaning ambiguous or uncertain, is the only case where interpretation is allowable; that contemporaneous history, or interpretation, can only be resorted to, to escape some absurd consequence, or guard against some fatal evil, etc.

He insisted that the meaning of the clause, "No person held to service or labor," etc., under which the power to legislate was claimed for Congress, was neither uncertain or doubtful; and that the maxim, "*It is not allowable to interpret what has no need of interpretation*," ought to apply; that the clause was a naked compact, the same as the two preceding clauses, which, while standing in the Articles of Confederation, had been named and regarded as mere compacts. He urged that power to Congress being expressed in section first and section third of article four, and not expressed in section second, the maxim *expressio unius*, etc., applied with double force. He insisted that the plain and obvious sense of the clause was simply a treaty stipulation, the same as the one providing that "The citizens of each State shall be entitled to all privileges and immunities of citizens of the several States," and was never intended, and could not have been understood, to be a cession of powers to Congress to legislate. He denied that contemporaneous history was admissible, inasmuch as the people adopted the Constitution, not upon history which was not submitted to them, but upon the letter of the text which was; and when submitted to them, they must be presumed to have read and understood it according to its obvious meaning.

Referring, however, to contemporaneous history, he showed very clearly that nothing could be gained from that source, even if allowable to refer to it, to show that it was either understood or intended that power should be delegated to Congress to legislate in relation to fugitives from service. The Fugitive law of 1793 was passed for the proposed object of reclaiming fugitives from justice, with very little attention given to the bill at the time, that the question of power was not considered. But the States, on the other hand, claimed and exercised the power of legislating upon the same subject; and the States continued to legislate upon the subject until the decision of the Prigg case in 1842.

He then remarked upon objectionable features of the Fugitive Law of 1850; the commissioners were vested with judicial powers unconstitutionally. By the provisions of the law the right of trial by jury and due process of law were denied in violation of express provisions of the Constitution; that the provisions of the Constitution guaranteeing these rights, being contained in the amendments of the Constitution, they must have full force, however they may qualify the right of the claimant to a summary removal of the person owing service. He remarked that the Fugitive Law of 1850 pro-

vided for the surrender of fugitives from service in other cases than that mentioned in the Constitution; that while the provision of the Constitution was only for the delivering up of fugitives "held to labor in one State *under* the laws thereof," the act provides for the surrender of fugitives "held to service or labor in any State," merely. The act was as general in its terms as any law upon the statute book, and its provisions were applicable to all other general laws, to every person within the State. It was, therefore, not only unconstitutional, in that it was enacted without power, and in authorizing unreasonable seizures, and in cases not provided for by the Constitution, withholding due process of law, and denying a right of trial by jury, etc., but was, in its provisions, a flagrant subversion of the municipal laws of the States for the protection of the personal rights of their citizens. In determining the constitutionality of the fugitive law under consideration, and upon which the conviction and sentence rest, the act is to be regarded as one equally applicable to any free citizen of the State against whom a claim for service may be preferred by the provisions thereof.

He referred to the various judicial opinions expressed, some incidentally, and others directly in favor of the authority of Congress to legislate upon the subject of fugitives. The case of Prigg v. Pennsylvania (16 Peters, 539), is the only case relied upon in which the Supreme Court of the United States has ever attempted to offer any reason for the claim of power in Congress on the subject. The question was not then necessarily before the Court for decision; their opinion expressed in that case was, therefore, necessarily, only an *obiter dictum;* and though expressed in favor of the power, it was only by an acknowledged disregard of the *general* rules of construction, applicable to the Constitution, and upon a mistaken statement of contemporaneous history; and this, too, when reference to contemporaneous history was not admissible, even if correctly stated. The Van Zandt case (5th Howard, 229) was only a reaffirmance of the former opinion; as is the opinion recently pronounced in the case of the United States v. Booth.

He also referred to the contrary opinions as maintained and expressed by Mr. Jefferson and Mr. Madison, in their resolutions of 1798, introduced into the legislatures of Virginia and Kentucky, in relation to the power of Congress to pass "an act concerning aliens." He also referred to the opinions of Chancellor Walworth, Chief Justice Hornblower, Judge Baldwin, and Mr. Webster, maintaining that Congress had no power to pass a fugitive law, insisting that the power belonged, under the Constitution, to the States alone to legislate upon the subject.

Speaking of the previous decisions of the Supreme Court upon the subject, and the relations of the State Judiciary to the Federal, he insisted that the State and Federal Judiciaries were each, by the Constitution, left independent, and ought to act with perfect independence; that it was not only the right but the duty of the Supreme Court of the State — in a case clearly of importance to the State or its citizens, sufficient to justify such a course, and under circumstances which would dictate such exercise of their discretion — not to suffer a question to be settled, as to any case coming before them, against their clear convictions of the constitutional rights of the State, or its citizens.

He urged that they would not suffer themselves to be thus governed by any adjudication made by the Federal Court in another case. This was not judicial insubordination, but the judicial independence contemplated by the Constitution of the United States, and which he believed it the duty of the Supreme Court of the State to exercise in this and all similar cases. It was the only position, in his judgment, peacefully and with due respect towards the Federal Judiciary, to maintain the independent State sovereignty contemplated by the framers of the Federal Government, and to avoid an unconditional surrender of the constitutional powers belonging to the States whenever usurped by the Federal Government.

Entertaining these views, he added, and, after carefully examining the Constitution and the Act of Congress in question, with the aid of all the reasons and light afforded by the various opinions and authorities referred to, having no reasonable doubt of the unconstitutionality of the act upon which the prisoners had been convicted and imprisoned, that, in his judgment, they ought to be forthwith discharged.

The petition of the relator from Cincinnati was dismissed, as the return showed that the proceedings against him in the United States Court were still pending and undetermined. The case was similar to the first application in behalf of Mr. Bushnell.

—— The opinions were scarcely read, before Marshal JOHNSON and District-Attorney BELDEN called upon Sheriff WIGHTMAN to say, that, as, according to the Booth decision, all interference of State Courts with United States prisoners, by *habeas corpus* or otherwise, was unwarrantable and illegal; the journey of Bushnell and Langston to Columbus was *constructive escape from jail*, and he must therefore add six days each to their sentences, to compensate for the time they had been "at large" before the Supreme Court.

The Sheriff being otherwise advised by his counsel, and assured that such conduct would render him liable for false imprisonment as well as for "constructive" contempt of the Supreme Court, declined obedience to this order, and discharged Langston on the following Wednesday, twenty days having elapsed since the date of his sentence.

CHAPTER FIFTH.

IN gratifying contrast with the charge of Judge Willson to the Grand Jury that indicted the Rescuers, we place on record here, as introductory to the

INDICTMENT AND ARREST OF THE KIDNAPPERS,

the manly charge of Judge Carpenter to the Lorain County Grand Jury.

CHARGE OF JUDGE CARPENTER.

Gentlemen of the Grand Jury: — Your Prosecuting Attorney, as a very pertinent part of his duty, has requested me to call your attention to the acts to prevent kidnapping. There is a statute against kidnapping white persons. Its provisions are plain and I need only mention it.

The Statute passed April 17, 1857, Sec. 1, makes it an indictable misdemeanor, to arrest and imprison or kidnap, or decoy out of this State, any free black or mulatto person, within this State; or to attempt to kidnap or forcibly or fraudulently carry off or decoy out of this State, any such free black or mulatto with the intention of having such person carried out of this State, unless in pursuance of the laws thereof.

It also (Sec. 2), makes it an indictable misdemeanor, to kidnap or forcibly or fraudulently carry off or decoy out of this State any black or mulatto, within this State, claimed as a fugitive from service or labor; or, to attempt to kidnap or forcibly or fraudulently carry off or decoy out of this State, any such black or mulatto, without first taking such black or mulatto before the court, judge, or commissioner of the proper circuit, district, or county having jurisdiction, according to the laws of the United States in cases of persons held to service or labor in any State, escaping into this State, and there, according to the laws of the United States, establishing by proof the claimant's property in such person.

It will be seen that this statute contemplates

two classes of blacks and mulattoes, the free and the not free: — that the first section provides for the protection of free blacks and mulattoes, and that the second section provides, first, for the security of the public peace against all provocation to break it in revenge, or prevention of any abduction from this State of any black or mulatto not yet legally proved to be a slave — and, secondly, for the protection of all free blacks and mulattoes in this State, against the hopelessness of proving their freedom in another State, where complexion is presumptive of their legal enslavement, — and against the hopelessness of any immunity to them from force, in a State where the legal status claimed against them, has its origin and maintenance, not in the law of nature, but in force alone.

The misdemeanor here defined, then, is the claiming of any black or mulatto, within Ohio, whether free or not free, to be a fugitive from service or labor, and the getting, or attempting to get him out of Ohio before such claim has been legally proved, with intent to enforce such claim. The gist of the offence is the getting, or attempting to get him out of the State before he is proved to be a fugitive slave, with intent to hold him as such.

The Constitution of Ohio inhibits slavery, and regards all persons as free except criminals. No doubt, however, the legislative intendment of the second section of this statute refers to slavery as the condition of certain persons in other States, and as the possible condition of such persons in Ohio, for the purpose of recaption and return only, in case of their escape from that condition in another State into this.

This, being a criminal statute, must be construed somewhat strictly against the State. Passing over the question, then (upon which much might be pertinently and strongly said), whether any person in Ohio, not charged with crime, can be legally otherwise than free, we must give to any one indicted under this statute, the benefits of this strict construction.

But this statute recognizing the possibility of finding a fugitive in Ohio liable to be seized and returned into slavery, it may become important in your inquest, to know when there arises a legal presumption of this liability, and what are the legal presumptions to the contrary. Who, then, is presumed to be free ? Everybody. Every man, woman, and child, in Ohio, of whatever birth, descent, parentage, complexion, or conformation, is presumed in law to be free. Whoever interferes with this freedom is presumed to do it in violation of law. Whoever is charged with such interference must deny the charge, or show his authority for the interference, or be held guilty. If the interference is proved against him, the legal presumption then is, that he has violated the law ; and it devolves on him to show his right to interfere.

It would not change this presumption, to show that the prisoner had been a slave in a slave State, and stop there. For, giving to the Constitution of the United States the loosest construction, the utmost latitude for slavery, which has ever been given it by any authoritative decision, the only possible case of a legal liability to be arrested and returned into slavery from within the boundary of Ohio, is that of a fugitive slave escaping out of a slave State into Ohio. He must come into Ohio in the act of escaping — a fugitive, — and this fugitive character must belong to him at the moment he enters the confines of Ohio, or he leaves the status of a slave where he leaves the slave State. For, by the decisions of all civilized nations, slavery is against natural rights, and can exist only by positive law. This, until very recently, has been the authoritative doctrine of our slaveholding States, as well as of all others. Slavery, then, being against the law of nature, and existing only by positive local law, it is clear that this positive local law cannot extend beyond the jurisdiction of the power which makes it. It is equally clear, that the right of this local law to hold a slave cannot go farther than this law can go itself; that the slave, having a natural right to freedom, and being held a slave only by a local law which violates that right, the moment he is beyond the arm of that local law, his natural right to freedom resumes its empire. The instant, therefore, the slave, by any means not as a fugitive, crosses our boundary, he is baptized in the air of freedom ; and that baptism is irrevocable.

The law of Kentucky cannot of itself reach into Ohio. The Constitution of the United States, according to the construction adopted by this statute, extends the slave law of Kentucky into Ohio, for the sole purpose of recaption and return in case of the slave's escape into Ohio, and only in such case — and that too, with such executory modifications as the State of Ohio has found it prudent to enact for the safeguard of its own citizens. But, that A is admitted to have been a slave yesterday in Kentucky and is found to-day in Ohio, raises no presumption that he came into Ohio by an illegal escape. Whatever a man does which in himself is not unlawful, the law presumes him to do innocently. We cannot, therefore, legally presume because he was yesterday a slave in Kentucky, and to-day is in Ohio, that he came here in violation of law — even of the slave law. The legal presumption is rather that he came here, as lawfully he might, by consent of his master. Or, if that presumption should be rebutted by evidence, then the legal presumption would be that he came here by the act of God — by the winds or the waves, in spite of himself — unless there were some evidence pointing to a different conclusion. For, I cannot hold the mere facts that a man was a prisoner in Kentucky yesterday, and is at large in Ohio to-day, to be any evidence that his enlargement is illegal.

Certainly, the slave's coming here by the act

of God, is not an escape. And since the slave status can exist only by the concomitancy of the Slave law, and since the Slave law can be concomitant with his person here only by the slave's escaping hither, his coming here by the act of God must leave his status as a slave behind him, and invest him with the inevitable status of a freeman.

Nor ought the master to complain of this inevitable. necessity. Ought he to complain of inevitable death? And, if not, he ought not to complain of an act of God which releases him with no worse result to the master, but a result always due a slave by the law of nature? Should the whirlwind which releases the slave by death be blameless, and the whirlwind which stops short of death, but drops him in a free State, be blamable? In each case, the Slave law would end because the slave was beyond its jurisdiction by the act of God.

Is there any thing, then, in the case, which should palsy our law, whenever the man thus freed might claim its protection? Neither the law of nature, nor the common law, nor any enactment, nor any comity of State, indicates any such thing.

If, then, the evidence should convince you of an attempt forcibly or fraudulently to carry off or decoy out of this State any black or mulatto, or to arrest or imprison any such person, with intent to have him carried out of this State, not in pursuance of the laws of Ohio, and if you do not find from evidence that he came into Ohio by an actual escape from service or labor, whatever the proof may be that he had been a slave, you will hold him to be free, and that the act described was a misdemeanor, for which you will indict whomsoever you find to have committed it.

In this position, that the law presumes every man in Ohio to be free, I am upheld by the Constitution of this State, as well as by that of the United States.

Our Bill of Rights begins, " Sec. 1. All men are by nature free and independent. Sec. 2. All political power is inherent in the people. Government is instituted for their equal protection and benefit."

Does any caviller pretend that the words, " all men," in the first section, and in the second, "people," for whose equal protection and benefit government has been instituted, were meant to exclude blacks and mulattoes? In article five, section one, we find, " Every white male citizen of the United States of the age of twenty-one years, who shall have been a resident of the State one year, ... shall . . . . be entitled to vote at all elections."

Now the word " white " here describes certain male citizens of the United States, and distinguishes them from certain male citizens of the United States of some other color. This conclusion is inevitable from the language. But neither, in their legislative nor in their judicial acts, nor in their common speech,

have the people of Ohio distinguished any other resident person in respect of color, than whites, blacks, and mulattoes. By necessary implication, those male citizens of the United States in Ohio who are not entitled to vote at all elections, are not whites, but are blacks or mulattoes. Did the people of Ohio, in adopting their Constitution, mean to exclude from their Bill of Rights men whom, in the same instrument, they declared to be citizens of the United States! Not at all. This construction is confirmed by article nine, section one, — " All white male citizens residents of this State . . . . shall be enrolled in the militia," etc. Now, here it is provided that those who are to be enrolled shall be made citizens, be residents, be whites. But this necessarily implies, first, that there are male citizens here who are not residents of this State; and, therefore, this word " citizens," must here probably mean citizens of the United States: and, secondly, that there may be citizens of the United States here who are not whites, and, therefore, are either blacks or mulattoes. Or if the word " citizens " here means citizens of Ohio, then blacks and mulattoes may be citizens of Ohio.

This presumption of universal freedom is supported by the common sentiment which gave our nation birth; and which, therefore, may well be regarded as a part of our common law. It is expressed in our Declaration of Independence, — a declaration of no new discoveries. It was but the utterance of principles so common, so pervasive and so long felt that they were there set forth as an indisputable law of human nature. I know that there is a puerile cavil, that the language — " All men are created equal, and are endowed by their Creator with certain unalienable rights — among these are life, liberty, and the pursuit of happiness " — was not intended to include black men. It requires more than ordinary patience to answer this cavil, when we remember that the very point in dispute between the colonies and the mother country was whether the sovereignty of Great Britain was illimitable, or was limited by the equal and unalienable rights of all mankind; the administration claiming that the sovereignty of the King and Parliament was without limitation over its subjects, and the colonists replying that human sovereignty was always limited by the equal rights of all its subjects, — the unalienable rights of all mankind.

They claimed that whenever human sovereignty so overstepped its lawful sphere as to trample upon these unalienable rights, it was itself a rebel against the law that limits it, and might be lawfully overthrown. And when argument was exhausted, and they stood upon their rights, they held forth these self-evident truths, and made their appeal upon them to all the world. If, from these unalienable rights, their language had excluded any part of the human race, their appeal would have been a mockery.

The second section of this statute, as before stated, provides for the case of one claimed as a fugitive from service or labor, and prohibits any attempt to get him out of the State, except as prescribed by the laws of the United States.

It is very probable the highest judicial authority of Ohio would hold so much of that United States statute, known as the Fugitive Slave Law, as authorizes the recaption and return of one claimed as a fugitive without the trial by jury, to be unconstitutional. But, as this criminal statute seems to recognize, that provision of the Fugitive Slave Law as valid, we pass by that question, to note what, if it is not more favorable to liberty, is, at least, less favorable to tyranny. The only person authorized by that act, to pursue and reclaim such fugitive, either by warrant, or by seizing him without warrant, is, first, the master, or, secondly, "his agent or attorney, duly authorized by power of attorney, in writing, acknowledged and certified under the seal of some legal officer or court of the State or Territory in which the same may be executed."

Any person but the master of the actual fugitive, or his agent or attorney, authorized in every particular as above stated — by power of attorney, in writing, acknowledged and certified under seal strictly as prescribed by the statute — any person, but the master, not thus fortified as agent, who, claiming such fugitive, has, within this county, done or attempted as expressed in this criminal statute by process of the United States or without it, violated the law of Ohio, and should be indicted at your hands.

He who handles edge tools must run the risk of cutting his own flesh. The severity of that old judge, who, if the extortioner would have his pound of flesh, because it was so nominated in the bond, would hold his life the forfeit if he shed one drop of blood, was but the severity of simple justice.

On the 15th of February, 1859, the Grand Jury, thus charged, returned a true bill against Rufus P. Mitchell, Anderson Jennings, Jacob K. Lowe, and Samuel Davis, for kidnapping and attempting to carry out of the State in an unlawful manner, a negro boy named John Price.

Upon this a warrant was issued to the sheriff of Lorain county, which he returned indorsed thus: —

State of Ohio,   } ss.
Lorain County, }

I executed this writ by taking the body of the within named Anderson Jennings, Samuel Davis, and Rufus P. Mitchell, May 11, 1859, and Jacob K. Lowe, April 4, 1859, and retained them in my custody for the period of nine days, when I brought them before the Cou-t as within I am commanded.

H. E. BURR, Sheriff.

This indictment being found defective in the orthography of Mr. Mitchell's first name, a new one was returned as follows: —

The State of Ohio, } ss.
  Lorain County, }

At a term of the Court of Common Pleas, begun and holden at the Court House, in Elyria, within and for the County of Lorain, and State of Ohio, on the seventeenth day of May, in the year of our Lord one thousand eight hundred and fifty-nine, the Jurors of the Grand Jury, good and lawful men of the county aforesaid, then and there duly returned, tried and sworn, and charged to inquire within and for the body of the county aforesaid, at the term of the Court aforesaid, upon their oaths aforesaid, and in the name and by the authority of the State aforesaid, do find and present, that Anderson Jennings, Jacob K. Lowe, Samuel Davis, and Richard P. Mitchell, on the thirteenth day of September in the year one thousand eight hundred and fifty-eight, with force and arms at the county aforesaid, unlawfully did arrest and imprison one John Price, the said John Price then and there being a free black person then and there within the State of Ohio, with intent then and there and thereby of having said John Price carried out of the said State of Ohio; the same not being in pursuance of any law of the State of Ohio, contrary to the form of the statute in such cases made and provided, and against the peace and dignity of the State of Ohio.

And the Jurors aforesaid on their oaths aforesaid do farther present and find that the said Anderson Jennings, Jacob K. Lowe, Samuel Davis and Richard P. Mitchell on the thirteenth day of September in the year one thousand eight hundred and fifty-eight, at the county aforesaid, one John Price then and there being, the said John Price being a black person then and there within the State of Ohio, and claimed as a fugitive from service, did then and there with force and arms unlawfully and forcibly attempt to kidnap and carry off out of the State of Ohio, without first taking him, the said John Price, before the Court, Judge, or Commissioner of the proper circuit, district, or county having jurisdiction according to the laws of the United States in cases of persons held to service or labor, in any of the United States, escaping into the State of Ohio, and then and there having jurisdiction according to said laws in the case of said John Price so claimed as a fugitive from service, and then according to the laws of the United States establishing by proof their property in him the said John Price, without the consent of the said John Price, and against his will, and contrary to the form of the statute in such cases made and provided, and against the peace and dignity of the State of Ohio.

W. W. BOYNTON, *Prosecuting Attorney.*

And hereupon a new warrant was issued: —

The State of Ohio, }
Lorain County, } ss.

To the Sheriff of said County of Lorain, GREETING:

[SEAL.] We command you that you take Anderson Jennings, Jacob K. Lowe, Samuel Davis, and Richard P. Mitchell, if they be found in your bailiwick, and them safely keep so that you have them before our COURT OF COMMON PLEAS at the Court House, in the Town of Elyria, in and for said County, on the 18th day of May, 1859, to answer an indictment for kidnapping John Price.

Herein fail not, but of this writ and your service thereof make due return. Witness Roswell G. Horr, Clerk of our said Court, at Elyria, this 18th day of May, A. D. 1859.

ROSWELL G. HORR, *Clerk.*

— which was indorsed in due form as having been served and returned on the day of its date.

The Journal entry of the Court is as follows: —

The State of Ohio, }
v. } May 19, 1859.
Anderson Jennings. }

This cause came up for hearing, upon defendants' motion for a continuance, upon consideration of which the Court overruled said motion, and set the case down for trial at the present term on the 6th day of July next. And thereupon came the defendants and moved the Court to grant them a separate trial, on consideration of which the Court overruled said motion. It was farther ordered that said defendants be released from custody on entering into bail for their appearance with good and sufficient surety in the sum of eight hundred dollars each.

O. S. Wadsworth, Joseph L. Whiton, and Malachi Warren thereupon became surety in the sum of $3,200 for the appearance of the defendants for trial on the day named.

To Roswell G. Horr, Esq., Clerk of the Court, we are indebted for certified copies of all the proceedings in this case.

We have next the history of another kidnapping case, which is of interest in this particular connection. It was compiled from original documents, or certified copies, by the Editors of the Cleveland *Leader*, and, making

due acknowledgments, we avail ourselves of the results of their labors.

We quote from the columns of the *Leader* without alteration: —

TRUTH OF HISTORY VINDICATED.

Being full accounts of U. S. District Judge Willson's connection with the Kidnapping of a colored boy in the year 1841 — a copy of the Indictment found against Jackson, Lindenberger, and Willson, for Kidnapping — and a copy of the Requisition made by the Governor of New York on the Governor of Ohio for the Kidnappers !

[From the Akron Beacon.]

FUGITIVES FROM JUSTICE AND FUGITIVES FROM SERVICE. — At the term of the United States District Court, at Cleveland, as our readers know, some thirty-seven citizens of Lorain county, were indicted for rescuing, or aiding and abetting in the rescue of a man claimed as a fugitive slave at Wellington. It is charged that one of the Grand Jury was the person who through the agency of his son, entrapped the negro in question, decoying him under pretence of employing him to work. The charge of Judge Willson to the Grand Jury was published in the Cleveland papers, and furnished the subject of not a little comment. The *Leader*, in connection with the proceedings, observed that "a tale could be unfolded touching an indictment in Erie county, New York, for violating the laws of that State, by aiding and abetting in kidnapping a colored man from Buffalo, for the purpose of returning him to slavery."

The facts referred to by the *Leader*, if fully narrated, tend to throw light upon some of the "antecedents" and "proclivities" of certain persons who have been and are prominent before the public.

In 1841, Henry B. Payne and Hiram V. Willson were practising law in Cleveland, under the firm name of Payne & Willson. J. W. Gray, now of the Cleveland *Plaindealer*, was a student of law in that office.

Henry Jackson, a mulatto, kept a barber shop in Cleveland. In the summer of that year, two fugitives from service, from Louisiana, we believe, were staying with Jackson, in his employ. They had confided their story and the name of the party from whom they escaped, to their employer, Jackson.

In consequence of some disagreement, they left Jackson and sought employment elsewhere; one of them, Alek, a likely mulatto, as a barber in Buffalo; the other as a cook on the steamer De Witt Clinton.

Enraged at their leaving him, Jackson went to the office of Payne & Willson, and disclosed their entire story, and, perhaps hoping to get a reward, procured a letter to be written to their owner or claimant in Louisiana.

The State fugitive law was then in force in Ohio: — "An Act in relation to fugitives from service and labor" passed by the Legislature of 1838–9. (In the Prigg case it was afterwards decided that all such legislation by the States was unconstitutional, and this act was repealed.) It was then a cheap and convenient process of rendition.

In due time Mr. Vernon Lintenberger, of Louisiana, appeared in Cleveland with the evidences of title, and with authority to reclaim the fugitives. The public mind was somewhat sensitive at such transactions then, and it was desirable to secure the two in the same boat, and dispose of both cases at once. Lintenberger found shrewd advisers. A warrant for the arrest of the boys was issued by Justice Hoadley, and placed in the hands of an officer, we believe, named Wait.

To get Alek from Buffalo to Cleveland required dexterous management. But Lintenberger, the barber, Jackson, and the attorneys, were equal to the emergency. The two first named and H. V. Willson, Esq., went to Buffalo. Arriving there, Jackson went to persuade Alek to come back to Cleveland with him on the De Witt Clinton; assuring him that Mr. Hanks, the painter, was anxious to take him as an apprentice, and that if he would go at once he would secure this desirable situation, and that the opportunity was too good to be lost by delay.

Alek's objections were overcome, Jackson promising to pay his passage money, etc., and thus he was decoyed on board the De Witt Clinton, his fellow fugitive being a cook on the same boat, and the whole party returned. Arriving at Cleveland, Jackson in a friendly way conducted Alek up the street, where, by preconcert, the officer was waiting for him, and securing him, they proceeded to the boat and arrested the other. Thus they were captured together, which was an important point gained. They were placed in the jail for safe detention, and the jailer was directed — so it was reported — to allow no person access to them. The arrest was made about the third of September, 1841.

A habeas corpus was sued out on their behalf by Thomas Bolton, Esq., now President Judge of the Common Pleas, who being then prosecutor of the County, had no difficulty in gaining access to the prisoners. The habeas corpus was returnable before Judges Josiah Barber and Fred. Whittlesey. For some reason, we do not recollect precisely what, the hearing upon the habeas corpus was postponed, and the boys held in $1,000 each. One of them, Alek, was bailed out temporarily by John Brown, a well-known barber in Cleveland, for the purpose, we think, of enabling him to go to Buffalo, to make complaint before the Grand Jury of Erie County, New York, against his abductors. Two gentlemen, whose names it is needless to give, went also to Buffalo upon the same errand. Mr. Rogers, of Buffalo, was then District-Attorney. A bill of indictment was found against Vernon Littenberger, Henry Jackson, and Hiram V. Willson, for kidnapping or aiding and assisting in the kidnapping of Alek.

A requisition was made by the Governor of New York upon the Governor of Ohio for the surrender of these three "fugitives from justice," and about the 15th day of September an officer came up from Buffalo to receive them.

By some means— supposed to be by a friendly whisper from one of the Deputy-Sheriffs — Lintenberger got wind of the proceedings, and disappeared. Jackson also vamosed. He afterwards located at Cincinnati, where he resided up to the time of his death, a year or two since. The proceedings as to Mr. Willson were dropped, the principal in the affair having escaped.

In a general jail breaking, Alek, who had been again put in jail, escaped without waiting for the hearing in habeas corpus. The other— if we mistake not — was discharged on account of some informality or defect in the title papers or proceedings.

Nothing is known of their fortunes thereafter. Lintenberger is equally unknown to present fame.

H. V. Willson is now Judge of the United States District Court for the Northern District of Ohio.

Jackson, as already stated, is dead.

The tale is told fairly, though, perhaps, in some points imperfectly. We do not know that it demands any comment from us, further than to say that it shows that the "fugitive from justice" clause, like the "fugitive from service and labor" clause, has sometimes, through connivance, failed of complete execution.

———

From the Cincinnati Philanthropist, of Nov. 10th, 1841.

BASENESS.

Cleveland, Oct. 12, 1841.

Dr. Bailey: — As much interest has been excited in the case of the two colored persons, recently kidnapped in the State of New York, I now forward you a short account of this atrocious transaction, with the names of those concerned.

In August, a fellow by the name of Lindenberger, from Louisiana, an expelled officer from the United States army, and a regular slave-hunter, came to this city. He called on one Jackson, a mulatto barber, and presented him with two dollars, thereby obtaining his confidence, and from him learned that he, Jackson, had employed a yellow boy by the name of Williams, then living in Buffalo, and also that the barber had assisted fugitives on the way to the land of liberty. The hunter now sought for and found suitable persons to aid him in his vile project, in the firm of Payne & Willson, (H. B. Payne and H. V. Willson, technically known by the name of "Fogg & Dodson.") ..

. . . . It is unnecessary to detail the black tissues of falsehood with which the yellow boy Williams, and another colored man were inveigled to this city. Upon landing, the yellow boy was directed to some distance, where he was seized by the jailer, whose christian name is "*Liberty!*" [Waite.] The victims were put into a carriage, and hurried to the house of Associate Judge Barber, who it was expected would order the boy into bondage. Fortunately, the Judge was absent. The county jail, built by the money of freemen, was now opened to secure these kidnapped victims of tyranny. On the following day they were brought before Judge Barber, when the Court adjourned for a fortnight. Messrs. Bolton, Foote, Stetson, Wade, and Welles appeared for the defence. Payne & Willson, and Horace Foote for the kidnappers.

A demand in due form had in the mean time been made by the proper authorities in Buffalo, for the slave-hunters and their accomplice, Jackson. A writ of *habeas corpus* was issued by Judge Barber, and the warrant of the magistrate for the arrest of the defendants, declared to be deficient, contrary to the opinion of both Associates, who advised with him, one of whom is a gentleman of legal attainments. This cause was now abandoned by the counsel for the oppressed, for obvious reasons, and Williams gave bail in the sum of one thousand dollars for his appearance on the following Friday. The bail were three colored men. One was ample. It was thought best to release the boy in the evening, when lo! "Liberty" [Waite], the turnkey, refused to let him out without the order of the Sheriff, and the Sheriff demanded a special order from Judge Barber. The Clerk made out and gave an order for carrying out the decision of the Court, regarding the boy, but Payne, the lawyer, opposed it so violently, that he finally took it back. The Judge was then called in, when he said that since he had accepted the bail, he had learned that they were colored persons, but that he would attend to it on Monday morning at 9 o'clock, although he had previously approved of the bail, as also had Judge Whittlesey, and the Prosecuting Attorney for the county. By this measure two days out of six were lost, which the boy expected to have to undertake a journey of 400 miles and appear before a grand jury in Buffalo, and have his wrongs redressed, and his oppressors punished. On Monday morning, Williams's friends disdaining to have him liberated by a man whose conduct every candid lawyer in the community deemed infamous, obtained a writ of *habeas corpus* from Judge Whittlesey, and obtained his discharge on bail, when he and one of his bail started for Buffalo. It happened that Payne embarked in the same boat, and accompanied them to their place of destination. An incident occurred on the boat which fully illustrates the correctness of the opinion of Judge Clay, of Kentucky. The Judge is said to have

declared when he read the black law of Ohio, "that if a man should return to him one of his fugitive slaves under this law, he should watch him, while in his house, for fear he would rob him!" The bail, who was on the boat, a pious and devoted member of the Baptist Church, says that Payne there told him that he had got from Lindenberger $100, and that he had done with the suit, thus violating the old adage, "honor among . . . . . . ," etc. Another colored man who was on board the boat, said that Payne mistook him for Williams, and advised him to flee to Canada and forfeit his bail. Was not Judge Clay correct in his opinion?

On the appointed day the parties again appeared in Court, and by their counsel prayed for an adjournment for one month, which was granted.

The counsel for the prisoners then applied to the Court for permission to visit the jail, a privilege they claimed, but one that had been denied them. The Sheriff then arose and denied that permission had been refused them — Messrs. Bolton, Welles, and John A. Foot then declared that they had severally applied for permission to enter, which was denied them.

A few nights after this, while "Liberty," the turnkey, was entering the cells, a white prisoner seized him and endeavored to escape. In the confusion, one of the fugitives escaped, and is now a free man in Canada.

The cashiered officer of the army felt it to be his duty, as well as his interest, to help the wretched Jackson away. Ignorant and unable to read, this miserable dupe of a designing knave, frightened into a course of kidnapping, was obliged to flee to avoid the walls of the New York Penitentiary, a punishment richly merited by his employers and deceivers.

Yours, etc., KNOX.

Copy of the Indictment.

At the term of the Recorder's Court of the City of Buffalo, holden at the Court House in the city of Buffalo, in and for the said city, on the 15th day of September, in the year of our Lord one thousand eight hundred and forty-one, before the Honorable Horatio J. Stow, Recorder of the City of Buffalo, assigned to keep the peace in the said city, and also to hear and determine divers felonies, trespasses, and other misdemeanors in the said city perpetrated.

County of Erie, }
City of Buffalo, } ss.

The Jurors for the people of the State of New York, in and for the said city of Buffalo, in the County of Erie aforesaid, to wit: Harry Daw, Cornelius A. Waldren, Nelson B. Palmer, Charles S. Pierce, Samuel C. Smith, Velones Hodge, John Prince, Albert J. Stow, William Haws, Hamilton Rainey, Daniel F. Kimball, Henry Scun, John D. Bemy, Morris O. Barnes, Giles G. Thomas, and George W.

Valentine, then and there being empanelled, sworn, and charged to inquire for the People of the State of New York, and for the City of Buffalo, in the County of Erie, upon their oath present, that Henry Jackson, Vernon H. Lindenberger, and Hiram V. Willson, late of the city aforesaid, heretofore, to wit, on the first day of September, in the year of our Lord one thousand eight hundred and forty-one, with force and arms at the place in the county aforesaid, feloniously and without lawful authority, did inveigle *one* Alexander Williams, then and there, being with intent to cause him, the said Alexander Williams, to be sent out of the State of New York, against his will, contrary to the form of the statute in such case made and provided, and against the peace of the people of the State of New York and their dignity.

And the Jurors aforesaid, upon their oath *aforesaid*, do farther present that the said Henry Jackson, Vernon H. Lindenberger and Hiram V. Willson, afterwards, to wit, on the same day and year aforesaid, with force and arms at the city and in the county aforesaid, feloniously and without lawful authority did inveigle one Alexander Williams, then and there, being with intent to cause him, the said Alexander Williams, to be held to service against his will, contrary to the power of the statute in such cases made and provided, and against the peace of the people of the State of New York and their dignity.

And the Jurors aforesaid, upon their oath aforesaid, do farther present that the said Henry Jackson, Vernon H. Lindenberger and Hiram V. Willson, afterwards, to wit, on the same day and year aforesaid, at the city and in the county aforesaid, with force and arms, feloniously, and without lawful authority, did inveigle one Alexander Williams, then and there, being with intent to cause him, the said Alexander Williams, to be sent out of the State of New York aforesaid, to the State of Louisiana, and to be there held to service against his will, contrary to the form of the statute in such case made and provided, and against the peace of New York, and their dignity.

And the jurors aforesaid, upon their oath aforesaid, do further present that the said Henry Jackson, afterwards, to wit, on the same day and year aforesaid, with force and arms at the city and in the county aforesaid, feloniously and without lawful authority, and with a view to wheedle, deceive, and inveigle one Alexander Williams, then and there being, and with intent, the said Alexander Williams to be sent out of the State of New York, to wit; to the State of Louisiana, against his will, to be held to service against his will, then and there did deceitfully pretend to the said Alexander Williams that one Jarvis F. Hanks, a Portrait Painter at the city of Cleveland, in the State of Ohio, had said to him, the said Henry Jackson, that he wanted the said Alexander Williams to go to the said city of Cleveland and live with him,

the said Jarvis F. Hanks, and learn to paint portraits, by means whereof, the said Alexander Williams was induced to and did go to the said city of Cleveland, to wit, on the same day and year aforesaid, whereas in truth and in fact, the said Jarvis F. Hanks did never at any time say to the said Henry Jackson, or to any other person, that he wanted, nor did he want, the said Alexander Williams to go to the said city of Cleveland and live with him, the said Jarvis F. Hanks, and learn to paint portraits, all which was then and there well known to the said Alexander Williams; and so the jurors aforesaid, upon their oath aforesaid, do say that the said Henry Jackson feloniously and without lawful authority, and by the deceptive means aforesaid, him the said Alexander Williams did then and there inveigle and induce to go to the said city of Cleveland with intent to cause him, the said Alexander Williams, to be sent out of the State of New York, to wit, to the State of Louisiana aforesaid, against his will, and to be held to service against his will, contrary to the statute in such case, made and provided; and the jurors aforesaid, upon their oath aforesaid, do further present that the said Vernon H. Lindenberger, and Hiram V. Willson, before the offence and felony was committed in form aforesaid, by the said Henry Jackson, to-wit: on the thirtieth day of August, in the year aforesaid, at the city of Buffalo, in the county aforesaid, did feloniously and without lawful authority incite, move, procure, aid, counsel, hire, and command the said Henry Jackson, the said offence and felony in manner, deed, form aforesaid, to do and commit, contrary to the form of the statute in such case made and provided, and against the peace of the people of the State of New York and their dignity.

And the Jurors aforesaid, upon their oath aforesaid, do further present that the said Henry Jackson aforesaid, to wit, on the first day of September, in the year aforesaid, with force and arms, at the city of Buffalo, in the county of Erie aforesaid, feloniously and without lawful authority, did wheedle, inveigle, and deceive one Alexander Williams, then and there being, with intent to cause him, the said Alexander Williams, to be sent out of the said State of New York against his will; and the Jurors aforesaid, upon their oath aforesaid, do further present, that the said Vernon H. Lindenburger and Hiram V. Willson, before the said crime was committed in form last aforesaid, to-wit, on the same day and year last aforesaid, at the city of Buffalo aforesaid, did feloniously and maliciously incite, move, procure, aid, counsel, hire, and command the said Henry Jackson, the said crime in manner and form last aforesaid, to do and commit, contrary to the form of the statute in such case made and provided, and against the peace of the people of the State of New York and their dignity.

And the Jurors aforesaid, upon their oath

aforesaid, do further present that the said Henry Jackson afterwards, to wit, on the same day the year last aforesaid, with force and arms at the place last aforesaid, feloniously and without lawful authority, did deceive, inveigle, and induce the said Alexander Williams, then and there being, to go to the city of Cleveland, in the State of Ohio, with intent thereby to cause him, the said Alexander Williams, to be held to service against his will.

And the Jurors aforesaid, upon their oath aforesaid, do further present that the said Vernon H. Lindenberger and Hiram V. Willson, before the said crime was committed in form last aforesaid, to-wit, on the same day and year, at the place last aforesaid, did feloniously and maliciously incite, move, procure, aid, counsel, hire, and command the said Henry Jackson, the said crime in manner and form aforesaid, to do and commit; contrary to the form of the statute in such case made and provided; and against the peace of the people of the State of New York and their dignity.

(Signed,) H. W. ROGERS,
District-Attorney.

Erie county, } ss.
City of Buffalo, }

I, Michenes Cadwallader, Clerk of the Recorder's Court of the City of Buffalo, do certify that the foregoing is a true copy of an original indictment on file in my office, as Clerk of the said Court — and further, that I have compared said copy with said original, and find it to be a correct transcript of the same and of the whole thereof.

In witness whereof, I have hereunto subscribed my name, and affixed the [Seal.] seal of the said Court the fifteenth day of September, A. D. 1841.

(Signed,)
M. CADWALLADER, Clerk.

County of Erie, } ss.
City of Buffalo, }

Henry W. Rogers, District-Attorney of said county, being sworn says — that Henry Jackson, Vernon H. Lindenberger, and Hiram V. Willson are now in the State of Ohio, as this deponent is informed and verily believes — and that they are the identical persons named as defendants in an indictment of which the within and foregoing is a copy.

Subscribed and sworn this ⎤
15th day of September, |
A. D. 1841. |
(Signed,) | (Signed,)
M. CADWALLADER, } H. W. ROGERS.
Clerk of the Recorder's |
Court of the City of Buf- |
falo. ⎦

Endorsed: " The People v. Henry Jackson, Vernon Lindenberger, and Hiram V. Willson, indictment—inveigling and kidnapping. H.

W. Rogers, District-Attorney, (A copy.) Filed September 15, 1841."

Copy of the Requisition.

William H. Seward, Governor of the State of New York : —

To His Excellency the Governor of the State of Ohio : —

It appears by the annexed papers duly authenticated according to the [Seal.] laws of our State, that Henry Jackson, Vernon H. Lindenberger and Hiram V. Willson (Signed,) stand charged in this State WM. H. SEWARD. with having without lawful authority inveigled and kidnapped a person with intent to cause such person to be sent out of this State and to the State of Louisiana, against his will, there to be held to service against his will, and it has been represented to me that they have fled from the justice of this State and have taken refuge within the State of Ohio.

Now, therefore, pursuant to the provisions of the Constitution and Laws of the United States in such case made and provided, I do hereby require that the said Henry Jackson, Vernon H. Lindenberger, and Hiram V. Willson be apprehended and delivered to George B. Gates and Joel W. Barton, who are hereby duly authorized to receive them and convey them to the State of New York, there to be dealt with according to law.

In witness whereof, I have hereunto affixed my name and the Privy Seal of the State, this twenty-fifth day of September, in the year of our Lord one thousand eight hundred and forty-one. By the Governor.

(Signed,) HENRY UNDERWOOD,
Private Secretary.

Endorsed: " Requisition of the Governor of New York for Jackson, Lindenberger and Willson." " Warrant issued to Sheriff of Cuyahoga, October 5, 1841."

The same paper furnishes us other refreshing reminiscences : —

Judge Willson a Candidate for Congress — What he said of the Fugitive Slave Act — The Empire Hall Meeting and Resolutions — His Connection Therewith — Why he had the Resolutions Published.

READ, PONDER, AND INWARDLY DIGEST!

The "*Waechter am Erie,*" German Republican, replies to the *Plain Dealer's* statement that Judge WILLSON was not present when the resolutions read in Court by Mr. Spalding were passed, as follows : —

" We will remind the principal editor of the Plain Dealer, that he, Mr. Gray, himself, with the present U. States Collector Parks, Colonel Mack, and Mr. Schuh introduced on the 4th day of October, 1852, to our office Mr. WILL-

SON, who at that time was a Democratic candidate for Congress. Mr. WILLSON did, then and there, and in the presence of the gentlemen aforenamed, answer directly and without ambiguity certain questions, the satisfactory answer to which was the condition made by us for our supporting Mr. WILLSON. These questions referred to the Homestead Bill, to the position of our Government in regard to revolutionary movements in Europe, and to the *Fugitive Slave Law.* Mr. WILLSON replied very sufficiently and entirely satisfactorily to all of these questions; in regard to the Fugitive Slave Law, he stated especially, *this Law was, in his opinion, unconstitutional, non-democratic, dangerous in its principle, and infamous; it must not be enforced, neither at present nor at any time.* As a confirmation of this assertion he promised to send us certain resolutions, *drawn with his assistance,* and about an hour later he sent the printed reports of the meeting held at Empire Hall, Oct. 11, 1850, containing the same resolutions lately read in Court by Mr. Spalding. These very resolutions were published in our paper Oct. 6, 1852, by the expressed desire of Mr. WILLSON, and for the purpose of defining his position. It is very evident, therefore, that the editor of the Plain Dealer has rather a short recollection; probably he has forgotten all his former democratic principles for the same reason."

THE UNITED STATES FEDERAL COURT APOSTATES!

The Hon. Joseph Cable, Editor of the Van Wert American, was formerly a Democratic Member of Congress from Ohio. Mr. Cable like a free, honest man, declined to keep pro-slavery step with his party at the command and lash of Southern masters, and spurned the bribes offered to secure degrading subserviency. His votes in Congress against the Fugitive Slave Act, the Texan Boundary, and Ten Millions Bill, the Territorial Law to Utah, etc., were warmly approved at the time by many of the leading Democrats of Ohio — some of the same Democratic politicians and place-men who afterwards joined in hunting him down for those very votes, and who have become eager " Government Pursuers" of the Jeffrey scent and odor, under the very Fugitive Act they denounced " as unconstitutional and insulting to Free States," and " ought never to be enforced."

Mr. CABLE has not forgotten the past: and in the last American he gives the names of the packed jurors who went through the farce of trying Bushnell, a jury which he pronounces "made up by a set of apostates, with the exception of two of whom we know nothing" — and he then presents the following loathsome picture of rewarded apostasy in higher places. Read, ponder, and inwardly digest. Says Mr. C.:—

Here the question arises — *who are the men who compose that court, and what was the price of their apostasy?*

It has been our good or bad fortune — as the case may be — to have an acquaintance with most of the prominent members of that court: Judge WILLSON, the presiding *deity* of that court, we became acquainted with some ten or twelve years ago; and meeting with him aboard of a steamboat on the Ohio River, we received a flattering encomium from him for having voted, while in Congress, against this Fugitive Slave Act, and in which vote he concurred. In the course of his remarks, he denounced that law as clearly unconstitutional; and that it never could be enforced. We reminded him that we were glad his name was identified with the proceedings of an INDIGNATION meeting at Cleveland, composed of all parties, a short time previously. He expressed his unalterable determination to oppose the enforcement of that unconstitutional act.

Since then the Northern District of Ohio was created, and the then Mr. Willson, has somehow become the judge of that new district. What influence the appointment has had on his mind, or whether apostasy was the condition upon which his appointment was confirmed by a fogy Senate, we leave others to determine.

Our intimacy with Judge BELDEN, now District-Attorney, was still more close. We have known him since he stood at the case as a printer. We have labored for his political promotion : — To make him Common Pleas Judge, which he filled with ability and honor to himself. We have been his friend, personal and political in several other contests; and for which, up to his apostasy, we have no regrets. When Gen. Cass, Gen. Taylor, and Mr. Van Buren were before the people for President, Judge Belden voted for Mr. Van Buren.

He, too, after we had voted against the Texan Boundary and *Ten Millions Bill* — against the Fugitive Slave Act — against Territorial law to Utah, *etc.*, Judge BELDEN, in the overflowing of a then honest heart, wrote us a long *eulogistic letter,* admiratory of our course in Congress generally, and especially in reference to the Fugitive Slave Act, denouncing it as unconstitutional and insulting to the Free States — it ought never to be enforced, said he.

Marshal JOHNSON is of like character on the act he now degrades himself to enforce. The only charitable and friendly conclusion we are able to arrive at is, that these men, with deputy Marshal C. N. ALLEN, who also wrote us a kindly letter approving our course on the same subject — have *thrown conscience to the dogs for office.*

We might go further into the list of the officers of that court, and they all show a like passiveness for emolument.

Hon. F. G. GREEN, the Clerk (if he yet be Clerk), is the only consistent man of the lot. He is a Marylander by birth and feeling. He was in Congress after the passage of the Fugitive act, was there in '54, and voted for the repeal of the Missouri Compromise and the extension of Slavery. He is much of a gentleman and entitled to more respect than apostates. He is consistent in error — they forsake a right to do wrong. How widely do Judge Willson, Judge Belden, Marshal Johnson and their apostate clan now differ with us — once of one sentiment on the tyranny of Slavedom! We, too, have had alluring and sweet-scented bait thrown to us as well as they, perhaps. We stand where we then had deliberately taken our position, and have suffered therefor.

They have changed and been benefited, if not blest thereby. They have their *reward*, and we are at *peace with ourself.*

MARSHAL JOHNSON AND HIS DEPUTY DAYTON.

The National *Democrat* copies from the *Leader* as follows: —

"Marshal Johnson visited Oberlin and consulted with a number of the leading citizens. With smooth and honeyed words he sought to allay the indignation of the people. The conduct of Dayton was disapproved, and assurances were given that farther trouble need not be apprehended. He expressed a strong repugnance to the execution of the law, and left a favorable impression on the minds of the citizens present."

And then says: —

"This is far from being a correct account of the interview which the Marshal had with some of the Oberlin people; he assured them that he would not send his Deputy, Mr. D., another warrant; should he get one, he would serve it himself."

To make this a "correct account," the Democrat should add that at the interview alluded to the Marshal took especial pains to have it understood that not only should he come himself, but that he should give such notice of his coming, and of the object of his visit, as would enable the fugitive to escape, intimating that such a result would be most gratifying to his feelings.

The Marshal also took occasion to say, then and there, that Deputy Dayton was distasteful to him, and that he had exhibited improper readiness to engage in taking fugitives by going to Painesville, as he had other deputies whose duty it would be to serve warrants in Painesville.

The Democrat publishes the following epistle in full · —

U. S. MARSHAL'S OFFICE, }
Cleveland, October 4, 1858. }

A. P. DAYTON, Esq.:

SIR, — Your favor of the 1st, is received and contents noted. You must not resign. I am not disposed to be driven by the violators of the laws and Constitution of the United States, to discharge a deputy for doing his duty, nor do I wish such a deputy to resign. You need fear no violence. It is all bravado — an effort to scare you into a resignation.

Yours, M. JOHNSON,
U. S. Marshal.

And adds: —

It will be seen that that letter was written after the Marshal had visited Oberlin, and we believe the public will honor the position taken in this case.

But the Democrat fails to state that another letter was written to Deputy Dayton, before the interview alluded to, which is not published — and further, that Marshal Johnson apologized for that letter to the men at Oberlin, saying that he wrote it in such a manner that while it seemed to require Dayton to serve the warrant in behalf of Mr. McMillan, it was not so intended by him; and when Marshal Johnson went to Oberlin to make the arrest of the indicted, he *denied in the most positive terms that he ever wrote Dayton* ANY *letter about his resignation or removal.* Did it publicly and repeatedly, and said if Dayton showed any such letters, they were *forgeries.*

Such has been the duplicity and double dealing of U. S. Marshal Johnson with the citizens of Oberlin touching his Deputy Dayton and the execution of the Fugitive Slave Act.

Since reference has been made to this "Deputy Dayton," justice demands that the public should know more of him. The following lines so accurately and happily advert to the leading exploits of his official career, that they are accepted with acknowledgments as furnishing the precise *multum in parvo* desiderated here.

DEAR LEADER: — The following melody, though in the style of Mother Goose, may, nevertheless, be relied upon as a truthful history of several remarkable passages in the life of a distinguished Deputy U. S. Marshal, by the name of Dayton. Q.

OUR MARSHAL.

BY AN OBERLIN MECHANIC.

Who sought this place when purse was low,
And he had nowhere else to go,
And strove his legal wit to show?
   Our Marshal.

Who sought for favors at our hand,
And tried to seem an *honest* man,
And *called* himself Republican?
   Our Marshal.

Who asked and got a recommend *
From our P. M. his worthy friend,
To do what *honest* men condemned?
   Our Marshal.

Who was the first to shake with fright,
When out a "little late" one night,
To see a figure robed in white?
   Our Marshal.

* Marshal Johnson says, " I did n't like his looks, but appointed him because he was so well recommended by Postmaster Munson."

Who was the first to break and run,
Though strongly armed and four to one,
From Wagner with his lockless gun?
     Our Marshal.

Who in his brave and daring mode,
Shot luckless chipmonks * by the road,
To get inured to deeds of blood?
     Our Marshal.

Who, bearing his revolvers twain,
Fled from a boy but with a cane,
And bawled for help with might and main?
     Our Marshal.

Who asked the Mayor for his aid,
To keep him from the colored maids,
Lest he might sometime be waylaid?
     Our Marshal.

Who fled from Painesville on the car,
Because he had no taste for war,
Or more especially for tar?
     Our Marshal.

Long live Old Buck in power and might,
To *punish* wrong and *guard* the right,
And longer live the Gallant Knight,
     Our Marshal.

When Liberty shall need a friend,
And threat'ning ruin shall impend,
May Government to rescue send,
     Our Marshal.

" To preserve from oblivion " two, as samples of the multitude of "memorable" speeches drawn out in a great number of localities by these " political trials," we insert the following: —

SPEECH OF HON. JOHN R. FRENCH,

At a Public Meeting held in Painesville, to consider the treatment of citizens of Lorain county by the Federal court.

JOHN R. FRENCH, Esq.:

SIR, — Believing that the circulation of your speech before the meeting in Painesville to consider the proceedings of the Federal Court in Cleveland, would aid to promote right views and feelings upon the subject, we respectfully suggest that it be published with the proceedings of the meeting.
  Yours, etc.,   A. MORLEY,
        T. ROCKWELL,
        WM. MATTHEWS,
        JOHN HOUSE,
        URI SEELEY.

PAINESVILLE, April 26, 1859.

Messrs. MORLEY, ROCKWELL, and others:

GENTLEMEN, — In the remarks I made at the meeting last evening (owing to the late hour when I spoke), I was obliged to take but a hurried glance at some very important points in this great controversy between Liberty and her ancient foe ; but if the printing can be of any service to the Right, I will write them out

* An Oberlin Democrat says he accompanied the courageous Deputy on a trip to Wellington to prepare for the kidnapping of " John," which was improved by "our Marshal" in shooting at chipmonks on the road-side, that he might become accustomed to blood.

as well as I may, and place the manuscript at your disposal.
  Your friend, JOHN R. FRENCH.

Mr. Chairman and Fellow-Citizens : —

I have no words suitable for the occasion. Twenty of our fellow-citizens — noble, excellent, Christian men — have been torn from their families, and, guiltless of all crime, are incarcerated in a prison. To express the sympathy you all feel for these men, and their wives and their little ones, one needs such kind words, such pitying words as only the angels have learned. And if I would give voice to the indignation that every true heart must feel when told that this GREAT WRONG is committed in the sacred name of " Law," I should need words as bitter as the dregs of a strong man's wrath. Ah, and who can command the trumpet tones that may arouse this slumbering nation to a sense of its danger.

Men in prison in Ohio, for violating the provisions of the Fugitive Slave Act! Has it, indeed, come to this, that in Ohio it is a crime to sympathize with the wronged and suffering? Are there men and courts still found in this State who believe in the constitutionality, the binding force of this statute, whose counterpart may not be found outside the statute-books of hell. The clause of the Constitution upon which they pretend to found this law, talks about " owing service." Certainly these cannot be slaves. A slave cannot *owe* service. A slave, in the eye of the law, is, to all intents and purposes, property; and property cannot make contracts, assume responsibilities, or owe service.

Mr. Chairman, can you talk of your horse owing service, or the table upon which you eat your dinner? The very first act of slavery, as it seizes its victim, its crowning, damning crime, is its total obliteration of the slave's personality, the wiping out of every vestige of his manhood, the herding of immortal beings with the beasts of the stall, the consigning of souls to the shambles. The slave is but merchandise, and when the framers of the Constitution talked about persons who " owed service," they could not have meant slaves, or horses, or household furniture.

But admitting, sir, the Fugitive Law construction of the Constitution — in spite of our common sense acknowledge that property may not " owe service "— and still you have not saved the constitutionality of this Law. This is an enactment of *Congress*, which has no right to interfere in the premises, for if there was a compact as claimed, it was a compact between sovereign States, and whatever legislation may be necessary to carry out the agreement, must come from the States. No where in the Constitution is this power delegated to the Federal Government, and all powers and rights not expressly delegated were reserved by the States.

But there is other ground upon which we of Ohio, who deny the binding force of the Fugitive Act, may stand. If there was a contract to restore Fugitive Slaves, it was a contract between the then thirteen States. Ohio and Kentucky were not there. They were not parties to the trade. And Kentucky cannot ask us to fulfil any contract which may have been made between Massachusetts and Carolina.

At the time of the adoption of the Constitution, slavery was looked upon by all parties as a temporary affair, soon to pass away. With this then universal sentiment, there could have been no legislation providing for future slavery in then unoccupied territories.

But the unshaken rock upon which we may all plant ourselves is this: The Fugitive Act tramples upon eternal and universally acknowledged RIGHT, and whatever statute violates RIGHT cannot be law, and so reads every acknowledged writer of the profession. The very office of Law is to protect Right, not to trample it in the mire of the street.

Sympathizing as I do, Mr. Chairman, with my entire heart with our friends in prison, and hating the doings of the Federal Court now in session at Cleveland, with as intense and holy a hatred as burns in any man's bosom, still I must confess that I am glad of this development of the spirit and determination of that Court.— It will turn the attention of the intelligent citizens of Ohio to the encroachments of the Federal Judiciary upon the sovereignty of the States and the rights of the People. Encroachments that have been accumulating stealthily, but uninterruptedly, from the commencement of the nation, until this department of the government threatens to assume to itself all power. Gentlemen may care nothing for the friendless negro, or for the " Oberlin Abolitionists," but do they care nothing for their own rights, or the sovereignty of their State? We have twenty millions of bank capital in Ohio — there is a dispute as to the just manner of its taxation. Certainly this is a question exclusively belonging to Ohio, to Ohio courts, and Ohio legislation, and Ohio citizens. But the Federal court steps in, and says this matter of levying taxes in Ohio, is a question for her disposal, and laughs your State courts to scorn. Two years ago the Ohio Legislature saw fit to declare certain Canal Contracts fraudulent, and therefore void. The highest court of the State passed upon the whole matter, and found the action of the Legislature legal and proper. That parties concerned might receive no harm, by special act of the Legislature they were allowed to come into our Courts and prosecute the State. Now, what power outside of Ohio had a right to interfere? But this very winter past, the Supreme Court of the United States has sent its mandate to our Supreme Court with a writ of error, requiring a copy of the canal contract proceedings, involving that whole subject which

had just gone through the departments of our Government, and been finally adjudicated in the State court of the last resort. In the Clark county rescue case a Sheriff of Ohio, in the proper discharge of his legal duty, was shot and beaten by a posse of Deputy U. S. Marshals until he was nearly dead, and when these men had been arrested, indicted for attempting to kill, and were in jail awaiting their trial, the Federal court steps in with its writ of *habeas corpus*, and sets the men at liberty. Now, men of Ohio, how do you like this trampling upon your State Rights and Sovereignty? One might think we were no longer an independent State, but a sort of colonial dependence upon the Federal Government.

In the midst of these accumulating outrages upon the sovereignty of the State, it is not strange that men are forgetting the true nature of our General Government. They forget that that Government is *Federal*, in contradistinction from National. That it sprang from the *States*, and not from the *people*. That it is a confederation of independent and sovereign States, for few and special purposes, and those purposes clearly defined and carefully set forth in the written compact. They confederated, as they said, " in order to form a more perfect union, establish justice, insure domestic tranquillity, provide for the common defence, and promote the general welfare, and secure the blessings of liberty to ourselves and our posterity." These were their objects, and the power to secure those granted to the Federal Government was limited and well defined. But the Federal Judiciary has been gathering to itself the power and rights of every other branch of both Federal and State Governments, until now, while Death on the pale horse, in its uncurbed haughtiness, it is galloping through every co-ordinate department, trampling all rights and sovereignties beneath its hoofs, while hell and destruction follow in its train. But there is an uprising of the people, there is a noble Republican party gathering in the free States, which will soon seize this horse by his bridle, and throw him upon his haunches.

Mr. Chairman, when we call in question the conduct of the President, or of Congress, or of the Federal Judiciary, ofttimes we are charged with talking " against the Union." But, sir, it should never be forgotten that these are not " the Union." The thirty-three independent STATES are the Union — and whoever, and whatever, denies the rights or tramples upon the sovereignty of these, he it is who is an enemy to the Union.

But, fellow citizens, the Republican party is not yet for two years in the possession of the Federal Government; and do you ask me where is our immediate and present escape from the oppressions of this Federal Judiciary? I answer that our hope is the Supreme Court of our State. And I believe we have sure protection here. Thank Heaven, that Court is a

REPUBLICAN COURT — every man of them. Last January the last of the doughfaces was made to walk the plank. Let us look, then, with all confidence to this Court, and the more so, as we have a man at the head of the executive department of the State, who has the heart and nerve to promptly execute its commands.

Mr. Chairman and fellow-citizens, when the State of Ohio, through the calm decision of her highest Court, shall take her place by the side of the gallant young State of Wisconsin, in repudiation of this cruel and wicked enactment, a proud day will have been reached in the progress of American civil liberty. And an example so potential will have been set, that within a twelvemonth it will have been followed by every free State of the Union.

Fellow-Citizens, we have another hope — like the Christian's "sure and steadfast"—the assurance of the early dissolution of that political body of men in our country, known as the "Democratic Party." Democrats, and yet aiding in all these attempts to consolidate all power in the hands of a grand central government. Democrats — and yet approving of all these outrages upon the rights and liberties of the State. Democrats — and yet finding it their highest ambition to go yelping, with tongue out and nose to the ground, upon the track of some fleeing fugitive. Why, sir, every man engaged in this Cleveland conspiracy, from the Judge on the bench down to the meanest (if there may be shades of meanness where all is superlatively base) pimp of the half hundred who were yesterday sworn in as special deputies, all, all are Democrats, and "National Democrats," at that. I do not learn, sir, that there has been so great a lie in the world since Cain denied all knowledge of his murdered brother, as this Democratic party. But it has got to die the death. The indignant scorn of the people has already dug its grave, a thousand fathom deep ; so deep, sir, that we need have no fear that the pestiferous exhalations of its putrefaction may pollute God's free air. Let the tidings of its speedy death, then, go forth. Proclaim it to the nations of the old world, that the tyrants and crowned heads, who have so long made a jest of American hypocrisy, may no longer hold us in derision. Let the news reverberate through the arches of heaven, that a new joy may be added to the rejoicings of that noble company of defenders of freedom, who have finished their labors on earth, and entered upon their reward. Aye, sir, let it bellow along through all the deep gorges of hell, where tyrants and slave-catchers most do congregate, for nowhere else may be found a larger company interested in the news.

Tom Moore somewhere tells of a vision in which he saw the Spirit of Liberty passing among the nations in the form of a lighted torch. He tells of the " expectant nations " anxiously awaiting its coming : —

> " And each as she received the flame
>   Lighted her altar with its ray,
> Then, smiling to the next who came,
>   Speeded it on its sparkling way."

So let these Meetings of the People be held, from town to town, until the old fires of Liberty are lighted in every breast. The people of Ohio must see to it that at their next election they return a Legislature which will pass a Personal Liberty Bill that shall put an end to slave-catching on Ohio soil, and disfranchise and outlaw any citizen who shall aid in enforcing within our limits the hated Fugitive Act.

But men tell us that we are contending against the laws of our country ; and the men engaged in enforcing the Fugitive Act plead, in justification of their conduct, that it is a " Law." So when the same class of men nailed Jesus to the cross between two thieves, they justified themselves by the same old plea, " WE HAVE A LAW, and by that Law he ought to die ; his blood be on us, and on our children." But those crucifiers of the Saviour were none the less guilty, and their pretended regard for the sanctity of law was loathsome hypocrisy and horrible impiety. These are the men, these who roll up their eyes in such mock astonishment and talk so flippantly about the duty of obeying the " Law," whenever the Fugitive Act is called in question, whom Whittier has gibbeted in his immortal verse where he asks : —

> Who knows not well these cankers of the North,
> These modern Esaus, bartering rights for broth?
> Taxing our justice with their double claim,
> As fools for pity, and as knaves for blame;
> Who, urged by party, sect, or trade, within
> The fell embrace of Slavery's sphere of sin,
> Part at the outset with their moral sense,
> The watchful angel set for Truth's defence;
> Confound all contrasts, good and ill; reverse
> The poles of life, its blessing and its curse;
> And lose thenceforth from their perverted sight
> The eternal difference 'twixt the wrong and right;
> To them the Law is but the iron span
> That girds the ankles of imbruted man;
> To them the Gospel has no higher aim
> Than simple sanction of the master's claim,
> Dragged in the slime of Slavery's loathsome trail,
> Like Chalier's Bible at his ass's tail!

> Such are the men who, with instinctive dread,
> Whenever Freedom lifts her drooping head,
> Make prophet tripods of the office stools,
> And scare the nurseries and the village schools
> With dire presage of ruin grim and great,
> A broken Union and a foundered State!
> Such are the patriots, self-bound to the stake
> Of office, martyrs for their country's sake,
> Who fill themselves the hungry jaws of Fate,
> And by their loss of manhood save the State:
> In the wide Gulf themselves like Curtius throw,
> And test the virtues of cohesive dough;
> As tropic monkeys, linking heads and tails,
> Bridge o'er some torrent of Ecuador's vales!

"SONS OF LIBERTY!"—REMARKS OF MR. GIDDINGS.

At the meeting of the people in Jefferson on the 7th, favorable to immediate and energetic action in reference to the trials pending before the U. S. District Court of Northern Ohio, for offences under the Fugitive Slave Act, the Hon. JOSHUA R. GIDDINGS introduced a constitution for the Order of the "Sons of Liberty" revived, of which order he gave the following historical sketch : —

It is important in times like the present, that we should look to precedents, to the action of our Revolutionary ancestors, men immortalized in history, their conduct will furnish safe rules for us to follow under like circumstances. They passed through scenes like these with which we are now surrounded, similar in principle, but differing widely in degree. I refer to the "Stamp Act," when an attempt was made to tax the colonists by compelling the people to buy stamped paper of the government. It was an encroachment upon their rights of property; but bore no comparison to the outrage upon liberty inflicted by this enactment; yet it was an encroachment upon their rights, an attempt to tax them without permitting them to be represented in Parliament. The Fugitive Law taxes us for purposes which we hold in abhorrence, in utter detestation. The compelling people of Ashtabula county to pay the expenses of seizing and carrying slaves from Ohio to Virginia and North Carolina, is a thousand times more revolting, than to pay the same amount to support a government in Germany. But this tax to carry back slaves is nothing compared to that provision which shocks our sensibilities at seeing a fellow man robbed of his liberty, ourselves compelled to aid in the perpetration of the crime, made to rivet the iron upon his limbs, and hand him over to his tormentors, and compel him to drag out a miserable existence, a thousand times more horrible than death itself.

But our fathers would not submit to the Stamp Act; shall we submit to the despotism of this slave act? We are greatly embarrassed in opposing the obnoxious law. So were they. There is a strong feeling, a deep hostility to this act. A gentleman from Portage county the other day, told me there were two thousand men ready to march, or do any thing else to relieve the prisoners at Cleveland, and put down this insult to our moral sensibilities; and such is the case here, and in all the counties of the Reserve. The popular heart swells with indignation, each individual feels and expresses it; but this feeling avails little until concentrated, united, and guided in some well-defined channel of operation.

Such was the case in New England in 1765. Our fathers were excited and indignant. They felt their rights were outraged. The "Stamp Act" had passed. Jared Ingersol of New Haven, happened at that time to be in London. He sought and obtained the appointment of stamp master. He landed at Boston on his return and bore himself as became a supercilious office holder. Soon as he had reached New Haven, a town meeting was called, as has been done here this evening. They passed resolutions requesting him to resign. Norwich, New London, and Wethersfield did the same; he refused. He probably felt as Judge Willson, District-Attorney Belden, and Marshal Johnson now feel, that the Government is on their side, and they hold the people in contempt. So said Ingersol. Our fathers saw the necessity of union, of concentrating the public indignation, the same as we feel it now.

To effect that object, Dagget and Thurman and other parties conceived and established the order called "The Sons of Liberty." It was composed of ardent Whigs; they had no tories among them. Each knew those who belonged to the order. They consulted together and *acted* together. Comparatively few were willing to unite and thereby incur danger of treason under British law. Thank God, we have no such fears. But a goodly number united, and *acted.*

Ingersol started from New Haven to go to Hartford at the convening of the Legislature. As he drew near to Westfield, he met four men riding two abreast, each holding a staff newly cut from the forest, peeled, and looking white. It was one of the insignia of the order, which Ingersol did not understand. Soon after he met sixteen others, riding two abreast, each with his peeled staff. They opened to the right and left, and Ingersol passed on his way. Soon after he met five hundred, preceded by three trumpeters and two officers in military dress. They opened right and left, Ingersol passed on to the centre, when they wheeled their horses and rode to the village with Ingersol in their midst. Then they halted, and ordered him to dismount, "The Sons of Liberty" also dismounting, gathered around him, and the leader informed him that he *must then and there resign his office.* "I will wait the orders of Government," said Ingersol. To which the leader responded in language worthy a "Son of Liberty," "*Here is the Government!*" The office-holder was astounded. He supposed that a feeble old man who sat on the throne at Westminster with a bauble on his head and a sceptre of less potency than a peeled cane in his hand, constituted the government. Such, too, is the view of office-holders at this day. They believe that James Buchanan *is the Government!* They think, at least, that he and his cabinet and the Supreme Court and Congress, constitute the Government. Poor "mistaken souls." They are all our servants; I have often told them, in the language of the Sons of Liberty, "*Here is the Government!*" that the People are the depositaries of power! Here resides the sovereignty of the nation. Each individual constitutes a component part of the government. I would that freemen should understand their dignity and power. The government is in *our hands*, and we are *not* in the hands of the government. Those farmers of Wethersfield had thought of this matter. They were conscious of their dignity; and Ingersol then saw their powers. "If I refuse, what will follow?" said he. "YOUR FATE!" said the leader of the patriots. These two monosyllables reached his heart. It was the determined language of the patriots; these words should reach the heart of Buchanan and every servile office-holder, who attempts to enforce this fugitive law. I would send these words thrilling through the heart of every slave-catcher, commissioned by James Buchanan, or acting upon the impulse of the Prince of Slaveholders. I would say to them, If you attempt to enslave a man here on this Western Reserve, "*your fate*" will follow. As I said in Congress, I say to-night, if the slave-catcher pollutes my threshold with his footsteps, I will strike him down; be he slave-holder or Deputy-Marshal, *his fate shall follow!* These two words will constitute one of the appropriate maxims for the "Sons of Liberty," whom I propose to organize to-night.

When Ingersol heard them, a new world seemed to open up to his frightened imagination. "The cause," said he, "is not worth dying for," — language which many slave-catching dough-faces and Deputy-Marshals of our State would utter if the people, or one tenth part of the people, would firmly and kindly whisper, "*your fate*" in their ears. "I resign," said Ingersol. "Swear to it," said the leader. Ingersol remonstrated. Then, said the leader, shout "*Liberty and Property*," three times; and Ingersol opened his profane lips, and, for the first time in his life, shouted "Liberty and Property," "*Liberty and Property*," "LIBERTY AND PROPERTY!" It should be borne in mind, that the mother government had not then so persecuted the colonists as to rob any of their lives. But five years afterwards, when the people in King street, Boston, were fired upon by the King's troops, and five of them killed, their motto was then amended by adding to it the word "*life*," so that, from 1770, "*life*, liberty, and property" became their motto, and will, I trust, be ours in coming time.

But Ingersol went to Hartford in company with the "Sons of Liberty," and there announced his resignation to the proper authorities, and retired to private life. The Order rapidly spread throughout New England. Patriots in every town, village, hamlet, and school district united with it. They had no tories in their ranks; public sentiment was guided in its proper channels. Its influence constrained the office-holders to send back to England the stamped paper forwarded to them, and to resign their offices. The King and Parliament opened their eyes to the great truth, that *the people constituted a power superior to themselves*, and they repealed the Stamp Act. Gentlemen, let the true "Sons of Liberty" in Ashtabula County manifest the same firmness exhibited at Wethersfield in 1765, and James Buchanan and his satraps would never be seen chasing slaves in Ohio, nor would they persecute our citizens.

The Order was kept up; and when the odious tax on tea was forced upon the pioneers, and the two ships loaded with it lay in Boston harbor in 1773, they again sat in council, and determined on their course. At nightfall, in disguise, they went on board, and, using the Atlantic ocean for a teapot, they got up the celebrated tea-party to which our friend (Mr. Simonds) alluded. This was the second and last exercise of force by the "Sons of Liberty." Their great usefulness consisted in giving direction to the popular mind which guided the provincial legislatures, and found an equally emphatic expression in Congress.

John Adams informs us that a deputation from the "Sons of Liberty" in Pennsylvania met him in New Jersey in 1776, when on his way to Congress. Their principal object was to induce him so to arrange matters as to have Mr. Jefferson write the Declaration of Independence, — a measure which Mr. Adams had brought forward and advocated. They thought by so doing they would secure the influence of Virginia and other Southern States. I now think the proposition wrong; that Mr. Adams should have pursued his own course and received the glory which he thus surrendered to another. But he being one of the Order, submitted to their advice, and Jefferson feeling the import of this phrase, adopted the natural rights of man to life, liberty, and property, as the basis of the new Government. He, however, changed the word "property," to that of "the pursuit of happiness," as a better mode of expression.

But so much had the people become attached to this maxim that they adopted it into the Constitution, which provides that "*no person shall be deprived of life, liberty, or property, without due process of law.*" This declaration, in the words used by the "Sons of Liberty" in 1770, and incorporated into the Constitution, I suggest as the proper basis of the Order which I now propose to revive. I hope that our friends in other counties and towns may unite in reviving this organization, and concentrating the popular mind upon the importance of maintaining the right of every human being to life, liberty, and property, until slave-catchers and slave-catching office-holders shall be driven from the Reserve, from the State, *from the Union*, FROM THE WORLD.

Mr. G. then presented the Constitution, etc.

"CONSTITUTION OF THE SONS OF LIBERTY."

WHEREAS, The authority of Britain over her American Provinces was first set at defiance by an association of patriots called "The SONS OF LIBERTY," who by their personal efforts concentrated the influence and gave direction to the popular voice, which is always powerful when guided by discretion and judgment: And whereas, the party that now controls the administration of the Federal Government has waged a cruel war against human nature, establishing an execrable commerce in the souls and bodies of men, a commerce so cruel that its victims often prefer death by their own hands rather than the degradation, the horrors to which it consigns them: employing the army and navy to butcher defenceless women and children on account of their love of liberty; enacting a fugitive law so barbarous that the tender mother is driven to the terrible alternative of slaying her own children rather than see them subjected to its cruelties; overruling the laws and trampling upon the rights of our State; protecting felons indicted in our courts; extending impunity to murderers who shed the blood of their fellow men upon our soil; arresting, imprisoning, and prosecuting our citizens for the exercise of virtues which constitute the true glory of our revolutionary ancestors:

Now, therefore, in order to reform the administration of our Government; to direct its energies to the *protection*, instead of the destruction of human rights; to put an end to this piratical war, we hereby revive the ancient order of "THE SONS OF LIBERTY," recognizing each other and those who shall hereafter sign this Constitution by that name; declaring our present purpose and ulterior design to inculcate and maintain the duty of human governments to protect human rights; that the violation of those rights by individuals, by officers, or by men acting as a Government, constitutes CRIME:

Appealing to the Supreme Judge of the world for the rectitude of our intentions, we declare that "*no person shall be deprived of life, liberty, or property, without due process of law,*" WHEN WE HAVE POWER TO PREVENT IT.

[The foregoing Constitution was then subscribed by nearly one hundred gentlemen, embracing the names of some of the most prominent and respectable citizens in the community.]—*Ashtabula Sentinel.*

OF THE COUNTLESS "MEETINGS held to consider the treatment of the Lorain citizens," with their stirring speeches and plain-spoken resolutions, we have room to notice only one; and of that we publish the proceedings in full, as reported in the daily papers.

The call, in response to which the masses gathered, was this:—

MASS CONVENTION.

In view of the impending crisis, which seems to admonish us that "LIBERTY IS TO BE PRESERVED BY CEASELESS VIGILANCE," it is deemed important that a general Mass Convention of the foes of Slavery and Despotism, and the friends of State and Individual Rights, be held in some convenient place on the Western Reserve without an unnecessary delay.

We do, therefore, earnestly request our Republican friends throughout the said Western Reserve, as well as all others who are in sympathy with us in our opposition to despotic usurpation of power, to meet in council in the City of Cleveland, on Tuesday, the 24th day of May, instant, at eleven o'clock A. M.

Arrangements have been made with all the Railroads for half fare tickets to and from the Convention.

C. W. Noble,	J. J. Ellwell,
H. F. Brayton,	B. Barker,
J. F. Keeler,	H. B. Spelman,
D. L. Wightman,	Jno. C. Grannis,
R. C. Parsons,	W. M. Corner,
J. S. Grannis,	James B. Wilbur,
R. P. Spalding,	John Coon,
D. R. Tilden,	and 500 others.
A. G. Riddle,	

Cleveland, May 12, 1859.

Of the meeting we read thus:—

GREAT MASS MEETING.
NORTHERN OHIO AWAKE.
THE FOES OF THE FUGITIVE ACT IN COUNCIL.

The great Mass Meeting of Republicans this morning has caused a cessation of all business, and the streets are full of strangers from all parts of the State. The influx from the surrounding country commenced at an early hour this morning, wagon loads of people arriving by all the streets leading in from the country villages. Preparations for a great meeting had been made on the Square. A large platform had been erected on the corner of the Square, near the United States building, and the regular music platform in the vicinity was set aside for the use of some of the bands.

THE RAILROADS.

The Cleveland and Pittsburg early train brought in about a hundred passengers for the Convention, and several came in last evening by the different railroads. About half past nine o'clock this morning, the Elyria train brought in six loaded cars, and in about half an hour afterwards the train from Oberlin brought in thirteen loaded cars. Seven crowded cars came in on the Cleveland, Columbus, and Cincinnati Railroad. From the Lake Shore Railroad came in sixteen car loads of delegates to the Convention. The Cleveland and Pittsburg Railroad brought in five car loads, and the Cleveland and Mahoning Railroad brought nine crowded cars. The railroads to-day did not bring less than 3,500 people to the Convention.

The Delegates from the Eastern lake shore towns, from Wellington, and from Oberlin, with their neighboring towns, formed in procession at the depots, and marched to the Public Square. As they passed up Superior street, the Lake and Ashtabula county delegations led the way, headed by a military band, and bearing a banner inscribed on one side,

ASHTABULA.
Regnanto Populi.

And on the other side —

SONS OF LIBERTY.
1765.
Down with the Stamp Act!
1859.
Down with the Fugitive Act!

As this part of the procession turned the corner from Water street, a handsome national flag, surmounted with a cap of Liberty, and bearing the legend —

"SONS OF LIBERTY
We Welcome you!"

was sent from one of the stores in the neighborhood.

Next came the Oberlin delegation, marching two abreast, and headed by the Oberlin Brass Band, playing the "Marseillaise." Conspicuous in the procession, was the venerable figure of Father GILLETT, seventy-four years of age, bearing aloft the "stars and stripes" with the inscription "1776."

They were followed by the Wellington delegation and an immense crowd of persons from all parts of Lorain county. This party carried a banner inscribed "LORAIN," and on the other side —

"Here is the Government,
Let Tyrants Beware."

ON THE PUBLIC SQUARE.

As soon as the crowd arrived at the square, a very large delegation went down to the jail to see the prisoners. Sheriff WIGHTMAN had caused that jail yard to be strictly closed, so that no ingress or egress could be had. The prisoners were allowed to be in the jail yard, and loud calls were made for PLUMB, PECK, and others of the prisoners. Short addresses were made by these gentlemen, avowing their determination never to flinch from the good cause in which they were engaged, but at the same time counselling moderation. After a round of hearty cheers, the crowd adjourned to the speakers' stand.

Here the Convention was called to order by the appointment of Hon. R. P. SPALDING as temporary President, and JOHN C. GRANNIS as Secretary.

Professor MORGAN invoked the Divine blessing on the proceedings of the day.

Hon. R. P. SPALDING addressed the meeting. He said they had met to consult on the best means to preserve the gift of liberty left us by our fathers. The founders of this Republic had left us valuable rights and privileges, and how long these privileges may be enjoyed depends entirely on ourselves.

The speaker referred to the action of the Colonial Congress of 1774, in which a resolution was passed providing for the abolition of the slave-trade, whilst now a recent convention at Vicksburg, passed resolutions condemning the laws for the prevention of the slave-trade.

Whilst men are prosecuted here to fine and imprisonment for obeying the natural instincts and dictates of our nature, the law against the slave-trade is treated with contempt at the South, and the offenders against the law are set at liberty.

Judge SPALDING concluded by saying that we have not met to set at defiance either the law or the officers of the law. We have met to manifest the will and determination of the people in a peaceful and constitutional manner. He counselled them to preserve order. Let us make known our rights, and our determination to maintain those rights, even to the last issue; but as you value your position as Republicans, as members of that great party of the right, let good order characterize your doings, and keep you from any illegal acts.

This address, which was listened to by at least ten thousand persons, was received with great enthusiasm.

The President then announced the following names as forming the Committee on Resolutions: —

John Coon, Cuyahoga; W. H. Upson, Summit; B. F. Wade, Ashtabula; James Monroe, Lorain; J. R. French, Lake; H. G. Blake, Medina; O. P. Brown, Portage; Wm. T. Boscom, Franklin; R. W. Taylor, Mahoning; Dr. George Howe, Trumbull; Peter Hitchcock, Geauga; William S. Miner, Erie; James M. Ashley, Lucas; Frank Sawyer, Huron; Jacob Heaton, Columbiana; J. W. Vance, Knox; W. T. Day, Hamilton; A. Burke, Stark; A. H. Palmer, Ashland; J. M. Keeler, Sandusky.

The Committee on Permanent Organization was then reported: —

Dr. Alvin Pomeroy, Putnam; John F. Converse, Geauga; N. P. Schuyler, Huron; J. M. Keeler, Sandusky; J. D. Cox, Trumbull; ——, Mahoning; Hon. H. Canfield, Medina; D. C. Allen, Ashtabula; Dr. R. C. Kirk, Knox; J. S. Herrick, Portage; Philemon Bliss, Lorain; A. D. Howe, Lake; H. D. Cooke, Franklin; N. Wentworth, Ashland; D. R. Tilden, Cuyahoga.

The Secretary read various letters received from gentlemen unavoidably absent: —

LETTER FROM HON. WM DENNISON, JR.

Columbus, May 20, 1859.

S. O. GRISWOLD, ESQ., and others: —

GENTS,— A prior engagement to attend a meeting of the Republican National Executive Committee, at Albany, New York, on the 25th inst., will prevent me complying with your kind invitation to attend the Convention you have called, to be held at Cleveland the preceding day.

Let me express my ardent hope that the proceedings of your Convention may be such as will permanently contribute to the advancement of the sacred principles of freedom, justice, and humanity, which have been so violently assailed by the imprisonment in your county jail of Messrs. Plumb and Peck, and their devoted colleagues, under the insulting provisions of the Fugitive Slave Act, and that in the contest between the antagonisms of freedom and slavery forced upon us by the Southern oligarchy and its Northern allies, we may at all times prove ourselves worthy descendants of the heroic founders of the Republic, who declared one of the great purposes of the Federal Constitution to be, the securing to themselves and their posterity "the blessings of liberty."

Accept the assurance of my sincere regard personally, and of my uncompromising hostility to slavery and despotism in every form.

Truly yours,
W. DENNISON, JR.

LETTER FROM THOMAS SPOONER.

Cincinnati, May 21, 1859.

S. O. GRISWOLD and others:—

GENTS,—Yours of the 16th inst., inviting me to attend a Mass Convention of all "Foes of Slavery and Despotism," to be held in Cleveland on the 24th inst., is before me.

I regret that I cannot be present to participate in the proceedings of the Convention.

It is high time that the people of the North had spoken boldly and fearlessly their true sentiments upon the only living political question of the day.

It is time that we had declared against a further extension of Slavery—that while we will not interfere with the rights of the States, we are determinedly fixed in our resolution, that the territories of our country shall be consecrated to free labor. That no longer shall the great groundwork of our declaration of rights—the basis of our laws—the natural impulses of man—the great law of right—the dictates of conscience—that no longer shall these be trodden down, be crushed out, a nullity in our land—that we will hold sacred and inviolable the rights of all to life and liberty who may obtain a foothold in the North-west—that no longer will we countenance a Judiciary who will under "safe precedents" give up to slavery those who are seeking freedom.

The sympathy of the State—of all lovers of self rights—is with Prof. Peck and others who are now incarcerated in the jail of Cuyahoga county, solely for aiding those who were fleeing from Slavery to Freedom.

Very truly,
THOS. SPOONER.

LETTER FROM PHILIP DORSHEIMER.

Buffalo, May 18, 1859.

S. O. GRISWOLD and others:—

GENTLEMEN,—I have the honor to acknowledge the receipt of your invitation to attend a Mass Convention to be held at Cleveland the 24th inst. I shall leave home to-morrow upon an engagement made some time ago, and shall not return in time to reach Cleveland on the day mentioned.

I agree with you that the aggressions of the Slave power "are sufficient to alarm every true patriot." Every concession the North has made seems to have emboldened the South to make new demands. Having defeated us in our efforts to prevent the extension of slavery, Southern politicians now seek to secure the National power for the sole purpose of extending the area of slavery; having abolished the Congressional interdiction upon the introduction of slaves into the Federal territories, they have now, with the assistance of the judiciary, proclaimed as a part of the fundamental law, that the Constitution carries slavery into every Territory; and finally Southern statesmen seek to engage the Republic in an infamous and piratical traffic by the repeal of the existing laws against the slave-trade. These abominable doctrines, and above all, the success which has hitherto attended them, may well excite the fears of the patriot.

I wish you that success which your cause deserves, and remain yours, etc.

PHILIP DORSHEIMER.

LETTER FROM T. H. COULTER.

S. O. GRISWOLD and others, Committee:—

GENTS,—If my business affairs were not absolutely compelling my constant attention, I should take great pleasure in complying with your invitation to attend a Mass Convention of all the foes of slavery and despotism, to be held at Cleveland on the 24th inst.

I should as soon think of chaining the lightning as to think of smothering the feeling of resentment aroused in your manly bosoms, by the recent outrages perpetrated in your midst, under the hypocritical cover of law.

I declared that we should reap bitter fruit as a party, when we first organized as Republicans, by not declaring against the constitutionality of the Fugitive Slave Law. Our position was too tame then, and events now prove it.

The proper attitude boldly taken then would have rendered our position as a party impregnable. But from our desire to conciliate conservatism then, we now have its strength doubled upon us. Thousands of men, who then declared this law an outrage upon the Constitution, are now meekly bowing to this usurpation of power, and some of them, like Judge Willson and Attorney Belden, are its willing instruments of execution. They are represented as having been its fierce denouncers, and are now its willing supporters.

Though no Republican is willing to sanction in any way the law, many allow it to be constitutional. This is what we have lost by our tameness, for not one in twenty, who now concede this, would have done so, if we had incorporated into our platform the opposite opinion. Hard work is now necessary to enable us to advance to that position as a party.

It must be done, however, and Ohio, more properly than any other State, should lead the column. Yours, etc.,

                              T. H. COULTER.
Columbus, May 23, 1859.

LETTER FROM CASSIUS M. CLAY.

GENTLEMEN, — Your favor of the 16th is received too late to accept it on my part. I deeply sympathize with you in your movement against the advances of " slavery and despotism." The scenes which are now being enacted in Cleveland, where men are fined and imprisoned for the exercise of the highest instincts of Heathen Philanthropy and Christian Morality in violation of the sacred principles of our government and the utter overthrow of our much vaunted *Constitution*, are well calculated to arouse a sluggish people to action, and awake the sleepiest from their fatal slumbers! I always hated and denounced the Fugitive Slave Law — not only because it violated the United States Constitution — the return of fugitives from labor being a duty imposed upon the States only, according to the unbought dicta of the " Expounder of the Constitution," Daniel Webster, and denied to Congress, — but because it violated all the safeguards of freedom, jeoparded the life, liberty, and happiness, not only of the humble and hated African, but of every proud Saxon in the land, and made justice a mockery in all its forms, and because it *humiliated and degraded our manhood*, and fitted us to be ourselves slaves, which our masters long since designed.

Gentlemen, allow me to be a little egotistical. In a letter to the members of the New York Legislature, dated January 9, 1846, more than thirteen years ago, I used these words: " This is no longer a question about Africans — whether they be beasts or men — a debate about maudlin philanthropy ! — *but whether* we, the eighteen millions of white men of these States, shall be free men or slaves !"

These sentiments and utterances were denounced as the most atrocious and fanatical all over the North; and what little reputation I had for common sense was, for long years, lost ! What say you now, men of Ohio ? What think you of the expulsion of the representatives of Massachusetts, seeking legal redress of wrongs in the Courts of the United States, from Charleston and New Orleans ? What think you of the army and navy present in Boston to enforce an unconstitutional law ? What think you of the trials of American citizens for their lives for " *constructive treason ?* " What think you of the selling Northern citizens into Southern slavery ? What think you of the Governmental murders in Kansas ? What think you of the military dictatorship there ? What think you

of the armed overthrow of the ballot-box by the national bayonets ? What think you of the political attempts to vote a minority Constitution over the heads of the freemen of Kansas, and to drive it down their throats with sword and ball ? What think you of the decision of the Supreme Court that the black man has no rights which the white man is bound to respect ? What think you of their dicta that citizens of the free States are not citizens of the *United States ?* What think you of the Dred Scott decision in its *real purpose* — that slavery is the only sovereignty in these States — in the language of the Kentucky and Kansas laws — a man's right to his slave " is higher than all laws and constitutions ? " What think you of that sort of a " Higher Law ? " What think you of the embryo political movement under " Democratic " (!) auspices, which will, in 1860, call upon you to invest Congress with the power to put it into practice in all the Territories, and then in all the States ? You can't see speculative opinions — you know nothing of the logic of principles — you ignore cause and effect by induction, making the past, future history ! But you see your good and true men now lying in prison ! You begin to understand that thing ! You call a convention on the 24th inst. You invoke the countenance and aid of " every true patriot and friend of freedom ! " Very good ! You intend to " resolve," to " protest," to " denounce." Is that all ? Then go home and wear your chains ! I say, *are you ready to fight?* Not to fight the poor Judge at Cleveland — not to fight the Marshal — not to fight the miserable packed Jury — not to fight the tools of the Despots — but the Despots themselves ! Not to violate the laws — not to make emeutes — not to produce anarchy, but to maintain constitutional liberty — peaceably *if we can — forcibly if we must !* Are you ready for that ? If not, give it up now ! Don't go into a National Convention to select a standard-bearer who is a " submissionist ! " Don't put up a " compromiser ! " Don't look out for a " conservative ! " They 'll all betray you, as they have done ! they all do that which you expected and desired them to do. They 'll all sell us out as we have been willing to be sold ! " The Union will be again in danger ! " I played prophet thirteen years ago — I 'll play the same part again.

Men do not lay down power voluntarily; our masters, the slaveocracy, are not going " to go out like a snuff." The " Democracy " intend to *rule the Union*, or *ruin the Union !* I don't intend, so far as I can prevent — so far as I can control or influence the Republican party, that they shall be allowed to do either. I want a man at the head of the party, who will be the *platform* of the party. I want now no cornstalk general, but a real general. I want a man whose banners bear no uncertain sign. When I see *slave propagandism* on the banners of the Democracy, I want to see, in legible colors, *liberty propagandism* on the flag of the Republicans. When I read "Slavery is higher than all laws and all constitutions," I want a scribe who will write under it and on it, in letters like those of John Hancock, *that is a lie!* When the slave-holders say if you elect a Republican President, we will dissolve the Union, I don't want any one to put off the evil day which would follow such event by saying, "let it slide!" but some one who would stand by the tomb of Andrew Jackson, and become infused to such extent with the spirit of that old patriot and hero — that he would be ready to cry out in the fulness of inspiration : " By the Eternal — the Union shall be preserved !" I would have no man to be precipitate — bandy no hard words — be by no means " fussy" — but standing upon the great rocks of *State Sovereignty* and *National Supremacy*, I would defy the canting traitors to Liberty, Law, Civilization, and Humanity! That 's what I mean by asking you, are you *ready to fight!* If you have got your sentiments up to that manly pitch, I am with you all through to the end! But if not, I 'll have none of your conventions — no more farcical campaigns; no more humbugs; no more Fourth of July orations — no more Declarations of Independence — no more platitudes — no more glittering generalities — no more rights of man — no more liberty, equality, and fraternity! In obscure places — in silence and humility, I will crush out the aspirations of earlier and better days — and attempt the dutiful but hard task of forgetting that I was *born free!*

Your Obedient Servant,
C. M. CLAY.

Messrs. S. O. GRISWOLD, etc., Com., etc., Cleveland, Ohio.

THE PROCESSION.

On the adjournment, until half-past one o'clock, a procession was formed under the direction of Marshal SPANGLER and his assistants. The Bands furnished fine music while the procession marched at times to the inspiriting music of Huntoon's drummers and fifers of Painesville. The cheerful looks of those composing the procession, with the Bands and the Banners which floated gaily in the breeze, rendered the spectacle a very pleasing and inspiring one. They were greeted with cheers all along the route, and marched through the principal streets.

Hon. E. WADE spoke, in the interim of other exercises, on the Fugitive Slave Law, its nature, its constitutionality, and its binding force. Because a Judge, not in the line of his judicial duty, pronounces an enactment law, that does not make it law. He is not to make the law, but to look at it as it has been made. What is the Supreme Court, and what is Justice Taney? Why ! I wish the crowd could look in upon the Supreme Court, as I have done, and I tell you your bump of veneration would fall right in. [Laughter.] You have seen, in passing by

farmers' barns in the early times of the country, the sides of his barn and outbuildings covered with the skins of coons, and other animals. The Supreme Court has much the same appearance and the same nature as these dried parchments. The Democracy of this day is opposed to civil and religious liberty. [Cries of " true, true."] In the Democratic party of this nation, eighty-five per cent. is put in by the party leaders.

AFTERNOON MEETING.

The temporary Chairman, Judge Spalding, called the meeting to order at half-past one o'clock.

Judge Tilden, from the Committee upon permanent organization, reported the following officers : —

Permanent Officers.

Hon. J. R. GIDDINGS, President.

Vice-Presidents. — John P. Converse, Geauga ; John F. Morse, Lake ; Geo. H. Howe, Trumbull ; Joseph DeWolf, Portage ; James Dumars, Mahoning ; J. W. Vance, Knox ; Jacob Heaton, Columbiana ; James Monroe, Lorain ; Herman Canfield, Medina ; Sidney Edgerton, Summit ; Dr. A. D. Skillenger, Huron ; N. Wentworth, Ashland ; Felix Nicola, Cuyahoga.

Secretaries. — John C. Graniss, Cuyahoga ; J. S. Herrick, Portage ; Augusta Thieme, Cuyahoga ; Joseph H. Dickson, Lorain.

The report of the Committee was accepted by three cheers, and the officers took their seats.

Judge TILDEN was then introduced to the audience and made a short and telling speech, full of appropriate and cutting allusions to the Federal Court and to the officers who have incarcerated these Oberlin men. After throwing hot shot into their castle and sufficiently punishing them for their infamous actions, he passed into the features of Congressional politics, showing that the Chairmen of all the important Committees, and the majority of these Committees were of the unterrified Democracy. Passing rapidly over these, he threw into his remarks many capital hits at the dominant party, which kept the immense audience in a roar.

He showed up the inconsistency of the officers of this Federal Court. Belden had been an Abolitionist, but had turned Democrat, but they could mark his words, Belden would come yet to the Republican party, but every man should have his boots ready nailed to kick him out of the party.

Outside of some cannibal and heathen countries he did not believe there was such an infamous Court as this.

Three hearty cheers thanked Judge TILDEN as he sat down.

J. W. VANCE, Esq., of Mt. Vernon, was next introduced.

He came here, as every man who has a mind

for freedom and is opposed to slavery should do, and he should be proud to speak a word for free principles. It was a fundamental principle of our government that all men had free and equal rights, and these principles are not confined to our government. They have their source in natural justice, the great source of all law and all rights. Shall we, as freemen, stand up for our rights and defend them as in the days of the Revolution, or shall we tamely submit to tyranny?

The Constitution gave us no right to make slaves of a part of our citizens; on the contrary, it provided that all should have equal rights to citizenship. It is true that we should, under the Constitution, let the owner of escaped slaves come and get them as they would a horse, but the slave-holders were not satisfied with this, they must have a law by which they could seize any colored man, woman, or child, and carry them into slavery. They call, too, upon us — upon all of us — to help them carry back into slavery these persons whom they seize, and will you do it? [Cries of " No, no, never ! "] We are here to-day, not only to treat of law for ourselves, but to force the administration to obey the laws. [Applause]. You have some men and brothers in yonder jail; now what shall we do? Let us exhaust every law and legal means in our power, and if then we should fail, which God forbid, let us show that Ohio *shall be free* by the right of the people. [Three cheers].

" Hail Columbia" by the Chagrin Falls band.

Hon. JOSHUA R. GIDDINGS was next introduced.

The old War Horse spoke as follows, being greeted with hearty applause : —

I have met many of you at different times, but this is the greatest occasion of all. Forty-seven years ago I first entered this territory. I bore my musket on my shoulder. The British fleet lay in the offing, and here on this ground on the 10th of Sept., 1812, many of my companions listened to the thunders of Perry's fleet, and the heroism of that day has not passed and gone. But this country for which so many of our fathers fought and bled, is now contaminated by the presence of tyrants, and here in this New England of the West, men have been arrested and imprisoned for aiding a fellow man to gain his freedom. This may be a common scene in Africa, but not here. Had this tyranny confined its operations to Congress, where it struck down your Senators and gagged the bold and fearless men who dared to raise their voice against this terrible wrong, you could do no more than to use your own influence in bringing about a better state of affairs. When it invaded our own State, and wrongs unheard of before were enacted in the southern part of our State, you could not go there to correct those wrongs. The people of the Western Reserve could only shudder at the wrongs and hope for better things.

But now the war is brought to our own door. Here among our own residences and homes, some of our most respected citizens have been thrust into a prison for doing what I thank them for from my inmost soul.

For thus obeying the high behests of Heaven's King, these men are now thrust into a gloomy prison which would disgrace the Southern portions of Africa.

But it is said that this man had no rights which we should respect. It was said that God had given to the doughfaces in Congress the power to turn him from one master to another with no voluntary act of the victim. All the nobleness of our nature rebels against such Atheism; all human beings have derived from their Creator a right to life, liberty, and the pursuit of happiness. You may brutalize him and abuse him; but no more can human government transfer the right of human liberty than they can put life into a corpse.

Now had Congress the right to consign this man, or any man, to everlasting slavery and bondage? No, never! and here we leave the Democratic party. If they held the doctrines which we do upon this point, there would be no point of disagreement between us. But one judicial decision that I know of has been given upon this fundamental point — the Dred Scott decision. I know that throughout Christendom there is a universal abhorrence of this doctrine. As early as 1765, John Adams announced that the right to human liberty was antecedent to all law or government. Only the tories of the Revolution denied this. They were the men who, like the pro-slavery party of this day, deny all human right against the will of tyrants. Not the Democracy of this or any other day, hold to this doctrine. No, such an imputation would put Democracy to the blush, it would insult hell itself to give it such an opinion and characteristic.

I tell you that all men are created free and equal, and that eternal truth I for one will stand by and abide by. Men talk of Constitutional laws. There stands a Constitution that declares that all have equal rights.

I have no hesitation as to the means for acting upon this great matter which is now before us. I would have a committee appointed to-day, to apply to the first and nearest officer who has the power, that he shall issue a writ for the release of those prisoners — not the men who have now been summoned to Columbus, but those who have not been sentenced. And I want to be appointed on that committee, and if so, I will promise you that no sleep shall come to my eyelids this night until I have used my utmost endeavors to have these men released. [Immense applause.] If it was not for the Supreme Court of the State, for which I have the utmost respect, I would ask for no judicial process, but those men should be brought before you to-day. [Vociferous applause.] I will, if such a committee be appointed, apply to Judge Tilden, and if he flinched in the exercise of his duty, and refused to issue this writ, I would never speak to him again or give him my hand. If he failed, I would go to another, and another, until death came to close my eyelids. I know that the Democratic press throughout the country has represented me as counselling forcible resistance to this law, and God knows it is the first truth they have ever told about me.

Now let me take a vote. I want all in this crowd who are ready to tamely and timidly submit to tyranny to speak out. [Not a voice replied.] Now let all those who are ready and resolved to resist when all other means fail — when your rights are trampled into the dust — when the yoke is fixed upon your necks — and when the heel of oppression crushes your very life out — all those who are thus ready to resist the enforcement of this infamous Fugitive Slave Law — speak out. [The roar which now arose from thousands of voices was deafening.] I would have this voice sound in the mouth of the cannon, and I would have it resound over every hill, through every vale, by every winding stream and rushing river. I would have it go roaring in every free mountain wind which rocks your forests, until all the world shall hear. [Cheers.]

And now let me say to the Democrats,· if there are any here, that so long as I have life and health, I will use all my influence, and all legal means to oppose the execution of this law, —and when all such means fail, then so long as I have strength to raise and wield an arm, so long I will resist unto death, and will work and pray for liberty with my latest breath.

Deafening and prolonged applause and cheers showed the interest taken by the vast audience in the remarks of Mr. Giddings.

The following resolutions were then presented and read by John Coon, Esq., chairman of the committee on resolutions, and adopted by a thundering vote.

DECLARATION.

This assembly of the people of the State of Ohio, holding : —

That, next to our duty to the Supreme Being, is our obligation to preserve our free institutions and our civil liberties;

That the greatest tyrants have been those whose titles have been least questioned;

That every violation of the Constitution should be watched with jealousy and resented with spirit;

That the history of every free people has shown the impossibility of a cordial compliance with laws which neither embody nor execute the public will;

That the enforcement of such laws against an unwilling people, is productive only of evils threatening public order and the stability of governmental institutions : and holding farthermore,

That the history of the government of the United States, as recently administered, is a history of repeated injuries and usurpations, all having in direct object the Africanization of this continent by the diffusion and establishment of slavery and the restriction and limitation of freedom, thus reversing the ancient policy of the founders of the Republic, which looked to the extinction of slavery and the extension of liberty ; and

That the Dred Scott decision, reversing all the well-established rules which for ages have been the bulwark of personal liberty, yields its legitimate fruits in the recent atrocities committed in the heart of the Western Reserve, and calls upon us for new efforts and new sacrifices for constitutional liberty, do, therefore, publish and DECLARE,

1st. That the several States composing the United States of America, are not united on the principle of unlimited submission to their general government, but that by compact, under the style and title of a Constitution for the United States, and of amendments thereto, they constituted a general government for special purposes, and delegated to that government certain definite powers, reserving each State for itself the residuary mass of right to their own self-government; and that whensoever the general government assumes undelegated powers, its acts are unauthoritative, void, and of no force, and being void, can derive no validity from mere judicial interpretation ; that to this compact each State acceded as a State, and is an integral party ; that this government, created by this compact, was not made the exclusive or final judge of the extent of the powers delegated to itself, since that would have made its discretion, and not the Constitution, the measure of its powers ; but that, as in all other cases of compact between parties having no common judge, each party has an equal right to judge for itself, as well of infractions, as of the mode and measure of redress.

2d. That the law commonly known as the Fugitive Slave Law of 1850, was, in the opinion of this assembly, passed by Congress in the exercise of powers improperly assumed; and had it been presented as an original question to a wise and impartial court, must have been held in conflict with the Constitution, and, therefore, *void*.

3d. That one of the most alarming symptoms of degeneracy in the General Government, is the pliant subserviency of the Supreme Court of the United States to the objects of party politics, thus greatly diminishing that public confidence in the judiciary so essential to good order ; that the extent to which the Supreme Court has thus compromised its character, renders it incumbent upon the people to consider what measures are necessary to restore that tribunal to its ancient estate.

4th. That, in the opinion of this assembly, an amendment of the federal judiciary system is indispensably necessary, so that the sovereignty of the States may be respected, and individuals guarded from oppression. As a means to this end, it is strongly recommended that the life tenure of judges be abolished, and that the judicial office be limited to a term of years; that Congress so remodel the judicial circuits that a majority of citizens of the United States shall have a majority of the justices of the Supreme Court.

5th. That the recent proceedings of the Federal Court for this District, in producing the conviction of persons indicted under the provisions of the Fugitive Slave Law, by the employment of the most disgraceful partisan means, is without a parallel even in the modern history of despotism; that the victims of that Court, now incarcerated in yonder prison, convicted or accused of "humanity to man," are entitled to, and we hereby tender to them, our cordial sympathy; and to make that sympathy effectual, we hereby recommend:

*. That a fund be raised to be called *The Fund of Liberty;* and to the end that every Republican on the Reserve may share in accumulating that fund, that the contributions be limited to *one dollar* each, the same to be collected under the direction of the several Republican County Central Committees of the Reserve; that three commissioners be appointed by this assembly, to be called *Commissioners of the Liberty Fund,* who shall receive said fund, disburse it for the objects named, and account therefor by periodical publications until their duties are performed; applying any surplus to the advancement of *Republicanism and Liberty.*

6th. That our fellow-citizens of Lorain county, who are now in jail waiting the pleasure of the U. S. District Judge, for their trial, are entitled to their liberty, and must have it, peaceably and in conformity with the rules of law;

In pursuit of this end it is

Resolved, That Joshua R. Giddings, of Ashtabula County, Herman Canfield, of Medina County, and Robert F. Paine, of Cuyahoga County, be constituted a Committee to sue out the writ of *habeas corpus* in behalf of said prisoners without unnecessary delay, and that they address the application at their discretion, to any judicial officer of the State of Ohio, having power to grant the writ.

7th. That the chief reliance of freedom in the American Republic rests in the great Republican party, to which the people and the age look for a restoration of every branch of the federal government to the pristine purity of *Jeffersonian Republicanism;* that, stimulated as well by the wrongs and outrages which were the immediate occasion of this vast assemblage, as by the late triumphs of the people over federal power and corruption, it is the manifest duty of Republicans everywhere to renew their united efforts with an energy not to be re-mitted until that great result be accomplished.

The Committee subsequently met, and Mr. Giddings dissenting, decided to await the decision of the Supreme Court in the cases of Bushnell and Langston.

Hon. JOSEPH M. ROOT, of Sandusky, was here introduced, and greeted with cheers.

He came down upon the Supreme Court of the United States with stern severity, and no less so upon the Federal Court of Cleveland. It was not much to be surprised at, that a Judge could be found who, hopeless of any honorable promotion or preferment, could only hope for it from executive favor; nor was it surprising that a District-Attorney could be found; but it was *our* shame, and *our* fault that a *jury* could be found such as had sat upon this case. The Court was too low to have any business brought before it except Slave catching. That should be their sole business; but to the State Courts we would go for the settlement of the cases of Bushnell and Langston, and let them grant the release of these men, and unless he was greatly mistaken, the executive of the State would see that it was done, and he trusted that there never would be an executive who would not do such a noble deed. We must apply to the Courts, and if they would grant this release, it was well. If not, we would have another meeting and talk it over. He thought that whatever else might happen, Ohio shall not, in God's name she *shall not,* be made a hunting-ground for slave-catchers. [Applause and cheers.] Stand steady,—trust in God and keep your powder dry, and look for the things that shall be.

Gov. CHASE was then received with hearty and tremendous cheers.

A few hours ago he was sitting in his office at Columbus, not expecting to be present to-day, but having received a summons to meet with them to-day, he had felt it his duty to come, but he had not come to advise them to do any thing which they hereafter might have occasion to regret. He had not come to counsel any violence. The American people, having the control of all power by the ballot boxes, it was for them to do it in their legitimate way.

It was not necessary that we, the sovereigns of the land, should resort to any measures which could not be carried out at all times and under all circumstances.

Some of the most respected citizens of the State whom he had known for years, had done what they believed to be right, and which not one man in ten thousand would look up into the blue sky with his hand on his heart and say was not right; they had been thrown into confinement. This was wrong, and what should we do? We exist under a State Government and a Federal Government, and if the Government does wrong, turn it out. Dismiss the unworthy servants and put in those who will do your will. So with the State Governments. Take the right course always and look to the Governments and reform them.

The Federal Government is now acting under the Fugitive Slave Law of which he had often expressed his opinion, and what is our redress for those who are imprisoned under that act? The first thing to do was to ably defend them, as had been done. It was said that this law was unconstitutional. If this be so, all done under that law is null and void. He believed when the law was passed, and believed now, that that act was intended rather as a symbol of the supremacy of the Slave States, and the subjugation of the Free. This case has been brought before the Courts of the State, and they are bound to carry out their duty under such a view of it. If the process for the release of any prisoner should issue from the Courts of the State, he was free to say that so long as Ohio was a Sovereign State, that process *should be executed.* He was in favor of reciprocity, but if the State Court issued papers and process, the Federal Court must show the same deference to the State Court that was at other times shown to the Federal Court. We can reform the Judiciary, the Congress and the Administration, and although the process may be too slow to suit some of the more excited of the audience, yet none of them were so old that they might not see the operation of this remedy. He did not counsel revolutionary measures, but when his time came and his duty was plain, he, as the Governor of Ohio, would meet it as a man.

He then reviewed the circumstances of the arrest and seizure of the negro boy John under a power of attorney, and this process of a power of attorney gave to the agents of the power the right to take John wherever he was found, although at that time he was a citizen of Ohio. Consequently that paper of authority was not peace, but war, against a citizen of Ohio.

His deliberate judgment was that no person could be seized and captured while he was a citizen of any sovereign State, under the Constitution of the United States. He entered into a brief analysis of the constitutionality of this law, showing it to be at variance with the letter and spirit of that document, giving, as it does, the power of the Judges to the Commissioners under this Act.

Who does not see in all these unrighteous accusations and persecutions the doom of this law? He remembered the statement of the *Plain Dealer* of a few years ago, which said that the origin of this law was infernal, and it must be repealed whether Constitutional or not. But it was never intended by this clause which permits slavery in the land, that it was to spread farther than the States in which it then existed, and had they believed otherwise, the Constitution would never have been enacted.

Let the Courts be appealed to, and let them act in accordance with their consciences and their duty between themselves and their God. The great remedy is in the people themselves, at the ballot box. Elect men with backbone who will stand up for their rights, no matter what forces are arrayed against them. See to it, too, what President you elect again. Let such a man be selected as will do as you desire — a man who will represent the people in the spirit of freedom and right, and administer the Constitution of our fathers, the securer of liberty and not the prop of slavery.

I have said just what I feel and think, just what I will live by, and just what I will die by. Go on and be faithful to your charge — do your duty to yourselves, your country and your God.

Gov. CHASE was frequently interrupted by cheers and applause.

Judge HITCHCOCK, of Lake county, was next introduced.

Little Lake was represented here to-day by men with true hearts, and he stood there but a moment to represent those true men. We are here to consult about those men who are arrested and punished without law. They could appeal to the State Courts for redress, and feel confident that they would do their duty according to the best of their ability.

In relation to the resolutions passed in this town years ago, and which were lately thrown like a bomb-shell into yonder Court, he would simply say that what District-Attorney Belden had said about their authenticity was wholly false. Those resolutions expressed the speaker's mind then, and he had the same mind now.

Hon. COLUMBUS DELANO, of Mt. Vernon, said he had come here to this meeting and had endeavored to keep out of sight and hear others, but some rascal had kidnapped him. He had long known the people of the Western Reserve, and had known them to be full of liberty and loyalty to human right. He had come to tell them that Central Ohio was ready to respond to them in the love of liberty. But he had not come to counsel violence. We never yet had perfect liberty, and were perhaps not yet prepared for it. But we have had forced upon us oppression after oppression until now we are accused of and punished for crime if we refuse to assist in carrying back to slavery a fellow man. We are told that we must obey all laws. There is a difference in refusing to obey a law and refusing to enter into the carrying out of an evil law.

We must refuse to obey such laws as this. We have refused and have been tried for that. Law first — law and patience — but with it all, a patience and perseverance that shall *never* die, for the suppression of wrong.

I come to-day to greet the spirit I see in your faces, that, like that in Independence Square when the Declaration of Independence was read in Philadelphia, turned in earnest prayer to God to give them strength to go in the right cause. If you have not such a Court as you want, *make* such a court by the ballot box, and your laws will be executed. You are here in solemn, thoughtful, earnest, manly, and solid determination to do right, and naught but right. Go on in that course, and God will be with you.

Hon. D. K. CARTTER said he merely expected to wind off abundant speaking. He could express his convictions in a very few words. First, he did n't believe that one man has a right to buy and sell another.

As a plain exposition of his platform, he believed that this law which would send back men to slavery, originated in hell, and was executed by poor miserable devils, who had sold themselves for a few base honors or dollars. The man who would assist to send back a fellow being to hopeless bondage, is, of all creatures this side of hell, the most to be commiserated. On the theoretical points, therefore, he thought he was sound on this law.

While he bowed with the utmost deference to all law, he held in supreme contempt any law that enslaved any human being. You have repealed this law in Ohio. There is only just enough of monumental relics of this law now left, to show that it exists somewhere else. Those men who say that these poor, robbed, down-trodden people are designed by the Creator to be slaves, are open blasphemers, and don't believe in God, hell, or immortality. That's his idea of the religious part of the law. He was the chief of sinners, but he would n't swap his chance of a decent immortality with one of those who help to sustain this law. He thought the audience would be satisfied with this *conservative* view of the subject, especially when he said that he was in favor of having those men out of that jail the best way they could be got out.

Mr. Cartter's remarks were received with frequent shouts of laughter and applause.

JOHN LANGSTON, Esq., of Oberlin, was next called to the stand. He said that he hated the Fugitive Slave Law as he did the Democratic party, with a deep, unalterable hatred. He then went on with a clear, noble, and bold utterance of sentiments which were clothed in as eloquent language as is often heard upon the floor of the halls of Congress. The listeners forgot that he was a black man — he spoke a white language such as few white men can speak. He trampled the Fugitive Slave Law under his feet, for it incarcerated his own brother and his friends and neighbors for disobeying its bloody commands. If you but hate slavery because it oppresses the black man in the Southern States, for God's sake, hate it for its enslavement of white men. Don't say it is confined to the South, here it is on our neighbors and citizens, and shall we say that slavery does not affect us? As we love our friends, as we love our God-given rights, as we love our homes, as we love ourselves, as we love our God, let us this afternoon swear eternal enmity to this law. Exhaust the law first for these men, but if this

fail, for God's sake, fall back upon our own natural rights, and say to the prison walls " come down," and set those men at liberty. [Cheers.]

Hon. O. P. BROWN, of Portage county, said he was one of the most fanatical men upon this fanatical Western Reserve. In yonder pile there is pure despotism. It makes no difference whether you call the tyrants Nicholas or Belden, whether you call the despot the Czar of all the Russians, or Willson. Infamous, corrupt, and devilish as the Fugitive Slave Law is, it is yet white and pure compared with the persons who have executed it in yonder building. It is Federalism which fines one man $ 1 for killing a man, and another $ 600 and long imprisonment for helping a man keep and save his life. I trust if the Federal Power is ever to make an issue and test the fact whether we will execute our laws, let them test it now. They know not how soon the smouldering volcano beneath them may burst under their rotten carcasses. We are ready for the question. Don't let them put off this question one moment for our convenience, and I say to you in conclusion, stand firm by the eternal landmarks which our fathers have planted, and your names shall be handed down when those poor miserable office-holders shall be forgotten. [Cheers.]

Judge CONVERSE, Vice-President, remarked that the ladies had a work to do in this matter. They should train up their husbands, and those who had no husbands should tell their lovers to go to the polls and do their duty, then come back and claim their reward.

President ASA MAHAN being called to the stand, rejoiced to know that some of the prisoners, whom he had instructed in years past and taught them principles of liberty, were still true to their duty. He felt that he had not lived in vain.

Langston had hated the Fugitive Slave Law, but the speaker liked it, for it was a monster, and he hoped the Devil, its father, would never beget any thing but monsters. He liked it, too, because it could not be executed; and again, because it was political death to the party that originated and executed it. When the news goes to Michigan, of what you have done here to-day, a voice will go up like the sound of many waters, that "the Lord God Omnipotent reigneth."

This closing the speeches, the Vice-President, Judge CONVERSE, announced the names of William Fuller, of Cuyahoga Co., Reuben Hitchcock, of Lake Co., and Philemon Bliss, of Lorain Co., as the Commissioners of the Liberty Fund, according to the resolution.

After the close of the public exercises, the Oberlin and Wellington bands went to the jail, and being admitted into the yard, played a number of inspiriting tunes for the special benefit of their brethren in bonds. A large concourse of people gathered upon the sheds, stones, and fences near by, to see and hear the proceedings, and greeted the prisoners and the musicians with cheers.

The number of persons present upon the square to listen to the speakers was, at the lowest estimate, from ten thousand to twelve thousand. From the speaker's stand an almost unbroken sea of heads covered the space all over that section of the Park from the fountain to the fences. The trees, fences, windows, and steps of the custom-house were crowded with interested spectators, the whole forming a congregation, equal to several Fourth of July celebrations, with this exception, that here the feeling that called the vast crowd together was a deep and strong love of liberty, and not a firecracker and firework effervescence. It was an earnest and working day, — a day to be marked as an epoch, — a day to inspire the attendants with zeal and stern enthusiasm for God and the right. The calm and unflinching eye, tone, and word of Gov. CHASE, the earnest fire of Judge SPALDING, the sarcasm and fearless denunciations of CARTTER, the humorous and open thrusts of TILDEN, the clarion rallying notes, the earnest expostulation and thundering anathemas of GIDDINGS, and the bold, manly, energetic counsels of HITCHCOCK, ROOT, DELANO, BROWN, MAHAN, VANCE, and WADE, all these will not soon be forgotten by the participants in the events of the Mass Convention of May 24, 1859. We have had a good meeting, one that we may be proud of as the gathering of the clans of independent freemen, and as such let us " sound its praise abroad."

THE MEN OF LORAIN AND THE PRISONERS.

When the Lorain procession, some two thousand strong, marched round the public square to the vicinity of the jail, in which their friends and neighbors are inhumanly incarcerated by the Government pursuers under the infamous Fugitive Slave Act, the greetings were hearty and vociferous. As soon as the long procession broke up, the jail yard was surrounded by a dense mass of the people, and the Oberlin victims of Federal Court persecution, kindly permitted by Sheriff WIGHTMAN to occupy the yard, shook hands over the rough fence with the freemen who pressed forward to cross palms with the moral heroes over whose heads waved the tattered stars and stripes which they had flung from the battlements of the prison. The scene has no parallel in the annals of the Republic, and it will be historic.

A personal greeting for all was impossible, and the cry rose for " LANGSTON." Messrs. LANGSTON, PECK, PLUMB, and FITCH were successively called out, and briefly responded in the spirit and words of Christian men and true patriots. Their remarks were loudly applauded, and made a deep impression. When Mr. FITCH concluded, the people quietly withdrew to the public square, though many sought and were permitted interviews with the prisoners inside the yard and jail. Indeed, the prisoners held a pleasant levee all day — ladies and gentlemen, acquaintances and strangers, from far and near, constantly thronging the prison.

MR. C. H. LANGSTON'S REMARKS.

GENTLEMEN, — I will not insult you. I will not come from the dungeon of the jail of Cuyahoga county to address free and honest citizens of Ohio. Imagine a thief, a counterfeiter, or a murderer coming forth from yonder grated cells to address honorable citizens — men guilty of no crime. How absurd. How ridiculous. I am a felon, tried, convicted and sentenced for wilful and malicious violation of the laws of this country. We live in a peculiar country, in a peculiar age, and now we exist under *very peculiar* circumstances. We are taught that this is the land of the free; yet we are imprisoned for breaking the bonds of the oppressor, giving liberty to the captive, and letting the down-trodden and the oppressed go free.

Shall we submit to this outrage on our rights? [Crowd shouted no!] Are you here to-day to obey the Fugitive Slave Law? [No!] Are you here to sustain the dicta of the Dred Scott decision? [No!] Are you here to support the decision of the United States Court of the Northern District of Ohio? [No! in thunder tone.]

The foul spirit of slavery has crushed the rights of the States beneath its iron heel, and led the Federal Judiciary captive at its despotic will. Shall it, too, crush out the spirit of the free citizens of Ohio? Will you tamely submit to this tyranny and despotism? Will you not defend your own rights, sustain your own liberty and roll back this tide of judicial usurpation which is sapping the very foundation of your country's liberty, so that being free and untrammelled yourselves, you may assist us who are groaning beneath the cruel weight of gigantic wrongs and brutal oppression? [Three cheers were given for Langston.]

PROF. H. E. PECK'S REMARKS.

FELLOW-CITIZENS, — It does us good to look upon your honest faces. We see in them signs at once of determination and sympathy. We learn from them that you are resolutely on the side of right, and that you are disposed to feel for those who suffer for the right.

The sympathy you express indicates an appreciation on your part of the trials to which we have been subjected. It will not be improper, therefore, for me to say in your presence, that much as our inconveniences are lightened by the generous kindness of the officers who have charge of us, and by the commiserating care of friends, our confinement is irksome and painful to us. To men of active habits like ourselves, life in a jail cannot but be oppressive. We miss exceedingly our usual duties, pursuits, and pleasures; and it is, as you will readily believe, a pressing grief to be separated from our homes and families.

But, gentlemen, irksome and painful as our present life is, it is not so trying as was the life we led when we were anticipating the assault which terminated in the arrest and rescue of John Price. To know that armed villains were skulking about our village, to be at every step importuned for counsel by poor wretches who lived in terror of arrest; to have our premises swarmed at night with those who clung to their neighbors for the protection with which they could not provide themselves, to be conscious that a storm of marauding violence was soon to burst upon us and to be in suspense as to where or when it was to fall, and whether its issue might not be one of blood, this was distress, this was discomfort to which even that of life in a jail makes but a poor comparison.

And it cheers us to be able to know that what we now suffer is doing something towards preventing a recurrence of those disgraceful scenes which occurred before and at the arrest of John Price. We believe, and your presence here to-day testifies to us, that the issue of our present griefs will be the making of man-hunting upon the Reserve a difficult and dangerous pursuit.

Let us in acknowledging your sympathy, urge you to bear your part towards ending the business of man-enslaving hereabouts. Let us charge you to fear no bonds, and to be terrified by no penalties when the law forbids you to give succor to the fugitive. Help him as he has need, and if you be imprisoned for the act, the consciousness of well-doing and the earnest sympathy of loving hearts will both cheer and reward you. So have we been abundantly cheered and rewarded, and never more than in meeting you to-day.

MR. PLUMB'S REMARKS.

Mr. Plumb, after being repeatedly called for, mounted the post of the jail-yard fence and said: —

GENTLEMEN, — I object to undertaking to make a speech from my present position, lest by some mishap I find myself " astride the fence," a calamity which hitherto has never befallen me. But I cannot forbear to say a word to this vast multitude of good men and true, gathered from every part of Northern Ohio, whose presence here to-day gives assurance that the great heart of the people is stirred as it never has been before. Gentlemen, you are here to-day because you have an intelligent appreciation of the important truth that the rights of the meanest inhabitant of our great State cannot be ruthlessly trampled under foot, without endangering your own.

You are here because you clearly apprehend the fact that a great political revolution is going forward, a revolution not second in importance to that of 1776, that being a conflict which resulted in deciding the question of National In-

dependence of a foreign tyrannical power, while this " irrepressible conflict " is to go on until the still greater question of personal freedom is settled, a question in which your children and your children's children have an untold interest.

It is enough for me to know that you apprehend these points, that you know your rights, and, knowing, dare maintain them. Your visit to this jail, gentlemen, is doubtless to extend to us the assurance of your approbation, for which you have our thanks, but you will soon repair elsewhere to hear from those who are prepared properly to address you, and I will not detain you longer.

For one I feel grateful that I have enjoyed the privilege of representing somewhat your opposition to unrighteous laws, and their attempted enforcement by the Federal court. The walls of a prison, though not to be coveted, by any manner of means, as an abiding place, have furnished me with suitable surroundings, wherewith to study over again the great principles of human rights and their practical application to the wants of man, so that I feel to-day strengthened by review to go forth better prepared for future conflicts with the giant wrong of our land.

And let me say in conclusion, that should our noble State now utter her sovereign voice through an undivided judiciary in favor of State rights, and the protection of the liberty of the citizen from the persecutions of the slave power, through a federal judiciary, I am content.

MR. J. M. FITCH'S REMARKS.

GENTLEMEN, — I cannot think the multitudes who compose this assemblage are prompted by the curiosity which they feel when visiting a menagerie, and yet I confess my feelings, while exhibiting myself to you, remind me of those I had as I stood in the Zoological Gardens of London last fall.

No, no, you are actuated by nobler motives than the gratification of curiosity. Gentlemen, I cannot make a speech to you on such an occasion. The very presence of these thousands of earnest souls is the grandest speech that can be uttered. You see us the inmates of a jail, *and not ashamed.* Still it is a serious thing to shut within prison walls citizens of the free State of Ohio, who are incapable of a crime. It is a serious thing when the little children to whom we have taught morals and religion in our Sabbath schools, inquire, with wondering eyes, the meaning, when their teachers are shut within a jail. Upon what times are we fallen, when our little children must call after us, as they stand weeping upon the threshold of our dwellings, and say as mine did, " Come back, Pa, *as soon as you can get out of jail.* I shall want to see you." And are we, then, criminals? Are we justly arraigned for a violation of the laws of the land? Can that be law which contravenes every principle of right, whether natural or revealed? Can a few graceless men who may meet at Washington, and by trickery and management secure the passage of an act like that, which we to-day denounce, bind it upon our consciences *by calling it a law?*

I read the answer in the earnest faces before me. It is a great comfort to us, while enduring this imprisonment, to know that when we, who are now incarcerated, have been sufficiently ground between the upper and nether millstones of Federal power, that there are hundreds of thousands more of just such in our noble State, who are ready to enter the hopper as future grists. No, Gentlemen, we have not violated law. Ours is not the status of felons; and, till we die, we will not admit it, in any degree, by giving a cent of bail. While there is any thing left of us we shall be found resisting. Why, Gentlemen, my feelings lead me to remember the farmer's pugnacious animal which was so determined to push for the right, that it was thought necessary to furnish him disciplinary exercise for his butting propensities. As the farmer assures us, this animal resolutely fought a beech maul suspended from a limb till nothing was left of him but the tip end of his tail; but this tip was so surcharged with the same determined resistance, that at every rebound of the maul, Mr. Tail pitched into it. Even so, if possible, do we feel like resisting the Fugitive Slave Law against all odds, and while a particle of our proper selves remains. We have trampled on this infamous enactment many a time in our day, and never while God shall spare us, will we yield obedience to its wicked demands. Pot-house politicians may utter *the law*, and pro-slavery Courts may try and sentence us if they please, but it shall be enough for us to know that the Great Master saith of all those who feed the hungry, clothe the naked, and help the poor: "Inasmuch as ye did it unto one of the *least of these my brethren* ye did it unto me."

LETTER FROM MR. GIDDINGS — CORRECTION.

ANGIER HOUSE, Wednesday Morning.

Editor of the Leader, — In your report of my remarks yesterday, I am made to say, "If it was not for the Supreme Court, I would ask for no judicial process, but these men should be brought before you to-day." The most casual reader will see that this remark is in conflict with other portions of my speech as reported. What I did say was — "I would not wait *one hour* for the decision of the Supreme Court, but *would obtain* process from the nearest judicial officer, and if I could direct its proceedings, would have the prisoners brought at once to the stand, and there, in the presence of the people would have them released, that all might witness the process by which citizens of Ohio are set at liberty when imprisoned under the Fugitive act."

I do not blame your reporters. I know the difficulty they meet in reporting me; but this remark, as it stands, may hereafter be quoted

separately from other parts of the speech, and made to imply an invitation to disregard law, and proceed in a form that would be revolutionary, while no such intimation ever escaped my lips or pen. But my position has been, now is, and probably will be while I live, that when the forms of law shall fail, and peaceful resources be exhausted, I would maintain the liberties of our citizens against the Fugitive act *by force*, and I said yesterday that so far as the Democratic press represented me as entertaining that view, it had done me justice.   J. R. GIDDINGS.

VISIT OF THE SABBATH SCHOOL.

One of the most touching of all the scenes in this exciting panorama, occurred on Saturday, July 2, when four hundred Sabbath School children applied at the jail to see their Superintendent! Month after month they had looked toward his wonted place for him in vain — a place from which he had not been so long absent for sixteen years; and now, no longer patient, they came trooping like little angels as they were, and beat with their very wings upon the prison door. A long account lies before us of the day's exercises and incidents, which it is difficult to refrain from quoting entire. But amid the press of good things, we must be content with extracts. We cut from the editorial columns of the Morning *Leader:* —

Four Hundred Sabbath School Children visit their Superintendent in Prison.

At 11 o'clock on Saturday morning, our streets were enlivened by a procession of Sabbath School scholars and teachers, who came on the Toledo train from Oberlin.

They were led by an escort from this city, who met them at the depot, when the procession was formed under the direction of Professor JOHN M. ELLIS. LELAND'S Band discoursed appropriate music as the little army marched in grand style up through Superior street to the Public Square.

At the head of the Procession was a splendid Banner, inscribed as follows: —

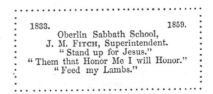

1833.   1859.
Oberlin Sabbath School,
J. M. FITCH, Superintendent.
"Stand up for Jesus."
"Them that Honor Me I will Honor."
"Feed my Lambs."

Each class bore a small banner, with the name of the School and of the Superintendent, as well as the number of the class.

The weather in the morning was hot, and the dust troublesome to the earnest little folk, but this was soon forgotten amid the enlivening scenes of the Park, and the children seemed anxious to press on to the jail, to greet once more their beloved Superintendent, whose imprisonment has for eighty days separated him from his little flock.

The throng of little feet soon pressed the prison floor, and the various rooms, stairways, halls, and cells were filled; each anxious to grasp the hand of one of the men of whom Judge WILLSON impiously said that they were "not good Christians."

After lunch in the Park, they were escorted by the Plymouth Sabbath School to the Plymouth Church, where a series of pleasant exercises were held, and the touchstone of the following sentiment applied, with such a result as might have been anticipated : —

"OUR SUPERINTENDENT. We respect him more, and love him better to-day than ever before ! "

The Oberlin School returned to the yard in front of the jail about 5, P. M., to listen to what the Superintendent and others of the prisoners had to say, and bid them " Good-by."

Prof. ELLIS called for Mr. FITCH, who came forward and addressed the children as follows : —

MY DEAR CHILDREN, — I am exceedingly glad to see you, and I am greatly gratified to observe the pains you have taken to visit your Superintendent in a body. These beautiful banners, and all these other evidences of your interest gratify me much. I mean, they make me glad, that is the better word. I cannot suitably express the happiness I feel on seeing you all once more. May God bless the precious children !

*   *   *   *   *

For sixteen years I have endeavored to be faithful in instructing you in morals and religion, and I have often especially warned you to be careful in your habits, and to avoid the great disgrace of *being sent to jail.* Hitherto scarcely a member of our dear school has ever disgraced us in such a way. But what do I now see ! What great evil has overtaken you ! What great crime have you now committed ! Here I behold you *all in jail !* How shall I account for it ? I remember my legal friend, one of our prisoners, says some people are brought to jail by the Marshal's warrant, and others *by an attachment.* Surely, this is the explanation. An *" attachment "* must have brought you here, for such precious children as those who now crowd around me, in this jail-yard, are incapable of a crime.

You must have noticed, my children, that two classes of people have in all ages been made the inmates of prisons. Wicked people, who harm the world, and the good and holy, who are so far in advance of their age that the wicked world misunderstands them. The Bible and history will assure you of the truth of what I say. To which class do your Superintendent and his companions belong ? I will not here say we are representatives of the good and holy. Let our past lives tell their own tale. But this I will say, — *our friends,* — those who uphold our sentiments, — those who applaud our course, and who spurn the infamous Fugitive Act under which we are imprisoned, as the devil's own instrument, are among the wise, the learned, the good, and the holy of earth. They are those who have despised personal ease, and worldly gain, and have, during their whole lives, devoted themselves, body and soul, to the work of doing good. I see just at my right hand our venerable father KEEP, a man with the weight of many years upon him. He has preached this gospel of Jesus for more than *fifty-five years,* and yet with a youthful spirit he mingles with the children to-day. On what times are we fallen when such men are considered felons, — fit tenants of a jail; but their persecutors, who, perhaps, have defrauded the halter of its due, go free as if they were the good !

Yet thus has it always been. The motto on this beautiful banner, which the excellent Mayor of our town is holding by my side, is the text for us all. " Stand up for Jesus." These words of the dying Tyng, are the words for us to-day. So will we do while life shall last.

We are compelled to endure painful imprisonment, but we have done no wrong. We appeal to God above and all the holy, that to feed the hungry, to clothe the naked, and to securely hide and safely convey away a poor and helpless brother, who is panting in his haste to escape from the hands of robbers, is to do right, and only right.

*   *   *   *   *

Before I close, I wish to read a sweet hymn from this little volume, which must, I think, have come down from heaven. I do not mean that it came down all bound in this way, but it was sent to Prof. PECK, from whom I know not, and its sentiments I am sure came down from heaven.

> " God made all his creatures free :
>   Life itself is Liberty;
>   God ordained no other bands
>   Than united hearts and hands.
>
> " Sin the primal charter broke;
>   Sin, itself earth's heaviest yoke;
>   Tyranny with sin began,
>   Man o'er brute and man o'er man.
>
> " But a better day shall be,
>   Life again be Liberty,
>   And the wide world's only bands
>   Love-knit hearts and love-knit hands.
>
> " So shall envy, slavery cease,
>   All God's children dwell in peace,
>   And the new-born earth record,
>   Love, and love alone, is Lord."

I close by uttering the sentiment which I have so often expressed in your hearing, and which I have earnestly endeavored to impress upon your minds, to wit: DO RIGHT! ALWAYS DO RIGHT! Nothing shall by any means harm you if ye be doers of THAT WHICH IS RIGHT.

At the close of Mr. F.'s remarks, a beautiful and appropriate hymn was sung by Prof. ELLIS, Mr. VETTER, Miss CHURCH, and Miss COWLES, each stanza ending with an exhortation to " Do Right."

Prof. PECK was called out and spoke as follows: —

MY YOUNG FRIENDS, — I have often *seen* you since we came here. At night-fall, as I have walked upon the house-top to enjoy the glories and beauties of sunset, it has occurred to me that those I love were enjoying the same glowing scene. The thought has tempted me to " go home." And I have done so. I have clambered up by one golden beam and let myself down by another, and so I have stood among scenes and friends dear to my heart. I have seen you and your parents, and the loved places in which I have been accustomed to associate with you and other friends. But it has been only in my spirit that I have thus made a journey and seen you. I have not been able to talk with you. *Now* I look upon you in very person, and am permitted to speak to you.

And how *shall* I speak to you? I am at a loss to know. But I may interest you somewhat if I tell you I have learned since I came here, what I never very much thought of before, that many parts of the Bible — the blessed book which you study from Sabbath to Sabbath — were written in prisons, and that all of it is grandly good reading for those who are cast into prison for doing right.

Has it ever occurred to you that Isaiah, whose style is so glowing, wrote many of his prophecies, and Daniel many of his, in prison? Have you ever reflected that Paul wrote some of his most useful epistles while bolts and bars shut him from the world, and that John was a prisoner when he penned the Apocalypse? It will interest you, I am sure, to take your Bibles and note how many passages were written in prison.

And I can assure you, my young friends, that whether much or little of the Bible was *written* in prison, it is all good for men who are " in bonds." Such *we* have many times found to be the fact since we came here.

I wish I could adequately set before you one instance of it which I shall never forget. It was the evening of the day on which we received the intelligence that the Supreme Court had decided against us in our " *habeas corpus* " case, of which all of you know. We had for days and weeks looked forward to this decision with most agonizing expectation. At length the telegraph informed us that we were *defeated.* Oh! what anguish came upon us then. For my own part, I suffered more on that dreadful night than I did when my dear first-born died in my arms. Well, a sorrowful group, we gathered ourselves that evening for our usual worship. It was my privilege to conduct the exercises. I opened the Bible, as I at first thought *accidentally*, but as I soon knew *providentially*, at the sweet Psalm which begins, " Fret not thyself because of evil doers." As I read that first verse, it seemed as if the words were written purposely for us. I paused an instant, and every syllable of the sentence went like a plummet to the bottom of our hearts. Then I read another verse, and that seemed better than the first. It was received with breathless silence from all. And as I read on, " Commit thy way unto the Lord, trust also in Him and He shall bring it to pass;" and " For yet a little while and the wicked shall not be;" and " The steps of a good man are ordered by the Lord, and He delighteth in his way;" " Though he fall he shall not be utterly cast down;" it seemed as if the whole Psalm had been *written for our special use at that particular time.*

And on several occasions, we have been struck with a like appropriateness in Bible narratives or truths to our cases. So, my young friends, I can commend the Bible to you as being a book eminently good for those who are in difficult places while doing right. And you know you may before long come into strait places while doing the will of God. Who knows but you may be cast into prison for obeying the law of Christ? I think some of you *will* be if our Government goes on in its present way of endeavoring to crush those who help the bondman to the liberty to which he is entitled.

Be ready for such an event. Make ready for it by acting as did the Irish boy, who fearing that the Catholic priest would take his Bible from him, fell to committing it to memory, so that when the priest did seize and burn the book, he was able to say, " There is one thing you can't burn, and that's them ten chapters I 've got laid up in my heart."

Do you lay up the word of God in your hearts, and in whatever strait you may be, even if you are cast into prison for obeying the law of God, you will enjoy constant comfort and peace.

After a beautiful address from Mr. PLUMB and a fitting response from Prof. ELLIS, the procession formed and marched to the depot on their homeward way, which we trust they pursued without accident. What a scene!

THE FINALE.

Slowly the weeks trode by, till the close of the month of June. The imprisoned Rescuers had quietly settled themselves each in his cell, having "labored," now to " wait" for the hour of honorable release. Systematic appeals had been made to the public in behalf of their wives and little ones, and prompt and heart-cheering responses had begun to come back. Every hope of speedy release having failed, each sent for the implements of his accustomed labor, and the prison became a workshop. One made shoes, another harness, another cabinet-ware, two set type, two edited, and others read Latin, Greek, and Metaphysics, that they might not fall behind class mates in college. A copy of "The Rescuer," dated July 4th, 1859, lies now before us. Collectors for antiquarian libraries seldom exhume choicer morceaux. The first page announces that : —

"THE RESCUER will be published at the Cuyahoga County Jail, every alternate Monday, by the Political Prisoners there confined. Five thousand copies of the first number will be issued. Price 3 cents per copy."

From the editorial columns we clip the following : —

THE RESCUER—HOW IT WAS PRINTED. —After the "political prisoners" had remained in jail for seventy-five days, they began to find themselves possessed of "thoughts that breathed and words that burned." We not only wished to utter them, but we wished to print them. Could the thing be done? We looked around for printers, and found among the "prisoners" two rusty and dilapidated "typos" one of whom had not handled a "stick" for fifteen years. Would the Sheriff allow us a corner of the jail for a printing-office? We asked him. Generous as ever, he replied — "Certainly, and I'll help you too, if I can." "O where shall TYPE be found?" we next inquired. The generous purchasers of our old printing-office responded by lending us a font of Small Pica, and the liberal Publisher of the *Cleveland Daily Leader* added more, with other things. For a "plane" we used a carpenter's with the irons knocked out. A policeman's club answered for a "mallet," in "taking proof," and for other purposes, we could select a pounding instrument from a large pile of *shackles* which lay at our feet. A fellow-prisoner supplied us with "side-sticks," "quoins" and "reglet," made from a white-wood board. Another prisoner sawed up a fence board to make a "rack." (Quite like a "felon" that, but we must settle it with the Commissioners.) For a "shooting-stick"— not the dangerous kind which we have understood "rescuers" sometimes use, but a simpler instrument — we hewed out a piece of stave, and the door-stone answered for a "table." Thus furnished, and with the ample space of just five feet by ten for a printing-office we proceed to establish the "Rescuer." If we labor under difficulties, it is but appropriate, for "rescuers" always do. We forgot to express

regret that we could not procure *italics*. Many were needed. We must ask our readers to supply the emphasis according to taste.

From the advertising columns, these : —

PRINTERS AND BOOKSELLERS!

FITCH & BUSHNELL

Are not in partnership and never were; but as they agree so perfectly as to what should be done with fugitives and fugitive slave laws, they are sure they can still do business together. They were lately removed by *Marshal Johnson*, from Oberlin, O., where they had been long engaged in the above business, and have established themselves in the front hall of *Cleveland Jail*, where the "Rescuer" is published every alternate week. Having been successful in securing a large share of *government attention*, we expect, presently, to be able to do a good deal of GOVERNMENT PRINTING, for which we have no doubt we shall get our *pay*. Indeed, one of us has already been *paid in advance*.

In our jail Bookstore will be found valuable works. Constantly on hand, as soon as published, a Narrative of the Oberlin Rescue Trials, 250 pp., full of curiosities.

At their branch establishment in Oberlin, they still keep a choice assortment of Anti-Slavery Literature, which they specially recommend to "Union Savers" as worthy their notice. Bibles and Testaments will be sold to Administration Democrats strictly at cost; and to Lower Law men generally at very low rates. Hoping to check the progress of barbarism *as well as of slave-catchers*, they have filled their shelves with many good books, which are real "Helpers." Hallam's Middle Ages is highly recommended as a valuable aid in settling the dispute as to whether Democratic America has yet advanced in civilization, beyond the Medieval Period. The attention of United States Judges, District-Attorneys, and others, is especially called to a neat little Manual which they offer, containing the Constitution of the United States, Declaration of Independence, Acts of Congress on Slavery, including the Fugitive Slave Act, and arguments showing the Constitution to be unconstitutional, and that negroes are "persons" now and "things" then, just as shall suit.

Their motto is,

"Consider well each deed you mean to do;
But, once resolved, *with earnest zeal pursue*."

UPHOLSTERERS AND MATTRESS MAKERS.

Henry Evans & Brother (late of Oberlin, O.), have removed to the shed one door west of J. Scott's Saddle and Harness-shop. All persons who would secure a visit from

"Tired Nature's sweet restorer, balmy sleep,"

will please call and examine their work.

You can rest on their beds, *if you can rest anywhere.* Government officials need not apply.

HOG-SKIN SADDLE AND HARNESS-MAKING.

John H. Scott, late of Oberlin, has opened a shop under the shed in the Jail Yard, in front of Wightman's Castle, Cleveland. Mr. Scott assures the public that hereafter he shall use hides of his own tanning, and will warrant his work to be thoroughly done.

N. B. Dog collars of all sizes made to order

BOOT AND SHOE SHOP.

James Bartlett, late of Royce's extensive Manufactory, Oberlin, Ohio, has opened a shop in cell No. 3, up stairs, Cuyahoga County Jail, where he will be happy to meet his patrons.

Mr. B. feels confident that he can be of great service to those who, from constant gyrations in the dirt, have damaged their soles.

Lower Law Ministers, Hunkers, and Cat-Footed Politicians of all parties are particularly invited to call.

P. S. Hides taken in exchange for work. Dark copper-color greatly preferred.

For data which enable us to furnish a complete account of the sudden interruption of these new business enterprises, we are indebted to the special kindness of Hon. Ralph Plumb.

Marshal Johnson and District-Attorney Belden had been to Washington for counsel, and returning, had declared that a Court term of ninety days continuance was to be commenced on the twelfth of July, and that all necessary funds would be at their command; that the Oberlinites were every one to be tried, *found guilty,* and sentenced to the end of the law.

Meantime, the Kentuckians, Jennings, Mitchell, Cochran, and Bacon, arrived, and the administration press boasted largely that the chivalry were " on hand, and ready to face the music like men." This was some ten days before the trials were to commence at Elyria.

But it soon transpired that Judge McLean had issued a writ of *habeas corpus* in behalf of Jennings, Mitchell, Lowe, and Davis, which Marshal Johnson had in his pocket and proposed to serve upon the Sheriff of Lorain county, so soon as their bail should technically surrender the defendants into custody. How these gentlemen could make the necessary oath to entitle them to this writ, alleging that they were "illegally restrained of their liberty," etc., while

altogether at large, is a query which may possibly suggest itself to the fastidious, but which we will not detain the reader to consider.

This writ was served upon Sheriff Burr, although the persons named in it were not in his custody. He returned it indorsed according to fact, and the return was accepted.

While this farce was being enacted, the Kentuckians and their accomplices, frightened to the last degree at so near a prospect of justice, were actively engaged by their counsel, Hon. R. H. Stanton, of Kentucky, in getting the U. S. Government to propose terms of capitulation of some sort, whereby they might parry, if not avert, the impending blow.

They complained of Belden; said he had betrayed them, had induced them to give themselves up by promising *habeas corpus* relief; and now that it had failed, there was nothing but the penitentiary in prospect.

Belden was inexorable. He had sworn to put Oberlin " through," and was purposed to do it, cost what it might. It is said that Mr. Stanton then told him that he *must* make terms with the Lorain officers, or, when he wanted his Kentucky witnesses, the subpœnas would infallibly be returned " *non est inventus.*" The fox was fast in his own trap, and there was no alternative but to " show the linen." With the best grace possible, therefore, terms were soon proposed to Hon. D. K. Cartter, associate counsel for the Lorain prosecution, which were as follows: — The United States were to enter *nolle prosequi* in all of the Rescue cases at once; and upon this condition the suits against Jennings, Mitchell, Lowe, and Davis at Elyria, were to be dismissed. On due consideration, the Lorain authorities generously acceded to these terms, and so ended " *The First Siege of Oberlin.*"

These arrangements were concluded on the 6th of July, and Sheriff Wightman was forthwith ordered to discharge his prisoners.

THE RESCUER'S RESOLVES.

At a full meeting of the " Oberlin Rescue Company," held in Cuyahoga County Jail immediately after their discharge from custody, it was unanimously

Resolved, That as we take leave of the prison in which we have been confined for the last three months, we cannot refuse to ourselves the privilege of giving public expression of our gratitude to God, who has been our constant keeper, and who, as we have passed through sore difficulties and trials, has well fulfilled the promise, "as thy day so shall thy strength be."

We also return thanks to Sheriff WIGHTMAN, and Jailor SMITH and family, whose kindness has greatly mitigated our troubles; and to the Attorneys who have nobly defended our cause; to the friends, far and near, who by prayer and act have remembered us, and to that portion of the Press which has given us constant and valuable aid.

Resolved, That after all the pains and penalties inflicted upon us by Government Officials in the attempt to enforce the Fugitive Slave Act, we feel it to be our duty to say, that our hatred and opposition to that unjust and unconstitutional law are more intense than ever before.

No fine or imprisonment however enforced by whatever Court, can induce us to yield it obedience. We will hereafter, as we have heretofore, help the panting fugitive to escape from those who would enslave him, whatever may be the authority under which they may act.

Resolved, That, in our opinion, when duties enjoined by the Word of God and illustrated in the example of Christ are punished in our country as *crimes*, it becomes all loyal citizens to ask themselves whether they have not lost the substance of their liberties, and whether they should not use instant and earnest endeavors to recover the rights which they have lost.

Resolved, That, for the sake of Liberty, Justice, and Right, we rejoice that the recent decision of our Supreme Court, affirming the constitutionality of the Fugitive Slave Act, has already met with emphatic public rebuke, and that we exhort the people of Ohio to protest against that decision until, by a reversal of it, the lost dignity and sovereignty of our noble Commonwealth shall be restored to her.

Resolved, That we furnish a copy of the above resolutions to the Daily Morning *Leader* for publication.   J. M. FITCH, Chairman.

S. M. BUSHNELL, Secretary.

CUYAHOGA CO. JAIL, }
Cleveland, O., July 6, 1859. }

CLOSING SCENE AT THE JAIL.

Just as the Rescuers were leaving for their homes, they stepped into the parlor of the jail, where were present their Attorneys, Messrs. R. P. SPALDING, A. G. RIDDLE, F. T. BACKUS, S. O. GRISWOLD, Sheriff D. L. WIGHTMAN, Jailor J. B. SMITH, and H. R. SMITH, Esq., who had rendered the Rescuers repeated services, with their wives, and numerous friends, when Mr. PLUMB, in behalf of the Prisoners, presented the Ladies for their husbands, each a beautiful Silver Napkin Ring, Fork and Spoon, engraved with the initials of their husbands, and "From Rescuers: Matthew 25: 36."

Mr. PLUMB, in a brief and happy vein, said, that the prisoners though poor were desirous of

presenting to them a small remembrancer, in token of the high regard in which they held them, and in acknowledgment of the valuable services they had rendered them during their imprisonment. To their counsel for legal aid, and to the others for services scarcely less valuable. And he wished to request the ladies to place the gift before their husbands, at meals, three times a day while they lived, that they might at such times, when surrounded by their families and those dear to them, when noble and generous feelings were sure to come, look upon the memento, and remember the exciting scenes through which they had just passed;—and that although they were intended for their husbands, like all other dear things they would be in the keeping of the Ladies.

Judge SPALDING then replied in behalf of the Ladies and their husbands, in a few eloquent and appropriate remarks.

He said, that it was certainly very cheering to them to know that they had been of service to the prisoners—that they had done what they had, without any expectation or desire of remuneration—but for the cause in which the Rescuers had suffered—that when first spoken to about defending them, he had said he neither asked nor would take pay for services in the case.

Judge S. said the memento so kindly presented would be highly prized, and left as a legacy to their children. He hoped that if ever they got into jail again it would be for no other cause than delivering the oppressed from the oppressor.

Prof. PECK remarked that a portion of the first hour in jail had been spent in imploring the blessing of God, and it would be consonant with their feelings to spend the last moments in thanksgiving to the Protector and Preserver of themselves and families, and the Good Deliverer who had been their hope and support during the many days and nights of their confinement. A fervent prayer by Prof. P. closed the affecting scene, one long to be remembered.

From the Morning *Leader*, of July 7th, we clip the following:—

THE RELEASE OF THE OBERLIN RESCUE COMPANY. Considerable excitement was created in this city upon the announcement being made in the *Leader*, that a proposition had been made by the Kentucky kidnappers to have mutual *nolles* entered in their own case and the case of the Oberlin Rescuers. The consequence was the most intense anxiety among men, both Black Republicans and Yellow Democrats, to learn the upshot of the whole matter. The negotiations between Judge Belden and the Kidnappers on one side, and the authorities of Lorain on the other (the Oberlinites refusing to be parties), were consummated yesterday in the forenoon, when Marshal Johnson called at the jail and announced to the Rescue prisoners that they were free.

The news spread rapidly that the Government officials had *caved*. Hundreds immediately called on the company, to tender their congratulations at this signal triumph of the "Higher Lawites," as the *Plain Dealer* is pleased to call them. In the afternoon, about 5 o'clock, a hundred guns were fired, and some several hundred of our citizens gathered at the jail to escort the Rescuers to the depot. At half past five, the whole company, headed by Hecker's Band, marched two and two to the depot, through Superior and Water streets, the Band playing "Hail Columbia," "Hail to the Chief," "Yankee Doodle," etc. On arriving at the depot, three stentorian cheers were given with a good-will for the Rescuers, when Judge Brayton, of Newburgh, was called upon for a speech, which he gave in his vivid and eloquent style. After this, the company bid farewell to their friends, and took their seats in the cars, and the train started, amidst the hurrahs of the people, the Band playing that peculiarly appropriate air for the occasion, "Home, Sweet Home." Thus has ended the great Oberlin Rescue Case. It was the unanimous opinion of the public in general, and of the *Plain Dealer* in particular, that it was a triumph, not a mere triumph, but a decided triumph, for the Rescuers. The prosecutor, kidnappers, Judge, "eminent counsel from Kentucky," and the Yellow Democracy and all, displayed an immense white feather.

The people of Oberlin were making preparations to receive the Rescuers yesterday afternoon. We doubt not that the returned husbands, fathers, brothers, and sons will have received such a welcome as the warm-hearted people of Oberlin know how to give.

The following account of the reception at Oberlin, was prepared and furnished to the *Leader* by Mr. J. M. Fitch, whose name by this time is in the heart of the reader. It was no sooner published than by its author placed at the writer's disposal. If passages in it seem warm, the critic has only to imagine himself in the author's place. After eighty-five days' imprisonment, to be thus welcomed HOME might not impossibly affect the blood of more phlegmatic temperaments.

THE OBERLIN RESCUERS AT HOME.

ENTHUSIASTIC RECEPTION.

SPEECHES AND SPIRIT OF THE JOYOUS OCCASION.

OBERLIN NOT "SUBDUED."

OBERLIN, July 7, 1859.

EDITOR LEADER, — You left the "Political Prisoners" at the Depot, and gave them your hearty congratulation as they pursued their way "home again," amid the roar of cannon, the peals of martial music, and the echoing shouts which came from a multitude of earnest friends of freedom. You heard Judge Brayton's eloquent speech in congratulation of the "prisoners," their friends and the nation; and then "you missed it" that you turned again to your labor and your sanctum. If you ever get an adequate idea of the glorious reception which awaited these humble and persecuted, but now famous, friends of freedom on their arrival at Oberlin — despised, persecuted Oberlin — you will regret to your dying day that you had not "been there to see."

The wives of Peck, Plumb, Fitch, and Watson, met the company at Grafton, and here arose the first shout that was, in twenty minutes more, to be taken up and borne along as "the sound of many waters and the roar of mighty thunderings." If the conquerors of the old world have, at any time, had a more numerous reception, not one of them ever had a reception half so hearty as greeted these "saints and sub-saints" on their arrival at their beloved Oberlin. The entire town was out to greet them. A sea of heads could be seen extending for a long distance on both sides of the track. Youth and beauty vied with men of venerable age in their endeavors to catch a glimpse of these but recently contemptible, these reviled and abused men; and when they alighted from the cars, the heavens rang again with the united and prolonged huzzas of nearly *three thousand* persons, who, though styled "fanatics," were not a whit behind the brightest ornaments of our country, in intelligence, purity, patriotism, and every excellence of which a nation should be proud. Joy beamed in every eye. Exultation marked every movement, and enthusiasm burst from every lip. But one discordant element, and that a *very little one*, could be detected in that vast throng. E. F. Munson, the Oberlin Postmaster — the man whose head was but recently as good as off, and who stuck it on again by the dirty work which he was able to do for the Government and the marauders who have lately disturbed the quiet of our peaceful town, — E. F. Munson stood motionless, grim, dark and dreary, like a bald eagle on a rock, or a stork on a seashore. "Poor fool," said I, "let him eat the fruit of his own doings, and be *filled* with his own devices."

The eloquent Prof. Monroe was called out, and from the platform pronounced the following thrilling speech in welcome of the prisoners: —

PROF. MONROE'S SPEECH AT THE CARS.

MY FRIENDS, — In behalf of this vast assembly, I am requested to express, in a word, the unqualified satisfaction, the heartfelt joy which we feel, on welcoming you once more to the bosom of this community and to your homes. From that sad day when you left us to the present time, we have never, for a moment, ceased longing for the sight of your faces among us, whenever you could return consistently with duty; and to-night we are glad, from the very bottom of our hearts, that that time has come. We rejoice, not only because you have come back to us, but also because you have come without the shadow of a stain upon that strict integrity which it is the duty and the privilege of a Christian anti-slavery man to cherish. You have made no compromises with slavery. There has been no bowing down of the body, no bending of the knee. Erect, as God made you, you went into prison; erect, as God made you, you have come out of prison. We come, then, once more, to Oberlin. In behalf of this assembly, in behalf of Oberlin, in behalf of Lorain county, welcome! thrice welcome! friends of Liberty!

The procession then formed, with Father Keep and Father Gillett (Matthew Johnson will remember him) in advance, and the vast throng, with banners flying, moved to the stirring music of the Oberlin Band, towards the great church. As the " prisoners " marched up the path towards the noble edifice, the fire companies, dressed in uniform, opened to right and left, and with heads uncovered, received the " Rescuers " with a right hearty greeting. The vast building was in a moment crowded to its utmost capacity. Scarcely less than three thousand persons were crowded within its walls. Here was such a scene for a painter as I cannot now describe. Two thousand in this great audience were men and women in the freshness, the beauty, and the vigor of youth. It was a grand and cheering sight. As the prisoners walked up the aisle, each was presented by some fair hand with a beautiful wreath, and bouquets and flowers danced and sparkled in all directions. The pulpit was elegantly decorated, and all the " Rescuers," with many of their friends, were seated on the rostrum. The venerable Father Gillett, the kind-hearted but firm and manly Sheriff Wightman, and the genial and generous H. R. Smith, our constant friend, were among those who occupied the stand. The great organ opened with the most enlivening strains, and a glorious choir of one hundred and twenty-five choice singers poured forth a flood of song which rolled over the vast congregation and away through the town its waves of heavenly melody.

The venerable Father Keep (may he live forever) took the chair at precisely eight o'clock.

Father Keep opened the exercises by an impressive prayer to that God who will " cause the wrath of man to praise him," and then addressed the meeting in the following impressive words : —

FATHER KEEP'S SPEECH.

Christian Friends and Fellow-Citizens : —

I devoutly congratulate you that our brethren, heroic men, persecuted for righteousness' sake, have now returned to our bosoms. On their countenances we, indeed, trace indications of a severe mental conflict; but, likewise, the divine favor in their personal vigor and health, — and in the flash of their eye, the spirit and purpose of men whom, in such a warfare, *tyrants* cannot subdue. In your behalf I tender them a cordial and joyous welcome, and in your name I assure them that they are now especially endeared to us all.

But, beloved sufferers, this welcome is not intended to cover the fact that you have come to us "jail-birds." You must ever bear this appellation. It, however, comforts us, and it must cheer you to know that you have earned the *title* after the example of the Prophets and Apostles, having been imprisoned for the act of witnessing for the *truth as it is in Jesus.*

In your persons, at this joyous interview, we thus publicly acknowledge the gift of God in answer to prayer. In all your confinement, our sympathies for you have been a deep flowing current. We have felt called of God to the special mission of prayer in your behalf. In the daily reports of your persistency in the " *Right,*" we have received the rich, sustaining answer to our prayer. We have been also strengthened and comforted to know that this sympathy is next to universal in the country. The press has given it voice. Its breath, to you in prison, to us in our watchings, has discoursed music along the telegraph wires.

We have felt honored that you have so faithfully represented the moral sentiment of this community, and of our fondly cherished College. Your firmness in this crisis, has sharply admonished us for our sluggishness in the present conflict for Liberty, and what is more, for our lack of moral courage; and still more, the obtuseness of moral sense in men who counselled compromise.

In your imprisonment you have nobly represented a *great principle.* The Divine Law supreme, everywhere; human enactments subordinate. Thus you have stood before the country the intelligent, sagacious, unflinching friends of human freedom.

Your testimony will live, a permanent record in history, — a memorial to preserve your names to the undying recognition of an approving posterity.

We thank you for your wisdom and firmness in the rejection of all compromise between right and wrong. In this whole movement, your instructive and impressive example is before the country as a model for Church and for State. God has given you the spirit and the courage for the crisis. Your reward is before you, and sure.

Let Politicians, Statesmen, and Christians, but follow this example, and our own Ohio shall be *free,* — personal rights will be held as sacred, and be sustained. *Our country shall be free !*

The Hon. Ralph Plumb was next called out.

He came forward amid immense and prolonged cheering, and said : —

HON. RALPH PLUMB'S SPEECH.

What a scene here greets the eye ! This vast multitude, — the whole population almost of this usually quiet village, filling every niche of this vast edifice with joyous countenances and glad hearts, are before us ; and for what do they come ?

They come to welcome us their neighbors, — their husbands, fathers, and brothers, back to this community, — to our dear families and our sweet homes ! They come, too, to learn not only that we, their representatives, have been released from the prison-walls that for eighty-five days have confined us, but to learn also whether this enlargement, so valuable to us and to them, has been purchased at the cost of one iota of principle, or one grain of self-respect.

Fellow-citizens, it gives me great pleasure to assure you that the band of Rescuers whom you greet stand before you to-night, with yourselves breathing the free air once more of free Oberlin, without having in the least degree compromised themselves or you.

Nay, permit me to go farther and say, that the officers of Lorain county, to whom the government pursuers proposed the entering of *nolles* in the cases, have throughout maintained the honor and the dignity of Lorain, so that we and they stand before you without having yielded dishonorably to any exaction of those who sought to humble us, and destroy the principle so clearly apprehended by your intellects, and so warmly cherished in your hearts. But I do not propose to make a speech to you now; but to give the key-note to your rejoicings by demonstrating what I have already stated, and for that purpose ask your permission to read what will be received by you all as sufficient proof, in the editorial of the Cleveland Daily Plain Dealer of this evening, which is as follows : —

From the Plain Dealer, July 6.

OBERLIN CASES NOLLED — HIGHER LAW TRIUMPHANT.

We learn with astonishment that the United States District-Attorney has nolled the indictments against the Oberlin Rescuers now in jail, on condition that the Oberlinites will nolle the indictments against the Kentucky witnesses who were under arrest on a trumped up charge of kidnapping. This arrangement, we understand, has been made at the solicitation of the four Kentucky gentlemen, who, while under recognizance of the United States Court to appear here and testify in these Rescue cases, were indicted by an Oberlin Lorain jury, and arrested while in the discharge of their duties, on a false charge of kidnapping. They were thrust into the Lorain county jail, but were subsequently released on bail. A special term of the Lorain County Court was to be held on the 6th inst., to try them, and a Lorain county jury was all in readiness to send them to purgatory or the penitentiary, without any regard to Constitutions, Courts, or the laws of the land.

An effort was made to get them out of the hands of the Oberlinites by a writ of *habeas corpus*, issued by Judge McLean, but the sheriff of Lorain hid himself for several days, and the Probate Judge ran away, to prevent the bail from surrendering the prisoners up, so that the writ could take effect, and in this way nullified the law and set at defiance that " Great Writ of Right " which these same Oberlinites have resorted to, and have had the full benefit of, on two occasions, since these arrests have been made.

Finding no law in Lorain but the Higher Law, and seeing the determination of the Sheriff, Judge, and jury to send them to the penitentiary any way, for no crime under any human law, but on a charge trumped up on purpose to drive them out of the country, and having been kept away from their families most of the summer, and away from their business, at great pecuniary expense to themselves, for the Government fees for witnesses do not pay board bills, they proposed to exchange nolles, and the District-Attorney consented to it. So the Government has been beaten at last with law, justice, and facts all on its side, and Oberlin with its rebellious Higher Law creed is triumphant.

The precedent is a bad one. All these factionists have to do in future, whenever any of their number is arrested for the violation of our statute law, is to pay no regard to the writs of the lower law courts; but threaten the witnesses with the terror of their own inquisition, and enforce the penalties of the higher law. This is Mormonism, with Prof. Peck acting the part of Brigham Young, and it will have to be put down, as Mormonism has been, by the strong arm of military power.

There will now be some unearthly shoutings by these triumphant myrmidons of Mormonism. Oberlin will blaze in her new won glory, and *Te Deums* will be sung in all her churches. There will be a great accession to her calendar of saints. Those immortal men, who, armed with muskets, mobbed the United States officials, while in the discharge of their sworn duties, will now be canonized, instead of cannonaded, and Saint Peck will be listed with Saint Peter, and as worthy to hold the keys of Paradise.

Mr. Plumb said in conclusion . —

Fellow-citizens, — It is meet that your rejoicings should be without restraint, for the victory has been complete. [Prolonged cheering.]

Prof. H. E. Peck next came forward, and was received with such a hearty greeting, with such enthusiastic and prolonged cheering, as we never before witnessed and never expect to hear again. The Professor, after long waiting for the resounding waves and the mighty thunderings to die away, addressed the audience in the following eloquent speech : —

PROF. H. E. PECK'S SPEECH.

An event like this is surely a marked occasion in one's life. It constitutes for him a standpoint from which his mental vision can take a wide reach, both backward and forward. Since I came into this house my mind has reviewed, in their order, various salient points of my life. My part in childhood at the bedside of my dying mother; the consecration of myself in the beginning of manhood, to the service of God; my marriage ; my reception of my first-born ; my parting with the dear child as it died in my arms ; the act of devotion, when with my wife and children at my side, I thanked God that John had been rescued ; my arrest ; my imprisonment ; the encounter I had with disappointment when the Supreme Court refused our application for discharge, and my deeper and woful grief when our second plea at the bar of the Supreme Court failed — all these momentous events have passed in solemn procession before me. And having reviewed them, I find myself taking part in this wondrous scene.

It seems to me, my friends, as if in naming to you the events I have set before you, I had suggested in outline, the history of my whole life ; and as if that history naturally divided itself into two parts, one reaching down to the hour when I thanked God that John was free, and the other coming to this glad moment. And it further seems to me as if in these two parts of my life I had realized the truth of the doctrine of the philosophers that man has two consciousnesses — his own proper one and a special one — and that he may leave the one for a time to dwell in the other, and then return to his original one, his state while in the abnormal condition seeming to him when he has come out of it only blankness and chaos. Since last September I have been, in a sort, in a state of special consciousness, so new has my experience been ; but now, as I stand in this familiar place and look upon this sea of familiar faces, and read in their kindling eyes the sympathy with which every heart is aglow, my normal consciousness seems to be restored. The will, intelligence, and above all, the affections which I once exercised again put themselves in motion.

I owe my renewed life to the generous greeting which you have given us. And now, as I turn my back upon that special state from which you have awakened me, I think I can, in a measure, compensate your kindness by indicating to you one of the great lessons which I have been studying while in that state. It is the lesson which Christ set forth in the words, " he that loseth his life for my sake shall find it."

In the months of trial now brought to a happy close, it has been the lot of myself and my associates to be called upon to make in behalf of the cause of God and humanity, frequent and practical surrenders of things dear to us. And in every case the thing surrendered has been more than restored to us. We have offered health and even life upon the altar of duty. The sacrifice has been restored to us in the consciousness we have had that our lives were being used to good purpose, and that in the privilege of looking iniquity " framed into law " in the face without quailing or faltering, we were being amply paid for our self-sacrifice. We have surrendered home with its daily comforts and constantly renewing endearments. But home and kindred, wives and children, have never before been so dear, and have never before so stirred our best affections and kindled our tenderest delights as while we were making the sacrifice of them. We have given up our usual associations, have separated ourselves from *you* whom we love so well. And yet we have found, in our isolation, closer affinities, warmer spiritual fellowship than we ever knew before. Never before, dear friends, have *you* been so near and precious to us as you have been while we were consenting to being separated from you.

So, in all respects, the words of our Lord which I have recited have proved to be true.

Let me and my associates, let this great multitude, let our hundreds of young people remember always, that he who is willing to lose his life for the truth's or Christ's sake shall surely find it. Let no fear of consequences ever persuade any of us to draw back from any consecration which a good cause may require.

Before I take my seat let me add, in such discursive method as I may choose to follow, one or two statements respecting our circumstances while in prison.

First, let me certify to you that we have enjoyed the comforts of religion. The spirit of God has been with us in our seasons of private devotion and social worship. The Word of God has been both open and illuminated for us, and its rich promises have cheered us abundantly. When tempting enemies have crowded about us, the Saviour who preceded us at the bar of unrighteous judgment, has presented himself to assure us that He who was for us was more than they who were against us, and in every dark hour the assurance that Jehovah reigns has made our hearts rejoice.

In the next place, let me gratefully acknowledge the fact that we have been favored with earnest and continued sympathy and approval from steadfast friends. If the tide of *popular* sympathy has seemed at times to ebb, the regard and practical approval of thoughtful, Christian men, have risen to the last hour. Not a breeze has blown from east, or west, or north, or even south, without bringing the tidings that wise and good men were taking up our cause and remembering it in a practical way. The incidents of the single hour which followed the coming of our mail on the last day of our stay in prison, illustrated the fact that sympathy for us was at once widely extended and profound. A modest letter from a member of the Society of Friends residing in Philadelphia, whose family name is honored in the annals of Christian resistance to federal tyranny, brought us, with words of cheer, a check for one hundred dollars. And while our eyes were yet moist with gratitude for the thoughtfulness of our benefactor, a citizen of Cleveland, distinguished for his years and his standing as a Christian, and a member of society, not less than for his wealth, came in, and after handing us a donation which exceeded all but one of the many gifts we had received, blessed us for what we had done, and assured us that God had made us the ministers of abundant good. And to prove how widely the influence of our struggle with oppression had reached, he rehearsed a recent conversation with the venerable Dr. Nott, of Union College, in which the now almost dying sage had tenderly spoken of us, and had expressed the hope that our firmness would stay the progress of tyranny towards the overthrow of our liberties.

Thus have wise and Christian men remembered us to the end. And in the sympathy we have thus enjoyed, we have had abundant proof that the Christian anti-slavery element of society is at length stirred, and that the change which must follow this quickening is close at hand.

And now, friends, to all the blessings which Heaven has sent us, has been kindly added this greeting. Surely our cup runs over with good things, and long will it be before we forget the mercies which in our imprisonment and in our release, we have been and are permitted to enjoy.

After the Professor had closed his remarks, the cheering was renewed. Such cheering it was good to hear. It was only equalled by the grand performance of the great organ and choir which followed. The Marseilles Hymn was sung as, we were about to say, that choir only can sing it, and then Mr. Fitch was called for, and was received with a cordial welcome which would have been gratifying to any man.

J. M. FITCH'S SPEECH.

Mr. Fitch said: — My heart beats tumultuously, and my joys are abundant, as I once more look upon the faces of my dear friends in Oberlin. Oberlin! The people most abused and insulted, yet the dearest to my heart of all the world besides. Oberlin! The name which for twenty-four years I have pronounced with the love, the veneration, the enthusiasm with which the old Jews were wont to say Jerusalem! Dear Oberlin! "Where thou goest, I will go. Thy people shall be my people, and thy God my God. Where thou diest I will die, and there will I be buried." When, unexpectedly,

my eyes were again delighted with a view of Oberlin in the distance, it was the most precious moment of my life. Glorious Oberlin! let thy rebuke of wrong be uttered, and the world shall hear thy voice.

I have had my seasons of deep sadness in Oberlin; I have had my share of affliction. When remorseless death has sent to yonder graveyard my parents and my first-born, — when a large family of dear brothers have melted away like the snows of early Spring, I have sometimes felt desolate and alone. But I see to-night that I am not friendless. This overwhelming jubilation is too much for poor sinful man to bear. Who am I, that I should be crowned as a conqueror? I have received a wreath from the hands of youth and beauty, and God forgive me if the tears I shed are not those of humble thankfulness, instead of pride. I have borne the token to this stand with difficulty, which I could not and would not have done, if I were not assured that these extraordinary attentions betoken your interest in THE GLORIOUS CAUSE, and not in the man. The language of my heart is, "God forbid that I should glory," save in the triumphs of truth and righteousness.

Eighty-five days' imprisonment have taught me many lessons, two of which I will recite, and if I should be as successful in my recitation as I have been in my study, I should receive the highest mark, for I have learned the lessons thoroughly.

First, I have learned in a sense never before so well understood, that *truth is mighty*, and that in a conflict with error, one "shall chase a thousand, and two put ten thousand to flight." Oh, that the leaders who are set for her defence could understand that when settled on *the rock of truth*, they want nothing more but boldness to lift up their heads against the storm! Oh, that they would disencumber themselves — that they would spurn all considerations of policy — that they would cease to ask how will it affect my standing — and *only* ask, am I right? — then in the name of God and of truth *I will go ahead!* They have in possession a sword of heavenly temper, but, I am sorry to say, many of them are afraid to draw lest its very flash in the sun should scare the people and create an excitement. So shall they never succeed. So shall truth never prevail. So have not the brave hearts of old done their work. Let us say, with the Hebrews — "God will deliver us — but it not we will not obey" wicked laws. Let us, like Daniel, open our windows towards Jerusalem, and publicly spurn the wicked enactment as aforetime. Like Nehemiah, let us say, "Shall such a man as I flee?" "Shall I go in (or 'give in') to save my life? *I will not*." Or like Luther — "Duty calls, and I will go if the devils are as thick at Worms as the tiles on the houses." Let our leaders boldly *cast all into the scale* — make an offering of self entirely, even to the extent of life, if necessary, and then their blows will "dash the enemy in pieces like a potter's vessel."

"Tho' sharp be the conflict 't will pass *before long*,
And then, O how pleasant, the Conqueror's song.

Again, I have learned another lesson, namely, that it is not a dreadful thing *to go to jail*. Our trials have been considerable ; our unfavorable situation and our various excitements by day, and our restlessness in close rooms and amid the noise of raving maniacs by night, have been, in one sense, hard to bear. We would blush to compare ourselves with the noble sufferers for truth who have gone before us, yet we have suffered enough to understand them. We don't wonder that the brave martyrs and a glorious host of " whom the world was not worthy" endured pains, torments, and death cheerfully, yea, triumphantly, for we can well understand that when sustained by the immortal hope that the truth which was in them should soon rise like a sun upon a darkened world, and shed a shower of gold upon the impoverished earth, such inspiration might easily lead them to say to the God of truth — " In thy service pain is pleasure." Physically, the prisoner for the truth suffers as well as others, but the " answer of a good conscience," the hope of usefulness, and the luxury of divine approval, assuage his griefs, and banish all his pains.

Never since I became a lover of truth have my hopes risen so high, and my confidence in her speedy triumph been so great. Courage and energy are all we want, *when warring for the Lord*. Slavery is a braggart. He is a coward. He foameth and maketh a noise, but he who meets him with the courage of a David, and says, " in the name of the Lord will I destroy you," shall soon see how unequal the conflict when truth and error meet. Oberlin alone, if baptized with the true spirit of martyrs, would be a match for the world. This glorious company of youths, clothed in the panoply of righteousness, strong in the boldness of truth, and fired with the zeal of the Lord, could soon send the huge but really weak monster, Slavery, howling to his native hell.

John Watson was next called out and was received with applause. His speech was listened to with marked attention.

JOHN WATSON'S SPEECH.

Friends and Fellow-Citizens, — I come before you to-night, under circumstances new indeed. And right gladly do I meet you. This is my heart's home. When I look on your familiar and loving faces, my heart flows with gratitude that I may see you once again. On the 13th of September last, when there came a rumor that one of my fellow men had been kidnapped, I left my little place of business to ascertain, if possible, his whereabouts. I went to Wellington, and did what I thought was my duty toward releasing the helpless victim of oppression. Little did I then think of being brought before the District Court of the United States. But I was not only taken there, but thence dragged to prison, along with these my brethren, and there kept in close confinement for eighty-five days; and when I look upon these my brethren in bonds, my heart gushes with gratitude to think that their friends are my friends.

I believe it to be the duty of every Christian — and every man should be a Christian — to help all who are oppressed, whatever may be the color of their skin. I believed so then, and it was from this conviction of duty alone that I acted. My friends, when I heard Mr. Fitch and Prof. Peck speak about the death of their mothers, brothers, children, and friends, my own mind was led to the contrast between the separation of mothers and children by death, and that unspeakably more awful separation at the Auction-block.

But the spirit of slavery is the same North and South, and even here it would rob us of our all as readily as in South Carolina. The Federal Government is possessed of this demon, and we have all seen within the last three months the graspings of its fiendish greed. Yes, and even here in Oberlin, have we wolves in sheep's clothing. They come to us with fawning fingers and smiling lips, while in their hearts they are plotting the most piratical and inhuman atrocities, and plotting them against us, their next-door neighbors, who never lifted a finger to harm them or theirs, and never would. Now, my friends, shall such men remain in our midst ? If we had not had these traitors here, we should never have seen such wretches as Lowe, Mitchell, Jennings, and Davis — yes, and even *Dayton* — prowling about our houses. I think that if emphatic leave of absence had been given these men long ago, we should have been saved all the trials of the last year. But if good has grown out of our sufferings, we ought to be content. My friends, as the hour is late, I will not detain you. I rest in this confidence, that your purpose is one purpose, and that it was never so fixed as now, that whatever you may have done in the past, henceforth you will show oppression *no quarter*.

The evening was by this time far spent, and the venerable chairman resigned his seat to Professor Monroe.

The Professor informed the audience that the County Clerk, Mr. Horr, of Elyria, was present, and would entertain them with an account of how the Kentuckians *did n't* succeed in Elyria, and how the writ *was n't* served. Mr. H. came forward, and met such a warm reception as must have been cheering. He spoke as follows : —

MR. HORR'S SPEECH.

Just before leaving home for this place, I met one of the prominent Hunkers of your county, and observing that he looked rather downcast and crest-fallen, I said to him, "What is the matter?" "Why," said he, "there has been a contest going on between Lorain County and the United States, and *Uncle Sam* has kicked the bucket!"

Poor man! how I pitied him in his affliction. But I have been asked to give some account as to how they "*did'nt* serve the *habeas corpus*" down at Elyria. Some two weeks ago it was rumored in our village that an attempt was going to be made to release the Kentucky kidnappers from our custody by the aid of a writ of *habeas corpus*, which would be issued by Judge McLean. In a conversation with our Sheriff as to what was best to be done in such an emergency, he informed me that when such a writ reached our town he should probably have business in the remote part of the county! On Saturday last the District-Attorney, marshal, and prisoners arrived in Elyria, just as our Sheriff *happened* to be leaving the same place. The marshal immediately despatched a *post-office* clerk with a message that Marshal Johnson, marshal of the United States, wished to see him, and that he should return as soon as possible to Elyria. The sheriff was in Amherst attending to the sale of some property, and sent back word to his honor, the marshal, that if he wished to see him he had better come where he was, as he might be detained *rather late*. The Sheriff reached town early in the evening. The Attorney Belden, the Marshal, and the kidnappers immediately repaired to the office of the Probate Judge, for the purpose of surrendering the prisoners into custody, the bail being present to make the application. But lo! and behold the Sheriff was missing! Then commenced a search for him that lasted until eleven o'clock. All hands turned in and searched for Burr. But wonderful to relate, no Burr could be found! Some of us had often heard the remark, that it was a great help for a person in searching for an individual whom he wished to find, to *know where* he was, but we had never before fully realized what an advantage it was, in a search for one whom we *did not* wish to find! But not being able to find the Sheriff, the matter was postponed until Sunday morning, when an attempt was made to get the Sheriff and Probate Judge together, and so do their work on the Sabbath. But both officers refused to open office on that day. Then came the game on the part of Belden and Johnson. They asked the Judge if he would be in his office in the morning? He replied that he should. They then informed several of our citizens that they should leave the town immediately, and not return until after the Fourth, and it was generally understood that they had gone. But instead of doing as they said they would, they confined themselves in their room, and no more was seen of them until evening. It was then rumored that they had been playing a double game, and that all the talk about going to Cleveland, was a mere ruse gotten up solely to throw the officers of our county off their guard. Under these circumstances it was thought advisable that Judge Doolittle should visit his friends in Painesville, whom we all knew he had *neglected* very much of late! The Judge objected on the ground that Belden and the Marshal expected to see him in the morning, but being informed by Judge Sheldon that they had both told him distinctly that they should leave, and that nothing more would be done in the case until Tuesday, he finally concluded to go, and that he might have a plenty of time to celebrate the Fourth, he took an *early start!*

On Monday morning Mrs. Doolittle was waited upon by Attorney Belden, between four and five in the morning, who inquired for Judge Doolittle. You may imagine how he looked upon being informed that Judge Doolittle had been gone some *two hours!* But, said Belden, "I had an appointment with the Judge." "True," replied Mrs. Doolittle, "he spoke of that; but Judge Sheldon informed him that you had told him that you should leave town and not be back until Tuesday, hence supposing that his services would not be needed, he concluded to visit his long *neglected* friends." Attorney Belden left, with that peculiar expression on his face that always attends an individual who has been caught in his own trap. The kidnapping squad then left for Cleveland, and returned again on Tuesday morning; but Judge Doolittle, very unfortunately (?) had been unable to "tear himself away from his friends," and Belden, Johnson & Co. were compelled to return, with the consciousness that unless something could be done, the kidnappers must be tried or forfeit their bail. But to complete the farce, Belden ordered Johnson to serve the writs on our Sheriff, but he not being inclined to take them, they afterwards served them on our jail, by leaving them at the residence of Sheriff Burr.

Here we have a United States Marshal serving a writ commanding an officer to bring certain prisoners to Cleveland, who he well knew had not been in that officer's custody for nearly two months. How the writ of *habeas corpus* was obtained is difficult to tell, unless it was by false affidavits. Tuesday evening Hon. D. K. Cartter arrived in town, who had been employed to assist in the prosecution. He said the Kentuckians were in great terror at the prospect of "facing the music." "Why," said Cartter (he stutters sometimes you know), "them scapegraces were so scart you could ha' wa-a-a-ashed your ha-a-a-ands in the sweat o' their faces!" He at once communicated the intelligence that he brought proposals for an unconditional surrender on the part of the General Government. The conditions you all understand, and the result of them is the spectacle now before us.

Many of us have come here to-night for the purpose of seeing the twelve men who stood up boldly for freedom, who have asked for no quarters from the enemy, who are here to-night, victorious, with no *nolle contendere* to dim the lustre of their fame. This should be a proud evening for them. They have taught the country a great lesson : they have shown to the world that men who would steal our citizens must do it at their peril. They have established the fact that henceforth in Lorain county the Fugitive Slave Law is a nullity, and for their reward thousands of hearts are to-night beating the response, " well done, good and faithful servants."

Mr. W. E. LINCOLN was called out, and was received by his fellow-students and the audience generally, in the warmest and most cordial manner.

W. E. LINCOLN'S SPEECH.

In the presence of slave-holders, when rebuking them from the pulpit in the South, for the sin of slave-holding, I have been undaunted ; but in the presence of so much intellect and sympathy, I strangely fear, and want in self-possession. In the democratic papers, we, the four naturalized citizens from England, have been denominated " Oberlin Jacks and Donkeys." This feeling and usage from the Democracy has not surprised us after the Cass letter ; but we accept the title, and being Bible men par excellence, as the Democrats own, we seek for our character there. Bible donkeys were not the degenerate, much abused animals you find now, but a right royal and king bearing quadruped. We find they laughed to scorn the speed of the hunter, and swiftness we find to be their predominant characteristic. We *were*, as Democratic evidence shows, for we got to Wellington, some nine miles off, in forty-five minutes. Ever swift and speedy will we be for the right and for freedom ; and if needs be to rescue our brother, we will equal the speed of the ball.

In olden times a stream rising from two mounds sent death and barrenness all along its course. The land that would have smiled with palm and cedar and waving corn, was bald and seared. Many trials were made to cure the barren waters ; what failures, what disappointment. Becoming wise from repeated failures, the men of Jericho came at last to the man of God, Elisha. When they took the course of true wisdom they soon heard the welcome, " Thus saith the Lord, I have healed, there shall not be from them any more death or barrenness."

Slavery is a fountain whose waters spread along all its course desolation, misery, despair, and stolidity more dire than the dreadful Upas shade.

We Americans have wondered at its death course from its fountain, at its deep springs in Covetousness and Lust to its " consummation of all villany." We have striven to heal its waters by compromises ; by Websterian Slave Laws ; by ignoring all the rights of colored men in Supreme Courts, and have miserably failed. We have called on the church of God for help, and

she, by calling good evil and evil good, hoped to purify and cleanse the abominable stream. She has trailed the banner of Love in the filth of sin, and amid the scorn and jeers of the ungodly she has failed, miserably failed, reaping a dragon-teeth harvest of scorning infidelity. We have tried political excitement, and have failed. Now wise, let us seek to God, and the waters shall be healed. Let us gird ourselves with truth and holiness, and then under the banner of the Almighty we shall move on to certain victory. We shall thus cast into the water salt from the new cruise which has ever healed the world's woes. This made the difference between the result of the labors of the ancients on the one hand, and of Luther, Cromwell, and the Puritans on the other. The ancients, with powers of intellect to which our masters bow as pupils, failed because there was no Christ, no God, only a Pater Omnipotens, a Jupiter to aid them. These noble moderns succeeded and founded the only liberties of earth, because they thus spoke and trusted : —

" Here I stand, I can do no other, God help me."

" Men, fear God and keep your powder dry."

Let us, then, with a gentle, firm spirit, be *suaviter in modo fortiter in re*, imitating the goodness of the Scotch wife, so well illustrated by the wives of the married of our party, and sweetly illustrated by the " *gentle friends* " of the non-married of our party ; let us with the cannie wife say, " Your majesty, rather than my husband should break God's law in obeying you, I would receive his head in my apron here."

The Chairman here remarked that he would ask the audience to excuse him for the introduction of another subject — the subject of finance. Expense is attendant upon all our doings, and we incur expense to-night. You remember when the slave woman was to be redeemed in Henry Ward Beecher's church, the pastor said " he did not like to hear a vulgar noise in church, but he had no objection to a godly clapping of hands." We have had various kinds of clapping here to-night, and the chairman would now suggest one additional kind, namely, clapping — their hands into their pockets.

Nimble youth moved through the audience as collectors, while Mr. JOHN SCOTT, who was called for, addressed the meeting in a few forcible and appropriate words.

JOHN SCOTT'S SPEECH.

We left our loved home ere the snows of early spring had melted, and we returned not till the gardens were filled with flowers, and the fields clothed with greenness. We have endeavored to maintain the truth, and we are not ashamed to send down our example to our children. God has been very merciful to us, and we and our families have been preserved in health. Surely God has encouraged us ever after this to "stand up for Jesus."

HENRY EVANS'S SPEECH.

Friends: when I use the term friends, I do not use it as a mere figure of speech. It comes from the utmost depths of my soul. Your presence here bears testimony of the fact that you are our friends. The care that you have taken to provide for our families during our imprisonment, proved your heartfelt sympathy, for which we are grateful. Never during our confinement have you been forgotten; in our daily devotions to Almighty God you have been remembered. We felt that your cause was our cause, and your presence in such numbers this evening more than substantiates the conviction. While in prison we were cheered by daily communication from your breathing a spirit of prayer in our behalf. I profess to be a believer in Christ, knowing that without prayer and His presence no great good can be accomplished. The Bible has been our guide. Through it we have realized the presence of the Holy Spirit, which has led us on in the discharge of our duty, and buoyed us up to faithfully accomplish the work that had been assigned us; the result of which is a victory on the side of truth, a triumph, indeed, over wrong.

For eighteen years, I have been seeking to know what the Lord would have me do in my humble position in life. During that time he has visited me with afflictions. He has taken from our earthly embrace a darling child; He has taken from me a loved and loving mother. All this I bore patiently in submission to his will. When I was cast into prison, my heart again said, let thy will, not mine be done. I need not tell you, my friends, that to suffer for humanity's sake has been to me a pleasure and not a pain. I rejoice to say that I had resigned myself into the hands of Him who is the wise disposer of us all. Every thing of an earthly nature my mind had given up. My soul had entered into the work that God had called me to accomplish.

I feel that we have discharged our duty; we have finished the work given us to do. The telegraph wires have flashed our victory through the country. It has gone up to heaven — angels and archangels are now singing hosannas to the Lord for our deliverance, and there are no words that better express my feelings than the following, which by way of conclusion I will repeat: —

"Praise God from whom all blessings flow,
Praise Him all creatures here below."

Mr. LYMAN was called out, and every one who heard the cheering was well assured that the audience were glad to see him.

A. W. LYMAN'S SPEECH.

Upon a scene like this language has no power. The occasion speaks for itself. My own heart is too full for utterance. I am glad to see you. I am glad to meet friends and associates. I am glad to meet the Fire Department upon this occasion, of which I am a member. I know there are true and devoted hearts to the great cause of freedom in that Department, who would sacrifice their lives and their all to the cause of liberty. What has brought about this great change? Was it a compromise upon our part? Did we get down upon our hands and knees, and crawl in the dust at the feet of the slave power? No! It was the government that wished to come to terms. They did not wish nor did they dare prosecute the matter any farther. They were not only afraid of having those Kentucky kidnappers sent to purgatory, but they were afraid that the whole Democratic party would be sent there. We have heard those that have visited us during our confinement say that we must not adopt any policy that would damage the Republican party. I would say if there is not power and virtue enough in the Republican party to repudiate the great evil of American slavery, and the infernal Fugitive Slave Act of 1850, then I say let the party go. I believe there is virtue enough left in the party to do it. Let us go to work and get rid of the conservative elements of the party, and those old fogy principles that stick tighter than a tick on a sheep's back. Our fathers fought at Bunker Hill and on the plains of Lexington for the rights and liberties which we this day enjoy. Liberties, did I say? No. We do not all enjoy liberty. It was the design of the fathers of this great Republic that all should enjoy the blessings of liberty without distinction in regard to birth, complexion, or conditions of men. I would say in conclusion, that we should all adopt the language of Patrick Henry, "Give me liberty, or give me death."

Mr. RICHARD WINSOR came forward in answer to an earnest call, and was received with as much enthusiasm as heart could wish.

RICHARD WINSOR'S SPEECH.

Beloved friends: — I feel that I must say a few words, for my heart is full. I with joy return again to the bosom of Oberlin. Oberlin, if not heretofore, now an *honor*, a *joy*, and *glory* to our State.

And you, my fellow-students, who, while this glorious strife has been waging, have been climbing the hill of science, we, who are young in this little band, trust that we have made some progress too; while you have progressed theoretically, we have in experience and rigid discipline. And you, my beloved class mates, who have been taught from the mouths of your teachers, we, too, have been taught, but by the silent, God-like *patience, energy, and perseverance* in the example of these, my elder brethren, who have been to us examples of *true men* during our imprisonment.

And now, as I stand here, my eye rests upon

that little *upper chamber* within the prison walls, where we have often sung and prayed together, and there, as we have consulted together concerning the glorious combat between *Freedom* and *Slavery*, I have seen the tear glisten in the eye, and heard the outgushing of hearts filled with the *love* of *truth*, as these dear brethren have consecrated their *wives*, their *little ones*, their *property, their lives, and all*, to God and *Freedom*. Ah, my friends, no language can portray the scenes that there have transpired within those prison walls. And now I close, my beloved friends and fellow-students, by saying, let us go and do likewise.

Sheriff Burr, of Lorain, after repeated and urgent calls, came forward.

SHERIFF BURR'S SPEECH.

He said: — Sham Democrats have raised a great hue and cry about my dodging. I dodged nobody. I had business to do, and I attended to it as though no Belden or kidnappers were about. I was in town for a considerable time, and when I got ready to go to another part of the county to sell some property, I went. Marshal Johnson sent for me to come home as quick as possible. [The Marshal is apt to *order* folks a good deal, and to add, with, O how much importance, "I am the United States Marshall."] But, continued the speaker, I sent word to the Marshal that if he wanted to see me more than I did him, he could come along if he liked. They had a writ which they could not have obtained without the perjury of somebody, which represented the kidnappers as in custody when it was notoriously true that they were at large. I did not care to trouble myself much under such circumstances. I made up my mind to put the matter through straight, if I should be compelled to lie in jail for the offence till the bars rusted off.

Sheriff Wightman was demanded (I can hardly say called for), and rose up before the audience. Never, in all my life, did I listen to a more hearty, spontaneous, and *tremendous* cheering than greeted him. He stood for a long time awaiting silence, but it seemed as though the people would never be satisfied. When the repeated bursts of enthusiasm were over, Mr. W. spoke as follows: —

SHERIFF WIGHTMAN'S SPEECH.

Sheriff Wightman said it would be impossible for him to express his feelings on beholding such a mass of people. He was no speaker, and should he tell people when he got home that he had addressed such an audience, they would be astonished. He loved and respected the prisoners, and had done what he could for them. He had been glad, also, to see their friends at the jail. They had always been welcome. There was but one thing to mar the pleasure of the evening — the absence of Simeon Bushnell. Let us all remember him. Let those wives who are permitted to enjoy the society of their husbands to-night, sympathize with his sad and lovely wife.

Mr. Wightman closed amid hearty expressions of applause from the audience.

Mr. Monroe said, " Our friend need not suppose for a moment, and I presume does not suppose, that we are in any danger, to-night, of forgetting Simeon Bushnell. As God lives, and as my soul lives, and as we all live, when Simeon Bushnell does come to town we'll give him a reception which will convince the tyrants who have oppressed him, that there are hearts here that love him."

Father Gillett — the grand old man — the white-haired patriarch, next rose. I will not attempt to describe the splendid reception he met. A life of faithful adherence to truth would be well rewarded by such a hearty greeting from such a glorious audience.

FATHER GILLETT'S SPEECH.

He spoke in a lively and witty manner. He said that after being taken out of jail the marshal told him not to go back to jail. I said, "I *will* go, I want to get my clothes; and beside, I *want to bid my friends good-by.*" So he took me down here. He took me in his carriage right beside him. ['T aint often I get a ride in a carriage.] While we were riding he said, "You see we want to get rid of you Wellington folks, and then — [don't say nothing 'bout it]." "O no," says I, "I ain't going to say nothing about it." But I suppose this is like all other things, when it is over with, you can tell out. "And then we will drive those Oberlin fellows *to the wall.*" Thinks I, then you'll have *something to drive*, that's all !

Never made a speech in my life; don't know how to make a speech, and I aint going to make a speech; but I'll just say that every thing *under the heavens* that I was taken down to jail for was just for being ketched down at Wellington; and that aint all. I hav n't confessed it all yet. I am ashamed that I did n't do more than just be ketched down there; and if there is ever another such a time I am going to have more to be accused of, and if other folks are cowards, I'll rescue the fugitive *myself*. I used to think Oberlin was a pretty bad kind of a place, but I've changed my mind about it now.

Prof. Monroe then rose and said: "When we see a good old block, we always want to ask if there are any more chips of the same kind. The other day, when I was at Wellington, a young man stepped up and handed me three dollars for the benefit of our friends here : and when I asked him his name he only smiled, and then disappeared in the crowd. But I asked a person who stood near me, and he told me his name was Gillett; and I understand that he is not the only one, but there are several more of 'em."

The Chairman then said, "We have given you to-night a specimen of an honest Professor of a college; and perhaps that is not the most remarkable thing in the world. We have also brought forward an honest Lawyer, and perhaps that will not surprise you. But we have another specimen to present — a real curiosity — I mean *an honest Postmaster!* [Cries of, " Bring him out!" "Let us see him!"] I introduce to you Mr. Henry R. Smith, whose unceasing efforts to make the prisoners comfortable have received their lasting gratitude. (Nearly two thousand letters have been sent from the jail during the confinement of the " Rescuers," and Mr. Smith's kindness in mailing them has secured him his office.)

Mr. Smith came forward. To give an account of his reception would be but to repeat — " the warmest and most enthusiastic." His little speech was just the thing.

Mr. Washburn, of the Elyria Democrat, was introduced to the audience and made a capital speech.

GEO. G. WASHBURN'S SPEECH.

Mr. W. said: — He was present at the great Convention of freemen in Buffalo, in 1848, and heard the eloquent Charles B. Sedgwick, as he gazed over the vast multitude, exclaim, " My friends, my eyes in their wildest dreams of fancy had never hoped to look upon a scene like this!" With truth, he could adopt the language of the eloquent orator. He had watched with deep solicitude the events connected with the prosecutions which had just been abandoned by the Government, and, although at times the future looked dark and gloomy, he had come here to rejoice that a glorious day had dawned upon our cause. He felt it was well the blow had fallen where it did — upon a community who had the boldness to meet it, the fortitude to endure it, and the discretion to act in such a manner as to result in the triumph they had met to rejoice over. He urged the friends of the slave to make a city of refuge for the oppressed in every township, and to permit no slave-hunter to enter it in pursuit of his victim.

It was now near the hour of midnight, yet the audience gave the profoundest attention to the very close of Mr. W.'s speech, of which we have given but a brief report.

Principal H. E. Fairchild next occupied a few moments in appropriate remarks, and then read the following resolution: —

RESOLUTION OF OBERLIN.

Resolved, That this meeting request the Town Council to enter the following minute upon the Records of the Village of Oberlin: —

The citizens of Oberlin assembled in Mass Meeting to welcome home our faithful representatives, Messrs. Peck, Plumb, Fitch, W. Evans, Winsor, Lincoln, H. Evans, J. Watson, D. Watson, Bartlett, Lyman, and Scott, who, rather than give the least countenance to the Fugitive Slave Act, have lain eighty-four days in Cleveland jail, under indictment for the rescue of a fugitive slave from the custody of a U. S. Marshal, give devout thanks to Almighty God for the grace which has enabled them patiently, faithfully, and firmly to maintain the contest against that impious enactment till the government has asked for quarter, and has volunteered the proposition to release the Lorain *criminals* under the Fugitive Act. on condition that Lorain will relinquish the U. S. *executors* of the Act.

To our faithful friends we express our warmest gratitude and our unqualified commendation for the firmness, the wisdom, and the fidelity with which they have maintained our common cause.

And finally, in view of all the consequences attendant upon this prosecution, and all the light shed upon the subject, we unanimously express our greatly increased abhorrence of the Fugitive Slave Act, and avow our determination that no fugitive slave shall ever be taken from Oberlin either with or without a warrant, if we have power to prevent it.

Passed unanimously July 6, 1859.

CLOSING SERVICES.

Dr. Morgan's prayer was eloquent and impressive. In closing, his great and noble heart reached out towards all, and he prayed that the day might soon dawn when all the world should be free, and when in all the earth should be found not one enslaved family, *nor one enslaved soul.*

It was then requested that the congregation would join with the choir in singing the Doxology, and not less than twenty-five hundred voices united in singing to the majestic tune " Old Hundred," the words: —

> " Praise God from whom all blessings flow,
> Praise Him all creatures here below ;
> Praise Him above, ye heavenly host,
> Praise Father, Son, and Holy Ghost."

The Benediction was pronounced by Dr. Morgan, while the vast congregation listened with the profoundest silence and most reverent attention. Throughout all the crowded galleries scarcely a sound was to be heard.

It was midnight before the vast audience broke up, and during the long exercises, scarcely a person moved from the church. In no other instance in all our life, have we known so large an audience held for so long a time in perfect quiet. It was an evening never to be forgotten by the thousands of youth who have caught the spirit and will carry the fire into all the earth.

THE RECEPTION OF BUSHNELL.

The last and crowning ovation to the triumphant Rescuers came off on Monday, July 11th, a day that will long be too bright for tyrant eyes to look calmly upon.

Again we recur to the editorial columns of

the *Leader*, extracting only the salient points from a full and accurate detail.

BUSHNELL AT HOME.

THE OBERLIN DEMONSTRATION.

Yesterday was a proud day for the " Oberlin and Wellington Rescuers." Previous notice had been given, that Bushnell, the last of the jail confined " Rescuers " and " Felons," was to proceed to his home in Oberlin ; and as the hour approached for his departure from the stone castle where for so many weeks he had been confined, an immense crowd gathered in and about the jail to see him off. Both jail and yard were densely crowded with the friends of the prisoner. Mr. John F. Warner was endowed by the Sheriff with the powers of Marshal, and under his guidance the procession was formed, headed by a guard of colored men with a banner inscribed " Oberlin and Wellington Rescuers."

Then followed the Chaplain, Rev. J. C. WHITE, and after him the Hecker Band in full uniform, discoursing lively and spirited national airs. Then came a long line of friends on foot followed by Mr. BUSHNELL in a carriage with his baggage; accompanied by the ladies of Sheriff Wightman's family. Several other carriages followed, decorated with banners and flags. A great crowd followed the procession to the depot, where there were gathered immense masses who welcomed the hero of the occasion with hearty cheers.

At 11:25 the train, with six crowded coaches, left the depot, the band playing national airs as they commenced the journey. On reaching Oberlin, the guns of Artillery Co. A., Captain W. R. SIMMONS, who had gone to that place on the early train, spoke forth in booming notes one hundred shots of welcome and triumph. That Company, with the Oberlin Hook and Ladder and Engine Companies were drawn up to receive the Clevelanders. Besides these, there were thousands of the Lorain citizens ready to grasp their fellow-citizen by the hand. One banner which they carried was curious and noticeable. An immense horn, labelled " U. S. District Court," was the principal feature, the " Rescuers" issuing from the large end, while from the little end of the horn the Officials were crawling out upon the " Democratic Platform," at which one was grinding at " Public opinion." At a little distance from the Rescuers were friends who greeted them with " Well done, good and faithful servants." Besides these there was a pair of scales, with " Higher Law " going down in one scale, while " U. S. Laws " were flying up, being weighed in the balances and found wanting. It was expressive.

On leaving the cars, Judge SPALDING said to the crowd, " My friends, Bushnell had no regrets to express that he had aided in rescuing the boy John ; WE have no regrets to express that he has been imprisoned."

Mr. BUSHNELL was then welcomed home by Rev. E. H. FAIRCHILD, as follows : —

Mr. BUSHNELL,

In behalf of this crowd of your fellow-citizens gathered to greet you on your return from jail. I am requested to extend to you the right hand of fellowship, and welcome you home. I esteem it a high privilege to discharge an office at once so agreeable and so honorable.

For many years we have known you only to respect and esteem you. We have known you as a citizen incapable of an act of injustice to a fellow man, or to your country. And this high estimation of you has by no means been damaged by the events of the few past months.

When on the evening of the 13th of September last, you returned with that rescued man, we were not ashamed of you. When the news came of your indictment by a grand jury selected from a small minority of the citizens of this district, we were not ashamed of you. And when we heard of your conviction by a jury of the same stamp, and of your sentence by a judge eager to execute the most impious of all laws, we were not ashamed of you. And now that you return to us unsubdued, ready to repeat the same act when opportunity offers, we are not ashamed of you. Again, I say, welcome ! thrice welcome to your home in Oberlin, and to the county of Lorain ! How general, and how hearty this welcome is, let the cheers of five thousand people assembled in the heat of harvest, on the first working day of the week, at the hour of dinner, bear testimony.

Yet, sir, we should do you and ourselves injustice, should we intimate that we have gathered here for the simple purpose of expressing our personal regard for you.

We are well aware that we cannot thus honor you on your return from prison, without making ourselves responsible for the act that sent you there. Indeed, for this very purpose we are here. What was your act ? The alarm was given and came to your ears, that a neighbor had fallen among thieves, who were dragging him South into life-long bondage. Without inquiring into the character, color, or condition of that neighbor, without asking whether the robbers were private or public robbers, whether they acted on their own responsibility, or by United States authority, you hastened to the spot, delivered the " spoiled from the oppressor," brought him to a friendly inn, " and took care of him."

For such an act we wish to be responsible before our country and the world. You could neither have been " a good Christian nor a good citizen," had you coldly witnessed such an outrage on a fellow man, and " passed by on the other side."

You raised no standard of rebellion against your country ; you simply violated an inhuman statute so base, that, on its engrossment, only two Northern Senators voted for it; and then you quietly submitted to its penalty. How long we will imitate you in this latter respect, we do not propose to say. We acknowledge our obligation to submit so long, and only so long as we lack the moral, political, and physical power to render the enforcement of that Act impossible.

We belong to no "modern school" of politics or theology, and lay claim to no new light on these subjects. We belong to the school of the Fathers, who having been driven from their native land by the persecutions of their government, taught their children that "resistance to tyrants is obedience to God;" or to the more ancient school, which exclaimed to the existing authorities, "Whether it be right to hearken unto you more than unto God, judge ye;" or to that still more ancient, which said to the king, "We will not serve thy gods nor worship the golden image which thou has set up." We crave the honor of some slight connection with the long line of prophets, apostles, reformers, and martyrs, who, by the governments of their time, were persecuted, imprisoned, and killed, " of whom the world was not worthy."

Three more cheers were then given, when the procession, headed by the Wellington Sax Horn Band, and including the Artillery, Fire Companies, the Elyria Band, the " Rescuers," visitors, etc., marched to the immense church, which was most densely crowded with thousands of the best citizens of Lorain county and vicinity. The spacious galleries of the church presented a beautiful spectacle, being almost entirely filled with the ladies of the college and neighborhood. These ladies held a prominent banner inscribed —

THE LADIES.
1000
WELCOME YOU.
Thrice Welcome.
GREETING.

Such a beautiful sight as those galleries presented one seldom sees. It was an exhibition surpassed nowhere " on this terrestrial ball."

A large choir of ladies and gentlemen occupied the front of the gallery, and by their execution added greatly to the interest of the occasion. The speakers and reporters occupied the pulpit.

Prof. MONROE opened the exercises at half past one o'clock, by calling upon the venerable Father KEEP to open with prayer, which he did in an eloquent and stirring appeal to the God of Heaven for his blessing upon the meeting, and rendering heartfelt thanks and gratitude for the blessings which had been poured forth on the " Rescuers," and enable them to go through that trying ordeal and despotic rule.

Prof. MONROE, as Chairman, first called upon Hon. D. K. CARTTER, who responded in his usual off-hand, sarcastic, and impetuous manner.

*   *   *   *   *

Mr. CARTTER closed amid the most enthusiastic cheers. His remarks having been frequently interrupted with shouts of laughter and cheers.

This speech was followed by singing by the choir of a magnificent quartette and chorus, entitled " The Gathering of the Free," by Prof. George N. Allen. This was splendidly performed by the choir, setting every heart beating with exultation and sympathy.

A. G. RIDDLE, Esq., was then called upon, and rehearsed with hearty eloquence the history of the trial and incarceration of those who had so long felt the force of a tyrant's prison. At one point the speaker brought Bushnell up to the stand, who was greeted with rousing cheers.

At the close of Mr. RIDDLE's remarks, which were heartily cheered, the Hecker band gave some of their unsurpassed music. After which Hon. R. P. SPALDING was introduced to the audience as the man who, when he was on the Supreme Bench of the State of Ohio, announced publicly, that should a fugitive slave be brought before him, he would set him free. He was received with cheers, and remarked —

When BUSHNELL was asked by the Judge if he had any regrets to express for his conduct, how would he have leaped from his seat and shouted, " No, sir'ee," could he have looked forward to this proud day, when five thousand citizens assemble to bid him welcome. The speaker gave a high tribute to the character of Father Gillett, who told him at Cleveland that should he plead " nolle contendere," his sons at home would shut the door against him. The speaker then gave a history of slavery from the fifteenth century to the present time, with appropriate and earnest comments.

Mr. BUSHNELL was then brought up to the stand. The applause and cheers that greeted him spoke truly of the sympathy and welcome which the audience felt for the noble " felon." He remarked, that while he had felt no regret when before the Court, he did now regret that he could not in fitting language respond to their call. He had been imprisoned for disobeying the Fugitive Slave Law, and Marshal Johnson told him that that law had been enforced on the Reserve; but this audience showed that it could not and should not be; and as for him, if a fugitive came to him for aid he should have it, though all the mortals in Ohio opposed it, so help him God. " Three times three " were then given with a will for Simeon Bushnell in " speaking tones."

Music by the Wellington band.

Hon. JOSHUA R. GIDDINGS was then brought forward.

[So well does literally " ALL THE WORLD " know JOSHUA R. GIDDINGS, and just what he would say on such an occasion, that we may perhaps be pardoned for omitting — since we have not space for all — his eloquent address, as we have also the scarcely less brilliant one of Mr. Cartter.]

The Marseilles Hymn was then executed by the choir, the solo being finely sung by Miss Church, and the full choir of one hundred and fifty ladies and gentlemen joining in the chorus with splendid effect.

Hon. Ralph Plumb (one of the Rescuers) was the next speaker. On the 13th of September last, just ten months ago, he had, it is true, been glad to know of the rescue of John Price ; but he was ashamed to say that he did nothing to aid in the rescue. It was not these men alone, but it was the spirit of Oberlin, which was opposed to all oppression, which was indicted. But years ago he had been guilty of rescuing slaves. [At this point Mr. Giddings arose and said that he remembered one Sunday morning, long years ago, when this man Plumb brought a whole wagon load of slaves to his house, on the way to freedom.] The speaker then went on to describe and speak of their prison lives of eighty-five days, of the feelings that actuated the imprisoned, and their trials when thinking of their families at home. He had felt cheered with the thought which his daughter had written him while in prison, " Father, it is a great boon to be the lever, or even the stone upon which that lever rests, which is to lift a nation and a whole people up into purer atmosphere where freedom can live and bless." They should go on, until Ohio should be, what she professes to be, a free State, and until our whole broad land is free from slavery's blighting curse.

Prof. Monroe announced at the close of Mr. Plumb's remarks, that it had been said that recent events had soured the temper of the Oberlin people; and he must confess that Prof. Fairchild, one of the most amiable of men, had become so soured that he was about to *cane* a person right there on the stage.

PRESENTATION ADDRESS BY PROF. J. C. FAIRCHILD.

Mr. President. It seems to be your prerogative to assign us our duties, at your pleasure, however grotesque they may seem, and we are not at liberty to decline them ; but, I take it, every man is by nature chartered with the privilege of performing his duties in his own way. You will expect me, then, to administer the *caning* which you have appointed me, in our plain Oberlin fashion — not with that display of refinement andchivalry which might be appropriate to the chamber of the United States Senate.

There are, probably, few in this vast assembly who need to be informed that our friends at Cleveland experienced much kindness from various sources, as an offset to the pains and penalties laid upon them by United States officials. At their first introduction to prison walls, they made the acquaintance of a Sheriff

whose manhood could not be overshadowed or perverted by his official character, — who, with the discernment which God gives to the true-hearted, could discover honest and upright men, even under the brand of indicted and convicted felons. Those committed to him as prisoners, he dared to receive as guests; and, from the first moment of their commitment to this present hour, he has made it his care to administer to their comfort and welfare.

Our friends were sought out and cared for by many others. Foremost among these, was one who did not merely come and look on them, to " pass by on the other side," but he came to them with such comfort and help as personal attention and personal resources could provide. He *took care* of them, and even went beyond the parable, in not leaving them until he saw them safely lodged in the bosom of their families.

[Now, Mr. President, do not permit the good people here to say that I have intimated that our friends had *fallen among thieves.* If they press the illustration to that extent, they must do it on their own responsibility ; I was brought up not to call bad names.]

Within the prison walls, our friends were introduced to a jailer — whom God made a man before he was made a jailer — and to his excellent wife and her two assistants, all of whom were unwearied in their attentions to the prisoners and their friends that visited them, and by their considerate kindness gave to the gloomy place as much the air of a *home* as a prison ever had.

The citizens of Oberlin, in whose behalf I speak, have not been insensible to this kindness, of which hundreds of them have been personal witnesses. Without the idea of repaying it, they have wished in a measure to relieve their sense of obligation, by a public testimonial of their gratitude ; and I will call upon our friend Mr. Grannis to accept and transmit to Mr. Sheriff Wightman this cane, presented by the citizens of Oberlin, and this — its fellow — to Mr. Henry R. Smith, the good Samaritan; a small token of our appreciation of their kindness. Assure them, sir, that these gifts have been selected with an eye to utility as well as comeliness — not that we would intimate that they are afflicted with any *spinal weakness*, or require any such support of their manhood. Nor have they enemies whose assaults they might repel, — nor is there any thing in human form against which *we* bear a grudge, upon which we would wish them to try the temper of these trusty weapons. But if, in their pilgrimage through the world, they should fall in with the monster which Mrs. Partington has called the fugitive slave *Bill,* " going about seeking whom he may devour," the mere sight of these two good sticks shall frighten him back to his native pandemonium, whence he is a fugitive, and where he " owes service and labor."

The matrons of Oberlin who have thus far

had the privilege of caring for their husbands at home, have provided for the gentle hostess of our friends, Mrs. John Smith, this set of spoons; for her assistants, Miss Eliza Morrill and Miss Lucy P. Wightman, this dress and this book; assure them that their kindness will be held in remembrance, and that they are among those whom we shall delight to honor.

Prof. FAIRCHILD then presented to John C. Granniss, Esq., to be presented by him to the parties named — a gold-headed cane for Sheriff Wightman; a similar one for Mr. H. R. Smith; a set of spoons for Mrs. Smith; a dress for her sister; and a book for Miss Lucy Wightman. These articles Mr. Granniss delivered, and responded for the recipients in a happy and fitting manner.

The canes are heavy ebony, with elegantly chased gold heads, inscribed to the recipients "from the citizens of Oberlin." They are valuable articles, both intrinsically and for their deeply interesting associations.

Prof. MORGAN then read the following resolution, which was carried with a will: —

Resolved, That the people of Oberlin in Mass Meeting assembled, tender to R. P. SPALDING, F. T. BACKUS, A. G. RIDDLE, and S. O. GRISWOLD, our heartfelt gratitude for the unwearied zeal and devoted self-sacrifice with which, refusing all compensation, they have conducted their very able defence of the Rescuers before the U. S. Court and the Supreme Court of the State. We feel that no fees could have bought such services, and that no gift can duly express our sense of the debt we owe; but by us and by countless others of the friends of right and freedom, the names of these able jurists and their noble services will be had in everlasting remembrance.

Esq. GOODWIN, of Sandusky, was then introduced, and spoke of the present contest between common and higher law — claiming that nothing was "law" save that which commanded what was right, and prohibited what was wrong. He spoke with words of counsel and hope for the future, and with a prophetic eye looking through the coming ages to the last day, when kings and beggars, black and white, bond and free, should meet together before the great white throne, to be judged for the deeds done in the body.

JOHN LANGSTON, Esq., rose in response to a call, to apologize for the absence of his brother Charles, and to speak a word for himself. In his characteristic bold eloquence, he spoke fearless and startling words in opposition to the Fugitive Slave Law. He paid a high and proud tribute to the speech of his brother in the United States Court, which was received with loud applause. He thanked his noble friends who had gone up to Cuyahoga county jail — thanked them in his character as a negro — as a white man — as one in whom the blood of both races joined — as a *man* — and

as an American citizen. We wished that the wide world could all have seen him standing there, pouring forth in clarion notes his noble, manlike, and godlike thoughts. No more eloquent speech was made yesterday than his.

Prof. MONROE then introduced Prof. PECK, expressing his doubt in the mathematical assertion that eight quarts were equal to one *Peck.*

Prof. PECK remarked that he had been put into intimate association with the noble men who had brought eloquence and talent to bear upon their defence, and expressed his gratitude to them in touching words and kind remembrances, and also in the highest and tenderest terms of Jailer Smith, his family, and those associated with him in imprisonment, expressing as his will and testament, that those brethren should be the first to follow his body to its burial, and the ones to offer up the last prayer over his lifeless clay.

Judge SPALDING and Mr. RIDDLE, for the counsel for the defence, expressed their thanks for the compliments paid them, but asserted that the Bar of Cuyahoga, with possibly a few exceptions, were entitled to equal gratitude, for all were ready and eager to leap forward for the defence of such men; — "so bring on your Rescuers."

With music by the Hecker Band, the immense congregation of not less than 3,000 persons was then dismissed, it being 6 o'clock, and at 7:50 the Cleveland delegation returned to the city, "satisfied."

The meeting was an earnest and a good one, — not less than five thousand persons gathered to do honor to the occasion. Notwithstanding the dust — the intense heat of the sun's rays — the time in the middle of harvesting — and the fact of its being the first working day of the week, the hosts of freedom came up and encamped in the strong-hold of liberty and equality. Oberlin is *not* "subdued," and *never will be.*

Of all the features of the day, there was nothing that was of more interest than the singing by the vast and well-trained choir. It was, without exception the most grand and glorious singing — the nearest to our conception of a grand choral harmony, of any thing we ever heard.

A lady remarked to us on the homeward passage, that she "didn't believe we would hear better singing in the other world." We do believe there is no choir like that one in the country. No words, no language can express the beauty and sublimity of the execution of the Marseilles Hymn, or the "Gathering of the Free," and so will not attempt it. It was beyond all praise.

After partaking of a bountiful supper at Prof. PECK's, we returned home, hearty cheers rising as the excursionists left the station, and when next Oberlin celebrates, and her eleven hundred students are "out of school," and the latch strings are out, "may we be there to see."

We are permitted to close this volume with the following beautiful and thrilling lines, the offering of a recent graduate of Oberlin College.

A SONG FOR FREEDOM.

EMILY C. HUNTINGTON.

A SONG for Freedom! let it ring
   In wild and stirring rhyme,
Fit for the glowing lips to sing,
   When beating hearts keep time;
For all the hills are flushing red,
   A glorious morn is breaking,
And earth is thrilling to the tread
   Of Freedom's hosts awaking.

Through the long night we only heard
   The distant warder's cry,
And here and there a soul gave back
   The watchword in reply :
Now, full and clear above them all,
   The bugle notes are sounding,
A thousand voices swell the call,
   A thousand hearts are bounding.

From lip to lip along the lines,
   The battle-cry rings out : —
" GOD SPEED THE RIGHT ! " then loud and high
   The kingly leaders shout : —
" Now with your good swords flashing bare,
   O host of GOD's anointing !
Look to the heavens ! and follow where
   The beacon star is pointing ! "

Ho, Tyrants! ye who dared to steal
   The pearl ye could not win,
Who thought to crush with iron heel
   The free-born soul within ; —
Bowed to the dust beneath your sway,
   Our hearts spring up the stronger;
Lo, FREEDOM takes the crown to-day
   And falsehood rules no longer.

We cannot fail, while day by day,
   In every cottage home,
Young children kneel, and softly pray,
   " Thy heavenly kingdom come ! "
So courage, heart ! for come it must,
   That kingdom high and glorious,
The tyrant's power shall fall to dust,
   And truth shall reign victorious.

Brooklyn, Conn. }
  July 4, 1859. }